ETHNICITY IN CONTEMPORARY AMERICA:
A Geographical Appraisal

Jesse O. McKee, Editor
The University of Southern Mississippi

Kendall/Hunt
Publishing Company
Dubuque, Iowa

Contents

Preface **v**

Foreword **vii**

Introduction **ix**

1. Humanity on the Move
   Jesse O. McKee **1**

2. The Native American
   James M. Goodman **31**

3. The Evolving Spatial Pattern of Black America: 1910–1980
   Harold M. Rose **55**

4. Mexican Americans
   Daniel D. Arreola **77**

5. The Cuban-Americans
   Thomas D. Boswell **95**

6. Puerto Ricans Living in the United States
   Thomas D. Boswell **117**

7. American Jewish Ethnicity
   Jonathan S. Mesinger
   Ary J. Lamme III **145**

8. Japanese Americans
   Midori Nishi **169**

9. The Chinese in America
   Catherine L. Brown
   Clifton W. Pannell **195**

10. The Indochinese
    Alice C. Andrews
    G. Harry Stopp, Jr. **217**

11. Rural Ethnic Islands
    Allen G. Noble **241**

12. Urban Ethnic Islands
    Donald J. Zeigler
    Stanley D. Brunn **259**

Preface

Ethnicity in Contemporary America is intended to serve as a text for college level courses in ethnic or minority studies. It can be used also as a supplementary reading text in other appropriate courses and by secondary school teachers as a reference book.

The National Council for Geographic Education presents this book as one of the volumes in its Pacesetter Series. The idea for such a volume was conceived more than six years ago by the editor of the Series, Clyde F. Kohn, but active work on the book did not begin until the summer of 1981. Once an editor was chosen, individual contributors were solicited for each of the chapters. Where possible, an attempt was made to choose an author from a particular minority group to write about that group. The chapters on Blacks, Mexicans, and Japanese were written by persons belonging to those specific groups. One of the co-authors of the chapter on Jews belongs to that particular minority.

The overall structure, selection of groups to be included, and the basic outline for each chapter was established, initially, by the editor of the volume. Most authors have conformed to established guidelines, thereby providing some continuity to a text that is multi-authored. Not all chapters, however, conform exactly to the originally proposed structured outline because of the varied nature of each minority or topic, and because each chapter is the individual author's expression of that minority. It is hoped that individual expressions presented by each author do not distract from the overall purpose and mission of the volume, that is, to provide a sampling of some of the major ethnic minority groups in the United States as to their origin, diffusion, and settlement patterns. Each chapter is an original contribution and was written specifically for this text. None of the chapters are reprints from previous research.

Nine of the first ten chapters of this book have been devoted to specific ethnic groups, the majority of which have been of non-European ancestry. Because of the complexity of the volume of migration and source areas of immigration, only slight attention has been given to specific groups from Europe. Admittingly whole books have been written on such groups as the Germans, Irish, Italians, and the Russians. Since it was not desirous to exclude these various European groups entirely, it was felt that one way to solve this problem was to include two additional chapters on "Rural Ethnic Islands" and "Urban Ethnic Islands" where the focus would be on the selection of specific immigrant groups, primarily of European heritage, and on a discussion of their various impacts on the cultural landscape of the United States.

In Chapter 11, specific groups such as the Germans, Belgians, Swedes, Finns, Norwegians, and the Amish, Cajuns, and Mormons are discussed. Emphasis is placed upon their material culture contributions, particularly their house types and barns.

In Chapter 12, examination is focused on the ethnic mixes (mainly European) in selected American cities, their urban settlement concentrations, and other such features as the foreign language press, foreign language broadcasting, and ethnic festivals.

The study of ethnic minorities is interdisciplinary in nature. Anthropologists, sociologists, historians, political scientists, economists, and geographers as well as scholars in other disciplines have written extensively on the subject. Admittedly, each discipline approaches the study of ethnic groups differently. Each distinguishes itself by the questions it addresses, and not necessarily by the phenomena it investigates. This text is a geographical appraisal of ethnicity in contemporary America. Geographers not only examine the character of places and people, but emphasize spatial relations of phenomena. They ask such questions as "How do humans organize their society in space in order to accomplish their needs and wants?" or, "How are minority groups related spatially to other groups within a society?" Hopefully, scholars in other disciplines will find this approach complementary to their own research and teaching pursuits.

The editor of the series together with the editor of this volume acknowledge the cooperation extended to them by the contributors. They wish to thank chapter authors for their patience, time and knowledge in making this text a reality. The volume editor accepts sole responsibility for errors of omission, but is not accountable for statements or opinions expressed by individual authors.

For each of the authors, the editor wishes to thank the respective universities for their cooperation and assistance. In addition, a word of appreciation is extended to all those who helped critique the text while it was in its early stages of development. Although all names of those involved cannot be mentioned, special recognition is given to Gary Taylor and Van Lowe for their cartographic assistance, and to Lena Sizemore and Betty Blackledge for their type and proofreading of portions of the original manuscripts.

Jesse O. McKee, Editor
University of Southern Mississippi

Foreword

A *minority,* in a general sense, means a number forming less than one-half of the whole. When applied to ethnic or social relations several characteristics appear. First, being a member of a minority not only indicates that one is a member of a social group, but frequently of a political unit as well. A dominant group in society normally shares a host of common traits such as language and religion, a common value system and history, and a common physical appearance or an identifiable "biological visibility." Cultural traits, value systems, and physical appearance of a minority are frequently devalued by the dominant group. Minorities are also conscious of themselves as a group, and usually resist intermarriage.

Ethnic is a term frequently used to refer to minority or racial groups. The word is derived from the Greek word *ethnos,* meaning a 'people' or 'nation.'[1] It is a very popular term which emphasizes the cultural ethnos of a group and to a lesser degree its physiognomic (racial) traits. An *ethnic group* has been defined as "a cultural group possessing a common tradition and strong feeling of belonging, living as a minority in a larger host society of a different culture."[2] Unlike a nationality group, an ethnic group usually does not possess a strong loyalty to a former nation-state. Usually, nationality also includes such meanings as the individual's place of birth, citizenship of the individual or group, or the ancestors' place of birth. Frequently, different ethnic groups may base their identity on different traits. For the Amish, it is religion; blacks identify with race; the French-Canadians use the mother tongue; Jews use religion; and folk culture is utilized by the Appalachian Southerner.

Race is used to refer to a group of persons connected by common physical and/or biological characteristics which are transmitted in descent. It is a term full of misunderstandings and myths. Race is not to be confused with culture or nationality. Culture is learned behavior, and the use of the term nationality may infer cultural traits. In a strict sense, race infers a biological connotation only, but use of the term frequently emphasizes the barriers often placed upon a minority race by a dominant group. For purposes of this book, the use of the term, race, has not been emphasized in favor of the more comprehensive and less discriminatory concept of ethnic minority.

The ethnic groups discussed in this book provide a sampling of some of the major ethnic minority groups in the United States. The Introduction discusses migration theory and acculturation processes. The essay is intended to provide a theoretical foundation to the other chapters. Chapter One discusses immigration to the United States from 1607 to the present, thus giving a background to the time of entry and spatial distribution of various groups. Separate chapters then follow on Native Americans, Blacks, Mexican Americans, Cubans, Puerto Ricans, Jews, Japanese, Chinese, and Indochinese. Because so many persons have emigrated from Europe to America, a separate book could have been written discussing just European groups. However, rather than having separate chapters on European groups and other smaller minority groups, they are discussed in the chapters on *Rural Ethnic Islands* and *Urban Ethnic Islands.*

NOTES

1. Terry G. Jordan and Lester Rowntree, *The Human Mosaic: A Thematic Introduction to Cultural Geography,* 2nd edition (New York: Harper & Row, Publishers): p. 295.
2. Ibid.: P. 327.

Introduction

Jesse O. McKee
University of Southern Mississippi

Human beings have always tended to be rather mobile. In societies experiencing advanced economic and technological progress, particularly in transportation and communication facilities, there is a corresponding increase in mobility and migration. The mobility of humans is evidenced by the linguistic, religious, social, and racial mixing of much of the world's population. In the United States for example, one-fourth of its residents do not reside in the state in which they were born, and every year about one out of five Americans moves to a new residence.

Migration is not random, nor is it just biologically determined. It is selective—frequently influenced by such demographic characteristics as race, age, sex, and a host of other variables including educational attainment, occupation, marital status, as well as economic and political pressures generally associated with specific geographical areas. Some migrate by free choice; others are forced. Migration is frequently thought of in terms of individuals exercising free choice, but the majority of worldwide migrations in the 20th century have been forced or impelled. Many persons emigrate in search of better jobs, higher wages, and general improvement in their quality of life. By some estimates, in contrast, more than 100 million persons have been forced to move because of environmental/ecological changes in their homelands, civil or international war, differences in political ideologies, or pressing economic conditions. These displaced persons or refugees are recognized as comprising a different type of migratory movement than those exercising free will. Some refugees realize that prospects of returning to their homelands are virtually nil and that their movements are permanent. Others see their moves as temporary and do expect to return at a future date.

Once an individual migrates, particularly to another country, there are usually enormous social and cultural adjustments to be made. A certain job skill may have to be acquired; one may encounter a language problem; gainful employment must be sought; housing is needed; and besides normal adjustment problems from the individual's standpoint, there may be the issue of acceptance into the host society.

To further understand the topics of migration and assimilation of an ethnic minority, this introductory chapter provides a theoretical and conceptual framework from which to examine and evaluate migration patterns and cultural adaptions of various ethnic minority groups. The chapter also provides a frame of reference from which to view the various ethnic groups discussed in the ensuing chapters of this text.

MIGRATION THEORY

The pioneer effort in establishing migration theory was developed and written by British demographer E. G. Ravenstein in 1885 and 1889. In his first paper, Ravenstein summarized five items. He added two more statements in his second paper. After studying migration in Britain, and then adding more than twenty countries for his second article, he reached the following conclusions:[1]

1) *Migration and Distance:* Most migrants travel a short distance, but those who travel farther show preferences to move to larger cities;

2) *Migration by Stages:* Migration produced "currents of migration," and persons surrounding cities move to them leaving gaps to be filled by persons from more remote districts;

3) *Streams and Counterstreams:* Each main current or stream of migration produces a counterstream;

4) *Urban-Rural Differences:* Persons living in towns or urban areas are less migratory than those inhabiting rural areas;

5) *Predominance of Females Among Short-Distance Migrants:* Generally, females tend to be predominate among short-distance migrants;

6) *Migration and Technology:* Improvements in technology regarding transportation and industrial development encourages an increase in migration; and

7) *Dominance of the Economic Motive:* Other variables such as climate, social and political pressures are important, but the desire to improve one's economic status is a dominant variable.

Everett S. Lee, writing in 1966, expanded upon some of Ravenstein's ideas. He felt that, "No matter how short or how long, how easy or how difficult, every act of migration involves an origin, a destination, and an intervening set of obstacles."[2] He believed that the factors which influenced one's decisions to migrate could be summarized under four headings:

1. Factors associated with the area of origin;
2. Factors associated with the area of destination;
3. Intervening obstacles; and
4. Personal factors.

He then summarized three of these factors in a schematic diagram (Fig. 1). The two circles represent places of origin and destination, separated by intervening obstacles. Those factors which cause potential migrants to respond favorably to an area are indicated by a plus. Negative factors are indicated by a minus. Those factors to which potential migrants tend to act indifferently are indicated with a zero. Usually, before moving, a potential migrant considers the positive and negative factors at the point of origin. Family ties may be a plus, but a cold climate and being unemployed may be minuses. At the point of destination, family ties may be negative, but a warmer climate and the opportunities for a job are pluses or pull factors. Migration can be thought of in terms of pluses and minuses, or "push and pull" factors. Usually, one or more negative variables exist at the point of origin which push the migrant from the point of origin, and one or more plus variables exist at the point of destination which tip the migrant's decision-making process and pulls the individual to the point of destination. Once these variables are evaluated, and a potential decision made, the final act of moving cannot be pursued until the intervening obstacles are surmounted. Financial and psychic costs, together with marital status, number of dependents, educational skills, age, health, distance involved, and many other personal and possible restrictive variables must be considered. Most moves cannot be completed until the intervening obstacles are surmounted. Even then, the decisions may not always be rational. Accidental occurrences may still account for a considerable proportion of total migrations.

Voluntary migration is selective rather than random with biological and cultural determinants, such as ethnic composition, sex, marital status, educational attainment and occupational skills. The interplay of these variables may shift when forced migration forces are at work resulting in many refugees and displaced persons. Certain life cycles or stages can also effect migration. Graduation from high school or college, marriage, entrance into the labor market, divorce, death of a spouse, or retirement, are all factors which may induce persons to migrate.

Lee also postulates about the volume of migration, development of streams and counterstreams, and the characteristics of migrants. With regard to volume, Lee states six major hypotheses.[3]

Volume of Migration:

1. "The Volume of Migration within a given territory varies with the degree of diversity of areas included in that territory." The higher the diversity, the greater the in-migration flow.
2. "The volume of migration varies with the diversity of people." The greater the diversity, the higher the rate of migration.
3. "The volume of migration is related to the difficulty of surmounting the intervening obstacles." Fewer obstacles may permit increased migration.
4. "The volume of migration varies with fluctuations in the economy." During periods of business expansion, in-migration is likely to increase in the affected areas.

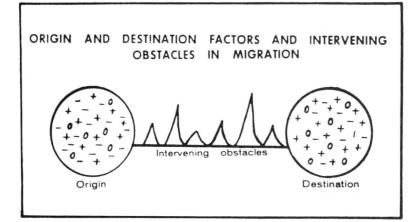

Figure 1. Origin and Destination Factors and Intervening Obstacles in Migration. Source: "A Theory of Migration" by Everett Lee, 1966. Reprinted by permission from *Demography*.

5. "Unless severe checks are imposed, both volume and rate of migration tend to increase with time." Once the set of intervening obstacles are surmounted, increasing migration is likely.

6. "The volume and rate of migration vary with the state of progress in a country or area." In developed nations people are very mobile in contrast to lesser developed nations. When persons change residences in lesser developed societies, frequently it is *en masse* and often under duress.

Stream and Counterstream:

1. "Migration tends to take place largely within well defined streams."

2. "For every migration stream, a counterstream develops."

3. "The efficiency of the stream (ratio of stream to counterstream or the net redistribution of population affected by the opposite flows) is high if the major factors in the development of a migration stream were minus factors at origin."

4. "The efficiency of stream and counterstream tends to be low if origin and destination are similar."

5. "The efficiency of migration streams will be high if the intervening obstacles are great."

6. "The efficiency of a migration stream varies with economic conditions, being high in prosperous times and low in times of depression."

Characteristics of Migrants:

1. "Migration is selective."

2. "Migrants responding primarily to plus factors at destinations tend to be positively selected."

3. "Migrants responding primarily to minus factors at origins tend to be negatively selected; or where minus factors are overwhelming to entire groups, they may not be selected at all."

4. "Taking all migrants together, selection tends to be bimodal."

5. "The degree of positive selection increases with the difficulty of the intervening obstacles."

6. "The heightened propensity to migrate at certain stages of the life cycle is important in the selection of migrants."

7. "The characteristics of migrants tend to be intermediate between characteristics of the population at origin and the population at destination."

In summary, the hypotheses established by Lee regarding volume, streams and counterstreams, and characteristics of migrants are significant, and provide a rather simple schema for examining migration at local, national, or international levels.

Types of Migration

There are three basic types of migratory movement; *cyclic, periodic,* and *migratory. Cyclic* movements are journeys that begin and eventually terminate at the ini-

tial place of origin. Typically, the daily "journey to work", or commuting trip, is an excellent example of this type; so too are the many shopping, social, and service trips taken by most Americans on a daily or weekly basis. Another form of cyclic movement is seasonal, which may involve traveling for leisure on holidays and vacations. Although many of the aforementioned types of movement can be thought of as regular, some cyclic movements such as business trips or week-end travel may be viewed as irregular.

Another type of movement is *periodic.* This type usually involves a temporary stay away from one's normal site of residence. Examples may include persons in military service, students in college, migrant laborers, or persons who move to the sunbelt states from northern states during the winter months.

The third, *migratory* movement, involves a permanent change in residence for a substantial period of time in a new political unit. This type of movement has a spatial requirement and a time component (usually a year—but not always), and involves a territorial/administrative change in a political unit. But, further clarification is needed. Persons who make a permanent change in their residence are considered movers not migrants, unless the move takes them into a new political unit (Fig. 2). Thus, all migrants are movers, but all movers are not migrants. There is little problem in understanding migration in terms of interstate or intercounty moves. However, there appears to be no general agreement as to what constitutes a political unit, particularly below the county level. So undoubtedly some confusion will persist over when to designate specific individuals officially as migrants or movers.

In further examination of migratory movements, it is useful to think of migration in terms of *total displacement migration* and *partial displacement migration,* particularly with regard to social and cultural

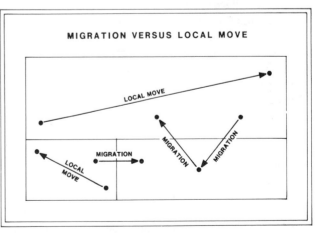

Figure 2. Migration Versus Local Move. Source: Modified from G. S. Lewis, *Human Migration,* (New York: St. Martin's Press, 1982): p. 10.

attachments to the place of origin and the new place of destination.[4]

Total displacement involves the move to a new residence, which will modify drastically the person's activity space of journey to work, school attendance, shopping patterns, and other social and leisure trips. Conversely, partial displacement allows individuals to continue to use much of their same activity space. Frequently, partial displacement is not caused by job relocation, but is constrained by it. In this instance, migrants change residences but are still able to maintain many of their former activity-space ties to shopping centers, churches, and social facilities.

Classification of Migration

William Petersen was one of the first to recognize most of the following different classes of migration: 1) primitive, 2) free-individual, 3) mass or groups, 4) restricted, and 5) impelled or forced.[5] *Primitive* migration involves persons who are unable to cope with certain natural forces such as geophysical, meteorological or ecological hazards related to the deterioration of their physical environment. One solution to coping or adjusting to the problem is to move.

Free-individual/group migration involves the movement of individuals or families acting on their own initiative without being compelled by official or governmental policy. Much of the immigration to the USA in the 18th, 19th and early 20th centuries might be categorized as this type.

Mass migration refers to a social group of persons larger than a family. Free migration can cause collective behavior, and when large numbers begin to migrate and migration streams or channels become refined and streamlined, it can be considered mass migration.

Restricted migration has rapidly started to replace free and mass migration. Since the early Chinese Exclusion Act of 1882, and particularly since 1921, the USA has placed restrictions on the number and ethnic composition of those seeking resident status. Similar legislation exists in most other nations. The restrictions may help to stem the tide of normal migration flows, but frequently the greatest migration problems involve refugees and displaced persons which can play havoc with normal migration legislation and regulations.

Impelled or *forced* migration is the fifth category. Impelled migration includes migrants who retain some power of decision and degree of choice, whereas forced migration refers to migrants who have no control or power of decision over their moves. For those who have fled their homelands, *emigres* regard their exile as temporary and plan to return at some date in the future, whereas *refugees* intend to settle permanently in a new country. Forced migration intended to remove a dissident population is frequently referred to as *displacement*. Although all displacement need not be forced,

some is impelled. The end result is the same in that these migrants feel that they cannot safely return to their homelands.

ACCULTURATION, ASSIMILATION, CULTURAL PLURALISM

How are Minorities Created?

A minority refers to persons who are members of a social group that comprise less than one-half of the total population. Usually they share a host of social and cultural traits, and in appearance they may be physically distinguishable. Minority groups emerge through four processes: 1) voluntary migration, 2) involuntary migration, 3) annexation, and 4) colonialism.[6] With regard to the USA, many minority groups have evolved from voluntary migration, some involuntary (such as blacks), and the American Indian has been the dominate group falling under the category of annexation. Colonialism has not been a major factor in the creation of minorities within the USA.

How Do Minorities Adapt?

The acculturation of minority groups into the mainstream of American society has always been of concern to the American public, particularly when the volume of migrants increases rather rapidly in a short time span. In the past, and still somewhat true today, more concern has been expressed over the willingness of these new immigrants to adopt the English language and a political ideology compatible with democratic ideals, than with the religious preference of these new arrivals. Religious choice is still a highly cherished freedom in the USA. Educational attainment, health condition, and occupational status of immigrants also have been frequent areas of concern.

Three basic concepts guide the process of migrants becoming Americanized: *Anglo-conformity, the melting pot,* and *cultural pluralism*.[7] The Anglo-conformity concept involves keeping English as the official language and adopting Anglo-culture norms as the standard of life. The Americanization of European ethnic groups has been rather successful, but non-European immigrants have frequently been denied full assimilation into the Anglo-culture because of their skin color and visibility. For these groups, some acculturation has occurred, but structural assimilation has not taken place. Prejudice, discrimination, and even segregation have kept these minority groups in a subordinate position.

The melting pot concept assumes that as different ethnic groups come to America they intermingle. Rather than conformance amalgamation occurs, thereby producing a new composite national stock and a new breed called the "American." In practice, the melting pot concept has become similar to that of

Anglo-conformity. Contributions by minorities have been ignored and through time have been lost in the "pot." Thus, both of these concepts in actuality are based on ". . . the absorption and eventual disappearance of the immigrant cultures into an overall 'American culture.' "[8]

A viable alternative to the two concepts discussed above is that of cultural pluralism. Cultural pluralism enables a minority group to keep its identity and to maintain its culture yet participate in the dominant society. But, cultural pluralism based on prejudice and inferiority of certain ethnic groups is not a sensible substitute. A workable relationship between the dominant and subordinate cultures whereby equality is assured and where some degree of collective societal goals can be agreed upon is probably the best alternative. Figure 3 is a schematic diagram which attempts to show that many groups have Americanized and are part of the mainstream (Canadians, Irish, Scots, etc.), whereas other ethnic groups have not been fully assimilated. They operate rather, as subcultures in a pluralistic society (i.e., blacks, Native Americans, Chinese). Some of these subcultures function close to the mainstream; others are on the margin of plural acceptance.

Researchers have developed other theories which explain how minorities usually adapt to "dominant-minority" relationships. These theories are generally referred to as "race relations cycles." One such cycle involves the alternatives of: 1) *separatism,* 2) *accommodation,* 3) *acculturation,* 4) *assimilation,* and 5) *amalgamation.*[9] *Separatism* refers to the geographical separation of a group so they can maintain their way of life. The early history and settlement pattern of the Mormons and the Amish exemplify this mode of adaption quite well. Some groups, upon arrival, tend to cluster to promote self needs and security, but this clustering should not be considered the same as separatism.

In *accommodation* the minority or subordinate group must, out of necessity, adopt various traits and conform to a certain degree to the wishes and behavior of the dominant group.

Acculturation is the process whereby individuals adopt traits from another group. Usually the adoption of material traits, language, and secular behavior are undertaken. Certain elements of the minority culture, however, may be maintained and practiced in a subcultural fashion. Later, cultural attitudes, values, and other non-material traits from the dominant culture are acquired. Most ethnic groups must acculturate to some extent with the dominant or host culture. In return, the dominant or host culture frequently makes accommodations and adopts some of the minority's cultural traits, thereby enabling both cultures to coexist.

Assimilation is when a minority individual or group adopts the cultural traits of the dominant group and identifies with that group, and the dominant group accepts the individual or group without discrimination. The assimilated individual must also be assured that intermarriage can occur without fear of being ostracized by the dominant group. When full assimilation occurs, the minority status ceases to exist.

Amalgamation is the biological merging of a distinct racial stock with the dominant racial group. Of course, some amalgamation will always take place between dominant and minority groups with or without formal approval should the two groups interact and live in close proximity to each other. This does not necessarily infer, however, that assimilation has occurred.

It is also quite presumptuous to infer that minority groups will follow the aforementioned five alternatives in a sequential fashion. For example, acculturation is not always followed by assimilation, nor is assimilation inevitably followed by amalgamation. Some minority groups may never fully assimilate. Traditionally, in American society, it can be stated that most minority groups have tended to achieve some form of accommodation, acculturation or assimilation. Separatism and even secession have been proposed by some groups, but this alternative has not been extremely successful.

Other types of race relation cycles have been proposed by Robert Park and Emory Bogardus. According to Park, there are four main cycles: 1) *contact,* 2) *competition,* 3) *accommodation,* and 4) *assimilation.*[10] After contact, competition between groups

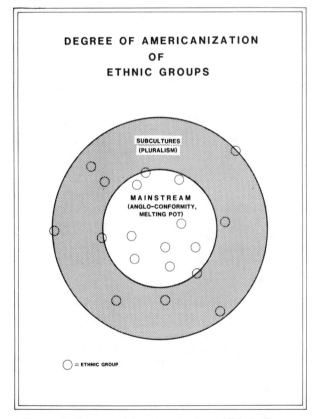

DEGREE OF AMERICANIZATION
OF
ETHNIC GROUPS

SUBCULTURES
(PLURALISM)

MAINSTREAM
(ANGLO-CONFORMITY,
MELTING POT)

◯ = ETHNIC GROUP

Figure 3. Degree of Americanization of Ethnic Groups.

for jobs, land, and other goals occur—violence may even breakout. One group then establishes dominance and the groups learn to accommodate each other. Eventually, assimilation may result. Emory Bogardus developed seven cycles: 1) *curiosity,* 2) *economic welcome,* 3) *industrial and social antagonism,* 4) *legislative antagonism,* 5) *fair-play tendencies,* 6) *quiescence,* and 7) *second generation difficulties.*[11]

Michael Banton in his research developed six orders of race relations.[12] These include: 1) *peripheral contact* (where groups remain independent), 2) *institutionalized contact and acculturation,* 3) *domination,* 4) *paternalism,* 5) *integration,* and 6) *pluralism* (Fig. 4). He then established a develop-

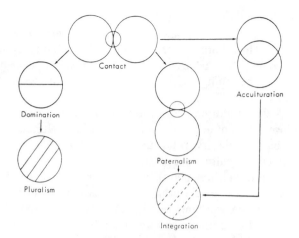

Figure 5. Sequence of Racial Orders. Source: *Race Relations* pp. 69–75 by Michael Banton. Reprinted by permission of Tavistock Publications, Inc.

mental sequence among the orders (Fig. 5). In the United States, sequence one of *contact, domination,* and *pluralism* is the most appropriate model of race relations. The *contact, paternalism,* and *integration* sequence best describes the experience of European-African relations. Part of it is exemplified in the South in the USA with regard to white-black relations, but the final order, integration, has not developed. The final order in the South is better categorized as pluralism. The third sequence: *contact, acculturation,* and *integration* has been the general pattern for many white migrants to the United States. Normally, except where race and/or color is a significant factor, these immigrants have become Americanized, or integrated by the third generation—the "three generation process." However, sometimes in the third generation ". . . the grandchildren of immigrants attempt to recover the heritage of the first generation."[13] The idea that the second generation tries to forget its heritage and the third to recover or revive it is often referred to as "Hansen's law" or thesis.[14]

For assimilation or Americanization to occur certain key factors encourage or discourage the process, these include:

> 1) similarity of the two groups culturally and physically, 2) the desire of the minority to assimilate and willingness of the majority to allow them to, 3) the nature of minority settlement, and 4) recentness of arrival and proximity to the homeland.[15]

If these factors are favorable, the Americanization process proceeds without too much complication, but for some it may not be achieved. Won Moo Hurh, in his study of Korean immigrants, developed seven critical phases in the adaption process[16] (Fig. 6). These phases include *excitement,* followed by *exigency* or disenchantment—a critical phase because the immigrant may leave. For those who stay a period of

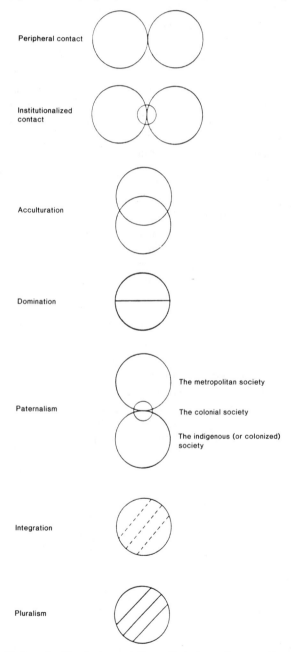

Figure 4. Six Orders of Race Relations. Source: *Race Relations* pp. 69–75 by Michael Banton. Reprinted by permission of Tavistock Publications, Inc.

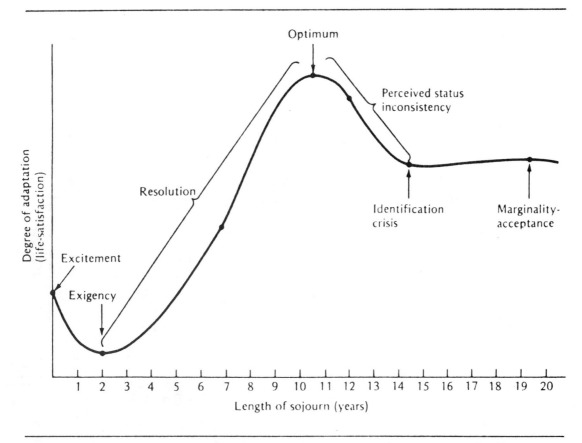

Figure 6. Critical Phases in Adaptation Process: A Hypothetical Model. Source: Won Moo Hurh, 1977, p. 46. (Used by permission).

resolution is established where the immigrant resolves to "make it." After reaching *optimism,* the immigrant may realize that he or she is being discriminated against and an *identification crisis* emerges before the immigrant finally accepts the role between a foreigner or outsider and a fully accepted member of society—*marginality acceptance.* In this model, assimilation is obviously not achieved.

Numerous migrants from Northwest Europe, as well as other white migrant groups have had an easier time of adapting and being accepted into the mainstream. Research efforts to document this include the use of a social distance scale, frequently referred to as the Bogardus scale.[17] The seven items used, with their corresponding distance score, are:[18]

To close kinship by marriage (1.00)
To my club as personal chums (2.00)
To my street as neighbors (3.00)
To employment in my occupation (4.00)
To citizenship in my country (5.00)
As visitors only to my country (6.00)
Would exclude from my country (7.00)

The survey, administered to white respondents as well as blacks, Jews, and Asians over forty years (1926,

1946, 1956, and 1966), reveals striking similarity in the hierarchy of acceptance of various groups. Although some groups have moved up or down in the scale (i.e. Japanese, Russians, and Italians), the general order has been for white Americans and persons of North European descent to be in the upper third of the distance scale, Eastern and Southern Europeans occupy the middle third, and racial minorities the bottom third (Fig. 7). When certain racial (i.e. blacks) and religious (Jews) minorities have been surveyed, they place their group high (i.e. egocentric and ethnocentric tendencies), but then they tend to follow a similar hierarchy as demonstrated in Figure 7.

How Society Removes the Minority Status

If a society recognizes the existence of minorities, then that society is confronted with the issue of possibly removing that status. Extermination, expulsion, and secession do not appear to be appropriate solutions. Assimilation, amalgamation, and Americanization may work for some groups but not all. For most minorities, participation in a pluralistic society seems to be a significant aspiration to attain. In a pluralistic society, minority groups retain certain traditions and cultural traits

Figure 7. Changes in Social Distance, 1926–66. Source: Bogardus, 1968, p. 152. (Used by permission).

I — Racial distance indices given racial groups in 1926 by 1,725 selected persons throughout the U.S.		II — Racial distance indices given racial groups in 1946 by 1,950 selected persons throughout the U.S.		III — Racial distance indices given racial groups in 1956 by 2,053 selected persons throughout the U.S.		IV — Racial distance indices given racial groups in 1966 by 2,605 selected persons throughout the U.S.	
1. English	1.06	1. Americans (U.S. white)	1.04	1. Americans (U.S. white)	1.08	1. Americans (U.S. white)	1.07
2. Americans (U.S. white)	1.10	2. Canadians	1.11	2. Canadians	1.16	2. English	1.14
3. Canadians	1.13	3. English	1.13	3. English	1.23	3. Canadians	1.15
4. Scots	1.13	4. Irish	1.24	4. French	1.47	4. French	1.36
5. Irish	1.30	5. Scots	1.26	5. Irish	1.56	5. Irish	1.40
6. French	1.32	6. French	1.31	6. Swedish	1.57	6. Swedish	1.42
7. Germans	1.46	7. Norwegians	1.35	7. Scots	1.60	7. Norwegians	1.50
8. Swedish	1.54	8. Hollanders	1.37	8. Germans	1.61	8. Italians	1.51
9. Hollanders	1.56	9. Swedish	1.40	9. Hollanders	1.63	9. Scots	1.53
10. Norwegians	1.59	10. Germans	1.59	10. Norwegians	1.66	10. Germans	1.54
11. Spanish	1.72	11. Finns	1.63	11. Finns	1.80	11. Hollanders	1.54
12. Finns	1.83	12. Czechs	1.76	12. Italians	1.89	12. Finns	1.67
13. Russians	1.88	13. Russians	1.83	13. Poles	2.07	13. Greeks	1.82
14. Italians	1.94	14. Poles	1.84	14. Spanish	2.08	14. Spanish	1.93
15. Poles	2.01	15. Spanish	1.94	15. Greeks	2.09	15. Jews	1.97
16. Armenians	2.06	16. Italians	2.28	16. Jews	2.15	16. Poles	1.98
17. Czechs	2.08	17. Armenians	2.29	17. Czechs	2.22	17. Czechs	2.02
18. Indians (American)	2.38	18. Greeks	2.29	18. Armenians	2.33	18. Indians (American)	2.12
19. Jews	2.39	19. Jews	2.32	19. Japanese Americans	2.34	19. Japanese Americans	2.14
20. Greeks	2.47	20. Indians (American)	2.45	20. Indians (American)	2.35	20. Armenians	2.18
21. Mexicans	2.69	21. Chinese	2.50	21. Filipinos	2.46	21. Filipinos	2.31
22. Mexican Americans	—	22. Mexican Americans	2.52	22. Mexican Americans	2.51	22. Chinese	2.34
23. Japanese	2.80	23. Filipinos	2.76	23. Turks	2.52	23. Mexican Americans	2.37
24. Japanese Americans	—	24. Mexicans	2.89	24. Russians	2.56	24. Russians	2.38
25. Filipinos	3.00	25. Turks	2.89	25. Chinese	2.68	25. Japanese	2.41
26. Negroes	3.28	26. Japanese Americans	2.90	26. Japanese	2.70	26. Turks	2.48
27. Turks	3.30	27. Koreans	3.05	27. Negroes	2.74	27. Koreans	2.51
28. Chinese	3.36	28. Indians (from India)	3.43	28. Mexicans	2.79	28. Mexicans	2.56
29. Koreans	3.60	29. Negroes	3.60	29. Indians (from India)	2.80	29. Negroes	2.56
30. Indians (from India)	3.91	30. Japanese	3.61	30. Koreans	2.83	30. Indians (from India)	2.62
Arithmetic mean of 48,300 racial reactions	2.14	Arithmetic mean of 58,500 racial reactions	2.12	Arithmetic mean of 61,590 racial reactions	2.08	Arithmetic mean of 78,150 racial reactions	1.92
Spread in distance	2.85	Spread in distance	2.57	Spread in distance	1.75	Spread in distance	1.56

with some degree of collective identity. The dominant group accepts the minority identity and assures equality and human dignity in the dominant-minority relations. The relationship between the dominant and minority groups should be agreeable to both parties involved. Thus, it may not be a desirable goal to remove the minority status from all groups. Indeed, to do so may even be an impossible objective to achieve. Minorities operating in a pluralistic society which attaches no negative stigmas to a minority status offer an achievable alternative to extermination, expulsion, secession or Anglo-conformity. But one should recognize that there are differences between cultural and social pluralism. "Although in practice both go together, cultural pluralism refers to the maintenance of ethnic subcultures with their traditions, values, and styles;"[19] whereas, "social pluralism refers to the extent that society is structurally compartmentalized into analogous and duplicatory, but culturally alike, sets of institutions and into corporate groups that are differentiated on a basis other than culture."[20]

NOTES

1. E. G. Ravenstein, "The Laws of Migration," *Journal of the Royal Statistical Society* 48 (June, 1885): pp. 167–227. Also "The Laws of Migration," *Journal of the Royal Statistical Society* 52 (June, 1889): pp. 241–301. These two articles have been summarized by Everett S. Lee, "A Theory of Migration," *Demography* 3(1966): pp. 47–57. Also see D. B. Grigg, "E. G. Ravenstein and the 'laws of migration'" *Journal of Historical Geography* 3 (1977): pp. 41–54.
2. Lee, 1966: p. 47.
3. *Ibid.:* pp. 52–57.
4. John A. Jakle, Stanley Brunn, Curtis C. Roseman, *Human Spatial Behavior: A Social Geography* (North Scituate, Mass.: Duxbury Press, 1976): pp. 151–155.
5. William Petersen, "A General Typology of Migration," *American Sociological Review* 23 (June, 1958): pp. 256–265.
6. Raymond W. Mack, *Race, Class and Power,* 2nd ed. (New York: Van Nostrand, 1968): pp. 227–28.
7. Milton Gordon, *Assimilation in American Life* (New York: Oxford University Press, 1964).
8. Harry H. L. Kitano, *Race Relations* (Englewood Cliffs: Prentice-Hall Inc., 1974): p. 59.
9. Charles F. Marden and Gladys Meyer, *Minorities in American Society* (New York: American Book Company, 1962): pp. 34–38.
10. Robert E. Park, *Race and Culture* (New York: The Free Press of Glencoe, 1964).
11. Emory S. Bogardus, "A Race Relations Cycle," American *Journal of Sociology* 35 (January, 1930): pp. 612–17.
12. Michael Banton, *Race Relations* (London: Tavistock Publications, 1967): pp. 68–76.
13. S. Dale McLemore, *Racial and Ethnic Relations in America* (Boston: Allyn and Bacon, Inc., 1980): p. 5.
14. *Ibid.*
15. Richard T. Schaefer, *Racial and Ethnic Groups* (Boston: Little, Brown, and Company, 1979): p. 43.
16. Won Moo Hurh, *Comparative Study of Korean Immigrants in the United States: A Typological Approach* (San Francisco: R and E Research Associates, 1977): pp. 46–52.
17. Emory Bogardus, "Comparing Racial Distance in Ethiopia, South Africa, and the United States," *Sociology and Social Research* 52 (January, 1968): pp. 149–156.
18. Schaefer, 1979: p. 64.
19. Kitano, 1974: p. 54.
20. *Ibid.*

1

Humanity On the Move

Jesse O. McKee

University of Southern Mississippi

During the 1970s, immigration became a critical issue in the United States. Concern over the rise of immigrants from Latin American and Asian countries, an increase in the number of undocumented workers, and the problem of refugees caused Congress and U.S. citizens to question seriously our policies on immigration. The USA basically clings to its humanitarian instincts and its concern for the socially, economically and politically depressed persons in the world. Yet, it is somewhat apprehensive about possibly becoming a "dumping ground" for the world's poor, particularly during periods of lag in the USA economy.

Population growth is also a concern of many Americans since it is estimated that 50 percent of the national population growth is attributable to immigration. Then there is the problem of the perceived rate of acculturation into American society of many of these non-European ethnic groups. Will cultural pluralism increase as a viable alternative to acculturation? Should the USA continue to promote bilingualism, or support the learning of English only?

Many questions are again being raised about current immigration in the U.S. which are reminiscent of the arguments presented in the early part of this century prior to the enactment of the quota laws in the 1921 and 1924. Not only are numbers and acculturation issues, but to some extent the spatial dispersal of these immigrants are causes for concern to the residents of the states where these persons are settling. For example,

"... 60.5 percent of all Cubans planned to settle in Florida; 46.4 percent of all Filipinos in California; 74.4 percent of all Mexicans in California and Texas; and 70.4 percent of all Dominicans in New York."[1]

It is important, therefore, to understand the present issues of immigration and to seek familiarity and an appreciation of past USA migration trends and immigration policies. Thus, this chapter is devoted to the historical development of immigration to the United States and will also serve as an introduction to the other ethnic groups discussed in this text.

IMMIGRATION TO THE UNITED STATES SINCE 1600

The chronicling of immigrants to America since 1607 is indeed a fascinating topic and is critical to the understanding of American history and the development of American culture. The processes whereby these cultures, transplanted from the Old World (particularly Europe) to America, began to transform the landscape into something distinctively American is in itself quite intriguing. But, the development processes of American culture have not been static. The nation continually changes. As new groups arrive, and the exchange of cultural traits takes place, and as the acculturation process is set into motion, a slightly different America emerges. To be sure, certain groups have had more impact than others, and their imprint upon the landscape has been more noticeable. Our ties to Europe are evident in our basic cultural traits of language, religion, political system, and technological achievement. The imprint of the various Asian groups, and to some extent those from Latin America, is presently developing. The contribution of these groups to American society has not yet been fully realized.

The immigration waves to America can be subdivided in many ways. A suggested division, which will be the basis for discussion in this chapter, appears in Table 1.1.

1607–1820: Colonial and Early U.S. Period

The settling of Jamestown marks the beginning of the stream of immigrants who eventually came to America from virtually all over the globe. In the early years (1607–1700), the English and the Welsh provided the initial wave together with Africans. Besides the Vikings, blacks may have been the first non-Indian permanent settlers in America when some fled from a Spanish colony to the Pedee River area in South Carolina in 1526.[2] However, the generally accepted date of blacks in America is 1619 when "twenty-Negroes were put ashore at Jamestown . . . by the captain of a Dutch frigate."[3] These early blacks were considered

TABLE 1.1 Immigration Periods

1607–1700:	Initial Wave. Strong English and Welsh, with a complement of Africans.
1701–1775:	Second Wave. Predominantly English, Welsh, and African, with strong Teutonic and Scotch-Irish components.
1776–1820:	Third Wave. Similar in composition of immigrants as in the second wave, but with a reduced number of arrivals.
1821–1880:	Northwest European Wave. Heavily Irish, German, British, French, and other Northwest Europeans, together with a complement of persons from Canada, China and the West Indies.
1881–1920:	Great Deluge. Large numbers of Southern and Eastern Europeans principally from Italy, Austria, Hungary, Russia (USSR), together with those from Northwest Europe, Canada, Mexico, West Indies, Asiatic Turkey and Japan.
1921–1930:	Transition Period. The Quota Acts are enacted. Migration is principally from Canada, Mexico, Italy, Germany, and the United Kingdom. The number of migrants declined from preceding decades, but still relatively large with more than 4 million entering the U.S.
1931–1960:	Immigration Bust. Principally from the Western Hemisphere nations of Canada and Mexico, Northwestern Europe (Germany and Great Britain), plus Italy, and a complement of Japanese after World War II.
1961–1980:	Immigration Boom: Largely Hispanic Americans from Mexico, Cuba, and other West Indies nations, together with Asians from the Philippines, Korea, China and Taiwan, India, and Vietnam.

Source: Wilbur Zelinsky, *The Cultural Geography of the United States* (Englewood Cliffs: Prentice Hall, Inc., 1973): p. 23. The classificatory scheme is modified from Zelinsky.

to be indentured servants and not slaves, but as their numbers grew, a Virginia slave code came into existence. As the need for laborers increased, Maryland, the Carolinas, Georgia, the Middle colonies, and New England became involved in slavery and the slave trade. By 1650 the estimated population in the colonies was 50,368, of which 1,600 were black.[4]

Between 1700 and 1775, migration to the United States continued to be predominantly English, Welsh, and African, together with Teutons and Scotch-Irish. Other small ethnic and religious groups of the seventeenth and eighteenth-century included the Spanish, Dutch, French, Swedes, Flemish, Jews, and Italians; but, the British accounted for the largest number of immigrants. Their superior military, economic and political strength enabled them to establish superiority in

eastern North America. In 1790, shortly after the suspension of major movements in 1775, the census reported a population of 3,929,214 persons of which 757,208 were black with 697,624 of this number as slaves. Of the remaining population, more than 75 percent was of British origin, 8 percent was German and the remainder were primarily Dutch, French, or Spanish. In addition, it is also estimated that about one-half million Native Americans lived within the present-day borders of the United States.

Because of military conflicts in America and Europe, immigration from abroad to the United States was light between 1776 and 1820. It did not resume until after 1820. Official immigration figures for persons entering the United States before 1820 are lacking, but between the end of the Revolutionary War and 1820, it is estimated that about 250,000 entered the U.S. Thus, this early period (1607–1820) had three rather distinct subdivisions: 1607–1700 (initial wave), 1701–1775 (second wave), and 1776–1820 (third wave).

Early Immigration Policy. Prior to the American Revolution, the United States obviously had no immigration policy. At the time of the founding of the new nation with the signing of the Treaty of Paris in 1783, British influence was dominant, but other ethnic groups had settled and pluralism was evident in American life.

During the 1790s, Congress was mainly concerned about regulating naturalization and citizenship. A series of acts were passed. The Naturalization Act of 1795 required a five-year residency, oath swearing attachment to the Constitution, and satisfactory proof of good character and behavior (Table 1.2). In 1798 another Naturalization Act was passed raising the residency requirement from five to fourteen years. In that same year Congress passed the Alien Enemies Act and the Alien Friends Act. Both Acts gave the president powers to deport any alien whom he considered dangerous to the welfare and security of the nation. When the two alien acts expired in 1802, a new Naturalization Act was enacted re-establishing the provisions of the 1795 Act.

Since the U.S. had not been collecting detailed and adequate data on immigrants, Congress passed a law in 1819 ("Steerage Legislation") requiring that select data be collected on immigration by nationality, sex, occupation, and age.

1821–1930: Maturation of Immigration.

Source of Migrants During this period, the number of immigrants, their country of origin, and the process of acculturation of these new arrivals differed rather vastly from the previous period when most were from Great Britain and their cultural adjustment and acculturation processes were minimal. Most nineteenth and early twentieth century migrants experienced more "culture

TABLE 1.2 Major Immigration Legislation

1795   *Naturalization Act*—required declaration of intent, five-year residency, oath swearing attachment to Constitution, satisfactory proof of good character and behavior

1798   *Alien Enemies Act, Alien Friends Act*—President may deport any alien whom he considers dangerous to U.S. welfare

1798   *Naturalization Act*—applicant for citizenship must reside 14 years in United States, 5 in state where naturalization is sought

1802   *Naturalization Act*—reestablished provisions of the 1795 Naturalization Act

1819   *Steerage Legislation*—regulated accommodations provisions; set minimum standards on transatlantic vessels; required ship captains arriving from abroad to compile lists of passengers and to designate age, sex and occupation of each

1875   *Immigration Act*—the first national restriction of immigration, banned prostitutes and convicts

1882   *Immigration Act*—increased lists of inadmissibles (those considered lunatics, idiots, convicts, likely public charges) and established head tax

1882   *Chinese Exclusion Act*—barred Chinese laborers (repealed in 1943)

1885   *Alien Contract Labor Law* (Foran Act)—barred importation of contract labor; intended to end employers practice of importing large numbers of low-paid immigrants, thus depressing the U.S. labor market

1888   *First Deportation Law*—authorized deportation of contract laborers

1891   *Immigration Act*—increased inadmissible classes (those considered to have loathsome or contagious diseases, and polygamists, paupers and those guilty of moral turpitude); Act also authorized deportation of illegal aliens

1903   *Immigration Act*—increased inadmissible classes (epileptics, those who become insane within five years of entry or have had two attacks of insanity, beggars, anarchists and white slavers)

1906   *Naturalization Act*—made English a requirement, provided for administrative reform

1907   *Immigration Act*—increased inadmissible classes (imbeciles, feeble minded, tubercular, suffering from physical or mental defects affecting the ability to earn a living; those admitting to crimes involving moral turpitude, women coming for immoral purposes, unaccompanied children under 16)

1917   *Immigration Act*—established literacy as basis of immigrant entry; increased inadmissible classes (those considered to have constitutional psychopathic inferiority, men entering for immoral purposes, chronic alcoholics, stowaways, vagrants, those with one attack of insanity); Asian exclusion affirmed

1921   *Emergency Quota Act*—limited annual immigration to 3% of national origin of foreign born in United States in 1910; European immigration limited to 355,000 per year—55% from northeastern Europe and 45% from southeastern Europe

1924   *National Origins Act*—(fully effective in 1929), assigned quotas to each nationality in proportion to its contribution to the existing U.S. population, based on 1920 census. (As an interim measure, reduced annual quota to 2% of national origin of foreign born in United States in 1890, nearly eliminating immigration from central and southern Europe). Other provisions: aliens ineligible for citizenship excluded; total quota of 150,000, plus unlimited entry by Canadians and Latin Americans; U.S. consuls abroad to issue visas; avowed aim of act was to maintain the "racial preponderance (of) the basic strain on our people."

1929   *National Origins Act*—enacted quotas now to be computed according to national composition of entire U.S. population in 1920, based on 1920 census

1942   *Bracero Program*—established bilateral agreements with Mexico, British Honduras, Barbados, and Jamaica for entry of temporary workers

1943   *Chinese Exclusion Laws*—repealed all such laws.

1946   *War Brides Act*—facilitated immigration of foreign-born spouses and children of armed services personnel

1952   *Immigration and Nationality (McCarran-Walter) Act*—codified immigration and naturalization statutes, national origins provisions retained; no limitations on Western Hemisphere immigration; preference system established

1965   *Immigration and Nationality Act Amendments of 1965*—repealed national origins provisions; created annual Eastern Hemisphere ceiling of 170,000 with annual per-country limit of 20,000; new preference system with labor clearance requirement; Western Hemisphere ceiling of 120,000 with no country limitations or preference system, but with labor certification requirement

1976   *Immigration and Nationality Act*—extended per-country limitation of 20,000 and preference system to Western Hemisphere

1978   *Worldwide Ceiling Law*—combined Eastern and Western quotas creating a worldwide ceiling of 290,000 immigrants

1980   *Refugee Act*—allocated 50,000 visas for "normal-flow" refugees and permitted the president, after consultation with Congress, to increase the annual allocation. Reduced worldwide ceiling to 270,000 immigrants annually

SOURCE: *U.S. Immigration Policy and the National Interest,* 1981, pp. 32–44.

shock," and had to work harder at learning the ways of life in America, frequently under difficult circumstances. Except for intermittent periods of war, economic depression, or immigration restrictions, the flow of migrants (mainly from Europe) continued to increase in numbers during most of this time period. This 110 year interval can be subdivided into three divisions: 1821 to 1880 when most migrants were from Northern and Western Europe; 1881 to 1920 when Southern and Eastern Europe predominated; and 1921

THE FIVE COUNTRIES WITH HIGHEST LEVELS OF IMMIGRATION TO THE UNITED STATES BY DECADE, 1821-1978

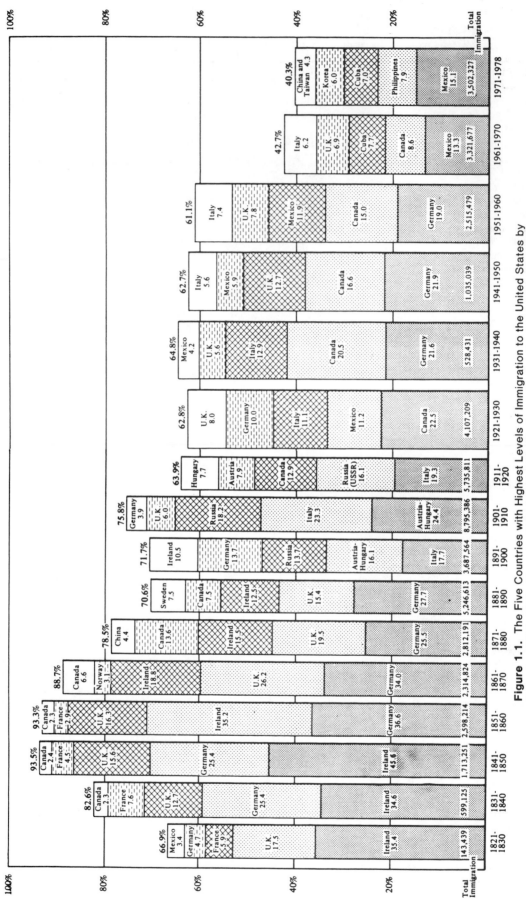

Figure 1.1. The Five Countries with Highest Levels of Immigration to the United States by Decade, 1821–1978. Source: *U.S. Immigration Policy and the National Interest,* 1981; pp. 230–231. Data are compiled from Tables 13 and 14, *Immigration and Naturalization Service,* Annual Report, 1978. Note: Reporting of immigration via U.S. landborders with Mexico and Canada was not fully established until 1908.

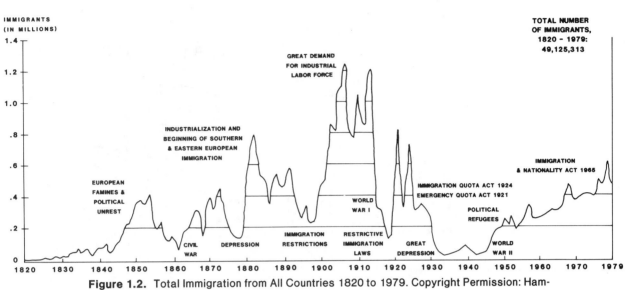

Figure 1.2. Total Immigration from All Countries 1820 to 1979. Copyright Permission: Hammond Incorporated, Maplewood, N.J.

to 1930 when the Quota Acts were put into effect and most migrants came from the Western Hemisphere nations and Northwest Europe. Figure 1.1 summarizes by decade the five countries with the highest levels of immigration to the U.S. since 1821.

From 1820 to 1979 sharp increases and periodic declines are readily visible (Fig. 1.2). During the 1820s and 1830s, 742,564 persons immigrated to the United States.[5] The total number of immigrants for the decade of 1840 (1,713,251) was more than double that for the previous two decades. Immigration continued to increase into the 1840s as potato famines in Ireland and political unrest in Europe provided a "push" to emigrate to America. Immigration then declined somewhat in the late 1850s and 1860s but resumed after the Civil War.

During the period 1821 to 1880, 86 percent of the immigrants were from North and West Europe (Fig. 1.3), mainly Germany, Ireland, and United Kingdom, with a lesser number from Norway, Sweden, Denmark, Netherlands, Switzerland, Belgium, and France. A total of 10,181,044 persons came to the USA during this period, an average of 169,684 a year. Ireland dominated the 1820s, '30s, and '40s. Germany dominated the 1850s, '60s, and '70s followed by Ireland, United Kingdom, Canada and Newfoundland (Fig. 1.1). Less than 250,000 came from Asia during this sixty year span. Most of these Asian immigrants were Chinese. Just slightly more than 1,000 persons came from Africa. The contribution from Africa was very small during this period. This is basically attributed to the

outlawing of the importation of slaves into the United States in 1808. Few Africans wished to emigrate to a nation which was still engaged in slavery.

Due to the large number of Catholic Irish immigrants, some anti-Irish feeling began to emerge in America. They were accused of bringing diseases to the USA and contributing to crime. The uproar over these immigrants spurred Protestant evangelicals and nativists to form associations and political parties such as the Native American Party in 1845, and later the American (Know-Nothing) Party in 1856 to preserve the nation's morals and ethnic purity. These groups sought to place a curb on immigration. After the Civil War, when the economy and the settlement of the West expanded, the need for labor increased and immigration rose correspondingly. Thus, these early political groups did not necessarily affect immigration policy, but they raised basic questions that Americans had to address later in the 19th and early part of the 20th centuries.

The period from 1881 to 1920 is frequently referred to as the Great Deluge. And in some respects, the Great Deluge period can be extended to 1930. Although the quota acts of 1921 and 1924 slowed down immigration immensely, many persons continued to come to the USA during the 1920s, particularly from the Western Hemisphere which had no quotas (Fig. 1.2). During this time period, 1881 to 1920, the shift from Northern and Western Europe to Southern and Eastern Europe was most notable. But, if the decade of the 1920s (the Transition Decade) is included with the Great Deluge (it is

U. S. IMMIGRANTS BY REGIONS OF ORIGIN,
1821 THROUGH 1979

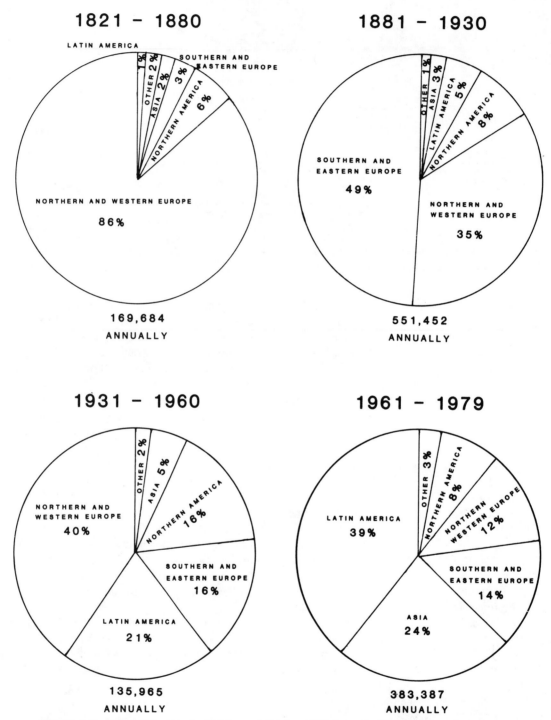

Figure 1.3. U.S. Immigrants by Regions of Origin, 1821 through 1979. Source: Compiled from *1979 Statistical Yearbook of the Immigration and Naturalization Service.*

included here with the Great Deluge primarily because of the number of migrants, not necessarily because of the source areas of migrants), a total of 27,572,583 immigrants entered the U.S. during this period, an annual average of 551,452 persons. Migration from Southern and Eastern Europe amounted to 49 percent of the total, Northern and Western Europe contributed 35 percent and Canada and Newfoundland 8 percent (Fig. 1.3). If one were to delete the decade of the 1920s from the Great Deluge period, then more than 50 percent of the immigrants originated from Southern and Eastern Europe.

During the period, 1881–1930, the volume of immigration varied. It declined slightly before the turn of the twentieth century when certain immigration restrictions were passed such as the Chinese Exclusion Act of 1882 and other Oriental Exclusion Acts between 1882 and 1907. These were designed to restrict immigration of Chinese to California. Other laws prescribed the physical and mental health, morals and financial status of immigrants. But, migration rose sharply from 1900 to the beginning of World War I. It rose again in the early 1920s, and then declined considerably by 1930 due to the quota acts and the Great Depression. Further examination of this period reveals that more than 5.2 million persons migrated to the United States between 1881 and 1890. Of these, 27.7 percent were from Germany, 15.4 percent from United Kingdom, 12.5 percent from Ireland, and 7.5 percent each from Canada and Sweden respectively (Fig. 1.1). Between 1891 and 1900, more than 3.6 million immigrated, largely from Eastern and Southern Europe (principally Italy, Austria-Hungary, and Russia), and from Germany and Ireland.

The largest decade with regard to numbers was 1901 to 1910, when more than 8.7 million immigrants entered the U.S. mainly from Eastern Europe, Italy, and Russia. In 1907 alone, nearly 1.3 million entered the U.S., the highest of any year in USA history. The decade, 1911 to 1920, was another period of large numbers of immigrants (more than 5.7 million), similar in source areas of the immigration of the previous decade except that a large group came from Canada and Newfoundland.

During the 1920s, after the Quota Acts of 1921 and 1924, the largest number of immigrants to the USA came from Canada, Newfoundland, and Mexico—nations which had had no quotas. These three nations contributed 33.7 percent of the immigration total. Italy and Germany together with Poland accounted for 26.7 percent. Thus, slightly more than 60 percent came from these six source areas.

The settlement patterns of these immigrants, resulting from the Great Deluge and the preceding decades, are indeed intriguing. Many of them gravitated to the larger cities and to the Northeast. But many, like the Germans and Scandinavians, sought the upper Middle West and North Central States. Very few settled in the South—the apparent explanations include: an inferior array of economic opportunity, even after Emancipation; a social climate that few immigrants found enticing; and a xenophobia that may have been both cause and effect of the low incidence of aliens.[6]

Immigration Policy. During most of the 1800s, which witnessed the expansion of the Western frontier, Indian removal and the Civil War, Congress paid little attention to enacting immigration laws. From 1821 to 1880, the migrants were primarily of Irish, German, and British descent.

To help control immigration in the latter part of the 1800s against certain undesirables, immigration acts were passed in 1875 and 1882 to restrict the admission of prostitutes, convicts, and lunatics. Racial restrictions were incorporated into law with the passing of the Chinese Exclusion Act in 1882 which restricted Chinese laborers. (See Table 1.2 for major immigration legislation between 1881–1930.)

The first Chinese arrived in the United States in 1847. They were young boys brought for schooling in Massachusetts by a missionary. Between 1860 and 1880, Chinese migrants came to work on the railroads and in mining. Anti-Chinese feelings began to develop in the West as many critics felt that the Chinese were slow to assimilate.

During the 1880s, additional legislation was passed regarding immigrant laborers. The Alien Contract Labor Law of 1885, which barred the importation of contract labor, attempted to end the practice of employers importing large numbers of immigrants. Then in 1888, the Deportation Law authorized the deportation of contract laborers. In 1891, another Immigration Act was passed which increased the list of inadmissible classes to include those having contagious diseases, polygamists, paupers and those guilty of moral turpitude. It also provided for medical inspection of all arrivals and the deportation of illegal aliens. As immigration increased near the turn of the nineteenth century, Ellis Island was established as an immigrant processing center in 1891.

From 1881 to 1920, more than 23 million immigrants arrived in the USA. Much concern was expressed over the number of incoming migrants, the perceived cultural inferiority of these persons, and their ability to assimilate into American Society. A feeling of xenophobia gripped many Americans. Discrimination against Jews, Italians and other Southern and Eastern Europeans became prevalent. Certain American groups fought to restrict open immigration. An Immigration Restriction League was formed in the mid-1890s. Many of its members centered their arguments against immigration on literacy and English-language abilities. Debate and controversy over immigration continued into the early 1900s. In 1903 and 1907 immigration acts were passed which further increased the list of inadmissible classes to include anarchists, beggars, white slavers, epileptics, imbeciles, and those who became insane within five years of entry, together with other categories relating to physical or mental defects.

In 1906, a Naturalization Act was passed making proficiency in English a requirement for citizenship. There was also widespread demand to establish a literacy test as a mechanism to screen migrants. The Dillingham Commission report published in 1911, and totaling 41 volumes, called for restrictions on Eastern and Southern Europeans—feeling that migrants from these areas were quite different religiously, linguistically, and culturally. It also endorsed the literacy test as a way to help stifle immigration of certain undesirable ethnic groups. After several unsuccessful tries, Congress finally succeeded over presidential veto in 1917 in establishing literacy as a basis for entry. Besides establishing a literacy test, the Immigration Act of 1917 also increased its list of inadmissibles to include alcoholics, vagrants, and stowaways; and it continued to affirm exclusion of Chinese laborers and placed further restrictions on Japanese immigration. Restrictions on Japanese immigration had been earlier established by the Gentleman's Agreement established in 1907. Then with World War I, and the period of isolationism in the USA, the Deportation Act was passed which provided for deportation of persons convicted of espionage and wartime offenses. Many Communists were deported as a result of this act.

After passage of the literacy test, a concerted effort was made to Americanize the foreign born. Opinions varied on the success of these programs and many groups called for restrictions or quotas to be placed on immigration. Finally in 1921, Congress passed the Emergency Quota Act. This act established annual quotas principally from European countries and allotted visas to each nationality—usually defined by country of birth—corresponding to the proportion of that group already in the United States. The law permitted immigration from each European country amounting to 3 percent of the corresponding number of foreign-born persons of that nationality living in America at the time of the 1910 census.

A few years later, in 1924, the National Origins act was passed. It became fully effective in 1929. At the time, this was probably the most important piece of immigration legislation passed since 1795. As an interim measure, the Immigration Quota Act of 1924 made adjustments to the 1921 act by using 1890 as the base year and lowering the quota from 3 to 2 percent. It established the annual immigration quota total at 150,000 persons. The result was a larger quota for groups from the British Isles and Northern Europe and smaller quotas for Southern and Eastern Europe. But the act did not place quotas on any nations in the Western Hemisphere. Then, in 1929, when the National Origins Law was put into effect, it tied immigration quotas to nationals living in the United States with the base year being 1920. In summary, this law numerically limited immigrants and attempted to preserve the Anglo-Saxon ethnic composition of the United States.

1931–1960—Immigration Bust

Source of Migrants During the 1930s and continuing until the ending of World War II, the flow of migrants dwindled before increasing during the 1950s. The Depression and World War II, together with federal restrictions were important factors in stemming the migration wave from Europe. It is quite possible that had the quota system not been enacted, that flow of immigrants would have ebbed on its own accord due to the somewhat sluggishness of the American "pull" in the 1920s and the 1930s for unskilled labor, and the weakening "push" factors which had previously caused many persons to leave Europe.

Because all these factors were at play, the number of migrants entering the United States between 1931 and 1960 was 4,078,949. The annual average declined to 135,965 a year. Since no quota restrictions were placed on Western Hemisphere nations, the proportion of migrants from this area increased dramatically. For example, between 1931 and 1940, 528,431 persons immigrated to the United States—30.2 percent were from the Western Hemisphere nations. Canada and Newfoundland accounted for the largest portion of this figure—20.5 percent, and Latin America for 9.7 percent. It should also be noted however, that Germany accounted for 21.6 percent, the highest of any country during this decade.

Between 1941 and 1950, migration from Latin America amounted to 17.7 percent. Canada and Newfoundland accounted for 16.6 percent, for a total of 34.3 percent from the Western Hemisphere. Germany accounted for 21.9 percent and Great Britain 12.7 percent. Because of the quota acts, it is evident that the sources of immigrants dramatically shifted back to Northern and Western Europe and the Western Hemisphere nations.

After the war, the migration pace quickened and a total of more than 2.5 million migrated to the USA between 1951 and 1960. The Western Hemisphere led the way with 39.6 percent of the total immigration, Latin America contributed 24.6 percent of that total, with the majority coming from Mexico and the West Indies. Germany contributed 19 percent, Great Britain 7.8 percent, and Italy 7.4 percent. Thus, between 1931 and 1960 data reflect a shift back to Northern and Western Europe and a sharp decline from Southern and Eastern Europe. Migrants from Northern and Western Europe amounted to 39.8 percent, 20.9 percent from Latin

America, 16.5 percent from Southern and Eastern Europe, and 16.1 percent from Northern America (Fig. 1.3). Since the quota acts did not affect the Western Hemisphere nations, an active recruitment of Mexican workers gained momentum during the 1920s and later in the '40s and '50s before burgeoning in the '60s and '70s. As early as 1918 the USA government exempted Mexicans from normal immigration requirements such as the literacy test, the prohibition on contract labor, and the head tax. This decision obviously increased the active recruitment of Mexican workers, and helped to explain the increase from the United States' neighbor south of the border.

To be sure, in addition to the active recruitment of Mexican workers, and with the cut-off of a labor supply from Europe due to World War I and the quota acts, a move also was made by Northern manufacturers to recruit blacks from the South to help fill the void vacated by a dwindling labor supply from Europe. These variables were important "pull" factors emanating in the North. Identifiable "push" factors in the South encouraging black migration were the mechanization of farms, changes in the managerial techniques of cotton production, the boll weevil, and a series of bad crop years. The earlier passage of Jim Crow laws, and other forms of segregation, discrimination, and injustices helped to contribute to the first large wave of blacks from the South to the North during the period from 1915 to 1925. While 89.7 percent of the black population resided in the South in 1900, it dropped to 77 percent in 1940. Then with the second wave of blacks migrating North after World War II, the percentage of blacks in the South dropped to 60 percent by 1960.

1961–1980—Immigration Boom

Source of Migrants. During these two decades, countries in Latin America and Asia provided the major source of migrants to the United States. Between 1961 and 1970, 3,321,677 persons entered the USA. Of these, 39.2 percent were from Latin America, 17.7 percent from Northern and Western Europe, 16.1 from Southern and Eastern Europe (includes the U.S.S.R.), 12.9 percent from Asia, and 12.4 percent from North America. They entered at annual numbers of 332,167 during the decade of the 1960s. From 1971 through 1979, 3,962,675 persons entered the USA, or 440,297 annually. Of these, 39.2 percent were from Latin America, 34.3 percent from Asia, 11.8 percent from Southern and Eastern Europe, and 6.5 percent from Northern and Western Europe. Although Latin American nations had the largest percentage, the 1970s can be viewed as the Asian decade since migrants from Asian countries increased from 12.9 percent to 34.5 percent during the 1960s and 1970s. From 1971 through 1979, slightly more than 1.5 million persons from Latin America entered the USA. Of this number,

approximately 41 percent were from the West Indies and 37 percent from Mexico. With regard to Asia in 1979, five countries accounted for 72 percent of the Asian immigrants. In rank order they included the Philippines (41,300), Korea (29,248), China and Taiwan (24,264), Vietnam (22,546) and India (19,708).

In summary, between 1961 and 1979, 7,284,352 persons entered the USA at an average of 383,387 persons per year (Fig. 1.3). The period was dominated by immigration from Latin American (39.2%) and Asian (24.5%) nations.

Immigration Policy Since 1930. The National Origins Act, together with the Great Depression, actually resulted in a net migration loss in the USA, when emigration exceeded immigration in 1932 at the height of the depression. The rise in the percentage of immigrants from Northern and Western Europe increased significantly from 1921 through 1950, although the total number of immigrants dropped drastically. World War II affected the USA in many ways, and immigration policy changes were affected as a result of the war. For example, with a shortage of labor in the U.S. during World War II, the U.S. enacted the bracero program in 1942. This program provided for the entry of temporary workers from Mexico, Belize (British Honduras), Barbados, and Jamaica. Because of our relationship with China in World War II, the Chinese Exclusion Laws were repealed in 1943.

Following the war the problem of refugees and war brides became critical. Congress passed the War Brides Act in 1946 permitting immigration of foreign-born spouses and children of armed services personnel. Then in 1948, President Truman was very influential in getting Congress to pass the Displaced Persons Act. More than 700,000 refugees and displaced persons from Germany and other European nations entered the USA during this four year program. The problem of refugees and displaced persons continued into the 1950s. After the expiration of the Displaced Persons Act, Congress passed the Refugee Relief Act in 1953 and 214,000 persons were admitted. Many were from Eastern Europe.

The major piece of legislation passed in the 1950s, the most important act to affect immigration since the National Origins Act in 1924, was the Immigration and Nationality Act of 1952, amended in that same year by the McCarran-Walter Act. The early 1950s when this act was passed, it was the era of McCarthyism, and there was much concern over Communist expansion. This anxiety concerning Communism dominated American thought.

The acts referred to above preserved the national origins quota and established a system of preferences for skilled workers. They also encouraged the strengthening of family ties by giving preference to relatives of USA citizens. A numerical limitation of 150,000 was placed on immigration from the Eastern Hemisphere, but the Western Hemisphere remained unrestricted except for a few colonies and dependent areas. These laws also addressed two groups of refugees that were eligible to come into the United States under regular immigration procedures. First, they permitted the entry of those from "any Communist or Communist-dominated country or from any country within the general area of the Middle East. . . ."[7] Secondly, they eliminated the clause excluding Japanese as immigrants and established a small quota for persons in the Asia-Pacific triangle. They also instituted the "parole" clause. In emergency situations, the "parole" clause authorized the Attorney General to admit persons temporarily for "emergent reasons." However, special legislation was required to grant immigration status to those so "paroled." The "parole" clause was used to admit more than 30,000 Hungarian refugees between 1956 and 1958, more than 650,000 anti-Castro Cubans in the early 1960s and over 100,000 in the late 1970s, Czechoslovakians in 1968, Chileans after 1973, more than 221,900 Indochinese as of mid-1979 following the fall of Ho Chi Minh City (Saigon) in 1975. In 1979, President Carter set the number of Indochinese to be paroled at 14,000 per month.

The problem of refugees continued to plague the USA, and the Refugee-Escapee Act of 1957 was passed to aid escapees from Communists countries and the Middle East. Then in 1960, Congress passed the Refugee Fair Share Law, a temporary program to aid in the admission of World War II refugees still remaining in camps.

One of the most recent major changes in USA immigration policy came with the passage of the Immigration and Nationality Amendments Act of 1965. The Civil Rights movement of the 1960s helped Americans and Congressional leaders to rethink the discriminatory national origins quota system. Also, concern over increased immigration from Latin America, particularly Mexico, together with a widening awareness of the worldwide "population explosion," helped to usher in a new immigration policy. This act accomplished several goals. It abolished the National Origins Quota System and replaced it by establishing numerical restrictions and a "preference system" emphasizing family reunification, needed professions, and skilled and unskilled workers in demand in the USA. An annual ceiling of 170,000 was established for the Eastern Hemisphere with no more than 20,000 a year from any one country. The ceiling for the Western Hemisphere was set at 120,000 a year on a first-come, first served basis, and no numerical limitations were placed on any one country. It should also be noted that the U.S. ended the bracero program in 1964, and that the Immigration Act of 1965 did not apply the preference system to Western Hemisphere nations.

In 1976, Congress limited the number of migrants from any Western Hemisphere nation to 20,000 and extended the "preference system" to Canada and Latin America. This action affected Mexico deeply since it had been supplying as much as 60 percent of the Western Hemisphere's ceiling of 120,000. Two years later, Congress enacted a Worldwide Ceiling Law. It set the ceiling at 290,000 annually and maintained the seven-category preference system. In addition to the preference system, some individuals are classified as "Special Immigrants" and are admitted without numerical limitation. These include such persons as those who were once citizens of the USA but now desire reacquisition of citizenship, or an employee of the USA Government abroad who desires to come to the United States.

In 1980, Congress again addressed itself to the refugee problem and passed the Refugee Act of 1980. The Act increased the "normal flow" of refugees from 17,400 to 50,000 a year. The bill also provided for "exceptional admissions" and mass admissions on an emergency basis. Should the quota of 50,000 need be exceeded, the Secretary of State and Attorney General are to advise the President of such action. The President is then to consult with Congress about the number of admissions necessary above the 50,000 quota. It also broadened the definition of a refugee to include persons other than those in a Communist or Communist dominated country or from the general area of the Middle East, and reduced the average ceiling of immigrants to 270,000. Under the 270,000 numerical limitation, the preference system is listed in Table 1.3.

TABLE 1.3 U.S. Immigration Preference System

First Preference: 20 percent or 54,000 of the total to be allocated to unmarried sons or daughters of citizens of the United States.

Second Preference: 26 percent or 70,000 to spouses and unmarried sons or daughters of permanent resident aliens.*

Third Preference: 10 percent or 27,000 to members of the professions of exceptional ability and their spouses and children.

Fourth Preference: 10 percent or 27,000 to the married sons or daughters of citizens of the United States, their spouses and children.*

Fifth Preference: 24 percent or 64,800 to brothers or sisters of citizens of the United States (at least 21 years of age) and their spouses and children.*

Sixth Preference: 10 percent to skilled or unskilled occupations in which laborers are in short supply, plus their spouses and children.

Non-preference: Other qualified applicants.**

---

*Numbers not used in higher preferences may be used in these categories.

**Any numbers not used in preferences 2, 4, or 5.

Source: *U.S. Immigration Policy and the National Interest,* Staff Report of the Select Commission of Immigration and Refugee Policy, April 30, 1981, p. 372.

As we look toward the end of the twentieth century it becomes evident that additional immigration laws will be passed as needs or events warrant them. There are still many unanswered problems needing attention. Proposals have been offered but none enacted upon regarding the flow of "illegal aliens" or the so called "undocumented workers." What should be done about the illegals already here? Do adjustments need to be made to raise or lower the numerical restrictions? Many questions such as these must be answered. But, the basic question remains, how to establish just and fair laws that can be enforced consistently and humanely.

Summary: 1821–1980

The heavy immigration from Germany and Northwestern Europe is evident from 1821 to 1880. From 1881 to 1920, Southern and Eastern Europe predominated. Beginning in the 1920s and extending to 1980, immigrants from the Western Hemisphere became numerous. Although the number of immigrants during the 1920s is quite high from the Western Hemisphere because of the lack of quotas, most were from Canada and Newfoundland. During the 1930s, '40s and '50s, migrants continued to come from the Western Hemisphere and immigrants from Northwestern Europe accounted for a larger percentage than at anytime since 1900. Since 1960, however, Latin American countries have comprised the bulk of immigration from the Western Hemisphere. The rise of migrants from Asia since 1960 together with the decline from Europe is the other quite obvious trend.

IMMIGRANTS BY TYPES OF ADMISSION

It should be noted that the Immigration and Naturalization Service of the United States breaks down its immigration statistics between new arrivals and those seeking adjustments to their status (Table 1.4). An immigrant is an alien admitted for permanent residence in the U.S. In 1979, 460,348 persons were admitted as immigrants, of which 279,478 were subject to numerical limitations, and 180,870 were exempt from them. Of those subjected to numerical limitations, 232,112 were "new arrivals," and another 99,635 "new arrivals" were exempted. In addition, 47,366 were already in the USA and had adjusted or changed their status to that of immigrant, but were subject to the numerical limitations. Another 81,235 persons changed their status but were exempt from numerical limitations. Therefore, of the 460,348 immigrants admitted into the U.S. in 1979, 331,747 were new arrivals, and 128,601 entered by adjusting their status. Table 1.4 gives the totals for the years 1971 through 1979.

In chronicling the immigration trends to the USA, most of the discussion and statistics given have been for *immigrants* or *permanent resident aliens* who, after arriving in the USA are eligible for citizenship in five years. Some of these immigrants have come under numerical limitations, and some have been exempt. All have been admitted legally, however, with the intention of residing in the USA and becoming citizens. *Nonimmigrant aliens* are persons who came to the USA for a temporary period. They may be tourists, business travelers, students, or temporary workers. However,

TABLE 1.4 Immigrants Admitted, by Type of Admission, Fiscal Years 1971–1979

Fiscal Year	Immigrants Admitted			New Arrivals			Adjustments of Status		
	Total	Subject to Numerical Limitations	Exempt from Numerical Limitations	Total	Subject to Numerical Limitations	Exempt from Numerical Limitations	Total	Subject to Numerical Limitations	Exempt from Numerical Limitations
1971	370,478	280,626	89,852	297,153	225,010	72,143	73,325	55,616	17,709
1972	384,685	283,666	101,019	295,504	220,420	75,084	89,181	63,246	25,935
1973	400,063	282,911	117,152	309,299	220,108	89,191	90,764	62,803	27,961
1974	394,861	274,131	120,730	318,763	224,447	94,316	76,098	49,684	26,414
1975	386,194	281,561	104,633	311,906	227,183	84,723	74,288	54,378	19,910
1976	398,613	284,773	113,840	316,632	226,667	89,965	81,981	58,106	23,875
1976 TQ*	103,676	72,511	31,165	84,082	59,113	24,969	19,594	13,398	6,196
1977	462,315	276,500	185,815	332,487	242,121	90,366	129,828	34,379	95,449
1978	601,442	341,104	260,338	371,029	281,900	89,129	230,413	59,204	171,209
1979	460,348	279,478	180,870	331,747	232,112	99,635	128,601	47,366	81,235

Source: *1979 Statistical Yearbook of the Immigration and Naturalization Service,* (Washington, D.C.: Government Printing Office, 1982), Table 2. *Transition quarter (TQ) for 1976, includes the 3-month period, July–September.

some of these nonimmigrant aliens, such as college students, may wish to change their classification from nonimmigrant to immigrant after entering the USA. As was shown in Table 1.4, several persons each year make these adjustments. The total number of immigrants admitted however, does not reflect the total number of persons entering the USA because it deletes *refugees*—persons admitted because of persecution for racial, political, or religious reasons. These migrants are admitted conditionally but are eligible to adjust their status to *permanent resident alien* after one year. Also, the figure does not include *asylees* who are defined the same way as refugees except for the fact they have not first been processed as refugees in some other country. When the total figures for Gross Immigration for the United States are assembled, they are much higher than when just immigrants are listed. Between 1976 and 1979 therefore, more than 2 million immigrants entered the USA, but an additional 222,000 were admitted as refugees and special entrants thereby increasing the total to more than 2.2 million (Fig. 1.4). The year 1980 was an exceptionally high year when it is estimated that 808,000 entered the USA—441,000 as immigrants and 367,000 as refugees. The estimated total for 1981 declined to 697,000 but still approximately 217,000 of this number entered as refugees—all legally.

Besides the problem of refugees, there is the issue of undocumented or illegal aliens who come to the U.S. without documents, enter illegally, or overstay the specified time of their nonimmigrant visa. Because many underdeveloped countries are confronted with economic, social and political problems, and because migration quotas from these countries are in effect in the United States, many persons decide to enter illegally. The number of illegal aliens currently residing in the United States is not known, but estimates place the figure between 6 and 10 million, and maybe as high as 12 million.

Mexico is the source nation that most authorities say accounts for many of the illegals. For example, of the 875,915 illegal aliens apprehended in 1976, 89 percent were from Mexico. Figure 1.5 plots the historical trend in Mexican migration since 1943. The establishment and termination of the bracero program is evident in the rise and decline of legal temporary workers. The number of legal immigrants is basically in accordance with Western Hemisphere ceilings that have been in effect since 1965. However, two distinct peak periods of undocumented apprehensions are evident—the early 1950s and the middle and late 1970s. Some authorities believe that 1 million or so Mexicans annually enter the U.S. illegally. The problem of illegal entry from Mexico and elsewhere continues to plague the U.S. as Congress and the President seek solutions.

DEMOGRAPHIC CHARACTERISTICS OF IMMIGRANTS

Besides national origin and number, the composition of immigrants is also significant. In the period 1975–1979, 47 percent of the entering immigrants were male, a sharp contrast to the first decade of this century when men accounted for 70 percent.[8] The median age of the immigrants has been increasing slightly during the past twenty-five years. In the 1975–1979 period the median age for males was 26.1, and 26.3 for females.[9] During this same period, ". . .49.4 percent of male immigrants and 54.7 percent of female immigrants were married"—and 60.7 percent of all women immigrants were of child-bearing age (15 through 44).[10]

"Between 1975 and 1979, an average of 60 percent of those coming into the country reported that they were either housewives or children, or they reported no occupation."[11] Of those who reported occupations, 31.6 percent were professional and managerial, 13.2 percent were clerical and sales workers, 11.7 percent were crafts workers, 24.9 percent were other blue collar, 13.7 percent were service, and 4.8 percent were farm workers.[12] The more stringent labor requirements of the 1965 Amendments Act is thought to be the major factor in contributing to the increase in the percentage of professional and skilled workers.

Immigrants can usually match the salary of native born Americans within 11 to 15 years after arrival, and in some cases, the figure may be as low as 6 to 10 years.[13] Most studies show that immigrants go through an initial period of disadvantage followed by upward mobility which is equal to or surpasses native born. However, it is much more difficult for refugees than the average immigrant to achieve salary parity in such a short period of time. Some refugees do achieve successful careers; some do not.

In a survey conducted in 1979, 30.4 percent of native born Americans had college degrees, 56.6 percent had high school diplomas, 12.5 percent had one through eight years of education, and only 0.5 percent had no education. For foreign born, 27 percent had a college degree, 38.9 percent had a high school education, 30.8 percent had one through eight years, and 3.3 percent had no education.[14]

PORTS OF ENTRY AND STATES OF INTENDED PERMANENT RESIDENCE

In 1978, of those migrants coming into the United States, 43 percent entered Atlantic Coast ports, 24 percent entered Pacific Coast ports, 16 percent entered via Mexican Border cities, 10 percent entered through the Canadian Border cities, 3 percent through ports bordering the Gulf of Mexico, and 4 percent came through

U.S. GROSS IMMIGRATION: 1976 - 1981

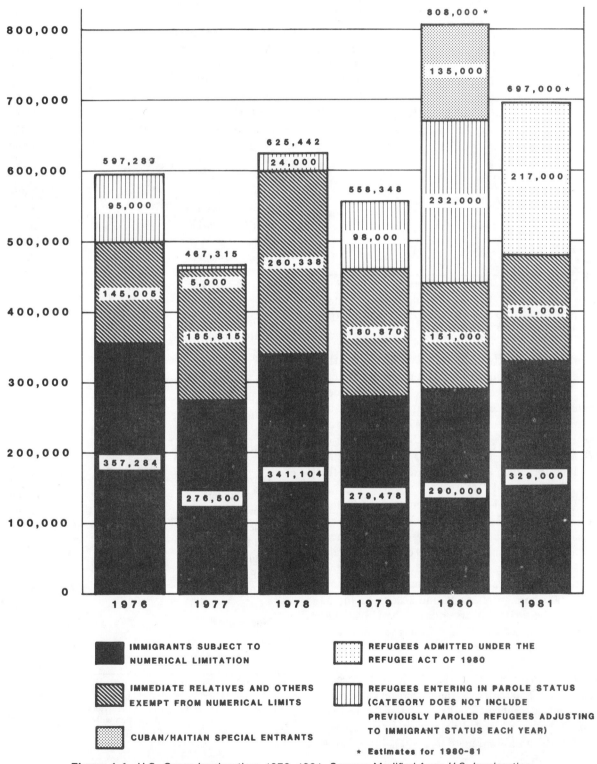

Figure 1.4. U.S. Gross Immigration: 1976–1981. Source: Modified from *U.S. Immigration Policy and the National Interest,* 1981; and *1979 Statistical Yearbook of the Immigration and Naturalization Service.*

13

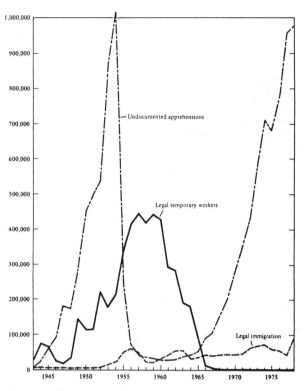

MEXICAN MIGRATION TO THE UNITED STATES
1943-1978

Undocumented apprehensions

Legal temporary workers

Legal immigration

Figure 1.5. Mexican Migration to the United States 1943-1978. Source: *U.S. Immigration Policy and the National Interest,* 1981; p. 471.

TABLE 1.5 Immigrants Admitted by Port: 1978

All Ports	*601,442*
Atlantic	259,099*
Atlanta, GA	5,547
Boston, MA	14,544
Charleston, SC	1,412
Hartford, CT	3,158
McGuire, AFB, NJ	1,061
Miami, FL	47,085
Newark, NJ	13,119
New York, NY	140,668
Norfolk, VA	1,106
Philadelphia, PA	8,489
San Juan, PR	6,464
Virgin Islands	2,586
Washington, DC	11,388
Gulf of Mexico	19,632
Houston, TX	7,608
New Orleans, LA	8,729
San Antonio, TX	3,094
Pacific	142,889
Agana, Guam	2,790
Honolulu, HI	50,997
Los Angeles, CA	45,387
Portland, OR	2,897
San Francisco, CA	27,912
Seattle, WA	12,599
Alaska	3,699
Anchorage	3,678
Canadian Border	58,223
Blaine, WA	2,031
Buffalo, NY	3,643
Champlain, NY	4,383
Chicago, IL	22,937
Cleveland, OH	2,296
Detroit, MI	8,314
Mexican Border	95,049
Brownsville, TX	1,599
Calexico, CA	4,766
Del Rio, TX	1,146
Eagle Pass, TX	2,463
El Paso, TX	14,598
Hidalgo, TX	2,563
Laredo, TX	9,801
Nogales, AR	1,069
San Luis, AR	1,137
San Ysidro, CA	32,649

Alaska and other ports. New York City was by far the leading port city accounting for 23.4 percent of the entrants. The other three leading ports of entry included Honolulu at 8.5 percent, Newark at 7.8 percent and Los Angeles at 7.5 percent. Thus, 47.2 percent of all immigrants in 1978 entered the U.S. via four major ports. Statistics also show that these were the leading port cities for much of the immigration during the 1970s. (Table 1.5 and Fig. 1.6).

In 1978, when 601,442 persons entered the United States, California (24%) and New York (17%) were the leading states where immigrants sought permanent residence. The remaining nine states of Texas, Florida, Illinois, New Jersey, Massachusetts, Pennsylvania, Virginia, Michigan and Washington admitted more than 10,000 immigrants each, and accounted for 33 percent of the total numbers entering the USA. Thus 11 states accounted for 77 percent of the immigrants seeking permanent residence.

In those 11 states, 60 percent of the immigrants chose to live in cities of more than 100,000, 39 percent chose cities of 2,500 to 99,999, and 1 percent chose rural areas. Table 1.6 reflects the 11 top states (more than 10,000 immigrants) and their respective cities (over 100,000) which received more than 1,000 immigrants.

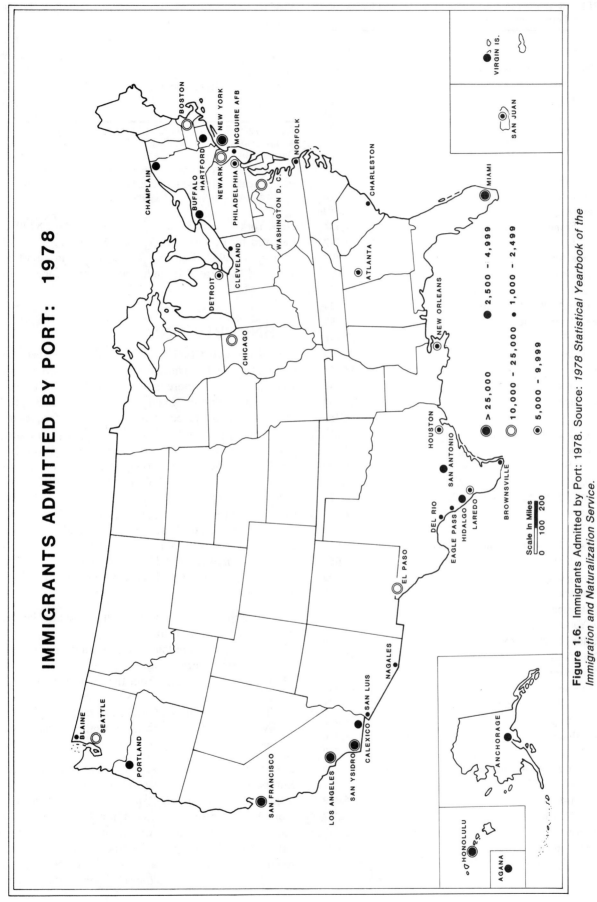

Figure 1.6. Immigrants Admitted by Port: 1978. Source: *1978 Statistical Yearbook of the Immigration and Naturalization Service.*

TABLE 1.6 Immigrants Admitted by State[1] and Cities[2] of Intended Permanent Residence: 1978

California	146,061
Under 2,500 Inhabitants	2,660
Anaheim	1,124
Fresno	1,652
Glendale	1,434
Long Beach	1,929
Los Angeles	28,141
Oakland	2,094
Pasadena	1,255
Sacramento	1,616
San Diego	8,180
San Francisco	11,434
San Jose	4,272
Santa Ana	2,202
Stockton	1,001
Florida	39,428
Under 2,500 Inhabitants	24
Fort Lauderdale	1,098
Miami	23,176
Tampa	1,509
Illinois	33,638
Under 2,500 Inhabitants	46
Chicago	20,932
Massachusetts	16,383
Under 2,500 Inhabitants	17
Boston	2,313
New Bedford	1,080
Michigan	11,520
Under 2,500 Inhabitants	21
Detroit	2,166
New Jersey	32,973
Under 2,500 Inhabitants	536
Elizabeth	2,084
Jersey City	2,205
Newark	3,172
Patterson	1,868
New York	100,542
Under 2,500 Inhabitants	56
New York	87,981
Rochester	1,168
Pennsylvania	15,342
Under 2,500 Inhabitants	91
Philadelphia	4,432
Pittsburgh	1,306
Texas	46,752
Under 2,500 Inhabitants	176
Dallas	3,811
El Paso	5,819
Fort Worth	1,292
Houston	12,418
San Antonio	3,093
Virginia	11,596
Under 2,500 Inhabitants	74
Alexandria	1,135
Arlington	1,599
Washington	10,952
Under 2,500 Inhabitants	31
Seattle	3,956

Source: *1978 Statistical Yearbook of the Immigration and Naturalization Service* (Washington, D.C.: Government Printing Office, 1980).
[1]Includes only states receiving more than 10,000 immigrants.
[2]Includes cities of more than 100,000 in population size which admitted more than 1,000 immigrants.

New York City received the largest number; 87,981, followed by Los Angeles 28,141, Miami, 23,176 and Chicago, 20,932. Figure 1.7 reflects the immigrants admitted by state of intended permanent residence in 1978.

ETHNIC REGIONS

It is estimated that more than 49 million persons immigrated to the United States between 1820 and 1979, and millions more have entered illegally. It is evident that much mixing and acculturation of these peoples have taken place. This mixing has frequently caused many persons to think of America as a "melting pot." This may not be an accurate term, however. Instead, the United States' ethnic mix might be likened to a "tossed salad"—each group reflecting distinctiveness; yet having overall cohesiveness within American society. Even so, there is an overall "glue" or "salad dressing" that holds American society and its culture together. The processes accounting for the ". . . massive transformation of Old World elements into the singular American compound" have been summarized best by Zelinsky.[15]

1. The importation of selected individuals and, hence, selected cultural traits.
2. The simple fact of long-distance transfer of people and their cultural freight.
3. Cultural borrowings from the aboriginal populations.
4. The local evolution of American culture.
5. A continuing interchange with other parts of the world.

In general terms, the sequence of migration within Europe ". . . moved steadily outward in wavelike fashion through time and space from a hearth area around the North Sea toward the north, east, and south, ..."[16] "A mirror image of the migratory impulse in the European subcontinent was the spatial zonation of ethnic groups in the United States and Canada, especially within the rural population."[17] The

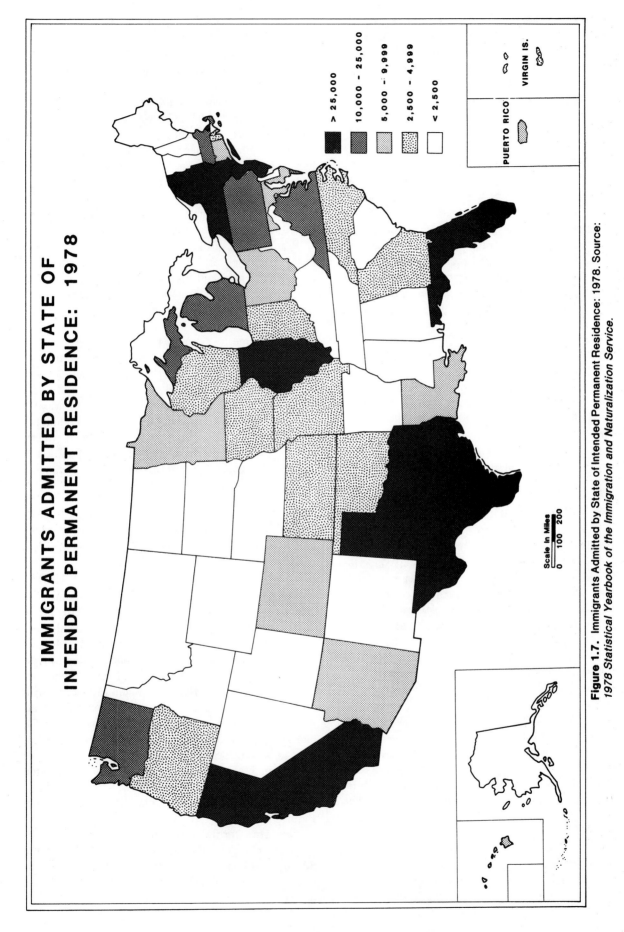

IMMIGRANTS ADMITTED BY STATE OF INTENDED PERMANENT RESIDENCE: 1978

> 25,000
10,000 – 25,000
5,000 – 9,999
2,500 – 4,999
< 2,500

PUERTO RICO

VIRGIN IS.

Scale in Miles

0   100   200

Figure 1.7. Immigrants Admitted by State of Intended Permanent Residence: 1978. Source: *1978 Statistical Yearbook of the Immigration and Naturalization Service.*

early arrivals in the 17th, 18th, and early part of the 19th centuries tended to settle in the East. The later arrivals in the 1800s and early 1900s tended to seek opportunities in the central and western third of the USA, in addition to cities in the East. For example, many Germans settled in the upper Mid-West, Scandinavians and Russians in the North-Central states, Italians in California and Nevada, and various Slavic groups on the Great Plains and in the Northwest. As the frontier moved westward, and immigrant groups moved with the frontier, change occurred in the size of ethnic blocs. Initially in New England and the South, however, these areas were rather homogeneous in ethnic composition. Later, as settlements developed in the Middle West, rural immigrant blocs emerged together with distinct ethnic neighborhoods in the urban centers. Finally, in the Far West, large rural blocs of a single European ethnic group are rather rare, and group dominance within the city seldom extends beyond a residential block.[18] In recent years, however, large urban populations of Asians and Latin Americans have become characteristic of many southwestern cities.

There is also a distance-decay effect. The importance of relative proximity when examining the settlement of specific immigrant groups is best exemplified by the Hispanics of the American Southwest, the early concentrations of the Chinese and Japanese on the West Coast, and the Cubans in Florida.[19]

Environmental affinity is another variable that may help to explain the settlement patterns of some groups. For example, Scandinavians are concentrated in the North-Central states, the Italians and Armenians in the Central Valley of California, the Dutch farmers in the polderizing of the Michigan marshland, the Vietnamese in the Gulf Coastal regions, Greek sponge-divers in the Tampa area, black population in areas earlier marked by the plantation system, and Cornish miners in southwestern Wisconsin. All of these examples are highly generalized, but serve to provide some examples of environmental affinity.[20]

What is obvious, is that some groups have tended to cluster whereas others have mixed and internalized more for a variety of different reasons. This pattern becomes more evident when one examines the spatial distribution and regional concentration of some groups in America. There are specific core areas or regions where particular ethnic groups are clearly identifiable. Some form broad generalized geographic areas; some form rural or urban islands. These pockets of ethnic distinctiveness are readily visible and distinguishable. The blacks form a sizeable number in the Southeast; Mexicans in the Southwest; Native Americans in Oklahoma, the Four Corners area of Colorado, Utah, Arizona and New Mexico, and the Northern Plains and Rocky Mountain areas; Chinese and Japanese on the West Coast; Filipinos, Asian Indians, Koreans, Vietnamese, Puerto Ricans in the urban cities of the North, principally New York and Chicago; Scandinavians in the Upper Mid-West; the Germans and Slavics in the Northeastern cities along with the Italians; Jews on the eastern Seaboard; and French in New England, Michigan, and Louisiana.

In 1980, there were 24,488,218 blacks in the United States. Of these, 14,041,379 were in the South.[21] The largest number of blacks is in New York state with 2,401,842. Eleven other states have more than 1 million blacks. The nation is 11.7 percent black, and five states are greater than 25 percent black. These include Mississippi (35.2%), South Carolina (30.4%), Louisiana (29.4%), Georgia (26.8%), and Alabama (25.6%) (Figs. 1.8 and 1.9).

Persons of Spanish origin[22] are largely concentrated in the Southwest and in the states of New York, Illinois, New Jersey, and Florida. Most Mexican-Americans reside in the Southwest, whereas Puerto Ricans predominate in New York and New Jersey, and Cubans in Florida (Fig. 1.10).

Native Americans totaled 1,361,869 in 1980, with 49 percent of them residing in the West. Six states contained more than one-half of the Native American population. These included California (198,095), Oklahoma (169,297), Arizona (152,610), New Mexico (104,634), North Carolina (64,519), and Washington (58,159) (Fig. 1.11). Percentagewise, Native Americans had the highest proportion of total population in New Mexico (8.0%), North Dakota (6.5%), Oklahoma (5.6%), Arizona (5.6%), and Alaska (5.5%).

A total of 3,500,636 Asian and Pacific Islanders are presently in the United States. Of the 806,027 Chinese,[23] more than half are in California (322,340) and New York (148,104) (Fig. 1.12). Filipinos comprise 774,640 persons, and reside primarily in California (357,514) and Hawaii (133,964) (Fig. 1.13).

More than 70 percent of the 700,747 Japanese reside in California (261,817) and Hawaii (239,618). The Asian Indians appear to be a little more evenly spatially distributed. This population totals 361,544 persons. Of this number, 60,511 are concentrated in New York, 57,989 in California, 35,711 in Illinois, and 29,507 in New Jersey. Koreans amount to 354,529, with approximately one-half of these being located in California (103,891), New York (34,157), Illinois (23,980), and Maryland (15,087). The 261,714 Vietnamese appear to be quite scattered spatially. Eleven states have more than 5,000, but more than 50 percent are located in the four states of California (89,587), Texas (29,112), Louisiana (10,877), and Virginia (10,000) as shown in Figures 1.14, 1.15, 1.16 and 1.17.

Core areas for five major minority groups are summarized in Figure 1.18. Blacks predominate in the Southeast, Mexican Americans in the Southwest, Native Americans in the West, and Chinese and Japanese on the West Coast.

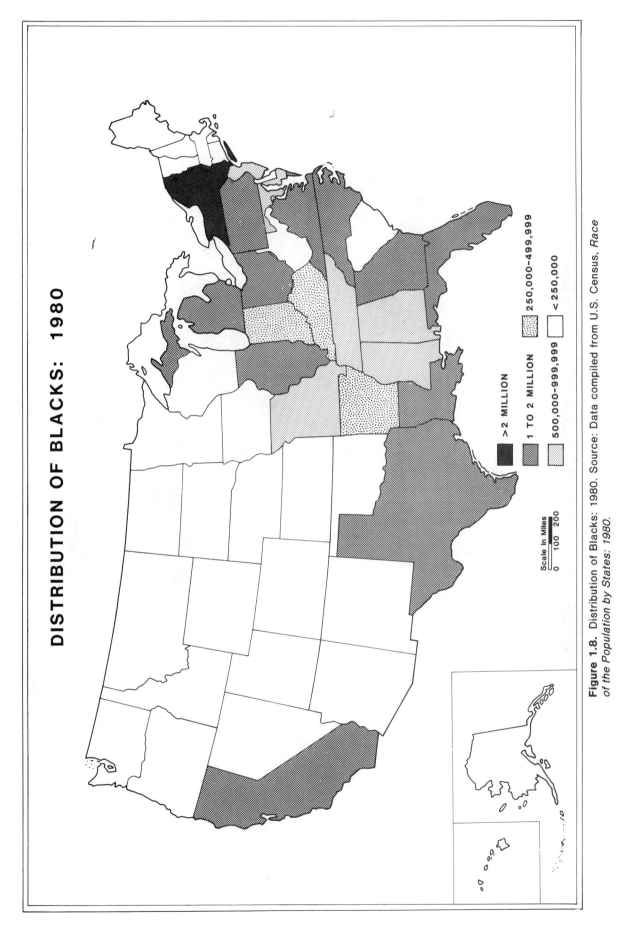

DISTRIBUTION OF BLACKS: 1980

> 2 MILLION

1 TO 2 MILLION

500,000-999,999

250,000-499,999

< 250,000

Scale In Miles

0   100   200

Figure 1.8. Distribution of Blacks: 1980. Source: Data compiled from U.S. Census, *Race of the Population by States: 1980.*

19

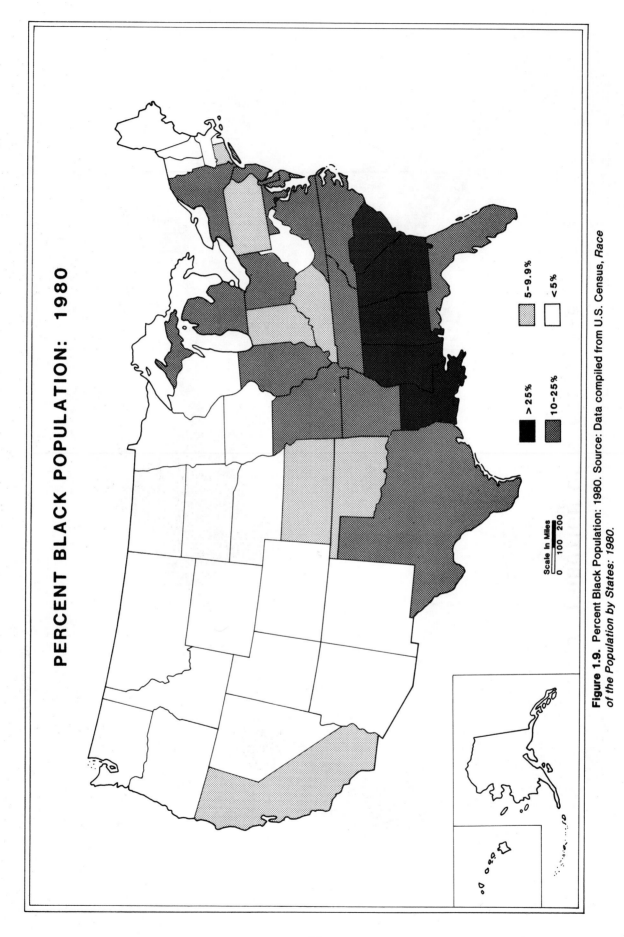

PERCENT BLACK POPULATION: 1980

> 25%

10-25%

5-9.9%

< 5%

Scale In Miles
0   100   200

Figure 1.9. Percent Black Population: 1980. Source: Data compiled from U.S. Census, *Race of the Population by States: 1980.*

DISTRIBUTION OF PERSONS OF SPANISH ORIGIN: 1980

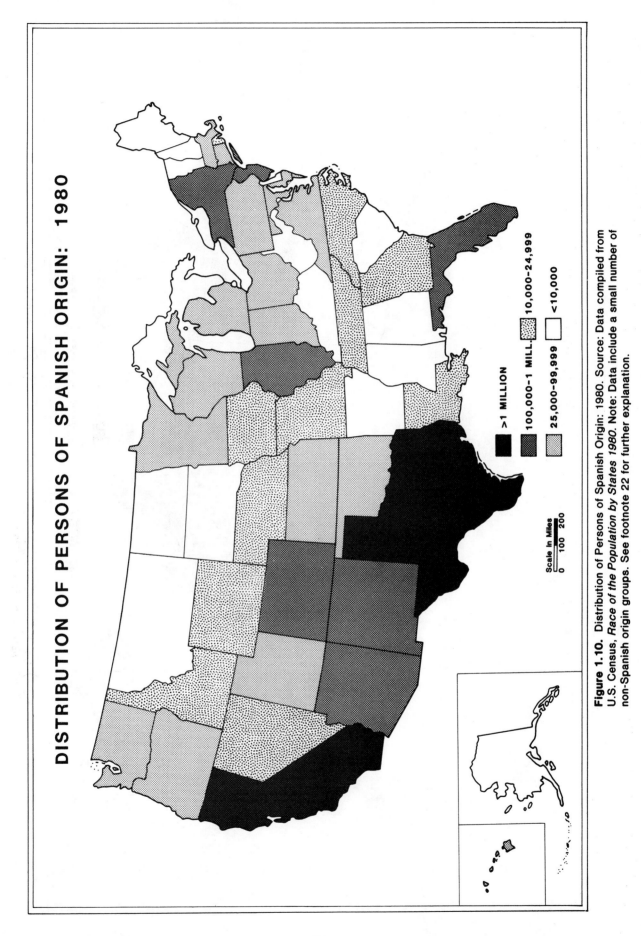

Figure 1.10. Distribution of Persons of Spanish Origin: 1980. Source: Data compiled from U.S. Census, *Race of the Population by States 1980.* Note: Data include a small number of non-Spanish origin groups. See footnote 22 for further explanation.

DISTRIBUTION OF NATIVE AMERICANS: 1980

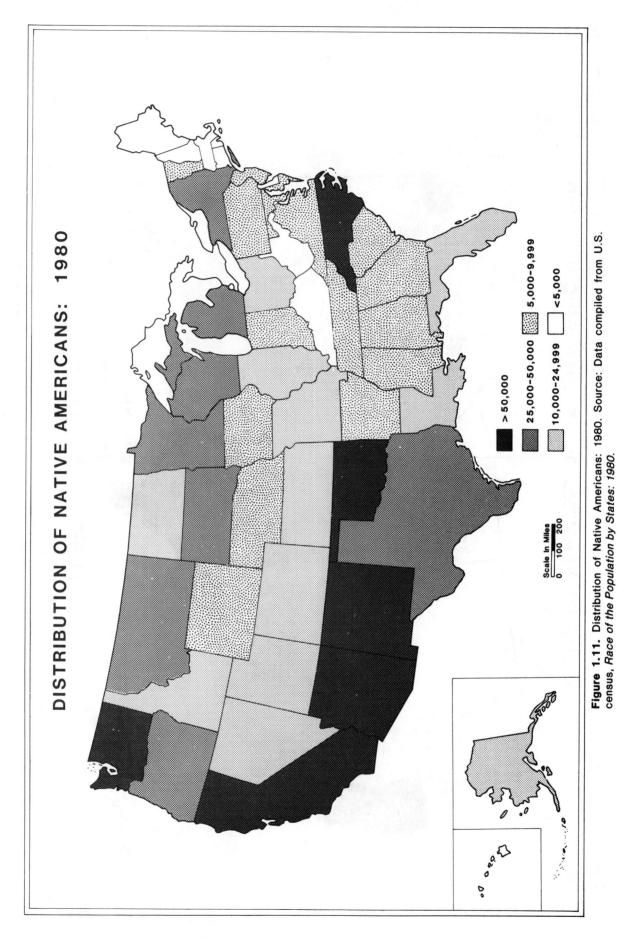

Figure 1.11. Distribution of Native Americans: 1980. Source: Data compiled from U.S. census, *Race of the Population by States: 1980.*

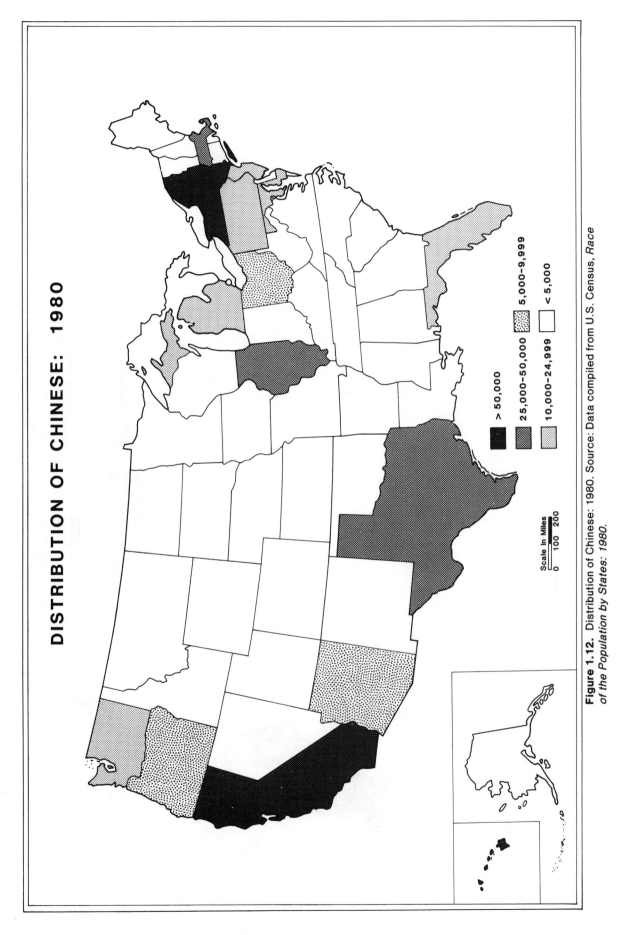

Figure 1.12. Distribution of Chinese: 1980. Source: Data compiled from U.S. Census, *Race of the Population by States: 1980.*

23

DISTRIBUTION OF FILIPINOS: 1980

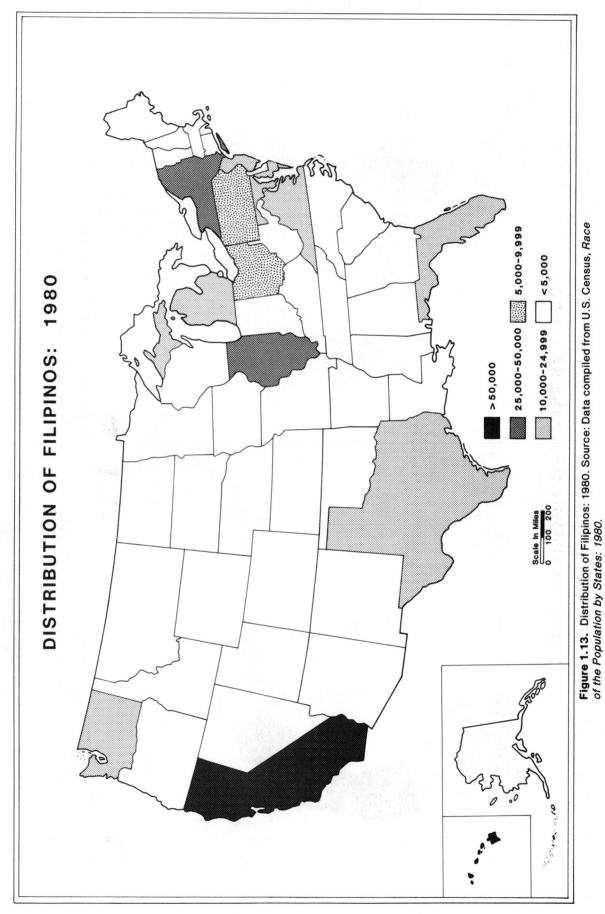

Figure 1.13. Distribution of Filipinos: 1980. Source: Data compiled from U.S. Census, *Race of the Population by States: 1980.*

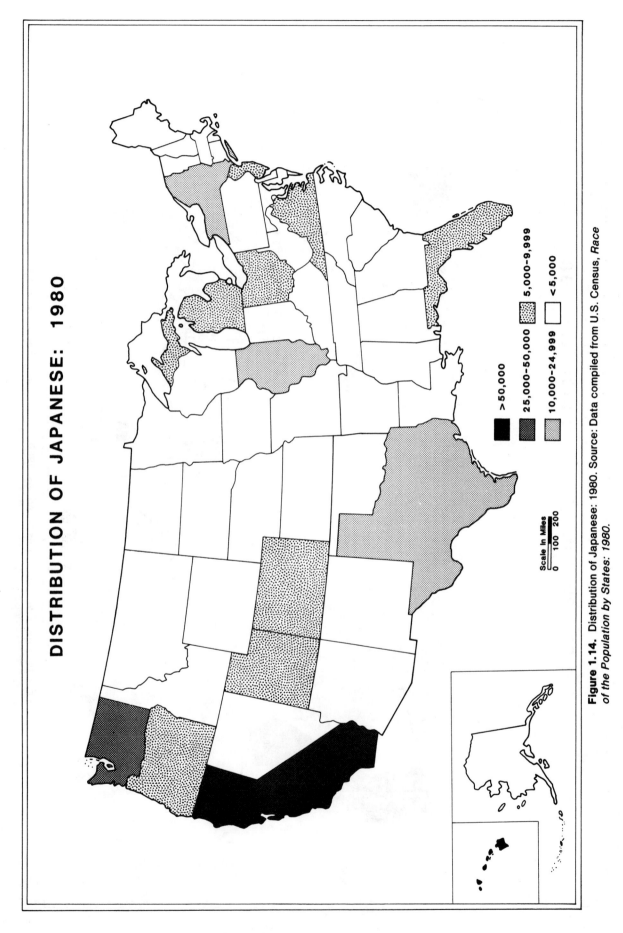

DISTRIBUTION OF JAPANESE: 1980

Scale in Miles
0   100   200

>50,000

25,000-50,000

10,000-24,999

5,000-9,999

<5,000

Figure 1.14. Distribution of Japanese: 1980. Source: Data compiled from U.S. Census, *Race of the Population by States: 1980.*

25

DISTRIBUTION OF ASIAN INDIANS: 1980

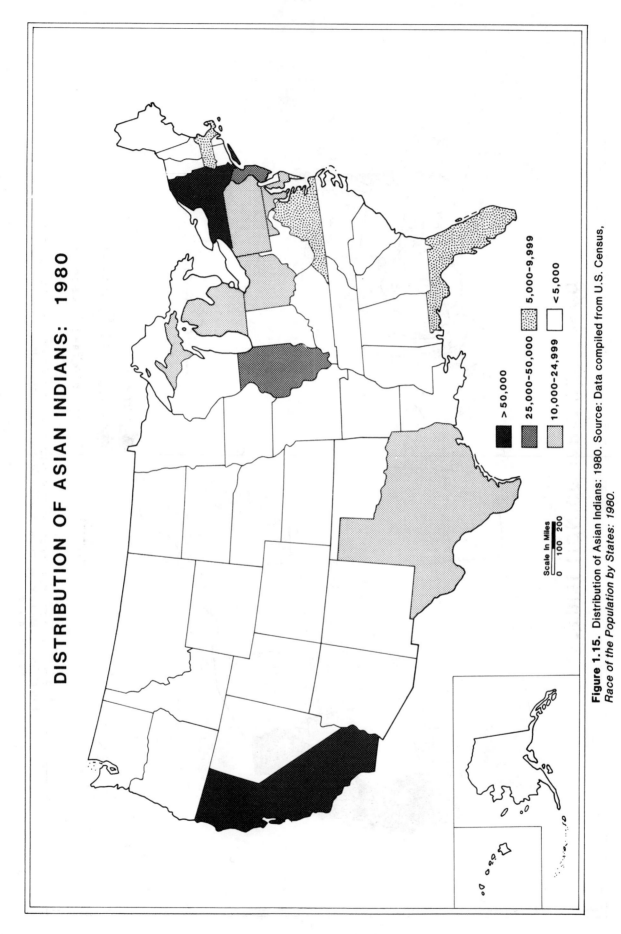

> 50,000

25,000–50,000

10,000–24,999

5,000–9,999

< 5,000

Scale In Miles
0   100   200

Figure 1.15. Distribution of Asian Indians: 1980. Source: Data compiled from U.S. Census, *Race of the Population by States: 1980.*

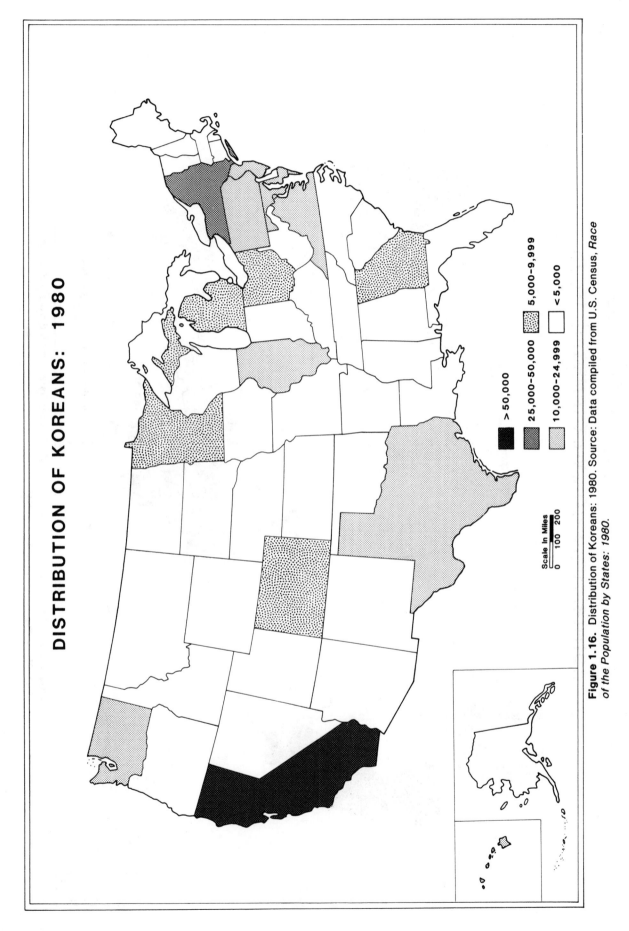

DISTRIBUTION OF KOREANS: 1980

Legend:
- > 50,000
- 25,000–50,000
- 10,000–24,999
- 5,000–9,999
- < 5,000

Scale In Miles
0 100 200

Figure 1.16. Distribution of Koreans: 1980. Source: Data compiled from U.S. Census, *Race of the Population by States: 1980.*

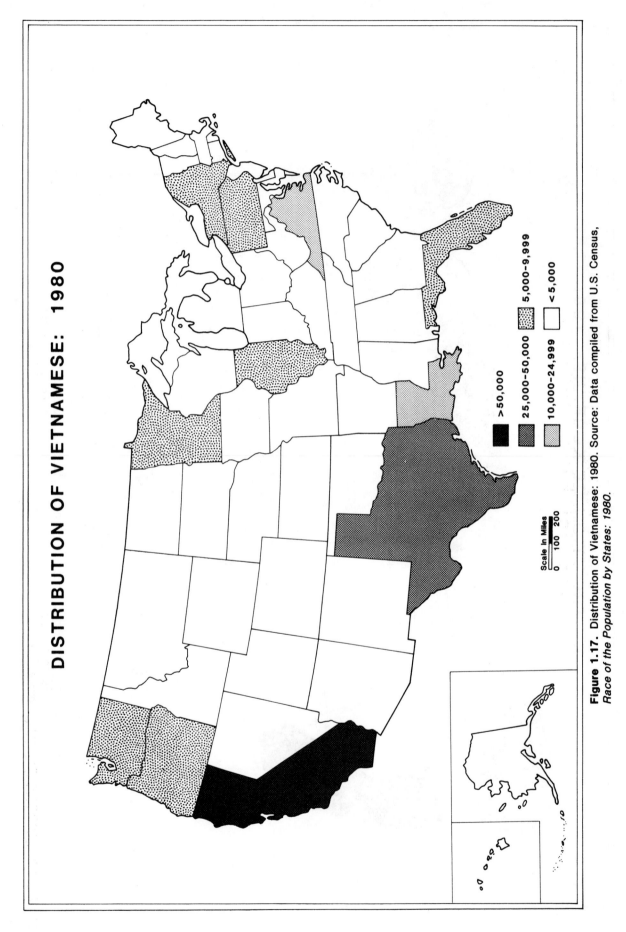

DISTRIBUTION OF VIETNAMESE: 1980

>50,000

25,000–50,000

10,000–24,999

5,000–9,999

<5,000

Scale in Miles
0   100   200

Figure 1.17. Distribution of Vietnamese: 1980. Source: Data compiled from U.S. Census, *Race of the Population by States: 1980.*

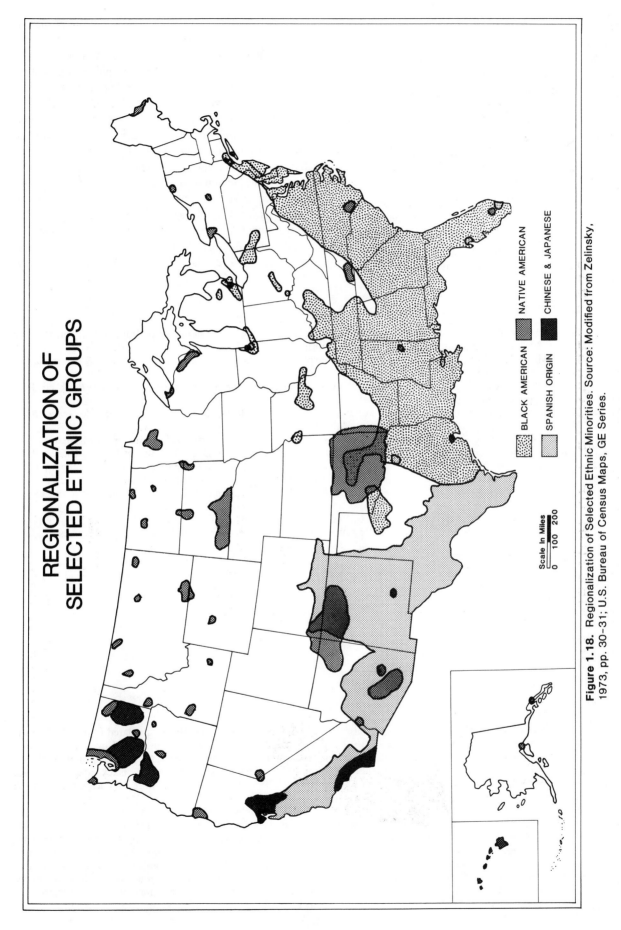

Figure 1.18. Regionalization of Selected Ethnic Minorities. Source: Modified from Zelinsky, 1973, pp. 30-31; U.S. Bureau of Census Maps, GE Series.

REGIONALIZATION OF
SELECTED ETHNIC GROUPS

NATIVE AMERICAN

CHINESE & JAPANESE

BLACK AMERICAN

SPANISH ORIGIN

Scale in Miles

0   100   200

CONCLUSION

It is evident from the information in this chapter that the USA is a "nation of immigrants," including Native Americans. Their origin can be traced to early migrations across the Bering Strait. That the USA is primarily an off-spring of Northwest European culture does not distract from the fact that many other ethnic groups have contributed cultural traits which have assisted in establishing a truly distinctive "American" culture. Admittingly, the adoption of southern and eastern European cultural traits and the acceptance of these European ethnic groups into American society have been easier than for many non-European people and their cultures. For many non-European and non-white people, discrimination, prejudice, ethnocentricism, and even violence have occurred in the USA despite democratic ideals that have led to the reduction of ethnic and racial tensions.

The flow of immigrants to the USA is closely connected to the nation's immigration policy. The Quota Act in 1921, the National Origins Act in 1924, the Immigration and Nationality Act of 1952, and the Immigration and Nationality Act Amendments of 1965 have been major immigration legislative acts. But the USA immigration policy presently needs major overhauling. The current Immigration Reform and Control Act of 1982, introduced by Senator Alan Simpson and Representative Romano Mazzoli, focuses on such key issues as legal immigration, illegal immigration, employer sanctions, and legalization of illegal aliens already in the USA. If passed by Congress and the President, this legislation will be the major act which will direct USA immigration policy in the 1980s.

NOTES

1. *U.S. Immigration Policy and the National Interest,* Staff Report of the Select Commission of Immigration and Refugee Policy, April 30, 1981 (Washington, D.C.: Government Printing Office): p. 237.
2. Richard A. Morrill, O. Fred Donaldson, "Geographical Perspectives on the History of Black America," 48 *Economic Geography* (January, 1972): p. 1.
3. John H. Franklin, "A Brief History of the Negro in the United States," in *The American Negro Reference Book,* ed. John P. Davis, (Englewood Cliffs, N.J.: Prentice Hall, 1966): p. 8.
4. Karl E. Taeuber, Alma F. Taeuber, "The Negro Population in the United States," in *The American Negro Reference Book* ed. John P. Davis, (Englewood Cliffs, N.J.: Prentice Hall, 1966): p. 100.
5. All immigration data, unless otherwise noted, were taken directly or calculated from U.S. Department of Justice, *1978 Statistical Yearbook of the Immigration and Naturalization Service* (Washington, D.C.: Government Printing Office, 1980). U.S. Department of Justice, *1979 Statistical Yearbook of the Immigration and Naturalization Service* (Washington, D.C.: Government Printing Office, 1982). U.S. Department of Commerce, Bureau of the Census, *Historical Statistics of the United States, Colonial Times to 1970, Bicentennial Edition,* 2 Vols. (Washington, D.C.: Government Printing Office, 1975).
6. Wilbur Zelinsky, *The Cultural Geography of the United States* (Englewood Cliffs: Prentice Hall, Inc., 1973): p. 32.
7. "Humanity on the Move" in *Great Decisions* 1980, ed. Wallace Irvin, Jr., (New York, New York: Foreign Policy Association, 1980): p. 53.
8. *U.S. Immigration Policy:* pp. 229–230.
9. Ibid.: p. 232.
10. Ibid.
11. Ibid.: p. 233.
12. Ibid.: p. 234.
13. Ibid.: pp. 249–250.
14. Ibid.: p. 260.
15. Zelinsky: pp. 5–9.
16. Ibid.: pp. 25–26.
17. Ibid.: p. 26.
18. Ibid.
19. Ibid.: p. 29.
20. Ibid.
21. Data on the 1980 distribution of ethnic groups discussed in this section are taken directly or calculated from U.S. Department of Commerce, Bureau of the Census, *Race of the Population by States: 1980* (Washington, D.C.: Government Printing Office, 1981). 1980 was a year the census concentrated on gathering detailed data on racial groups, and the data gathered on race for 1980 is classified slightly different than it was in the 1970 census. Basically in 1980, the black category includes black Americans, but it also includes such persons who categorized themselves as black but were Jamaican, black Puerto Rican, West Indian, Haitian, or Nigerian.
22. In the 1970 census, many persons of Spanish origin were included in the "white" category. However, in the 1980 census, persons listing themselves as Cuban, Puerto Rican (white), Mexican, or Dominican were included in the "Other" category. However, a problem does exist in that the "Other" category may also include such non-Spanish origin groups who were not listed as black, American Indian, Eskimo and Aleut, or as an Asian and Pacific Islander (this category includes only Chinese, Filipino, Japanese, Asian Indian, Korean, Vietnamese, Hawaiian, Samoan or Guamian). Non-Spanish origin groups may include such groups as Cambodian, Laotian, Pakistani, and Fiji Islander that were not given a separate category under Asian and Pacific Islander and are therefore listed under "Other." Thus, the "Other" category includes predominantly persons of Spanish origin but other small groups of non-Spanish origin are also included in the "Other" category.
23. Includes Taiwanese and Cantonese.

2

The Native American

James M. Goodman
University of Oklahoma

INTRODUCTION:

The Original Americans

The inhabitants of the Americas prior to the arrival of Europeans in the late 15th Century are the ancestors of today's Native Americans—they were the *Original Americans*. In the beginning, these natives of the New World were a majority group numbering, perhaps as many as 80 to 100 million on the twin continents of North and South America. In the nearly 500 years that have followed the initial European contact, Native Americans have been reduced in rank to one of the smallest of the American minorities. They constituted only 0.6 percent of the total 1980 population of the United States.

The original Americans occupied lands that now form the conterminous United States and Alaska. Most of their descendants are now either intermingled with non-Indians in urbanized landscapes, or reside on reservations. These reservations represent about 2.5 percent of the national land area. Those places where notable numbers of Native Americans live are not uniformly distributed within the nation. The modern distribution of Indian people reflects historical patterns of national growth of the United States and federal government policies that were developed to deal with its aboriginal inhabitants.

A Minority With Minorities

Native Americans are, in a modern sense, a minority within minorities. Although once the dominant population of Western Hemisphere, disease, war, famine, and interracial mixing have reduced their numbers and diluted the purity of bloodlines. Various demographic studies estimate populations of the pre-Columbian United States at 900,000 to 4,000,000 people. The 1980 Census of Population lists 1,418,195 American Indians, Eskimos, and Aleuts. It may be concluded then that, despite the high birth rate among Indian people, drastic population reductions between the time of initial European contact and the present

have resulted in a populace that is about the same size now as it was 500 years ago. Native American populations now appear to be growing at a relatively rapid rate. When compared to other racial and ethnic minorities, however, the Native American ranks a distant fourth after Hispanics, Blacks, and Asians. The Native American represents only one of every forty persons classified as an American minority!

The unavoidable and most devastating impact of the peopling of the New World by Europeans was the introduction of diseases to which the Native Americans had no resistance. Smallpox, malaria, typhus fever, yellow fever, syphilis, measles, hookworm, and dysentery swept rapidly through segments of Indian populations reducing their numbers alarmingly. Whole villages died; large regions lost as much as 75 percent of their populations. S. F. Cook estimated that the Indians of the northern San Joaquin Valley of California lost about three fourths of their population between 1830 and 1850 due to epidemics, starvation, and exposure produced in part by warfare with non-Indians.

The impacts of epidemics were reinforced by endemic diseases that slowly debilitated their victims. In some areas the result was a gradual reduction in population. These diseases, such as tuberculosis, diabetes, diarrhea, and hyperglycemia, offset the growth potential from high birth rates by reducing life expectancy. High infant mortality rates have always been common, and continue to be so on many Indian reservations. Although most of the endemic diseases are controlled today, the social stresses of modern life make the Native American particularly susceptible to alcohol and drug related problems.

A reversal of population trends has come with the introduction of extensive health care and improved sanitary conditions. Diet changes have also helped. In addition, the intermarriage of Indians between tribes and between races has strengthened the genetic pool; however, at the same time it has diluted the cultural roots of each tribe. Only those Indian tribes with sizeable numbers in relatively homogeneous demographic environments can hope to achieve an increased tribal population growth. Many Native American tribal elements have disappeared, or will disappear, as their numbers and the integrity of the bloodlines diminish.

Uniqueness of the Native American Minority Group

The Native American minority group has a number of characteristics that make it distinct and unique among other minority groups in the United States. Native Americans, even 500 years after Columbian contact, retain a certain cultural character that separates them from mainstream American society: retention of non-European languages, behavioral and religious traits that are of non-Old World origins, and ecological-land use principles that are non-Anglo American in practice.

Native Americans display great diversity in languages. Around 150 different Indian languages are spoken at the present. There were probably more than 200 in pre-Columbian times. Communication between Anglo Americans, the dominant single language majority, and the numerous Indian groups, with their complex oral (unwritten) languages has always been difficult. Throughout the years this poor communication has resulted in faulty understanding of the social and cultural characteristics of both groups. The lack of communication between Indian groups has contributed in part to the lack of a unified resistance to non-Indian aggressions in territorial expansion in the Americas. Furthermore, the rather small numbers of Native American peoples speaking some of the less common languages meant that ethnic survival has been precarious. Indeed many groups have become extinct.

Native American religious beliefs were not compatible with the Christian ethics of European settlers. As a result Indians were frequently treated as "savages" who challenged the missionary zeal of the encroaching frontier of an expanding nation. This missionary fervor resulted in religion playing a great role in an effort to reshape the culture and social outlook of the Native Americans—in fact, a remarkable role in a nation based on the separation of church and state. The pressure to Christianize the Indian undoubtedly resulted in the disintegration of native religious identity and contributed to the demise of some Indian cultures.

The early Native Americans were settled widely over a land that provided them with a rich resource base. They subsisted in a vast variety of physical environments. Some of the people maintained fixed settlements in well defined areas; other engaged in seasonal migrations within larger areas. This way of life was shattered as non-Indian America crowded in about them pushing them into smaller and smaller land areas. Relocation frequently saw Indian people removed to areas with environments they were unfamiliar with and

did not understand. The communal use of land is a common principle among Indian groups and differs greatly from the land use practices of Anglo Americans. Individual ownership of land and the title to land are foreign ideas to the Indian, and the failure of non-Indians to understand or accept this principle resulted in loss of tribal lands. Many Native Americans were bilked out of lands that were legally assigned to them; many tribes were forced onto reservations. Those on reservations were placed in a special relationship with the federal government—a relationship that even today sets them aside as a unique communal landed minority.

The Geographer's View of the Native American

The geographer is concerned with interactions between natural and human entities over the earth's surface. These interactions provide a character to areas that allow the geographer to delimit and analyze regions. Regions of unique and homogeneous qualities may then be used as the space within which the perceptions and attitudes of the human inhabitant are studied. The goals, policies, and priorities developed by the governing system of the region that modify the natural environment through resource utilization can be examined as an ecological system.

The study of the Native American within the United States affords the geographer an opportunity to integrate a small, but significant, component of regional landscapes into a larger mosaic—a mosaic that frequently reveals the rich cultural diversity of a nation that also possesses a rich diversity of physical environments. Viewing Native Americans within this context aids those who seek an understanding of today's Indians and their role in American society.

The following sections will consider the origins of the modern Native Americans, the ways in which they lost their original lands, the means which were developed by the federal government to deal with the Indian problem, and the demographic and social-economic character of these people. The nature of modern Indian settlement character will be reviewed, the character of the lands remaining to the Native American will be surveyed, and the nature of their natural resources examined.

THE NATIVE AMERICAN: ORIGINS AND ROLES IN AMERICAN DEVELOPMENT

The people that occupied the American continents before the arrival of Europeans in the 15th Century had a diverse origin. Archaeological, physiological, and linguistical evidence suggest that the Americas were peopled by numerous waves of immigrants from Asia. The migrations probably occurred over thousands of years and the migrants were unlikely to have been from the same racial stock. Physiognomic variation has suggested to some researchers that various stages in the evolution of Mongoloid stock within waves of migration that required long periods of time led to the distinctive physical types within the Native American group. Languages also display the great variety that might result from multiple origins through time and in place. These diversities were to compound the difficulties that Indians and white Americans alike experienced in their attempts at coexistence.

The initial impact of European presence in the new continent was the reduction of Indian populations due to exposure to Old World diseases. This was followed by a loss of lands due to the increasing non-Indian populations that claimed lands as a conquering nation would, and later through treaties that were frequently flawed by the poor comprehension of both parties, but especially because these agreements were concluded in English.

Native Americans utilized most, if not all, of the space that now constitutes the United States, but their recognition of land use rights was totally different than those that the new nation of the United States employed. Individual ownership of specifically defined plots of land was as foreign to most Indians as the communal sharings of parcels of undelimited lands was to most non-Indians. This difference in the philosophy of property rights coupled with a lack of understanding of each others land use concepts led to a series of poorly conceived "agreements" couched in the form of treaties. The treaties drafted as formal documents that registered agreement between nations were frequently misunderstood by both parties. The advantage, of course, went to those with the boldness and technological superiority to enforce their perceptions upon the other. The Native Americans thus saw their numbers, their lands, and their rights reduced as the non-Indian flourished by asserting their treaty gained "rights."

The Development of Indian Lands

The Native American is the only minority that did not become an integral factor in the growth and expansion of the United States. Blacks were imported to sustain economic requirements and, following the Civil War, a liberated but oppressed minority functioned as a sub-culture of the major U.S. society. Mexican and Spanish Americans were absorbed as territorial expansion occurred. Hispanics and Blacks were part of the wave of immigration, whether voluntary or not, and their cultural adaptations have not placed them too far from the majority population. In contrast, the Indian was never a complement to the economic structure of the country, and when their lands were absorbed by territorial expansion they were either relocated to undeveloped lands or confined to reserves of land (reservations) that were administered by the federal government. In the process they were disenfranchised and became wards of the state. Civil rights have always come slowly to minorities; thus, the Indians were first on this land, but they were the last to be given citizenship and voting rights.

Federal and state governments have always displayed ambiguity in their practices of dealing with the *Indian Problem*. This problem is defined here as "those issues concerned with the 'proper', i.e. ethical or moralistic, policies and methods of treating a people who occupy lands that a nation claims for its own." In essence, the problem involves the majority who wish to be fair and of good conscience in their displacement of a people who they generally view as inferior, in need of cultural and social change, or in need of protection. The Indian Problem also involves the notion that the Native American should be integrated into the society at large.

Historically, the Indian Problem involved skirmishes along a frontier that lay very close to all major settlement sites. As the frontier was pushed farther to the west and became more remote to centers of government, the sense of urgency that arose from hostile actions was reduced. Pro-Indian sentiments increased, in a general way, as the distance between Indian settled areas and the centers non-Indian populace increased. At a distance the Native American was sometimes viewed in an idealistic, romantic fashion; on the frontier at near range there were those who viewed Indians as a contemptuous and weak people.

In colonial times, the Native Americans were treated as members of independent states (nations) by several European countries. The British entered into trade agreements and granted individual allotted lands to Indians (in 1633) in the Massachusetts Colony. Land grants were made by the Spanish royalty to Indians; the French treated the Indians as partners in trade. Prior to the American Revolution, the British crown established "reserved lands" for some Indians, and by 1764 developed plans for an Imperial Department of Indian Affairs. Interestingly, concepts of reservations and special government agencies to deal with Indian affairs developed before the United States became a nation.

The northeastern quadrant of the conterminous United States was the scene of complex intrigues between two European colonial powers (France and England), the American colonists, and numerous Indian tribes. Indian tribes allied with either the French or the British in the establishment of trade areas. Frequently intertribal hostilities led to the gain or loss of trade advantages for the European competitors. Eventually, with Indian assistance, the British gained territorial supremacy as the French were expelled from North America. During the American Revolution, Indian tribes along the western frontier of the Colonies were treated with favor by the revolutionaries to prevent them from allying with the British.

Shortly after the American Revolution, the young nation of the United States looked forward to settlement beyond the Appalachian Mountain barrier that had retained its people within the littoral zone for several centuries. The Northwest Ordinance, written in 1787, stated policy toward the Indian as westward expansion started:

> The utmost good faith shall always be observed toward the Indians; their land and property shall never be taken from them without their consent; and in their property, rights and liberty, they shall never be invaded or disturbed unless in just and lawful wars authorized by Congress; but laws founded in justice and humanity shall from time to time be made for preventing wrongs done to them, and for preserving peace and friendship with them.

But, as westward expansion into the Trans-Appalachian west proceeded, Indians were forcibly removed and pushed westward to the prairies west of the Mississippi River where spatial competition arose between the displaced Indian groups. Since Indian groups were numerous and usually not unified in their dealings with the federal government, a consistency in dealing with problems associated with the settlement of non-Indians within Indian territories was never realized. In essence, however, the language of the Northwest Ordinance was ignored and areas were removed from Indian control by military action. In some cases Indians and their lands were absorbed and incorporated in organized territories and populaces. In most instances, Indian groups were moved en masse to another location beyond the path of white settlement.

Prior to 1849, the military branch of the federal government, the War Department, was responsible for Indian affairs. Although interactions between Indians and non-Indians were on a frontier and did at various times involve skirmishes, some of the problems faced involved commerce and education, two areas the military was ill-prepared to handle. Congress created the Department of the Interior in 1849 and Indian affairs were passed to civil control. This event corresponds with the addition of large areas to the western United States through treaties with Great Britain for the Oregon Territory, and with Mexico for a large area of the southwest that became the territories of New Mexico and Utah, and the state of California. At the same time the western half of the 1803 Louisiana Purchase, that is the Great Plains portion, was still unorganized. Thus, by mid-nineteenth century, that section of the country that was eventually to contain most of today's Indian lands (reservations) was passed to civil control. The Department of the Interior from that time on developed the *civilizing* processes and policies that linger in Indian affairs to this day.

Pressure for land in southeastern United States led the Congress to pass into law the Indian Removal Act of 1830. Lands of several southeastern Indian tribes were exchanged for lands west of the Arkansas Territory (organized in 1828) within the Louisiana Purchase. Although several attempts were made to organize pan-Indian resistance to land cession to the expanding United States, none were successful. Thus, by the mid-nineteenth century all the area east of the Mississippi was organized by states. A tier of states, from Iowa southward to Louisiana, along the western edge of the eastern woodlands represented the starting line of the race of American settlers across the grassy plains (the Great American Desert) and the Rocky Mountains, to the gold of California and the lush lands of Oregon.

The scene of Indian affairs within an expanding national territory next shifted away from the wooded landscapes of the American Midwest and South into the country of the wide ranging, mobile plains tribes, the mountain tribes, the Pueblos, the arid, semi-arid nomadic tribes of the Southwest, and the hunters and fishers of the Pacific Coast region. A whole new set of people had to be dealt with! Some were peaceful, others were talented warriors; some were settled in fixed villages, others ranged over sizeable areas; some claimed lands in well watered sites, others lived in arid barren lands. Some tribes were located along the major corridors between departure points in the east and the western destination of white settlers, while others occupied areas that were relatively isolated—remote from non-Indian interests. A major factor in the treatment of the Indian Problem evolved: as the national conscience freted with the treatment of the Indian, space for tribal relocation was diminished. The quality of that space was not capable of supporting the Native American population within an ecological subsistence system of the pre-European (American) period.

The latter half of the Nineteenth Century saw the further reduction of Indian lands as large areas were ceded to the United States by treaty. Indian wars continued throughout much of this time and led the federal government to adopt a policy for the achievement of peace through the restriction of Indians to reservations. The reservation concept was possible because relatively large areas of land, unattractive to non-Indians, were available in the public domain. The reservation provided a means of bringing the Indians into dependency upon the United States because the land area generally would not provide the space and environment for the maintenance of traditional subsistence practices. Thus, the federal government was able to keep the tribes subservient by becoming their major source of food and other life supporting materials. The Indians' resistance to the encroachment of non-Indians upon their lands was broken for many when they became totally dependent upon the United States for their subsistence.

In the closing decades of the 1800's, some reservations were dissolved by the granting of individual land titled to heads of Indian families. This policy, referred to as *allotment,* resulted in further reduction of Indian lands, and continued erosion of the traditional Indian patterns of communal land holdings. Boundaries often meant little to the Indian land owner.

From the very earliest period of contact between Europeans and Native Americans, efforts were made to modify the lifestyles of the Indians. Strong missionary leanings were common among the non-Indians whether English, Spanish, or French. A common goal within the developing social structure of the country was to cause the Indians to abandon their traditional religious views in favor of Christianity. In doing so, the Native Americans were supposed to "rise above their savagery" and to become "useful" citizens. One way this could be accomplished, according to policy makers, was to have the Indians become farmers, thus tying them to a place and occupying their time. Many Indians were, of course, successful farmers well before allotment practices were initiated, but many had never engaged in these activities. To give them a parcel of land, a plow, and a sack of seeds was no guarantee of their becoming "useful citizens"; in fact, it was a sure way to further disaster for many.

In 1924, Native Americans, in recognition of their service to the nation during World War I, were granted United States citizenship—the final minority group to achieve this status. At about the same time the Meriam Report, a study by the Brookings Institute of the "Indian condition" as of the 1920s, was published. This study initiated many policy changes in the 1930s, especially the passage of the Indian Reorganization Act of 1934 (IRA). As a result, allotment policies that had reduced tribal land holdings some sixty percent, from 140 million acres in 1887 to fifty-two million acres in 1932, were eliminated. Procedures were developed to allow tribes a representative form of government, rather than permitting the appointment of tribal leaders by the Bureau of Indian Affairs. Investigations were set in motion that collected information on Native American culture and social conditions in the hope that there would be a more rational approach toward the improvement of the Indians' poor economic, health, and social conditions.

Just as the 1930s and 1940s were times of gain for Native Americans, the post World War II decade of the 1950s saw attempts to reduce Indian land holdings by termination of reservations and the encouragement of Indian people, especially young and middle-aged adults, to relocate from their rural reservations and small towns to metropolitan areas where greater opportunities for employment existed. These actions, initiated by the United States Congress, may have represented the frustrations of government officials to the long period of the Roosevelt administration's efforts to improve the Indian condition—efforts that

seemed to display few tangible results despite sizeable expenditures of funds and bureaucratic reorganization. Legislative reactions to these frustrations removed 1.5 million acres of land from reservation status and tried to move 11,500 Native Americans into the American mainstream as "full tax paying citizens." However, the termination of some federal reservations, such as the Menominee Reservation in Wisconsin, worked major hardships on county and state governments. Reluctantly the federal government, which had hoped to be free of these responsibilities, reentered the scene by providing financial assistance to the states.

In retrospect, the complete reversal of federal Indian policy that occurred between the 1920s and 1930s, and the series of legislative acts in the 1950s and 1960s demonstrate the convulsions of public conscience to the Indian problems that have plagued Indian treatment from the beginning of European settlement of the Americas. Just as the Meriam Report noted the failure of allotments and led to legislative reform in the Indian Reorganization Act, the carrying forth of this law was closely monitored by a later Congress that viewed the IRA as "communistic" and "antireligionistic."

By 1970, Congress had rejected termination and, in doing so, the Menominee Indians were restored as a tribe. Indian people were returned to a condition more favorable to survival of their cultural-traditions by the passage of the Indian Self-Determination and Educational Assistance Act of 1975.

The concepts of termination and assimilation that were so widely accepted in the 1950s have from time to time in the 1970s resurfaced. These concepts, which are so widely opposed by Native Americans, offer a solution to the Indian Problem that would result in the loss of cultural and political identity that has nourished an American minority through centuries of severe trials. In addition, termination and assimilation violate a special relationship between Indians and the federal government that has evolved through many centuries. The government of the United States has pledged itself to ensure certain standards among the Indians in health and education, and to assist them in the improvement of social and economic conditions.

The shifts in federal policy from Congress to Congress has stymied a smooth, gradual progress toward a betterment of the Indian Problem. Given the nature of the problem, a solution may always be elusive. But, therein lies one of the major traits of a minority; a trait which may be tremendous point of pride, a strength that sustains a cultural-ethnic identity.

Native Americans today are much better educated than their predecessors. Communication problems are not nearly so common as those that their ancestors faced. Numerous men and women who are well respected and strong spokesmen for their people are recognized today. Although progress remains to be made in many areas, the Native American is well represented and has become a visible minority.

On the other hand, Native Americans are plagued by high unemployment, low educational attainment, low standards of living, and numerous social problems related to their position between traditional cultural character and a modern American lifestyle. Indians are still subject to racial and cultural prejudices. Resentment toward their "special relationship" to the federal government strongly influences political stances and attitudes of the general public. The Native American is too often viewed in stereotypical romanticism as a person who communes with nature in simple surroundings. The same view suggests to some that the person is not industrious, and is content to live as a welfare recipient. These prejudices translate too frequently as "inferior" and "unequal."

A Land-based Minority

Native Americans have a strong cognizance of their relationship to the land. Current demographic patterns, however, indicate that the Indian has belatedly joined in the mainstream American's drift to the city. Strong attachments, nonetheless, bind them to environments that display much lower levels of human modification. Since the Indian has advanced very rapidly from a low technology form of subsistence into an urban-industrial age, they generally retain that sentimental and emotional attachment to their place of their origin.

Just as the settlement patterns of the Native American of the past have been related to federal policies related to reservations, relocations, and allotment of individually owned parcels of land, so too is the current trend of rural to urban movement of people. The federal government initiated a series of programs in the 1950s that were designed to provide employment and residences for Indians in urban areas. In part the programs were designed to create economic improvement, but to many Indian people it was a sinister ploy to terminate federal reservations. The immediate net outcome of the program was positive in relatively few cases. The return migration of Native Americans was great; social adjustment problems and a general lack of support systems produced by a generally unenlightened planning had severe impact upon many of the persons involved.

Attempts at relocation, in part, arose from the economic conditions of the Native American. As late as 1970, the average family income on reservations was $4,326, and more than half of these family incomes were classed as being below the poverty threshold. Unemployment rates remain extremely high on reservations, and most housing is inadequate by non-Indian standards. The attraction to the urban area is then one of economic improvement.

The disrupting effect of World War II on the populace of the United States, following a decade of economic and social despair, initiated a trend of rural to urban migration for many segments of population including American Indian. Early results of this migration were not favorable for those who participated in the shift. Older Indians, often returned to the reservations because urban job opportunity favored younger persons. Those who remained in the new environments found themselves exploited by landlords. They lived in poverty neighborhoods and mingled with other minority groups in overcrowded conditions that were worse than those they had left behind on the reservation. Help from the Bureau of Indian Affairs was lacking in the preparation of Native Americans for employment in the cities. Jobs that were entered by early participants were those that allowed no opportunity for advancement.

Regardless of the many problems associated with adaptation to an urban area, the trend continues and a greater number of individuals succeed in the rehabitation each year. Central to the improvement of this rate of success is an ever improving network of support factors for Indians within the cities. Indian centers now provide a means of economic and cultural support, and Indian communities within the urban complex provide a basis for emotional support. But, education, health, and housing support for new urban Indian population has not been fully developed. Until these new support bases are developed the Native American will continue to have problems with this type of massive rehabilitation of an ethnic group that represents a third world environment within the United States.

DEMOGRAPHIC AND ECONOMIC PROFILES

Statistics on Native American populations are not reliable. There has been no commonly accepted definition of "Indian". Census data collected by enumerators suffered either because many Indians do not speak English, or many Indians are never located to be interviewed. Data collected by mail are frequently missed because the addressee is not literate. Invariably, demographic and socio-economic information differs from source to source.

Despite problems of reliability, some general pattern can be detected with regard to the distribution of modern Native Americans and their social and economic condition. The general population may be divided into three groups: urban, reservation, and non-urban/non-reservation. About half of the total 1980 Indian population of 1,200,425 are urban residents. Most of these urban dwellers are located in the metropolitan areas of Los Angeles, Tulsa, Oklahoma City, San Francisco and Oakland, and Phoenix. These urban locations agree closely with the states that have the largest Indian populations: California (17 percent of USA total), Oklahoma (14 percent), and Arizona (13 percent). The population of reservations constitutes between twenty-five and thirty percent of the total. The remaining twenty to twenty-five percent of the population is settled in communities or on rural, non-reservation sites. These figures, however, do not reveal that many of the non-reservation dwellers maintain a strong and continuing contact with the reservation or with their former home sites that may have been on allotted land, and hence former reservation sites. Native Americans generally have a much stronger place identity and sense of place than non-Indians.

Current information on a number of social and economic characteristics of the Native American is generally unavailable. However, by examining figures collected during the past decade, the following general statements can be made:

1. Incomes for Native Americans are significantly lower than the U.S. population at large—the median income may be half that of the total populace.
2. Life expectancy has increased sharply since the establishment of the Indian Health Service in 1955, but remains lower than any other population group in the United States.
3. Native Americans as a group are undereducated. Only sixty-three percent of Indian men finish grade school, thirty-four percent high school, and four percent college (for the same time total USA figures were, respectively, 73%, 54%, and 13%). Indian women were about one percent higher in the first two categories and one percent lower at the college level.
4. Unemployment rates run two to four times greater among Indians than the total population. Unemployment, in recent years, on some reservations has exceeded fifty percent.
5. Rural Indians, reservation and non-reservation, live in a high degree of poverty. In the 1970s 14 percent lived in crowded housing, 67 percent of these houses were without running water, 48 percent without toilets, and 32 percent of the occupants were without transportation. For the total USA rural population the figures are, respectively, 10%, 9%, 14% and 12%.
6. Rural Indian women face the greatest difficulty. Widowed, divorced, and aged women usually live in tragic poverty especially if abandoned by the family support system of their offspring.

It would be improper to suggest that all Native Americans fit the socioeconomic traits just listed. Some elements of the Indian population have achieved a typical USA lifestyle, hold responsible jobs, and are inconspicuous in their daily routines. Many have entered professions and serve as role models for Indian youth. But the process of transition into an effective role within the predominant Anglo-American society, while retaining cultural elements of their heritage, has made the path of the Native American slow and difficult.

DISTRIBUTION OF NATIVE AMERICANS

The Native American is a minority within minorities. The United States Census of 1980 counts one Indian for every 167 other persons. Of the 166 non-Indians, 139 are Whites, 20 are blacks, and 3 are Asians and Pacific Islanders. Of the total 1980 Native American population 96 percent are identified as American Indian, 3 percent as Eskimo, and 1 percent as Aleut. Between 1970 and 1980 the Native American population count rose from 827,268 to 1,418,195. The group's percentage share between the same two census counts increased from 0.4 percent to 0.6 percent of the total population, hardly a major gain in percentage points, but an indication that there is growth and a higher degree of recognition (some demographers believe that the Native American has been undercounted in pre-1980 censuses).

Some Native Americans live in each of the fifty States. Their distribution is not uniform; five States—all within the southern tier of States—contain about one-half the total population. In rank order these States are: California (first), Oklahoma, Arizona, New Mexico, and North Carolina. The top four of these States plus Texas (ninth in total population) emphasizes the major concentration of Indian people in the southwestern quadrant of the United States. A northern fragmented tier of States contains almost a fifth of the total population. Alaska, with its large Eskimo and Aleut population has just less than five percent. The remaining States all have less than 2.5 percent each of the total Native American population.

From a historical perspective, Native American populations have changed quantitatively and spatially. As previously noted disease and warfare initially reduced the numbers of Indians and later, relocation policies and practices gradually shifted the Indian to the western portions of the country. In the past several decades, Indian populations have increased, but Indian settlements remained concentrated in the western portions of the country. Importantly, however, these patterns of settlement show a shift from the rural West to the urban West.

In the decade beginning with 1950 the number of Indians living in rural settings dropped below 75 percent. By 1980 the number of urban Indians (53 percent) exceeded the number living in communities less than 2,500 and other non-urban settings. The notion that Indians live in the wilderness has not been true for many years. In the following sections, three questions will be addressed: Where is the Indian today? In what kind of environment does the Indian live? What are the trends in Indian settlements?

The Current Distribution of Native Americans.

Where are Native Americans located today? The 1980 population census of the United States, at the time of this writing, remains incomplete, but a view of the distribution of Native Americans can be presented on a state by state basis.

For purposes of the 1980 census, Native American populations are subdivided into three groups: American Indians, Eskimos, and Aleuts. American Indians form 96 percent of the total Native American population; Eskimos represent 3 percent, Aleuts account for the remaining 1 percent. Eskimos and Aleuts are located primarily in Alaska where they make up 66 percent of the Alaskan Native population (Eskimos, 53%; Aleuts 13%; and American Indians, 35%).

Regional Distributions.

Distinct regional patterns can be recognized in the distribution of Native Americans. If those states with greater than 2.5 percent of the total 1980 American Indian population are examined, two regions emerge as important areas of Indian settlement (Fig. 2.1). Approximately 47 percent of Native American residents live in the southern tier of the conterminous United States. A second tier of states, extending discontinuously from Washington to New York, contains 18 percent of the total. Two outlying states, Alaska and North Carolina, collectively equal another 9 percent. Almost 75 percent, then, of the Native Americans are located within 13 states.

Small, but significant, numbers of American Indians reside in the intermountain west between the two major regions identified on Figure 2.1. Five states, Oregon, Idaho, Nevada, Utah and Wyoming, fill in a space (Fig. 2.2) that links the southwest and northern Indian regions when one views American Indian populations as minority elements of individual state populations. Only four states have especially strong minorities of Indians, three of these are in the southwestern region—Oklahoma, New Mexico, and Arizona, whereas South Dakota represents the northern region. Interestingly, in California, the most populous state in the country, as well as the state with the largest Native American population, the American Indian minority group is small compared to other minorities. Native Americans in California are outnumbered by blacks 9 to 1 and Asian-Pacific Islanders 6 to 1.

Alaska has the largest Native American minority; some 16 percent of the states total population are Alaskan Native (Eskimo, Aleuts, and American Indians). The uniqueness of Alaska's native population is discussed further in a later section of this chapter.

Urban Native Americans.

Less than 10 percent of the 1940 Native American population was classified as urban; by 1980, Native Americans living in towns and cities of more than 2,500 population accounted for 53 percent of their total population. The population shift to urban areas became particularly noticeable in 1950 when the percentage doubled over the 1940 figure to reach 16 percent. By 1960 the figure rose to 28 percent and in 1970 it reached 45 percent.

Those states with either important numbers of Native Americans and/or significant numbers of Native Americans living in urban areas are presented in Figure 2.3. In those states having at least one percent of the total American Indian population one could deduce that in the more populous, industrial states, such as California, Texas and Illinois, larger proportions of Indians are situated in urban environments. On the contrary, in those states where the American Indian represents an important minority of the state's total population, such as Arizona, New Mexico, Oklahoma, North Dakota, South Dakota, and Montana, the proportion of urban dwelling Native Americans is less. Many states that earlier did not have large Indian populations on reservations, such as California, Texas, and Colorado, and Illinois, became attractive to urban migrations of Indian people during the decades of the 1950s, 1960s and 1970s.

Slightly more than one half of the urban American Indian population is contained within 22 Standard Metropolitan Statistical Areas (SMSA's) and Standard Consolidated Statistical Areas (SCSA's). The four largest urban areas are located in California and Oklahoma, the number one and two ranked states in total Native American populations (Fig. 2.4). The large Los Angeles SCSA (LA+, first in rank) and San Francisco (SFO, fourth) SMSA contain over 7 percent of U.S. Native American; Tulsa (TUL, second) and Oklahoma City (OKC, third) SMSA's have almost 5 percent of the urban Indians. Phoenix (PHX, fifth), Albuquerque (ABQ) and Tucson (TUC) complete the strong concentration of urban Indians in the American Southwest.

Five urban areas are located in states with minor numbers of Native Americans (Fig. 2.1 and 2.2), the SMSA's of Dallas-Fort Worth (DFW), Houston (HOU), Denver (DEN), Salt Lake City (SLC) and Kansas City (KC) are peripheral to the southwestern and northern regions of Native American concentrations.

The Seattle-Tacoma (SEA) and Portland (PRT) SMSA's are the only major Indian urban centers in the northwest. A block of states from Idaho in the west to North and South Dakota has few urban Indians (Fig. 2.3).

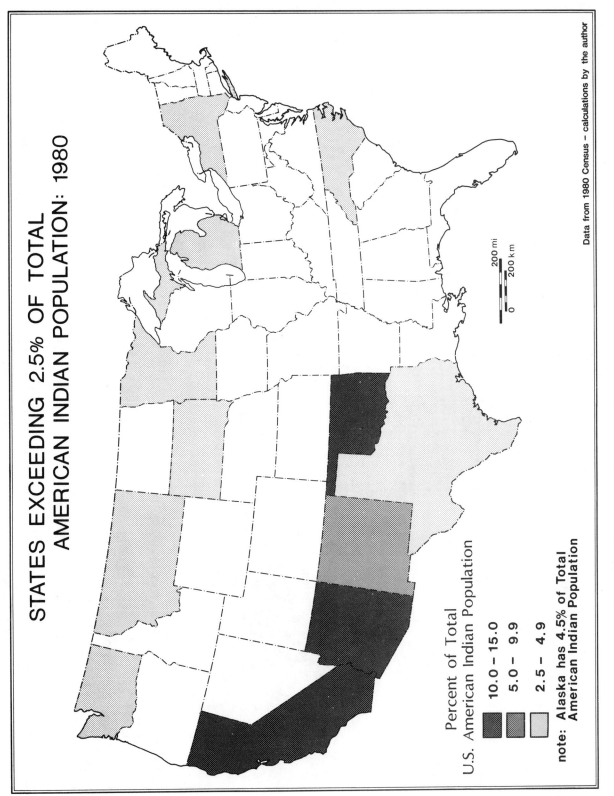

STATES EXCEEDING 2.5% OF TOTAL AMERICAN INDIAN POPULATION: 1980

Percent of Total
U.S. American Indian Population

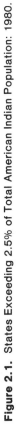

10.0 – 15.0

5.0 – 9.9

2.5 – 4.9

note: Alaska has 4.5% of Total
American Indian Population

200 mi
200 km
0

Data from 1980 Census – calculations by the author

Figure 2.1. States Exceeding 2.5% of Total American Indian Population: 1980.

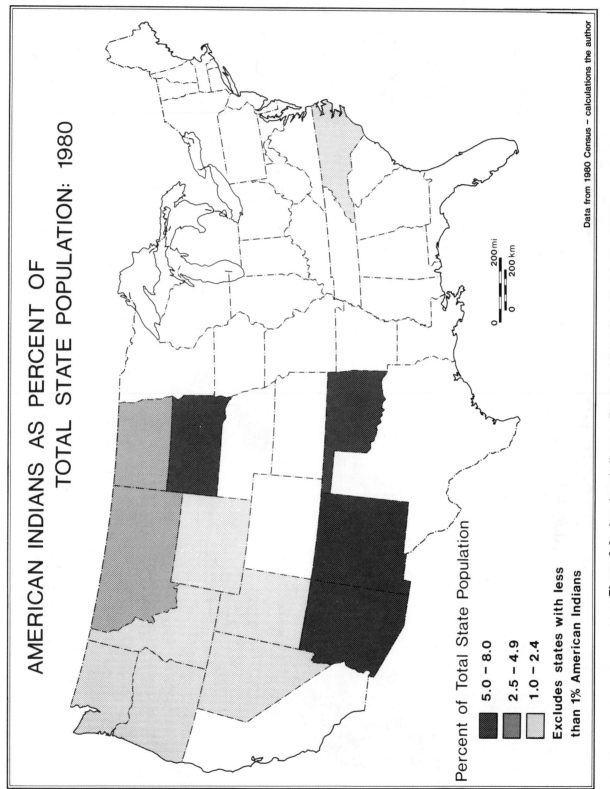

AMERICAN INDIANS AS PERCENT OF TOTAL STATE POPULATION: 1980

Percent of Total State Population

5.0 – 8.0

2.5 – 4.9

1.0 – 2.4

Excludes states with less than 1% American Indians

200 mi

200 km

0

0

Data from 1980 Census – calculations the author

Figure 2.2. American Indians as Percent of Total State Population: 1980.

40

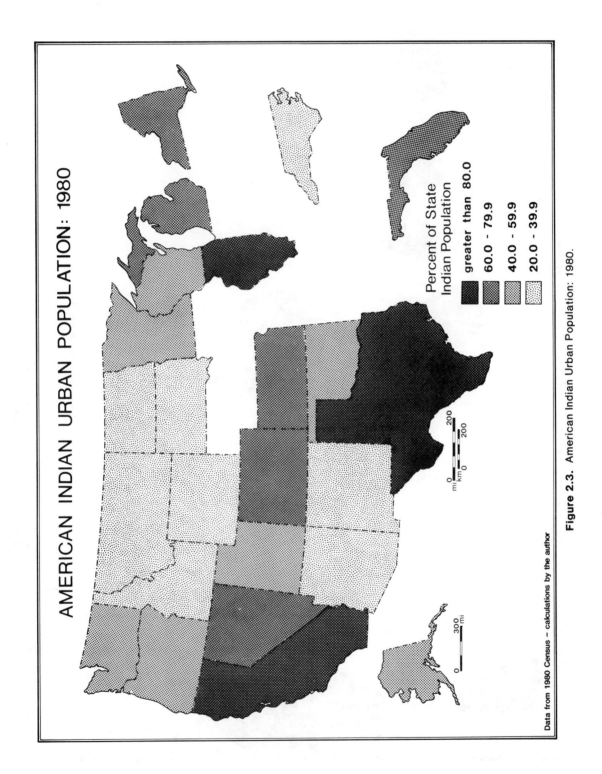

AMERICAN INDIAN URBAN POPULATION: 1980

Percent of State
Indian Population

greater than 80.0

60.0 - 79.9

40.0 - 59.9

20.0 - 39.9

Data from 1980 Census – calculations by the author

Figure 2.3. American Indian Urban Population: 1980.

41

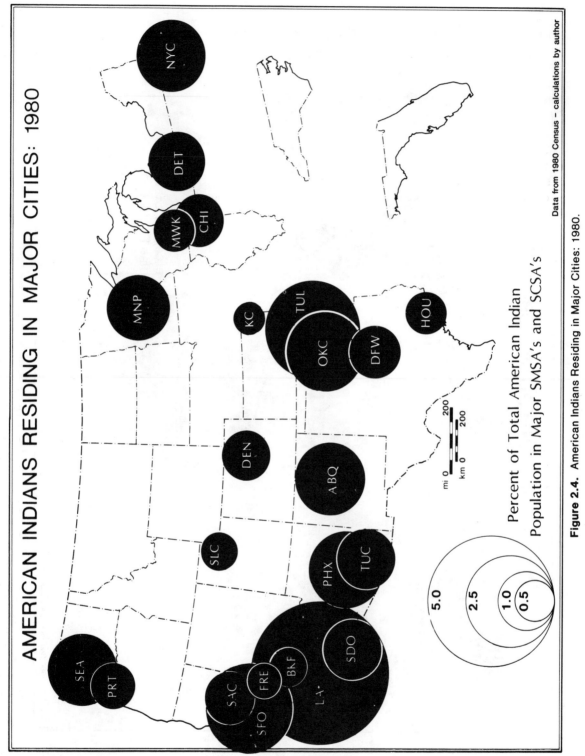

Percent of Total American Indian
Population in Major SMSA's and SCSA's

Figure 2.4. American Indians Residing in Major Cities: 1980.

More than half of the Native Americans residing in Minnesota, Michigan, and New York and Illinois are located in urban areas. Illinois and Wisconsin have even fewer American Indians than their neighboring states in the northeast region (Fig. 2.1). Their two major urban centers, Chicago (CHI) and Milwaukee (MWK) differ in the character of their relationship to the remainder of the State (Fig. 2.3). Chicago has 86 percent of Illinois Native American population, whereas only 46 percent of Wisconsin's American Indian population lives in urban areas.

The movement of the Native American from rural to urban environments has established a momentum that will undoubtedly continue for some time. The movement was initiated by the federal government as an effort to improve the economic conditions of Native Americans. The Employment Assistance Program, initiated in 1952, was designed to relocate individuals or families from reservations and rural areas to urban centers where employment opportunities existed.

The preparation of Native Americans for relocation involved some job training, financial assistance in the move, and aid in job placement. Critics of the program—and there were many—maintained that job training resulted only in employment with minimal opportunities for advancement. Further, the federal sponsors of the program were charged with not providing adequate support for the new urban dweller: no social-cultural oriented counseling programs were made available; no medical subsidization was provided once the person moved from the areas served by the Indian Health Service; and no assistance was offered to individuals who were unfamiliar with personal financial management and negotiations in an urban environment.

Because of the shortcomings in the early phases of the program, many Indian people returned to their former places of residence. Those who remained in the cities experienced varying degrees of success. Some fell into deep poverty, some became derelicts, and some succumbed to addictive drug and alcohol practices; others achieved some success in social adaptation and economic status. The last eventually became the nucleus of a group that offered counsel and emotional support for migrants that followed. As larger numbers of Native Americans assembled in an urban center, opportunities became greater for a lasting migration.

Much of the improvement in the urban environment for Native Americans, according to Indian leaders, can be traced to the development of Indian community centers, or urban centers. These centers are organized by Indian groups and offer assistance ranging from advisement for job opportunities through general education, health care and psychological support. Regardless of improvements in their conditions, however, one must be mindful of the fact that Native Americans retain very low status in the economic and social spectrum of the city.

The continuing trend of migration to urban areas is strong evidence of the terrible economic plight of most reservations and rural areas. Unemployment is exceptionally high (frequently exceeding 50 percent of the working age population) on Indian reservations. Non-reservation, rural dwelling Native Americans face many of the same problems that non-Indian citizens have faced when they seek a means of support in rural environments. The stereotypical image of the quaint citizen of the wilderness is a deceiving and cruel perception of a people who have been swept into the current of abrupt social and cultural change.

Reservations and Allotments.

The majority of non-urban Native Americans reside on lands reserved by the federal government for tribal use. Others are on lands that were alloted by the federal government to an individual and their heirs.

The federal government has from time to time adopted policies aimed at the reduction of Indian lands. Two of these programs, allotment and the Employment Assistance Program, have had a profound effect upon the patterns of Native American land holdings and populations. Most remaining reservations and allotted lands are located in eleven western states (Fig. 2.5 and 2.6, Table 2.1). The bulk of the remaining allotted lands, not accounted for in Table 2.1 are in Oklahoma, the former Indian Territory.

Cartographic display of Indian land is difficult because large scale maps are required to show the fractional nature of allotments that fall within areas depicted as reservations. Consequently, the highly generalized map of reservations (Fig. 2.5) only shows the larger reservations; some of these areas may contain a large proportion of the alloted lands listed in Table 2.1.

The importance of the reservations as the home for the Indian is further emphasized by noting the proportion of a state's total Indian population that lives on the reserve (Fig. 2.6). Six states clearly represent the remaining strongholds of these Indians. Two of them, Arizona and New Mexico, are located in the southwestern region; the remaining four, Montana, South Dakota, North Dakota and Wyoming, are in the center of the northern region. Of the two sets of states, the most uniform Native American reservation population is in the Southwestern region (Fig. 2.7).

Contrary to popular belief, those residing on reservations are not exclusively Native American (Fig. 2.7). Only five of the fifteen states in the western and north central portions of the United States have more American Indians on their reservations than non-Indians. Lands that are located within the bounds of reservations have frequently been allotted to individual Native American title and then passed by transfer of title to

TABLE 2.1 Indian Lands in Eleven Western States

State	Area: Square Miles		Percent of USA Total		
	Reservation	Allotted	Reservations	Allotments	Total Indian Lands
Montana	2,800	5,244	4.5	31.4	10.2
North	237	1,082	0.4	6.5	1.7
Dakota	3,189	4,209	5.1	25.2	9.4
South	2,777	169	4.5	1.0	3.7
Dakota	3,462	86	5.6	0.5	4.5
Wyoming	1,172	8	1.9	0.05	1.5
Utah	30,256	405	48.8	2.4	39.0
Colorado	9,596	1,064	15.5	6.4	13.6
Arizona	646	584	1.0	3.5	1.6
New Mexico	809	263	1.3	1.6	1.4
Idaho	2,931	911	4.7	5.4	4.9
Oregon					
Washington					
Total	57,875	14,025	93.3	84.0	91.5

(Data abstracted from T. W. Taylor, *The States and Their Indian Citizens* U.S. Department of the Interior, BIA, 1972): pp. 176–177.

non-Indians. Only two states, Arizona and New Mexico, have minor non-Indian elements within their bounds.

The Native American in Alaska: Alaskan Natives

The composition of the Native American population in Alaska is unique among the states. Whereas the American Indian dominates the Native American population in the conterminous United States*, only one of three Alaskan Natives is classed as Indian.

Alaskan Natives were spared the traumatic and social impacts that affect the American Indian on the western frontier of the conterminous United States. The few numbers of non-Native Americans and the size and remoteness of Alaskan sheltered many of the ancient lifestyles, customs and cultures of the aboriginal Alaskan. Some exposure to the external Alaskan world did end tragically for some, but in a broad sense impact on the Alaskan Native was small compared to that suffered by the American Indian.

The Alaskan Native, in a sense, joined the modern world in the 20th Century. The United States acquired the Alaskan Territory by purchase from Russia in 1878. Some ninety years later, in 1959, Alaska was proclaimed a State. During the territorial period, Alaskan Natives were at times assaulted, along coastal areas, by contacts with fishermen and hunters, and in the interior by gold prospectors and other who set out to develop Alaskan natural resources. Although the federal government attempted to allot lands to individual na-

tives and to organize reservations, the Alaskan Native was never maneuvered to the extent that the American Indian was through relocation and termination of reservation lands.

Alaskan Natives, like the American Indian, were traditionally not unified in their efforts to address the changes brought forth by Russian occupation of coastal Alaska and later by the United States' administration of the territory. The first effort at organization for political response beyond a local area was the Alaska Native Brotherhood (ANB). Founded in 1912, the ANB was followed three years later by the creation of the Alaskan Native Sisterhood (ANS). One of the chief goals of the ANB and ANS was the recognition of Alaskan Natives as citizens of the United States. The fact that the Alaskan Natives retained a majority of the total population of Alaska until about 1900 allowed them a strong potential in territorial affairs, although the growth of non-native population reduced them to a minority role. At the present only 1 of 6 Alaskans is a Native.

Alaskan Native rights had been specified in several documents. The first two were the treaty between the United States and Russia, and the First Organization Act of 1884. The status of Native lands was not directly confronted, however, until the period following the Act of Congress in 1958 that made Alaska a state. Alaskan Natives began pursuing a series of claims to their aboriginal lands that culminated in the Alaska Native Claims Settlement Act of 1971 (ANCSA). The Act had two major components: one was to protect and establish legal title to lands for the benefit of Alaskan Natives; the second was to conserve and protect some Alaskan lands through the possible inclusion—after

*The 48 adjacent, conterminous, States are home for 19 percent of the total Aleut population. Within the conterminous United States the Native American population is composed of 0.6 percent Eskimo, 0.4 percent Aleut and 99.0 percent American Indian.

AMERICAN INDIAN RESERVATIONS

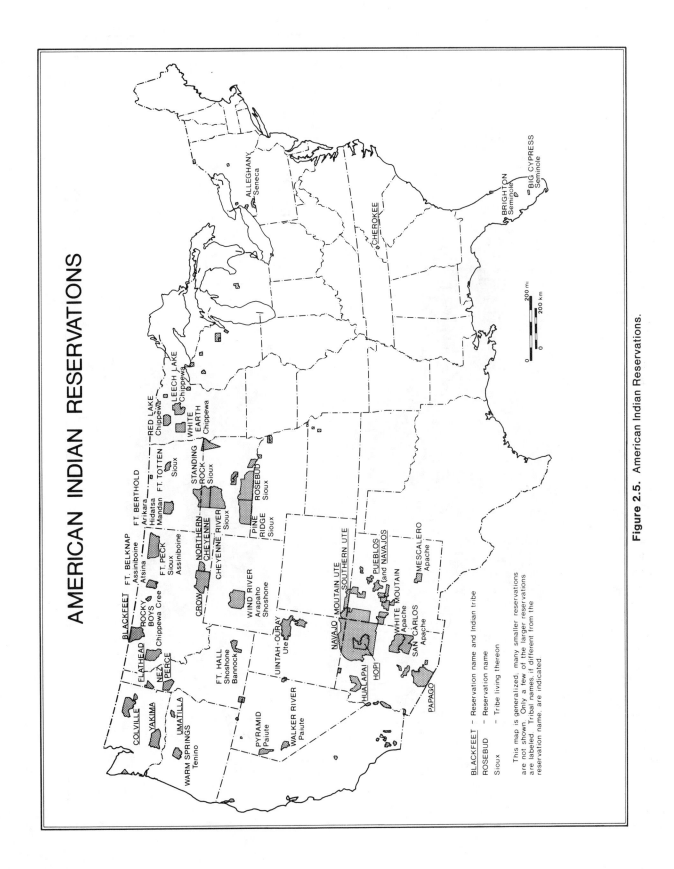

BLACKFEET – Reservation name and Indian tribe

ROSEBUD – Reservation name

Sioux – Tribe living thereon

This map is generalized; many smaller reservations are not shown. Only a few of the larger reservations are labeled. Tribal names, if different from the reservation name, are indicated.

Figure 2.5. American Indian Reservations.

45

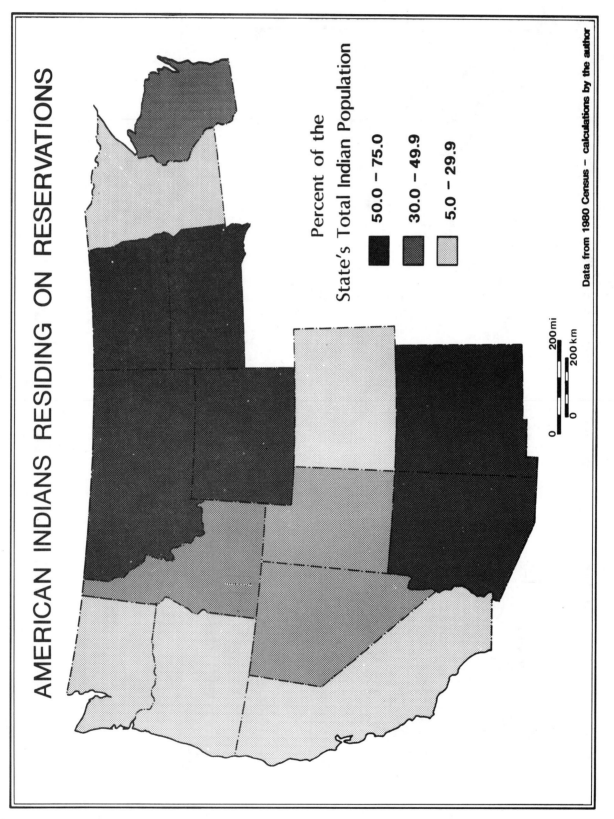

AMERICAN INDIANS RESIDING ON RESERVATIONS

Percent of the
State's Total Indian Population

50.0 – 75.0

30.0 – 49.9

5.0 – 29.9

200 mi

200 km

0

0

Data from 1980 Census – calculations by the author

Figure 2.6. American Indians Residing on Reservations.

POPULATION OF INDIAN RESERVATIONS: SIZE & COMPOSITION

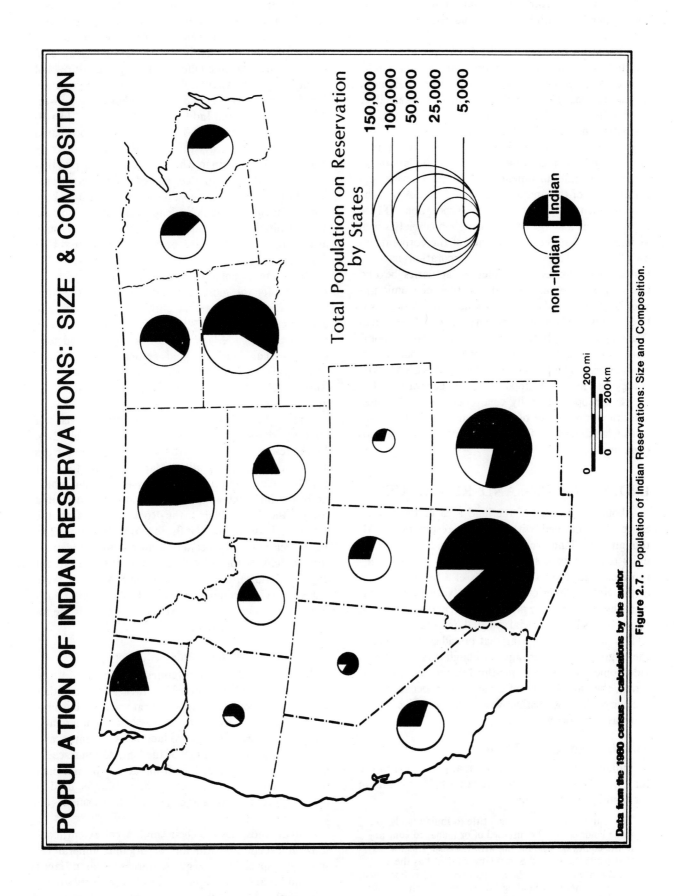

Figure 2.7. Population of Indian Reservations: Size and Composition.

47

study by the Secretary of Interior—into the national forest, parks, wildlife refugees and wild-scenic river systems.

Alaskan Natives prior to ANCSA, had legal or restricted title to only slightly more than 24 square miles in Alaska. Another 6250 square miles were designated as reservations. The majority of Native Alaskans lived at that time upon lands designated as public domain; a smaller number lived in urban areas.

ANCSA set aside 62,500 square miles for Alaska Natives and provided almost one billion dollars in return for the extinguishment of all Alaskan native land claims. One of the unique aspects of ANCSA was the establishment of regional native corporations. These organizations manage the resources—financial as well as natural—that the beneficiaries of the corporations own. Many of the twelve regional corporations have invested their monies in commercial activities beyond their regional bounds. As a result, their economic impact is extensive. Shares of stock held by Alaskan Native members (U.S. citizens with at least one fourth Alaskan Eskimo, Indian or Aleut blood) of corporations have placed them squarely in the modern economic world. The process provided by ANCSA, while supplying a means of support of future generations, has thrust a people generally conditioned by subsistence activities into a state of high finance business operations where cleavage from past cultures is sharply noticeable.

INDIAN LANDS AND RESOURCES:

About 2.5 percent of the land area of the United States is contained within Indian reservations. Although these lands represent only one of every forty units they retain a special significance because they represent the residual or remains of a former domain of the Native American. Since the Native Americans were the only minority group to claim aboriginal lands, these parcels hold a special spiritual importance to some Indian people; a wellspring that provides an avenue to the origins of their heritage. Although these lands provide home for less than one-third of the Indian population, they are worthy of consideration because they are one of the most distinctive aspects to Native Americans as a minority group.

The Nature of Indian Lands

Indian lands that remain in tribal possession in the form of federal reservations are lands held in common for certain Indian groups.

> The United States holds legal title to Indian lands, yet those lands cannot be disposed of or managed contrary to the equitable title resting with Indians. This means that while the United States Government has the appearance of title as the nominal owner of Indian trust lands, it is actually holding title entirely for the benefit and use of the Indian owners.

Other Indian lands fall into the categories of state reservations, allotted lands, and ceded lands. State reservations form a very small fraction of the total of modern Indian land holdings. Allotted lands were issued to individual title holders, although the Bureau of Indian Affairs may still hold in trust some of the titles. Much of the allotted land was purchased by non-Indians once individual Indians were given title. Most allotted lands that remain in Indian names are now shared by descendants, each with a small fraction of commonly held ownership in what was originally a plot that averaged 160 acres in size. Ceded lands were transferred from areas with vague limits that constituted the domain of the Native American to the public domain of the United States, and hence to another status such as private, corporate, state, or lands administered by a federal agency.

Reservations held in trust by the federal government are, for the most part, located west of the Mississippi River. Most are in climatic zones that have deficiencies of moisture; many straddle lands that rise to high elevations. Many of these lands were undoubtedly viewed as inferior to lands settled by non-Indians. In general, the lands that became Indian reservations were barren and remote, away from well-traveled trails and major communities.

Greater than 90 percent of Indian lands reserved and allotted are located in 11 western states (Table 2.1). Indian reservations—relatively large, contiguous areas as opposed to parcels of allotted lands—are for the most part situated within four major physical regions which lie in the interior and western portions of the United States: the Great Plains, the Rocky Mountains, the Colorado Plateau, and the Basin and Range. (Fig. 2.8) Each area has a distinct set of environmental characteristics, chiefly topographic and climatic, that present certain limitations on use of the land. Many of these lands, however, contain valuable resources that may provide an economic base that has potential for the revitalization of these lands.

Resources of Indian Lands

Indian lands generate revenues in a variety of ways. Some of the lands are mined for their minerals; other lands may be rented for agricultural use or as business sites. Still other areas are mantled by commercially important forests. Crop production is common and livestock is grazed on much of the land. Often sizeable quantities of water that flow from, across, or marginal to Indian lands have been claimed, and can be used to enhance local resources or can be sold to consumers off the reservations.

Indian lands, despite their small areal extent, contain an exceptional amount of organic mineral resources, especially energy resources. Indian lands account for about one square mile of every forty square miles in the United States, yet one of every five square

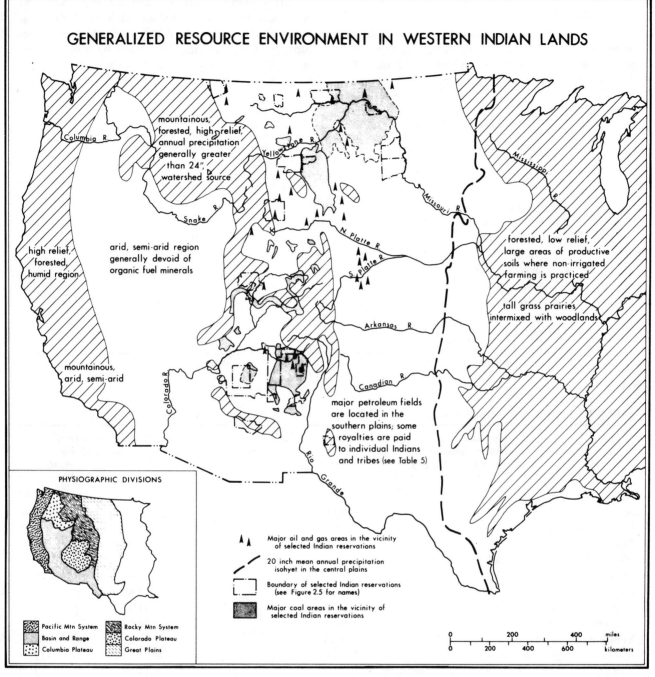

Figure 2.8. Generalized Resource Environment in Western Indian Lands.

miles underlain by coal is on Indian land, and one of every two square miles of land containing uranium ore is on Indian land. The Indian coal reserves represent one-third of the total low sulphur strippable coal deposits in the United States. The major source of mineral production income is derived from oil and natural gas production. Indian lands have about one-twentieth of the petroleum reserves of the nation.

Organic fuel minerals are not evenly distributed on Indian lands. Some reservations have none; others are abundantly rich. As a result some tribes derive sizeable incomes from the royalties paid by production companies. Indian income, by state, generated by energy mineral production is listed in Table 2.2. The income is partially produced on reservation lands and partly on allotted lands held in trust by the Bureau of Indian Affairs. From Table 2.2 it can be deduced that 98.5 percent of all income from oil and gas leases on Indian lands in the United States is produced in the eight states listed; 95.5 percent of all income from other minerals is accounted for by Indian tribal lands in these eight states; and 98.0 percent of all mineral income from the total tribal lands within the United States comes from these eight states.

Agriculture plays a major role on many reservations in providing subsistence support or cash income support for many Native American families (Table 2.3). Agriculture has been important to the Indian for many centuries; domestication of such plants as corn and beans occurred in the Americas well before Columbus. Many practices, developed in very early years of occupancy of the American Southwest by tribes such as the Pueblos of New Mexico and Arizona, survive today. Most Indian lands are located in areas that are either

TABLE 2.2 Indian Tribe Income by State from Subsurface Leases 1978

State	Oil & Gas Leases (%)	Other Minerals Coal, Uranium, etc. (%)	Percent of Total USA Indian Income
Oklahoma	40.5	—	30.3
New Mexico	13.6	37.7	19.5
Utah	19.0	—	14.2
North	11.5	—	8.6
Dakota	9.9	—	7.4
Wyoming	—	26.5	6.8
Washington	—	22.7	6.1
Arizona	4.0	8.5	5.1
Montana			

"Surface Leases and Permits, Subsurface Leases and Permits" (United States Department of Interior, BIA), Sept. 30, 1978.

TABLE 2.3 Income from Indian Surface Land Rental for Agriculture and Business by States—1978

State	Percent of Total Indian Agricultural Land Rented in U.S.	Percent of Total Rented Land in State That is Agricultural	Income per Acre of Rented Lands for Agriculture	Income per Acre of Rented Lands for Business
Alaska	—	—	—	$ 25.07
Arizona	3.7	69.5	$34.04	60.30
California	0.3	46.3	68.27	335.86
Colorado	0.8	84.5	0.26	82.90
Florida	0.2	55.1	3.55	1,277.15
Idaho	7.3	96.1	20.67	6.18
Iowa	0.02	99.6	33.93	—
Kansas	0.5	97.3	11.17	—
Michigan	0.01	84.5	15.07	—
Minnesota	0.1	42.3	6.27	201.21
Montana	36.6	98.8	3.26	22.03
Nebraska	1.1	100.0	19.50	12.43
Nevada	0.3	71.2	2.39	27.25
New Mexico	0.8	44.2	0.63	90.60
North Carolina	—	—	—	1,176.79
North Dakota	5.0	98.5	6.18	8.29
Oklahoma	15.4	98.6	10.64	36.16
Oregon	1.1	96.8	25.39	31.78
South Dakota	20.1	98.5	4.22	6.31
Utah	0.8	82.0	6.70	17.50
Washington	4.5	92.6	12.87	111.65
Wisconsin	0.01	2.6	7.12	191.65
Wyoming	1.2	94.2	3.44	16.99
Average			8.28	105.23

"Surface Leases and Permits, Subsurface Leases and Permits" (United States Department of Interior, BIA), September 30, 1978.

50

too dry or too cool to support extensive farming operations. Crop cultivation has been developed on a large scale commercial basis in projects such as the Navajo Indian Irrigation Project in northwestern New Mexico. In this case, water impounded in the Navajo Reservoir on the upper San Juan River is distributed by canal and tunnel into a 339 square mile development that eventually may contain 172 square miles of irrigated fields, feed lots, and agribusiness operations whose profits will benefit a largely Navajo labor force and the Navajo Tribal treasury. Opportunities to develop similar projects on other reservations will be expensive and will obviously require sources of water that are uncontested. Clearly, water rights are the key to any development for it is the resource upon which most other land use is based.

Livestock play a central role to many reservation economies. Too great a dependency upon some range lands have resulted in a deterioration of this phase of agriculture. Overgrazing promotes soil erosion, which in turn reduces the potential of the range to recover. Livestock may be sold to provide an income; but it also serves as a subsistence base for many Indian people.

Animal byproducts, such as wool, are placed in the commercial marketplace whether directly through sales of wool, or indirectly through the manufacture of saleable terms by Indian artisans.

Commercially significant forests thrive in some Indian country. Many of the reservations in the Rocky Mountain region, on the Colorado Plateau, and in some sections of the Basin and Range region have extensive forests of Ponderosa pine, Douglas fir and other valuable trees. Sawmills and wood byproduct plants are located on several reservations providing job opportunities for local residents.

The title to lands that were allotted to heads of households, and now held in trust by the BIA, have passed through generations of heirs. Many of those areas are rented for agricultural use by non-Indians. Table 2.4 shows the income derived from rental of lands used for agriculture and business. Since the ownership is so fragmented as title is passed along from generation to generation, the value to an individual is usually quite small. As time passes and future inheritances occur, these undivided interests will continue to fractionalize, administrative costs of tracing ownership and

Table 2.4 Income to the Top Twenty Indian Reservations from Mineral Production

Reservations (Tribes)	Income, 1978 (millions of $)	Percent of Total Indian Mineral Production
Osage Tribe, OK	25.4 *	18.9
Navajo Reservation, AZ, NM, UT	22.0 **	16.4
Ft. Berthold Reservation, ND	11.5 *	8.5
Wind River Reservation, WY	10.0 *	7.5
Laguna Pueblo, NM	9.5	7.0
Uintah-Ouray Reservation, UT	9.2 *	6.8
Colville Reservation, WA	8.5	6.3
Jicarillo Apache Reservation, NM	7.1 *	5.3
Cheyenne-Apache Tribes, OK	4.5 *	3.4
Wichita-Caddo-Delaware Tribes, OK	3.8 *	2.8
Five Civilized Tribes, OK	3.4 *	2.5
Kiowa-Commanche-Apache-Ft. Sill Apache Tribes, OK	2.9 *	2.2
Crow Reservation, MT	2.9 **	2.1
Blackfeet Reservation, MT	2.3 *	1.7
Papago Reservation, AZ	2.0	1.5
Ft. Peck Reservation, MT	1.3 *	1.0
Hopi Reservation, AZ	1.2	0.9
San Zavier Reservation, AZ	1.2	0.9
Ft. Hall Reservation, ID	1.1 *	0.8
Mountain Ute Reservation, CO	1.0 *	0.7
Totals	130.8	97.2

Note: The BIA lists ten additional tribes as having income from subsurface mineral leases.

* indicates that income is primarily from oil and gas production.

** indicates that income is from oil and gas and coal production.

"Surface Leases and Permits, Subsurface Leases and Permits" (United States Department of the Interior, Bureau of Indian Affairs), September 30, 1978.

TABLE 2.5 Known and Potential Resources of Members of the Council of Energy Resource Tribes

Tribe	Coal	Uranium	Geothermal	Natural Gas	Oil	Oil Shale
Acoma Pueblo (NM)	X	X	X			
Blackfeet (MT)	X			X	X	
Cheyenne River Sioux (SD)	X	X		X	X	
Chippewa-Cree (MT)	X		X	X	X	
Colville (WA)		X	X			
Crow (MT)	X			X	X	
Fort Belnap (MT)	X		X	X	X	
Fort Berthold (ND)	X			X	X	
Fort Hall (ID)			X	X	X	
Fort Peck (MT)	X		X	X	X	
Hopi (AZ)	X	X	X			
Jemez Pueblo (NM)		X	X			
Jicarilla Apache (NM)	X	X	X	X	X	
Laguna Pueblo (NM)	X	X	X			
Navajo (AZ, NM, UT)	X	X	X	X	X	
Nez Perce (ID)	X		X			
Northern Cheyenne (MT)	X			X	X	
Santa Ana Pueblo (NM)		X	X			
Southern Ute (CO)	X	X	X	X	X	
Spokane (WA)		X	X			
Uintah-Ouray (UT)	X	X		X	X	X
Ute Mountain (CO)	X	X	X	X	X	
Wind River (WY)	X	X		X	X	
Yakima (WA)			X			
Zia Pueblo		X	X			

distributing the incomes from the rentals will increase. Individual Indians will receive less and less benefit from their land.

The most important resources to the future economic gain of Indian tribes are the mineral resources. Table 2.4 lists the top twenty tribes in income from mineral production. Most of this income is derived from energy minerals—oil, natural gas, coal, and uranium.

Because of the relatively large proportion of energy reserves on Indian lands, twenty-five tribes have joined together as the Council of Energy Resource Tribes (CERT). This group (Table 2.5) has organized a series of services to provide the expertise needed by individual tribes to develop their resources. CERT also acts as a public relations effort between the tribes and the marketplace. Financial revenues that could be used to improve various components of tribal economy and society may be generated by these efforts.

Non-reservation tribes, such as those in Oklahoma (Table 2.4), divide royalties paid from mineral production among qualified members of the tribe. This income is derived from retained mineral rights, a heritage of former surface lands that belonged to the tribes.

Economic opportunities are relatively limited on Indian reservations. Unemployment is very high, sometimes running in excess of fifty percent of the available labor force. Job training may be gained on the reservation or in nearby communities. Jobs are often not available, however, near a reservation home. Usually the single largest employers of the Indian is government; either tribal government, the Bureau of Indian Affairs, or a government sponsored program.

The absence of a trained labor pool to serve in a variety of labor niches is a basic problem for most reservations. Although the number of skilled people usually increases annually, the improvement of economic opportunities on the reservation advances very slowly, if at all. Consequently, many of the young, trained Native Americans leave the reservations. The impact that resource development on the reservation will have on economic opportunities remains to be determined.

Adjustment to non-reservation life varies from individual to individual and from generation to generation. Within urban areas there are no traditions of Indian ghettos. Individuals without peer support who arrive in an urban area face numerous difficulties in adjusting to and accepting city life. On the other hand if one has family or relatives for emotional support, adjustment may come more easily. The relocation of Indians in the 1950s to cities was not always successful, however, in the 1980s with better educated individuals and more collective experiences in the urban place, the chances for successful adjustment are greater.

SUGGESTED ADDITIONAL READINGS

American Indian Policy Review Commission, *Final Report* (Washington, D.C.: US Government Printing Office 1, 1977).

Vine Deloria, Jr., *Behind the Trail of Broken Treaties* (New York: Delacorte Press, 1974).

Charles Hamilton, ed., *Cry of the Thunderbird: The American Indian's Own Story* (Norman: University of Oklahoma Press, 1972).

Alvin M. Josephy, Jr., *Now That the Buffalo's Gone: A Study of Today's American Indian* (New York: Alfred A. Knopf, 1982).

U.S. Civil Rights Commission, *Indian Tribes: A Continuing Quest for Survival* (Washington, D.C.: US Government Printing Office, June, 1981).

Christopher Vecsey and Robert W. Venables, eds., *American Indian Environments; Ecological Issues in Native American History* (Syracuse: Syracuse University Press, 1980).

Jack O. Waddell and O. M. Watson, eds., *The American Indian in Urban Society* (Boston: Little, Brown and Company, 1971).

3

The Evolving Spatial Pattern of Black America: 1910–1980

Harold M. Rose
University of Wisconsin—Milwaukee

INTRODUCTION

The black population in the United States now numbers in excess of 26 million persons, or 11.7 percent of the nation's total population. At present that population is larger than was the nation's population in 1850. But what is important is the developmental sequence that has led that population to acquire an internal identity that is rooted in a sense of peoplehood. Blacks today not only represent a population group distinguishable in terms of a set of biological traits, but more importantly it represents a population whose experiences in America have promoted a social bonding that has led to the development of a unique group culture. This process has fostered not only a racial identity, but an ethnic identity as well. It is not possible to indicate when an ethnic identity began to emerge. But, by the close of the Civil War it became obvious that blacks no longer represented a population group that had simply evolved from a common racial stock.

Because race in the United States has historically represented a more powerful social construct than has ethnicity, the ethnic qualities of the black population have been given only limited attention by scholars. This chapter will not directly address the question of ethnic status and the position of blacks in American society, but will do so indirectly by highlighting those forces promoting spatial isolation during the 20th century. The extent to which the social millieu of black Americans is severely constrained by external factors will influence the promotion and maintenance of that population's ethnic status. Therefore, a spatial-temporal treatment of how blacks have responded to the American opportunity structure during the 20th century should provide a background to an understanding of the continuing evolution of a black ethnicity.

Black Americans represent one of the original population groups involved in the making of America. Their presence in North America, according to Bennett[1] dates back to 1619. The first blacks in the United States were indentured servants, and it was not until the middle of the 17th century that their status was altered to that of permanent bondage. The growth of that population was replenished through importing slaves from Africa, but after 1720 natural increase exceeded importation as the primary source of population growth.[2] Thus, the percentage of foreign-born black Americans became nominal by the end of the 18th century, a condition that is in sharp contrast to the pattern of origin of America's European population.

Because black Americans were introduced to the Americas as an agricultural labor source to be employed in the production of tropical and subtropical crops, it was only logical that their ports of entry were basically confined to then existing southern coastal states. The introduction of blacks to the southern subtropics has been variously explained, but a more recent contention is that their immunity to selected tropical diseases to which Europeans were susceptible was the principal factor leading to their enslavement.[3] Thus, blacks were thought to represent an ideal southern labor force.

PRE- AND POST-EMANCIPATION DISTRIBUTION: TO 1910

The spatial distribution of American blacks was essentially confined to the Chesapeake Bay area from the period of their introduction to the beginning of the 19th century. Virginia and Maryland were centers of concentration, with secondary centers occurring in the Carolinas. From 1790 to 1860, there was a sharp increase in the size of the black population. Johnson and Campbell[4] indicate blacks increased during this period from approximately 700,000 to 4,000,000 and that the increase was associated with the development of a plantation economy. Cotton, not tobacco, became the crop demanding ever-increasing quantities of slave labor.

The evolution of a system of plantation agriculture was responsible for the pattern of black population distribution that could be observed at the beginning of the 20th century. The ever-increasing demand for cotton led to a redistribution of the slave population from the upper South to the lower South. The interregional migration of the slave population was directed to the cotton-producing states of Alabama, Mississippi, Louisiana, and Texas. By the beginning of the Civil War, the cultural hearth of the nation's black population had its boundaries fixed, boundaries that basically coincided with those of the Confederacy. Within this territorial configuration, Africans, who represented many distinctive groups, were transformed into Americans. Thus, Americanization of the nation's black population took place under the constraint of bondage associated with the labor demands of a plantation economy.

During the first 250 years that blacks were present in what now constitutes the United States, they had little control over their lives or their movements. The spatial pattern of black population distribution was determined, therefore, by a set of exogenous forces dictated by labor demand. It is, however, the pattern of distribution that has emerged since 1865 which is of primary interest in this essay. Moreover, emphasis will be basically placed on the geography of black America during the 20th century, for it is during this period that blacks have had to adapt to a series of major changes in the nation's economy. These changes have subsequently had an impact upon the geographic distribution of that population.

Geographers, unlike historians, have devoted only limited effort in detailing changes in the spatial distribution of black Americans, and did not begin to show interest in the mobility characteristics of this population until after 1950. Even today sociologists conduct most migration studies that focus upon black Americans. Nevertheless, patterns of black migration are well documented; but the work of several geographers, including that of Calef and Nelson,[5] Hart,[6] Lewis,[7] and Morrill and Donaldson,[8] is instructive in helping us to understand selected forces in the redistribution of black Americans. The writings of Hart and Lewis are especially instructive in allowing us to identify the cultural hearth of black America. The cultural hearth embraces most counties whose populations were at least 33 percent black in 1910.

The first generation following emancipation resulted in some interregional movement of the newly freed population. The most notable of these movements was to Kansas in the 1870s and to several northeastern states toward the end of the period. More noticeable, however, was the initiation of an urbanization process that drew blacks into both southern small towns and cities. By 1910 almost one-fifth of the region's black population could be identified as urban, whereas at the beginning of the period only ten percent of the population resided in urban places.[9] Between 1870 and 1910, there was only negligible change in the percent of the black population residing in the South, with almost nine-tenths of the population present in both time periods. Thus, during the first generation following slavery, the black population evolved a pattern of redistribution within the region leading to minimum urbanization and a preponderant continued involvement in the agricultural sector.

Incipient Regional Shifts in the Black Population

By the turn of the century, blacks had experienced one full generation as free persons, but freedom actually produced much less than it had promised. During the era following the war, the South instituted various oppressive measures that lent continuing protection to a white supremacy system and at the same time maintained its prime agricultural workforce in place. An agricultural tenancy system continued to allow the region to satisfy a growing demand for cotton on the world market. Within this context, ex-slaves and the children of ex-slaves fashioned a bondage-free culture. But, one could hardly expect the many dimensions of slave culture to disappear within a single generation. Nevertheless, within the group of counties that Lewis[10] identified as the core of the Negro region, important aspects of 20th century black culture evolved.

The Exodus from the South Begins

During the second generation following the Civil War a pattern of population redistribution was initiated that continued for almost 60 years. Migration from the South was spurred by the termination of the massive European immigrant flow occurring as a result of the outbreak of war in Europe. Labor shortages took place in the nation's manufacturing belt when the immigrant flow was interrupted. Southern blacks already in the North, northern black newspapers distributed in the South, and labor agents prompted blacks to leave the southern region. A steady deterioration of both social and economic conditions within the region aided and encouraged blacks to sever their ties with the South. Not all movement during the period, however, was interregional. This was also the period of take-off in southern growth.

The first major movement of blacks out of the South was disproportionately confined to a selected set of core counties in the eastern South. Selected border state counties also represented early leaving targets of northern-directed migrants. Numerically, the largest migrant group originated in Alabama, Virginia, Georgia, North Carolina, and Mississippi.[11] This migration was directed toward a limited number of urban centers in the Middle Atlantic and East North Central census divisions. Thus, after less than two generations following the termination of slavery, major changes took place that led to an alteration in the established pattern of black population distribution.

The South's Pre-World War I Black Population

On the eve of the Great Migration, which was to lead to a net loss of almost a half million blacks from the region, 8.7 million of the nation's 9.8 million blacks resided in the South (Table 3.1, Fig. 3.1). More than one-third of the region's population was concentrated in Georgia, Mississippi, Alabama, and South Carolina, states where rural density reached its peak. Also in these states the intensity of black occupancy was highest. The good cotton soils occurring in an almost continuous band from South Carolina through Mississippi were responsible for providing a context in which a black core culture evolved and subsequently became diffused over a larger territory, only to be modified in the process.

Hart[12] defined black core areas in terms of intensity of occupancy at the county level. In 1910 more than 100 counties included 50 percent or more blacks as residents. These counties represented a discontinuous band extending from the tobacco-producing regions of Virginia and North Carolina to the premier cotton counties from South Carolina through northern Louisiana. In such an intensely occupied black milieu, it is only logical to assume that aspects of black culture would originate, to maintain an extended life, and to diffuse outward from its origin. Movers from these core counties might be expected to engage in practices different from those developed in counties remote from the core.

Although less than 25 percent of the region's population were urban in 1910, the rise of New South industries led to urban growth in which blacks were inextricably involved. Few southern cities were less than 25 percent black at this date. By 1910, 19 southern cities had populations of more than 50,000 (Fig. 3.2), an urbanization level coinciding with the current metropolitan area population threshold. In environments satisfying this level of urbanization it is appropriate to assess the existence of black territorial communities that might be viewed as possessing a ghetto or pre-ghetto scale.

Incipient Urban Growth

Fifteen primary black urban concentrations had evolved in the South by the early 20th century. They were basically associated with the rise of southern commercial centers and therefore tended to have either river or ocean port locations. There were few exceptions to this rule, the most notable being Birmingham. Washington (94,000), New Orleans (89,000), and Baltimore (84,000) were the most populous black urban centers in the region, outstripping in size (in 1910) both the larger northern centers, New York (91,000) and Philadelphia (84,000). This set of urban centers were the first urban environments of black entry. But, given their limited size and the nature of their economies, e.g., service centers, they could hardly accommodate the vast rural populations whose economic state had changed very little since blacks were granted freedom. Rural poverty, viewed by most analysts as the chief motivation for moving out of the region, was everywhere.

The size of these larger southern urban concentrations provides one the opportunity to examine their spatial patterns as a means of addressing the validity of the notion of the existence of southern ghettos. It should be noted that the term "ghetto" was not used to describe southern black urban concentrations until recently. No doubt the absence of large southern and eastern European clusters in southern cities was responsible for the retardation in the use of this terminology to describe zones where unassimilated urban populations were concentrated. The physical character of these places as well might have led to the failure to adopt this terminology. Or, it could be that it was simply an inappropriate social construct within the southern region.

TABLE 3.1 The South's Black Population in 1910

Census Division	South Atlantic		East South Central		West South Central	
States	Delaware	31,000*	Kentucky	262,000	Arkansas	443,000
	Maryland	233,000	Tennessee	473,000	Louisiana	714,000
	Virginia	671,000	Alabama	908.000	Texas	690,000
	W. Virginia	64,000	Mississippi	1,009,000	Oklahoma	138.000
	N. Carolina	698.000				
	S. Carolina	836,000				
	Georgia	1,177,000				
	Florida	309,000				
Divisional Totals:		4,112,000		2,653,000		1,984,000

*All values have been rounded off to the nearest 1,000.

Source: Robert B. Grant, *The Black Man Comes to the City* (Chicago: Nelson Hall Publishers, 1972): pp. 16–17.

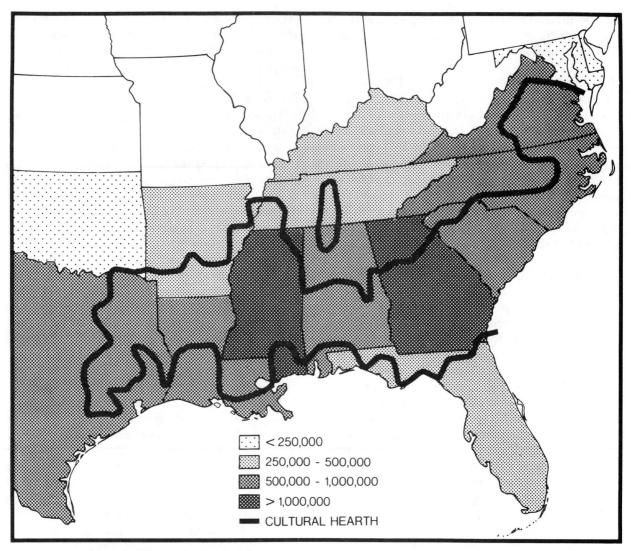

Figure 3.1. Black Population in the South, 1910. (Courtesy of the University of Wisconsin-Milwaukee Cartographic Services.)

The latter explanation appears to have greater intuitive appeal. If ghettos in the American context were viewed simply as zones where immigrants would be transformed into Americans, and in the second or later generation to seek their position in American society as individuals, then the concept was inappropriate. Although there were black residential concentrations in all southern cities, the spatial pattern and intensity showed much variation. Nevertheless, Kellog[13] demonstrated that in postbellum cities black communities most often grew up on the edge of town. Moreover, numerous clusters often existed. These were not communities where blacks succeeded previous white residents, but instead, were territories explicitly set aside for black occupance.

Dog run and shotgun houses, commonplace in the rural countryside, were often replicated in the cities. Over time, however, the urban housing stock was upgraded and the amenities present in urban settings became far superior to those generally available in the rural South. But the central issue seems to revolve around a state of permanence or transience. Immigrant ghettos were viewed by many as simply transient entities that could be expected to provide both shelter and communal resources to persons entering American society from the outside. In many respects, the urban quarters established for southern blacks represented the relocation of rural villages to the city. These zones of permanent occupancy, which could be employed to sustain a black culture, had their origins in a set of rural core counties.

Assimilation was unnecessary because blacks and whites in the South had a fixed relationship. Therefore, black urban clusters in the South were simply zones where black culture could flourish, where a set of black-controlled institutions could emerge, and where one's social world would be totally circumscribed. The contention here is that it would be inappropriate to use the term ghetto to describe urban black concentrations in southern cities satisfying a metropolitan population def-

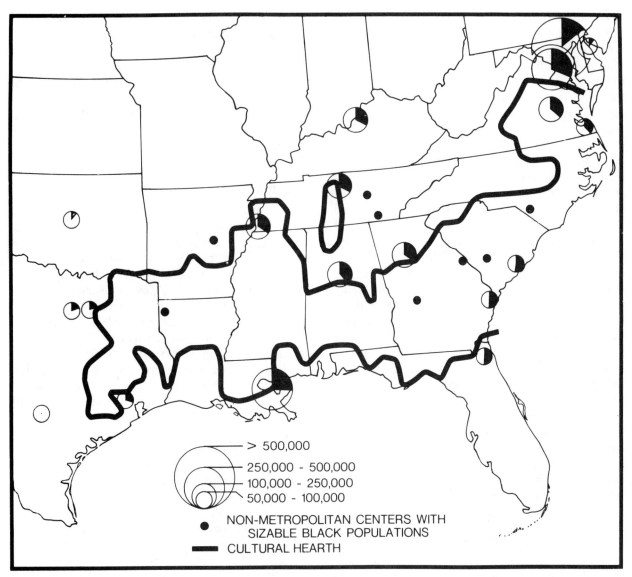

Figure 3.2. The South's Urban System, 1910. (Courtesy of the University of Wisconsin-Milwaukee Cartographic Services.)

inition in 1910. Although in that year only fifteen such places existed with black populations in excess of 10,000, numerous other southern urban centers had black populations that exceeded this threshold. Thus, sizeable urban villages also existed in such places as Little Rock, Arkansas; Augusta and Macon, Georgia; Lexington, Kentucky; Charlotte, North Carolina; Columbia, South Carolina; Chattanooga, Tennessee; and Portsmouth, Virginia. The size of the black population was partially circumscribed by the size of the total population and the center's role in the urban economy.

FIRST GENERATIONAL PATTERNS OF INTERREGIONAL MOVEMENT: 1910–1940

In 1910, the South's black population had a spatial pattern similar to that recorded in the 1870 census. But,

this date represented the eve of the beginning of a redistribution pattern that eventually led blacks to settle throughout the rest of the nation. The initial movement is generally said to have gotten underway in 1915. In just five years, approximately one-half million blacks left the South. This movement led to an intensification of the urbanization process as most blacks who left the region settled in the then largest urban centers of the Northeast and North Central regions. The process of urban ghettoization took off during this period, resulting in the formation of large contiguous spatial clusters where blacks represented the majority population.

The Great Migration

As indicated earlier, the advent of World War I and the subsequent termination of European immigration served as the initial impetus for the "great migration."

59

Once underway, however, the depression of the thirties slowed down the migration stream. Blacks arriving in northern cities entered the urban economy on the lowest rung of the ladder as people from southern and eastern Europe had almost a full generation head start. This led to the latter groups' more favored position in the opportunity structure once the war emergency had ended.

Blacks were especially attracted to cities where manufacturing employment was easily available. In these cities first generation ghettos expanded abruptly and new ghetto configurations came into being. The black population in Chicago, Detroit, and Cleveland more than doubled from 1910 to 1920, while that of New York, Philadelphia, St. Louis, Cincinnati, and Indianapolis grew at less than one-half this rate. Among the larger southern cities, only the growth rate in Houston's black community could compare favorably with the growth rate in the slower growing northern centers. In fact, both Nashville and Louisville experienced an absolute loss in their black population during this decade. By 1920, the largest black urban concentrations were no longer in Washington, New Orleans, and Baltimore, but in New York, Philadelphia, and Chicago.

It should be remembered that at this date both black and white southern populations were also moving from the rural countryside to southern towns and cities. It required another twenty years, however, before the urban population of blacks became larger than the rural population. Furthermore, white migrants had a greater affinity for southern cities than did blacks. Also, because blacks had been cut off from some of the skilled jobs they performed during the reconstruction period, whites were more likely to secure the desirable jobs. Thus, the move to southern cities, save a few, simply assured blacks continuing employment in the low-wage service economy. Even this was an inducement to move away from the almost certain poverty and fear of repression that characterized segments of the rural South.

During this period also more white southerners than blacks migrated to northern cities. Old hostilities accompanied these migrants. At this time, however, black migrants to northern cities entered occupations previously closed to them, although the jobs were among the least attractive ones. Although most emphasis has been directed to the economic factors contributing to migration, there is some evidence that social forces played a strong secondary role,[14] and were far more important than they have generally been reported.

The Post World War I Flow

The end of the war did not terminate the flow of black migrants to Middle Atlantic and Great Lakes cities. There was a speed up in the process during the twenties, when approximately twice as many migrants moved during the previous ten years. But, the ravages of the depression led to a slowing of the rate of outmigration and subsequently to a sizeable return flow;[15] but, even during the worst of times,[16] this latter movement was not sufficiently adequate to offset the continued migration of blacks out of the South. By 1940, a full generation of black movers had departed from the cultural hearth and had subsequently established a secondary black population concentration in the Northeast and in the North Central region.

From 1910 to 1940, eight southern states were sources of almost two million black migrants (Fig. 3.3). The principal contributors were Georgia and South Carolina, followed by Mississippi and Alabama. As is shown in Table 3.2, the impact on the contributing states and receiving ports of entry was substantial.

The states of the South Atlantic division, despite their high fertility, were unable to maintain their population at the 1910 level; and all except North Carolina were inhabited by fewer blacks on the eve of World War I than in the initial time period. The secondary movement from Alabama and Mississippi during this interval was not enough to prevent these states' populations from growing.

TABLE 3.2 Black Population in 1910 and 1940 in Primary Sending States and Primary Ghetto Centers (in 1000's)

States	1910	1940	% Change 1910–1940	Ghetto Centers	1910	1940	% Inc. 1910–1940
Virginia	671	661	− 0.01	New York	92	458	+ 251
North Carolina	698	981	+40.0	Philadelphia	84	251	+ 209
South Carolina	836	814	− 0.3	Chicago	44	278	+ 531
Georgia	1,177	1,085	− 0.7	Detroit	6	149	+1,662
Alabama	908	983	+ 0.8	Cleveland	8	85	+ 975
Mississippi	1,009	1,075	+ 0.6	Pittsburgh	26	62	+ 134
Arkansas	444	483	+ 0.09	Indianapolis	22	51	+ 131
Louisiana	714	849	+17.0	St. Louis	44	109	+ 145

Source: U.S. Bureau of Censuses of 1910 and 1940.

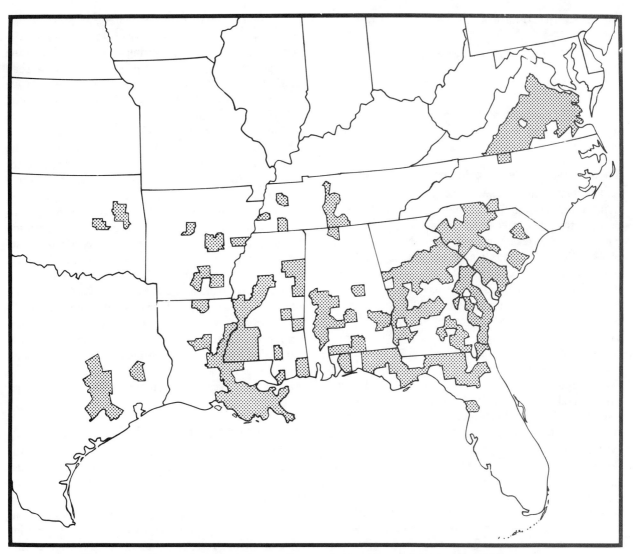

Figure 3.3. Black Population Losses, 1910–1940. (Courtesy of the University of Wisconsin-Milwaukee Cartographic Services.)

Black movement out of the South represents one of the primary movements in American migration history during the twentieth century. Because the depression sharply slowed black migration, the first phase of the migration movement was completed before 1940. But, during this thirty-year period, more than 1.7 million blacks had departed from the cultural hearth and were forging new lives for themselves in the Northeast and North Central part of the nation. Because prejudice was rampant and satisfactory residential accommodations were difficult to obtain, blacks encountered much difficulty in the new environment.[17] Fortunately, wages were higher and institutional constraints were lower. As a result, others were urged to join the migrants in what some were calling "the promised land."

WORLD WAR II USHERS IN A NEW MIGRATION PHASE: 1940–1970

The advent of the second major war in this century served as the impetus that catalyzed the depression-retarded flow of blacks from the South. The severe labor needs characterizing the period 1942–1945 did much to induce new movement. Since most of the war industries were concentrated in the American manufacturing belt, which had converted its peacetime facilities to war materials production, urban centers in the Northeast and North Central regions were again the principal targets of the migrant flows. The West, too, was a locus of aspects of war material production, especially aircraft and shipbuilding. Thus, for the first time, a sizeable number of black migrants were destined for selected western urban centers (Table 3.3). Prior to 1940, only Los Angeles, among western cities, was the place of residence of more than 25,000 blacks.

TABLE 3.3 The Destination of Southern Black Migrants from Southern Core States, 1940–50

Total Net Migrants	Northeast	North Central	West
1,244,792	411,766	528,675	304,351

Source: Conrad Taeuber and Irene B. Taeuber, *The Changing Population of the United States* (New York: John Wiley & Sons, Inc., 1958).

The Opening of New Employment Opportunity

The distribution of employment in war-related activity did much to influence the volume and direction of migration, as can be observed in the choice of specific migration target communities. Not only were blacks being drawn to urban centers that served as the primary ports of entry during the previous thirty years, but they were also attracted to places where there was only a nominal black presence in 1940. Cities such as San Francisco, Milwaukee, Boston, Buffalo, and Rochester were among the newer urban magnets that had not by 1940 qualified as ghetto centers. Thus, the war was primarily responsible for ushering in a third set of ghetto centers.

Although as a result of the war, blacks were settling in a larger number of urban centers, the primary contributors to the growth process were first and second generation ghetto centers. They were as a rule the largest urban centers in the nation and were subsequently able to absorb and house large numbers of migrants. But, when we consider the existence of the spatial pattern of racial restrictive covenants on housing, extraordinary pressures were placed on the housing stock in some of these centers. Seldom was housing available to blacks outside of the context of racial succession in the new environments. Because of the magnitude of migration to larger urban centers and the constraints on housing access, conversions were frequently necessary to satisfy part of the housing demand.[18]

Southern Cities Bypassed

By the end of the forties, the black population had grown to sizeable levels in the traditional migration target centers. All but a select set of southern cities were bypassed in this new movement wave. As a matter of fact, net migration out of a number of leading southern cities was the rule, with selected southern coastal cities serving as the only significant regional magnets. Among the 24 urban centers in the nation to attract more than 10,000 black migrants during this decade (the forties), only five were located in the South: Washington (65,000 net migrants), Baltimore (35,000 net migrants), Houston (25,000 net migrants), Norfolk (18,000 net migrants), and New Orleans (12,000 net migrants). None of the southern centers were among

the primary migration target centers, although Washington was a leading secondary center. Eventually the movement that occurred during this decade led to the largest concentration ever of blacks in northern urban centers, and the subsequent decline in the relative ranking of early black urban concentrations in Birmingham, Jacksonville, Richmond, and Louisville.

Not only were the migrant destinations altered during this period, but so were migrant origins. In the decade following World War I, the South Atlantic states were the principal contributors to the South-to-North migration stream and the subsequent growth of northern urban centers along its course. Although this area maintained its relative position as a migration source region during the more recent decade, it was seriously challenged by the East South Central division, largely on the basis of massive migration from Mississippi and Alabama. The West South Central division states of Arkansas and Louisiana also became significant contributors to regional abandonment. The contributions to migration from an expanded southern migration field were responsible for the sharp increase in the size of the black population in selected North Central and Western urban centers during the forties (Fig. 3.4).

The Role of Agricultural Mechanization

The decline in agricultural labor demand in the cotton South, as an outgrowth of reduced crop acreages and agricultural mechanization, freed sharecroppers from the land. Fligstein specifically states, "The introduction of cotton pickers in the late 1940's made the rural non-farm population a total surplus population and left them no choice but to migrate."[19] On the other hand, tobacco production was mechanized more slowly and possibly retarded the black outflow from North Carolina's bright-leaf tobacco producing counties. It has been previously pointed out that in some North Carolina rural counties there was an absolute increase in the black population during this decade, constituting a pattern not observed elsewhere.[20] Thus, with the expansion of opportunity in northern and western urban centers, which was motivated by the need to accelerate war production, many blacks left the South. Others left because of declining opportunity in southern agriculture, especially after the war's end. Shimkin[21] has made a distinction between persons who were pushed out of southern agriculture and persons who migrated because they perceived alternative opportunities. The former he described as refugees. In the next decade, the number of refugees in black migration streams no doubt increased as agricultural mechanization continued apace.

Generational Change in the National Economy

The movement that got underway during World War II continued almost unabated for 30 years. During those

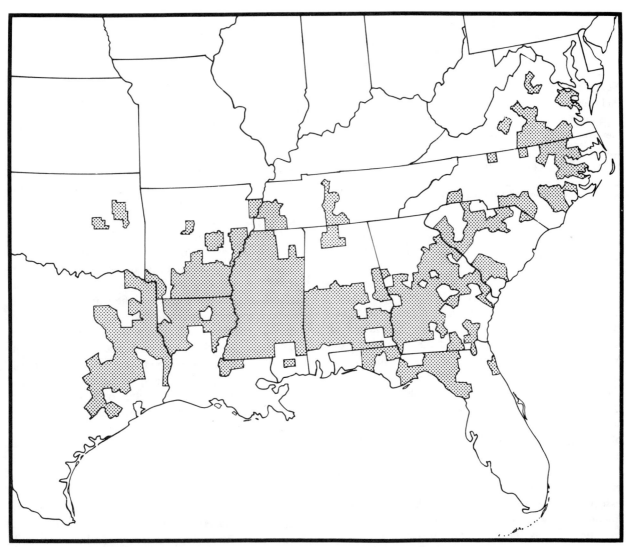

Figure 3.4. Black Population Losses, 1940–1970. (Courtesy of the University of Wisconsin-Milwaukee Cartographic Services.)

years more than four million blacks left the South to settle in the large urban centers of the North and West. By the end of the period, the South's share of the Nation's black population was reduced from 77 percent to 53 percent. The urban proportion of the population increased from less than 50 percent to more than 75 percent. Since the black population outside of the South was already overwhelmingly urban, the percentage increase also indicates a growing southern urbanization. Needless to say, the growth of southern urban centers was inadequate to stem the tide. It has been estimated that only 29 percent of southern black migrants during the fifties remained in the region, whereas 71 percent became part of interregional migration streams.[22] Thus the decline in demand for agricultural labor, coupled with growing tensions associated with the civil rights movement concentrated in southern cities, led many to seek opportunity and equality outside of the region.

Nevertheless, as a result of higher than average fertility, the southern black population grew by more than two million persons from 1940 to 1970.[23]

Major economic changes were to appear in the primary target zones, the Northeast and North Central regions, before this period was to come to a close. After 1960 it was clear that manufacturing was to play a declining role in the American economy. Not only was manufacturing growth decreasing, but the manufacturing belt states were unable to capture an equitable share of incremental growth. Thus black Americans were being attracted to manufacturing belt cities during a period when this activity was becoming relatively less important in the American economy, but at the same time manufacturing growth was beginning to take place in the region of abandonment. This did not become apparent, however, until the last decade of the generation.

TABLE 3.4 Changes in the Size of the Black Population in First and Second Generation Non-Southern Ghetto Centers: 1940–1970 (in 1000's)

	1940	1970		1940	1970
New York	504	1667	Cleveland	85	238
Philadelphia	251	654	St. Louis	166	254
Pittsburgh	62	105	Indianapolis	56	134
Newark	52	207	Cincinnati	51	125
Chicago	278	1103			
Detroit	149	660			

Source: USA Censuses of 1940 and 1970.

GHETTO DEVELOPMENT DURING THE SECOND GENERATION: 1940–1970

Movement since 1940 has led to massive ghetto formation. By the end of the period, first and second generation ghetto centers were the places of residence of no fewer than 200,000 black residents, with both New York and Chicago black communities housing in excess of one million persons (Table 3.4). Not only had the population grown absolutely, but the proportion of blacks in the city had changed as well, most often resulting in blacks constituting a minimum of one-third of the city's population. Among first and second generation centers, Los Angeles represents the sole exception, with a proportional population share of less than one-fifth. But, the changing proportions were primarily associated with the rate at which whites were abandoning the city for residence in metropolitan ring communities.[24] Thus the number of blacks entering the central city during this period was much smaller than the number of whites exiting. This movement subsequently led to a decline in both core city populations and jobs.

The Seeming Permanence of Ghetto Spatial Configurations

Ghetto formation permitted blacks from diverse origins to develop sanctuaries in the city during their period of initial arrival, but a continuous flow of migrants resulted in ghettos becoming permanent fixtures in American urban centers. Needless to say, this statement oversimplifies the problem. Moreover, the refusal of whites to share social space with blacks and the codification of that refusal in the establishment of racial restrictive covenants is well known. The latter did much to channel growth in the first generation to a set of rigid corridors.[25] Thus it was not until after the previous generation of migrants had carved out a residential niche for themselves were racially restrictive covenants outlawed. But, by 1948, the year the decision was rendered, the ghetto pattern was already fully developed.

Hence, a comparison of black and European ethnic ghetto development patterns prior to this period represents a comparison of an involuntary versus a voluntary development.

Throughout this period, blacks acquired housing through the racial succession process, and only recently has that pattern begun to show signs of modification. The nature and quality of the black residential environment is, therefore, a function of the nature of available housing in the wake of black expansion. During periods of surplus construction, the quality of black residential space is likely to be enhanced,[26] but during downturns in housing construction, trickle-down housing is unavailable to satisfy demand.

Unlike the fifties, the building boom in American metropolitan areas during the sixties loosened demand in core cities. Subsequently, blacks were able to upgrade their housing stock, and once this housing construction boom got underway, the transition of border markets to ghetto space accelerated. By the end of the interval, the flow of black migrants to a number of the previous target cities had slackened, but the absolute size of the black population was sufficiently large to propel expansion of ghetto space beyond the political limits of the core city. From 1965 to 1969 this spill over effect was to account for a large share of black movement to select suburban areas.

Black Residential Development in Southern Cities

Black population growth in southern cities occurred more slowly during this developmental period. Prior to the 1950s, blacks were seldom involved in the racial residential succession process. Housing was built, rather, to satisfy the demand on a race-specific basis. At the beginning of the interval, therefore, southern cities were likely to contain a number of pockets of black residential development, with additional units often built adjacent to existing pockets. The ghettoization process did not appear to get underway in southern cities until the fifties when economic and social changes in the South led to modifying the racial housing allocation process. Once the modified process got underway, a filling-in of spaces separating individual pockets of black residences was initiated, and racial residential succession began.

Earlier it was indicated that the ghetto concept as employed here was inapplicable to black residential concentrations in southern cities prior to the recent period. That position was based on the general absence of racial residential turnover as the predominant mode of allocating housing to blacks. This is not to say that blacks and whites did not reside in racially segregated communities, but only to point out early differences that often led to a different spatial pattern of residential segregation. In the South, moreover, social distance between blacks and whites was not determined by propinquity. As institutional barriers began to decline, however, and as the threat of institutional sharing became more prominent, convergence toward the northern pattern of black residential allocation began to appear.

From 1950 to 1956, Coe[27] reports that none of the non-white housing units added in Atlanta were previously occupied by whites. But by 1970, the previously existing pattern had been modified. Kenyon writing almost two decades later, described the Atlanta situation in the following way:

> Although Atlanta, like other southern cities, is still characterized by a number of small, as well as large black neighborhoods and communities, the rapid growth and consolidation of these sections is leading to a pattern increasingly similar to the massive ghetto belts of the large northern city.[28]

It appears currently that a mixed racial residential allocation process operates in southern cities, where both new construction in black social space and racial residential turnover are principally responsible for satisfying incremental demand. Long and Spain,[29] employing sample survey data, indicate that from 1967 to 1971 only one-sixth of black demand in southern cities was satisfied via racial succession, whereas more than two-fifths of the units occupied by blacks in the Northeast were acquired by way of racial turnover. Thus, in attempting to evaluate the impact of migration-inspired housing demand on the ghettoization process, one should be constantly aware that the housing allocation mechanism in southern and non-southern cities did not begin to converge until after 1950.

The slower rate of migration to southern cities generally led to less pressure on the existing housing supply. In locations where growth was rapid, however, a combination of residential turnover and new construction in black residential space satisfied demand. The strong tradition of supporting a separation of the races in the South, coupled with an absence of political clout in the black community led new construction, whether privately or publicly financed, to take place in settings designed to attract one racial group or the other. Blacks who gained access to new housing were often better housed than persons possessing similar socioeconomic rank outside of the South. Under the circumstances, demand for housing in previously white areas was tempered by the lower intensity of demand and access to an alternative supply. Thus, although it is no longer improper to describe southern black communities in a metropolitan context as ghetto communities, it would be shortsighted to think of them as being historically equivalent to similar communities that have evolved outside of the region. Although convergence has been underway for almost a generation, it is not yet complete.

The Black Migrational Response to Incipient Post-Industrial Development

The last decade of the 1940–70 period was one of great social upheaval and economic change. Older core cities were characterized by population decline and subsequent erosion of their tax base. Jobs that had been easily available during a previous period were now shifting to the suburbs, and small towns were becoming accessible by completion of the National Defense Highway System. Lower income blacks were trapped in environments of limited opportunity, whereas their middle income counterparts were actively involved in gaining access to housing along the white-black border.

The pattern of acquiring housing in urban centers outside the South led to a socio-spatial stratification of the population within black communities, in many ways similar to that prevailing in the larger society. When the size of the black population became sufficiently large, it created the basis for extending the ghetto into contiguous suburban communities. Thus, by 1970, the largest metropolitan areas in the country, which also happened to represent the place of residence of the nation's largest black population concentrations, were also places where the largest black suburban ring populations were to be found. Needless to say, these new suburban ring populations, although much smaller in size, were almost as rigidly segregated as central city populations. Therefore, suburbanization was seldom tantamount to dispersion.

By the end of the second generation of 20th century black migration, the national pattern of black population distribution had been radically altered from that existing in 1910. A rural population had gone to the city with the expectation that their life chances would be improved. When blacks chose to migrate to places with income levels significantly higher than those in the area of origin, they logically expected improved wages. The nature of the economy supporting such income differences was however, in the throes of transition toward the end of this period. The ushering in of a post-industrial economy was to have an impact on second generation movers and their offspring in ways that could not have been foreseen in the forties or fifties. By 1970 it was evident that major changes were underway and that some black migrants who had earlier chosen to leave the South for the non-South were beginning to reverse their course.

LARGE METROPOLITAN CENTERS AS POTENTIAL MIGRATION BASES

By 1970 the black population nationally had become overwhelmingly urban. There had developed a sizeable increase in the number of blacks who were residents of the national system of ghetto centers with black populations of 50,000 or more. Smaller ghetto centers—with fewer than 50,000 blacks but more than 25,000 blacks—were also frequently in evidence and growing. But the larger centers in this network constituted a population base that led to intermetropolitan migration becoming the modal origin and destination of black migrants. This is not to imply that non-metropolitan to metropolitan migration was not occurring, but that its contribution had been dampened. Non-metropolitan migrants were most often destined for the largest urban centers in the nation, whereas intermetropolitan destinations were more diffuse. The growth of non-southern metropolitan black populations over two generations had established a migrant population base that approached the southern base in size, and this growth largely fostered the transition to intermetropolitan dominance.

The Role of Non-Southern Migrants on Changing Migration Patterns

There is an extensive literature describing both black rural to urban migration and migration from the South to the non-South. But interregional flow data emphasizing the movement pattern of black migrants of non-southern origin is almost non-existent. Yet, from 1965 to 1970, non-southern black migrants were found to contribute substantially to the total of black migration to the principal non-South migration targets. Table 3.5 compares southern migrants to the leading migrant targets of both migrant groups. In one-third of the targets, non-South migrants constitute the majority, but they account for more than two-fifths in an additional

TABLE 3.5 Southern and Non-Southern Contribution to Primary Non-Southern Migration Centers: 1965–70

Target Centers	Non-Southern Migrants	Southern Migrants	Non-Southern Migrants as % of Total
New York	17,661	38,206	32.0%
Los Angeles	38,575	34,370	53.0%
Chicago	16,512	33,325	33.1%
Detroit	22,788	33,081	40.8%
Philadelphia	17,661	17,885	49.7%
San Francisco	18,935	13,907	57.7%
Newark	9,308	12,015	43.7%
Cleveland	8,281	10,820	43.4%
St. Louis	7,613	9,088	45.6%
Boston	4.757	6.198	43.4%
San Diego	7,150	5,276	57.5%
Milwaukee	4,356	4,764	47.8%
Indianapolis	4,377	4,411	49.8%
Columbus	5,037	4,222	54.4%
Kansas City, Mo.	4,416	4,320	50.5%

Source: U.S. Department of Commerce, Bureau of the Census, *Mobility for Metropolitan Areas* (U.S. Census of Population 1970, Final Report PC(2)-2C).

eight centers. Only in Chicago and New York did non-southern migrants represent as few as one-third of all migrants. Non-southern migrants were the predominant group in each of the western centers as were they in Columbus, Ohio, and Kansas City, Missouri. Only in centers where the vast majority of the migrants are from the South does non-metropolitan migration origin become the dominant one. Thus, New York and Chicago continue to represent the primary target destination of migrants from states where the non-metropolitan population continues to be larger than the metropolitan populaton; e.g., Mississippi and North Carolina.

The contribution of non-southern migrants to principal metropolitan complexes within the region is approximately 80 percent of that of southern migrants to center growth. Non-southern migrants, however, were far less likely to migrate to southern metropolitan areas, although Washington, Baltimore, Atlanta, Houston, Memphis and Dallas are exceptions. Nevertheless, the volume of flow from the non-South to these centers is only one-third to one-fourth as large as the southern flow. An exception is Washington, where the southern flow is only twice as large as that from the non-South. One of the problems with attempting to specify the magnitude of the non-southern flow is our inability to specify what part of this represents return migration. Returnees could seriously inflate the proportion of non-southern migrants destined for southern migrant targets.

THE POST-CITY AGE AND THE NON-METROPOLITAN TURNAROUND

A number of geographers have chronicled the changing spatial pattern of population shifts in the United States since 1970. Brunn and Phillips[30] postulate that we have now entered a fifth major epoch of urban systems development. They describe this new epoch as "Slow Growth" or Post-City age, which they attribute to the widespread adoption of birth control technology, the alterations in energy availability, and the "rural renaissance" that has occurred in the United States since 1970. The last factor they attribute to major developments in electronic communications technology.

A similar theme has been promoted by Fisher and Mitchelson,[31] but with greater emphasis being placed on what they term the population turnaround, which refers to the positive net migration occurring in non-metropolitan areas from the nation's urban core. Other than Berry and Dahmann,[32] little attention has been devoted to changes in the black population in particular, or the implications of these changes on the well-being of blacks in economically declining environments.

Changes in the Recent Pattern
of Black Migration

Some of the more notable features of recent United States migration history were the turnaround involving movement from metro to non-metropolitan environments during the seventies, and the major change in the regional focus of migrants. The changing structure of the economy seems to now favor southern or Sunbelt growth and development. An expressed preference for small town living and the increasing potential for acting on that preference has led to major adjustments in the historic pattern of black migration.

During the early seventies, Campbell and Johnson,[33] using Current Population Survey (CPS) data, reported that more blacks migrated to the South than left the region. Because the CPS sample was small and the difference in the size of the in-and-out southern movement was also small, the authors were uncertain at the time whether this marked the beginning of a new trend. Even as recently as 1977, Current Population Survey reports indicated "From March 1975 to March 1977 the number of blacks moving from the South was not significantly different from the number moving to that region." Now that the 1980 census results are available, it is possible to estimate what actual changes have occurred in the migration behavior of blacks under an altered set of constraints. This preliminary assessment will be based on a forward projection of the known aggregate rate of natural increase of the black population during the decade. Because rates of natural increase vary across a number of dimensions, the projected increase will vary substantially from the actual increase from place to place. Despite this weakness, the approximate dimensions of the net change in the number of black migrants from place to place can be estimated.

Return Movement to the South

By 1970 it was evident that a growing number of blacks were moving back to the South and that the percentage of black return migrants during 1965–70 was greater than during the period 1955–60. Twenty percent of the blacks leaving the South during this interval had returned by 1970.[34] During the second half of the sixties, returning blacks set the stage for the pattern that was to evolve in the seventies. Most returnees were young, better educated than black migrants in general, and held higher status jobs than did southern non-migrants.[35] Nevertheless, returnees did not earn as much as non-returnees, although they earned more than blacks who had remained in the South.[36]

Although evidence shows that black migrants to the South have been selective on a number of dimensions, it is still unclear what provoked this growing return flow. There are strong indications, however, that the downturn in the economy of the economic core region during the seventies was an important factor in the alteration of the pattern of black interregional flow. Moreover, at various times during the decade, several core region cities bordered on the abyss of fiscal collapse. Unemployment levels rose and labor force participation rates continued to decline. The Northeast was the hardest hit financially, while the North Central region seemed better able to hold its own. But, by the end of the decade, the relative position of the North and Northeast compared to the South and the West was economically unfavorable. During this period changes occurring in regional economic development led to the use of the Frostbelt/Sunbelt designations to highlight the environmental context in which economic change was taking place. How have blacks been affected by these changes, especially in terms of their migration propensities?

PRESENT MOBILITY STATUS

In 1980, the nation's black population totalled 26 million, unadjusted for the undercount. The growth rate declined from the previous decade: 20.0 percent to 17.3 percent. This change largely reflected a continuing decline in black fertility rates, with only limited change in mortality rates. The 17.3 percent increase in the black population during the decade may be used to project the size of the 1980 black population at the county level in those 645 counties that constitute the cultural hearth, and at the city, metropolitan ring, and regional levels as well. Using this technique makes it possible to uncover the basic dimensions of black mobility during the seventies.

It is clear from viewing Table 3.6 that the nation's black population growth varies widely on the basis of region of residence. From 1970 to 1980, the South, for the first time in this century, was a net recipient of black population; the Northeast was a net loser. The magnitude of southern gain was modest, agreeing with the pattern shown in Current Population Survey data during the early seventies. Later Current Population Survey data indicate the magnitude of black movement to the South during the second half of the decade was much greater than during the first half. The North Central region had a small net loss. The big gainer, however, was the West, which absorbed almost 300,000 blacks. These crude estimates imply that movement has become more diffuse and that the origins of in and out movers are so disguised in these net data that a clear pattern of interregional movement cannot be easily deduced.

Changing Regional Linkages

Given the observed net differences at state and county levels, some additional insights can be gained. Previous migration linkages between census divisions in the South and the non-South also provide clues in

TABLE 3.6 Regional Black Population Changes: 1970–80

Region	Population 1970	Population 1980	Percent Change Resulting from Net Migration
The South	11,957,055	14,041,374	+ 0.4
South Atlantic	6,381,843	7,647,743	+ 2.8
East South Central	2,569,625	2,868,268	− 5.4
West South Central	3,005,587	3,525,363	+ 0.3
The Northeast	4,336,913	4,848,786	− 5.2
Middle Atlantic	3,950,356	4,374,237	− 6.0
New England	386,557	474,549	+ 5.8
North Central	4,565,413	5,337,542	− 0.1
East North Central	3,857,653	4,547,998	+ 0.6
West North Central	697,760	789,544	− 3.8
The West	1,690,434	2,261,516	+16.8
Pacific	1,512,018	1,992,856	+14.8
Mountain	178,416	286,660	+33.6

Source: 1970 and 1980 Census of Population and Housing (Advance Reports)

deducing the magnitude and direction of migration flows. What becomes clear from reviewing change at a subregional scale is the continuation of the previous pattern of net outmigration from those non-metropolitan counties that constitute the cultural hearth. Given the general absence of economic opportunity in most of these locations, this comes as no surprise. Approximately one-fifth (3,471,906) of the nation's black population was found in this setting in 1970. Moland describes these persons as "the people left behind" and goes on to describe them as poor people who continue to suffer "unemployment, underemployment, inadequate housing, isolation from community services, and lack of access to resources and leadership to meet these and other needs."[37] But, even within this setting, differential opportunity and variations in the intensity of poverty prevail.

If size of population loss in individual non-metropolitan counties is an index of an absence of hope, then what happens in these counties during the 1980s provides some indirect evidence on the changes that are occurring in the opportunity structure. Figure 3.5 depicts the major losing counties during the seventies. A review of the changes in volume of net migration shows that in each state there has been a sharp decline in the volume of loss from counties registering excessive losses. Only in Mississippi were losses similar to those occurring during the previous decade sustained in more than 25 percent of the losing counties. What becomes evident is, although non-metropolitan black populations are not growing as a result of net migration, they do not continue to sustain losses of the magnitude of the recent past. Only selected Delta counties of Mississippi and Arkansas have continued to have losses similar to those of the previous decade.

Are these smaller net losses the result of a continued return flow of individuals who were previous residents of the region, or is there a general retardation in leaving rates? On the basis of preliminary data this question cannot be answered (unequivocally). In the past, Delta counties do not appear to have attracted a significant return flow when one considers the volume of outmovement. The return flow described earlier was selective in its target destination, with the principal targets being selected locations in Maryland, Virginia, North Carolina, and South Carolina.

Large net outmigration levels from the Northeast, a division with strong ties to the South Atlantic division, could possibly have led to a sizeable return flow to that division. But, the level of net migration from the North Central region was estimated to be nominal and thereby limited the magnitude of the return flow to East South Central division states. Thus, it can be deduced that there has been a slowdown in net outmigration from the South's non-metropolitan counties in general, and with only modest return flow to the previously heavy-losing Delta counties, but possibly a larger return flow to counties in North Carolina, South Carolina and Virginia.

Has There Been a Non-metropolitan Turnaround?

The population turnaround in southern non-metropolitan counties is not the result of a large scale movement back to the region, but rather the result of a retarded outflow that permitted most such counties to experience an increase in their black population during the seventies. The movement of blacks to non-metropolitan counties in the South during the seventies does not appear to represent a meaningful element in the

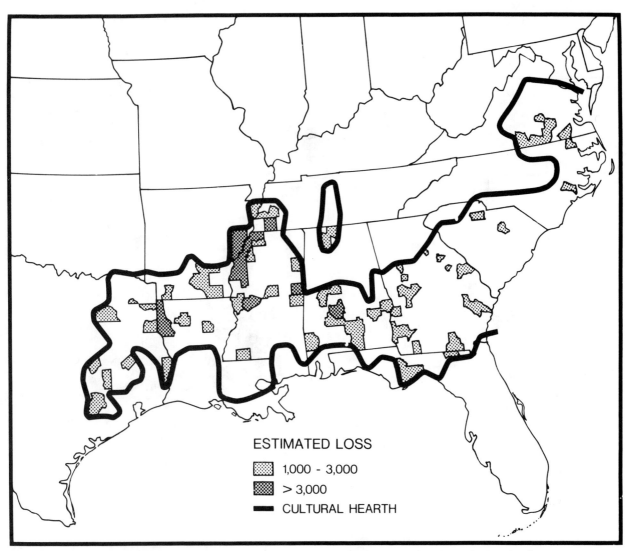

Figure 3.5. Primary Black Population Loss in the Non-Metropolitan South During the Seventies. (Courtesy of the University of Wisconsin-Milwaukee Cartographic Services.)

ESTIMATED LOSS
- 1,000 - 3,000
- > 3,000
- CULTURAL HEARTH

pattern of regional redistribution, a factor distinguishing it from the non-metropolitan turnaround characterizing white migration behavior over the same interval. The continuing absence of opportunity in the core of the cultural hearth still permits those counties to serve as a seedbed for regional outmigration. Numerous writers have suggested that the manufacturing expansion underway in the non-metropolitan South has simply bypassed counties where blacks constitute a significant element in the population.

Estall[38] indicates that more than 200,000 manufacturing jobs were created in the South between 1970–1977. This growth in manufacturing activity has contributed to promoting turnaround in non-metropolitan counties. But Walker states that "The Southern turnaround counties that have been the primary beneficiaries of industrial decentralization are overwhelmingly white in racial composition."[39] On the other hand, Hart and Chestang[40] have provided a contrasting

scenario in describing the absorption of former black farm workers into the manufacturing economy of numerous eastern Carolina tobacco counties. One can only conclude from this evidence that non-metropolitan counties with large black populations are seldom chosen as plant site locations; in the few instances where this has occurred, blacks have been successfully absorbed into the economy.

The Renewed Growth of Southern Urban Centers

It must be assumed that if black outmigration from non-metropolitan counties is continuing, then intra-regional metropolitan centers are serving as the locus of intervening opportunity. As older southern metropolitan areas have grown during the recent period and new ones have come into existence, they are more attractive to a segment of non-metropolitan movers than are a growing number of urban centers outside of the region. Such a pattern can be deduced by simply observing the

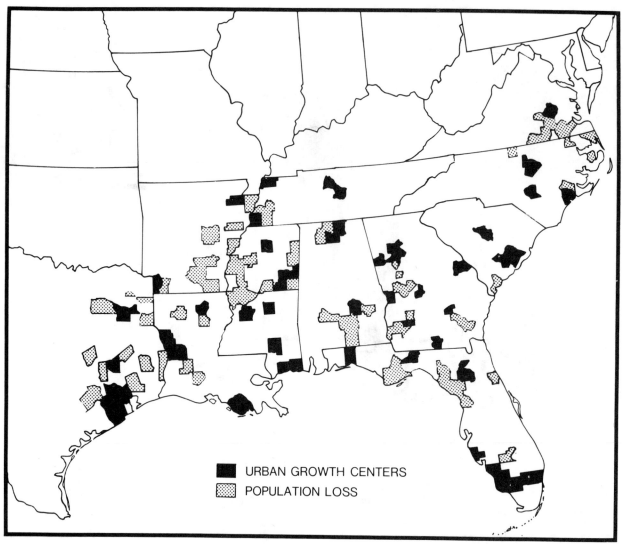

Figure 3.6. Black Population Loss in Counties Contiguous to Urban Growth Centers, 1970–1980. (Courtesy of the University of Wisconsin-Milwaukee Cartographic Services.)

URBAN GROWTH CENTERS

POPULATION LOSS

net migration characteristics of non-metropolitan counties in the vicinity of southern metro areas (Fig. 3.6). In most instances, net in-migration characterizes southern central cities, whereas the surrounding non-metropolitan field is characterized by a net outflow.

Migration to southern and western metropolitan areas during the most recent decade does much to highlight the plight of the metropolitan economy in the Northeast and North Central regions. A turnaround in migration to these regions has indeed occurred. They are becoming net migration dispensers as opposed to receivers.

The primary destination of black migrants during the seventies is not easy to deduce. But, if the projection method employed here does not seriously distort reality, the largest volume of net migration has been directed towards a selected set of central cities in the South and West. The primary target cities are tentatively identified in Table 3.7. Among the top ten cen-

tral city targets, only Milwaukee was not located in the Sunbelt. A note of caution is, however, in order. All of the central cities shown in Table 3.7, with the probable exception of Birmingham and Oakland, have no significant metropolitan ring population. Ring growth was very sizeable in some metropolitan areas; and since its origin cannot be specified, there is no way to identify its inter- and intra-regional components. In some instances, persons who might have in the past settled in the central cities may now be by-passing them for life in the suburban ring.

The Relative Decline of First and Second Generation Ghetto Centers

As a result of altered migration patterns, first and second generation ghetto centers in the Northeast and North Central Census divisions have been the principal losers. This may prove somewhat misleading, however, when one views the pattern of mobility at a larger scale;

TABLE 3.7 Primary Destination of Black Migrants to Central Cities

City	1970 Population	1980 Population	Estimated Net Migration
Houston, TX	316,551	440,257	70,000
Memphis, TN	242,513	307,702	24,000
Milwaukee, WI	105,008	146,940	24,000
Jackson, MS	61,063	95,357	23,000
Dallas, TX	210,038	265,594	20,000
San Diego, CA	52,691	77,000	16,000
Oakland, CA	124,710	159,234	14,000
Charlotte, NC	72,972	97,627	12,000
Shreveport, LA	62,152	84,627	12,000
Birmingham, AL	126,388	158,223	11,000

Source: *Data User News,* (Bureau of Census, United States Department of Commerce), October, 1981. Net migration figures derived by author.

that is, if one shifts to the metropolitan area rather than simply focusing attention on central cities, a different view emerges. Rapidly increasing black populations in these metropolitan areas (first and second generation centers) during the period 1940–70 have made it virtually impossible for the central cities of these metropolitan areas to accommodate the diverse housing needs of this population and those of competing populations at the same time. Thus, during the seventies, although numerous ghetto centers experienced net outmigration from central cities, their suburban ring communities experienced net in-migration. The results of this process are highlighted in Table 3.8.

If the estimates are reasonably accurate, it becomes clear that two processes are at work. In New York, Philadelphia, Cleveland, and St. Louis there has been a net loss of both blacks and whites from the metropolitan areas, reflecting the inability of these economies to provide the desired level of economic support. But in each instance, there was net in-migration to the suburban ring, although inadequate in volume to prevent a net loss from the metropolitan area. Nevertheless, with the exception of Houston, the scale of suburban movement in a set of predominately non-southern metropolitan areas exceeds that characterizing the leading net central city gainers. This fact reflects a difference in the stage of the mobility process that distinguishes ghetto centers on both a regional basis and age of the black community in developmental terms. Suburbanization represents the most recent stage of development and is essentially confined to first and second generation ghetto centers. Ghetto centers in the previously cited stage of development are beginning to manifest mobility characteristics that were previously associated with older central cities in general.

The lesser discrepancy in the magnitude of estimated net change in Detroit, Chicago, and Cleveland no doubt reflects the continuing central city in-migration to those centers, although on a much reduced scale.

TABLE 3.8 Net In- and Out-Migration Patterns Within the Spatial Structure of Selected Metropolitan Areas: 1970–80

Ghetto Center	Central City Net Migration	Suburban Ring Net Migration
New York	− 165,000	+ 43,000
Newark	− 51,000	+ 50,000
Philadelphia	− 125,000	+ 23,000
Cleveland	− 91,000	+ 60,000
Detroit	− 14,000	+ 15,000
Chicago	− 93,000	+ 80,000
St. Louis	− 91,000	+ 55,000
Los Angeles	− 83,000	+157,000
Washington	− 180,000	+194,000
Baltimore	− 91,000	+ 44,000

Source: Estimates derived by author based on changes in size of population between 1970 and 1980.

Under the circumstances, one can only speculate at this point about the distinguishing characteristics of movers involved in centripetal and centrifugal flows to selected ghetto centers. Implicitly these movement patterns, if they are largely characterized by suburban spillover, provide support for Deskins'[41] contention that the current stage is metropolitan ghettoization rather than the previously described stage of central city ghettoization.

The latter stage of development reached its apex in first and second generation non-southern and southern border centers. This pattern is also evident in Atlanta, Miami, Richmond, and New Orleans. In most southern centers net out-migration from the suburban ring represents the modal pattern, reflecting both the more recent development of suburban ring communities in southern metropolitan areas and the presence of blacks in rural settings in metropolitan counties.

In some instances the recent rapid expansion of suburban developments in newer southern centers has led to black displacement; in other instances it has led to rural blacks in ring counties abandoning these locations for central city life. The latter pattern seems to be at work in southern counties characterized by absolute black population losses during the most recent decade when found in close proximity to counties characterized by black net in-migration. At this point, it is unclear what the role of small metropolitan centers and non-metropolitan counties with small urban centers has been in attracting black migrants to their sphere of influence. It should be noted, however, that a small number of counties suffering absolute population losses were not located in close proximity to growth center counties. Nevertheless it is possible that smaller urban places in the South may become increasingly important as migration targets for interregional migrants.

FUTURE IMPLICATIONS OF MIGRATION STRATEGIES AS A PROMOTER OF ECONOMIC OPPORTUNITY

This chapter has focused attention on the movement pattern of blacks in the United States during the 20th century. Movement represents a single strategy that might be employed to enhance opportunity and/or to escape oppression. Because social and economic conditions prevailing in the rural South at the turn of the century were destined to keep most blacks mired in poverty, blacks were motivated to move by both of the foregoing stimulants. Likewise, to understand more fully the present position of blacks in America, it becomes necessary to provide a temporal-spatial backdrop that reflects the principal economic and social changes that have taken place throughout the 20th century. Therefore, a non-static but continuously changing set of circumstances has guided the actions of the nation's largest minority as they have attempted to alter their status.

The Role of the Changing Complexity of the American Economy

The geography of black America has changed continuously, going from a single-region population to a multi-region population on the macro scale, and from a rural population to an urban population on the micro scale. But, as we approach the 21st century, it appears even greater changes can be anticipated if blacks continue to depend on migration strategies as a means of adjusting to changes in the national and international economies.

Yet, because of the complexities of the changes occurring in the economy and the lag in timing between economic and social change, the movement strategies are unclear at this time. For example, it is often said that blacks can more easily engage in interregional moves than in some intra-metropolitan moves, i.e., the movement to non-black suburbs. Social barriers continue to be high even as economic barriers fall. The future geography of black America will be strongly conditioned, therefore, by these two sets of forces.

Ethnicity and Economic Competition

The previously described movement strategies have allowed blacks to reduce the proportion of their population described as living below the poverty line and at the same time to elevate the percent of the population whose earnings place them in the middle class. Nevertheless, problems still abound. Progress for blacks has been slow when compared to that of other groups entering the northern industrial system at about the same time, or only somewhat earlier, and possessing similar handicaps.[42] By 1970, the immigrants or European ethnics who arrived at the turn of the century had essentially escaped their earlier poverty status and entrapment in inner city ghettos. Furthermore, their children and/or grandchildren no longer have their identities operate as major barriers to upward economic and social mobility.

Despite the claims of "the declining significance of race,"[43] there is widespread evidence that race continues to affect important decisions having an impact both on employment opportunity as well as on one's position in social space. Berry and Kasarda[44] have indicated that some employers are strongly motivated to relocate their administrative offices in order to minimize the number of black applicants in the labor pool. Thus, in attempting to account for the present economic status of blacks in American society, it becomes very difficult to disentangle the role of social and economic factors.

It should be clear that although a set of social forces has produced conditions favoring the evolution of a black ethnicity—leading to internal group cohesion—it is race that motivates an external response that places blacks in an economically disadvantaged position. To be sure, differences are more stylistic than substantive, e.g., the North versus the South. But, if further group progress is to be anticipated before the turn of the 21st century, it will be necessary for both the economic and the social systems to show greater openness.

Changing Economic Organization and Its Impact on Intragroup Linkages

Changes in the organizational structure of the American economy have affected the status of America's black population in both positive and negative ways.[45] These changes have allowed a growing number of blacks to enter the ranks of white-collar employment, accompanied by a corresponding change in class position. Yet, on the negative side, an increasing number of individuals are being trapped in poverty and welfare dependency.[46] Until we are able to more fully understand the impact of the forces that produce this conflicting set of conditions, it will be difficult to outline the prospective future of black America. A question that might be legitimately raised is the following. How will the future of blacks be affected by geography and how will it affect geography?

There is growing evidence that the changing geography of economic opportunity is likely to play as crucial a role as it has in the past. For instance, will the continued movement of blacks to the suburbs, as occurred during the seventies, drive a wedge between black have- and have-not communities (anchored in core cities)? Or, do the communities constitute single economic and social entities that are mutually dependent upon each other?

The foregoing discussion specifically raises the question of the extent to which the growing black middle class has attained its status by providing service to a stable or expanding lower class. If the black middle class has experienced only limited success in penetrating the private sector, white-collar labor field, then its future status is likely to be highly problematic and bound up in the ghetto configurations described throughout this essay. On the other hand, a weakening of the links between these communities will no doubt lead to a heightened probability for violent conflict on the part of segments of the population permanently trapped in the worst of inner city environments. The strength of race as opposed to ethnicity, however, will quite likely influence future changes in the economy and how they affect the socio-spatial character of the nation's black population, both at macro (regional) and micro (neighborhood) levels.

Perceptions and Choice of Migration Strategies

From the perspective of geography a number of actions, based on migratory behavior, could significantly influence the well-being of the nation's black population. Among them are the receptivity of small urban centers outside of the South to a black presence; the willingness of northern-born blacks to migrate to southern growth centers; and the feedback associated with post-1968 international migration patterns. With regard to the first item, if blacks perceive small non-southern urban areas to be hostile places, then they might refuse to settle in environments of expanding economic opportunity. Likewise, as indicated earlier, the largest potential black migrant pool exists in northern ghetto centers. The majority of these persons are native to the northern urban region. The question becomes the following: To what extent will earlier images of the South influence their decision to migrate to the South if opportunity is to be found there? And, finally, what will be the likely impact of unskilled Asian and Latin immigrants on low-income black populations in those urban centers where these groups most

often settle? Will they replace blacks as the new generation of inner city poor? Or, will these groups simply intensify the competition for scarce resources and therefore initiate a new round of urban violence?

The current status of the nation's black population represents a vast improvement over their status in 1910, but so does that of the nation. Moreover, black progress has moved at a much slower pace and, therefore, has been the recipient of both the good and the bad associated with the faster pace of national economic development.

For the segment of the black population that has suffered most as a result of the negative feedback associated with an increasingly secularized society, it is unclear if any migration strategy will lead to softening the blow. Nevertheless, migration will continue to represent a strategy to facilitate an effective adjustment to changes in economic development. The extent to which these strategies prove effective, at least in terms of migrant destinations, will largely revolve around a set of social decisions that continue to be undergirded by racial considerations.

SUMMARY AND CONCLUSIONS

A brief assessment of the movement pattern of black Americans focusing on 20th century movements illustrates one facet of economic change upon the lives of the nation's largest racial minority. From 1910 to 1980, the pattern of black population distribution has undergone major change as it has shifted from a regional concentration in the South to a national distribution in which each of the nation's major regions has a significant black presence. The movement has not been uniform, however, but has been associated with major changes in national economic development.

Two major wars and changes in the structure and technology of southern agriculture provided the primary impetus for many of the moves. The pre-1910 black population was overwhelmingly southern and rural, such that more than 600 contiguous counties, plus a few others, evolved as the cultural hearth of black America. During the 20th century, the intensity of settlement in non-urban hearth counties has continuously declined, although they have remained a seedbed for a national black population. Now, more than two generations later, secondary regional clusters have evolved, which are almost totally urban, having only limited contact with the South. Only a minority of persons in the North and West today were born in the South.

The timing and direction of movement have led to a staged evolution in the national settlement pattern. A national system of ghetto centers has emerged as the most obvious element of recent black migration history. That system was essentially confined to the Northeast and North Central region during the first generation of movement. In the second generation, it expanded to include major urban centers in the West and secondary centers in the North. During the more recent period, the pattern of urban residence in the metropolitan South took on many characteristics of ghetto centers elsewhere. By 1980, the national network had become coextensive with the location of large and intermediate metropolitan areas.

Much of what has transpired during the first two generations of movement has been well documented, although much of that work has focused on interregional flows at the expense of intraregional and intermetropolitan flows. More importantly, an attempt has been made here to illustrate the importance of structural changes in the United States economy upon the character, volume, and direction of black population movement. It is generally concluded that the United States developed into a post-industrial economy sometime during the post-World War II period. It was not until the seventies, however, that black migration patterns first began to reflect this change. Thus, a third generation of black migration got underway and is already beginning to modify the settlement system that emerged after 1910.

The principal dimensions of settlement which are beginning to emerge that reflect both a break with the past, as well as a continuation of the past, are the following: 1) rapid suburbanization in the larger first and second generation ghetto centers; 2) net outmigration from the core cities in a number of first and second generation ghetto centers; 3) absolute population decline in selected first and second generation centers; 4) rapid population growth in large and intermediate southern ghetto centers; and 5) the continued net outmigration from non-metropolitan counties of the cultural hearth. Many of these changes simply represent a late response to general changes that have been underway for some time. The non-metropolitan turnaround, which has recently received extensive attention, does not appear to be underway in southern counties which have a significant black presence.

This essay has not explicitly grappled with the complex problems associated with the status change of blacks during this century. Implicitly, however, that is what this discussion is all about. Migration simply represents one strategy used to minimize the level of status inequality. There is little question that this strategy has produced pronounced reductions in the level of inequality, but a significant gap continues to remain. Migration can only be expected to reduce status inequality within limits established by the larger society. As long as a move is perceived to produce some advantage, it will be made; yet the central issue becomes, where are the perceived locations of advantaged environments for the largest number of potential movers?

Black migration and movement patterns will continue to be dominated by economic considerations with social considerations playing a secondary role. Will young blacks born in the North seriously consider a move to the South? Or will blacks who moved to northern cities in the forties and fifties retire to the non-metropolitan South in the eighties and nineties? These are questions which should now be answered, but the decision to move is likely to be motivated by both social and economic interpretations. It is quite possible, however, that other far-reaching and unexpected changes will occur in the propensity and direction of black migration during the remainder of this century.

NOTES

1. Lerone Bennett, *Before the Mayflower* (Chicago: Johnson Publishing Co., 1967).
2. Robert W. Fogel and Stanley L. Engerman, *Time on the Cross* (Boston: Little, Brown and Co., 1974).
3. Kenneth F. Kiple and Virginia H. King, *Another Dimension to Black Diaspora* (New York: Cambridge University Press, 1981).
4. Daniel M. Johnson and Rex R. Campbell, *Black Migration in America* (Durham, North Carolina: Duke University Press, 1981).
5. Wesley C. Calef and Howard J. Nelson, "Distribution of Negro Population in the United States," *The Geographical Review,* 46 (January, 1956): pp. 82–97.
6. John Fraser Hart, "The Changing Distribution of the American Negro," *Annals of the Association of American Geographers,* 50 (September, 1960): pp. 242–266.
7. G. M. Lewis, "The Distribution of the Negro in the Conterminous United States," *Geography,* 54 (November, 1969): pp. 410–418.
8. Richard L. Morrill and O. Fred Donaldson, "Geographical Perspectives on the History of Black America," *Economic Geography,* 48 (January, 1972): pp. 1–23.
9. Daniel O. Price, *Changing Characteristics of the Negro Population* (Washington: Bureau of the Census, 1969).
10. Lewis, 1969.
11. Johnson and Campbell, 1981.
12. Hart, 1960.
13. John Kellog, "Negro Urban Clusters in the Post-Bellum South," *The Geographical Review,* 67 (July, 1977): pp. 310–321.
14. Florette Henri, *Black Migration: Movement North 1900–1920* (Garden City: Anchor Press/Doubleday, 1975).
15. Henry S. Shryock, Jr., *Population Mobility Within the United States* (Chicago: University of Chicago Press, 1964).

16. Gunnar Myrdal, *An American Dilemma* (New York: Pantheon, 1972); Robert C. Weaver, *The Negro Ghetto* (New York: Harcourt, Brace and Co., 1948).
17. Henri, 1975.
18. Paul F. Coe, "The Nonwhite Population Surge to Our Cities," *Land Economics,* 35 (August, 1959): pp. 195–210.
19. Neil Fligstein, *Going North, Migration of Blacks and Whites From the South* (New York: Academic Press, 1981): p. 148.
20. Calef and Nelson, 1956.
21. Dimitri B. Shimkin, "Black Migration and the Struggle for Equity: A Hundred Year Record," in *Migration and Social Welfare,* ed. James W. Eaton (New York: National Association of Social Workers, 1971).
22. C. Horace Hamilton, "The Negro Leaves the South," *Demography,* 1 (1964): pp. 273–295.
23. Brinley Thomas, *Migration and Economic Growth* (Oxford: The University Press, 1973).
24. Larry H. Long, "How the Racial Composition of Cities Changes," *Land Economics,* 51 (August, 1975): pp. 258–267.
25. Donald R. Deskins, Jr., "Morphogenesis of a Black Ghetto," *Urban Geography,* 2 (April-June, 1981): pp. 95–114; and Willard T. Chow, "The Context of Redevelopment in Oakland," *Urban Geography,* 2 (January-March, 1981): pp. 41–63.
26. Brian J. L. Berry, "Short-Term Housing Cycles in a Dualistic Metropolis," in *The Social Economy of Cities,* eds. Gary Gappert and Harold M. Rose (Beverly Hills: Sage Publications, 1975).
27. Coe, 1959.
28. James B. Kenyon, "Spatial Associations in the Integration of the American City," *Economic Geography,* 52 (October, 1976): p. 292.
29. Larry H. Long and Daphne Spain, "Racial Succession in Individual Housing Units," *Current Population Reports,* Special Studies, Series P-23, No. 71, (September, 1978).
30. Stanley Brunn and Philip D. Phillips, "Slow Growth: A New Epoch of American Metropolitan Evolution," *The Geographical Review,* 68 (July, 1978): pp. 274–292.
31. James S. Fisher and Ronald Mitchelson, "Forces of Change in the American Settlement Pattern," *The Geographical Review,* 71 (July, 1981): pp. 298–310.
32. Brian J. L. Berry and Donald C. Dohmann, "Population Redistribution in the United States in the 1970's," *Population and Development Review,* 3 (December, 1977): pp. 443–471.
33. Rex R. Campbell, Daniel M. Johnson and Gary Stangler, "Counterstream Migration of Black People from the South: Data from the 1970 Public Use Sample," *Public Data Use,* 3 (January, 1975): pp. 13–21.
34. Anne S. Lee, "Return Migration in the United States," *International Migration Review,* (Summer, 1974): pp. 283–306.
35. Rex R. Campbell, Daniel M. Johnson, and Gary Stangler, "Return Migration of Black People to the South," *Rural Sociology,* (Winter, 1974): pp. 514–527.
36. Larry H. Long and Kristin A. Hansen, "Trends in Return Migration to the South," *Demography,* 12 (November, 1975): pp. 601–614.
37. John Moland, Jr., "The Black Population," in *Nonmetropolitan America in Transition,* eds. Amos H. Hawley and Sara M. Mazie (Chapel Hill: University of North Carolina Press, 1981): p. 477.
38. Robert Estall, "The Changing Balance of Northern and Southern Regions of the United States," *American Studies,* 14 (December, 1980): pp. 365–386.
39. James L. Walker, "Industrial Development and Race in the Nonmetropolitan South," *The Review of Regional Studies,* 9 (Spring, 1979): p. 39.
40. John Fraser Hart and Ennis L. Chestang, "Rural Revolution in East Carolina," *The Geographical Review,* 68 (October, 1978): pp. 435–458.
41. Deskins, 1981.
42. Stanley Lieberson, *A Piece of the Pie, Black and White Immigrants Since 1880* (Berkeley: University of California Press, 1980).
43. William J. Wilson, *The Declining Significance of Race* (Chicago: University of Chicago Press, 1978).
44. Brian J. L. Berry and John D. Kasarda, *Contemporary Human Ecology* (New York: McMillan Publishing Co., 1977).
45. Marvin Harris, *America Now: The Anthropology of Changing Culture* (New York: Simon and Schuster, 1981).
46. Ken Auletta, *The Underclass* (New York: Random House, 1982).

4

Mexican Americans

Daniel D. Arreola
Texas A&M University

The ancestors of Mexican Americans were the first Europeans to settle what is now the southwestern United States. A majority of their descendants still reside in the borderlands that stretch from Texas to California.

The Mexican American minority is the second largest in the United States and its numbers are growing more rapidly than the greater population. Despite early rural roots, the minority today is more urban than the general population. In 1980, approximately eight of every ten Mexican Americans lived in cities, with Los Angeles having the largest single nucleus of Mexican Americans in the United States. Cities like San Antonio and El Paso are predominantly Mexican American.

This chapter will examine the geographical evolution of the Mexican American population, from the minority's origins in the borderlands to patterns of immigration, population distribution, landscape, and social characteristics. Since most of this population lives in cities, the geographic patterns of urban Mexican Americans will be stressed.

ORIGIN IN THE BORDERLANDS

Mexican American populations had their origins in the borderlands that stretch from California in the west to Texas in the east. Between 1598 and 1821, parts of the states of California, Arizona, New Mexico, Colorado, and Texas were settled by Spanish-speaking peoples from New Spain, present-day Mexico. After 1821, portions of this region became part of the Republic of Mexico, and each of the settled areas developed its own regional identity. Since 1848, the major settled areas have come under Anglo influence, both political and cultural. Today, these five states remain the principal subregions where the Mexican American people are located. The transformation of these areas from Spanish outposts to Mexican provinces to Mexican American subregions represents the planting, germination, and rooting of Mexican American culture in the United

States. The origins of many of the features associated with Mexican American culture from place names to architecture and numerous social customs can be traced to this early period of settlement in the borderlands.

Patterns of Settlement

The initial settlement of the borderlands was in New Mexico (Fig. 4.1). This colonization followed the successful sixteenth-century settlement of the mining and livestock frontier of northern Mexico. In 1598, Juan de Oñate guided colonists to the upper drainage of the Rio Grande Valley to settle among the Pueblo Indians. In 1610, Santa Fe was founded as the provincial capital and principal center of the region. Missions and presidios were established between Taos and Socorro and down river at Paso del Norte near present El Paso. Albuquerque was founded in 1706 following a Pueblo Indian revolt that temporarily forced the Spanish out of the northern settlements. At the close of the Spanish period in 1821, most of the borderlands population resided in New Mexico. A road connecting New Mexico with Chihuahua in northern Mexico was the principal link between the frontier and Mexico City farther south.[1]

Southern Arizona was a second region of Spanish settlement in the borderlands (Fig. 4.1). Like New Mexico, the Spanish presence in Arizona was an extension of a settlement effort that originated in Mexico. During the 1600s, Jesuit missionaries penetrated Mexico's northwest lowlands and the few settlements established in Arizona were the northern-most reach of this frontier. Southern Arizona became known as Pimería Alta, or the upper Pima Indian area. The most successful settlements—the mission at San Xavier del Bac (1700), and the presidios at Tubac (1752) and Tucson (1776)—were situated along the Santa Cruz River. Settlements were extended to the San Pedro Valley to the east and for a short time on the Colorado River near Yuma. In both areas, Indian hostilities prohibited successful colonization. In the Santa Cruz Valley, Apache raiding continued to be a threat to pop-

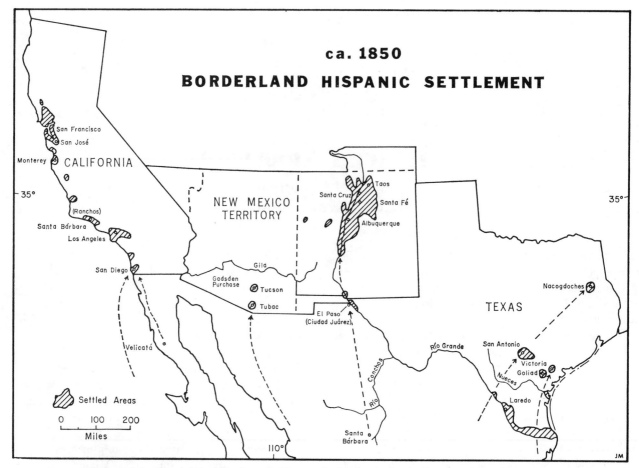

ca. 1850

BORDERLAND HISPANIC SETTLEMENT

Figure 4.1. Spanish and Mexican Settlement in the Borderlands. Reprinted from Nostrand, *Annals of the Association of American Geographers* 60 (1970), Figure 1, p. 645, with the permission of the Association of American Geographers.

ulations well into the nineteenth century. These conditions made difficult any firm footing in Pimería Alta where populations never exceeded 2000 during the Spanish and Mexican periods.[2]

Texas became a third area of Spanish settlement in the borderlands (Fig. 4.1). Colonization was prompted by the desire to confront French influence in the lower Mississippi River valley. Settlements in Texas were also an extension of the northern Mexico mining and livestock frontier. Three major mission-presidio complexes were founded in the Texas area: 1) Nacogdoches west of the Sabine River in 1716; 2) San Antonio situated between the central plateau and the gulf coastal plain in 1718; and 3) La Bahía near present-day Victoria in 1722. This last settlement was relocated to the lower San Antonio River near present Goliad in 1749. Another community, Laredo, was founded in 1755 on the north bank of the Rio Grande. By the late 1700s, San Antonio had become the major provincial settlement of Spanish Tejas (Texas). Road connections with northern Mexico and few Indian hostilities allowed for

permanence in the Texas borderlands. By 1850, some 14,000 Mexican Americans populated the region.[3]

California was the last of the borderland outposts to witness Spanish and Mexican settlement (Fig. 4.1). Although explorations and coastal reconnoitering had taken place along the Pacific coast as early as 1542, permanent settlement did not commence for over two centuries. The threat of Russian and British intrusion into California finally led to its settlement in 1769. In that year, land and sea parties converged on San Diego where a mission-presidio complex was built. Within twenty years, additional settlements were established at the provincial capital of Monterey (1770), and in San Francisco (1776) and Santa Barbara (1782 and 1786). By the early 1800s, a chain of twenty missions connected the settlements of coastal California, including two civil communities founded at San José (1777) and Los Angeles (1781). Sea and land connections between the California settlements and an ocean link to Mexico insured this region's viability. By 1850, over 9,000 Californios inhabited this part of the borderlands frontier.[4]

78

Figure 4.2. Mission San Buenaventura, Ventura, California. Photo by Author.

Settlement Institutions

Spanish settlement in the borderlands, as elsewhere in the New World, was dictated by the Laws of the Indies (1573). These legal codes set forth in theory how new lands should be settled. As a result of practical problems encountered in each settlement area, not all regions of Spanish-Mexican settlement complied precisely with these laws. The institutions that developed, however, were remarkably similar from one end of the borderlands to another.

The mission and presidio were the initial frontier institutions. The mission was, in essence, an extension of the religious agreement made by Spain with the Catholic church to convert Indian populations. Missions were usually established where Indian populations were concentrated. In the borderlands, both Jesuit and Franciscan religious orders were involved in mission founding, although at different times and in different regions. The priests converted Indians to the Catholic faith, with varying degrees of success. In addition, Indians were trained to the ways of the Spaniard and employed as laborers to make the missions viable. They erected buildings, dug irrigation ditches, planted and harvested crops, cared for livestock, and performed work essential to the success of a mission.

The presidio was a military settlement or garrisoned fort. Presidios were sometimes founded in conjunction with missions. Often, they were located at strategic points along a line of transport or situated to defend a mission from native or foreign attack. Many missions and presidios were abandoned as the settlement frontier fluctuated. Some persisted and became centers around which population grew. The presidio in Tucson, Arizona and the mission at Ventura, California, for example, survived as settlements through the Mexican period and today are American cities (Fig. 4.2).[5]

The pueblo or town was a third Spanish settlement institution brought to the borderlands. While the mission and presidio were religious and military respectively, the pueblo was a civil community. According to the Laws of the Indies, the civil settlement was the climax institution whereas missions and presidios were, theoretically, only temporary frontier settlements. Pueblos were to be situated on a grant of land four square leagues or approximately forty-two square miles. The center of the pueblo included a plaza, surrounded by government offices and a parish church. A rectangular grid of streets emanating from the plaza accommodated houses. Surrounding these were lands for cultivation, pasture, and woodland. The pueblos became major nuclei of population and attracted merchants, artisans, and farmers. Los Angeles, California and San Antonio, Texas, for example, were founded as pueblos.[6]

A final means of settlement introduced by the Spaniards to the borderlands was the land grant. This form of settlement persisted in the border region during the Mexican period after 1821. Parcels of land were granted to private individuals. Land grants were allocated as an economic incentive to settle areas and make them productive. These lands were transformed into livestock *ranchos* where cattle, and sometimes sheep, became the economic mainstay of the settlement unit as in California and parts of Arizona. In other areas, where sufficient water could be controlled for irrigation, land grants became farmsteads where wheat and corn were cultivated as in New Mexico. Today, many land grants remain as legal definitions of property in the borderlands. They persist also as place names, and stand as examples of the legacy of Spanish and Mexican imprints in the border region.[7]

The Hispanic-American Borderland

After the United States-Mexico war, much of the borderland became United States territory. By the Treaty of Guadalupe-Hidalgo, signed in 1848, many of the resident Mexicans of these borderlands became Mexican Americans. After the Gadsden Purchase in 1854, Arizona south of the Gila River became United States territory as well.

In 1850, there were perhaps 80,000 Mexican Americans.[8] In a short time, the rapid influx of Anglos began to transform the borderlands into an American province, culturally as well as politically. The proportion of Mexican Americans to Anglos continued to decrease during the latter nineteenth century as the American population increased.

Today, the preponderance of the Mexican American minority resides in the five southwestern states that have been called the Hispanic-American borderland.[9] Parts of California, Arizona, New Mexico, and Texas are the major cores of this province, but a portion of southern Colorado is also part of the region. These areas represent the early nuclei of Spanish and Mexican settlement and expanded areas of the earliest colonizations. Many of the Mexican immigrants who have entered the United States since the early twentieth century also inhabit parts of this region.

Although Mexican Americans are considered the dominant Hispanic group in this province, there are distinct regional identities. This differentiation originated with the varied periods of Spanish-Mexican settlement in the borderlands, and the development of

separate self-referents. In Texas and California during the Mexican period, the appellations Tejano and Californio were used respectively. In New Mexico and parts of southern Colorado, much of the Hispanic population refers to itself as Hispano or Spanish American, not Mexican American. This subgroup claims ancestry from the earliest Spanish colonists of the region and considers itself culturally distinct from the Mexican or *mestizo* groups that constitute the majority of the Mexican American population.[10]

In the 1970s, Nostrand found that "Mexican" was not only the self-referent used by Mexico-born persons in the borderlands, but also the prevailing term among the native-born in much of Arizona and eastern Colorado.[11] The primary self-referent in Texas was "Latin American" or "Latin." In California both "Mexican American" and "Chicano" were primary terms, the latter popular among the young. Significantly, these two terms appear to be diffusing to other areas of the borderlands from Arizona to Texas.

Other differences testify to the diversity of the Mexican American population in the borderlands. Cuisine, religious affiliation, vernacular architecture, and music are just some of the categories that exhibit regional variation. The Hispanic-American borderland is certainly the hearth area that has given rise to and continues to nourish the majority of Mexican Americans, but it is also a region that is changing as the culture that occupies it changes.

IMMIGRANTS AND IMMIGRATION

Immigration has been and continues to be an important contributor to the Mexican American population. From the middle of the nineteenth century to the present, Mexican immigrants have been an important source of labor north of the border. Their availability helped make possible the economic development of agriculture and industry in the southwestern United States and their continued immigration, both legal and illegal, provides a labor pool to agriculture, manufacturing, and the service sector of urban economies throughout the Hispanic-American borderland and beyond.

An Immigrant Tradition

Mexican labor migration to the United States dates to the middle of the nineteenth century. The early Mexican migrants foreshadowed the coming of "wetbacks," "braceros," and others in the twentieth century. Together these streams have been part of a larger historical process of labor scarcity in the United States and a surplus of underemployed labor in Mexico. Arthur Corwin[12] has argued that there has been a long tradition of a migrant subculture in Mexico, marginal populations that moved seasonally with economic opportunity. When opportunity emerged in the United States, migrant Mexicans moved to satisfy the labor demand. Slowly at first as specific economic circumstances pulled migrants to regional nodes during the nineteenth century, then en masse during the twentieth century with the swelling of population in Mexico, changes in transport technology on both sides of the border, and the development of the southwestern United States.

Mexican immigration in this century has occurred in two distinct waves. The first took place from approximately 1900 to 1930, after which the Great Depression reduced the flow. The second was initiated by the war economy of the 1940s, and continues undiminished to this day. Between 1910 and 1930, Mexican immigrants to the United States averaged 30,462 per year with the greatest number (87,648) coming in 1924 and the lowest number (10,954) entering in 1913. Between 1953 and 1973, Mexican immigration averaged 44,329 annually, the high 70,141 and the low 18,454 entering in 1973 and 1953, respectively.[13] From 1975 to 1979, an average 61,700 Mexican immigrants entered the U.S. The high for this period was 92,400 in 1978 and the low was 52,100 in 1979.[14]

The mining frontiers of the western United States were the first major attraction for Mexican migrant labor. Mexican laborers from the northern states of Sonora, Chihauhua, Durango, and Zacatecas responded to the demand for workers in California, Nevada, and Arizona.[15] Practically every mining community in the West had a Mexican district. Jerome, Arizona, for example, was a copper mining town where Mexican labor was used from the late nineteenth century to the peak of the production years just before the Depression. The town became a major destination for Mexican immigrants and a jump-off point for migration to other parts of the West.

Railroads became the primary means for dispersing Mexican migrants in the United States. The rails bridged the expanses of the West and effectively shortened distances between population centers. In 1884, El Paso became connected by rail to Los Angeles and Chicago, and to Chihauhua and Mexico City. In the following decades, Nogales, Arizona was linked by rail to Hermosillo, Mexico, and San Antonio and Corpus Christi were joined to Monterrey, Mexico by way of Laredo. Spur lines, like capillaries, grew from these main arteries and brought Mexican migrants everywhere the railroad went. By 1930, colonies of Mexican migrants could be found in nearly every town and city along the rail routes. The railroads were also conduits to the inner cities where migrants could be recruited by contractors who sought other types of labor.[16]

The economic development of the Southwest was facilitated by the northward drift of Mexicans. Railroads integrated the Southwest into the nation's industrial economy and Mexican labor became the means for factory and mining employment as well did as railroad construction and maintenance. When federal legislation encouraging western irrigation projects was passed in 1902, Mexican labor again proved important to the success of citrus and cotton cultivation in California, Arizona, and the lower Rio Grande Valley in Texas. The mobility of Mexican labor likewise became vital to the beet sugar industry in Colorado, Kansas, and Nebraska and to the expansion of truck-farming in southern California, Arizona, and Texas.[17]

The Depression of the 1930s slowed the flow of Mexican migrants to the United States. High unemployment north of the border initiated a reverse movement of Mexican migrants back to Mexico.[18] From 1931 to 1943, an average of 2,013 Mexicans per year migrated to the United States, representing a considerable ebbing of the previous twenty year flow. In 1942, the American government instituted a contract farm labor agreement with Mexico commonly referred to as the Bracero Program. Under this agreement, Mexican laborers were transported to agricultural areas in this country to bolster the labor shortage brought on by the Second World War. The program served agricultural interests well since farmers were supplied with a steady and inexpensive source of labor. The Bracero Program also benefited Mexican migration. It pointed the way to "El Norte" (the north, or United States) and provided a view of the economic opportunities that awaited legal and illegal migrants to this country.

Closing the "Golden Door"

Today the migration of Mexicans to the United States is a headline social, economic, and political issue. While the numbers of legal entrants have been reduced, illegal immigrants continue to migrate to the United States. The termination of the Bracero Program in 1964 and the quotas set for legal immigration changed the circumstances of Mexican immigration. Illegal immigration grew as a consequence of the restrictions of legal entrance. The apprehensions of Mexican illegals rose from 55,000 in 1965 to 90,000 the next year and to 200,000 by 1969. These numbers climbed to 710,000 in 1974 and 978,000 in 1979.[19]

The illegal Mexican immigrant situation has received much publicity in the borderlands and across the country. Newspapers, magazines, and television have done countless specials on the immigrant dilemma, and words like *mojado* (wetback or illegal immigrant), coyote (illegal immigrant smuggler), and *la migra* (the Immigration and Naturalization Service or I.N.S.) have become part of the media language. The situation has also become heavily politicized. A frequently heard argument against illegal Mexican immigration is its alleged tendency to depress wages and increase unemployment. Undocumented or illegal Mexicans are often found performing low skilled tasks shunned by American workers. The fact that Mexicans have little difficulty finding these jobs in the United States might suggest that they do not displace American labor to any great extent. Also, it must be remembered that illegal Mexicans do not, by themselves, depress wages. Rather, employers offer pay scales well below what United States citizens might accept if they were willing to work these low skilled jobs, and illegal Mexicans fill the labor demand. As in other periods of American immigrant history, public pressure is usually directed against the migrant who is merely seeking to better his livelihood. Rarely is attention focused on the employer who hires the migrant. If illegal Mexican migration to the United States were stopped completely, one result might be higher prices for goods and services now produced by illegal workers.

A second charge against illegal Mexican immigrants is that they "freeload" on community services. This has not been well documented, and the evidence suggests the contrary. Illegal Mexican workers pay state and local taxes, and must have federal income and social security taxes deducted from their earnings. Field studies suggest that illegal Mexicans make very little use of social services. In San Diego, for example, undocumented Mexicans are estimated to have used $2 million of services per year, yet contributed nearly $50 million annually to the support of local services.[20] Also, researchers have indicated that many illegal immigrants are only here temporarily and ultimately return to Mexico. Their use of local services in many cases is occasional, whereas they contribute greatly to a fund that benefits the total population.

The total number of illegal Mexicans in the United States is unknown. Published estimates are usually based on the apprehension of illegal aliens. These estimates may be misleading, and the basis for them varies widely among sources. A 1975 estimate prepared for the I.N.S. concluded that 5.2 million illegal Mexicans resided in the United States. Fogel believes the number closer to 3 million, including immigrants who overstay their non-immigrant or tourist visas. Illegal Mexican immigrants in the United States are located in the same areas where Mexican American populations are highest. The 1975 I.N.S. study "estimated" 1.3 million in greater Los Angeles, 600,000 in Houston, and 500,000 each in San Antonio, San Francisco, and Chicago.[21] These "estimates," if accurate, would mean there are more illegal Mexicans in some of these cities than legal immigrants and Mexican Americans combined, an unlikely situation. Although illegals are likely to be in rural areas as well, they tend to concentrate in cities because Mexican American districts provide cultural familiarity and familial or friendship ties. Ultimately, however, job opportunities attract the illegal immigrant. Industries that often employ Mexican illegals include apparel, furniture, manufacturing, and food processing. The I.N.S. is known to frequently "survey" (raid) these industries, round-up illegals and return them to Mexico. Studies have shown, however, that apprehended illegals often find their way back to similar types of employment.[22]

A DEMOGRAPHIC PORTRAIT

The 1980 census designated Mexican Americans as part of the "Spanish origin" population. The Spanish origin population numbered 14.6 million and included Puerto Rican, Cuban, and "other Spanish" as well as Mexican. Mexican Americans numbered 8.7 million or nearly 60 percent of the Spanish origin group.[23] In 1970, the census counted 4.5 million people of "Mexican origin or descent."[24] The difference suggests that the Mexican American population increased 4.2 million or almost 100 percent between 1970 and 1980. While these figures may reflect an undercount of Mexican Americans in 1970, they reveal the growth of the Mexican American population, now the second largest minority group behind Blacks.[25]

The Mexican American population is largely concentrated in the borderlands, yet areas outside of this hearth region house significant numbers. The population as a whole is young, characterized by large families and rapid growth.

Population Distribution

The Mexican American population in the states that are considered part of the Hispanic-American borderland totaled 7.2 million in 1980 (Table 4.1). California ranked highest in the nation with 3.6 million Mexican Americans followed by Texas with 2.7 million. Arizona, New Mexico, and Colorado counted 396,410, 233,772 and 207,204 Mexican Americans respectively. In 1970, California counted 1.8 million Mexican Americans, Texas 1.6 million, and Arizona, New Mexico, and Colorado 240,025, 119,049, and 103,584 respectively (Table 4.1).

Mexican Americans are located in four regional concentrations outside of the borderlands: the upper Midwest, the Mountain West, the Pacific Northwest, and the South. The upper Midwest, comprising the states of Illinois, Indiana, Michigan, Ohio and Wisconsin, counted 672,518 Mexican Americans in 1980 (Table 4.1), as compared with 300,904 in 1970. Economic opportunity first brought Mexicans to this area during the First World War. Railroads, steel mills, and meat packing houses provided employment to these immigrants. The industries continued to draw immigrants during the Second World War as migrants established large permanent populations in the industrial cities of the Midwest.

TABLE 4.1 Mexican Americans by Prominent Regions, 1970 and 1980

Region	1980[a]	1970[b]
Borderlands	7,227,339	3,939,751
California	3,637,466	1,856,841
Texas	2,752,487	1,619,252
Arizona	396,410	240,025
New Mexico	233,772	119,049
Colorado	207,204	103,584
Midwest	672,518	300,904
Illinois	408,325	160,477
Michigan	112,183	65,329
Indiana	57,625	30,034
Ohio	53,318	26,795
Wisconsin	41,067	18,269
Pacific Northwest	126,282	44,749
Washington	81,112	33,483
Oregon	45,170	11,266
Mountain West	121,248	44,888
Utah	38,021	14,560
Nevada	32,681	9,486
Idaho	28,143	10,478
Wyoming	15,940	6,628
Montana	6,463	3,736
South	282,067	56,760
Florida	79,392	20,869
Louisiana	28,558	7,300
North Carolina	27,818	5,093
Georgia	27,647	5,850
Virginia	24,104	5,953
Alabama	18,869	1,401
Tennessee	18,577	2,301
South Carolina	17,523	1,804
Mississippi	14,543	966
Kentucky	14,150	2,942
Arkansas	10,866	2,281
U.S. Total	8,740,439	4,532,435

Source: [a]U.S. Bureau of the Census, *Census of Population: 1980, Persons of Spanish Origin by State: 1980*, Supplementary Report PC80–S1–7 (Washington D.C.: U.S. Government Printing Office, 1982); Table 1.

[b]U.S. Bureau of the Census, *Census of Population: 1970, Persons of Spanish Ancestry*, Supplementary Report PC(S1)-30 (Washington D.C.: U.S. Government Printing Office, 1973); Table 1.

The Mountain West and Pacific Northwest had nearly equal numbers of Mexican Americans in 1980, approximately 121,000 and 126,000 respectively. In 1970, each region counted approximately 45,000 persons of Mexican origin. In the Northwest, Washington state had nearly twice as many Mexican Americans as Oregon in 1980, whereas in the Mountain West Utah and Nevada had 50 percent more Mexican Americans than Idaho and Wyoming. Montana was the only state in the western continental United States that had less than 10,000 Mexican Americans (Table 4.1). Unlike the Mexican migrants who moved to the cities of the upper Midwest, Mexican American populations in the far western regions had their origins in rural activities. As miners, livestock herders, and agriculturalists, Mexican and Mexican Americans migrated to these areas as economic activities began to demand their labor in the second half of the nineteenth century. Agricultural labor, for example, was in high demand during the twentieth century and Mexican migrant laborers largely filled this need. Over time, temporary rural centers developed services that catered to Mexicans and permanent populations became established. The Yakima Valley and parts of southeastern Washington, as well as the fertile Willamette Valley of Oregon have been major agricultural districts that have accommodated Mexican migrant labor, creating satellite communities far from the borderland states.[26]

The South grew rapidly in the decade from 1970 to 1980, and the Mexican American population expanded considerably in this region. The arc of states from Virginia to Florida, west to Louisiana, and including the states of Arkansas, Tennessee, and Kentucky, counted 282,067 Mexican Americans in 1980 (Table 4.1). These same states had only 56,760 Mexican Americans in 1970. Florida is the nucleus in this group, having counted nearly 80,000 Mexican Americans in 1980. The reasons for the dramatic change in Mexican Americans in this region are not completely clear, but the census indicates that most of this group live in places of less than 10,000 people. This might suggest an agricultural orientation, although industrialization has brought on some of the region's recent growth. A misreporting of Mexican origin by non-Spanish persons in some states may also explain the large numbers counted for this region in 1980.

In addition to the primary core of the borderlands and the secondary spheres outside of this hearth, Mexican Americans can be found in rural and urban districts in many other states. Kansas, Oklahoma, and Missouri, for example, each had between 50,000 and 30,000 Mexican Americans in 1980. These states counted between 29,000 and 14,000 persons of Mexican origin in 1970. Minnesota had 11,000 persons of Mexican origin in 1970, and this increased to roughly 20,000 in 1980. Similarly, New York state's population of Mexican Americans increased from approximately 22,000 to nearly 39,000 between 1970 and 1980. As agricultural or industrial laborers, and as railroad workers or service sector employees, Mexican Americans migrated to these areas seeking economic opportunity. In each area, they have persisted and their numbers have grown considerably.

Population Characteristics

The Spanish origin population in 1980 was younger, on the average, than the entire United States' population. About 41 percent were under eighteen years old, whereas only 28 percent were in this age bracket for the general population. The census also showed that the median age for persons of Spanish origin was 22 years compared with a median age of 30 years for the total population.[27] While appropriate data were not available from the 1980 census at this writing, the 1970 census suggests that the Mexican American population remains younger than the general population.

In 1970, the median age of Mexican Americans was 19.3 years. The fertility rate, the number of births per 1,000 women in the 15–44 age group, has been higher for Mexican American women than Anglo women since the nineteenth century.[28] Also, since 1920, the growth of the Mexican stock population has been largely a function of natural increase.[29] High fertility rates in a population are usually evidenced by large families, and according to the 1980 data, Spanish origin families were larger than families for the general population. Only 17 percent of all United States' families consisted of five or more persons, yet 30 percent of all Spanish origin families, including Mexican Americans, had five or more persons. Also, whereas nearly 40 percent of the nation's families were two person families, among Spanish origin populations, only 24 percent were two person households.[30]

The character of the Mexican American population can be summarized by reading the group's age-sex population pyramid. In both the Mexican American and the general U.S. populations for 1970, females slightly outnumbered males, so that the pyramids were nearly symmetric (Figs. 4.3 and 4.4). The age structures of the populations, however, were significantly different. Fifty-one percent of the 1970 Mexican American population was under the age of twenty and only 2 percent was over seventy years old (Fig. 4.3). This compared with only 38 percent of the total United States population under twenty years and 6 percent of that population over seventy years (Fig. 4.4).

What these patterns tell us is that the Mexican American population, as compared to the total U.S. population, has a much greater potential for future growth with more than half of its numbers in age groups under twenty years of age. The pyramids also suggest that the dependency ratio, the number of the total population that is of working age as compared to the number of the population that is not likely to work, is higher among the Mexican Americans than the total population. The large numbers of dependent young as well as old in the Mexican American population suggests the economic burden that must be assumed by the working population. It is less than half the dependent total.

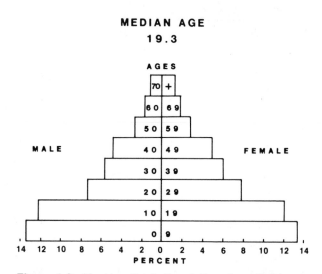

Figure 4.3. Mexican Origin Population. Compiled by author from U.S. Bureau of the Census, *Census of Population: 1970, Subject Reports, Persons of Spanish Origin,* Final Report PC (2)-1C (Washington D.C. U.S. Government Printing Office, 1973): Table 3.

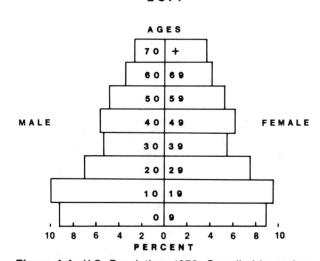

Figure 4.4. U.S. Population, 1970. Compiled by author from U.S. Bureau of the Census, *Census of Population: 1970, Subject Reports, National Origin and Language,* Final Report PC(2)-1A (Washington D.C.: U.S. Government Printing Office, 1973), Table 1.

AN URBAN PEOPLE

Despite the rural origins of their past, Mexican Americans in 1980 were overwhelmingly an urban people. The census showed that 83 percent of persons of Spanish origin, which includes Mexican Americans, lived in metropolitan areas. This percentage was higher than the corresponding proportion for the overall 68 percent of the USA population. In 1970, 86 percent of the Mexican American population lived in cities. Moreover, the 1980 census indicated that about one of every two persons of Spanish origin resided in the central cities of their metropolitan areas.[31] But, although these areas contain large numbers of Mexican Americans, in recent decades, there has been a population dispersion to suburban locations in some cities. In addition, the landscapes of urban Mexican American districts can be distinguished from other urban cultural landscapes.

The Urban Heirarchy

In 1980 the Mexican American population in the states of the borderlands was nearly 90 percent urban (Table 4.2). In California, Texas, Arizona, and Colorado, more than eight out of every ten Mexican Americans lived in cities. Only New Mexico had less than three-quarters of its Mexican Americans in urban areas.

Eighteen S.M.S.A.s had greater than 100,000 Mexican Americans in 1980 (Table 4.3). Many of the major cities in these regions had Mexican American populations greater than 50,000 in the same year (Table 4.4). All cities, with the exception of Chicago, were located in the Hispanic-American borderland. The city of Los Angeles was the single largest concentration of Mexican Americans in the country with nearly 616,000 counted. San Antonio had almost 400,000. Chicago, El Paso, and Houston each had approximately 250,000 Mexican Americans. Five other cities, San José, San Diego, Phoenix, Corpus Christi, and Dallas had Mexican American populations greater than 100,000. East

TABLE 4.2 Urban Mexican Americans in Borderland States, 1980

State	Mexican Americans	Urban	Percent Urban
California	3,637,466	3,382,673	92.9
Texas	2,752,487	2,364,800	85.9
Arizona	396,410	341,826	86.2
Colorado	207,204	178,627	86.2
New Mexico	233,772	174,346	74.5
Borderlands	7,227,339	6,442,272	89.1

Source: U.S. Bureau of the Census, *Census of Population: 1980, General Population Characteristics: California, Texas, Arizona, New Mexico, Colorado* PC80–1–B6,B45,B4,B33,B7 (Washington D.C.: U.S. Government Printing Office, 1982); Table 16 for each state.

TABLE 4.3 S.M.S.A.s with Greater than 100,000 Mexican Americans, 1980

S.M.S.A.	Mexican Americans
Los Angeles-Long Beach, CA.	1,650,934
San Antonio, TX.	447,416
Houston, TX.	374,510
Chicago, IL.	368,981
El Paso, TX.	282,001
Riverside-San Bernardino-Ontario, CA.	252,513
Anaheim-Santa Ana-Garden Grove, CA.	232,472
San Diego, CA.	227,943
Dallas-Ft. Worth, TX.	223,105
McAllen-Pharr-Edinburg, TX.	221,971
San Francisco-Oakland, CA.	189,742
Phoenix, AZ.	177,546
San José, CA.	176,838
Corpus, Christi, TX.	151,126
Fresno, CA.	140,976
Brownsville-Harlingen-San Benito, TX.	138,509
Denver-Boulder, CO.	108,697
Tucson, AZ.	100,085

Source: U.S. Bureau of the Census, *Census of Population: 1980, General Population Characteristics: California, Texas, Illinois, Arizona, New Mexico, Colorado* PC80–1–B6,B45,B15,B4,B7 (Washington D.C.: U.S. Government Printing Office, 1982): Table 16 for each state.

TABLE 4.4 Cities and Places with Greater than 50,000 Mexican Americans, 1980

City/Place	Mexican Americans	Total Population	Percent Mexican American
Los Angeles, CA.	615,887	2,966,850	20.7
San Antonio, TX.	394,331	785,880	50.1
Chicago, IL.	255,802	3,005,072	8.5
El Paso, TX.	252,609	425,259	59.4
Houston, TX.	248,881	1,595,138	15.6
San José, CA.	113,979	629,442	18.1
San Diego, CA.	106,274	875,538	12.1
Phoenix, AZ.	104,274	789,704	13.1
Corpus Christi, TX.	102,863	231,999	44.3
Dallas, TX.	101,943	904,078	11.2
E. Los Angeles, CA.	98,619	110,017	89.6
Santa Ana, CA.	82,652	203,713	40.5
Laredo, TX.	81,211	91,449	88.8
Tucson, AZ.	74,441	330,537	22.5
Brownsville, TX.	61,381	84,997	72.2
Denver, CO.	60,341	492,365	12.2
Austin, TX.	58,948	345,496	17.0
Albuquerque, N.M.	50,528	331,767	15.2

Source: U.S. Bureau of the Census, *Census of Population: 1980, General Population Characteristics: California, Texas, Illinois, Arizona, New Mexico, Colorado* PC80–1–B6,B45,B15,B4,B33,B7 (Washington D.C.: U.S. Government Printing Office, 1982): Table 16 for each state.

Los Angeles, Santa Ana, Laredo, and Tucson each counted between 70,000 and 99,000 Mexican Americans. Brownsville, Austin, and Alburquerque ranked between roughly 50,000 and 60,000 each. Of cities greater than 200,000, El Paso had the largest percentage of its population Mexican American, 59 percent. Taking the total group of cities with Mexican American populations greater than 50,000, only East Los Angeles (90 percent), Lardo (89 percent), Brownsville (72 percent), and San Antonio (50 percent), in addition to El Paso, ranked as predominantly Mexican American cities.

The pattern of cities with intermediate size populations of Mexican Americans reinforces the urban character of the population in the borderlands. Table 4.5 shows that California had nearly four times the number of cities with Mexican American populations between 20,000 and 50,000 than did Texas, the next highest ranking state. Colorado had one city in this intermediate size category, whereas New Mexico and Arizona had none. Table 4.6 illustrates a similar pattern for borderland cities with Mexican American populations between 10,000 and 20,000. California, again, ranks highest, but only slightly more than twice the

number of such cities in Texas. Arizona, New Mexico, and Colorado each had less than five cities in this category.

What these numbers for large, intermediate, and small cities indicate is that the borderland states with the largest Mexican American populations, California and Texas, have the largest cities and greatest number of urban places with significant Mexican American populations. In Arizona, New Mexico, and Colorado, where Mexican Americans are less than one-half million, the populations are clustered in fewer places.

Mexican American populations outside of the borderlands are also largely urban. The largest concentrations of Mexican Americans are in the cities of the upper Midwest: Chicago (255,802), Detroit (19,052), Milwaukee (15,363), East Chicago City 12,733), and Aurora (11,325). Outside of the Midwest cities, only New York (22,577) and Kansas City (12,173) have more than 10,000 Mexican Americans in 1980.[32]

Residential Structure

In most cities, Mexican Americans are a minority population and live in distinct districts within the urban region.[33] Before the second half of the nineteenth century, borderland cities were predominantly Mexican and populations were concentrated around the plazas that were established with a town's founding. When railroads entered these cities and Anglo populations increased, Mexican American districts became isolated as the city expanded around or away from the old nucleus. This pattern is evident in the 1893 town plan of Tucson, Arizona (Fig. 4.5). The irregular streets west of the railroad track date from the early Spanish-Mexican period while the standard grid to the north and south resulted largely from Anglo subdivision after 1880. The Mexican American district became known as a *barrio,* by literal translation, a neighborhood.

Barrios, sometimes referred to as *colonias* (suburbs) because they were located far from the center of town, were also formed in the borderlands as urban expansion engulfed agricultural settlements housing Mexican American workers. In southern California, Pacoima was one such colonia. The town became enveloped by the urbanization of the San Fernando Valley, a once fertile agricultural district northwest of the Los Angeles city center.[34] Still other rural communities like railroad worker settlements or labor camps followed a similar pattern, evolving into urban barrios. In his study of a Mexican American neighborhood in a Texas city, Arthur Rubel described the barrio of "Mexiquito" and its perception by residents and outsiders. The author suggests that the north and south sides of the railroad tracks are more than geographical zones, they are also societies with separate characteristics and traditions.

TABLE 4.5 Borderland Cities and Places with 20,000–50,000 Mexican Americans, 1980

State	Number of Cities	Example/Population
California	22	Fresno/46,964
Texas	6	McAllen/44,991
Colorado	1	Pueblo/22,395
Arizona	0	—
New Mexico	0	—

Source: U.S. Bureau of the Census, *Census of Population: 1980, General Population Characteristics; California, Texas, Colorado, Arizona, New Mexico* PC80–1–B6,B45,B7,B4,B33 (Washington D.C.: U.S. Government Printing Office, 1982): Table 16 for each state.

TABLE 4.6 Borderland Cities and Places with 10,000–20,000 Mexican Americans, 1980

State	Number of Cities	Example/Population
California	39	Bakersfield/14,085
Texas	17	San Angelo/15,834
Arizona	4	Nogales/12,718
New Mexico	2	Las Cruces/16,173
Colorado	1	Colorado Springs/10,375

Source: U.S. Bureau of the Census, *Census of Population: 1980, General Population Characteristics: California, Texas, Arizona, New Mexico, Colorado* PC80–1–B6,B45,B4,B33,B7 (Washington D.C.: U.S. Government Printing Office, 1982): Table 16 for each state.

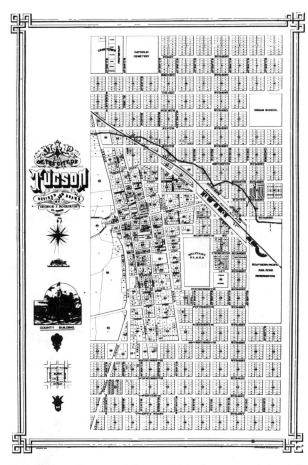

Figure 4.5. Tucson, Arizona 1893. Courtesy of the Arizona Historical Society, Tucson, Arizona.

New Lots is a city bisected by the railway of the Missouri Pacific. In 1921, the town's first year, the north side of the tracks was allocated by municipal ordinance to the residences and business establishments of Mexican-Americans, and to industrial complexes. Mexican-Americans refer to the north side of the tracks as Mexiquito, *el pueblo mexicano, nuestro lado;* even the traffic light north of the tracks is referred to as *la luz mexicana.* The other side of the tracks is spoken of as *el lado americano, el pueblo americano,* and other similar terms. Those who live south of the tracks also distinguish the two sides: "this side" and "the other side," "our side," and "their side," and "Mexican town" are all descriptive terms heard in the city of New Lots.[35]

Geographic isolation, housing restriction, and voluntary congregation have perpetuated residential segregation in the cities of the borderlands.[36] Mexican Americans are often segregated in the central cities of their metropolitan areas. There are two general explanations for this pattern. First, barrios became engulfed as the city expanded, as described above. A second process that helps explain the central city concentration is the filtering down of housing from one group to another. As central city areas are vacated by Anglos or other minority groups, lower income populations, including Mexican Americans, move into the inner city

neighborhoods. Many of the east side districts of Los Angeles such as Boyle Heights, City Terrace, and Lincoln Heights became populated by Mexican Americans in this manner.[37] Similarly, in Chicago, the Mexican American population grew by 84 percent between 1960 and 1970, expanding mostly into older ethnic neighborhoods that once housed Czechs and Poles.[38] A survey of thirty-five borderland cities in 1960 indicated that the mean index of residential dissimilarity between Anglo and Spanish surname populations was 54.5 based on a maximum segregation measure of 100. From this survey, the degree of segregation between the two populations ranged from highs of 75 and 72 in Odessa and Corpus Christi, Texas, to a low of 30 in Sacramento, California.[39]

Since the Second World War and particularly in the decade 1960–1970, the Mexican American population in cities has dispersed into suburban areas. In Los Angeles County, for example, there were twenty-three municipalities in 1970 in which Mexican Americans accounted for 10 to 20 percent of the population, and twenty-five cities or unincorporated areas in the county in which they made up 5 to 9 percent of the total.[40] Table 4.7 shows ten suburbs in the county where Mexican Americans increased significantly between 1960, 1970, and 1980. Similar studies in Texas and Arizona have found that dispersal from traditional barrios into the suburbs of cities escalated after the Second World War and the Korean conflict as veterans took advantage of federal legislation that allowed low interest loans and participation in the new housing market.[41] This movement to the suburbs was also an indication of the upward economic mobility achieved by Mexican Americans.

TABLE 4.7 Mexican Americans in Selected Los Angeles County Suburbs, 1960, 1970 and 1980

Suburb	Percent 1960	Percent 1970	Percent 1980
Montebello	18.4	44.2	89.9
Pico Rivera	26.4	59.2	69.9
Huntington Park	4.5	35.9	66.7
Baldwin Park	8.7	30.0	51.5
Paramount	7.8	17.9	41.6
Lynwood	3.5	16.1	38.0
Norwalk	15.0	25.7	34.5
Monterey Park	11.6	18.1	33.5
Alhambra	4.3	17.4	29.5
Pomona	9.2	16.3	27.2
Los Angeles County	9.1	18.3	22.0

Source: Francine F. Rabinovitz and William J. Siembieda, *Minorities in Suburbs: The Los Angeles Experience* (Lexington, Mass.: D. C. Heath, 1977); U.S. Bureau of the Census, *Census of Population: 1980, General Population Characteristics,* California PC80–1–B6 (Washington D.C.: U.S. Government Printing Office, 1982): Table 16.

Urban Cultural Landscapes

An axiom of human geography holds that landscape is a clue to culture. By analyzing the patterns of the built environment, an understanding may be gained of the culture that constructed or contributed to a landscape. The cultural landscapes of Mexican American barrios are distinct, and differ from the landscapes of Anglo communities or those of other minority communities. Barrios surveyed in Texas, Arizona, and California included particular landscape elements; for example, a preference for pastel house colors, the persistent use of fencing to enclose houses, and the incidence of colorful murals in residential and commercial areas.

Houses are important elements of the material landscape, and offer clues to the cultures that occupy them. A geographer, Peirce Lewis, has suggested that houses are more than mere shelters, they are personal and social testaments to those who live inside.[42] In most barrios, Mexican Americans did not build the homes they now occupy. In fact, in many urban barrios, the housing stock is older than in other parts of the city. Old houses, however, have not kept Mexican Americans from embellishing their residences. Houses in urban barrios are

often painted in pastel blue, green, yellow, or pink. This landscape trait is not completely understood, but the use of these colors appears to be a long standing Mexican tradition. This preference has persisted and is evident in the vernacular landscaping of barrios in the borderlands.

Yard fencing is another trait found in barrios. The persistent use of fences in residential landscaping has been studied in Tucson's Mexican American neighborhoods.[43] In these areas, fences and fence types were found to be keys in identifying Mexican American households. The pattern of fence use indicates a traditional attitude toward enclosed space in the urban landscape. Houses in urban Mexico were often built flush to the street with open space in the interior. The preference for fences as property markers in barrio districts illustrates the persistence of this landscape feature.

Street murals have become significant elements of the vernacular landscapes of barrios (Fig. 4.6). The street art movement in Mexican American districts is considered to have started in Chicago in 1967, and spread quickly to other cities with large Mexican American populations.[44] Today, highly stylized wall

Figure 4.6. Street Mural, East Los Angeles, California. Photo by Author.

paintings that reflect the mural traditions of Mexico can be seen in many barrios in the borderlands. Often, the murals are created by community artists. The street art movement has heightened neighborhood identity by decorating barrio landscapes. In San Diego, geographers Ford and Griffin found that murals "personalized" otherwise sterile institutional landmarks like freeway pillars and thus marked these landscapes as symbolic places for barrio residents.[45]

In many cities with large Mexican American populations, distinct immigrant quarters have become part of the cultural landscape. These smaller barrios are distinguishable from the larger Mexican American communities in that they house principally Mexican nationals or immigrants. In Los Angeles, these immigrant quarters, often a single apartment complex, have multiplied with the growth of migration from Mexico. Sawtelle, a middle-class community in West Los Angeles, houses a number of apartment complexes that have been transformed into immigrant villages.[46] Cozy Court is a 121–unit complex located near the busy intersection of Sawtelle and Olympic boulevards. Between 5 and 9 a.m., the sidewalks in front of the Cozy Court apartments are filled with Mexican men who wait to be picked-up by temporary employers. Many work as laborers and can earn up to $30 a day. The one-room apartments in the complex rent for $200–300 a month. Tenants describe the living arrangement as village-like where friends socialize in the parking lot, children play on the dirt roadways, and vendors hawk *tortillas* and other goods. A Mexican immigrant colony in the San Francisco Bay area revealed a similar village atmosphere.[47]. Immigrant families found to reside on the same street or on several nearby streets. The Mexicans maintained village cultural patterns that reinforced their identity as immigrants from a particular province of Mexico, and they distinguished themselves from Mexican Americans and other Mexican immigrants.

SOCIAL ECONOMIC GEOGRAPHY

The economic character of the Mexican American population differed from the total population in 1980. Individual and family income was lower, on the average, than that for the majority of Americans. Indices of income and employment also vary among Mexican Americans across the country. Average incomes from Mexican Americans were higher in midwestern and eastern cities than average incomes among Mexican Americans in most of the urban borderlands. The measurement of these variables combined with certain population and education indices can be mapped to show the variability among Mexican American subgroups. These patterns illustrate a regional social and economic geography for the Mexican American population.

Economic Patterns

In 1978, the median income of Mexican American families, $12,835, was nearly $5,000 less than that of all U.S. families, $17,640.[48] At the low end of this scale, 21 percent of Mexican American families had incomes below $7,000 compared to only 14 percent for all families in the United States. At the highest income levels, roughly 14 percent of Mexican American families had incomes above $25,000; for all Americans nearly twice this percentage of families were in the upper income levels.

In 1975, the median income of Mexican American families was $9,546 while $13,719 for all American families. If these data are compared with the 1978 data cited above, it is evident that Mexican American median family income grew faster (35 percent) between 1975 and 1978 than for all families in the United States (29 percent). In addition, the percentage of Mexican American families with incomes below $5,000 declined from 26 percent to 19 percent between these same years.[49]

The variability of income levels among borderland cities gives an indication of the geographical differences in per capita earnings among Mexican Americans. Generally, incomes increased from east to west in the border region. For example, in 1977, per capita annual income was $4,253 in Brownsville, $5,071 in El Paso, and $7,070 in San Diego.[50]

The occupational characteristics of Mexican American males in the borderlands has shifted from chiefly laborers to craft and operative occupations. In 1930, 63 percent of Mexican American male workers in the region were laborers and farm laborers, whereas in 1978 only 20 percent of the male population was counted in these occupations. For the same time periods, craft and operative occupations increased from 16 to 50 percent among Mexican American male workers. Mexican Americans were underrepresented in professional, technical, and managerial occupations—11 percent compared to 30 percent for the total population.[51]

Regional Variations

As we have seen, the distribution of the Mexican American population has been a function of historical inertia and migrations to areas of economic opportunity. The borderlands states and outlier communities of Mexican Americans have evolved under differing social and economic circumstances and at different times in the nearly four hundred years of Hispanic occupance in North America. This differential process of cultural adaptation and economic development has resulted in varied population groups within the larger Mexican American minority. Thus, Mexican Americans in south Texas are somewhat different from Mexican Americans in Chicago, and in turn, both are different from the Mexican Americans of Oregon and the Pacific Northwest.[52]

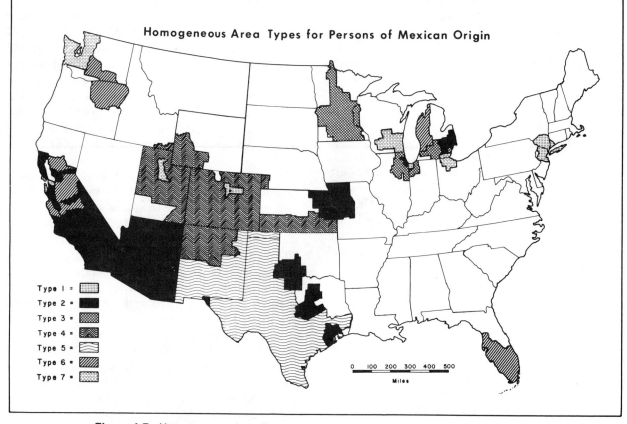

Figure 4.7. Homogeneous Area Types for Persons of Mexican Origin, 1970. Reprinted from Boswell and Jones, *Geographical Review,* Vol. 70, 180, with permission of the American Geographical Society.

Geographers Boswell and Jones analyzed the patterns of social and economic diversity among these various subgroups and regionalized the Mexican American population of the United States using 1970 census data.[53] Their study was based on a sample of Mexican Americans in USA counties, and analysis of six major socio-economic variables. These included median personal income, percentage of the population which was steadily employed, mean highest educational level, fertility ratio, percentage of the population over 14 born in another state, and percentage of foreign-born population. Computer analysis revealed seven separate population area types and these were mapped accordingly (Fig. 4.7). The study illustrates the regional variation in the socio-economic geography of Mexican Americans in 1970.

Type 1 areas totaled 118,700 persons of Mexican origin, representing only 2.8 percent of the total Mexican American population in 1970. These areas included the city of San Francisco and nearby counties, the suburban counties of Denver, the Gary-Hammond-East Chicago S.M.S.A., and the general metropolitan area of New York City and surrounding counties. Type 1 areas were found to have the lowest fertility ratios, highest levels of schooling, greatest percentage of

steadily employed workers, above average mobility, and the greatest percentage of foreign-born population. Their income levels ranked second highest among the seven area types. Mexican Americans in these areas appear to have a very high standard of living based on the indices measured and compared to Mexican Americans in other areas. The combination of high socio-economic status and high percentage of foreign-born might suggest that Mexicans of some affluence migrated to these areas and have become naturalized citizens.

Type 2 areas included Arizona, southern California, the Salinas and Santa Clara valleys, as well as Fresno and surrounding counties (all in California), several counties north and east of San Francisco, the city of Denver, metropolitan El Paso, Houston, Dallas-Ft. Worth, and Wichita Falls-Lawton in Texas, the Kansas City and Topeka regions of Kansas and Missouri, the city of Chicago, and the suburbs of Detroit outside of Wayne County. This type class was the largest revealed by the study and counted 2,472,800 persons of Mexican origin, 57.5 percent of the total Mexican American population in 1970. The populations in these areas ranked slightly above the mean value for all the indicators calculated for the total Mexican American population. In these areas, Mexican Americans had high fertility ratios, generally had earned higher income, had completed more years of school, were more mobile, and had higher numbers of foreign-born than the nation's Mexican Americans considered as a group.

Type 3 areas included four major midwestern urban districts: Minneapolis-St. Paul, the suburbs of Chicago, Kalamazoo-Lansing, Michigan, and the suburbs of Detroit in Wayne County. Only 61,000 or 1.4 percent of the Mexican American population resided in these areas in 1970. By the measurement of key variables, Mexican Americans in these areas ranked close to Mexican Americans in type 1 areas. Populations in type 3 areas had a high education, mobility and income, and high levels of steady workers. The population counted below average foreign-born populations, and a significantly higher fertility ratio than that recorded by those in type 1 areas.

Type 4 areas were found in Utah, Colorado, northern New Mexico, southern Kansas, and parts of Idaho, Wyoming, and Nebraska. The populations in these areas totaled 125,100 in 1970, 2.9 percent of the total ethnic group population. With few exceptions, such as Alburquerque and Colorado Springs, Mexican Americans in these areas were rural and generally poorer than in other area types. Income averages were below the national mean for the minority, but education, work permanency, and mobility were slightly above this mean. Fertility ratio and foreign-born population were significantly below the mean for the group.

Type 5 areas encompassed southern and eastern New Mexico, and most of central and western Texas, including San Antonio and the lower Rio Grande Valley, but excluding El Paso. This contiguous area was the second largest concentration of Mexican Americans among the type areas, accounting for 1,218,400 or 28.4 percent of the population in 1970. On the basis of income, educational level and mobility, the populations in type 5 areas ranked lowest of all area types. Fertility ratio and work permanency were near the mean for all Mexican Americans, whereas the percentage of the population foreign-born was well below the national mean for the group, despite the proximity to the border.

Type 6 areas included the third largest numbers of Mexican Americans behind type areas 2 and 5, totaling 239,600 or 5.6 percent of the population in 1970. Type 6 areas were found in southern Florida, western Michigan, southeastern Washington and northeastern Oregon, the northern San Joaquin and southern Sacramento valleys, and Monterey County in California. These areas generally ranked below the total mean for the variable indices except mobility and foreign-born. These two variables measured high compared to populations in other type areas. Specialized agriculture is practiced in each area and migratory laborers are numerous, thus accounting for the high mobility and foreign-born characteristics.

Finally, type 7 areas included metropolitan Toledo, southeastern Wisconsin, the urbanized areas of Everett, Seattle, and Tacoma in Washington, and the S.M.S.A.s of Ogden, Salt Lake City, and Provo-Orem, Utah. The combined population of type 7 areas ranked next to type 3 areas as the smallest percentage of the total Mexican American population, 1.4 percent or 61,200 persons in 1970. Education and income levels measured high for Mexican Americans in these areas, but fertility and mobility were the highest found in all type areas. High fertility is uncharacteristic of populations that are urban and highly educated and perhaps is explained by the migration of young adults to these regions.

This regionalization shows the subgroups of Mexican American populations that existed in 1970, when measured by key social and economic variables. Two area types, 2 and 5, accounted for almost 86 percent of the Mexican American population in 1970, most of which was concentrated in the borderland states. The Mexican Americans in type 2 areas, generally ranked higher in all categories, except fertility, than their counterparts in type 5 areas. Roughly the same numbers of Mexican Americans resided in type 1 and 4 areas as lived in areas designated type 6. However, the type 1 populations were urban and scored higher than either type 4 or 6 area populations by the variables measured. Finally, type 3 and 7 areas combined for approximately 3 percent of the population in 1970, and ranked nearly comparable by the social indicators.

CONCLUSION

Mexican American culture emerged in the borderlands where Spanish and later Mexican settlement made the first European imprints on the landscapes of the region. The legacy of this early colonization remains evident in the states of California, Texas, Arizona, New Mexico, and Colorado. These Hispanic-American borderland states contain close to 83 percent of the total Mexican American population. Outside of the border states, Mexican Americans are concentrated in parts of the Midwest, the Mountain West, the Pacific Northwest, and the South. The Mexican American population as a whole is younger, characterized by larger families, and is growing more rapidly than the general U.S. population.

During the twentieth century, two major social processes have been important in the spatial evolution of the Mexican American people: immigration and urbanization. Immigration has occurred in two separate phases from 1900 to 1930 and since the 1940s to the present. In both instances, Mexican immigrants have responded to the economic opportunities available in the United States. Their labor contributions to the economic development of the southwestern United States have been substantial. They continue today to provide steady and inexpensive labor in many of the cities of the West and Midwest, and elsewhere across the country. Largely because of changes in legal emigration from Mexico and as a result of continued underemployment in that country, the majority of Mexican migrants to the United States enter illegally. This situation will not likely change in the near future, unless by political agreement between the United States and Mexico. As long as Mexico's population remains chronically underemployed and American industries and service sector economies demand labor, the push-pull factors of migration will perpetuate this phenomenon.

What this continued migration portends for the United States is a greater plurality within the Mexican American minority. If large numbers of illegal Mexican laborers decide to remain in this country, they will certainly change the ratio of foreign-born Mexicans to native-born Mexican Americans. Over time, the children of foreign-born migrants that are born in the United States will themselves become Mexican Americans and fuel the already rapidly growing native-born population of resident Mexican Americans. It is conceivable that the nation's second largest minority could become the nation's largest minority, surging past the black population, if population growth rates in the Mexican American group remain high and immigrants continue to feed this population.

Urbanization has also been an important process of change for Mexican Americans. The Mexican American population was predominantly urban in 1980. As Mexican American populations grow, they will continue to transform the ethnic character of cities.[54] The major Mexican American cities of the country such as Los Angeles, San Antonio, Chicago, Houston, and El Paso will likely become more Mexican American. This process will probably affect intermediate and small urban areas where Mexican Americans are significant as well.

In many metropolitan areas with large Mexican American populations, the central cities showed the greatest concentrations of the group. In these areas, preliminary study suggests that a Mexican American landscape is evident and can be distinguished from other urban cultural landscapes. In some cities, Mexican Americans are dispersing out of traditional barrios and into suburbs. Ernesto Galarza sees this as an inevitable development of the process of cultural evolution for the Mexican American population.[55] As economic prosperity improves, the process of acculturation to the dominant Anglo society tends to accelerate, and Mexican Americans will become more like Anglo Americans in traditions and values. Further studies are needed, however, of the influences of changing economic situations on the social values and landscapes of Mexican American communities before any conclusions can be reached about urbanization and the Mexican American minority.

The regional implications of these changing social processes are equally significant to the future of the Mexican American group. The survey of key economic and population variables for the minority in 1970 revealed a mosaic of area types across the country. While the majority of Mexican Americans still reside in the borderlands, the populations inside and outside of this hearth show considerable socio-economic variation. This variation has its roots in the early plurality of the borderlands where different population cores have developed separate regional identities. As these regions developed differentially, the populations in some cases have preserved particular folk traditions and in others have more quickly adapted to changing circumstances. Thus, Mexican Americans have evolved independently in these regions. This regional variation is likely to persist into the future, perhaps to the dismay of politicians who would like to sway the minority to vote as a single bloc.

Despite these internal variations within the Mexican American minority, a distinct regional pattern may be evolving in the borderlands. Some scholars and recently some observers in the popular press have been speculating upon the regional dimensions of the future Mexican American population.[56] Popular writers are suggesting, for example, that the 2000 mile-long boundary between Mexico and the United States is emerging as the main axis of a new cultural province, called "MexAmerica" by one author.[57] This hybrid area represents what Nostrand has called the major zone of Anglo-Latin "cultural convergence" in the hemisphere.[58] It is a region where Mexican American cultural influences are intermingled with Anglo traditions and spiced with Mexican traits as immigrants move into and across the borderlands. Geographers Griffin and Ford have documented something of the hybrid nature of the landscapes that are spawned from the union of two of these cultures on the Mexico side of the border.[59] The ongoing changes in the urban areas of the Hispanic-American borderlands are likely to prove our best clue to the future population characteristics and landscape influences of the nation's second largest minority.

NOTES

1. Richard L. Nostrand, "Spanish Roots in the Borderlands," *Geographical Magazine,* 51 (December, 1979): pp. 203–209; Arthur L. Campa, *Hispanic Culture in the Southwest* (Norman: University of Oklahoma Press, 1979); and Carl O. Sauer, *Sixteenth Century North America: The Land and the People as Seen by the Europeans* (Berkeley, Los Angeles, and London: University of California Press, 1971).

2. D. W. Meinig, *Southwest: Three Peoples in Geographical Change, 1600–1970* (New York: Oxford University Press, 1971); Henry F. Dobyns, *Spanish Colonial Tucson: A Demographic History* (Tucson: University of Arizona Press, 1976).

3. D. W. Meinig, *Imperial Texas: An Interpretive Essay in Cultural Geography* (Austin and London: University of Texas Press, 1969); Terry G. Jordan, "Population Origins in Texas, 1850," *Geographical Review,* 59 (January, 1969): pp. 83–103; and Arnoldo De León, *The Tejano Community, 1836–1900* (Albuquerque: University of New Mexico Press, 1982).

4. Nostrand, 1979; Leonard Pitt, *The Decline of the Californios: A Social History of the Spanish-Speaking Californians, 1846–1890* (Berkeley, Los Angeles, and London: University of California Press, 1971); and David J. Weber, *The Mexican Frontier 1821–1846: The American Southwest Under Mexico* (Albuquerque: University of New Mexico Press, 1982).

5. Nostrand, 1979.

6. Ibid.

7. David Hornbeck, "Land Tenure and Rancho Expansion in Alta California, 1784–1846," *Journal of Historical Geography,* 4 (4) (1978): pp. 371–390; David Hornbeck, "Mexican-American Land Tenure Conflict in California," *Journal of Geography,* 75 (April, 1976): pp. 209–221.

8. Richard L. Nostrand, "Mexican Americans Circa 1850," *Annals of the Association of American Geographers,* 65 (September, 1975): pp. 378–390; Oscar J. Martínez, "On the Size of the Chicano Population: New Estimates, 1850–1900," *Aztlan,* 6 (Spring, 1975): pp. 43–67.

9. Richard L. Nostrand, "The Hispanic-American Borderland: Delimitation of an American Culture Region," *Annals of the Association of American Geographers,* 60 (Decmeber, 1970): pp. 638–661.

10. Nancie L. Gonzaléz, *The Spanish-Americans of New Mexico: A Heritage of Pride* (Albuquerque: University of New Mexico Press, 1967); Richard L. Nostrand, "The Hispano Homeland in 1900," *Annals of the Association of American Geographers,* 70 (September, 1980): pp. 382–396.

11. Richard L. Nostrand, " 'Mexican American' and 'Chicano': Emerging Terms for a People Coming of Age" in Norris Hundley, Jr. ed. *The Chicano* (Santa Barbara and Oxford: Clio Books, 1975): pp. 143–160.

12. Arthur F. Corwin ed., *Immigrants—and Immigrants: Perspectives on Mexican Labor Migration to the United States* (Westport, Conn.: Greenwood Press, 1978); Harry E. Cross and James A. Sandos, *Across the Border: Rural Development in Mexico and Recent Migration to the United States* (Berkeley: Institute of Governmental Studies, 1981).

13. Corwin, 1978.

14. U.S. Bureau of the Census, *Statistical Abstract of the United States: 1981* (Washington D.C.: U.S. Government Printing Office, 1981).

15. Carey McWilliams, *North from Mexico: The Spanish-Speaking People of the United States* (New York: Greenwood Press, 1968).

16. Mario T. Garcíia, *Desert Immigrants: The Mexicans of El Paso, 1880–1920* (New Haven and London: Yale University Press, 1981).

17. Alvar W. Carlson, "Seasonal Farm Labor in the San Luis Valley," *Annals of the Association of American Geographers,* 63 (March, 1973): pp. 97–108; McWilliams, 1968.

18. Abraham Hoffman, *Unwanted Mexican Americans in the Great Depression: Repatriation Pressures, 1929–1939* (Tucson: University of Arizona Press, 1974).

19. *Statistical Abstract,* 1981; Walter Fogel, *Mexican Illegal Alien Workers in the United States,* Institute of Industrial Relations Monograph Series: 20 (Los Angeles: University of California, 1979); Paul R. Ehrlich, Loy Bilderback, Anne H. Ehrlich, *The Golden Door: International Migration, Mexico, and the United States* (New York: Ballantine Books, 1979).

20. Manuel Vic Villalpando, et. al., *A Study of the Socioeconomic Impact of Illegal Aliens on the County of San Diego* (San Diego: County of San Diego Human Resources Agency, 1977).

21. Fogel, 1979.

22. Ehrlich, et al., 1979.

23. U.S. Bureau of the Census, *Census of Population: 1980, Persons of Spanish Origin by State: 1980,* Supplementary Report PC80–S1–7 (Washington D.C.: U.S. Government Printing Office, 1982), Table 1; Jose Hernández, Leo Estrada and David Alvírez, "Census Data and the Problem of Conceptually Defining the Mexican American Population," *Social Science Quarterly,* 53 (March, 1973): pp. 671–687.

24. U.S. Bureau of the Census, *Census of Population: 1970, Persons of Spanish Ancestry,* Supplementary Report PC(S1)-30 (Washington D.C.: U.S. Government Printing Office, 1973): Table 1.

25. Leo Grebler, Joan W. Moore, Ralph Guzman, *The Mexican American People: The Nation's Second Largest Minority* (New York: The Free Press, 1970).

26. Joan W. Moore, *Mexican Americans,* Second Edition (Englewood Cliffs, N.J.: Prentice-Hall, 1976).

27. U.S. Bureau of the Census, *Census of Population: 1980, Population Profile of the United States: 1980,* Current Population Reports, Series P-20, No. 363 (Washington D.C.: U.S. Government Printing Office, 1981).

28. Benjamin S. Bradshaw and Frank D. Bean, "Trends in the Fertility of Mexican Americans: 1950–1970," *Social Science Quarterly,* 53 (March, 1973): pp. 688–696.

29. Thomas D. Boswell, "The Growth and Proportional Redistribution of the Mexican Stock Population in the United States: 1900–1970," *Mississippi Geographer,* 6 (Spring, 1979): pp. 57–76.

30. *Population Profile of the United States: 1980,* 1981.

31. Ibid.

32. U.S. Bureau of the Census, *Census of Population: 1980, General Population Characteristics: Illinois, Michigan, Wisconsin, Indiana, New York, Missouri* PC80–1B15,B24,B51,B16,B34,B27 (Washington D.C.: U.S. Government Printing Office, 1982): Table 16 for each state.

33. Shirley Achor, *Mexican Americans in a Dallas Barrio* (Tucson: University of Arizona Press, 1978); Albert Camarillo, *Chicanos in a Changing Society: From Mexican Pueblos to American Barrios in Santa Barbara and Southern California, 1848–1930* (Cambridge, Mass.: Harvard University Press, 1979); Richard Griswold del Castillo, *The Los Angeles Barrio, 1850–1890: A Social History* (Berkeley, Los Angeles, London: University of California Press, 1979); Julian Samora and Richard A. Lamanna, *Mexican Americans in a Midwest Metropolis: A Study of East Chicago,* Advance Report 8, Mexican-American Study Project, U.C.L.A.; Division of Research, Graduate School of Business Administration (Los Angeles: University of California, 1967).

34. Joan W. Moore and Frank G. Mittelbach, *Residential Segregation in the Urban Southwest: A Comparison Study,* Advance Report 4, Mexican-American Study Project, U.C.L.A., Division of Research, Graduate School of Business Administration (Los Angeles: University of California, 1966).

35. Arthur J. Rubel, *Across the Tracks: Mexican-Americans in a Texas City* (Austin and London: University of Texas Press, 1966): p. 3.

36. W. Tim Dagodag, "Spatial Control and Public Policies: The Example of Mexican-American Housing," *Professional Geographer,* 26 (August, 1974): pp. 262–269; Ellwyn R. Stoddard, "The Adjustment of Mexican American Barrio Families to Forced Housing Relocation," *Social Science Quarterly,* 53 (March, 1973): pp. 749–759.

37. Moore and Mittelbach, 1966.

38. Brian J. L. Berry, *et al, Chicago: Transformation of an Urban System* (Cambridge, Mass.: Ballinger, 1976).

39. Moore and Mittelbach, 1966.

40. Francine F. Rabinovitz and William J. Siembieda, *Minorities in Suburbs: The Los Angeles Experience* (Lexington, Mass.: D.C. Heath, 1977).

41. William Madsen, *The Mexican-Americans of South Texas,* Second Edition (New York: Holt, Rinehart, and Winston, 1973); James E. Officer, "Sodalities and Systemic Linkage: The Joining Habits of Urban Mexican-Americans," unpublished Ph. D. dissertation, University of Arizona, 1964.

42. Peirce F. Lewis, "Axioms for Reading the Landscape: Some Guides to the American Scene," in D. W. Meinig, ed. *The Interpretation of Ordinary Landscapes: Geographical Essays* (New York: Oxford University Press, 1979): pp. 11–32; Peirce Lewis, "Common Houses, Cultural Spoor," *Landscape,* 19 (January, 1975): pp. 1–22.

43. Daniel D. Arreola, "Fences as Landscape Taste: Tucson's *Barrios," Journal of Cultural Geography,* 2 (Fall/Winter, 1981): pp. 96–105.

44. Eva Cockcroft, John Weber, and Jim Cockcroft, *Toward a People's Art: The Contemporary Mural Movement* (New York: E. P. Dutton, 1977); Jacinto Quirarte, "The Murals of El Barrio," *Exxon USA,* 13 (1974): pp. 2–9; Shifra M. Goldman, "Resistence and Identity: Street Murals of Occupied Aztlán," *Latin American Literary Review,* 5 (Spring-Summer, 1977): pp. 124–128.

45. Larry R. Ford and Ernst Griffin, "Chicano Park: Personalizing an Institutional Landscape," *Landscape,* 25 (2) (1981): pp. 42–48.

46. Michele Markel-Cohen, "Port of Entry: Sawtelle Area Carries on Long Tradition as Migrant Labor Colony in Heart of Middle-Class West L.A.," *Los Angeles Times* (January 9, 1983) part X: pp. 1 and 10.

47. Laura Zarrugh, "Home Away from Home: The Jacalan Community in the San Francisco Bay Area," in Stanley A. West and June Macklin, eds., *The Chicano Experience* (Boulder, Colo.: Westview Press, 1979): pp. 145–163.

48. Niles Hansen, *The Border Economy: Regional Development in the Southwest* (Austin: University of Texas Press, 1981).

49. Ibid.

50. Ibid.

51. Vernon M. Briggs, Walter Fogel and Fred H. Schmidt, *The Chicano Worker* (Austin: University of Texas Press, 1977); Hansen, 1981.

52. Madsen, 1973; Louise Año Nuevo de Kerr, "Chicano Settlements in Chicago: A Brief History," *Journal of Ethnic Studies,* 2 (Winter, 1975): pp. 22–32; Richard W. Slatta, "Chicanos in the Pacific Northwest: An Historical Overview of Oregon's Chicanos," *Aztlan,* 6 (Fall, 1975): pp. 327–340.

53. Thomas D. Boswell and Timothy C. Jones, "A Regionalization of Mexican Americans in the United States," *Geographical Review,* 70 (January, 1980): pp. 88–98.

54. Ray Herbert, "Vast Shift Noted in L.A. Ethnic Makeup," *Los Angeles Times* (February 27, 1978): Part II, pp. 1 and 4.

55. Ernesto Galarza, "Mexicans in the Southwest: A Culture in Process," in Edward M. Spicer and Raymond H. Thompson, eds. *Plural Society in the Southwest* (Albuquerque: University of New Mexico Press, 1972): pp. 261–297.

56. Stanley R. Ross, ed. *Views Across the Border: The United States and Mexico* (Albuquerque: University of New Mexico Press, 1978); Tom Miller, *On the Border: Portraits of America's Southwestern Frontier* (New York: Harper and Row, 1981).

57. Joel Garreau, *The Nine Nations of North America* (Boston: Houghton Mifflin, 1981).

58. Richard L. Nostrand, "The Borderlands in Perspective," in Gary S. Elbow, ed. *International Aspects of Development in Latin America: Geographical Perspectives,* Proceedings of the Conference of Latin Americanist Geographers, 6 (Muncie, Indiana: C.L.A.G. Publications, 1977): pp. 9–28.

59. Ernst C. Griffin and Larry R. Ford, "Tijuana: Landscape of a Culture Hybrid," *Geographical Reveiw,* 66 (October, 1976): pp. 435–447.

5

The Cuban-Americans[1]

Thomas D. Boswell
University of Miami, Florida

Cuban-Americans represent the third largest component of persons of Latin American origin living in the United States, being surpassed only by Mexican-Americans and Puerto Ricans. Currently, there are approximately one million Cuban-Americans.[2] Although this accounts for less than one-half of one percent of the United States' total population, Cubans living in the United States represent a significant minority worthy of study. They are an especially interesting American ethnic group for at least seven reasons. First, the number of Cuban-Americans is equal to approximately ten percent of all Cubans currently residing in Cuba.[3] Thus, although they represent an insignificant proportion of the United States' population, this is not true with respect to the population of Cuba. Second, emigrants from Cuba have not, until recently, been representative of Cuba's total population. The earliest waves were especially selective of professionals and entrepreneurs, thereby creating a serious "brain drain" in Cuba. Such a concentration of particular socioeconomic groups intensified the impact of emigration on Cuba's population structure, beyond what normally is suggested by a figure of ten percent. Third, the selectivity characteristics of the Cuban migrants has exhibited a dynamic quality, so that the most recent arrivals are significantly different from those who arrived earlier. Fourth, the socioeconomic concentration of Cuban migrants has been accompanied by a spatial concentration in their American destinations. Close to three out of every four live in the two metropolitan areas of Mami, Florida and Union City-West New York, in New Jersey.[4] In these two areas their economic, political, and social influence has been greatly amplified. Fifth, Cubans represent the first large group of *refugees* who have moved to the United States as their country of first asylum.[5] In the past most other refugees have come to America indirectly, after spending time in an intervening third country. Although some Cubans have also entered this way, the vast majority have moved directly from Cuba to the United States. As a consequence, they have been accepted automatically, until recently, as refugees who have been motivated by political persecution in a communist country. This status has entitled them to federal government benefits that were not available to most other immigrant groups who have migrated primarily for economic reasons. There is a considerable body of literature that suggests that migrants who move as political refugees are often considerably different from those who move in response to economic opportunities.[6] Sixth, Cuban-Americans have made remarkable progress in adjusting to living conditions in the United States. It is probably correct to say that there has never been a large non-English speaking immigrant group in this country that has exhibited more rapid upward socioeconomic mobility than the Cubans. A seventh reason for interest in persons of Cuban descent is that their large-scale movement to the United States is of recent origin and is a newsworthy problem that is being grappled with by the United States Immigration authorities, urban planners, and purveyors of social services *today*.

HISTORY OF CUBAN MIGRATION TO THE UNITED STATES

The history of Cuban emigration to the United States took place within seven distinct phases. The first was represented by a trickle movement that, for all intents, began in the middle 1800s and continued until the Castro takeover in 1959. The second was a large scale movement that occurred between 1959 and 1962, as Fidel Castro's revolution was being consummated. The third was characterized by a hiatus in the movement, that was initiated by the Cuban Missile Crisis in 1962 and lasted until 1965. During the latter year Castro changed his migration policy and ordered that Cuba be opened once again for a fourth phase of emigration to the United States. This was to last until 1973 and became known as the period of the Freedom Flights. Again, there was a temporary interlude in the movement to the United States between 1973 and 1980, that was to represent the fifth phase. In 1973 Castro again decided to close Cuban ports for direct passage to American destinations. Unexpectedly, in April, 1980 a veritable flood of Cuban migration was unleashed (as the sixth phase) through the small northern port of Mariel. Although it lasted only five months, approximately 125,000 Cubans participated in this wave. Since September, 1980 emigration has declined once again, as both the Cuban and United States governments have adopted stricter migration policies. This represents the seventh phase, which has continued to the time of the writing of this chapter.

The Early Trickle

The first year for which census data are available for determining the magnitude of the presence of Cubans in the United States is 1870 (Table 5.1). At that time there were a little over 5,000 persons living in the United States who were born in Cuba. By the mid-1800s there had developed a sizable exodus of Cubans in response to political turmoil on the island. Key West, Tampa, and New York City became particularly notable as places of refuge for Cuban political exiles who

TABLE 5.1 Estimates of the Cuban-American Population 1870–1982 (Numbers in Thousands)

Year[a]	Foreign Born	USA Born of Cuban Parents	Total
1870	5.3	NA	NA
1880	6.9	NA	NA
1890	NA	NA	NA
1900	11.1	NA	NA
1910	15.1	NA	NA
1920	14.9	NA	NA
1930	18.5	17.0	35.5
1940	18.0	NA	NA
1950	33.7	NA	NA
1960	79.2	45.3	124.5
1970	439.0	122.0	561.0
1980[b]	NA	NA	831.0
1981[c]	NA	NA	1,000.0

NA Means data are not available

[a]For the 1870 to 1970 period the figures are derived from: A. J. Jaffe, Ruth M. Cullen, and Thomas D. Boswell, *The Changing Demography of Spanish Americans* (New York: Academic Press, 1980): p. 247.

[b]The 1980 figure is for all persons who considered themselves to be of Cubam descent. It contains some individuals who were born in the United States with American born parents. The USA Bureau of the Census, *Current Population Reports,* Series, P-20, No. 361: "Persons of Spanish Origin in the United States," March, 1980 (Advance Report), (Washington, D.C.: U.S. Government Printing Office, 1981): p. 5.

[c]Estimate obtained from: Antonio Jorge and Raul Moncarz *International Factor Movement and Complementary: Growth and Entrepreneurship Under Conditions of Cultural Variation* (The Hague, Netherlands: Research Group for European Migration Problems. R.E.M.P. Bulletin, Supplement 14, 1981): p. 4.

were plotting the overthrow of their Spanish rulers.[7] In addition, during the 1860s and 1870s several cigar manufacturers moved their operations from Havana to these three cities, thereby providing additional employment opportunities for Cuban immigrants.[8] A slow growth pattern emerged that was temporarily interrupted by World War I and the Great Depression of the 1930s. Miami did not begin to appear as a center of Cuban influence until the 1930s when exiles fled the effects of the revolution against Gerardo Machado. Another spurt in the stream to Miami occurred from 1953 to 1959 as would-be revolutionaries fled the Batista regime.[9] From the beginning of the 20th century until the Castro revolution in 1959 immigration fluctuated, varying with changing political and economic conditions on the island.[10]

The early experience of Cubans living in New York and Florida proved crucial for the ability of future generations of Cuban immigrants to adjust to life in the United States. Cuban history books, songs, folktales, and poetry often provided moving accounts of living conditions in America. The exiles who emigrated after the introduction of communism in Cuba were at least partially aware of the Latin cultural concentrations in New York and Miami and were familiar with the geographical and climatic similarities between Cuba and southern Florida.

Period of the "Golden Exiles"

Historically it has been the case throughout the Caribbean that when one dictatorship is replaced by another, especially through use of force, the opponents of the victor became political exiles. This happened many times in Cuba before the advent of Castro. Therefore, it was not surprising that when Fidel Castro's forces overthrew the government of Fulgencio Batista in January 1959, an out-migration of backers of the ousted government occurred. The magnitude of this exodus, however, was not anticipated. During the 22 year period between 1959 and 1980, approximately 794,000 Cubans emigrated to the United States (Table 5.2). Except for Puerto Rico, no other island in the Caribbean has experienced a comparable outpouring in such a short period of time.

The key to understanding the reasons behind this remarkable exodus lies in developing an appreciation for the pervasiveness and speed of the societal changes that took place as Castro consolidated his power between 1959 and 1962. In contrast to all other changes in dictatorships that have taken place in the Caribbean, Castro's efforts left no social sector untouched. Fagen *et. al.* state that the period between 1959 and 1962 can be properly termed "cataclysmic."[11] The social structure, economic life, and political institutions were radically and rapidly altered. Those who were able and willing to adjust were welcomed into the new order.

Persons who could not, or would not, accommodate to the system were rudely shouldered aside and often treated harshly. A considerable amount of confusion, suspicion, and uncertainty accompanied these changes. There were many, perhaps a majority, who perceived themselves as benefiting from these changes. Included are the vast majority of the rural masses, blacks, perhaps the indoctrinated youth, and members of the new managerial and political class of elites.

More than 215,000 Cubans migrated to American between 1959 and 1962 (Table 5.2). In the beginning, the majority were members of the economic and political elite openly affiliated with the government of Batista. By the middle of 1959 members of the landholding aristocracy began to leave as an agrarian reform law was instituted in June, with the stated purpose of breaking up large land holdings. In July, 1960 a law was passed authorizing the expropriation of all American-owned property. In the same year an urban reform law was enacted in October that was designed to con-

TABLE 5.2 Cuban Emigration to the United States 1959 to 1980

Year	Number
1959 (January 1–June 30)	26,527
1960[a]	60,224
1961	49,961
1962	78,611
1963	42,929
1964	15,616
1965	16,447
1966	46,688
1967	52,147
1968	55,945
1969	52,625
1970	49,545
1971	50,001
1972	23,977
1973	12,579
1974	13,670
1975	8,488
1976	4,515
1977[b]	4,548
1978	4,108
1979	2,644
1980	122,061
Total, January 1, 1959 to September 30, 1980	793,856
Total, April 1, 1980 to December 31, 1980	125,118

[a]For 1960 through 1976 the figures are for fiscal years beginning July 1st and ending June 30th.

[b]For 1977 through 1980 the figures are for fical years beginning October 1st and ending September 30th.

Sergio Diaz Briquets annd Lisandro Perez, *Cuba: The Demography of Revolution* (Washington, D.C.: Population Reference Bureau, 36, No. 1, April, 1981): p. 26.

fiscate rental property in the cities.[12] By this time the Revolution was also felt by middle class entrepreneurs; thus widening its impact. In 1960 the number leaving expanded to approximately 60,000.

Relations between the United States and Cuba began to cool rapidly in early 1961. On the third of January diplomatic relations with Cuba were broken by the American government. The ill-fated Bay of Pigs invasion was launched in April. Castro announced in December that he was a Marxist-Leninist and that Cuba was destined to become a socialist state. Severe restrictions were placed on the amount of property and money that could be taken out of the country. Finally, in October 1962, the Cuban missile crisis resulted in termination of air traffic to the United States. Legal emigration to America remained suspended for about three years until September, 1965.[13]

The 1959 to 1962 era of Cuban immigration to the United States is often referred to as the wave of "Golden Exiles." This implies that the vast majority were former members of the elite classes in Cuba. The data in Table 5.3 suggest that this concept is only partly correct. When the occupational structure of Miami Cuban refugees (at the time they left Cuba) is compared to that of the population living in Cuba (at the time of the 1953 census)[14] it is clear that the refugees were overrepresented, especially in the legal and white collar professions. Conversely, they were underrepresented in the extractive occupations (such as agriculture and fishing) and in blue collar jobs. It is also relevant, however, to note that the refugees were a highly diverse group. Virtually all occupations were represented among the immigrants. Therefore, it is incorrect to think of all of them as having been elites in Cuba prior to their arrival in Florida. In fact, less than 40 percent should be so considered. Nevertheless, it is correct to state that, when considered as a whole, the refugees for the 1959 to 1962 interval were positively selected from the entire Cuban population.

The Miami Cuban refugee study also determined that a much larger share of the emigrants were from urban origins in comparison with the total 1953 Cuban population. For instance, 87 percent of the refugees lived either in Havana (62 percent) or some other large city (25 percent) in Cuba before leaving for Florida, whereas only 31 percent of Cuba's population lived in the same areas. On the other hand, 69 percent of all Cubans resided in small towns or rural areas. The figure for the refugees was 13 percent.[15]

Missile Crisis Hiatus

The missile crisis and United States military blockade of Cuba in October, 1962 brought to an abrupt halt all direct legal transportation between the two countries. A hiatus in legal migration to the United States was to ensue for a three year period until September, 1965. This was not to be the only time that the

TABLE 5.3 Comparison of the Occupational Structure of Cuba in 1953 with the Occupations of Cuban Refugees at the Time They Emigrated to Miami, Florida Between 1959 and 1963

Occupation	1953 Cuban Census	Percentage of Census	1959–63 Cuban Refugee	Percentage of Refugees	Ratio: Percentage of Refugees to Percentage of Census
Lawyers and Judges	7,858	.5	1,695	3.0	7.8
Professional and Semi-professional	78,051	4.0	12,124	22.0	5.5
Managerial and executive	93,662	5.0	6,771	12.0	2.5
Clerical and sales	264,569	14.0	17,123	31.0	2.3
Domestic service, military, and police	160,406	8.0	4,801	9.0	1.1
Skilled, semiskilled, and unskilled	526,168	27.0	11,301	20.0	.7
Agricultural and fishing	807,514	41.5	1,539	3.0	.1
Total	1,938,228		55,354		

Richard R. Fagen, Richard A. Brody, and Thomas J. O'Leary, *Cubans in Exile: Disaffection and the Revolution* (Stanford, California: Stanford University Press, 1968):p. 19.

Castro government quickly reversed its position on emigration. Rather, it was the harbinger of future similar sharp reversals in emigration policy.

Despite the fact that direct legal transportation was stopped between Cuba and the United States, it has been estimated that close to 56,000 still managed to migrate. This includes about 6,700 who were able to escape in boats and a few in planes. A little over 6,000 additional persons were allowed to leave directly for the United States during this period. These were former prisoners from the Bay of Pigs expedition and members of their families. They were released in exchange for a ransom consisting of shipments of badly needed medicines and medical supplies for Cuba.[16]

The vast majority of the remaining 43,300 who were able to reach the United States from Cuba during this three year period did so indirectly through intermediate countries, most frequently through Spain or Mexico.[17] However, this was a costly and enervating process. Persons who arrived in either New York or Miami directly from Cuba were automatically granted immediate legal entry. Yet, those who sought entry from a third country were considered aliens by the United States Department of Immigration and Naturalization Service, and were therefore subject to all existing immigration restrictions. Often the wait in Madrid or Mexico City lasted well over a year before clearance was obtained.[18]

Period of Freedom Flights

On September 28, 1965 Fidel Castro announced he would permit Cubans with relatives living in the United States to emigrate beginning on the following October tenth.[19] The departures would take place by boat through the small port of Camarioca on the northern coast of Matanzas Province. Immediately, hundreds of boats departed southern Florida for Cuba to pick up friends and relatives. Unfortunately, not all the crafts were seaworthy and a number of tragedies occurred. The chaos that ensued, as a result of the panicky rush and accompanying accidents, created a source of embarrassment for the Cuban government. As a consequence, United States and Cuban authorities signed a "Memorandum of Understanding" which established arrangements for an airlift between Miami and a Cuban airport located east of Havana, in the town of Varadero. The agreement was organized through the Swiss Embassy in Havana and the flights became variously known as the "Freedom Flights", "Aerial Bridge", or "Family Reunification Flights."

Air transportation was initiated on December 1, 1965 and continued until April 6, 1973. Normally two flights a day, five days per week, were operated between Miami and Havana, carrying 3,000–4,000 persons per month.[20] It has been estimated that 297,318 persons arrived during the seven-year airlift. In addition, 4,993 came by boat during the two-month boatlift from Camarioca. Thus, a little over 302,000 Cubans migrated directly to the United States between October 10, 1965 and April 6, 1973.[21] A few also continued to travel indirectly from Cuba via third countries, such as Mexico and Spain, to Miami and New York.

The airlift did not result in a free exodus from Cuba. Relatives of persons already living in the United States were given priority according to closeness of the family relationship. Thus, members of nuclear families were accorded the highest preference. Males of military age (17 to 26 years old) were not usually allowed to leave, and few skilled and highly trained individuals working in critical occupations were granted exit visas until replacements could be found and trained. The elderly and sick were more likely to receive clearance to leave, since there was a greater likelihood that they would become dependent on the Cuban social security system for their support. Persons who filed exit applications frequently lost their jobs and were required to perform agricultural labor until plane space became available. It was not uncommon for an adult male to spend two or three years working in agricultural fields for minimal wages before being allowed to exit.[22]

The Interlude from 1973 to 1980

Beginning in August 1971 the Cuban government started creating occasional interruptions in the Freedom Flights. Castro had decided by the end of May 1969 to stop accepting new applications for leaving the island. In September 1971 he announced that the list of people who had requested exit permits was getting smaller and that the exodus would end soon. It was claimed that the intention of the "Memorandum of Understanding", which was to reunite separated families, had largely been fulfilled. As a result the number of arrivals by way of the airlift began to slacken towards the end of 1971 and continued to decrease throughout 1972, until the last flight was made on April 6, 1973.[23]

From July 1, 1973 to September 30, 1979 a total of just under 38,000 Cubans arrived in the United States (Table 5.2). This was less than 13 percent of the number that arrived during the period of the Freedom Flights and the Camarioca boatlift. Those who were able to emigrate during this seven year interlude did so primarily through third countries, just as migrants had done during the Cuban missile crisis hiatus earlier. Again, Mexico and Spain served as the primary stepping stones on the way to the Miami or New York metropolitan areas, with smaller numbers being channeled through Jamaica and Venezuela.

The migration selectivity processes and trends that operated in earlier phases of the Cuban emigration waves were also in effect during the 1973 to 1980 interval. Studies of Cubans living in West New York[24] and Miami[25] indicate that although the new immigrants were better off in terms of their occupational and income status than the majority left behind in Cuba, the degree of positive selection was declining. As was the case during the 1965 to 1973 period, this most recent wave came closer to being representative of the Cuban population. It also became apparent that economic motives were beginning to play a larger role in affecting the decision to leave Cuba, certainly more so than had been the case in the early 1960s.[26]

An interesting change began to emerge during the 1970s with respect to the emigrants' origins in Cuba. As mentioned earlier, Havana had dominated as the leading sender, with Las Villas Province being a distant second. By 1979 Las Villas had surpassed Havana as the leading origin for Cubans going to West New York and was apparently having more of an influence as an origin for persons going to Miami as well. Furthermore, small cities, towns and rural areas began to account for a larger proportion of the refugees. In 1968, 56 percent of the Cubans living in West New York had come from large cities in Cuba. In 1979 the comparable figure had declined to 40 percent[27] This general shift in origins toward smaller settlements in Cuba is part of the same trend noted previously with respect to occupation and income, namely a tendency for the immigrants over time to take on characteristics more similar to the population living in Cuba.

The Flood from Mariel

In April 1980 Cuban history repeated itself, as once again mass emigration was allowed to the United States in a manner reminiscent of what occurred during the boatlift from Camarioca harbor in 1965. Again the mode of transportation was by sea and this time the place of departure selected by Castro was the small port of Mariel, located on the northern coast approximately 20 miles west of Havana. There was, however, one major difference between this exodus and the one from Camarioca that took place fifteen years earlier. The Camarioca boatlift lasted for about two months and involved approximately 5,000 Cubans; the Mariel diaspora lasted for close to five months (April 21 to September 26, 1980) and included 124,779 people. During the single month of May, the number leaving for the United States was 86,488.[28] This was more than the number who left the island during the entire year of 1962 (78,611), which until 1980 was the year characterized by the largest outflow of Cubans to America (Table 5.2).

To understand the mechanisms behind the Mariel exodus it is necessary to go back to December, 1978, when President Castro announced that he would allow Cuban-Americans to return to Cuba for one-week visits with their families.[29] Throughout 1979 and early 1980 about 100,000 persons took part in these sojourns, spending perhaps $100 million on the island. This stream of visitors has often been referred to as being the "blue-jean revolution" because returning émigrés usually brought gifts, such as designer jeans, for their relatives living in Cuba.[30] There were at least three motives for allowing these visits. First, the money spent in Cuba by the visitors helped the ailing Cuban economy. Second, by allowing the former Cuban residents to return, Castro hoped to demonstrate that his government was in firm control and that further attempts by Cuban exiles to dislodge him from power would prove futile. Third, Castro figured that his actions would improve his government's human rights image in other countries. What Castro and his advisors did not foresee was the "demonstration effect" that the returnees would have on their relatives still living in Cuba. Suddenly, twenty years of anti-American and anti-exile propaganda subsided as the visitors provided evidence of a much higher life style in the United States that contrasted sharply with the austere living conditions which existed under the direction of the totalitarian government of Cuba.[31] Perhaps, the tales of

99

opportunities and material benefits of life in the United States were sometimes overstated. Nevertheless, the effect was clearly to promote, or increase, the desire among many Cubans to leave.

In addition to the impact of the "blue-jeans revolution" there were several other factors that influenced the decision by many Cubans to migrate to the United States. Cuba's economy was experiencing a serious recession. The two major export crops, sugar and tobacco, were being riddled by diseases. Inflation and unemployment were beginning to emerge as major problems.[32] There were still many family members in Cuba who wished to join their relatives living in the United States but who were unable to do so during the earlier Freedom Flights. Some of these were males who were obliged to participate in the military services; others were persons working in certain skilled occupations who were not allowed to leave until replacements could be found. Also, 1979 was a year during which political dissent increased as a result of government austerity programs. When 400 Mariel immigrants in Miami were asked why they left Cuba, 79 percent said they did so for political reasons. Another 12 percent cited economic reasons for their decision to leave and six percent claimed that family reunification was their primary goal.[33]

Over one percent of the Cuban population left for the United States during the Mariel boatlift. In the process, this partially relieved an acute housing shortage and the widespread unemployment that was characterizing the island at the time. Furthermore, it allowed the government to rid itself of (or identify) dissidents who were prone toward not supporting the communist regime. It also provided Castro with "escape goats" who could be blamed for undermining the Cuban economy and would be used to infuse more spirit into the revolution that was showing signs of stagnation.[34] It has been estimated that more than one million additional Cubans would have left the island had Mariel not been closed by Castro in September, 1980.[35]

Once it became apparent that the number of persons who wanted to leave Cuba was a lot larger than the Cuban government had originally predicted, Castro tried to turn an embarrassing situation to his advantage. He decided to force many of the captains of the boats that had been sent from Florida to pick up family members also to take back to the United States many of Cuba's social undesirables. Included in this were a number of persons with criminal records, homosexuals, patients from mental institutions, and even deaf-mutes and lepers. In addition to trying to rid the island of many of what were considered to be its anti-social elements, there is little doubt that the Cuban government was trying to taint the reputation of the Cuban-Americans. Approximately 26,000 of the Mariel refugees had prison records, but many had been jailed for political

reasons or for minor crimes, such as stealing food or trading on the black market for a pair of blue-jeans.[36] Although estimates vary, perhaps 5,000 (or 4 percent) were hard-core criminals.

An opinion poll conducted by *The Miami Herald* in May, 1980, determined that 68 percent of the non-Latin whites and 57 percent of the blacks surveyed felt that the Mariel refugees have had a largely negative impact on Dade County.[37] In addition to the perception that the Mariel sealift was being used by Castro to empty his jails and mental institutions, there are at least four other reasons why the "Marielitos" were not welcomed upon their arrival in Florida. First, the suddenness and massive size of the influx intensified problems in helping them become settled. Many who did not have relatives or friends to help them adjust were temporarily housed in military camps in Florida, Arkansas, Pennsylvania, and Wisconsin. One estimate is that it has already cost the United States Government close to $1 billion to provide for the Mariel exiles, including the budgets for the Navy and Coast Guard operations that took place during the flotilla.[38] A second reason for refugees from Mariel not being welcomed, is that the United States' economy in 1980 experienced a recession, accompanied by inflation. In Dade County it has been estimated that the unemployment rate jumped from about five percent to 13 percent, primarily due to the Mariel influx. Also, the apartment vacancy rate was reduced to less than one percent, creating an acute housing shortage and high rents.[39]

A third reason for the cool reception given the "Marielitos" was that by 1980 public opinion was in favor of reducing immigration, as a result of attention given by the news media to the problems encountered during the migrations of Vietnamese, Mexicans, and Haitians to the United States.[40] A fourth factor was that between 70 or 75 percent of all the Mariel émigrés settled in southern Florida, especially in Dade County. This degree of concentration was greater than for the earlier Cuban waves and thus made adjustment problems more visible and newsworthy. Had the migrants been evenly dispersed throughout the 50 states, they probably would not have been noticed. The three largest cities in Dade County all experienced increases in their Latin populations as a result of the Mariel flotilla. The percentage of the population of the city of Miami that was Latin increased from 56 percent to 59 percent. For Hialeah the growth was from 74 to 78 percent; for Miami Beach the increase was from 22 to 27 percent.[41]

Unfortunately, the unwelcome attitude toward the "Marielitos" has diffused to many of the Cuban-Americans who arrived prior to 1980. It is now common to hear members of the Cuban Community in Miami speak in terms of "new" and "old" Cubans. The "old" Cubans are among the harshest critics of the "new" ones. This is a tendency that has been noted historically among other immigrant groups in the United States, but has been especially aggravated by the special set of circumstances that have accompanied the Mariel wave, particularly the forced inclusion by Castro of the criminal element.[42] Many of the "old" Cubans fear that the "new" will tarnish their reputation, just as Castro had hoped they would.

Unlike the emigrants from Cuba who preceded them, the Mariel refugees were characterized by an unbalanced sex structure. Approximately, 70 percent were males. There are two reasons for the male majority. First, most of the criminals and social misfits that Castro forced aboard the Mariel boats were males. Second, many of the young men who were unable to travel aboard the Freedom Flights between 1965 and 1973, because of required military service, were able to leave in 1980. The "Marielitos" also differed from earlier streams, since a larger percentage (about 20 percent) were blacks and a somewhat greater proportion arrived as single adults.[43] These are significant characteristics because the Cuban Refugee Resettlement Center has experienced its most trouble in finding help for the settlement of single, black, adult, Cuban males.

Occupationally, the Mariel flow can best be represented as a continuation of the trend previously noted during earlier Cuban emigration stages. Again, there was an increase in the representation of the working classes and a decline in the percentage that were categorized as professional and managerial workers. They came closer to being representative of the population in Cuba. Still, despite this trend and the criminal and misfit elements, the "Marielitos" (as a whole) enjoyed a somewhat higher socioeconomic status than the population left behind in Cuba. It is clear that these most recent emigrants were not marginal to the Cuban economy, nor are they unemployable in the United States.[44] Despite some of the problems created by a reputation sensationalized by both the Cuban and American presses, it is the collective wisdom of most who have studied them that the Mariel refugees will quickly and effectively accommodate themselves to life in the United States.

DISTRIBUTION AND MOBILITY PATTERNS OF CUBAN-AMERICANS

It is estimated that between 85 and 90 percent of all Cubans who have emigrated since the Castro revolution in 1959 have moved to the United States.[45] If there are approximately one million Cubans presently living in this country, an additional 111,000 to 176,000 must be living outside both the United States and Cuba. Other countries that have received notable numbers of these émigrés are Spain, Mexico, Puerto Rico, Canada, Venezuela, Costa Rica, and Peru.

It is reasonable to ask why the United States has become the home of the vast majority of the Cuban emigrants, rather than one of the nearby Latin American countries that has more in common with Cuba in terms of language and other cultural characteristics. The answer is found in terms of the cultural and economic ties that bound Cuba to the United States from the middle 1800's until 1959. The long term migration of political exiles to cities such as New York City, Key West, Tampa and later to Miami have been noted earlier in this chapter. In addition, American entrepreneurs and businessmen played a major role in resuscitating the Cuban economy after the Spanish-American War and Cuba's independence from Spain. Between 1898 and 1959 Cuba became as economically dependent upon the United States as it is dependent today on the Soviet Union. Most of the clothing worn by urbane Cubans, much of the food they ate, virtually all the cars and trucks they drove, and most of the radios they listened to came from the United States. Thus, depite language differences, many Cubans acquired tastes for American life and were aware of living conditions in the United States. This was especially true of the better educated and more highly skilled Cubans who accounted for a disproportionate share of the earliest wave of "Golden Exiles". Once these people led the way, the momentum of the stream quickly became oriented in the direction of the United States.

Concentration in Large Cities in a Few States

Cuban-Americans are highly concentrated in a few areas of the United States. In 1970, 87.5 percent were located in five states: Florida (46.0 percent), New York (16.5 percent), New Jersey (12.5 percent), California (8.7 percent), and Illinois (3.8 percent).[46] Furthermore, within these states they are found almost exclusively in large cities. The U.S. Census Bureau determined in 1980 that 96.7 percent of all families of Cuban descent were living in metropolitan areas.[47] Estimates provided by the Cuban National Planning Council for March, 1981 (after the Mariel boatlift) indicate that 98.9 percent of the Cuban origin population live in 14 cities (Table 5.4).[48] The outstanding growth of the Cuban populations in several of Florida's cities are readily apparent. As a result, the state has assumed even more of a position of preeminence than it had in 1970. Its location close to Cuba, its climate, and its history of Cuban settlement have been influential in this regard.

The emergence of the Union City-West New York metropolitan area in New Jersey, as the second leading concentration of Cuban-Americans, is due to a small cluster of Cuban families who lived here prior to Castro's assumption of power in Cuba. They served as an attraction for the in-migration of other Cubans coming both directly from Cuba and indirectly via a stage process through New York City during the 1960s and

TABLE 5.4 Estimates of Cuban-Americans by City of Residence, March, 1981

City (Metropolitan Areas)	Number of Cuban-American Residents in 1981
1. Miami	585,000
2. Union City-West New York	100,000
3. New York City	91,000
4. Los Angeles	30,000
5. Chicago	24,000
6. Orlando	15,000
7. Fort Lauderdale-Hollywood	15,000
8. Boston	13,000
9. Atlanta	10,000
10. Washington D.C.	8,000
11. Tampa	8,000
12. Dallas-Fort Worth	5,000
13. Key West	5,000
14. New Orleans	2,000
15. Other Cities	10,000
Total	921,000

Guarione M. Diaz, Executive Director, Cuban National Planning Council, Miami, Florida, personal interview, March 27, 1981. The figures do not include Cubans who were in refugee camps at this time.

1970s.[49] In addition, there were jobs available in blue collar occupations that provided economic opportunities, since Union City and West New York are essentially centers of light industry, warehousing, and transportation. By the late 1970s two-thirds of West New York's population was accounted for by persons of Cuban descent.[50]

New York City's position as one of the leading cities of residence for Cuban exiles can be traced back to the nineteenth century. Its history of opportunities for immigrants from other parts of the world and its reputation as a haven for political dissidents have undoubtedly contributed to its attraction for Cuban exiles. Unlike the concentrations in Miami and Union City-West New York, Cubans in New York City have not formed any outstanding core of settlement. Instead, they are diffused more widely throughout the city and do not dominate any particular neighborhoods.

The Cuban Refugee Program has had a major effect on the distribution of Cuban émigrés outside the state of Florida. When it was established in 1961 by President Kennedy, its purpose was to help the Cuban immigrants adjust to living conditions in the United States through job placement, temporary financial assistance, and other welfare benefits. In addition, another of its primary goals was to lessen the burden of concentration on South Florida by redistributing "relocatable" Cuban families to areas outside the state. Individuals with higher education levels and skills, and those with some knowledge of English, were considered to be most easily resettled. If individuals were offered an opportunity to relocate outside of South Florida but refused, then they were denied further federal government assistance and were considered to be on their own.[51] Of the 494,804 Cubans who registered with the Cuban Refugee Program between February, 1961 and October, 1981, approximately 61 percent were resettled in this manner.[52]

The Return Flow to Miami

Since the late 1960s a return flow of Cubans to the Miami metropolitan area from areas outside the state of Florida has become apparent. At first it started out as a trickle,[53] but by the middle 1970s it became a major migration stream. A survey of a sample of Cuban immigrants living in Miami in 1972 determined that 27.4 percent lived elsewhere in the country before returning to Dade County. A similar survey conducted in 1977 increased the percentage to 34.6 percent.[54] In 1978 *The Miami Herald* commissioned a telephone survey that found that about 40 percent of Dade County's Cubans were persons who had returned from living in other parts of the country.[55] Clearly the proportion of Dade County's Cubans that are returnees has been increasing and is likely to continue to do so, at least in the near future.

Most of the persons of Cuban descent who have recently returned to Miami were settled originally in other parts of the country through the Cuban Refugee Program. Once they were able to adjust to living in the United States, save some money, and learn English they became independent of government financial assistance. Many decided to move back to Miami, their original port of entry. When questioned about their reasons for moving back to Miami, the vast majority mentioned the climate of South Florida and a desire to be near relatives and friends who were living in Dade County. Surprisingly, less than 20 percent mentioned economic opportunities as a specific motive for returning.[56]

There is a clear relationship between the states outside of Florida that received the greatest number of Cubans under the Cuban Refugee Program's resettlement efforts and the states that sent the greatest number of returnees back to Miami. For instance, between 1961 and 1981, 46.7 percent of all Cubans who resettled outside the state of Florida located in New York and New Jersey.[57] A survey conducted by the Dade County Manager's office found that 61.1 percent of the returnees it questioned originated from these same two states.[58] The survey undertaken by *The Miami Herald* tends to support these findings.[59] The return of Cubans from these origins confirms the well-known proposition that for each major migration stream there develops a counterstream movement in the opposite direction.[60]

Upon returning to Dade County most settled in the western suburbs, rather than in the central city of Miami,[61] The years spent adjusting to American life styles outside Florida equipped these people with abilities to live comfortably near, but not in, the major Cuban concentration of Little Havana. In addition, the skills they had developed and the money they had saved enabled them to afford suburban housing.

The Expansion and Suburbanization of Cuban-American Settlement

Prior to 1959, there were no major concentrations of Latins living in Dade County. Although it has been estimated that there were approximately 20,000 Cubans living in metropolitan Miami at that time, they were generally a middle-class population that was scattered throughout the urban area. Once Castro seized power and began to limit severly the amount of money that Cuban emigrants could take out of the country, most of the refugees to Miami arrived virtually penniless. Despite the fact that some had relatives who could help them become established in their new homes, most resided in an area located on the southwestern edge of the city's central business district. This area had begun to deteriorate both as a residential and retail district prior to the arrival of the Cubans. Relatively inexpensive housing was available here and it was close to the transition zone that surrounded the central business district and contained the types of business establishments that offered the emigrants the best employment opportunities. In a short period of time the Cubans were able to invade, and then dominate, this area through their numerical increase. As a result, it became known as *Little Havana*. Its landscape acquired a definite Cuban cultural appearance, as it began to develop an improved image.[62]

The present distribution of persons of Cuban descent can be seen in Figure 5.1. The original core is located in Little Havana and provides the basic function of providing cheap housing and serving as a "port of entry" for many of the more recent immigrants. The areas that are 50 to 84 percent Cuban are generally characterized by better quality housing and more space per family. The fringe includes the outer edges, where Cuban families are presently invading but have not yet established numerical dominance. In these areas Cubans represent 25 to 49 percent of the population. Several outlying clusters have developed as detachments from the main body of the Cuban settlement zone. The most obvious is the concentration of Cubans in Hialeah, northwest of Little Havana. This area had many of the same advantages that Little Havana originally had for Cuban settlement and, as a result, has developed into a second focus of Cuban activity. Hialeah is Dade County's second largest city and contains a population that is about 78 percent Latin, taking into account the recent arrival of "Marielitos".[63]

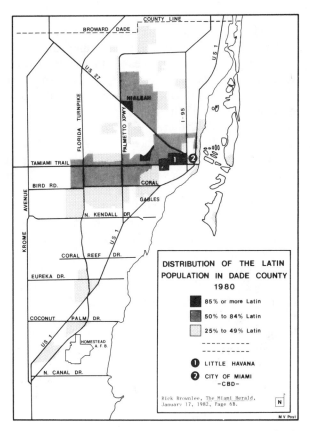

Figure 5.1. Distribution of the Latin Population in Dade County 1980.

A recent study of Miami's Little Havana suggests that most of the Cuban residential areas are expanding by a contagious diffusion process.[64] Generally, the areas closest to the main Cuban concentration of settlement are the next to be encompassed by the expansion process. One exception, of course, is the Hialeah area, which was settled by a "leap-frog" or hierarchical process. Where expansion of the Cuban ethnic area has been constrained, one of two types of barriers has been found to exist. First, neighborhoods that are dominated by blacks tend to be avoided by most Cubans, such as the gap in the growth of Little Havana to the north. Second, very wealthy areas have land values that are priced beyond the reach of most Cubans and also provide a barrier function. This has happened to the south of Little Havana in the exclusive residential areas of Coral Gables.[65] Despite these barriers, it is clear that generally a distance-decay relationship exists between the distance that neighborhoods are located away from the core of Little Havana and the proportion of their population that is comprised of Cubans. Usually, the greater the distance away, the lower the percentage that is Cuban.[66]

Evidence of a suburbanization trend in the residential patterns of Cuban-Americans is provided by a recent United States Census Bureau survey. It determined that only 39.5 percent of all families of Cuban descent live in the central cities of metropolitan areas. On the other hand, 57.2 percent live outside central cities but still within metropolitan areas.[67] A panel study of a sample of newly arrived Cuban immigrants in Dade County found that in 1973, 51.7 percent lived in the central city of Miami. Six years later, in 1979, only 38.8 percent remained in the central city. Most of the rest were living in the suburbs of Hialeah or unincorporated Dade County.[68] As suggested earlier, it appears likely that the core of Little Havana served as a "port of entry" for these exiles when they first arrived. Later many moved out to the middle or fringe areas.

Another study found that the suburban population of metropolitan Miami has grown primarily by two types of population infusion. The first is intraurban migration from the central city to the suburbs. The second is interurban return migration from cities outside the state of Florida to the suburbs of Dade county. Furthermore, when the socioeconomic status of suburban Dade County Cubans was compared to that of Cubans living in the central city, it was clear that (when collectively considered) the former were better off. Furthermore, the Cubans living in Hialeah appeared to occupy an intermediate position between the higher ranking suburban Cubans and the lower ranking Cubans who lived in Little Havana.[69]

Ethnic Segregation

The body of literature dealing with studies of assimilation of various ethnic groups indicates that people sort themselves residentially and socially into groups that are generally homogeneous with respect to both ethnic affiliation and socioeconomic rank. This notion is known as the *ethclass* concept.[70] It has already been determined that Cubans in Dade County appear to segregate themselves from one another according to socioeconomic status within the core, middle, fringe, and outlying cluster areas. A study of Cubans living in West New York alludes to a similar finding.[71] The question that remains is: To what degree are Cubans segregated residentially from the non-Cuban population?

It has been shown that the area of Cuban residential concentration in Dade County has spread outwards, from its Little Havana core, through a fringe sector that is ethnically mixed. Still there is considerable evidence that the Cuban population is notably segregated from other ethnic classes living in metropolitan Miami. One study has noted that Latins living in Dade County are strongly segregated from blacks and Jews when considered on a census tract scale. They are also moderately segregated from non-Latin whites. For instance, in 1970, 86 percent of the black population would need to be redistributed among the census tracts for it to exhibit a percentage distribution identical to that of Latins. The comparable figure for Jews is 72 percent. For whites it is between 55 and 60 percent, depending

on age class. It was further found that the differences in distribution had generally increased between 1950 and 1970.[72] A second study has determined that Dade County's Cuban population was notably segregated from the county's Mexican and Puerto Rican populations in 1970. It also found that there was considerable segregation within the Cuban population according to family income classes.[73] Thus, both studies demonstrate that the concept of *ethclass* is generally applicable to the residential patterns displayed by Miami's Cuban-Americans.

The massive influx of Cubans to Dade County and the high level of segregation between Cuban-Americans and blacks, Jews, and non-Latin whites has been blamed for aggravating ethnic tensions. The expansion of neighborhoods dominated by families of Cuban origin has been associated with a non-Latin white exodus from Dade County.[74] It has been estimated that Dade County has experienced a decline of at least 30,000 non-Latin whites between 1970 and 1980.[75] This "white flight" has had even more of an impact on the ethnic mixture of Dade County's public schools than it has on the total population. In 1974 the student population percentages were 44 percent non-Latin white, 26.5 percent black, and 29.5 percent Latin. In 1982 they were 31 percent non-Latin white, 31 percent black, and 38 percent Latin.[76] It is certainly too simple to blame the immigration of Cubans as the sole cause affecting the exodus of whites from greater Miami. After all, Dade County has experienced other problems during the past decade. Still, the Cuban increase is frequently stated as being one of the causes affecting the "white flight" that is helping to alter radically the ethnic composition of metropolitan Miami.

A DEMOGRAPHIC PROFILE OF CUBAN-AMERICANS

The structure and composition of a population can be very revealing in providing clues about the factors that have influenced it over time. Thus, to a considerable extent the present demographic characteristics of an ethnic group provide a mirror of past historical tendencies. The demographic characteristics of Cuban-Americans have been particularly influenced by the recent history of their migration to the United States. Both the emigration policies of the Cuban government and the "natural" selectivity of the types of Cubans who chose to migrate proved crucial in determining the characteristics of Cuban-Americans. These can be analyzed by examining the age and sex composition; racial characteristics; employment, occupation, and income tendencies; and fertility levels of the Cuban-American population.

Age and Sex Composition

When the age structure of the Cuban descent population is compared to those of the total Spanish origin and non-Spanish origin populations, some significant differences become immediately apparent (Table 5.5). The median age for the Cubans is more than eleven years higher than for the total Spanish descent population and almost three years older than for non-Spanish descent persons. Despite the fact that most have lived for a relatively short period in the United States, the age structure of the Cuban-Americans more closely resembles that of non-Spanish persons than it does the Spanish descent population. The fact that the Cuban origin population is considerably older in the age composition than the total Spanish-American population is related to two primary factors.[77] The first are the very low fertility patterns exhibited by the Cubans, when compared with most other ethnic components of the United States population. More will be said regarding this important tendency later in this chapter. Suffice it to say, at this point, that lower birth rates tend to depress proportional representation in the lower age classes. As a result, the population appears to "age" with declining fertility.

The second factor that helps account for the older character of the Cuban-Americans has to do with the selectivity of migrants who moved from Cuba to the United States. From the earlier discussion of the history of Cuban emigration flows, it will be recalled that the Castro government was unwilling to allow most young adult males to leave the island until they had satisfied their military obligation. This was especially true during the Freedom Flights between 1965 and 1973 and helps to explain why the Cuban population in Table 5.5 has smaller percentages in the 21 to 24 and 25 to 34 year age classes, when compared to either the Spanish origin or non-Spanish populations. It was also mentioned earlier that elderly persons were allowed to leave more freely because it was believed that many would become dependent upon the state if they remained in Cuba.[78] This helps account for the fact that close to ten percent of the Cuban-Americans are 65 years of age or older; whereas, less than five percent of the total Spanish-Americans fall in this age class.

Prior to the Mariel boatlift in 1980, a slight majority (50.2 percent) of the persons of Cuban descent living in the United States were female.[79] The very minor predominance of females also was related to the migration policies of the Cuban government. The reluctance to allow males of military age to leave during the Aerial Bridge of 1965 to 1973 had an affect, as did the greater freedom for the elderly to emigrate.[80] Since women usually exhibit greater longevity, it is to be expected that they would be overrepresented in the oldest age classes. Since the Mariel exodus was heavily dominated by males, it is apparent that the balance has swung in the direction of a male predominance. It can be estimated that males now represent somewhere between 50 to 55 percent of the total Cuban-American population.[81]

Racial Characteristics

The vast majority of Cubans living in the United States are considered to be white. The most recent year for which racial data are available for Cuban-Americans is 1970. In that year, 96.0 percent were classified as white, with 3.1 percent as black, and the remaining .9 percent as other categories.[82] For the entire population of the United States, a little over eleven percent is black. The overwhelming proportion of the Cuban-Americans who are white is not representative of the population remaining in Cuba. For instance, the 1953 Cuban Population Census shows that about 27 percent of the island's population was at that time black or mulatoo. This is about nine times the percentage for the Cubans living in the United States.[83]

Five reasons have been suggested for explaining why Cuban-Americans have a smaller proportion of their population as nonwhite.[84] First, the Castro revolution was designed primarily to benefit the poorer classes of Cuban society. Since blacks were more concentrated among the poor, presumably a larger percentage of them were able to obtain more opportunities under the new government. Second, the Castro government has expended major efforts to depict the United States as racist society, as part of its anti-American propaganda policy. Third, much of the Cuban flow to the United

TABLE 5.5 Age structure of Cuban-Americans Compared to the Total Spanish Origin and Non-Spanish Origin Populations in the United States: 1980

Age Classes (Years)	Cuban-Americans (%)	Total Spanish Origin[a] (%)	U.S. Non-Spanish Origin (%)
under 5	7.2	12.9	6.9
5 to 9	7.7	11.3	7.2
10 to 17	14.8	17.0	13.5
18 to 20	5.0	6.5	5.6
21 to 24	5.9	7.7	7.2
25 to 34	11.1	16.5	16.1
35 to 44	16.8	11.1	11.7
45 to 54	14.1	7.9	10.5
55 to 64	7.6	4.8	9.9
65 and over	9.7	4.2	11.3
Median Age	33.5	22.1	30.7

[a]Incudes person of Cuban origin.

U.S. Bureau of the Census, *Current Population Reports*, series P-20, No. 361: "Persons of Spanish Origin in the United States," (Advance Report), March 1980, (Washington, D.C.: U.S. Government Printing Office, 1981): p. 5.

States has been promoted and assisted through family ties with relatives already living in the United States. Fewer Cuban blacks have moved to the United States because a smaller proportion of blacks have relatives living in America on whom they can rely for assistance. Fourth, the immigration policy of the United States, since 1965, has generally favored the legal immigration of Cubans who have close family members already residing on American soil. Thus, not only were the kinship networks of whites not as readily available to them, but Cuban blacks also found that it was harder to gain entry through the American council in Havana because of this scarcity of American relatives. Fifth, there is evidence of resentment on the part of a minority of the white Cuban-American exiles living in the United States towards black Cubans because of a suspicion that many of the blacks welcomed the Castro revolution. Evidence in support of this hypothesis is manifested in Miami's Little Havana, where in 1970 less than one percent of the resident population was black.

A recent comparative study of Cubans living in the metropolitan areas of Miami and Union City-West New York found that a slightly larger proportion of the latter's population was black. This difference was attributed to differing perceived levels of discrimination.[85] It has been previously noted in the literature that the majority of Cuban nonwhites live in the northeastern United States, where the reputation for racial tolerance is better than in the South.[86]

Earlier in this chapter it was noted that approximately 20 percent of the Cubans who immigrated via the Mariel boatlift in 1980 were black. This represents a proportion that is about five times higher that has been characteristic of past Cuban migration waves. But even this new figure is only about three fourths of the percentage of the present black population in Cuba. Nevertheless, the fact that a larger proportion of blacks left Cuba during this last exodus, than ever before, has been heralded by some as being a sign that the Castro government is beginning to wear thin, even with the types of people it was supposed to benefit the most.

Employment, Occupation, and Income Tendencies

When the working force and income characteristics of Cuban-Americans are compared with those of the total Spanish-American population (Table 5.6) it is clear that the Cubans have achieved a remarkably high level of socioeconomic status. This is particularly noteworthy when their relatively short length of residence in the United States is considered. In terms of occupational distribution, employment levels and income, they are considerably better off than most other persons of Hispanic origin living in America. In fact, their economic achievements approach those of the non-Spanish descent population in the United States. Currently Cuban-Americans are represented by an intermediate position, in terms of their socioeconomic status,

TABLE 5.6 Occupation, Employment, and Income Characteristics of Cuban-Americans Compared to the Total Spanish Origin and Non-Spanish Origin Populations in the United States (Persons 16 Years Old and Over)

Occupation Classes[a] 1980	Cuban-Americans (%)	Total Spanish Origin (%)	USA Non-Spanish Origin (%)
Professional, technical and kindred workers	12.4	8.5	16.8
Managers and administrators, except farm	9.0	6.6	11.4
Sales workers	5.9	3.8	6.3
Clerical and kindred workers	14.4	16.1	18.9
Craft and kindred workers	12.4	14.0	12.7
Operatives, including transport	28.4	23.7	13.7
Laborers, excluding farm	6.1	7.9	4.3
Farmers and farm managers	0.2	0.3	1.5
Farm laborers and supervisors	0.0	3.0	0.9
Service workers	11.3	16.2	13.4
Percent unemployed, 1980[a]	5.0	8.9	6.5
Percent of males in labor force, 1979[b]	83.3	80.5	76.0
Percent of females in labor force, 1979[b]	53.1	47.4	50.9
Median family income, 1979[a]	$17,538	$14,569	$19,965
Median personal income, 1978[b]	$6,352	$5,893	$6,864

[a]U.S. Bureau of the Census, *Current Population Reports,* series P-20 No. 361: "Persons of Spanish Origin in the United States," March 1980 (Advance Report), Washington, D.C.: U.S. Government Printing Office, 1981): p. 5.

[b]U.S. Bureau of the Census, *Current Population Reports,* series P-20, No. 354: "Persons of Spanish Origin in the United States," March 1979 (Washington, D.C.: U.S. Government Printing Office, 1980): pp. 10 and 29.

between the Spanish-American and non-Spanish population. When compared to Puerto Ricans and Mexican-Americans within the Spanish descent class, it is clear that the Cubans are much better off economically.[87]

Although the figures displayed in Table 5.6 have been derived from the most recent available data, they present the characteristics of Cuban-Americans as they existed immediately prior to the wave of Mariel immigrants which arrived in South Florida between April and September, 1980. If the characteristics of the "Marielitos" were added to these figures, they would cause somewhat of a "dampening effect" on the economic position of the persons of Cuban descent because of their higher unemployment rates and lower skill levels. However, even with this impact, Cuban-Americans still occupy an intermediate position between all Spanish-Americans and Americans who are not of Spanish origin.

The current occupational composition of the population of Cuban-Americans is a product of four major trends that have characterized the labor force history of these émigrés. The first has been the tendency, noted earlier in this chapter, for persons with higher education levels and skills to be overrepresented in migration flows to the United States. Second, as also previously stated, there has been a tendency for this selection process to decline over time, so that the most recent Cuban immigrants are more similar to the population left behind in Cuba than was the case of the earlier migrants. There are a couple of reasons for the decline in the proportion of professionals among the later emigration waves. Many of the better educated and more highly skilled who wanted to leave have already done so. Thus, there are fewer remaining in Cuba to supply future streams to the United States. In addition, because the Cuban government is reluctant to see them leave, the remaining professionals have been accorded a privileged position in the socialist society of the island. Thus, there is less of an incentive for them to emigrate now, than in the past.[88]

A third trend that has affected the occupational characteristics of Cuban-Americans has been the tendency for most to experience a decline in status with their *first* job in the United States. Often they had to take whatever type of work was available when they first arrived. Their lack of facility with English was a major factor that affected their employment opportunities. In addition, many professional occupations require citizenship or formal licensing procedures that can take years to satisfy.

A fourth factor that has affected the labor force characteristics of Cuban-Americans has been their tendency towards upward mobility as their length of residence in the United States increased.[89] A study of Cubans living in the city of West New York found that although the last job held in Cuba prior to emigration had very little influence on the first job obtained in the United States, it did affect the potential for eventual upward mobility. Those who had higher status jobs in Cuba were more likely to become upwardly mobile in the United States. In addition, younger migrants and those who were better educated have also exhibited more success in climbing the occupational ladder.[90]

Fertility Levels

A number of fertility studies have found that middle class families in western societies tend to have smaller numbers of children than either the poor or wealthy classes. Apparently wealthy couples can comfortably afford to have as many children as they want, whereas the standard of living for the very poor is not likely to be altered much through the addition of another child.[91] Given the fact that most Cuban-American families are middle class in terms of their socioeconomic status, it is reasonable to find that they have characteristically exhibited very low fertility patterns while living in the United States. In fact, a very low birth rate characterizes Cuba.[92]

A recent study comparing various demographic characteristics of several components of the Spanish-American population found that the persons of Cuban descent have exceptionally low birth rates.[93] The number of births per 1,000 population for the Cuban-Americans was found to be 16. For the white population of the United States it was 17, whereas for Mexican-Americans and Puerto Ricans living in the United States it was 27 and 30, respectively. When controlled to take into consideration such factors as older age structure of the Cuban-Americans, their higher education levels, and higher female labor force participation rates, the differences became even more pronounced. When thus standardized, women of Cuban descent exhibited a fertility rate that was 23 percent lower than that of non-Spanish white women living in the United States. When compared to Mexican-American and Puerto Rican women living in the United States, the rate for Cuban women was 47 and 28 percentage points lower, respectively.[94] The lower fertility performance of the Cuban descent women can be attributed to their higher education levels, higher labor force participation rates, and generally higher aspirations.

CULTURAL CHARACTERISTICS OF CUBAN-AMERICANS.

The concept of culture is defined by social scientists to include all the learned characteristics of a given society, but only a few aspects of the culture of Cuban-Americans will be here discussed. The attributes selected for discussion are those that are thought to be particularly relevant for illustrating the differences of persons of Cuban origin from most Americans, and the changes in the cultural characteristics of Cuban-Americans over time.

The Cuban-American Family

Prior to the socialist revolution in 1959, the traditional family structure in Cuba was typical of that for most of Latin America. There was a sharp distinction between the role of men and women, with a double standard being applied in work, play, and sex. The wife was expected to stay at home and attend to the running of the household and care of children. A pattern of male-dominance prevailed, and most of the major family decisions were made by the husband. The tradition of *machismo* dictated that males demonstrate virility through physical strength, courage and business success. It was common, and considered proper, for males to have extra-marital affairs. Whether or not a husband had a regular mistress was frequently more affected by economics than conscience. Daughters and wives, on the other hand, were protected against temptation. A strict tradition of chaperoning was in effect for respectable, unmarried women who dated.[95]

Sociologists have developed a concept known as *Resource Theory* for explaining the position of decision-making power that the members of any particular family have relative to each other. An individual gains in power if the resources that he or she contributes to the family increases. These resources may be economic, intellectual, or emotional in nature.[96] Economic difficulties that many Cubans faced upon their arrival in the United States affected their adjustment. Often the husband was unable to find work, or found work at a lower status level than he had experienced in Cuba. As a result, it became necessary for many wives to enter the labor force to help contribute to the support of the family. In 1980, slightly over half of all women of Cuban descent in the United States who were 16 years of age or older were in the labor force (see Table 5.6). A survey of women in West New York found that less than one-fourth had worked in Cuba before coming to the United States.[97] Thus, as the wife's resource contribution to the family became greater through her employment, usually her power to help make decisions also increased, whereas that of her husband declined. A recent study of Cuban women in Washington D.C. reaches the conclusion that their entrance into the labor force is the single most important change in their lives as immigrants.[98] As a result, the traditional patriarchal family structure for Cuban-Americans began to change towards greater equality in decision-making abilities for husbands and wives. Also, a lessening of the former double standard began to take place. A study of Cuban families living in Miami determined that both wives and children gained greater power in making their own decisions when they obtained employment and contributed to the family income. In addition, length of residence in the United States and degree of association with Americans were also positively associated with level of equality or independence within the family.[99] As a result, Cuban-American families are less male dominated and the roles of husbands and wives are less segregated than the traditional Latin American family norm that typified Cuba before 1959.

Despite the fact that Cuban family structure has changed in the United States from what it was in Cuba, it is still different enough from the American norm to cause some conflict between the first and second generation Cuban-Americans. Studies of acculturation stresses among Cubans living in the United States have found that the second generation, which was the first to be born in America, generally has adopted Anglo attitudes and behavior patterns more quickly than their first generation, immigrant parents. Sometimes a crisis in authority emerges, as the parents find themselves being led and instructed in new ways by their children. Many of the traditional norms of the Cuban family became labeled "old-fashioned". Chaperoning for dating, as an example, has become a focal point of tension in many families. Many second generation Cuban-Americans feel they are caught between two cultures, by being neither completely Cuban nor American. They want to maintain selected aspects of both cultures, and as a result feel that they do not belong to (or are not completely accepted by) either.[100]

Another aspect of the Cuban-American family that distinguishes it from the contemporary American family is the tendency for Cuban households to include relatives in addition to members of the nuclear family. The United States Census Bureau indicates that about nine percent of all persons of Cuban descent live in households where these are "other relatives" (other than wife or child) of the head of the household. The corresponding figure for all persons of Spanish origin is about six percent; for the non-Spanish it is approximately four percent.[101] Often this additional relative is a widowed and dependent grandparent who came to the United States after the nuclear family had arrived. Because so many Cuban-American women work, the elderly have become important as housekeepers and babysitters. They also have passed on elements of their culture and language to the new generation children.[102]

One important indicator of the assimilation of an ethnic group is the degree to which it is characterized by the marriage of its members to persons outside the group. For 1970, when all women of Cuban descent are considered, 17 percent had married non-Cubans.[103] However, many of the marriages to Cubans took place in Cuba before arrival in the United States. When only second generation American-born women are considered, it was found that 46 percent of those married had married non-Spanish husbands. The comparable figures for women of Puerto Rican and Mexican descent are 33 and 16 percent, respectively.[104] Thus, second generation Cubans have exhibited an extraordinarily high rate of outmarriage, a fact which appears to indicate a very rapid tendency toward assimilation. A recent comparative study of outmarriage patterns for Hispanic groups living in New York City determined that Cubans had the highest outgroup marriage rates. It also found that the degree of outmarriage is much higher among second generation, American born children, than for their foreign born Hispanic parents. In addition, persons with higher socioeconomic status, those who are older at the time they marry, and those who had been married more than once all show higher outmarriage rates. Finally, the relative degree of spatial concentration proves to be the strongest determinant of exogamous marriage rates. Groups that are more dispersed residentially throughout New York City exhibited higher outmarriage rates.[105] It is also noted that the rate of intergroup marriage is considerably higher for Cubans living in New York than for those living in New Jersey and Florida. The lower rates for the latter two states is attributed to the greater concentration of Cubans residing in the metropolitan areas of Union City-West New York and Miami.[106]

Citizenship and Political Tendencies

Many of the Cuban refugees who arrived in the United States during the early 1960's figured that their stay in this country would be of short duration. They were convinced that Castro would soon lose control and that they would be able to return home to Cuba. As time wore on, however, it became apparent that their stay in the United States would be longer than originally expected. They began to adjust to American life styles and their desire and hope for returning to their island of origin decreased. Studies in both West New York and Miami clearly show that the desire to return to Cuba to live decreases as length of residence in the United States increases.[107] By the 1970s it was clear that the vast majority of Cuban-Americans planned to remain in the United States, even if the Castro government were to be overthrown.[108]

The increasing preference for remaining in the United States is paralleled by a growing desire for American citizenship. Again, length of residence is directly related to both the achievement of citizenship and the desire to attain citizenship status. One obvious reason for the link between length of residence and becoming an American citizen is that the United States government requires that once an individual receives legal permanent residency status, a five year wait is necessary before that person can apply for citizenship. The decision to become an American citizen is another important indicator of assimilation because it requires

that the person becoming naturalized renounce any previous citizenship. To a Cuban, this usually formalizes the realization that returning to Cuba to live is no longer practical or desirable. In 1970, approximately 25 percent of all Latins living in metropolitan Miami were citizens of the United States. By 1978 the figure had risen to 43 percent. Furthermore, of those who were not yet citizens, 77.2 percent planned to apply for this status.[109] In West New York, none of the Cubans questioned in a 1968 survey were American citizens. At that time 44 percent wanted to become citizens; 33.9 percent did not want citizenship status; and 22 percent could not make up their minds. In 1979 there was a dramatic change in these figures. By that time 40.3 percent had attained citizenship status; 43.7 percent wanted to become citizens; 6 percent did not want citizenship; and 10 percent had no preference.[110] In conclusion, Cuban-Americans are very rapidly attaining American citizenship and can be expected to continue to do so in the near future.

Once citizenship has been achieved, the political behavior of Cuban-Americans can be described as being participatory, personal, anti-communist, and conservative. It is participatory in the sense that an exceptionally large percentage of Cuban-American citizens both register to vote and exercise their voting rights at the polls. In 1978, 84.3 percent of the Cubans living in West New York who were eligible to vote registered to vote. In this same year, only 62.6 percent of the total eligible-to-vote population for the United States registered. In addition, the Cubans' voting participation rate was about ten percentage points higher than for the entire American population.[111] In November, 1981 the city of Miami held a mayoral election. Of those eligible to vote, the voter turn-out rates were 58 percent for Latins, 38 percent for Anglos, and somewhat more than 50 percent for blacks.[112] These participatory percentages suggest that Cubans will exert even more influence in future elections in both Miami and the Union City-West New York areas as more of the persons of Cuban descent become eligible to vote.

Cuban-American politics are personal, in the sense that most Latin American politics are personal. It represents a refusal to deal with a government that is bureaucratic and impersonal. It is a face-to-face approach, in which there is a belief that to obtain a favor a person needs to show (or have access to) a contact, someone who personally knows someone else in a position of power. In English the system is known as "power brokering," in Spanish it is called "personalismo." Most Cuban-American politicians are well aware of the political expectations that friends and relatives have once they achieve an elected position. How they react to such pressures varies, but it is true that it helps to have friends and relatives in influential positions.[113]

Persons of Cuban descent tend to be both strongly anti-communist and conservative in their political learnings as a result of their experiences with the Castro government in Cuba. Both tendencies favor membership in the Republican Party. A study of voting patterns in neighborhoods in Dade County, both before and after they became dominated by Cuban residents, showed a marked shift in voting preferences, first for Democratic Party candidates and later in favor of the Republican Party. In addition, a survey of over 500 Cuban emigrants in Miami found that 73 percent supported the Republican Party and most favored conservative policies. The general preference for the Republican Party has significantly changed the reputation of Miami which used to be known as a staunchly liberal enclave that traditionally could be counted on to vote in favor of the Democrats. The Cuban-American support of Republicans has been linked to its strong feelings against communism and the Bay of Pigs fiasco. The latter was blamed on the lack of support from the Democrat presidential administration of John F. Kennedy.[114]

Language and Religion

Language and religion are two cultural attributes that most ethnic minorities are very reluctant to abandon. Where different from those of the host society, they increase the visibility of the minority group. The degree to which an ethnic group maintains distinct language and religious patterns is often regarded as being an important indicator of acculturation and assimilation.

Language. Virtually all first generation Cuban immigrants living in the United States speak Spanish as their mother tongue.[115] Like most other immigrant groups who have come to America, it is common for the first generation Cuban-Americans to teach their native language to the second generation. This is particularly the case where both parents are of Cuban origin, or where one parent is from Cuba and the other is an immigrant from another Spanish speaking country. The Spanish that is learned in the home by the second generation is usually very basic and elementary. More often than not, the second generation children converse with neighborhood friends in a mixture of Spanish and English, called "Spanglish." In short, they learn a poor quality of Spanish that often serves as a source of embarrassment for themselves and for their parents. Furthermore, their ability to speak English may also be impaired, especially if they live in a predominantly Cuban neighborhood where little English is spoken. Mixed marriages that involve an immigrant Cuban spouse and a native Anglo seldom produce children who are truly fluent in Spanish. One exception to this generalization is encountered when the mother works and the children are raised by a Spanish-speaking relative.

Since by far the majority of Cuban-Americans are still members of the first or second generation, it is somewhat speculative to predict the language abilities of the third generation. However, limited evidence suggests that the majority of these grandchildren of the Cuban immigrants will be fluent only in English. This implies that by the third generation, facility with Spanish will be a legacy of the earlier two generations. This does not mean that Spanish will no longer be heard in areas of Cuban concentration in the near future. There are still many young first and second generation Spanish-speaking persons of Cuban descent living in Miami, Union City-West New York, and New York City who have many years to live. It will take at least four or five more decades for the Cuban population to become assimilated linguistically. Of course, this process can be delayed even longer by any future large-scale immigration waves from Cuba.

Where Cuban-Americans are heavily concentrated, as in metropolitan Miami and West New York, speaking Spanish can become an emotional issue. According to a recent survey conducted by *The Miami Herald*, language was the main obstacle to harmony between Anglos and Cubans living in Dade County. The Anglos felt that it was becoming necessary to be bilingual, in Spanish and English, to be in a position to compete for local jobs. They were afraid that second generation Cubans were in a more favorable position because of their knowledge of both languages. It was widely believed that Spanish was being forced upon the Anglos by the large number of first generation Cubans who, they thought, were not making a serious effort to learn English. The survey found that 79 percent of the non-Latins questioned agreed that students in Dade County schools should not be required to become proficient in Spanish. On the other hand, 70 percent of the Latins felt that proficiency in Spanish should be required.[116] In 1973 the Dade County Commissioners passed an ordinance that officially declared the county to be bilingual. Seven years later, in November, 1980 (just after the Mariel exodus), the electorate of Dade County repealed the ordinance in a referendum by a voting ratio of three to two. The new ordinance stipulated that public funds were not to be used to teach languages other than English or "to promote a culture other than the culture of the United States."[117] Many Miami businessmen fear that this action may have a damaging effect on South Florida's lucrative trade with Latin America.

When asked what is the most important problem posed by living in the United States, first generation Cubans most frequently cite the language barrier. Their lack of facility with English hinders their employment opportunities and affects their abilities to obtain government services. Since first generation immigrants still comprise a majority among Cuban-Americans, the language problem is magnified. A survey of Hispanics living in Dade County in 1978 determined that 43.2 percent judged their English speaking ability as being poor or nonexistant.[118] This is a much higher percentage than for most other ethnic groups who have a longer history of residence in the United States.

Religion. Most Cuban-Americans are at least nominally Roman Catholics. Their arrival in Miami and Union City-West New York has had a major impact on the membership of many local parishes. Virtually all Catholic churches in both urban areas have priests who can give mass, hear confessions, and offer council in Spanish. In Cuban neighborhoods, the Catholic church has become one of the key ethnic institutions of self-identity and a center of community life.

There is some evidence that the domination of Roman Catholicism has been declining among Cuban-Americans. Between 1968 and 1979 the percentage of Cubans living in West New York who expressed a preference for the Catholic faith decreased from 91.5 percent to 78.3 percent; whereas those with no particular religious preference increased from 1.2 to 11.3 percent. In addition, attendance rates dropped. the proportion who attended church at least once a month went down from 79.0 percent to 47.1 percent. Those who never attended increased from 5.0 percent to 19.6 percent. Despite these declining attendance rates, almost three-quarters indicated that religion was still a very important part of their life.[119] An explanation for the decreasing religious participation ratios of Cuban-Americans is necessarily speculative. Two factors are probably involved. First, it is possible that they are being influenced by the lower participation levels of non-Spanish Americans; and second, Castro's efforts to rid Cuba of religion may have reduced the religiosity of some of the Cuban immigrants, especially those who arrived during the later waves.

In addition to those professing the Catholic faith, there are a sizable number of Cubans who are members of various Protestant sects and a lesser number of Cuban Jews. However, one of the more unique religions practiced by Cuban-Americans is an Afro-Cuban cult faith known as *Santeria*. Referred to as an Afro-Christian syncretic religion because it combines aspects of Catholicism with African magical practices, it is believed to help cure illnesses, assist in finding jobs, bring good luck, and even exorcise evil spirits.[120] Because of its magical beliefs and its practices of chanting and animal sacrifice, there is a reluctance shown by many Cubans to admit that they follow *Santeria*. Still it is believed that many use it. For instance, a survey of Cubans living in Miami and Union City found that only 1.2 percent of the households in both cities reported practicing this religion. On the other hand, 7.1 percent of the Miami respondents and 23.5 percent of the Union City respondents said they would use a *san-tero* (a priest for the *Santeria* faith) if they felt they needed help.[121] One well-educated, prominent Miami Cuban leader recently explained that practicing *Santeria* is like an insurance policy. He hopes that he will never have to use it and he does not know how well it will work if he does try it. Nevertheless, if it is known that an important event is about to occur, everything that logically can be done to ensure a favorable outcome will be tried, and as added spiritual assistance *Santeria* may also be used.

An Economic Enclave

There are two traditional views of the ways new immigrants are incorporated into the United States labor market. The first is called the *assimilationist view* and assumes that immigrants start in the lower paying jobs and gradually move up the occupational ladder until they become indistinguishable, in terms of their employment characteristics, from the host population. The second perspective is termed the *internal colonialist view*. It holds that some ethnic groups are "unmeltable" and are therefore subject to exploitation in the labor market through continued employment in the lowest paying jobs with few opportunities for advancement.[122] Versions of this latter view have most often been used as an explanation for the continued disadvantaged economic position of black Americans. They have also been applied to several other traditionally disadvantaged ethnic groups, such as the Mexican-Americans and Puerto Ricans living on the mainland of the United States.

The labor force experiences of Cuban-Americans who live outside of metropolitan Miami most closely fit the assimilationist model. However, the Cubans living in Miami (and to a lesser extent those who live in Union City-West New York) do not appear to parallel either of the two models. A recent study of Miami suggests that Cubans have established their own economic enclave that caters particularly to a Cuban-American and Latin market. In this enclave it is possible to transact all business negotiations in Spanish and to use Cuban business customs, thus making it easier for newly arrived immigrants to become incorporated quickly into the economic mainstream. The initial capital and entrepreneurial skills that were used to establish the enclave were provided by the earliest waves of immigrants that left Cuba in the early 1960s. The later flows of refugees sustained its growth and allowed it to reach a sufficient size for economies of scale to be developed. As the more recent waves contributed immigrants who were somewhat less educated and less skilled, they provided a cross section of laborers who allowed for a more vertically integrated local ethnic economy to develop. In this way a laboring class of Cubans was provided to work in the Cuban-owned businesses. The return migration of Cubans, settled elsewhere in the United

States through assistance provided by the Cuban Refugee Program, contributed additional capital and labor for further growth.[123]

The Cuban economic enclave in Miami does not exist independently of the rest of American economy. In fact, the two are functionally integrated. The Cuban component has had a major impact on expanding South Florida's trade with Latin America. By 1978 the United States Custom District, in which Miami is included, accounted for 31 percent of all the United States' trade with Latin America. Aggregate exports from this District in 1979 amounted to approximately $6 billion, of which about 80 percent went to Latin America.[124]

While most businesses in the Cuban economic enclave are small, some are large and employ hundreds of workers. Enclave firms tend to concentrate on construction, finance, textiles, leather, furniture, and cigar making. There are more than 18,000 Cuban owned businesses in Dade County. Cuban-Americans account for about 25,000 garment workers, 3,500 doctors, over 500 lawyers, and about half of the aircraft repair and maintenance labor force in Dade County. There are 16 Cuban-American presidents of banks and approximately 250 vice presidents. Cubans own over 60 new and used car dealerships, about 500 supermarkets, and close to 250 drug stores. It has been estimated that the Cuban community of Dade County earns an aggregate annual income of over $2.5 billion.[125]

CONCLUSIONS

The Cuban-Americans have made remarkable progress in their adjustment to life in the United States. The first immigrants to arrive from Cuba after the Castro takeover in 1959, were positively selected in terms of their educational backgrounds and entrepreneural skills. They were able to establish an economic and cultural base that would ease the difficulties of adjustment for later waves of Cuban refugees who were not so positively selected. The Cubans who chose not to locate in the ethnic enclaves of Miami and Union City-West New York settled mainly in other large cities where they received considerable government assistance under the Cuban Refugee Program. By almost any measure it is apparent that the Cubans are becoming rapidly assimilated into American society, although they are still readily visible as an ethnic minority.

Residentially, during the early 1960s, the Cubans living in metropolitan Miami were concentrated in the Little Havana area. By 1980 they had dispersed widely throughout Dade County.[126] Although there is still a tendency for Cubans to live in Cuban dominated neighborhoods, there are many exceptions, especially in the outer fringe of the Cuban enclave. A poll conducted by the *Miami Herald* in 1978 of 500 Latins and 500 non-Latins living in Dade County determined that 71 percent of the non-Latin whites and 57 percent of the blacks lived in areas where they had Cuban neighbors.[127]

In addition to their residential patterns, Cuban-Americans are also becoming more similar to Anglo Americans in terms of their occupational patterns. After a usual decline in occupational status upon their initial arrival in the United States, most have experienced considerable upward mobility as their length of residence has increased. The younger and more highly educated Cuban immigrants have been especially successful in approaching the American occupational norms.

The fertility patterns and family structure of Cuban-Americans provide further evidence of their convergence towards non-Latin Anglo culture. The birth rates of Cuban females are now somewhat below those of white American women. The labor force participation rates for women of Cuban descent suggest that there are many working Cuban mothers, as is the case for many Anglo mothers. The patriarchical character of the traditional Cuban family is becoming weakened in the United States, as it evolves towards the American model and away from the Latin American model. American-born children of Cuban immigrants are intermarrying at exceptionally high rates with non-Hispanic whites. This is perhaps the strongest piece of evidence of their American assimilation.

Most Cuban immigrants have given up the desire to return to Cuba, even if Castro were to be overthrown by a democratic regime. As a result, most either have or would like to have United States citizenship status. Those who possess citizenship exhibit high levels of participation in the American electoral process. Politically, they have become very well integrated into the American system.

In terms of language, Cuban assimilation appears to be occurring primarily along generational lines; that is, the second and third generations of Cuban-Americans have developed the greatest facility with English. Typically, the second generation is bilingual, whereas the third usually is only fluent in English. Although the first generation is more comfortable when speaking Spanish, an increasing percentage is learning English. Their difficulties with understanding English is usually considered to be one of the most severe problems they have had to face while living in the United States. Nevertheless, there is an unmistakable drift towards the use of English and away from the use of Spanish as the generations incrase.

Some studies of immigrant groups living in the United States have noted a tendency for the third generation to try to recapture some of the elements of the culture of their immigrant grandparents. The second generation often rapidly abandoned the cultural traits of their parents because they were viewed as a handicap towards their upward social mobility in American society. This tendency is embodied in the sociological concept known as the *three generations concept*.[128] Although the third generations of Cuban-Americans is only beginning to appear, there is no evidence to suggest that the three generations hypothesis will apply in the case of Americans of Cuban descent. All available evidence seems to indicate the opposite. The assimilation momentum built up by the first generation and increased by the second will probably be sustained during the third and subsequent generations. Eventu-

ally, the Cuban element in the United States will become indistinguishable from the rest of the American population. The rapid rate of assimilation will be retarded only if there is another large wave of cultural infusion from Cuba through renewed immigration. Where heavy concentrations of Cubans occur, as in the metropolitan areas of Miami and Union City-West New York, the evidence of Cuban culture may linger and the rate of assimilation of the first and second generation may not be quite so rapid. Nevertheless, even in these areas, the results by the third generation will be the same—almost complete assimilation.

NOTES

1. The terms "Cuban descent," "Cuban origin," and "Cuban-American" will be used synonymously in this chapter and will refer to individuals who consider themselves to be of Cuban background, either by birth or parentage. This terminology concurs with that used by the U.S.A. Census Bureau. The United States Bureau of the Census, *Current Population Reports,* series P-20, No. 354: "Persons of Spanish Origin in the United States," March, 1979 (Washington, D.C.: U.S. Government Printing Office, 1980): pp. 1 and 57.
2. The 1980 United States Census data for persons of Cuban origin were not available at the time this chapter was written. When the 1980 population census was taken during the first week in April, it missed the massive wave of approximately 125,000 Cubans who left Cuba from Mariel Harbor beginning on April 21, 1980 and continued until September of that year. Jorge and Moncarz state that a figure of 1 million is a good "ball park" estimate of the number of persons of Cuban origin living in the United States. This considers: (1) an estimate of 794,000 Cuban-Americans, as of March, 1979, derived from the United States Census Bureau's Current Population Survey, (2) the possibility of a 10 percent population undercount, and (3) addition of the number of Cubans arriving through the 1980 Mariel boatlift. Antonio Jorge and Raul Moncarz, *International Factor Movement and Complementarity: Growth and Entrepreneurship Under Conditions of Cultural Variation* (The Hague, Netherlands: Research Group for European Migration Problems, R.E.M.P. Bulletin, supplement 14, 1981): p. 4. Also see: United States Bureau of the Census, *Current Population Reports,* Social Studies, P-23, No. 82, by Jacob S. Siegel and Jeffrey S. Passel, "Coverage of the Hispanic Population of the United States in the 1970 Census" (Washington, D.C.: U.S. Government Printing Office. no date): pp. 35–37.
3. The Population Reference Bureau estimates that the mid-year 1981 population for Cuba was 9.8 million. See *1981 World Population Data Sheet* (Washington, D.C.: Population Reference Bureau, Inc., April, 1981).
4. This three-fourths figure is based on an estimate provided by Guarione M. Diaz, Executive Director, Cuban National Planning Council, Miami, Florida on March 27, 1981.
5. Rafael J. Projias and Lourdes Casal, *The Cuban Minority in the United States: Preliminary Report on Need Identification and Program Evaluation* (Boca Raton: Florida Atlantic University, 1973): p. 1.
6. William S. Bernard, "Immigrants and Refugees: Their Similarities, Differences and Needs," *International Migration,* 14 (no month listed), 1976: pp. 267–280; and Egon F. Kunz, "Exile and Resettlement: Refugee Theory," *International Migration Review,* 15 (Spring-Summer, 1981): pp. 42–52.
7. Patrick Lee Gallagher, *The Cuban Exile: A Socio-Political Analysis* (New York: Arno Press, 1980): pp. 23–36.
8. A. J. Jaffe, Ruth M. Cullen, and Thomas D. Boswell, *The Changing Demography of Spanish Americans* (New York: Academic Press, 1980): pp. 246–248.
9. Gallagher, 1980: pp. 34–35.
10. Lisandro Perez, "Cubans," in *The Harvard Encyclopedia of American Ethnic Groups,* ed. Stephan Ternstrom (Cambridge: The Becknap press of Harvard University Press, 1980): p. 256.
11. Richard R. Fagen, Richard A. Brody, and Thomas J. O'Leary, *Cubans in Exile: Disaffection and the Revolution* (Stanford, California: Stanford University Press, 1968): p. 100.
12. Gallagher, 1980: pp. 37–39.
13. University of Miami, *The Cuban Immigration, 1959–1966, and its Impact on Miami-Dade County, Florida* (Coral Gables, Florida: Research Institute for Cuba and the Caribbean, Center for Advanced International Studies, University of Miami, July 10, 1967): p. 1, Appendix A.
14. The 1953 Cuban population census was the one that was the most recently available at the time Fagen, Brody, and O'Leary conducted their investigation.
15. Fagen, Brody, and O'Leary, 1968: p. 13.
16. Juan M. Clark, "The Exodus from Revolutionary Cuba (1959–1974): A Sociological Analysis" (unpublished Ph.D. dissertation, Department of Sociology, University of Florida, Gainesville, Florida, 1975): p. 75.
17. It has been reported that 1,612 persons (638 of whom had United States citizenship) were transported from Havana to Miami on an American Red Cross sponsored aircraft. Virginia R. Dominguez, *From Neighbor to Stranger: The Dilemma of Caribbean Peoples in the United States* (New Haven: Antilles Research Program, Yale University. Occasional Paper No. 5, 1975): p. 22.
18. Gallagher, 1980: pp. 39–42.
19. Dominguez, 1975: p. 22.

20. Barent Landstreet, "Cuba," in *Population Policies in the Caribbean,* ed. Aaron lee Segal (Lexington, Massachusetts: Lexington Books, 1975): pp. 140–141.

21. Clark, 1975: pp. 85–98.

22. Alejandro Portes, Juan M. Clark, and Robert L. Bach, "The New Wave: A Statistical Profile of Recent Cuban Exiles to the U.S.," *Cuban Studies,* 7 (January, 1977): p. 17.

23. Landstreet, 1975: p. 141.

24. Eleanor Meyer Rogg and Rosemary Santana Cooney, *Adaptation and Adjustment of Cubans: West New York, New Jersey* (Bronx, New York: Monograph No. 5, Hispanic Research Center, Fordham University, 1980): pp. 35–46 and 72.

25. Alejandro Portes, Juan M. Clark and Manuel M. Lopez, "Six Years Later, A Profile of the Process of Incorporation of Cuban Exiles in the United States," forthcoming in *Cuban Studies* (July 1981): pp. 15–57.

26. Portes, Clark, and Bach, 1977: pp. 2 and 30–31.

27. Rogg and Cooney, 1980: pp. 18–19; and Portes, Clark, and Bach, 1977: p. 11.

28. For a listing of the numbers of Cubans arriving in the United States by individual months during the Mariel boatlift see: Juan M. Clark, Jose L. Lasaga, and Rose S. Reque, *The 1980 Mariel Exodus: An Assessment and Prospect* (Washington D.C.: Council for Inter-American Security, A Special Report, 1981): p. 5.

29. Sergio Diaz-Briquets and Lisandro Perez, *Cuba: The Demography of Revolution* (Washington, D.C.: Population Reference Bureau, Vol. 36, No. 1, April, 1981): p. 28.

30. Guy Gugliotta, "How a Trickle Become a Flood: Origins of the Freedom Flotilla," *The Cuban Exodus, The Miami Herald,* Special Reprint, 1980: pp. 8–10.

31. Clark, Lasaga and Reque, 1981: p. 2.

32. Gugliotta, 1980: p. 10.

33. Clark, Lasaga and Reque, 1981: p. 9.

34. *Ibid.:*p. 6.

35. Guillermo Martinez, "Mariel Refugees: A City Within a City," *The Miami Herald,* December 14, 1980: p. 1A.

36. Clark, Lasaga and Reque, 1981: p. 7.

37. Richard Morin, "Deluge Adds to Fear in Uneasy Miami," *The Cuban Exodus,* see footnote 30: p. 11. The attitudes towards the Cuban refugees who came during the twenty years before the Mariel exodus were more favorable to the same poll. About 50 percent of the non-Latin whites and 48 percent of the blacks felt that they had a largely positive impact on Dade County.

38. Clark, Lasaga and Reque, 1981: p. 15.

39. *Ibid.:* p.12.

40. In June, 1980, the Roper Poll surveyed the American public concerning its attitudes towards controlling immigration. The results showed that 80 percent agreed that the quota for legal immigration should be lowered. Furthermore, there was strong agreement among ethnic and socioeconomic groups. "What Americans Want," *The Other Side* (Newsletter of the Environmental Fund, Washington, D.C. Number 22, Spring, 1981): p. 4.

41. Fredrick Tasker, "Refugees Have Revised Census Data," *The Miami Herald,* January 31, 1981: p. 1B.

42. Guillermo Martinez, "Cuban Miamians Prone to Highlight How they Contrast with Marielitos," *The Miami Herald,* May 26, 1981: p. 7A; and Zita Arocha, "Mariel's Scorned, Youths Feel Sting of Rejection," *The Miami Herald,* March 23, 1981: p. 2B.

43. Guy Gungliotta, "Who are They? Boatloads Salted With Criminals," *The Cuban Exodus,* see footnote 30: p. 12.

44. Robert L. Bach, "The New Cuban Immigrants: Their Background and Prospects," *Monthly Labor Review,* 103 (October, 1980): pp. 39–46.

45. Landstreet, 1975: p. 141.

46. U.S. Bureau of the Census, *Census of Population: 1970,* Subject Reports, Final Report PC(2)-1C, "Persons of Spanish Origin" (Washington, D.C.: U.S. Government Printing Office, 1973): p. 4.

47. U.S. Bureau of the Census, *Current Population Reports,* Series P-20, No. 361: "Persons of Spanish Origin in the United States: March 1980 (Advance Report)," May, 1981 (Washington, D.C.: U.S. Government Printing Office, 1981): p. 5.

48. These estimates were provided by Guarione M. Diaz, Executive Director, Cuban National Planning Council, Miami, Florida, through a personal interview on March 27, 1981. They do not include the Mariel Cubans who were in refugee camps at this time.

49. Eleanor Meyer Rogg, *The Assimilation of Cuban Exiles: The Role of Community and Class* (New York: Aberdeen Press, 1974): pp. 25–27.

50. Rogg and Cooney, 1980: p. 11–14.

51. Projias and Casal, 1973: pp. 102–117.

52. *Fact Sheet,* Cuban Refugee Program, U.S. Department of Health and Human Resources, Miami, Florida, October 31, 1981.

53. Projias and Casal, 1973: pp. 117–120.

54. Aida Thomas Levitan, *Hispanics in Dade County: Their characteristics and Needs* (Miami, Latin Affairs, Office of County Manager, Metropolitan Dade County, printed report, Spring, 1980): p. 18.

55. "Latins Now Are Living All Over Dade," *The Miami Herald,* July 2, 1978: p. 22A.

56. Levitan, 1980; p. 19; and Juan M. Clark, "Los Cubanos de Miami: Cuantos Son y de Donde Provienen," *Ideal,* January 15, 1973: pp. 17–19.

57. *Fact Sheet,* 1981, in footnote 52.

58. Levitan, 1980: p. 20.

59. *The Miami Herald* survey found that 56 percent of the returnees it questioned came from the New York City-New Jersey area. "Latins Now Are Living All Over Dade," see footnote 30, p. 22A.

60. Everett S. Lee, "A Theory of Migration," *Demography,* 3 (No. 1, 1966): pp. 47–57.

61. Levitan, 1980: p. 18; and Dade County Planning Department, "Mobility Patterns 1964–1969" (Miami: Dade County Planning Department, Memorandum Report, Work Element VII, Housing in the Metropolitan Plan, Dade County, Florida, April, 1970): p. 43.
62. Gallagher, 1980: pp. 48–51.
63. Tasker, 1981: p. 1B
64. Kimball D. Woodbury, "The Spatial Diffusion of the Cuban Community in Dade County, Florida" (unpublished M.S. thesis, Department of Geography, University of Florida, 1978): pp. 67–69.
65. *Ibid.:* p. 36.
66. Thomas D. Boswell, Afolabi A. Adedibu and Kimberly J. Zokoski, "Spatial Attributes of Social Areas Dimensions in Miami, Florida SMSA: 1970, *The Florida Geographer,* 14 (February, 1980): pp. 7–10.
67. U.S. Census Bureau, 1981, in footnote 47: p. 5.
68. Portes, Clark, and Lopez, 1981: p. 5.
69. Franklin P. Eichelberger, "The Cubans in Miami: Residential Movements and Ethnic Group Differentiations" (unpublished M.A. thesis, Department of Geography, University of Cincinnati, 1974): pp. 67–93.
70. Milton M. Gordon, *Assimilation in American Life* (New York: Oxford University Press, 1964).
71. Rogg, 1974: pp. 136–137.
72. Morton D. Winsberg, "Housing Segregation of a Predominantly Middle Class Population: Residential Patterns Developed by the Cuban Immigration Into Miami, 1950–74," *American Journal of Economics and Sociology,* 38 (October, 1979): p. 416.
73. B. E. Aguirre, Kent P. Schwirian and Anthony J. LaGreca, "The Residential Patterning of Latin American and other Ethnic Populations in Metropolitan Miami," *Latin American Research Review,* 15 (No. 2, 1980): pp. 46, 48–49.
74. Morton D. Winsberg, "Housing Segregation of a Predominantly Middle-Class Population: The Case of the Miami Cubans" (Unpublished paper read at the Annual Meeting of the Association of American Geographers, Los Angeles, California, April, 1981).
75. Fredric Tasker, "Anglo Flight Is a Two-Way Street," *The Miami Herald,* November 16, 1980: p. 1B.
76. Jeff Golden, "Schools Hit by 'White Flight,' Enrollment Off by 8,499 in Last Year," *The Miami Herald,* January 10, 1982: p. 1B.
77. Thomas D. Boswell, Guarione M. Diaz and Lisandro Perez. "The Socioeconomic Context of the Cuban American Population," *The Journal of Cultural Geography,* forthcoming in 1982.
78. Diaz-Briquets and Perez, 1981: pp. 30–31.
79. U.S. Bureau of the Census, 1981, in footnote 47: p. 5.
80. Diaz-Briquets and Perez, 1981: pp. 31–32.
81. The most recent published U.S. Census Bureau figures for Cuban-Americans are for March, 1980. At that time (before the Mariel boatlift) it was estimated that there were 414,000 males and 417,000 females in this population. If there were 125,000 Cubans in the Mariel exodus, and if (as reported earlier) 70 percent were male and 30 percent were female, the appropriate number of males (87,500) and females (37,500) can be added to the Census Bureau's 1980 figures to obtain a revised estimate of the sex composition for the current Cuban descent population. This procedure yields a figure of 52.5 percent for males and 47.5 percent for females.
82. U.S. Bureau of the Census, 1973, in footnote 46: p. 9.
83. Benigno E. Aguirre, "Differential Migration of Cuban Social Races," *Latin American Research Review,* 11 (No. 1, 1976): p. 104.
84. *Ibid.:* pp. 111–114.
85. Boswell, Diaz and Perez: 1982.
86. Aguirre, 1976: p. 115.
87. Jaffe, Cullen and Boswell, 1980: pp. 51–62.
88. Gugliotta, 1980: p. 12.
89. Portes, Clark and Lopez, 1981: pp. 15–19.
90. Rogg and Cooney, 1980: pp. 46 and 70–72.
91. William Petersen, *Population* (New York: Macmillian Publishing Co., Inc., 1975): pp. 528–530.
92. Diaz-Briquets and Perez, 1981: pp. 12–24. In 1981 Cuba's crude birth rate was 15 births per 1,000 persons and Cuba was tied with that of Canada as being the lowest in the Western Hemisphere. Population Reference Bureau, Inc., see footnote 3.
93. Jaffe, Cullen and Boswell, 1980: pp. 40–51 and 252–254.
94. *Ibid.:* pp. 40–41.
95. Marie LaLiberte Richmond, *Immigrant Adaptation and Family Structure Among Cubans in Miami, Florida* (New York: Arno Press, 1980): pp. 33–39.
96. R. O. Blood and R. L. Hamblin, "The Effect of the Wife's Employment on the Family Power Structure," *Social Forces,* 36 (May, 1957): pp. 347–352 and S. J. Bahr, "Comment on the Study of Family Power Structure: A Review 1960–1969," *Journal of Marriage and the Family,* 34 (May, 1972): pp. 239–243.
97. Rogg and Cooney, 1980: p. 4.
98. Margaret Stanley Boone, "Cubans in City Context: The Washington Case" (unpublished Ph.D. dissertation, Department of Anthropology, Ohio State University, 1977): p. 18.
99. Rogg, 1974: p. 134 and Rogg and Cooney, 1980: p. 4.
100. John Dorschner, "Growing Up Spanglish in Miami," *The Miami Herald,* Tropic Magazine, September 11, 1977: pp. G-13.
101. U.S. Bureau of the Census, 1980, in footnote 1: p. 42.
102. Perez, 1980: p. 259.

103. Joseph P. Fitzpatrick and Douglas T. Gurak, *Hispanic Intermarriage in New York City: 1975* (Bronx, New York: Monograph No. 2, Hispanic Research Center, Fordham University, 1979): pp. 23–25.
104. Jaffe, Cullen and Boswell, 1980: pp. 63–68.
105. Fitzpatrick and Gurak, 1979: pp. 83–86.
106. *Ibid.:* pp. 24–25.
107. Rogg, 1974: pp. 37–138; and Gallagher, 1980: pp. 72–79.
108. Rogg and Cooney, 1980: p. 18; Portes Clark and Lopez, 1981: p. 10; and Levitan, 1980: p. 20.
109. Levitan, 1980: p. 23.
110. Rogg and Cooney, 1980: p. 29.
111. *Ibid.:* p. 29.
112. "Trouble in Paradise," 1981: p. 32.
113. William R. Amlong, "Politics Cuban-Style Rule Miami," *The Miami Herald,* May 5, 1981: p. 1B.
114. Paul S. Salter and Robert C. Mings, "The Projected Impact of Cuban Settlement on Voting Patterns in Metropolitan Miami, Florida," *The Professional Geographer,* 24 (May, 1972): pp. 123–131.
115. For the purposes for this discussion, first generation Cuban-Americans are all those persons of Cuban origin living in the United States who were born in Cuba, regardless of their age upon arrival in America. Their American born children represent the second generation and their grandchildren born in the United States are the third generation.
116. Sam Jacobs, "Language: Main Obstacle to Harmony," *The Miami Herald,* July 3, 1978: p. 1A.
117. Diaz-Briquetz and Perez, 1981: p. 35.
118. Levitan, 1980: pp. 25–29 and 33–36.
119. Rogg and Cooney, 1980: pp. 25–26.
120. James R. Curtis, "*Santeria:* Presistence and Change in an Afrocuban Cult Religion," in *Objects of Special Devotion: Fetishes and Fetishism in Popular Culture,* ed. Ray Browne (Bowling Green, Ohio: Bowling Green University Popular Press, 1982); and James R. Curtis, "Miami's Little Havana: Yard Shrines, Cult Religion and Landscape," *Journal of Cultural Geography,* 1 (Fall/Winter, 1980): pp. 1–15.
121. Guarione M. Diaz (ed.) *Evaluation and Identification of Policy Issues in the Cuban Community* (Miami: Cuban National Planning Council, 1981): pp. 123–124.
122. Kenneth L. Wilson and Alejandro Portes, "Immigrant Cubans in Miami," *American Journal of Sociology,* 86 (September, 1980): pp. 295–319.
123. The Cuban Refugee Program has spent approximately $1.6 billion on its assistance for Cuban refugees. Jorge and Moncarz, see footnote 2: pp. 14–17.
124. Jorge and Moncarz, 1981: pp. 21–25 and 56.
125. Carlos J. Arboleya, "The Cuban Community 1980. Coming of Age, As History Repeats Itself" (self published letter by the President and Chief Operating Officer of Barnett Bank, Miami, 1980).
126. Fredrick Tasker and Helga Silva, "Latin Centers Spread, Transforming County," *The Miami Herald,* February 14, 1982: p. 1B.
127. Morris S. Thompson, "Cubans Fare Better, Black Family Says," *The Miami Herald,* July 5, 1978: pp. 1A and 20A.
128. Bernard Lazerwitz and Louis Rowitz, "The Three Generations Hypothesis," *The American Journal of Sociology,* 69 (March, 1964): pp. 529–538.

6

Puerto Ricans Living in the United States

Thomas D. Boswell
University of Miami, Florida

Puerto Ricans represent the second largest contingent of persons of Latin American origin living in the United States. In March, 1980, the United States Bureau of the Census estimated that there were 1.8 million persons of Puerto Rican descent living in this country, outside of the Commonwealth of Puerto Rico. This number represented 13.8 percent of the United States total Latin American population, second in number only to the Mexican-Americans.[1] Preliminary returns from the 1980 Population Census indicate that there are an additional 3.2 million Puerto Ricans living in Puerto Rico.[2] Since all Puerto Ricans, whether living in Puerto Rico or in one of the fifty United States, are considered to be American citizens, the total Puerto Rican-American population is approximately five million, with 36 percent living on the U.S. mainland and the remaining 64 percent residing in Puerto Rico.

Although the number of Puerto Ricans living in the United States represents less than one percent of the country's total population, their significance is greater than their numbers alone might suggest for at least five major reasons. First, they are the only large group of persons to come to the United States as American citizens from a distinctly different cultural background. Because of this they have complete freedom to move back and forth between Puerto Rico and the United States mainland without being affected by immigration restrictions. Therefore, they are the only Latin American component of the United States population that does not contain a significant element of illegal aliens.[3]

A second important distinguishing characteristic of Puerto Ricans living in the United States is that they represent the first large group of American immigrants who are predominantly of mixed black and white racial background. Puerto Ricans span the racial continuum between black and white. Some exhibit totally Caucasian characteristics; others are almost of pure black descent; but most have some mixture of the two. In addition, a few exhibit Indian features. It has been suggested by some researchers that the experience of the

Puerto Rican tolerance for social differences may be one of their major contributions to American society.[4]

A third crucial characteristic of Puerto Rican migration to the United States mainland is that it represents the first large air-borne movement of people from abroad. Because most travel by air from San Juan to New York City, the trip is only a 3.5 hour journey and represents an investment of an average of about one week's pay. It is a fact that a person can travel from Puerto Rico to New York City in less time than it took a New Yorker to travel from Coney Island to Times Square on Manhattan Island a century ago.[5] Thus, the physical act of moving to the United States is relatively easy and cheap, especially when compared to most other immigration waves that have characterized much of American history. Some writers have suggested that traveling between Puerto Rico and the United States is physically more like commuting, rather than immigrating. Such ease of movement promotes a greater magnitude of migration and makes it easier for Puerto Ricans living in the United States to return home for visits, thereby strengthening the maintenance of cultural ties with the island and promoting the additional migration of friends and relatives.

A fourth way in which Puerto Rican migration experiences are different from those of other migrants to the United States has to do with the role that the Puerto Rican government has played in facilitating moves to the mainland. Once it became apparent that the rapid increase in migration, after World War II, caused serious problems of adjustment, the Puerto Rican government created a Migration Division in its Department of Labor. This agency maintains offices in a number of cities in the United States and serves as an employment and orientation office for new migrants. It has negotiated contracts for Puerto Ricans traveling seasonally to work in American agriculture and has been concerned with helping organize Puerto Rican communities on the mainland. It also has become involved in public relation efforts to supply information and correct misconceptions about Puerto Ricans living in the

United States. In addition, it supplies information to Puerto Ricans who are contemplating a move to the United States and provides counseling services to those already living here.[6] There is no doubt that this agency has helped migrants from Puerto Rico to adjust to the American ambiance. On the other hand, there are some researchers who suggest that this paternalistic guidance, although well-intended, has helped to retard the development of powerful grass-root organizations among the Puerto Rican Americans, such as those that developed historically among a number of other American immigrant groups.[7]

A fifth distinguishing characteristic of the Puerto Rican migration experience involves the changing characteristics of the New York metropolitan area, historically the primary destination for most Puerto Rican in-migrants. Although a number of other immigrant groups selected New York City as their first area of concentration, the environment of this city has changed a great deal from what it was 75 years ago when large numbers of Irish, Italians, and Jews arrived. Automation has created a new type of economy that relies less on unskilled and blue collar labor which was furnished by the earlier immigrants. Urban renewal and public housing projects during the last 30 years have made it difficult for Puerto Ricans to establish the degree of numerical dominance in New York neighborhoods that typified some of the earlier arrivals. In addition, the Puerto Ricans have arrived when the city and federal governments are providing a wide range of services, such as health and welfare benefits, that did not exist 75 years ago. As a result, although there are some similarities, the Puerto Rican experience is not a simple repetition of the past experiences of other ethnic groups who earlier moved to the United States.[8]

BACKGROUND IN PUERTO RICO

Although this chapter concentrates on the characteristics of Puerto Ricans living on the United States mainland, it is appropriate to discuss briefly the characteristics of Puerto Rico. One reason for this is that somewhat more than half of all mainland Puerto Ricans were born in Puerto Rico and most were strongly influenced by their homeland prior to their arrival in the United States.[9] Second, available evidence indicates that the movement from the island to the mainland will continue for some time into the future. Third, the island of Puerto Rico is currently, politically and legally, a part of the United States.

Physical and Human Ecology

The island of Puerto Rico is located in the northeastern corner of the Caribbean Sea, east of the Dominican Republic and west of the Virgin Islands (Fig. 6.1). It lies 1,662 miles southeast of New York City, 1,050 miles southeast of Miami, and 550 miles north of Caracas, Venezuela. Its location between North and South American at one of the main entrances to the Caribbean Sea has provided it with considerable strategic significance. During the Spanish conquest of Latin America in the sixteenth century, Puerto Rico became one of the main fortresses against European competitors for control of the Caribbean. During World War II and throughout the cold war of the 1950s the United States built several military installations on the island that became primary links in the United States global defense system.[10] Today its location has proved beneficial for the development of trading and tourist activities with mainland United States.

Puerto Rico is the smallest of the four islands included within the Greater Antilles.[11] It averages a little over 100 miles in length and about 35 miles in width for a total area of 3,435 square miles, about the size of the state of Connecticut. Geologically, it is part of an ancient volcanic mountain range which is surrounded by a narrow coastal plain. Only about 30 percent of the island can be considered as level or undulating. A mountain range runs in an east-west direction through its center. The highest elevation (4,389 feet) is found in the Cordillera Central (Fig. 6.1).[12]

By virtue of its tropical location in the Caribbean, Puerto Rico is characterized by mild climatic conditions. There is only slight seasonal variability in temperature, with the hottest summer average monthly temperature being only three to seven degrees (Fahrenheit) warmer than the coolest winter monthly average. At sea level during an average summer day the highest temperature is in the high 80s or the low 90s; whereas the coolest temperature is in the high 70s. An average winter daily high is in the low to middle 80s, whereas the low is in the low 70s. At higher elevations in the mountains the temperature averages five to ten degrees cooler. Thus, there is no true winter season as experienced in most of the United States. One of the most frequently mentioned complaints that Puerto Rican migrants to the mainland have, especially those who live in the Northeast and Middle West, is that they have a hard time becoming accustomed to the cold winter temperatures because they never experienced anything similar while living in Puerto Rico. Rainfall is considerably more variable than temperature. The highest amounts are found in the mountains, especially in the northeastern Sierra Luquillo where the average is close to 200 inches. The lowest rainfall is around 30 inches and occurs in the southwestern coastal lowland.[13]

The topography and climate conditions of Puerto Rico have influenced the island's prevailing land use patterns (Fig. 6.2). Sugar cane is grown along most of the level to undulating coastal plain that surrounds the island's mountainous core and in the Caguas Valley.

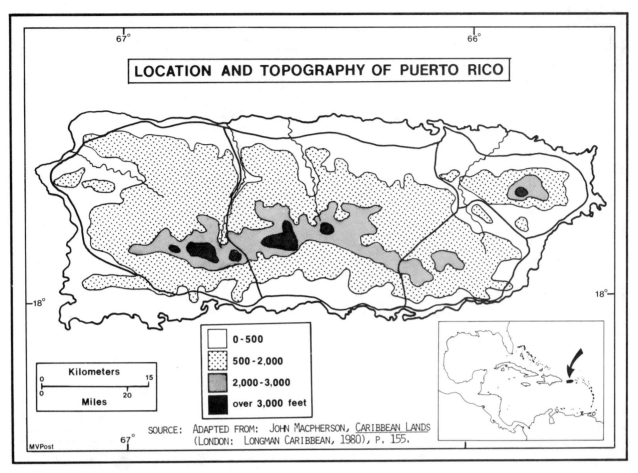

Figure 6.1. Location and Topography of Puerto Rico.

Coffee is a specialty crop produced in the western half of the Cordillera Central at elevations above 1,500 feet where it is commonly grown on small to medium-sized family farms. The growing of tobacco is concentrated in the eastern section of the Cordillera Central, surrounding the Caguas Valley. Pineapples and vegetables are grown in patches along the northwestern coastal plain and in the irrigated Lajas Valley in the southwestern corner of the island. Citrus and tropical fruits, as well as bananas and plantains, are grown throughout the island with no particular concentration. The raising of cattle, hogs, and poultry are also dispersed throughout the island.

Due to lack of available level land in the mountains, the majority of the major urban centers are located along the surrounding coastal plain. One major exception is Puerto Rico's third largest city, Caguas, which is located in the large Caguas Valley about 15 miles southeast of San Juan. Fifty-two percent of the island's population lives in the four major metropolitan areas of San Juan (1,083,664), Ponce (252,420), Caguas (173,929), and Mayaguez (132,814).[14] A total of 70 percent of the population is classified as living in urban centers[15] and perhaps three-fourths of the island's inhabitants live somewhere along the coastal plain.

Political History

The written history of Puerto Rico began when Christopher Columbus discovered the island during his second voyage to the New World in 1493. At that time the island was occupied by perhaps 25,000 to 30,000 Indians, known throughout the Caribbean as Tainos.[16] These Indians called their island homeland Borinquen, a name that is sometimes used affectionately today by Puerto Ricans living both in Puerto Rico and on the United States mainland. By the end of the sixteenth century almost all the Indian population had either been killed, died of disease, frightened off, or absorbed by the Spanish colonists.[17] Only infrequently are Indian physical traits recognizable among today's Puerto Ricans. Beginning in 1511 black slaves were brought to the island to replace the Indians as laborers. Slavery remained as an important part of the Puerto Rican economy until it was abolished in 1873. Today the predominant racial features of most of Puerto Rico's people are the result of either Spanish or black descent, or some combination of the two.[18]

Spain ruled Puerto Rico for nearly 400 years until the Spanish-American War in 1898. As a result of the Spanish defeat, the island was transferred to United states sovereignty by the Treaty of Paris on December

119

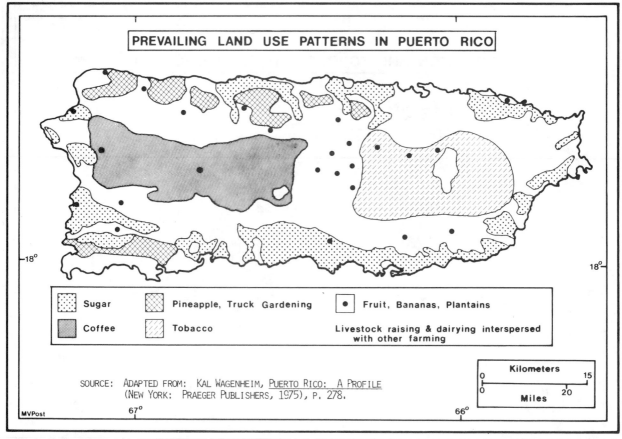

Figure 6.2. Prevailing Land Use Patterns in Puerto Rico.

10, 1898. After being administered by the American military for two years, a civilian government was established by the Foraker Act of 1900. Virtually all governing power was placed in the hands of the President of the United States who appointed the island's Governor. The legislature was composed of an Executive Council and a House of Delegates. The Council contained an American majority, the members of the House were elected by Puerto Rican voters. Any laws passed by the House were subject to veto powers of the United States Congress. Many Puerto Ricans were disappointed with this arrangement because they had hoped for a larger degree of local autonomy, such as Cuba had received shortly after the Spanish-American War. Furthermore, in 1897, just before Spain lost sovereignty over the island, the governing of Puerto Rico had been considerably liberalized to allow for more local control.[19]

In 1917 United States citizenship was conferred on all Puerto Ricans by the Jones Act, except for those who explicitly refused it.[20] However, Puerto Ricans living in Puerto Rico were not allowed to vote in American elections and adult males became subject to obligatory military service, both of which created some resentment. In 1948, Puerto Ricans were permitted to elect their own Governor (Luis Munos Marin) for the first time.

In 1950, the United States Congress passed Public Law 600 (also known as the Puerto Rican Federal Relations Act) which authorized Puerto Rico to draft its own Constitution, so long as it did not violate any of the rules contained within the Constitution of the United States. On July 25, 1952, the Puerto Rican Constitution was inaugurated and the island became known as *estado libre asociado* (free associated state), or as it is also frequently called, a commonwealth. Under this new arrangement, the island acquired much more local autonomy. It continued to elect its own Governor and Resident Commissioner to the United States Congress, but without voting rights. Puerto Ricans could now elect all members of their bicameral legislature, composed of a Senate and a House of Representatives. All judges, cabinet officials, and lesser officials of the executive branch were to be locally appointed. The Puerto Rican Government also established its own budget and amended its own civil and criminal laws. On the other hand, Puerto Rico remains a United States possession subject to all federal laws, including military conscription. Its native residents still cannot vote in elections in the United States. They also do not pay federal taxes. The United States Government has retained responsibility for their military defense, postal service, and foreign affairs. In addition, there is free movement of people and most goods between the island and mainland.[21]

Although the relationship between the United States and Puerto Rico has remained unchanged since 1952, it has not escaped heated political debate. Three distinct factions have evolved. First, there are those who would like to keep the present commonwealth system. They see it as a creative achievement that allows Puerto Rico to maintain a specific culture with its own language and traditions, while at the same time enabling benefits to be derived from a close identity with the United States. Second, there are the proponents who favor United States statehood. They believe that only by becoming a state will the island be able to receive all the benefits that the other fifty states receive, including the right to vote for Federal Government officials. They are convinced that through statehood Puerto Rico will have economic and political security along with freedom. The third political faction is composed of a diverse group who prefer complete political independence. They are of the opinion that only through independene will Puerto Rican culture continue to exist. They are convinced that, if they remain affiliated with the United States, Puerto Ricans will lose their language and will suffer abuse as second class citizens.[22] The pro-independence sympathizers have always been represented by a very small minority in Puerto Rico elections since 1948.[23] For instance, in 1967 a plebiscite on political status was held. Nearly 60 percent voted in favor of continuing the present commonwealth status. Close to 39 percent voted for statehood and less than 1 percent voted for independence. It has been stated that many independence supporters have abstained from participation in elections in Puerto Rico, but nobody knows for certain the numbers that have done so.[24] The proponents of independence are represented by several parties with different political philosophies, so it has been difficult to unify their efforts. Nevertheless, they have been very vocal in expressing their beliefs, despite their small percentage figures. Their tactics have ranged from election boycotts, to demonstration, and to violence and terrorism both in Puerto Rico and on the U.S. mainland.

Economic Development

The Spanish have never been known for promoting economic development for the benefit of their colonies; Puerto Rico was no exception in this regard. By the late 1800s, just after the United States takeover, the economy of the island was dominated by subsistence farmers and the growing of coffee, tobacco, and sugar for export. Unfortunately, during the first 44 years of their occupation the Americans did not do much better than the Spanish. By the 1920s Puerto Rico had developed a virtual monocultural economy based on the production of sugar cane. Most of the capital, land, and processing mills were owned by large American corporations. Several hurricanes and the Great Depression of the 1930s severely damaged agricultural production and wrecked havoc on the Puerto Rican economy. By 1940 it was common to hear the island being referred to as the "Poorhouse of the Caribbean." If someone were looking for potential sources of new immigration to the United States, Puerto Rico might easily have caught their attention.

In 1942 the Puerto Rican government created the Economic Development Administration, known locally as "Fomento."[25] It was decided that the greatest efforts for development would be directed towards the promotion of manufacturing, since the future dvelopment of agricultural production on the island did not look encouraging. During the 1940s the government tried to build an industrial infrastructure by opening some of its own plants to make key products from local raw materials. However, it was soon found that it did not have enough capital to carry out the kind of program that was needed. In addition, the government had experienced difficulties in the area of labor relations with its factory employees. As a result, in 1948 efforts towards economic development were reorganized under a plan known as "Operation Bootstrap." The objective was to send emissaries to visit corporations on the mainland to promote investments in the manufacturing, tourist, and rum industries in Puerto Rico. To prime the economic pump for manufacturing investments, the Puerto Rican government constructed buildings for new factories that would be sold or leased at modest rates. It also offered tax-free periods that would last from 10 to 25 years, depending upon where the businesses were located on the island. In addition, the government provided marketing data, offered to help train new personnel, and sometimes gave low-interest loans to new investors. Free access to the American market and the labor cost differential between Puerto Rico and the United States was also heavily advertised.[26]

These efforts towards industrialization had a profound impact on Puerto Rico. The number of persons employed in manufacturing increased by 85,000 between 1940 and 1970; the number working in agriculture declined by 156,000. By 1955 income generated by manufacturing surpassed that derived from agriculture. In 1940 about 43 percent of Puerto Rico's labor force was employed in farming pursuits and only 10 percent worked in industry. In 1970 only 10 percent worked in agriculture and about 19 percent were employed in manufacturing. Now the leading sectors of the Puerto Rican economy, according to money generated, are manufacturing, tourism, and agriculture, in that order. Between 1940 and 1970 net per capita income increased from $121 to $1,417.[27] Until the recession of the middle 1970s the island's annual economic growth rate was about 10 percent, one of the world's highest sustained rates.[28]

The social consequences of this economic development have also been immense. Rural to urban migration within Puerto Rico has become a basic factor affecting population redistribution on the island, as has emigration to the United States. In 1940, 72 percent of the population lived in rural areas; in 1980 the figure was about 30 percent. Education is rapidly eliminating illiteracy and a sizable middle class has begun to emerge. Still, there are some cracks in the showcase image of the island. Although the per capita gross national product in 1980 was $3,010 this is only about 60 percent what it is in Mississippi, the poorest of the states in the United States. About two-thirds of all Puerto Rican families still live below the poverty level, based on criteria established by the United States government. Many live in urban slums. Due to heavy population growth, it has been estimated that at least 1,000 squatter slum shacks spring up each year in urban areas and the government is not close to satisfying the demand of the poor for housing through its public housing projects. The official unemployment rate has waivered between 10 and 20 percent, primarily as a result of the decline in agricultural employment. If one includes the chronically unemployed, most of whom have given up hunting for a job so they do not get counted in the official figure, the real unemployment rate is closer to 30 percent. This is considerably higher than the rate that prevailed in the United States during the Depression of the 1930s.[29]

One of the strategies that many Puerto Ricans have employed in an attempt to increase their economic opportunities is to migrate to the mainland of the United States. In doing so, they have carried the experiences and cultural baggage acquired while living on the island. Where they come from in Puerto Rico can have a major influence in their adjustment to life on the continent. For instance, a Puerto Rican who grew up in the metropolitan area of San Juan is likely to face somewhat different problems adjusting to living in New York City or Chicago than one who originated from a rural *barrio* in the coffee region of the western Cordillera Central. Of course, some of the problems faced will be similar. Both will have to adjust to the cold winters and will find it useful to become familiar with the new language. Although most Puerto Rican migrants will have witnessed some of the processes of modernization prior to their move, they will find that the pace of life and competition for jobs is considerably different in large American cities. If they faced an identity problem in Puerto Rico because of the conflict in the political philosophies of those supporting either statehood, independence or commonwealth status, they are likely to be further confused by being a member of a disadvantaged minority living on the United States mainland.

With these thoughts in mind, the next topic covered in this chapter will be the history, causes, and consequences of the mass migration of more than one-third of Puerto Rico's population to the United States.

MIGRATION TO THE UNITED STATES

Some Puerto Ricans like to joke that Ponce de Leon, who founded the initial European settlement in Puerto Rico in 1508 and then searched for "The Fountain of Youth" in Florida, was the first Puerto Rican to migrate to the United States. Certainly, Puerto Ricans have been living in New York City since the 1830s. During the latter half of the nineteenth century there were a few students from wealthy Puerto Rican families attending universities on the mainland. In addition, there was a handful of Puerto Rican revolutionaries periodically living in New York City and plotting (often with Cuban exiles) against the Spanish government that then controlled Puerto Rico.[30] Shortly after the American occupation of the island in 1898, Puerto Ricans were recruited to work in the sugar cane fields of Hawaii. By 1901 there were 6,000 of these people. Some subsequently resettled in California and New York.[31]

The first year in which the United States Census Bureau listed Puerto Ricans as a separate group in its publications was 1910 (Table 6.1). At that time there

TABLE 6.1 The Puerto Rican Population Living in the United States: 1910–1970*

Year	Born in Puerto Rico	Born in United States	Total
1910	1,513	N.A.	1,513
1920	11,811	N.A.	11,811
1930	52,774	N.A.	52,774
1940	69,967	N.A.	69,967
1950	226,110	75,265	301,375
1960	615,384	272,278	887,662
1970	783,358	646,038[a]	1,429,396[b]
1980[a]	N.A.	N.A.	1,823,000[b]

*The figures for 1950 and 1960 in the "Born in the United States" Column refer to the second generation only (persons born in the United States with one or both parents born in Puerto Rico).

[a]This figure includes the second and subsequent generations of persons born in the United States who considered themselves to be of Puerto Rican descent.

[b]These figures include all persons who considered themselves to be of Puerto Rican descent.

N.A. means not available.

The figures for 1910–1970 come from Kal Wagenheim, *A Survey of Puerto Ricans on the U.S. Mainland* (New York: Praeger Publishers, 1975): p. 71; and the figure for 1980 comes from United States Bureau of the Census, *Current Population Reports,* Series P-20, No. 361, "Persons of Spanish Origin in the United States: March 1980 (Advance Report)," May, 1981 (Washington, D.C.: U.S. Government Printing Office, 1981): p. 5.

were just over 1,500 persons who were born in Puerto Rico and living in the United States, with 37 percent of them residing in New York City. Between 1910 and 1920 about 10,000 more were added to the United States population. There are two reasons why more did not migrate during this decade. One is that it was still difficult and expensive to travel the 1,662 miles to New York City from San Juan. Second, this was a period of heavy immigration to the United States from Europe and blacks were beginning to move northward out of the South, both of which increased competition for available jobs.

Emigration to the mainland picked up during the 1920s when about 41,000 new Puerto Rican residents were added to the United States population. The economic boom that followed the end of World War I and the strong curtailment of European immigration through enforcement of the United States Immigration Act of 1924 were factors prompting this surge. The decade of the 1930s witnessed a significant decline in the flow of Puerto Rican migrants. During this period the Puerto Rican component increased by slightly over 17,000 persons. The rate of increase in the mainland Puerto Rican populaton for the 1920s was 347 percent, while for the 1930s it was only 33 percent. This decline was caused by a decrease in the number of job opportunities as a result of the Great Depression. In fact, between 1931 and 1934 there was a net return migration of 8,694 persons to Puerto Rico.[32] By 1940 New York City had established its maximum degree of dominance as the primary residence for Puerto Ricans living on the mainland. At this time 88 percent of all the persons born in Puerto Rico but living on the mainland were residing in this city.[33] Between 1940 and 1945 the rate of flow picked up a little (Table 6.2) due to jobs created by the effects of World War II. The rate of flow was not greater because most Puerto Ricans traveled by boat to New York and the Atlantic was patrolled by German ships that posed a dangerous threat to their safe passage.

When compared to the heavy European immigration that influenced United States history from the 1800s to the early 1920s, Puerto Rican movements were insignificant until 1946. Immediately after World War II, however, the flow of Puerto Ricans grew rapidly. There were a number of reasons for the tremendous increase that was to follow. First, there was a backlog of persons who would like to have moved from the island during the early 1940s but could not because of the War. Second, many Puerto Rican men had fought in the Second World War and had been trained in the United States and, as a result, had developed an awareness of the opportunities on the mainland. Third, by 1946 there were already over 100,000 Puerto Rican born residents of the mainland who served as a "family intelligence service" for friends and relatives back home. They provided information, helped find jobs, and

TABLE 6.2 Net Migration from Puerto Rico to the United States: 1940–1980*

Years	Annual Numbers	Decade Totals	Years	Annual Numbers	Decade Totals
1940	1,008		1965	10,758	
1941	500		1966	30,089	
1942	928		1967	34,174	
1943	2,601		1968	18,681	
1944	8,088		1969	− 7,047[a]	
1945	11,003				144,724
1946	24,621		1970	44,000	
1947	35,144		1971	2,525	
1948	28,031		1972	−23,648[a]	
1949	33,086		1973	37,069	
		145,010	1974	24,971	
1950	34,155		1975	5,430	
1951	41,920		1976	− 36,201[a]	
1952	61,658		1977	4,610	
1953	74,603		1978	20,282	
1954	44,209		1979	6,078	
1955	31,182				85,116
1956	61,647		1980	16,101	
1957	48,284				
1958	25,956				
1959	37,212				
		460,826			
1960	23,742				
1961	13,800				
1962	11,363				
1963	4,798				
1964	4,366				

[a]A minus sign (−) denotes net return migration to Puerto Rico.
*Figures are for fiscal years from July 1 to June 30.

From 1940 to 1969 *Puerto Ricans in the Continental United States: An Uncertain Future* (Washington, D.C.: United States Commission on Civil Rights, 1976): pp. 26–27; and from 1970 to 1980 from a phone conversation with Jennifer Marks, National Population Estimates Branch, United States Bureau of the Census, Washington, D.C., March, 1982.

frequently offered a place to stay and food for the new migrants. Fourth, as mentioned earlier in this chapter, the Puerto Rican government created a Migration Division within its Department of Labor that facilitated movement to the mainland and assisted the new arrivals in making the necessary adjustments. Fifth, the cost and effort of traveling to New York City were drastically reduced. By boat the trip had formerly taken a minimum of four days and cost close to a month's pay. After the war surplus aircraft were available and air fares were lowered to as little as 35 dollars for a six-hour one-way trip, closer to a week's salary. Furthermore, financing was frequently available so passengers could make a five dollar down payment and the rest could be paid through installments after their arrival in New York. Sixth, heavy population growth in Puerto

Rico was creating population pressure and heavy strains on the island's labor force capacity. Seventh, a shift was beginning to take place that would significantly alter the island's occupational structure during the 1950s and 1960s. As a result, there was about to be a radical decline in agricultural employment. Both the increasing population pressure and declining agricultural employment provided strong incentives to leave the island, especially its rural areas. In conclusion, each of these seven factors promoted emigration, especially when it is recalled that: (1) since Puerto Ricans are United States citizens they have freedom to move to the mainland without any legal restrictions, and (2) there was a very large gap between the economic opportunities that prevailed on the mainland and Puerto Rico at this time.[34]

From 1946 to 1950 the number of Puerto Ricans residing in the United States increased by almost 121,000 persons (Table 6.2). By 1950 it became apparent that a second generation of Puerto Ricans born on the mainland was becoming numerically significant (Table 6.1). Even so, 75 percent of all Puerto Ricans were born in Puerto Rico. The decade of the 1950s represents the period of heaviest flow toward the United States. The total increase (including both the first and second generations) between 1950 and 1960 was almost 600,000 persons. In 1953 alone, 74,603 Puerto Ricans moved to the mainland.

During the decades of the 1960s and the 1970s, the rate of flow to the mainland began to ease progressively (Table 6.2). Between 1960 and 1970 the net flow was 144,724, whereas between 1970 and 1980 it was down to 85,116 persons. There are three main reasons for this decline: (1) there was a narrowing in the income differentials between the United States and Puerto Rico; (2) the "push" factors in Puerto Rico that helped motivate emigration were reduced as per capita income and the standard of living on the island rapidly improved, primarily as a result of the efforts of Operation Bootstrap; and (3) a significant amount of return migration to Puerto Rico from the mainland developed that partially offset the emigration in the opposite direction.[35]

There are two other trends worth noting that became apparent during the 1960s and 1970s in the mainland Puerto Rican population. First, the domination of New York City as the home of most Puerto Ricans in the United States has declined as this population disperses to other cities and states. From a high of 88 percent in 1940, the percentage of mainland persons who were born in Puerto Rico and living in New York City decreased to 70 percent in 1960 and then to 58 percent in 1970. Although the 1980 census data for mainland Puerto Rico are not yet available, an educated guess places the 1980 figure between 50 and 55 percent. The second trend that can be identified is that

by 1970 the second and third generations of Puerto Ricans living in the United States were beginning to approach the size of the immigrant component (Table 6.1). In that year 45.2 percent of all persons who identified themselves as being of Puerto Rican descent were of a second or subsequent generations. Furthermore, it is also clear that most of the numerical increase in the mainland Puerto Ricans was due to the growth, by natural increase, of those born in the United States.[36] This is an important point because it is well-known that second generation mainland Puerto Ricans generally enjoy higher socioeconomic status than their immigrant parents, as has been the case historically with virtually all other American immigrant groups.[37]

Return Migration

It is a well-known fact that most mainland Puerto Ricans desire to go back to the island, at least for a visit, if not to stay permanently. In a New York City study conducted in 1948 it was found that 22 percent of a sample of Puerto Rican migrants expressed some desire to return to live on the island.[38] Another study conducted in the 1960s noted that 33.5 percent planned to return.[39] Hernandez-Alvarez estimated that in 1960 there were 75,000 return migrants from the mainland living in Puerto Rico, representing about 3.2 percent of the island's population. For 1965 he estimated that the number had grown to 145,000 or 5 percent of the island's inhabitants.[40] The 1970 Population Census for Puerto Rico indicated that 13 percent of all those 14 years of age or older had been living on the mainland in 1965.[41] Another estimate for 1972 indicates that 372,000 or 14 percent of the island's population were return migrants.[42] Clearly, the trend has been upward since 1955, indicating that return migration is becoming increasingly important. Although figures for 1980 were not available at the time this chapter was being written, it can be estimated that in that year 15 to 20 percent of the island's population was composed of migrants returning from the mainland. Since there are roughly half as many Puerto Ricans living on the mainland as are living in Puerto Rico, it can be projected that somewhere between one-third to one-fourth of the Puerto Ricans who migrated to the United States had returned by 1980. As a standard of comparison, it has been estimated that about 25 percent of all the immigrants from Europe who arrived in the United States between 1908 and 1923 returned home.[43]

A study conducted during the 1960s indicated that most of the return migrants had started their migration process from a rural or small town origin in Puerto Rico.[44] Only about one-third of these persons moved from one place to another within the island prior to their trip to the mainland. Thus, the majority moved directly, instead of by a step process, to the mainland. Also about one-third of those who returned did so to a residence that was not the same as they left when they initiated their move to the mainland.[45] Approximately 42 percent returned to the San Juan metropolitan area, whereas another 10 percent returned to the other two metropolitan areas of Ponce and Mayaguez. Only 30 percent returned to rural areas. Thus, most return migrants started out in a rural area of Puerto Rico, moved directly to a large northeastern city on the mainland, and finally returned to an urban location on the island. It appears that migration to the mainland contributes to the general urbanization process that characterizes Puerto Rico's population, as people move internally within the island from rural and small town areas to the cities.[46]

It is interesting to note that there is some evidence that suggests that the migrants who return home to Puerto Rico do not do so primarily for economic reasons.[47] A study of prospective return migrants in New York City found that the most attractive qualities that they perceived in Puerto Rico, when it was compared to New York City, were friends, home life or family, climate, and neighbors.[48] Other factors that have also been mentioned as being influential in motivating a return are (1) retirement, (2) a desire to raise one's children in the more wholesome environment of Puerto Rico, (3) a desire to escape the drug and crime problems encountered in large mainland cities, (4) the more personal atmosphere of the island, (5) an inability to cope with American lifestyles, (6) the changing job situation on the mainland, especially in New York City, (7) a belief that skills acquired on the mainland will make it easy to find a job in Puerto Rico, and (8) homesickness.[49]

Migrant and Return Migrant Selectivity

Migrants in free societies almost never are representative of the populations they left behind. Thus, the importance of a mass migration flow goes well beyond the significance of only the numbers. In addition to adding numbers to the destination's population and subtracting people from the origin, migration also affects the composition of the population involved. This section will compare the characteristics of three classes of Puerto Ricans: (1) immigrants living on the United States mainland; (2) return migrants living in Puerto Rico; and (3) the nonmigrant population residing in Puerto Rico. Many of the figures to be used come from the 1960 census for the United States and Puerto Rico. Although these data are over 20 years old, this is the only source of information that allows for the comparison of these three populations.[50]

Origin Characteristics. It has already been determined that the majority of return migrants started their migration histories in rural areas of Puerto Rico. The origin of the nonmigrant population living in Puerto Rico is not relevant because they have, by definition, not migrated to the United States, although the Puerto Rican population census for 1960 indicates that about nine percent of all Puerto Ricans over the age of five years did migrate internally, within the island, between 1955 and 1960.[51]

There has been a change over time in the predominant types of origins of the Puerto Ricans who have migrated to the United States mainland. Prior to the 1950s most came to the mainland from urban areas in Puerto Rico. A study of New York City's Puerto Ricans conducted in 1948 indicated that 91 percent had originated from urban centers on the island, especially from the cities of San Juan and Ponce.[52] Another study shows that of the migrants who left Puerto Rico for the United States during the decade of the 1940s, about 67 percent came from urban origins. However, this latter study also indicates that the comparative figures for the 1950s and 1960s were 28 percent and 6 percent, respectively.[53] This dramatic turn occurred because, during the 1940s, all of Puerto Rico was poor, including both cities and rural areas. However, the economic development that characterized the island during the 1950s and especially during the 1960s was concentrated in the cities, so there was less incentive for people to migrate from the cities of Puerto Rico to the United States. Although the rural areas also saw some improvements during these two decades, they were still poor enough to be unattractive to many of their residents. As a result large numbers left rural areas. During the 1940s most migrants from rural areas moved internally to one of the island's cities because they were too poor to move to New York City, and many did not have friends or relatives living there to help them adjust. By the 1950s their incomes had risen above the per capita income threshold that would allow migration,[54] the cost of transportation to the mainland had declined, and many now had friends or relatives living in New York City who could assist them in making the move.

Sex Characteristics. In 1960 the Puerto Rican migrant population was almost exactly equally divided between males and females. However, it has not always shown this balance. The 1948 study of New York City's Puerto Rican migrants, mentioned earlier, found that 61 percent of its sample was composed of females. The 1940 United States population census shows that at that time about 52 percent of the nation's Puerto Ricans were female. In 1950 the percentage figure was the same. Thus, there was a slight predominance of females in the migration flow up to 1950. For the males to catch up with the females by 1960 implies that there was a slight male dominance during the 1950s. By 1970 there was again a slight female majority of 52 percent. By 1980 the majority climbed to approximately 56 percent. Thus, there has been a double turnaround in the selection process. The reason for the female dominance before 1950 is likely related to the fact that most migrants before this time came from urban areas in Puerto Rico, and the urban areas had a slight female majority. During the 1950s, as stated previously, the migration stream became characterized by a dominance of rural residents who had a slight male majority which, in turn, produced a male majority of migrants. The switch back to a female majority from 1960 to 1980 has probably been a function of occupational changes in New York City that tend to favor the employment of Puerto Rican females. For instance, between 1969 and 1974 this city lost 194,000 jobs in manufacturing, while it gained many clerical and secretarial jobs that usually favor female employment.[55]

Whereas the sex ratio of the Puerto Rican migrants on the mainland fluctuated, the ratio for the total population living in Puerto Rico remained stable, with an approximate balance between the sexes. On the other hand, there was a clear majority of females (about 55 percent) among the return migrants.[56] In fact, this may have been another factor that helped the males to catch up numerically with females among the Puerto Rican population living on the mainland in 1960. Perhaps the reason for the predominance of females in the return flow to the island had to do wth the nature of the jobs that were created by the industrial growth promoted by Operation Bootstrap. Most of the factories that were created during the 1950s and 1960s employed more females than males.

Age Structure. The median age for persons living in Puerto Rico in 1960 was 18.5 years, whereas for Puerto Rican migrants living in the United States it was 27.9 years and for return migrants it was 30.1 years.[57] The lower average age for Puerto Rico was a result of two factors: (1) high fertility, which created a large proportion of children thus drawing down the average for the total population; and (2) emigration to the United States mainland, selective of young adults. It has been estimated that 85 percent of all Puerto Rican emigrants during the 1940s and 1950s were in the 15–45 year age class, with a majority being in the 20–24 year group.[58] It is also apparent that the selectivity of emigration accounts for the older average age of the migrant population living on the mainland. As the adolescent and young adult migrants left for New York, they lowered the average age of the population in Puerto Rico and increased it for the migrants living on the mainland. It is reasonable that return migrants would be the oldest of the three populations being compared because, by definition, they must have spent some time on the mainland prior to their return to the island. One researcher found that the average stay on the mainland for his sample of return migrants was almost 6 years.[59]

The age characteristics of the nonmigrant, migrant, and return migrant populations suggests that the typical return migration sequence is related to stages in the family formation cycle. People traveling north from Puerto Rico to live on the mainland for the first time tend to be adolescents or young single adults. While on the mainland they form families by getting married and begin childbearing. If they return to Puerto Rico they often do so in their late 20s or early 30s, during the childbearing phase of their family cycle.[60] What has just been described is a generalized model to which there will be many individual exceptions. For instance, quite a number of persons who migrate to the mainland do so after they have already started their families. Sometimes the whole family moves together, but often either the husband or wife will go first and try to establish a household base and secure a job before the rest of the family moves. Occasionally, children will be sent back to Puerto Rico to be raised by relatives. This practice is especially prevalent when the wife works and the neighborhood lived in is characterized by crime and drug problems. Another exception to the model occurs because there is a moderate bulge in the age structure of the return flow to Puerto Rico of persons who have reached their 60s and are beginning to retire. In any case, the model is a general description of the relationships between age, family cycle stages, and migration behavior existing for the majority of the migrants.

Socioeconomic Characteristics.[61] When measuring the socioeconomic status of a population, the variables of education, occupational structure, and income are most often used in the literature. Therefore, this section will compare the Puerto Rican nonmigrant, migrant, and return migrant population in terms of these three variables.

When considering achieved education levels, return migrants are in the most favored position, followed by migrants living in the United States and nonmigrants residing in Puerto Rico. For persons 25 years of age or older, return migrants had a median education level that was about half a year higher than Puerto Ricans living on the mainland, and about three to four years higher (depending on sex) than those living on the island. The percentage figures for those who had less than five years of schooling and those who had completed at least high school show the same relative differences between the three Puerto Rican populations. Clearly, the return migrants are only slightly better off, in terms of their education levels, than the migrants living on the mainland, and both these populations are considerably better educated than the nonmigrant population living in Puerto Rico.

When considering occupational structure, again the return migrants clearly enjoyed the highest status with 44 percent employed in white collar occupations, 49 percent in skilled and semi-skilled jobs, and only 7 percent in unskilled positions. The comparable figures for Puerto Rican migrants living on the mainland were 17 percent, 75 percent, and 8 percent; for the inhabitants of Puerto Rico they were 33 percent, 41 percent, and 26 percent, respectively. A comparison of the latter two populations shows that those living in Puerto Rico are more concentrated in both the higher and lower status classes of occupations, whereas the migrants living on the mainland are more represented in the middle level occupational category.

The income structure of the three populations shows that the Puerto Rican migrants living on the mainland are in the most favored position. Their median personal income was 61 percent higher than for the return migrants and three times higher than the income of the inhabitants of Puerto Rico. The fact that return migrants, despite their higher educational and occupational status, have lower incomes than the migrants living in the mainland is a reflection of the much higher wages paid on the mainland in 1960. Since this gap has narrowed (but not closed) since then, further research is needed to determine the extent to which these conditions still exist. Nevertheless, these findings lend support to the statement made earlier in this chapter that the Puerto Rican migrants who return to the island commonly do so for noneconomic reasons. Further evidence of this is provided when it is noted that the return migrants also had the highest unemployment rates when compared to the other two poulations.

In her study of Puerto Rican migrants to and from the mainland, Sandis summarizes her findings by stating that it appears safe to conclude that a positive selection process characterizes the socioeconomic status of the migrants prior to their departure from the island. Upon their arrival on the mainland, many experience downward occupational mobility, but their earnings usually increase substantially. Those who return to Puerto Rico are characterized by higher educational and occupational levels, but have lower incomes than those who remained in the states. It is possible that return migrants are persons who were occupationally downwardly mobile on the mainland and returned to Puerto Rico to assume white collar or skilled blue collar careers, even though they paid lower salaries than the lower status jobs on the mainland. Another possibility is that the return migrants were upwardly mobile in terms of their acquisition of skills and knowledge on the mainland, and then returned to the island.[62] It is most likely that both possibilities have operated simultaneously to produce the characteristics of the return migrants, as they existed in 1960.

Farm Labor Migration

Except for working in the Hawaiian sugar cane fields at the turn of the century, Puerto Ricans did not begin to play a significant role in American agriculture until the early 1940s. With the manpower shortage created by World War II, American employers started recruiting Puerto Ricans to work on mainland farms. The American agricultural season fits in well with that of Puerto Rico because the island's sugar cane season normally lasts from January to June. During the rest of the year many Puerto Rican cane cutters are out of work. On the island this period is known as the "Tiempo Muerto" or dead time. Since this is the period of maximum activity on farms located in the American Middle West and North East, the recruitment of Puerto Ricans helped the island during its season of highest unemployment and provided low cost labor for American farms when it was most needed.

Seasonal agriculture has almost always had a tainted reputation for labor abuse in this country, and by the middle 1940s reports began to be heard about this in Puerto Rico. The Puerto Rican government passed a law that required all mainland farm employers who wanted to recruit laborers on the island to do so through use of a contract that was approved by the Puerto Rican Department of Labor. The contract contains provisions that guarantee such benefits as transportation to and from the farm, a 160 hour work month, suitable housing, food, health care, insurance, and death benefits.[63] The program was run through the Labor Department's Migration Division.

Presently an average of close to 20,000 seasonal farm laborers are coming from Puerto Rico to work under contracts on American farms. It has been estimated that an additional 20,000 to 30,000 come on their own as the result of the confidence and trust they have of specific farmers.[64] They help harvest sugar beets in Michigan and tobacco in Connecticut; tend vegetable production in New Jersey; cultivate potatoes on Long Island, and pick a range of crops north from Virginia to Massachusetts and west to Illinois. Many of these seasonal laborers eventually become permanent residents on the mainland. Some of the original Puerto Rican communities located in the American North East started out as clusters of farm contract laborers who stayed on the mainland. Examples of this are the Puerto Rican populations of Camden and Trenton, New Jersey; Springfield, Massachusettes; Detroit, Michigan; Rockland County and eastern Long Island, New York.[65]

Since the middle 1960s the contract labor program has come under attack from radical, and often militant, Puerto Ricans who charge that it is another manifestation of a colonial capitalistic system.[66] They claim that it is a way of providing cheap labor for American agriculturists. The government, they charge, uses it as a way of exporting their unemployment problem rather than making the structural changes in Puerto Rican society that would create greater equality. Demonstrations have been directed against the government's Migration Division both in New York City and on the island. Most of the participants are supporters of the small, but vocal, Puerto Rico independence movement.

Conclusions Regarding the Migration Processes

The migration of Puerto Ricans to the United States has been a dynamic process affected by a variety of factors. The movements have ebbed and flowed as conditions have changed. However, it was not until 1946 that conditions fell into line so that a mass migration developed. During the 1940s and 1950s the stream reached its maximum strength. Then it progressively declined during the decade of the 1960s and 1970s. One of several factors that prompted this decline was a sizable amount of return migration to Puerto Rico that became significant around 1955. After this date, it became apparent that there were significant differences between the migrant Puerto Rican population living on the mainland and the return migrants to the island. The migration to the mainland was primarily motivated by the availability of economic opportunities. Noneconomic factors seemed to be more important to the return migrants. For instance, when a group of New York City Puerto Ricans who planned to return to the island to live were interviewed, 91.6 percent said they thought there were more job opportunities in New York City than in Puerto Rico.[67] Even so, they wanted to go home.

The return migrants generally did not represent a group of failures who could not make it living on the mainland. In fact, they were better educated and held higher status jobs, but they had lower incomes because of the lower salaries paid in Puerto Rico compared to those in the mainland. Some of the characteristics of the Puerto Rican migrants changed over time. Up to 1950 most were females and came from urban origins on the island. During the 1950s it appears that males were in the majority, but during the 1960s and 1970s females once again predominated. Also, during the 1950s and 1960s more migrants came from rural areas.

Emigration to the mainland has had a major impact on the economy and demographic structure of Puerto Rico. If the 36 percent of all Puerto Ricans who currently live on the mainland were returned to Puerto Rico, its population would climb from 3.2 million to about 5.0 million, an increase of 56 percent. In the process its population density would increase from 932 to 1,456 people per square mile; thus, giving it one of the world's highest densities. If the United States had a density this high, it would contain more people than the entire world does today. A study of the impact of emigration to the mainland on the economy of Puerto Rico, during the 1940 to 1960 period when the rate of flow was at its highest, reached some interesting conclusions. Had emigration not occurred the population would have had an additional 1.3 million people and the annual growth rate would have been 3.3 percent, instead of the recorded 1.2 percent. In fact, during the decade of the 1950s it would have been 3.5 percent. Such a growth rate, if continued into the future, would have resulted in a doubling of the population in a little

less than 20 years. Emigration reduced the population growth rate both by directly subtracting migrants who moved and indirectly by helping to reduce the birth rate, since most of the migrants were young adults who were potentially fertile. As another benefit derived from the age selectivity that characterized the migrants the size of the labor force was reduced by almost 50 percent. With emigration, the unemployment rate averaged about 13 percent during the 20 year period. Without it, unemployment would probably have been somewhere between 25 and 33 percent. Furthermore, emigration to the mainland also helped improve the quality of the Puerto Rican labor force, since many of the migrants were working in agriculture and as unskilled laborers prior to their departure for the mainland. Partly as a result of this, the ratio of unskilled to skilled workers decreased from 5.0 to 2.1. The addition of return migrants who were also selected from the higher status occupation categories also helped to continue this trend.[68]

DISTRIBUTION OF PUERTO RICANS IN THE UNITED STATES

Like virtually all immigrant groups before them, Puerto Ricans living on the mainland are highly concentrated in a few areas. In 1980 approximately 95 percent of all mainland persons of Puerto Rican descent lived in large cities (50,000 or more population). This figure compares with that of 67 percent for all persons living in the United States. Furthermore, about 75 percent of the Puerto Ricans were concentrated in the central cities of large metropolitan areas, with only 20 percent living in their suburbs. The remaining five percent lived in smaller urban centers and rural areas.[69]

Considered collectively, the eleven states with the largest Puerto Rican populations, contained 95 percent of all first and second generation Puerto Ricans living on the mainland in 1970 (Table 6.3). The largest single concentration is in the North East, with New York and its neighbors of New Jersey and Connecticut forming the main cluster. Together, these three states contain approximately three out of every four mainland Puerto Ricans. A second cluster is found in Illinois, mainly in the industrial corridor of the metropolitan area of Chicago and adjacent northwestern Indiana. California and Pennsylvania also had minor clusters, as did the states of Florida, Massachusetts, Ohio, Indiana, and Texas. In fact, there is no state in the United States that is totally without Puerto Ricans. Still, the figures in Table 6.3 clearly indicate a particularly heavy concentration in the area surrounding New York. Both first and second generation Puerto Ricans exhibit the same patterns, at least on a state scale. A statistical study of the distribution of Puerto Ricans living in the 48 contiguous states determined that the greatest numbers lived in

TABLE 6.3 Distribution of Persons of Puerto Rican Birth and Parentage in the United States: 1970

States	*Persons of Puerto Rican Birth and Parentage*		*Persons of Puerto Rican Birth*		*Persons of Puerto Rican Parentage*	
	Numbers	*Percent*	*Numbers*	*Percent*	*Numbers*	*Percent*
1. New York	878,980	63.2	505,908	62.5	373,072	64.2
2. New Jersey	136,937	9.8	83,518	10.3	53,424	9.2
3. Illinois	88,244	6.3	53,664	6.6	34,580	5.9
4. California	46,955	3.4	23,670	2.9	23,285	4.0
5. Pennsylvania	44,947	3.2	25,339	3.1	19,608	3.4
6. Connecticut	38,493	2.8	24,883	3.1	13,610	2.3
7. Florida	29,588	2.1	18,578	2.3	11,010	1.9
8. Massachusetts	24,561	1.8	16,743	2.1	7,818	1.3
9. Ohio	21,147	1.5	11,298	1.4	9,849	1.7
10. Indiana	9,457	.7	4,881	.6	4,576	.8
11. Texas	8,311	.6	5,077	.6	3,234	.6
12. Rest of the States	63,843	4.6	36,528	4.5	27,310	4.7
TOTAL	1,391,463	100.0	810,087	100.0	581,376	100.0

United States Bureau of the Census, *Census of Population: 1970,* Subject Reports, Final Report PC(2)-1E, "Puerto Ricans in the United States" (Washington, D.C.: U.S. Government Printing Office 1973): pp. 1–3.

states that (1) had higher per capita incomes, (2) were located close to either New York City or Miami which served as ports of entry, and (3) had large total populations.[70]

Appropriately 93 percent of the state of New York's Puerto Ricans live in New York City. It was pointed out earlier in this chapter that the New York metropolitan area has played a dominant role throughout much of the history of Puerto Rican migration to the United States. The main attraction that it originally held was economic opportunity in the form of jobs and higher wages, just as it did for many immigrant groups who came before them. In 1910, there were only 554 Puerto Ricans living in New York City.[71] It was not until the time of World War I that the Puerto Rican element became noticeable in the city's population. The first settlement with significant numbers occurred in the area of Brooklyn Heights (see Fig. 6.3), next to the Brooklyn Navy Yard, in response to a demand for workers during the war years. At about the same time a cluster of Puerto Ricans also began to develop in southern Harlem, just to the north of Central Park and east of Morningside Park.

By 1930, the number of Puerto Ricans in New York City had increased to almost 45,000 with southern Harlem clearly emerging as the leading concentration with approximately 80 percent of the city's Puerto Ricans. The area around Brooklyn Heights was second with about 16 percent. Migration slowed during the depression years of the 1930s and almost stopped during World War II. After the war it again picked up very rapidly. Quickly the population overflowed from southern Harlem to East Harlem and across the Harlem River to South Bronx. From Brooklyn Heights the

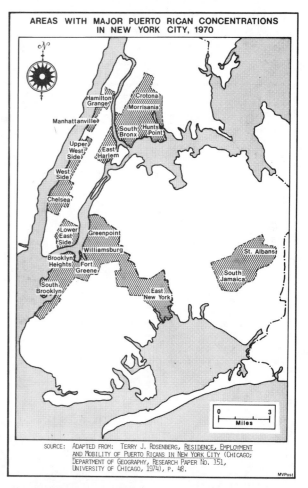

Figure 6.3. Areas with Major Puerto Rican Concentrations in New York City, 1970.

growth spread northward to Williamsburg and southward to South Brooklyn.[72] In 1940, about 70 percent of New York's 61,000 Puerto Ricans lived in Manhattan, with the largest concentration being in East Harlem. The latter became known as *El Barrio* "The Neighborhood"). Puerto Rican organizations sprang up in this area, as had happened with the German, Irish, Italian, and Jewish immigrants who preceded them. An open-air market, *La Marqueta,* was established to supply all the special goods and services that Puerto Ricans could not find elsewhere in the city. Although the Brooklyn settlement expanded simultaneously, it did not develop the ethnic flavor of East Harlem.[73]

The Puerto Rican population in New York City had grown to 245,880 by 1950, including 58,460 who were second generation Puerto Ricans born on the mainland. By this time, however, it became apparent that a shift away from Manhattan Island was beginning to take place, as its share of the city's Puerto Rican population declined to about 56 percent.[74] This trend was even more clear in 1970 when Manhattan's share had dropped to only 23 percent. By then, the Bronx contained the largest of the city's Puerto Rican population with 39 percent. Brooklyn was second with 33 percent and the boroughs of Queens and Richmond trailed

Manhattan with a total of five percent. In fact, between 1960 and 1970 the Puerto Rican community of Manhattan declined by 18 percent.[75]

While the Puerto Ricans within New York City were dispersing out of Manhattan and into the other four boroughs, they were also moving to locations outside the city. As previously mentioned, the percentage of all mainland Puerto Ricans living in New York City declined from 88 to 58 percent between 1940 and 1970. New Jersey's Puerto Rican population more than doubled between 1960 and 1970 with notable communities developing in such cities as Newark, Jersey City, Patterson, Camden, and Passaic (Fig. 6.4). In New England sizable concentrations evolved in Boston, Bridgeport and Hartford. Moving westward, communities developed in Rochester, New York and in Philadelphia to provide labor for manufacturing enterprises. In the Middle West heavy industry attracted Puerto Ricans to Cleveland and Loraine, Ohio and to Chicago. In the South, Miami developed a sizable Puerto Rican community, but this has been overshadowed by the city's much larger Cuban community. In California, Los Angeles has the only notable Puerto Rican concentration, and here they are not easily noticed because of the more numerous Mexican-Americans. In most cases, the

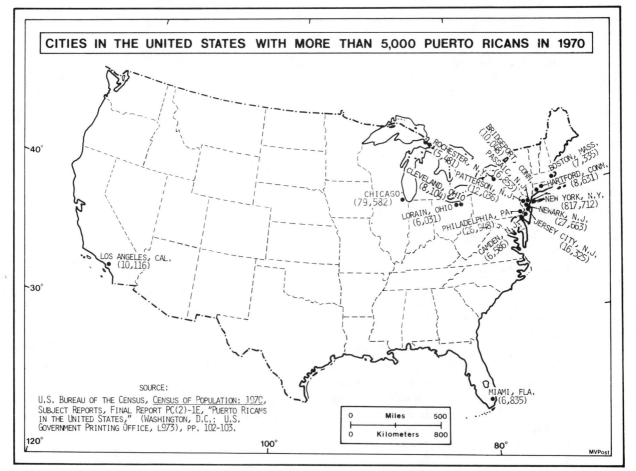

Figure 6.4. Cities in the United States with More Than 5,000 Puerto Ricans in 1970.

Puerto Ricans settlements that have developed outside of New York City have exhibited a similar evolutionary process. Usually, they started out as very small settlements of migrants born in Puerto Rico who were recruited from the island or New York City to work in factory jobs or as migrant laborers. A small base was then established that provided information for friends and relatives back home, who were soon to follow. A community began to develop with a definite Puerto Rican flavor, called a *colonia* (colony). In the beginning this was primarily composed of first generation migrants; but as it began to mature, a second generation of American-born Puerto Ricans became conspicuous. These people were often more upwardly mobile, in a socioeconomic sense, than their parents. As they became adults some left the *colonia* to become residentially more integrated with the rest of the city's population. This dispersion to areas outside the *colonia* has been termed a *diaspora*.[76]

Puerto Ricans represented a little over 10 percent of the total New York City population in 1970. In addition, they comprised about two-thirds of the city's total Hispanics,[77] and were the city's third largest minority, following Jews and blacks. Their presence, however, is of greater significance than their numbers might suggest, primarily because of their disadvantaged position in a highly competitive society. Even more than blacks, they are forced to take low-level jobs because of their limited education and their lack of ability to speak English. As a result of their youthful age structure and high fertility, their children account for about one-fourth of the city's public school enrollment. It has been estimated that 40 percent of the recipients of welfare in the form of Aid to Dependent Children and close to one-fourth of the heroin addicts are Puerto Rican.[78]

The Puerto Ricans who have migrated to New York City are probably similar, in terms of their educational and occupational profiles, to the majority of European immigrants who arrived in the city during the early part of this century. Such a comparison is virtually meaningless, however, since the situation is so different today from what it was then. When immigrants from Eastern and Southern Europe were arriving, they found both employment opportunities and available housing conveniently located in the central city. Conversely, since the later 1950s, Puerto Ricans have encountered more competition for housing, particularly from blacks immigrating from the South. In addition, many of the types of jobs for which Puerto Ricans might best be able to compete were moving out of the central city and into the suburbs. In part, these were being replaced in the inner city by white-collar occupations which had higher skill requirements.[79]

A more detailed investigation of the distribution of Puerto Ricans in New York City reveals three interesting attributes. First, the primary areas of concentration tend to be adjacent to the major areas of black settlement within the city. In fact, it has been hypothesized by one researcher that non-white Puerto Ricans may link the black and Puerto Rican clusters.[80] Clearly, the residential proximity of blacks and Puerto Ricans is a reflection of their disadvantaged economic state and consequent need to compete for the city's lowest quality housing. Second, Puerto Ricans do not numerically dominate the neighborhoods in which they live to the same degree that other immigrant groups have in the past. In the majority of the census tracts in which they live they make up less than 50 percent of the total population. In only a few does their percentage majority reach as high as 70 percent.[81] They have generally located in scattered housing sites, such as a block or an apartment building, rather than taking over an entire neighborhood. Moreover, they have frequently settled among other minorities, such as blacks and Italians. There are three factors that have influenced the low degree of neighborhood domination by Puerto Ricans: (1) a general housing shortage which makes it necessary for Puerto Ricans to live wherever there is available space which they can afford; (2) slum clearance that causes them to leave neighborhoods which they might begin to dominate; and (3) the availability of public housing which is offered at relatively low rents to other minority groups as well as to Puerto Ricans.[82]

The third detailed attribute of Puerto Rican settlement in New York City that is of interest is the amount of segregation within the Puerto Rican population based on different levels of economic achievement.[83] Wealthier Puerto Ricans tend to live in such areas as the better suburban neighborhoods of the Bronx and Queens, whereas the poor are more concentrated in central city areas like East Harlem and the Lower East Side. This situation is not unique to New York's Puerto Ricans; it is also characteristic of the city's blacks and other white ethnic groups.[84]

A POPULATION PROFILE OF MAINLAND PUERTO RICANS

The demographic characteristics of the Puerto Ricans living on the United States mainland reflect three primary influences: (1) their island backgrounds, (2) migration selectivity, and (3) their mainland experiences. Earlier in this chapter a comparison was made of nonmigrants living in Puerto Rico with migrants living in the United States and with return migrants to Puerto Rico. In this section, the population characteristics of Puerto Ricans living in the United States will be compared with those of the total Spanish origin population living in the United States, as well as with the mainland population that is not of Spanish origin. This will provide an understanding of the two major contexts in which the Puerto Ricans on the mainland find themselves with respect to the rest of this country's population. The following components of their population structure will be discussed: (1) age and sex composition; (2) education levels; (3) fertility levels; and (4) employment, occupation, and income tendencies. In addition, comments will be made regarding comparisons between the first and second generation Puerto Ricans and between those living in New York City and those living in the rest of the United States.

Age and Sex Composition

The Puerto Ricans are a young population when compared to the rest of the United States. In 1980 the median age for all mainland persons of Puerto Rican descent was 20.7 years. The average for all persons living in the United States who were not of Spanish origin was 30.7 years. The comparable figures for Cuban-Americans and Mexican-Americans were 33.5 and 21.4 years, respectively.[85] The youthfulness of the mainland Puerto Ricans is the result of two factors—their high fertility and the age selectivity of those who have moved to the mainland. Their high fertility, which is a product of their relatively low socioeconomic status, produces a population pyramid with a wide base that results from a high proportion being children. The selectivity of a majority of young adults as migrants adds an element to the population that is potentially high in fertility. Furthermore, as stated earlier in this chapter, a sizable component of the return migrants to Puerto Rico is composed of elderly persons of retirement age. If the latter are subtracted from the mainland population, average age is lowered.

When the first and second generation mainland Puerto Ricans are compared, it is clear that it is the age structure of the second generation that pulls down the overall average. The median age in 1970 for the first generation was about 30 years; whereas for the second generation it was about 10 years.[86] It is because of the recency of the Puerto Rican movement to the mainland that the second generation is so young. Within the next couple of decades the second generation can be expected to age, so the overall age structure should come closer to approximating that of the population for the rest of the United States. In the meantime, the fact that almost half of all mainland Puerto Ricans are of school age means that their burden of dependency will be felt in the cities in which they are concentrated more than their overall numbers might at first suggest.

It has already been mentioned in this chapter that approximately 54 percent of all mainland Puerto Ricans are females. About 51 percent of the total United States population is composed of females. The comparable figures for Cuban-Americans and Mexican-Americans are 50 and 49 percent, respectively.[87] The higher preponderance of females among the Puerto Ricans was explained earlier by their selectivity as a result of the types of jobs available in New York City, which tend to favor the employment of women. The predominance of females, especially in New York City, has resulted in a greater percentage of mainland Puerto Rican households being headed by females. The significance of this is that women usually earn less than men, so these families are more likely to be characterized by lower incomes and exhibit a greater tendency to receive some form of welfare assistance.

Education Levels

When compared to the rest of the United States population, mainland Puerto Ricans are characterized by low education levels. The only group within the Spanish origin population that has lower levels of schooling are the Mexican-Americans. Among the Puerto Ricans who are 25 years of age or older and living on the mainland, only 39 percent have completed high school and four percent have completed college. Among all persons living in the United States who are not of Spanish descent, the respective figures are 69 and 17 percent. For Cuban-Americans 25 years of age and older about 50 percent graduated from high school and 12 percent have a college degree. The Mexican-Americans are only slightly below the Puerto Ricans in terms of their levels of schooling.[87]

The median level of completed schooling for mainland Puerto Ricans who are 25 years of age or older is about 10 years. While this is considerably higher than that for the population living in Puerto Rico, it is well below the comparable figure for the rest of the United States population. As a result, even though Puerto Rican migrants are positively selected from the island population, they are in a disadvantaged position in terms of their education levels when it comes to competing for employment opportunities on the mainland. This disadvantaged position will be reflected in their occupational structure and income levels when compared to those of the rest of the United States population.

Fertility Levels

Puerto Rican women living in the United States have high fertility rates when compared to the nation's population as a whole. In 1979 the crude birth rate for the Puerto Ricans was 22.6 births per 1,000 persons in the nine states that contained the majority of persons of Spanish descent. For non-Hispanic women it was 14.7, and for Cuban-American and Mexican-American women it was 8.6 and 29.6 births per 1,000 persons, respectively.[88] When these rates are standardized for age structure, marital status, education level, and the degree of female participation in the labor force, it was found that the fertility performance of mainland Puerto Rican women is very similar to that of the general United States population.[89] In fact one study found that, when thus standardized, mainland Puerto Rican women have about the same fertility rate as both Puerto Rican women living in Puerto Rico and non-Spanish white women living on the mainland. The significance of this finding is that it indicates that there is nothing about Puerto Rican culture (by itself) that necessitates high fertility rates. It is clear the Puerto Rican birth rates have been declining recently on both the mainland and in Puerto Rico. The conclusion reached is that the fertility behavior of Puerto Rican women is rapidly approaching that of all white American women.[90] Still, it is likely that the higher fertility performance of mainland Puerto Rican women will continue to be felt in the cities where they are concentrated for another two or three decades, until they have reached a socioeconomic status comparable to that of the rest of the United States population.

Employment, Occupation, and Income Tendencies

The labor force characteristics of mainland Puerto Ricans (Table 6.4) clearly indicate their relatively low socioeconomic status. When compared to the United States non-Spanish origin population, they are underrepresented in white collar occupations and overrepresented in the manual labor jobs. If it were decided to alter the occupational structure of the mainland Puerto Ricans so that they exhibited the same percentage occupational distribution as that of the nation's non-Spanish population, it would be necessary to have 22.4

percent of the Puerto Ricans change jobs. The Puerto Ricans are much more similar to the Mexican-Americans, in terms of the types of jobs they have, than they are to the non-Spanish Americans. A study of New York City's Puerto Ricans found that close to 40 percent experienced downward occupational mobility upon their arrival from the island when a comparison was made with the types of jobs they held in Puerto Rico prior to their immigration. Only about 10 to 15 percent obtained jobs that were of higher status than the ones they left in Puerto Rico, and approximately 45 to 50 percent held jobs that were of the same status level in both places.[91]

In 1980 the official unemployment rate for mainland Puerto Ricans was 11.7 percent (Table 6.4). The rate for the non-Spanish population was 6.5 percent and for Cuban-Americans and Mexican-Americans it was 5.0 and 9.4 percent, respectively.[92] Again, this illustrates the disadvantaged position of mainland Puerto Ricans. Unfortunately, the situation is considerably worse than these figures indicate because of the method used by the United States Department of Labor in measuring unemployment. The official unemployment figures only count those people who either have a job, or are actively looking for one, as being in the labor force. Not included are persons who would like a job but have given up looking because they are discouraged. One observer has estimated that if these people

TABLE 6.4 Occupation, Employment, and Income Characteristics of Mainland Puerto Ricans Compared to the Total Spanish Origin and Non-Spanish Origin Populations in the United States (Persons 16 Years Old and Over)

Occupation Classes[a] 1980	Mainland Puerto Ricans (%)	Total Spanish Origin (%)	U.S. Non-Spanish Origin (%)
Professional, technical and kindred workers	8.9	8.5	16.8
Managers and administrators, except farm	3.7	6.6	11.4
Sales workers	3.4	3.8	6.3
Clerical and kindred workers	19.1	16.1	18.9
Craft and kindred workers	10.4	14.0	12.7
Operatives, including transport	29.8	23.7	13.7
Laborers, excluding farm	5.0	7.9	4.3
Farmers and farm managers	0.0	0.3	1.5
Farm laborers and supervisors	1.1	3.0	0.9
Service workers	18.6	16.2	13.4
Percent unemployed, 1980[a]	11.7	8.9	6.5
Percent of males in labor force, 1979[b]	72.1	80.5	76.0
Percent of females in labor force, 1979[b]	33.4	47.4	50.9
Median family income, 1979[a]	$9,855	$14,569	$19,965
Median personal income, 1978[b]	$5,131	$5,893	$6,864

[a]United States Bureau of the Census, *Current Population Reports,* Series P-20, No. 361: "Persons of Spanish Origin in the United States," March 1980 (Advance Report), (Washington, D.C.: U.S. Government Printing Office, 1981): p. 5.
[b]United States Bureau of the Census, *Current Population Reports,* Series P-20, No. 354: "Persons of Spanish Origin in the United States," March 1979 (Washington, D.C.: U.S. Government Printing Office, 1980): pp. 10 and 29.

were included, the "real" unemployment rate for mainland Puerto Ricans would be closer to 33 percent.[93]

The income levels of mainland Puerto Ricans are a reflection of their low education levels and occupation status. In 1980 the median income for Puerto Rican families was just under $10,000 (Table 6.4). For United States families that were not of Spanish origin, the comparable figure was almost $20,000, whereas for Cuban-American and Mexican-American families the median incomes were approximately $17,500 and $15,000, respectively.[94] Per capita income figures tell essentially the same story. About 39 percent of all Puerto Ricans who worked in 1978 had an annual income below $4,000. Less than ten percent earned $15,000 or more.[95] Despite these low incomes, it should be recalled that Puerto Ricans still earn substantially higher salaries on the mainland than they do in Puerto Rico. Nevertheless, it is also undeniably true that, in the context of United States society, they represent one of this nation's most disadvantaged ethnic minorities.

First and Second Generation Mainland Puerto Ricans

Earlier in this chapter it was noted that the percentage of the mainland Puerto Rican population born in Puerto Rico has been declining, from 75 percent in 1950 to approximately 55 percent in 1970. It has been found for most immigrant groups in the United States that the children of the first generation usually achieve higher socioeconomic levels than did their immigrant parents. Since they have grown up in American society they have been able to benefit from being better educated and being more fluent in their use of English. This same intergenerational upward mobility is also characteristic of the mainland Puerto Rican population. The significance of this is that as the percentage of mainland born among this group increases, it is expected that their socioeconomic characteristics will approach those of the general American population.

As a means of illustrating the intergenerational differences within the mainland Puerto Rican population, comparisons can be made between the characteristics of those born in Puerto Rico and those born on the mainland, using 1970 census data. For instance, for mainland Puerto Rican men between 20 and 24 years of age, 59 percent of those born on the mainland had completed high school; whereas only 37 percent of those born in Puerto Rico had achieved the same educational level. The unstandardized fertility rate of mainland Puerto Rican women born on the island was 97 percent higher than that of those born on the mainland. Approximately eight percent of the mainland Puerto Rican men 25 to 44 years of age who were born in Puerto were employed in better paying white collar occupations; whereas the comparable figure for mainland born

Puerto Rican men was 22 percent. The median family income for Puerto Rican families living on the mainland that had a Puerto Rico born head was $6,000; whereas those with a mainland born head had a median income of $7,520.[96]

Puerto Ricans Living in New York State vs. Those Living in the Rest of the United States[97]

Earlier in this chapter it was pointed out that close to six out of every ten mainland Puerto Ricans live in the state of New York, and that most of these live in New York City. However, there are some significant differences between the Puerto Rican population living in New York and those living in the rest of the nation. Generally, mainland Puerto Ricans living outside of New York are more similar demographically to the United States non-Spanish white population. The Puerto Ricans living in New York tend to be poorer and more disadvantaged.

The New York Puerto Ricans tend to be somewhat older than those living in most of the other states. For instance, of the Puerto Rico born, those living in New York had a median age of 32 years in 1970; whereas those living elsewhere averaged a little over 27 years of age. This difference is probably a reflection of the fact that the migration stream to New York City is of longer duration than those to the other states. Those residing in the other states are more recent arrivals, both directly from Puerto Rico and via a step process through New York City.

The New York Puerto Ricans exhibit a 55 percent majority of females; those in the other states had a slight male majority of approximately 52 percent. The different job opportunities in New York City and the other areas where the Puerto Ricans have concentrated is probably the cause for the differences in sex composition. The job opportunities in New York City favor the employment of Puerto Rican females; whereas those in many of the other cities exhibit a slight tendency toward favoring male workers.

Puerto Rican women living in New York have lower fertility rates than those living in the other states. The difference is equivalent to about one-half child by the end of the childbearing period. The lower fertility of New York women is most likely related to the problems of poverty, scarce housing, and crime that characterize many Puerto Rican neighborhoods in New York City and make it difficult to raise children.

The Puerto Ricans living outside New York have both higher education levels and higher labor force participation rates. About 55 percent of the Puerto Rican born men in the 20 to 24 year age class, living in New York in 1970, had completed high school. The figure for the other states was 66 percent. Approximately 81 percent of all Puerto Rican men in the 20 to 64 year age group living in New York were participating in the labor force. For those living in all other states, the comparable figure was 88 percent.

A larger proportion of the New York Puerto Rican workers are employed as clerical workers and service workers; a larger share of the Puerto Rican workers living in the other states are employed in high level white collar jobs and as operatives. Primarily as a result of their more favorable occupational structure and higher education levels, the income for non-New York mainland Puerto Ricans is higher than that for the New Yorkers. In 1969, the mean family income for New York families whose heads were born on the island was $6,200, while for similar families living in all other states it was $9,600.

In summary, when New York Puerto Ricans are compared with Puerto Ricans living in other states, the former (1) are older, (2) have a higher proportion of females, (3) exhibit lower fertility rates, (4) have lower levels of achieved schooling, (5) show lower labor force participation rates, (6) exhibit lower occupational status, and (7) tend to have lower income levels. Clearly, the New York Puerto Ricans are typified by lower socioeconomic status than those living elsewhere on the mainland.

SELECTED CULTURAL CHARACTERISTICS

Although the concept of culture embraces a wide variety of learned characteristics that typify any society, this section is selective and discusses four aspects of Puerto Rican culture that are of particular importance in establishing the character of mainland Puerto Ricans. The attributes to be studied are (1) family structure, (2) religious background, (3) language problems, and (4) attitudes toward race.

Family Structure

Generally speaking, the family plays a more important role in Puerto Rican society than it does in non-Puerto Rican American society. A Puerto Rican's self-confidence, sense of security, and identity are established primarily through family relationships. In contrast to other Americans, who value an individual in terms of his/her ability to compete independently for socioeconomic status, the culture of Puerto Rico views life as a network of personal relationships. Puerto Ricans rely on and trust persons. They know that in times of trouble a close friend or relative can always be counted upon for needed assistance. A Puerto Rican relies less on impersonal secondary relationships and generally does not trust or place much faith in large organizations. Such an attitude is not unique to Puerto Ricans but is typical of most Latin American societies.

One way in which the greater emphasis that is placed on the Puerto Rican family can be illustrated is through a description of its use of surnames. English custom in United States society dictates that family names be derived patrilineally. In Puerto Rican society it is more common for a person to have two surnames, representing both the father's and mother's sides of the family. For instance, a man with the name of Ricardo Gomez Gonzales had his name derived in the following way. His given name is Ricardo and his two surnames are Gomez and Gonzales. Gomez was his father's family name and Gonzales was his mother's family name. Suppose that a woman by the name of Maria Garcia Rivera married Mr. Gomez. Her new name would be Maria Garcia de Gomez. She would retain her father's surname, drop her mother's name, and add her husband's father's name after the "de". In fact, for formal occasions, even more complicated combinations of names frequently are used.[98] To avoid confusion, many mainland Puerto Ricans have adopted the American custom of using only the surname of the father.

Another characteristic of Puerto Rican society that illustrates a reliance on personal relationships is the institution known as *compadrazgo*. It is somewhat similar to the tradition of godparents in the United States, except that it is usually taken more seriously in Puerto Rico and often involves a higher level of personal obligation. Under the *compadrazgo* system a set of *compadres* are selected for each child. These are best thought of as being "companion parents" with the child's natural parents. Sometimes they are selected at the time the parents were married, but they might also be decided upon at the time the child was baptized or perhaps confirmed as a member of the church. The *compadres* are sometimes relatives, but often they are not. If they are not blood relatives, they become de facto members of the family upon becoming *compadres*. The purpose of a *compadre* is to offer both economic and moral assistance to the family whenever it is needed. He or she may feel freer to give advice in regard to family problems than a brother or sister of the father or mother would. It is essential that *compadres* live close to the family with which they are associated so that frequent contact can be made and the necessary obligations be honored.

The type of relationship that exists between husband and wife in a traditional Puerto Rican family is very similar to that described for the Cuban family in chapter 5. Basically, the husband is considered the superior authority. He expects to be obeyed and treated with respect by his wife and children. He often makes decisions affecting the family without consulting his wife. In addition, a double standard of morality exists regarding sexual behavior. It is regarded as normal behavior for the husband to have extramarital affairs, whereas the wife is expected to remain chaste and true to her husband. These attitudes carry over into the raising of the children. Daughters are strongly encouraged to remain virgins until they marry and their fathers and brothers feel an obligation to protect them.

When dating, a "good" girl is traditionally accompanied by a chaperone. Sons, on the other hand, are accorded much more freedom to explore sexually and lead much less sheltered lives. They are imbued with the spirit of *machismo,* which is associated with sexual prowess and influence over women and a jealous guarding of a sweetheart or wife.

The traditional Puerto Rican husband and wife relationships are changing, both in Puerto Rico and on the United States mainland. In both cases the main causes of change are urbanization and the emergence of a middle class. Female entrance into the labor force is perhaps the most important component of both modernization and urbanization that has influenced a redefinition of the wife's role in family decision making. This is especially true in New York City where women often have an easier time securing employment than Puerto Rican men. In addition, the modern welfare system has made it easier for women to become less dependent economically upon their husbands.[99] Also, laws have now made it more difficult for husbands to abuse their wives and children physically as a way of ensuring their respect. In short, the Puerto Rican family appears to be evolving towards the American norm.

Considerable evidence suggests that Puerto Rican family bonds are weaker on the mainland than they are in Puerto Rico, due to the sometimes traumatic changes experienced with living in large American cities. In a study of 50 Puerto Rican families living in New York City slums conducted during the middle 1960s, it was found that the percentage of couples living in free or consensual unions and the number of women who were divorced, separated, or abandoned increased in New York when compared to families living in Puerto Rican slums.[100] In 1970 about 24 percent of all mainland Puerto Rican families were headed by a woman. For the total United States population, the figure was close to 12 percent; for residents of Puerto Rico it was about 16 percent. Commonly, families that are headed by a female are ones that have experienced some form of marital discord.[101] In 1979, the United States Census Bureau estimated that the proportion of mainland Puerto Rican households that were headed by a female, with no husband being present, had risen to 40.1 percent. As standards for comparison, the figures for all persons of Spanish origin and for Mexican-Americans were 19.8 and 15.5 percent, respectively. [102]

One way of determining the degree to which the mainland Puerto Rican family is becoming Americanized is to look at their outmarriage rates. In 1979, about 22 percent of all husbands of Puerto Rican descent living on the mainland were married to non-Puerto Rican women; and approximately 24 percent of mainland Puerto Rican wives were married to non-Puerto Rican men.[103] The slightly higher outmarriage rate for the woman is due to the fact that there are more Puerto Rican females than males living on the mainland.

Data for 1970 indicate that there is a major difference between the outmarriage rates of first and second generation mainland Puerto Ricans. For first generation Puerto Rican male migrants only 18 percent were married to non-Puerto Rican women. On the other hand, 57 percent of all second generation males had outmarried.[104] Such an intergenerational difference in outmarriage rates between first and second generations has been a common experience for most of the European immigrants who preceded the Puerto Ricans during the late 1800s and the early part of this century.

It also has been determined that there are significant differences between the outmarriage rates of second generation Puerto Ricans living in the state of New York and the rest of the country. For instance, in 1970 about one-third of the second generation Puerto Ricans living in New York were married to non-Puerto Ricans; whereas for the rest of the states the comparable proportion was about two-thirds.[105] The lower rate of outmarriage for New York's component is primarily a reflection of its large concentrated Puerto Rican population, making it easier to find a spouse of Puerto Rican descent. It may also be that there is a selective outmigration of Puerto Ricans from New York City, with the more assimilated second generation Puerto Ricans being more likely to leave the city to establish residences in other states.[106]

Religious Background[107]

Religion has played a major role historically for many immigrant groups who have migrated to the United States. The congregation or parish often became the focus of social organization and provided support and security for these people, thus easing their adjustment to American society. Unfortunately, there is considerable evidence that religion is not playing the same role for Puerto Ricans living in the United States. To understand why this is so, it is necessary to first describe the religious background in Puerto Rico. Then their experiences and adaptations on the mainland will be described.

Religion in Puerto Rico. There are three major types of religions that have evolved in Puerto Rican society and all three have been transferred to the United States mainland with modifications. These are (1) Catholicism, (2) Protestantism, and (3) spiritualism. Virtually all Puerto Ricans are, at least nominally, Christians. About 80 percent are Catholic with the remaining 20 percent being members of one of the Protestant faiths. An unknown number practice spiritualism in conjunction with either Catholicism or Protestantism.[108]

Puerto Rican Catholicism has two major characteristics that distinguish it from mainland American Catholicism: (1) a *pueblo* aspect and (2) a personal aspect. The word *pueblo* is used to refer to both a town (or city) and the people who live in it. Most settlements in Puerto Rico were established by the Spaniards according to a rigid plan that provided for a focus of activity around a central plaza. The most prominent building that faced on this plaza was the Catholic church, symbolizing the importance of the church in the social organization of the community. The entire population of the *pueblo* worshipped God in the same way. Virtually all festivals were religious events. Each town had its own patron saint and special holidays. Schools were run by the church and the local priest played a prominent role in almost all events. To be Catholic was to belong to a Catholic community, and was a community manifestation, and not a matter of personal choice as it is in mainland United States.

The personal aspect of Puerto Rican Catholicism meant that religious practice was characterized by a perceived intimate relationship between individuals and their personal saints and the Virgin Mary. They were viewed as close friends who could be counted on during times of need. They were prayed to; candles were lit for them; their likenesses were carried in parades; small shrines were built to them in the home; amulets were hung around their necks; magnetic medallions were kept in their cars; and pictures were hung in their homes and places of work. These rites could be performed apart from formal worship, and at least one observer has suggested that they would continue to be practiced even if Catholicism were to suddenly disappear.[109]

Despite these overt signs of faith, many Puerto Ricans do not adhere to all the teachings of the organized church. That is, they seldom attend mass and receive confession. Many couples live in consensual unions, rather than being married by a priest. Also, perhaps one-fourth of the women of childbearing age have been surgically sterilized, which is against the teachings of the church.[110] In many cases, Puerto Ricans have a hard time identifying with the organized structure of the Catholic church due to a number of factors. First, Catholicism has never been controlled by Puerto Ricans in Puerto Rico. During the days of Spanish rule, the majority of the priests were from Spain. Today, close to two-thirds of the clergy are from the United States mainland.[111] Second, Catholic schools usually charge tuition and are quite selective in their admission of students. This tends to limit their enrollments to students from privileged backgrounds. Most poorer children must attend public schools. Third, the church has alienated some of the population by taking an active stand against birth control through use of contraceptives, although it is less vociferous today than it was several years ago in this regard. Fourth, the official Catholic position in the 1800s was against independence from Spain and did not favor the abolition of slavery. Fifth, in 1960 the church organized a political party, called the Christian Action Party, in opposition to the island's

Popular Democratic Party, the party that had created the impressive economic and social gains since the 1940s. The church's party lost badly, receiving only about eight percent of the votes. This left Catholicism discredited not only as a political influence but also as a moral factor in public life.

Protestantism became a significant religious force in Puerto Rico after the United States took possession of it in 1898. However, of the estimated 30,000 persons that are members of these sects, only about 70,000 belong to the major faiths such as the Methodists, Baptists, and Episcopalians.[112] These three religions have become popular, through American influence, primarily among the middle classes. The rest of the Protestants belong to revivalist movements such as the Pentecostals, the Seventh Day Adventists, and other Evangelical sects. The Pentecostals have proven to be particularly popular and are found widely dispersed throughout the island. They offer group singing, emotional testimony, and also are strict regarding the use of language, tobacco and alcohol. This is truly a grass-roots religion that appeals especially to the poor. It is relatively easy to become a Pentecostal minister and to open a church. Usually they are small-scale operations which are housed in storefronts in the inner city or in small houses in the suburbs or rural areas, with thirty or forty families providing their membership.

Spiritualism is practiced by many Puerto Ricans in conjunction with the more orthodox religious practices. There are many spiritist beliefs. One is that it is possible to make contact with the spirit world and that spirits can be helpful in bringing about a desired action, such as good luck for a friend or harm for an enemy. It is also believed that the spiritualist medium has the ability to contact the dead and can analyze a client's troubles. Often psychological advice is given. Closely allied with spiritualism is the practice of using herbs, oils, potions, incense, charms, and candles in a form of folk medicine. Sometimes voodoo dolls can also be bought that are thought to possess mystical qualities. These and many more bizarre items are sold in stores called *botanicas* that are widely scattered throughout the island. Spiritualism is not only practiced by the poor and uneducated; it also has quite a following among the better educated and wealthy classes. It is treated as an insurance policy that backs up and compliments traditional religious and medical practices.

Religious Practices in the United States. Most evidence indicates that mainland Puerto Ricans are somewhat less religious than those living on the island. A study of the heads of a sample of Puerto Rican families in New York City determined that 56 percent attended church at least once a week while living in Puerto Rico; whereas only 38 percent said they attended church this often in New York.[113] One researcher estimates that about 20 percent of New York City's Puerto Ricans are practicing Catholics and that approximately 6 percent are active followers of one of the various Protestant sects. Thus, although most of the remaining 74 percent of Puerto Ricans are nominally Catholics, they are not regular practitioners of the faith.[114]

There are at least two major reasons why Catholicism is not more widely practiced regularly on the mainland. One is that it does not have the "pueblo" aspect in the states that it does in Puerto Rico. Because Puerto Ricans do not generally dominate numerically the mainland neighborhoods where they live, Catholicism (and especially their type of creole Catholicism) is not a universal focus for community organization as it is in Puerto Rico. For instance, in New York City Puerto Rican festivals do not dominate the activities of any of the city's five boroughs.

A second factor that limits the influence of the Catholic church among mainland Puerto Ricans is that they have not developed "ethnic" parishes like the southern and eastern European immigrants before them did. Instead, the Catholic church has adopted a policy of attempting to serve the religious needs of Puerto Ricans through the use of "integrated" parishes. For example, when the Italians and Irish were immigrating in large numbers to the United States the Catholic church made major efforts to import an Italian and Irish clergy to service them. Since 1939 in New York City, the policy has been to accommodate all new immigrant groups with the clergy and facilities that are already in place. One reason for this is that there were not any spare Puerto Rican priests to bring to New York City, since only one-third of the clergy on the island were natives of Puerto Rico. Also, it was found that by the third generation most persons of southern and eastern European descent no longer spoke the native language, and most had adopted American customs and were moving out of their former neighborhoods. As a result, clusters of old ethnic churches were left behind serving only a handful of members. These could be used more efficiently if they were recycled for use by the new immigrant groups. A third factor that made it inefficient to provide Puerto Ricans with their own churches was their dispersed settlement among other minorities. These other groups also have to be served, so the Catholic church tries to serve them all together. The result is that services may be conducted in several different languages. Often the services in Spanish for the Puerto Ricans are held in a basement chapel, school hall, or a small chapel soomewhere else in the parish. Thus, the Puerto Ricans do not feel that they have their own church, and the Catholic faith has not become a major force in maintaining their cultural identity while living on the mainland.

The major Protestant denominations have experienced many of the same problems as the Catholic church. A major exception, however, are the Pentecostal churches which are flourishing. One writer has estimated that perhaps as much as ten percent of all Puerto Rican families in New York City belong to, and help support, one of the Pentecostal churches.[115] They are attractive on the mainland for the same reasons that they are in Puerto Rico. In addition, because they are small-scale operations they have no trouble accommodating small clusters of Puerto Rican families. There may be several in a given neighborhood operating out of small storefront chapels. In addition, they are almost always directed by a minister who was born in Puerto Rico. Often families coming from the same town or neighborhood in Puerto Rico will attend the same chapel in New York City. Thus, the Pentecostal churches have been successful in being able to satisfy some of the needs for security and cultural maintenance that the Catholic church has been unable to provide. There is some evidence, however, that they have been more successful in this regard with respect to the first generation of Puerto Ricans. The second generation tends to gravitate back to the Catholic church and the major Protestant denominations.[116]

The folk medicine aspect of spiritualism is widely used by mainland Puerto Ricans. This is evident from the large number of *botanicas* that are found in such cities as Chicago, New York and Miami. Often they are also used by other ethnic groups, such as Cubans, Haitians, Dominicans and West Indians from the Caribbean. Although there is some use made of spiritual mediums, this does not appear to be as widespread among the mainland population as it is in Puerto Rico.

Language Problems

Almost all Puerto Ricans living on the mainland speak Spanish as their mother tongue. The 1970 census shows that slightly over 92 percent of all persons living in the United States who were of Puerto Rican descent were raised in a family where Spanish was spoken in the home. For the first generation migrants the percentage was 97 percent; whereas for those born on the mainland the figure dropped to 86 percent.[117] If the Puerto Ricans follow the intergenerational trends displayed by most prior immigrant groups, it can be expected that by the third generation Spanish will be of much less importance as both social and economic assimilation take place on the mainland.

Most mainland Puerto Ricans speak at least some English, but many of the first generation do not speak it fluently.[118] Lack of facility with English is a major barrier for the acquisition of managerial and white collar jobs. Until 1965, a literacy test in English was required before a person was allowed to register to vote in New York City, so most of those who were born in Puerto Rico could not take part in elections until then. The language problems of Puerto Ricans in schools are very serious. Millions of dollars are spent each year on bilingual programs in New York City's schools because it has been found that if students learn to read and write well in their native language, then they tend to do better in English as well. In some respects, the language problems that the migrant Puerto Rican students have are greater than was true with some of the immigrant groups who came before them. For instance, when the Italians and Jews were arriving in large numbers in New York City, it was possible for them to leave school at an earlier age, often as early as 12. The current legal requirement for school attendance until 16 years of age prolongs the problems with English usage in the schools.[119] In addition, as the occupational mix of New York City has changed, the interrelated problems of language and education make it more difficult for Puerto Ricans to compete for employment opportunities.

Speaking Spanish has become both an emotional and political issue with many Puerto Ricans. The Spanish language is considered to be one of the highest forms of expression of Puerto Rican culture. Communicating in Spanish creates a feeling of security and identity for mainland Puerto Ricans, especially for those belonging to the first generation. Darker colored Puerto Ricans will sometimes make a point of speaking in Spanish around black Americans to make certain that they are not mistaken as being blacks. When the United States took over Puerto Rico in 1898, an attempt was made to impose English as the language of instruction in the schools on the island, even though most of the teachers and students did not understand it. Two years later it was decided to use Spanish as the medium of instruction in the first eight grades and to use English from the ninth through twelfth grades. Five years later it was decided again to use English for all grades. The policy was to change back and forth several more times until 1948. In that year it was decided finally to use Spanish as the main language in the schools, with English as a required second language to be taught on a daily basis.[120] Not only was the requirement to speak English a frustrating experience but it was very much resented by many Puerto Ricans who viewed it as an attempt to destroy the island's culture. In fact, this action is frequently used as evidence by supporters of Puerto Rican independence who predict that if the island becomes the 51st American state that its distinctive culture will be lost. Militant students and independence supporters on the mainland also place a heavy emphasis on the use and retention of Spanish as a traditional mark of their identity and cause.

Attitudes Toward Race

The 1970 census of the United States indicated that 93 percent of all mainland persons of Puerto Rican descent considered themselves to be white. In 1950 the comparable figure was 92 percent. In other words, the percentage that is classified as being white among the mainland Puerto Ricans has remained fairly stable at a little over 90 percent. In 1950 about 80 percent of the population living in Puerto Rico was classified as white. It is, therefore, tempting to conclude that the migration stream to the United States has been dominated somewhat more by whites than the population in Puerto Rico. Such a statement, however, would be an oversimplification of the true racial characteristics of the Puerto Ricans living both on the mainland and in Puerto Rico. In fact, most are a mixture of black and white. As mentioned in the introduction to this chapter, Puerto Ricans range in color along a continuum from being completely white to totally black. Since so many are in between the extremes, the United States Census Bureau quit distinguishing between blacks and whites on the island after the 1950 census.

The Puerto Ricans represent the first large group of immigrants to the mainland who are largely a mixture of blacks and whites. The fact that there has been a great deal of interracial mixing among Puerto Ricans indicates that their attitudes towards social distinctions are far different from those of most Americans. To understand the reasons for this difference in attitude, it is helpful to review briefly the historical background of racial attitudes in Puerto Rico.

The Spaniards first introduced black slaves to Puerto Rico in the early 1500s. Spain had just finished expelling the dark colored Moors from the Iberian Peninsula at about the same time that Columbus set sail to discover the New World in 1492. As a result of the more than 700 year Moorish occupation of parts of Spain, the Spaniards had a long experience of living and intermarrying with dark people before they colonized Puerto Rico. Laws had been developed for the protection of slaves that were somewhat similar to today's international agreements that govern the treatment of prisoners of war.[121] Although these rules did not guarantee civil rights as they are known today, they did serve to soften somewhat the harsh treatment of the slaves in Spanish colonies. Once slavery was established in Puerto Rico it was common for white men to father children born to black women. Frequently upper class fathers would legally recognize their illegitimate children by giving their freedom at baptism. It also was common for white men to become *compadres* (godparents) for black children which, as stated earlier in this chapter, created a set of economic and social obligations that were generally taken seriously. This was a relationship which did not exist for black children on the mainland.

In 1770 the governor of Puerto Rico declared that all free children, black or white, should be educated. Once slavery was abolished in 1873, the law opened public places to all people, regardless of color. There were no separate drinking fountains, rest rooms, or rear sections of public vehicles for segregated blacks in Puerto Rico, unlike the United States at that time.[122] Still, blacks on the island have always been overrepresented among the poorer classes of Puerto Ricans. The numbing experience of slavery had deprived many of the blacks of the skills needed to compete in a free society. Nevertheless, it was not impossible for blacks to rise to prominent positions in Puerto Rican society and there are a few examples of where this happened.

It would be incorrect to assume that there is no consciousness of color among Puerto Ricans. In fact, their awareness is both more subtle and more detailed than that of most Americans. On the mainland a person is usually thought of as being either all white or all black. Rarely are the shades in between recognized. In Puerto Rico, on the other hand, there are a number of terms that have been coined in the vernacular to refer to the specific characteristics of persons of mixed origin. To Puerto Ricans living on the island, however, color is only one aspect of class. For instance, there is very little residential segregation based on race in Puerto Rico as there is on the mainland.

The degree of color prejudice that exists varies among Puerto Rico's three major classes. In the lower class, where there is the largest concentration of Negroid features, there is almost no discrimination. Negroid traits can be completely outweighed by other characteristics, such as a higher income, education, or social standing within the community. Even though there are some blacks among the upper class, they are excluded from a few elite social functions. A small number of social clubs and fraternities still exclude blacks, but most do not. In business and political offices, however, blacks are treated as equals. It is among the middle class that discrimination according to color is most overt, but again it is more subtle and less severe than on the mainland. It is undoubtedly most characteristic of this class because it is here that the people are most upwardly mobile. Although there are many exceptions, this is the Puerto Rican class that tends to be most competitive in trying to achieve higher social and economic status, and some of its members wish to grasp at any possible advantage.[123]

When Puerto Ricans move to the mainland of the United States they encounter a culture that places a greater emphasis on color. They feel an increase in social pressure for several reasons. First, they find that the intermediate categories recognized in Puerto Rico do not exist on the mainland. They will be classified in American eyes simply as being either black or white. Second, they quickly notice that being perceived as black by Americans hinders their social acceptability. Third, they soon realize that being white has many economic advantages over being black. As a result, the darker colored Puerto Ricans, especially, try to distinguish themselves from American blacks so they will be recognized as Puerto Ricans. Some emphasize speaking in Spanish; some wear different types of clothes; and some associate as little as possible with black Americans.

Generally, mainland blacks and Puerto Ricans do not care much for each other. In addition to the friction created by the obvious desire of many Puerto Ricans not to be mistaken for blacks, there has been almost every conceivable type of competition between these two minorities. They compete for the lowest paying jobs, the poorest and cheapest housing, public funding for neighborhood projects, and political power. They even compete for the time of doctors and nurses in public health clinics. Some of their youth belong to competitive gangs. Whenever possible they try to segregate themselves residentially, although (as stated earlier) this has been made difficult by scarce housing, slum clearance programs, and public housing projects.

Among themselves, most mainland Puerto Ricans appear to treat color differences much the same as they did in Puerto Rico. It is the mainland blacks whom they treat differently. A 1957 study of marriage patterns among Puerto Ricans according to color designation in New York City found that 22.6 percent were judged to be racially mixed.[124] The author of that study concluded that there is a possibility that, if this pattern continues, the racial intermingling of Puerto Ricans could hasten the integration of the entire white and black populations of those cities where they form a numerically significant minority. But will this pattern of interracial marrying continue within the mainland Puerto Rican population? The answer is uncertain. Some scholars predict that within a generation or two persons of Puerto Rican descent will split into two groups. One will assimilate with white Americans and the other will identify with American blacks. They base this on historical evidence that the children and grandchildren of West Indian blacks who have moved to large American cities have married mostly American blacks.

CONCLUSIONS

The well-known anthropologist, Oscar Lewis, has described most Puerto Ricans as living in a culture of poverty. Many of his generalizations provide a good summary of what has been said in this chapter.[125] The culture of poverty is not uniquely characteristic of Puerto Ricans because it cuts across ethnic and international boundaries. Still, not all poor people are characterized by the culture of poverty, although being poor is one of its requirements. Lewis suggests that only about 20 percent of the people who lived below the poverty level in the United States in 1965 could properly be said to be living in the culture of poverty. In this category he placed many of this country's poor blacks, Mexican-Americans, Indians, and some Southern poor whites, in addition to Puerto Ricans.

Lewis calls his concept the "culture of poverty" because it can be passed between generations and the people who belong to it possess a set of recognizable characteristics. Groups that are represented by the culture of poverty lack effective participation and integration in the major institutions of the larger society in which they live. This results from a variety of factors that lessen the group's power such as lack of economic resources, discrimination, segregaton and isolation, and the development of local temporary solutions for problems. These are all characteristics of many of the poorer Puerto Ricans. They have low voter registration levels on the mainland and often do not participate in elections as an effective voting black. Although a large share of Puerto Rican workers are members of labor unions, they have been effectively barred from management positions and are generally poorly represented in the union hierarchies.

At the local neighborhood or community level, the culture of poverty is characterized by a minimum level of organization. The focus tends to be on the nuclear and extended family. Occasionally there are some informal (usually temporary) organizations that emerge, such as youth gangs. More often, however, there are few secondary group associations that are specifically designed to promote the members' self interest. For instance, although there are some exceptions, mainland Puerto Rican parents have exhibited low levels of participation at school PTA meetings. The tendency to change residences is frequently one of the major factors that limit group organization in Puerto Rican neighborhoods. The 1970 census indicates that only 32.7 percent of all mainland Puerto Ricans five years of age or older were living in the same house in 1970 and in 1965.[126]

On the family level, free or consensual unions are common and illegitimacy rates are often high. It has been estimated that in the early 1970s more than one-quarter of all mainland Puerto Rican unions were of the consensual type.[127] In 1977 about 48 percent of all live births to Puerto Ricans living in New York City were to women who were not married.[128] In the culture of poverty, free unions often make a lot of sense. Many Puerto Rican women feel that a consensual union gives them a better break because it provides them with some of the freedom that men have under the double standard that typifies many Latin marriages. By not giving the fathers of their children legal status as husbands, they have stronger claim on their children should they decide to leave their mates. It also gives women exclusive rights to any property they may own.[129]

At the level of the individual the culture of poverty is characterized by a feeling of marginality, dependence, and frequently fatalistic outlook. A feeling prevails among these people that there is little hope for changing things in their favor. They tend to live for the present and often make little effort to plan for the future. They are quite parochial in their outlook in that they have little knowledge of most areas outside their neighborhoods. The mainland Puerto Ricans may be somewhat of an exception to this latter point because of their ties with their homeland in Puerto Rico.

There are many mainland Puerto Ricans who have been able to escape the culture of poverty but there is no doubt that there are at least as many who still live in it. In most cities where they live in sizable concentrations they vie with American blacks for the lowest socioeconomic levels. Even though the second generation Puerto Ricans are generally better off than their immigrant parents, they still are typified by lower than average standards of living.

There are at least four major factors that have served as major deterrents to the rapid assimilation of Puerto Ricans into dominant American society. One is their notable concentration in the New York Metropolitan Area, and in *colonias* in other cities, which makes it easier for them to associate with fellow Puerto Ricans and thus have less contact with Anglos. Second, the cultural infusion that they receive from the continued influx of migrants from Puerto Rico also allows them to maintain their cultural ties longer than they might otherwise have. Third, the fact that Puerto Rico has legal status within the jurisdiction of the United States makes it easier to keep contact with Puerto Rico for return visits and facilitate arrangements to have relatives and friends follow in the stream to the mainland. A fourth factor that has slowed the assimilation of many Puerto Ricans is their mixed racial lineage.[130] Some researchers have predicted that those who are intermediate in color will have the most difficult time assimilating because they will find it hard to be accepted by either white or black Americans.

Although Puerto Ricans have not moved as rapidly into the mainstream of American society as Cuban-Americans have, there is little doubt that they will do so sometime within the next two or three generations. Furthermore, the Cubans who migrated during the 1960s were much more positively selected than the Puerto Rican migrants, in terms of their education, income, and skill levels. Thus, the Cubans were able to establish an economic enclave and numerical dominance in Miami that helped to absorb future waves of Cuban immigrants. Given their fewer economic resources and the changing occupation and housing conditions of New York City, Puerto Ricans do not have a chance to develop as rapidly. Nevertheless, there should be no doubt that they will soon enter the mainstream of American society, although it is going to take a little longer than it did for the Cubans and some other immigrant groups.

NOTES

1. United States Bureau of the Census, *Current Population Reports,* Series P-20, No. 361, "Persons of Spanish Origin in the United States: March 1980 (Advance Report)," May, 1981 (Washington, D.C.: U.S. Government Printing Office, 1981):p. 5.

2. U. S. Bureau of the Census, *1980 Census of Population and Housing,* PHC80–P-53, "Puerto Rico (Preliminary Reports)," February, 1981 (Washington, D.C.: U.S. Government Printing Office, 1981): p. 2.

3. The Cuban population living in the United States also contains very few illegal aliens. However, Cuban-Americans are exceptional because the United States Immigration and Naturalization Service has, until recently, accorded them special immigration privileges as a result of the Communist take-over in Cuba. For further information on this topic see the chapter on Cuban-Americans in this book.

4. Joseph P. Fitzpatrick, *Puerto Rican Americans: The Meaning of Migration to the Mainland* (Englewood Cliffs, New Jersey: Prentice-Hall, Inc., 1971): pp. 101–114.

5. Joseph P. Fitzpatrick, "Puerto Ricans in Perspective: The Meaning of Migration to the Mainland," *International Migration Review,* 2 (Spring, 1968): pp. 7–19.

6. Clarence Senior, *Our Citizens from the Caribbean* (New York: McGraw-Hill, 1965): p. 90–91.

7. Nathan Glazer and Daniel P. Moynihan, *Beyond the Melting Pot* (Cambridge, Massachusetts: The M.I.T. Press, 1970): pp. 109–110.

8. Fitzpatrick, 1968: p. 9.

9. The 1970 Population Census indicates that 54.8 percent of all Puerto Ricans living in the United States at that time were born in Puerto Rico. The United States Bureau of the Census, *Census of Population: 1970,* Subject reports, Final Report PC(2)-1C, "Persons of Spanish Origin" (Washington, D.C.: U.S. Government Printing Office, 1973): p. 46.

10. Kal Wagenheim, *Puerto Rico: A Profile* (New York: Praeger Publishers, 1975): pp. 23–24.

11. The Greater Antilles include the islands of Cuban, Hispaniola (which contains both Haiti and the Dominican Republic), Jamaica, and Puerto Rico.

12. The best description of Puerto Rico's topography is found in Rafael Pico, *The Geography of Puerto Rico* (Chicago: Aldine Publishing Comapny, 1974): pp. 25–79.

13. The best description of Puerto Rico's climate characteristics is found in Pico, 1974: pp. 143–176.

14. U.S. Bureau of the Census, 1981: p. 11.

15. *1982 World Population Data Sheet* (Washington, D.C.: Population Reference Bureau, Inc., 1982).

16. Pico, 1974: p. 223.

17. Wagenheim, 1975: pp. 37–40 and 160–162.

18. Joseph P. Fitzpatrick, "Puerto Ricans," in *The Harvard Encyclopedia of American Ethnic Groups,* ed. Stephen Thernstrom (Cambridge: The Belknap Press of Harvard University Press, 1980): p. 859.

19. *Puerto Ricans in the Continental United States: An Uncertain Future* (Washington, D.C.: United States Commission on Civil Rights, 1976): p. 12.

20. Only 288 Puerto Ricans chose not to become citizens of the United States. Clarence Senior, *Our Citizens from the Caribbean* (New York: McGraw-Hill Book Company, 1965): p. 16.

21. One exception to the free movement of goods between the United States and Puerto Rico is rum, which is subject to an import tax when sent from the island to the mainland. However, the funds thus derived are returned to the Puerto Rican Treasury to be spent on island development projects.

22. Fitzpatrick, 1971: p. 46.

23. For figures on the number of Puerto Rican votes cast for each of the political parties in Puerto Rico between 1948 and 1972 see: United States Commission on Civil Rights, 1976, in footnote 19: p. 14.

24. United States Commission on Civil Rights, 1976, in footnote 19: p. 15.

25. A. J. Jaffe, *People, Jobs and Economic Development* (Glencoe, Illinois: The Free Press, 1959): pp. 29–31 and 277–286.

16. Wagenheim, 1975: p. 106.

27. United States Commission on Civil Rights, 1976, in footnote 19: p. 16.

28. Wagenheim, 1975: p. 102.

29. Ibid: p. 6.

30. Adalberto Lopez, "The Puerto Rican Diaspora: A Survey," in *Puerto Rico and Puerto Ricans,* eds. Adalberto Lopez and James Petras (New York: John Wiley, 1974): p. 316.

31. Senior, 1965: p. 77.

32. United States Commission on Civil Rights, 1976, in footnote 19: p. 26.

33. Senior, 1965: p. 76.

34. When Puerto Ricans are asked why they migrated or planned to move, the vast majority usually respond that they were influenced by economic opportunities. For instance, see: (1) C. Wright Mills, Clarence Senior and Rose Kohn Goldsen, *The Puerto Rican Journey: New York's Newest Migrants* (New York: Harper and Brothers Publishers, 1950): p. 49–50; and (2) Jose Hernandez-Alvarez, *Return Migration to Puerto Rico* (Berkeley: Institute of International Studies, Population Monograph Series, No. 1, University of California, 1967): p. 91. Several studies that have scientifically investigated the specific economic factors influencing Puerto Rican migration to the United States tend to stress either unemployment or income differentials between the island and mainland. For instance, Fleisher and Maldonado have found the unemployment variable to be most important; whereas Friedlander and Galloway and Vedder place their emphasis on income: (1) Belton Fleisher, "Some Economic Aspects of Puerto Rican Migration to the United States," *Review of Economic and Statistics,* 45 (August, 1962): pp. 245–153; (2) Rita M. Maldonado, "Why Puerto Ricans Migrated to the United States in 1947–73," *Monthly Labor Review,* 99 (September, 1976): pp. 7–18; (3) Stanley L. Friedlander, *Labor Migration and Economic Growth* (Cambridge, Massachusetts: The M.I.T. Press, 1965): pp. 125–128; and (4) Lowell E. Gallaway and Richard K. Vedder, "Location Decisions of Puerto Rican Immigrants to the United States," *Social and Economic Studies,* 20 (June, 1971): pp. 188–197.

35. Friedlander lists these three reasons, plus a fourth. The latter was a reduction in the disguised unemployment rate in Puerto Rico, but this no longer appears to be true because of the island's current high rate of unemployment: Friedlander, footnote 34: p. 160.
36. Wagenheim, 1975: p. 5.
37. Nathan Kantrowitz, "Social Mobility of Puerto Ricans: Education, Occupation, and Income Changes Among Children of Migrants, 1950–1960," *International Migration Review,* 2 (Spring, 1968): pp. 53–71.
38. Mills, Senior and Goldsen, 1950, in footnote 34: p. 47.
39. George C. Myers and George Masnick, "The Experiences of New York Puerto Ricans: A Perspective on Return," *International Migration Review,* 2 (Spring, 1968): pp. 81–82.
40. Hernandez-Alvarez, 1967, footnote 34: pp. 15–17.
41. This figure was quoted in Fitzpatrick, 1980,: p. 860.
42. Maldonado, 1976, in footnote 34: p. 13.
43. Myers and Masinick, 1968: p. 80.
44. Jose Hernandez-Alvarez, "Migration, Return, and Development in Puerto Rico," *Economic Development and Cultural Change,* 16 (July, 1968): p. 575.
45. Hernandez-Alvarez, 1967, footnote 34: p. 23.
46. Ibid. pp. 28–29 and 40.
47. Maldonado, 1976, footnote 34: p. 13.
48. Myers and Masnick, 1968: p. 88.
49. Maldonado, 1976, footnote 34: p. 13.
50. The data to be used were derived from a special set of custom cross tabulations performed on the 1960 census results by the United States Census Bureau and are available in: Hernandez-Alvarez, footnotes 34 and 44, various pages.
51. Thomas D. Boswell, "Inferences Concerning Intermunicipio Migrations in Puerto Rico: 1955–1960," *The Journal of Tropical Geography,* 45 (December, 1977): p. 3.
52. Mills, Senior, and Goldsen, 1950, footnote 34: p. 33.
53. Wiliam D. Mosher, "The Theory of Change and Response: An Application to Puerto Rico, 1940 to 1970," *Population Studies,* 34 (March, 1980): p. 50.
54. Friedlander, 1965, footnote 34: pp. 28–30.
55. United States Commission on Civil Rights, footnote 19: p. 57; and Terry J. Rosenberg, *Residence, Employment and Mobility of Puerto Ricans in New York City* (Chicago: University of Chicago, Department of Geography, Research Paper No. 151, 1974): pp. 202–203.
56. Hernandez-Alvarez, 1968: p. 576.
57. Ibid: p. 576.
58. Friedlander, 1965, footnote 34: pp. 56–59.
59. Hernandez-Alvarez, 1967 footnote 34: pp. 27–28.
60. Ibid. p. 42.
61. Most of the information in this section comes from the following source: Eva E. Sandis, "Characteristics of Puerto Rican Migrants to, and from, the United States," *International Migration Review,* 4 (Spring, 1970): pp. 22–43.
62. Sandis, 1970: p. 36.
63. Fitzpatrick, 1971: pp. 15–19.
64. United States Commission on Civil Rights, footnote 19: p. 5.
65. Fitzpatrick, 1971: p. 17; and for a more detailed discussion of the relationships between contract labor and Puerto Rican communities in the United States see: Edwin Maldonado, "Contract Labor and the Origins of Puerto Rican Communities in the United States," *International Migration Review,* 8 (Spring, 1979: pp. 103–121.
66. Ibid: pp. 18–19.
67. Myers and Masnick, 1968: p. 84.
68. Friedlander, 1965, footnote 34: pp. 157–166.
69. United States Bureau of the Census, 1981, footnote 1: p. 5.
70. Gallaway and Vedder, 1971, footnote 34: pp. 193–197.
71. United States Bureau of the Census, *Census of Population: 1950,* Special Reports, Vol. IV, Part 3, Chapter D, "Puerto Ricans in Continental United States" (Washington, D.C.: U.S. Government Printing Office, 1953): p. 30–4.
72. Fitzpatrick, 1971: pp. 53–55.
73. Rosenberg, 1974, footnote 55: p. 47.
74. Robert T. Novak, "Distribution of Puerto Ricans on Manhattan Island," *Geographical Review,* 46 (April, 1956): pp. 182–186.
75. United States Commission on Civil Rights, footnote 19: p. 21.
76. J. Hernandez-Alvarez, "The Movement and Settlement of Puerto Rican Migrants Within the United States, 1950–1960," *International Migration Review,* 2 (Spring, 1968): pp. 40–51.
77. Jose Oscar Alers, *Puerto Ricans and Health: Findings from New York City* (New York: Hispanic Research Center, Monograph No. 4, Fordham University, 1978): p. 2.
78. Fitzpatrick, 1971: pp. 70–71.
79. Thomas D. Boswell, "Residential Patterns of Puerto Ricans in New York City," *Geographical Review,* 66 (January, 1976): pp. 92–94.
80. Nathan Kantrowitz, *Negro and Puerto Rican Populations of New York City in the Twentieth Century* (New York: American Geographical Society, Studies in Urban Geography, No. 1, 1969): p. 1.
81. Kantrowitz, 1969, plate 4.
82. Glazer and Moynihan, 1970: pp. 94–95.
83. Nathan Kantrowitz, *Ethnic and Racial Segregation in the New York Metropolis: Residential Patterns Among White Ethnic Groups, Blacks, and Puerto Ricans* (New York: Praeger Publishers, 1973): pp. 42, 48 and 52–53.

84. This same pattern of segregation, according to socioeconomic status, has been noted among the Cubans living in Miami, see chapter 5.
85. United States Bureau of the Census, 1981, footnote 1: p. 5.
86. A. J. Jaffe, Ruth M. Cullen and Thomas D. Boswell, *The Changing Demography of Spanish Americans* (New York: Academic Press, 1980): pp. 192–194.
87. United States Bureau of the Census, *Current Population Reports,* Series P-20, No. 354, "Persons of Spanish Origin in the United States: March, 1979" (Washington, D.C.: U.S. Government Printing Office, 1980): p. 5.
88. Stephanie J. Ventura, "Births of Hispanic Parentage: 1979," *Monthly Vital Statistics Report,* National Center for Health Statistics, Vol. 31, No. 2, Supplement, May 13, 1982, Public Health Service, Hyattsville, Maryland: p. 7.
89. Ronald R. Rindfuss, "Fertility and Migration: The Case of Puerto Rico," *International Migration Review,* 10 (Summer, 1976): pp. 191–203.
90. A. J. Jaffe and Ruth M. Cullen, "Fertility of the Puerto Rican Origin Population—Mainland United States and Puerto Rico: 1970," *International Migration Review,* 9 (Summer, 1975): pp. 193–209.
91. Mills, Senior, and Goldsen, 1950, footnote 34: pp. 68–73.
92. United States Bureau of the Census, footnote 1: p. 5.
93. Wagenheim, 1975: p. 200.
94. United States Bureau of the Census, 1981, footnote 1: p. 5.
95. United Sttes Bureau of the Census, 1980, footnote 87: p. 10.
96. Jaffe, Cullen and Boswell, 1980: pp. 21, 201, 214 and 222.
97. The information for this section came from :Jaffee, Cullen, and Boswell, 1980: pp. 228–238.
98. Fitzpatrick, 1971: pp. 78–80.
99. In 1970, 32.4 percent of all mainland Puerto Rican families were receiving either social security income (8.1 percent) or some form of public assistance or welfare income (24.3 percent.) United States Bureau of the Census, 1973, footnote 9: p. 135.
100. Oscar Lewis, *La Vida* (New York: Random House, 1966): pp. xxxviii-xxxix.
101. Karl Wagenheim, *A Survey of Puerto Ricans on the U.S. Mainland in the 1970's* (New York: Praeger Publishers, 1975): pp. 12–13 and 76–77.
102. United States Bureau of the Census, 1980, footnote 87: p. 41.
103. Ibid.: p. 44.
104. Joseph P. Fitzpatrick and Douglas T. Gurak, *Hispanic Intermarriage in New York City: 1975* (New York: Hispanic Research Center, Monograph No. 2, Fordham University, 1979): p. 6.
105. Jaffe, Cullen and Boswell, 1980: p. 232.
106. Fitzpatrick and Gurak, 1979: pp. 86–88.
107. Much of the information for this section comes from: Fitzpatrick, 1971: pp. 115–129.
108. Wagenheim, 1975: p. 164.
109. Fitzpatrick, 1980: p. 865.
110. Wagenheim, 1975: p. 175.
111. Fitzpatrick, 1980: p. 865.
112. Wagenheim, 1975: p. 167.
113. Lewis, 1966: p. 196.
114. Fitzpatrick, 1971: p. 128.
115. Wagenheim, 1975: p. 168.
116. Fitzpatrick, 1971: p. 129.
117. United States Bureau of the Census, *Census of Population: 1970,* Subject Reports, Final Report PC(2)-1E, "Puerto Ricans in the United States" (Washington, D.C.: U.S. Government Printing Office, 1973): p. 32.
118. Lewis, 1966: pp. 185–191.
119. Fitzpatrick, 1971: p. 142.
120. It has been estimated that about 45 percent of all Puerto Ricans living on the island can at least understand some English, even though they may not be comfortable or fluent speaking it. Wagenheim, 1975: pp. 170–173 and 213.
121. Fitzpatrick, 1971: p. 104.
122. Wagenheim, 1975: p. 162.
123. Sidney W. Mintz, "Puerto Rico: An Essay in the Definition of National Culture," in *The Puerto Rican Experience,* eds. Francesco Cordasco and Eugene Bucchioni (Totowa, New Jersey: Littlefield, Adams and Co., 1975): pp. 56–59.
124. Fitzpatrick, 1971: pp. 111–112.
125. Lewis, 1966: p. xlii-lii.
126. United States Bureau of the Census, 1973, footnote 117: p. 39.
127. Glazer and Moynihan, 1970: p. 89.
128. Ian A. Canino, Brian F. Earley and Lloyd H. Rogler, *The Puerto Rican Child in New York City: Stress and Mental Health* (New York: Hispanic Research Center, Monograph No. 4, Fordham University, 1980): p. 41.
129. Lewis, 1966: p. xlvi.
130. Jaffe, Cullen and Boswell, 1980: p. 18–20.

7

American Jewish Ethnicity

Jonathan S. Mesinger
University of Cincinnati

Ary J. Lamme III
University of Florida

THE MEANING OF JEWISH ETHNICITY

Like other ethnic groups in the United States, Jewish Americans are a diverse people with a wide range of socioeconomic characteristics, ancestral places of origin, degrees of acculturation or ethnic maintenance, and patterns of settlement. Even within the realm of religion, ostensibly the cement that holds the ethnic group together, Jews have evolved a rich variety of practices. This diversity suggests two questions which need to be confronted before examining the American Jewish community: (1) How is the ethnic group defined by individual Jews, the Jewish community, and by outsiders; and (2) what does it mean to be a Jew in America?

The role of religion in the life of a Jewish person has varied with the time and place in which the person lived. For some Jews coming to America from Germany in the early nineteenth century, cultural distinctiveness rapidly disintegrated, leaving them with only a Jewish religious identity. They saw themselves as a "community of Americans differing from other Americans in little but religion."[1] For the more Orthodox German Jews and for later immigrants from Eastern Europe, religion and daily life were more closely integrated. In the Jewish small town (stetl) or urban ghetto in Eastern Europe, Jewishness was a way of life—a complex of cultural values and customs, many of which had their origins in religious practices. Clearly, this Jewish lifestyle was different from that of the surrounding society, and Jews were not distinguished solely by their religious affiliation. A few American Jews have succeeded in maintaining parts of that traditional way of life, despite the pressures of acculturation and without the "protection" of enforced ethnic segregation. In twentieth-century America however, with increasing secularization and a blending of many different Jewish cultural threads, being Jewish has taken on new

meaning. For most Jews, secularization has meant a separation of religion and other aspects of life. For some, who otherwise view themselves as typical Americans, religion once more is the central focus of their Jewishness. For others who are not religiously observant, some other aspect of Jewish ethnicity must be the key to their sense of belonging to the group. However, it has also been said that ". . . a religiously inactive person is . . . identified as Jewish by the following rule of thumb: the religion he does not practice is Judaism rather than Christianity."[2]

Although the Jewish religion only partially explains Jewish ethnicity and, although the degree of observance of religious ritual and affiliation with formal religious institutions vary considerably among American Jews, religion continues to be viewed by many as the essence of Jewish identity. References to "Protestant, Catholic, and Jew" or the "National Conference of Christians and Jews," reflect the labelling of Jews as a religious category. However, if Jewish religious adherence is a necessary condition for Jewishness, many people who consider themselves American Jews would have to be excluded from the ethnic group.

Ethnicity and Association

How can a Jewish ethnicity which encompasses more than a religious definition be understood? The answer may be that, as a result of acculturation over a period of generations, the emphasis in Jewish ethnic identity has shifted from Jewish religion to association patterns, which reinforce a "recognition for the legitimacy of ethnic group separateness."[3] In other words, being an American Jew may be more a matter of choosing to associate with certain institutions or with a Jewish community, than sharing certain characteristics or observing particular customs. The important thing is perhaps the sense of belonging, even if the basis for that feeling is ambiguous.

For other Euro-American ethnic groups, this sense of belonging frequently is rooted in the ancestral place of origin. Even if a surname of a few family recipes are the only tangible remnants of an ethnic past, attachment to a home country seems to provide a focus for ethnic association for some time after the immigrant generation is gone. But, Jewish immigrants arriving in the United States came from many different countries and regions including various German states, England, France, Holland, Poland, the Austro-Hungarian Empire and the Russian Empire. In those places they rarely enjoyed the full privileges of citizenship. Jews living in different regions of the continent also developed distinct variations in customs in response to local opportunities and circumstances. This meant that whereas the ancient historical and religious heritage was shared by Jews in all parts of Europe, several different "Jewries" developed with their own dialects and rituals, as well as different economic, political, and social experiences. As a result, many Jews coming to America initially associated with specific regional-origin Jewish ethnic communities, while still being loosely identified with the broader ethnic group. Such distinctions within the ethnic group eroded only very gradually, as the second and third generations experienced the evolution of a new, hybrid ethnicity—"American Judaism."[4]

Ethnicity and Jewish Religion

Late twentieth-century American Judaism brings together traditions from many different European heritages, but it is also a response to the specific conditions of a pluralistic, modern, dynamic American society. The ethnic group is by no means monolithic. Within the Jewish community one can find three major and a number of minor forms of religious observance, rich people and poor people, political liberalism and political conservatism, urban, surburban and small town lifestyles, and new immigrants as well as generations-old American families.

Perhaps the most critical distinction among American Jews today has to do with the balance between religious tradition and secular modernism. In the United States one can find the full range of Jewish religious behavior from a strict adherence to the traditional modes, called Orthodoxy, to a total abandonment of religious practice per se. It has been estimated that only about half the Jewish population is affiliated with any religious congregation, although this is considerably more than the one-third estimated for 1930.[5] The remainder may include some who observe religious rituals sporadically, but many probably share a Jewish ethnicity which is devoid of specifically religious content. The three main versions of American Jewish religion—Orthodox, Conservative, and Reform—have institutionalized certain forms of ritual observance and theology. They have as their adherents, however, people

who practice their religion at a personal level with many different styles and intensities. Of those who are synagogue-affiliated, perhaps fifteen per cent attend religious services regularly. They traverse the spectrum from the more "traditional" congregations to the more "modern."

The Orthodox end of this spectrum of religious practice may contain between ten and twenty percent of the synagogue-affiliated American Jews.[6] Some people in this group belong to Orthodox sectarian communities, like the Hasidic group in New York and elsewhere, in which attempts are made to preserve a way of life transplanted from Europe. For them religious practice and other daily activities are most strongly integrated, making it important for them to live in small, self-contained, largely urban communities. Even within these communities, some people venture into the modern secular world to earn a living. Other Orthodox Jews participate in this secular milieu to a greater extent, but continue to lead a traditional lifestyle based on religious observance at home and in the synagogue. Still more Jews who are affiliated with Orthodox congregations do not observe traditional rituals with total regularity and lead lives in which religion is not an integral part of daily life.

About one-third of the synagogue-affiliated population are Reform Jews, part of a movement which had its roots in Germany, but flourished in America beginning in the mid-nineteenth century.[7] The Reform movement, during its history, has attempted to reconcile traditional Jewish values and religious observance with a modern and changing secular reality. This has led to alterations in the form of religious ritual, such as increasing use of the vernacular (English) in place of the customary Hebrew, as well as much deeper departures from traditional religious thought and Jewish law. The trend toward secularization and abandonment of rituals within Reform Judaism peaked in the late nineteenth century, at a point where it appeared to some to be only nominally Jewish. Even then, however, ". . . it could also be seen that the members of the dignified Reform congregations, in which the ministers spoke of a universal religion and social justice, were still made up largely of Jews who had no intention of being anything else . . ."[8] Since that time, Reform Judaism has become considerably less radical in its break with religious custom, has returned to a more mainstream Jewish position, and has developed its own traditions and a large following.

In reaction to the Reform movement during its most radical phase, a group of rabbis began to organize yet a third major stream within American Judaism. Conservative Judaism, which actually was not firmly established until the twentieth century has grown to be the largest of these streams. As many as forty percent of religiously observant Jews belong to this branch of the Jewish religion.[9] Unlike the Reform movement, which had its foundation in the old German-Jewish congregations and its focus in Cincinnati's Hebrew Union College, Conservative Judaism centered on the Jewish Theological Seminary in New York City and drew its main strength from the massive Eastern European Jewish population which resided there. Many of these people found Orthodoxy too severe and unresponsive to their new American environment. They also found Reform too "unJewish" or "distant from anything they knew as Jewish." Thus Conservatism has taken a middle course between the two, offering a more traditional Judaism than Reform in a more modern context than Orthodoxy.

For many American Jews, perhaps even the majority, identification with one of these denominations is not essential to their ethnicity. They are the secular, or non-religious Jews, whose Jewishness may be manifested by membership in non-religious Jewish organizations (community centers, charitable organizations, clubs), social networks consisting of Jewish friends, or occasional observance of traditional practices for non-religious reasons. These are frequently the Jews who are the most difficult to identify. Because of the customary methods of calculating Jewish population, through synagogue membership and charitable contribution lists, it is the presence of this large body of non-synagogue-affiliated Jews that renders most of the available statistical information on American Jews unreliable. Nevertheless, this information is useful for reconstructing the historical geography of the American Jewish ethnic group and assessing its character and situation in the late twentieth century.

THREE CENTURIES OF JEWISH IMMIGRATION AND SETTLEMENT

Colonial Immigration and the Early Community

The spatial patterns of Jewish settlement in the United States from colonial times until after the Civil War were strongly influenced by three factors. (1) Changing social environments in Europe; (2) Evolving settlement patterns in North America: and (3) The communal and economic institutions that Jews established in the new world.

Although there may have been individual Jews in North America from the earliest days of exploration, the first group intent on establishing a community arrived in the Dutch colony of New Netherlands in 1654. Most scholars believe that this group of 23 settlers came from Brazil. The stimulus for this movement and for the immigration of others who followed shortly can be found in European social history.

Jews had gone through periods of persecution in Europe ever since they had dispersed in large numbers from their Palestinian homeland in the Middle East.

Jews who found their way to North America came from two different European traditions. The settlers from Brazil were Sephardim, whose ancestors had lived in the Iberian peninsula. Under the Moors they had flourished for over 500 years, but conditions deteriorated as Christian rulers took over in the 1400s, culminating in 1492 with a royal edict that forced Jews either to convert or leave.

The building of colonial empires, the Protestant Reformation, new political ideas, the emerging foundations of industrialism, and the development of modern science made 16th and 17th century Northwestern Europe an exciting place. Jews from Central Europe, with a tradition of hard work and commercial experience, found places to live and opportunities for making a living. Some locations were better than others. The Netherlands, with its cosmopolitan traditions, and expanding significance as a trade center, developed as one of the favored locations. Jews settled in Holland, and some traveled with Dutch colonizers. It was a small group of Jews who had gone with the Dutch to Brazil. They left when the Portuguese took over, and arrived in New Amsterdam in 1654.

In the Europe of 1600, there were estimated to have been three quarters of a million Jews.[10] About 500,000 were found in Eastern Europe centered in the Jewish community in Poland. The rest were scattered in Central and Western Europe, and in North Africa and Asia. During this period of continental ferment, living conditions for Jews were constantly changing. Certain times and places would allow considerable freedom and opportunity, only to change dramatically after a war or a shift of position by a royal house. Jews learned to adjust, to be conspicuous, and to move. In Europe they were not allowed to own land in many countries, so few became farmers. Prohibitions on money lending by Christians to fellow Christians presented an economic opportunity to some Jews. Guilds often restricted their membership, but crafts could be carried on in homes and products peddled from door to door. Some managed to do well in business, so that as stock holders in the Dutch West India Company they could prevent the colonial governor in New Amsterdam from expelling Jewish settlers. Clearly life for a Jew in Europe was not easy and some chose to come to the New World which was characterized by a combination of religious tolerance and economic freedom.[11]

Most of the earliest Jews who came to the American colonies arrived from the Netherlands and were of the Sephardic tradition. Most were involved in commercial activity. They were well educated for the day, and were strict in terms of their religious observance. As members of a prosperous middle class they became involved in the life of the host community. A general pattern of acculturation emerged in relation to the dominant Anglo-American group. Colonial Jews never constituted more than one tenth of one percent of the colonial population of North America.[12] By 1700, they are estimated to have numbered 250, a number which increased to 2500 by the time of the American revolution.[13]

During the colonial era the population of North America was mostly confined east of the Appalachian Highlands. While one can assume that some Jews were found in the settled interior regions, most were located in coastal cities that served as centers of colonial economic and social life. Five congregations, all of the Sephardic tradition, were founded during the colonial era.[14] They were at New Amsterdam (1656), Newport Rhode Island, (temporarily in 1678 and permanently in the 1750s), Savannah (1733), Philadelphia (1745), and Charleston (1750).[15]

During the early 18th century, Jews of German and Polish ancestry began arriving in North America. These Ashkenazic Jews employed different liturgical forms than the Sephardim. By the end of the colonial era, Ashkenazim outnumbered Sephardim. In spite of that, there was a notable lack of schism in the religious community. The Ashkenazim joined the Sephardic congregations. It may have been that since they were such a small minority, theological divisions among Jews didn't make much sense. In addition, while most Jews were observant, acculturation tended to obscure the ritualistic differences among them. In any case, the five colonial congregations continued to employ the Sephardic rites.

There were no ordained rabbis in colonial America, but there were professional cantors who functioned as rabbis. Although they were observant, one does not get much sense of religious vigor among colonial Jews, at least in comparison to their ethnic and economic vitality. By 1740 Jews had acquired the civil rights enjoyed by all the citizens of British North America, but few political rights.[16] They did not abandon their heritage, but as successful shopkeepers and merchants they filled an important niche in the economic life of the colonies.

The German Jews in America

Although social conditions in Europe gradually improved in the 18th century, liberal reforms to protect groups such as Jews were not consistently or universally established. The end of the Napoleonic era in the early 19th century saw things get worse for Jews in many areas, particularly Germany.[17] Typical discriminatory laws against Jews, such as those in Bavaria, included heavy taxes, denial of citizenship, controls on business and travel, and restriction of the right to marry.[18] These conditions prompted large numbers of Jews from Germany and Poland to emigrate to the United States. In addition to Bavaria many came from Baden, Württemberg and Posen in Prussian Poland. One hundred years after the revolution American Jews

numbered approximately 250,000.[19] Most of this growth was attributable to immigration of Ashkenazim in the last 60 years of that period.[20]

Settling the Interior. By the end of the 18th century Americans were free to attempt a national movement to the West. From the Great Lakes to the Gulf of Mexico people headed for newly opened lands.[21] Initially settlers moved into the Ohio River Valley and the basins of Kentucky and Tennessee. Transportation availability played an important role as movement along trails changed to turnpikes, canals and railroads. Of particular importance to Jewish settlement was the development of canal and rail connections to the towns and cities of the Upper Midwest during the second quarter of the 19th century. The new cities there and the older cities of the Ohio Valley received increasing numbers of Jewish settlers, many of whom had recently arrived as part of a larger wave of German Jewish immigrants.

By 1880 the Jewish population of the United States was concentrated in over 300 different congregations (Fig. 7.1). These congregations were found in urban areas from coast to coast. As one might expect, heavier concentrations of Jews were found in the industrialized and urbanized Northeast quadrant of the country. However, outlying communities were found in all sections, especially the South. Some Jews lived in smaller communities within the hinterlands of larger places. They might not have organized congregations, but could travel to larger urban places for religious celebrations. The Jewish population of the United States was well situated in relation to the transportation system of 1880, a factor which played an important role in nineteenth century Jewish economic life.

The Syracuse Community. It is instructive to review patterns of Jewish settlement at the local level. Syracuse, New York, typifies the pattern of Jewish settlement in the third quarter of the 19th century. By 1880, Syracuse was a well established city along the Hudson-Mohawk-Ontario lowland route to the Midwest, but canal transportation in the 1820 to 1840 period had yielded to railroads. The city had a relatively large hinterland northward along the western edge of the Adirondacks and the St. Lawrence River as well as southward toward the southern tier of counties.

By 1880, the Jewish community of Syracuse was well established.[22] German immigrants to the United States settled in Syracuse while the city was growing as a transportation center, and here a typical and most important aspect of German Jewish economic life became established as it did in cities across the country. Itinerant merchants, or peddlers, were for a time a principal component of the Jewish working force. For instance, in 1850 two-thirds of the working Jews in Syracuse were peddlers. Advantages accrued to both

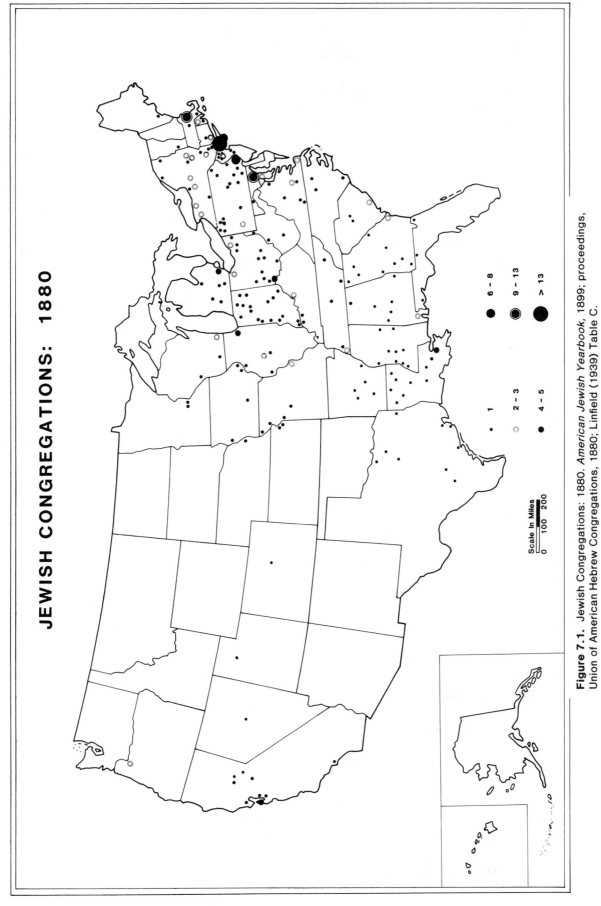

JEWISH CONGREGATIONS: 1880

Scale In Miles
0   100   200

• 1	● 6 – 8
○ 2 – 3	◉ 9 – 13
● 4 – 5	⬤ > 13

Figure 7.1. Jewish Congregations: 1880. *American Jewish Yearbook,* 1899; proceedings, Union of American Hebrew Congregations, 1880; Linfield (1939) Table C.

the country and the immigrant community from peddling. Rural areas had a need for increased access to consumer goods that were being produced as America industrialized. While the transportation system of the United States could get these goods to cities, an efficient system of distribution to the hinterlands was not always available. Meanwhile, the new Jewish immigrants needed jobs which required relatively little capital investment. Itinerant merchandizing was the perfect solution. The peddlers bought as much as they could carry on their backs, and were able to live in close-knit ethnic neighborhoods. They progressed in their careers from walking, to owning a horse and wagon, and eventually purchasing a store. Other Jews acted as suppliers, manufacturers of dry goods, and wholesalers. Gradually, as the prosperity of the immigrants increased and the distribution systems improved, peddling came to an end.

In 1880, the Jews of Syracuse lived in an ethnic neighborhood to the southeast of the city center (Fig. 7.2). In spite of having decreased in numbers from previous decades, peddlers were clearly an important segment of the community. They lived throughout the neighborhood with other Jews who had been in the United States longer and had other occupations. This ethnic neighborhood or ghetto was typical of those found in many cities of the United States at that time.

The businesses of the Jewish community in 1880 were concentrated in two nodes (Fig. 7.3). One node was the ethnic neighborhood; the other was in the central business district of Syracuse. Movement from home to business, whether to store or a train station, was not a problem for residents of the neighborhood. Throughout the country Jews were found in businesses that produced consumer goods for the public. Dry goods, clothes, shoes, tailoring, and general merchandizing were typical specialties. In the South before the Civil War Jews were important cotton brokers and commission merchants. In the West they were active in similar patterns of economic activities.

Religious Practices. Any social geography of 19th century American Jews must note that changes in religious activity strongly affected the ethnic group. A pattern emerged that was to be repeated several times in terms of religious practices. Jews who had been in the United States for some time tended to favor an evolution of religious practices suitable for the American scene. Newcomers to this country favored retention of the traditional practices, at least until they became established. Each wave of Jewish immigration brought this issue to the fore.

The Sephardic rite synagogue of colonial times had evolved by the 19th century into an inherently American institution.[23] Relatively affluent, long-established and acculturated Jewish families controlled synagogues that seemed foreign to newly arrived Ashkenazim. Like other immigrants most were poor, spoke English poorly if at all, and were homesick for a time. They desired a religious service similar to the one they had known. In the early years of the 19th century this led to the establishment of multiple synagogues in certain cities.

During the period 1820 to 1850 the German Jewish community became more comfortable in the United States. While the number of Jews in the country increased dramatically, they were still a relatively small minority. The 1850s saw efforts to find common religious bonds for the entire American Jewish community. Liturgical and organizational changes were common in many synagogues. The arrival of progressive rabbis from Germany added another element pressing for change. By the 1880s many synagogues in the United States were called "Reform." English was used in parts of the service, organs were installed in synagogues, men and women were seated together, some rites were changed, and progressive social thought of the late 19th century was influential in congregation and ethnic community affairs.

The quarter million Jews of 1880 America enjoyed what has been called a "period of confidence."[24] Economically, they had become prosperous and lived in cities and smaller places from coast to coast. Ethnically, they had maintained important elements of their cultural heritage. Religiously, they had reformed their practice into alignment with the American cultural scene. Socially, many had become important and respected members of their urban communities. A long period of stability and tranquility seemed to be in the offing for American Jews in 1880.

The Great Eastern European Immigration

The American Jewish Community of 1880 included people from Central and Eastern Europe (particularly Germany and Poland), as well as from England and France. The bulk of the community, by this time, was composed of native-born Americans—the children of immigrants. Jews generally lived in communities scattered across the vast spaces of American settlement. Some of these communities were larger than others, but there were not disproportional imbalances between the coastal and interior cities.

The tone of Jewish life was set by the German Jews, who had dominated American Judaism throughout much of the nineteenth century. But, the flow of new German Jewish immigrants into the United States had diminished considerably by 1880. Although they and their children may have continued to dominate the ethnic group numerically, the trend in immigration during the period after the Civil War was clearly in favor of the Eastern Europeans. This immigration began to reach major proportions after 1881, as anti-Semitic violence (pogroms) and official anti-Jewish decrees within the Russian Empire instigated a forty-year

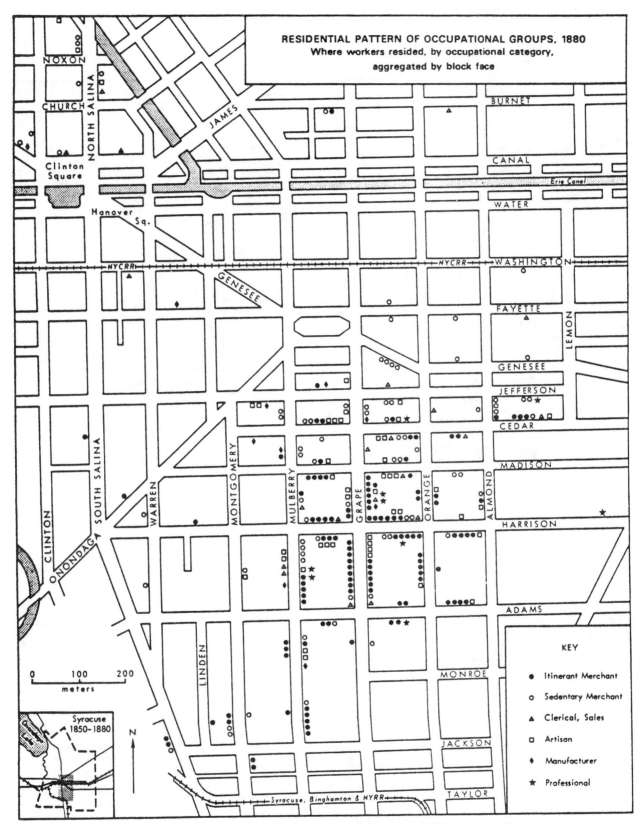

Figure 7.2. Residential Pattern of Occupational Groups, 1880. J. Mesinger, *Peddlers and Merchants: The Geography of Work in a Nineteenth Century Jewish Community.* Syracuse University in Discussion Papers, 1977.

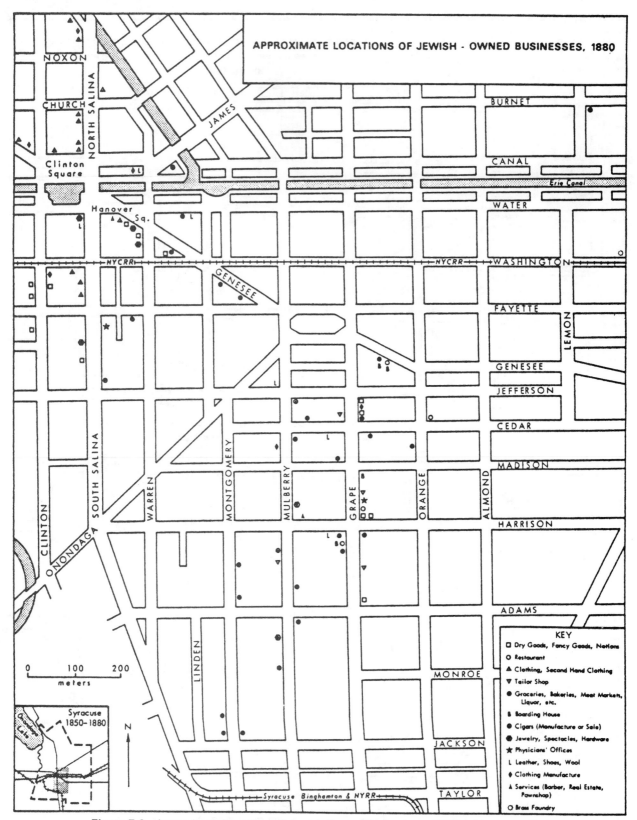

Figure 7.3. Approximate Locations of Jewish-Owned Businesses, 1880. J. Mesinger, *Peddlers and Merchants: The Geography of Work in a Nineteenth Century Jewish Community.* Syracuse University Discussion Papers, 1977.

period of Eastern European Jewish emigration. Over one-third of the Jews in Eastern Europe emigrated during that period. About 90 percent of them came to the United States.[25] The period of heaviest influx was from 1899 to 1914, when over 1.5 million Jews entered the United States. By 1924 there were nearly 4.2 million people in the American Jewish ethnic group, about 17 times as many as had been estimated in 1880. Five out of every six were of Eastern European stock. Jewish immigrants generally came to America to stay. In the first quarter of the twentieth century, the rate of reverse migration for Jews was about five percent, compared to 35 percent in the general immigrant population.[26]

New Character of Jewish Ethnicity. In the decade of the 1880s alone, over one-half million new Jewish immigrants, most of them from Eastern Europe, tripled the size of the American Jewish community. Although people from Poland and Russia had been present within the community for many years, it was during this period that the composition of the ethnic group began to shift from German to Eastern European. It could be argued that for a while there actually were two ethnic groups. Except for some charitable activities, the older immigrant group made every effort to distance itself from these poorer, "greener" newcomers. The religious link was there, and the ancient heritage which accompanied it, but even this was diminished in importance by the separation of German and Eastern European Jews into distinct congregations. The older, established congregations were not particularly eager to accept these "distant cousins" into their midst, and many of the new immigrants were uncomfortable with the form which Jewish worship had taken in America. Instead, they established their own synagogues ("shuls"), religious schools, newspapers and other cultural institutions which reflected their Eastern European life.

That life was quite different from the one which had evolved within the German-dominated American Jewish community. The new immigrants spoke Yiddish, a vernacular language based in German with Hebrew and other influences and written in Hebrew characters. Their predecessors, who spoke German or even "Judaeo-German" (akin to Yiddish) when they arrived, had all but abandoned the old language in their rush to become Americans. But Yiddish thrived in the densely-settled neighborhoods of the new immigrants, and became the centerpiece of a flourishing culture. "A well-defined Yiddish-speaking Jewish ethnic group emerged, very different in self-understanding and social conformation from the Jews of Sephardic and German origin who had preceded them."[27]

A New Settlement Pattern. This new element in American Judaism was felt at some level in virtually every sizable Jewish community. But nowhere was it more evident than in the large cities of the northeast,

especially in New York City, which served as the primary port of entry. Whereas earlier immigrants had fanned out across America to establish Jewish communities in Syracuse, Cincinnati, St. Louis, New Orleans, and Port Gibson in Mississippi, the newcomers seemed more reluctant to venture beyond the portals. It has been estimated that about two-thirds of all the Jews who entered the United States between 1880 and 1920 remained in the large coastal ports. By 1920, 60 percent of all American Jews lived in the cities between Boston and Washington. It is estimated that 45 percent of American Jews lived in New York City by the end of the period, compared to 25 percent in 1860 and 35 percent in 1880.[28]

There is no simple explanation for this pattern of settlement. One obvious factor was the availability of employment opportunities in these large cities. This fact was related to the specific skills and occupational propensities among Eastern European Jews, the industrial character of certain cities, and the presence of established Jewish employers. In the early part of this century, the new immigrants were generally young workers, skilled or semi-skilled, with distinctly urban backgrounds. As Ward has pointed out, Russian Jews preferred large metropolitan cities on the Middle Atlantic coast because of the diversified employment opportunities they presented.[29] New York was especially favored, however, because of its growing garment industry, which by the turn of the century became a virtually all-Jewish activity, with perhaps 90 percent of the city's wholesale clothing firms under Jewish ownership. By 1913, three-quarters of the labor force in the industry were Russian Jews.[30] The Jewish-dominated garment industry also became a focus for the organization of unions in the United States in the early 1900s, and Jewish unions were at the forefront of the American labor movement in its formative years. Many Jews arriving from Eastern Europe during this period had had experience in clothing manufacture and found similar work in New York. It also helped that so many of the factory owners were Jewish. They were inclined to hire the new immigrants and respond sympathetically to their special needs.

Formation of the Ghetto. The fact that so many of these employers, as well as landlords, were Jews is also important because it reflects the value of ethnic bonding as another explanation for the concentration of the new Jewish immigrants in these large cities. Jews tended to settle in areas where there were a sufficient number of other Jews who could provide them with the emotional and cultural support they needed; hence providing a comfortable feeling in a generally hostile environment. It also helped to ease their transition to American life.[31]

The large numbers of Jewish immigrants arriving in New York in a very short period necessitated the development of a complex set of cultural institutions, making the city familiar and hospitable for the Jewish inhabitants. In many ways their new home was what Louis Wirth called a "village world"[32]—a virtual re-creation of the old-world community with traditional ties to the old social networks transplanted from Europe. In turn, this development of ethnic culture islands made the largest cities even more appealing to new arrivals by ameliorating their culture shock and by isolating them from mainstream American society. Such enclaves sprang up in places like Chicago's West Side, Boston's North End, Cincinnati's West End, and of course New York's Lower East Side.

These urban, ethnic culture islands, which were called *ghettos,* were the spatial manifestation of ethnic bonding. The Jewish ghetto was both a form of accommodation to a new social milieu and a bulwark against assimilation, and it fostered the survival of the ethnic group. In a sense, the ghetto was a product of external pressures and discrimination.[33] But, it was also an outgrowth of the nature of Jewish culture which called for proximity to religious institutions and for communal self-sufficiency.

The American Jewish ghetto was in many ways similar to the original ghettos in European cities. Within the new ghetto neighborhood, one could find the same institutions and social networks operating. The old Jewish ghettos, however, were generally bounded quarters, often restricted by law both physically and socially. They were walled places with limited access. The American version was more open and susceptible to ethnic invasion and Jewish out-migration. Also, the society of the European Jewish ghetto was a tightly-knit, closed, and culturally homogeneous one, whereas the New World ghetto was a collecting pool for Jewish immigrants from diverse regional backgrounds with varied customs. Within the American ghetto, only at the block or small neighborhood level did one find homogeneity. Indeed, in spite of the general feeling of ethnic unity and community which pervaded the ghetto as a whole, the fragmented social structure of the Jewish community was reflected in a complex internal spatial structure. The large Jewish ghettos contained smaller enclaves representing common regional or even common village origins in Europe.[34] Within the Lower East Side ghetto in New York for example, one could find a Romanian Jewish block, a Polish Jewish neighborhood, a Lithuanian Jewish neighborhood, a block where most people came from the city of Lvov, and so forth. In each, the specific lifestyle of a particular source was transplanted. Overlaying this complexity was an ambiguous "Jewishness," which over a period of years gradually absorbed the provincial sub-ethnicities.

The German-East European Dichotomy. The ethnicity which ultimately bound together Eastern European and German Jews in America was not, however, forged in the ghetto. Rather, it was a product of the upward eco-nomic mobility of many second- and third-generation Eastern European Jewish Americans and their inter-minglining with the previously established American Jewish community in the suburbs and small cities. Until this mixing occurred, the rift between German and East European Jews was considerable. These broad regional-origin distinctions were perceived as important, but they tended to obscure the underlying socioeconomic differences which kept the two group apart, especially relative prosperity and recency of immigration. The German and Eastern European Jews maintained two distinct communities during this period of mass immigration, in part because of the differences in religious practice and cultural traditions mentioned earlier in this chapter, but also as a result of the class distinctions which emerged in a rapidly mobile Jewish society.

German-Jewish Americans, especially of the second and third generation, worked hard to establish themselves as a thoroughly American group. Many were distinctly middle class or upper middle class merchants or professionals and their families who retained only some vestiges of their religion as a link with their ethnic past. Their social and economic success and their cultural assimilation stood in sharp contrast to the "foreignness," poverty, religious and political extremism, and working-class character of the Eastern Europeans who followed them.

The disdain with which they viewed these newcomers was reflected in the resulting social geography of the urban Jewish community during the late nineteenth and early twentieth centuries. As new immigrants arrived, they continually replaced established Jews who abandoned older, lower quality housing as their economic circumstances improved. This succession satisfied some of the need for low-cost, abundant, preferably Jewish-owned accommodations, but it also tended to segregate the two communities residentially into higher- and lower-class areas. A few Eastern European Jews of the second generation who were economically successful in this early period did manage to join the German Jews in their flight from lower-class areas. This segregation process was experienced in communities as small as Syracuse's and, of course, as large as New York's. In the latter, ". . . the 'uptown-downtown' dichotomy was fostered by those who had managed to migrate uptown or move up the social ladder and who resented the tendency of the ghetto 'to catch up with them,' as well as by those who remained behind and viewed their more fortunate co-religionists with both contempt and envy."[35] Successive waves of new immigrants into the ghetto during this period pushed increasing numbers of marginally prosperous Jewish families out into "better" neighborhoods, who in turn pushed the more established Jews farther outward from the ghetto.

American Jewry Comes of Age

The residential succession pattern changed dramatically as the massive waves of immigrants were curtailed in the early 1920s by federal immigration quota legislation. With no large numbers of newcomers to fill the residential vacuum created by upward mobility and class separatism, the older ghetto areas began to lose Jewish population. New York's Lower East Side Jewish population declined from 353,000 in 1916 to 121,000 in 1930; similar effects were felt in the old neighborhoods of Chicago, Boston, Philadelphia, and Baltimore.[36] This process diminished the distinction between "uptown" Germans and "downtown" Eastern Europeans, as the latter moved outward and began to mix more thoroughly with the former.

Although the ghetto concentrations had begun to diminish, Jews had come to be a significant presence in large American cities by 1920. Over a quarter of the New York City population was Jewish, as were between nine and thirteen percent of the people in Cleveland, Newark, Philadelphia, Boston, Baltimore, Pittsburgh and Chicago.[37]

Stages of Settlement. Nathan Glazer has developed a highly simplified, but useful model of the internal structure of these Jewish communities in the period between the World Wars. They were composed of ". . . rapidly emptying areas of first settlement (slums), of rapidly growing areas of second settlement (middle class apartment houses or two-family houses or, least frequently, single-family dwellings), and areas of third settlement (expensive apartment-house areas or suburban developments of single-family houses)."[38]

This model suggests that the movement of the Jewish community from the downtown ghetto to the suburbs took place in stages. Initially, it appears that in both small communities and large ones, certain affluent families moved to areas of better housing, already occupied by non-Jews, but still relatively close to the downtown area. Traditional Jewish law would have inhibited Orthodox Jews from making such a move because they needed to be within walking distance of their synagogues. The first movers were generally Reform Jews who were not so constrained. In the Jewish communities of the interior United States, this stage seems to have occurred during the first two decades of the twentieth century, especially in the period from 1910 to 1915. When a sufficient number of influential members had moved to an area of second settlement, their synagogue migrated with them and other congregants followed. In some instances, the synagogue may have been moved in anticipation of its congregants' migration. More traditional Jews tended to move in groups, taking their synagogues or at least their congregations with them. Religious observance was often conducted under less than optimum conditions until a formal structure could be built or acquired.

In Cincinnati, Syracuse, and other medium-size cities, outward movement of the Jewish community often followed a single transportation artery. As new neighborhoods along the artery farther from the center of the city began to be settled by Jewish residents in the 1940s and 1950s, the older neighborhoods closer to downtown were progressively abandoned. This process was partially a result of upward economic mobility and a search for an increasingly higher standard of living. It also was related to the expansion of black neighborhoods. In many cases this expansion seems to have followed the same path as the Jewish migration, although the reasons for this are not clear. One theory is that blacks encountered less resistance to their expansion in these than in other white neighborhoods. On the other hand, it could probably be shown that this was because Jews, at least as much as any other group, experienced "white flight" in advance of that black expansion.[39] The pattern of Jewish movement from central city to suburbs has been described this way: ". . . a relatively small number of Jews moves out of a neighborhood of high Jewish concentration into an area where it is low; then within ten years, large numbers of Jews from the more segregated areas follow them and the new area becomes an area of high concentration and segregation, while the earlier area becomes abandoned by Jews; then the cycle begins all over."[40]

In their rush to move outward from the areas of first and even second settlement, American Jews left behind the hearth of their ethnicity. At first, only the poorest, oldest or most recently immigrated remained in the old ghettos. By the 1970s, only New York City had Jews still living in the original ghetto neighborhoods, probably because it was the only Jewish community with a sizable working-class population. Still, in most of the old neighborhoods, Jewish landlords and merchants continued to operate long after the Jewish residents had been succeeded by blacks and other disadvantaged groups.

The rich architectural cultural landscape created by Jewish communities in their old neighborhoods, if it survived the wrecking ball of urban renewal, was adapted by the new residents for their own needs. In many black neighborhoods today one can observe churches of many denominations which were once Jewish synagogues. Some of these imposing, neoclassical or modernistic structures still bear the symbols of their past—for example, the Star of David, the Tablets of the Ten Commandments, or some Hebrew inscriptions. American Jews left behind a trail of such artifacts in their migration from one settlement area to the next.

Generational Changes. The successive stages of Jewish settlement mirrored in some ways the changing values and circumstances from one generation to the next within Jewish communities during the 1920s and later periods. The immigrant or "survivalist" generation was the generation of the ghetto. Clinging to the past, especially through religion and a traditional lifestyle, Jews of this generation experienced minimal acculturation in their protected ghetto environment. Most remained in areas of first settlement, while attempting to build a future for their American-born offspring.

The second or "escapist" generation experienced considerable "Americanization," but nonetheless was raised in the milieu of the ghetto. "The second generation was torn between two worlds—the world of the ghetto, foreign to America, limiting social and economic expression and advancement, and the new world of America with unlimited economic opportunity and the apparent welcome sign to become American."[41] Many reacted to the dissonance of their two worlds by rejecting the life of the ghetto and, to some extent, the traditional religion of their parents. But this rejection was frustrating because acceptance by the non-Jewish society in areas of second and third settlement was not always forthcoming. Jews experienced discrimination in housing, employment, college admission, and club membership during this phase, especially in the 1920s and 1930s. In their desire to be fully "American," but in reaction to a sense of alienation, they frequently established new institutions, like clubs, country clubs, and schools, which were fundamentally Jewish but which paralleled those of the non-Jewish majority from which they had been excluded.[42] In addition, ". . . for a considerable number, residing in a Jewish neighborhood was the sole manifestation of ethnic identification."[43] Jews in this cohort began to develop a new Jewish identity which was quite distinct from that of their parents' generation, but which became more firmly established in their children's generation.

The third generation, free from the conflict between old world and new, raised largely in middle-class surroundings, was less inclined to reject the lifestyle of their parents. Instead they were able to integrate their Jewish identity into a way of life marked by greater interaction with non-Jews and greater integration into American society.[44] At the same time, some participated in a Jewish revival, going beyond the escapism of their parents in a search for ethnic continuity with the immigrant generation.

Patterns of Intraurban Migration. These depictions of the generational differences within the Jewish ethnic group are, of course, highly generalized. Individual Jews and Jewish families responded in a variety of ways to the challenges of minority group status in an overwhelmingly Christian social environment. Yet, research on the residential movement patterns of American Jews after the 1920s had revealed a remarkable consistency. Throughout the period since the end of mass immigration, large numbers of Jews have chosen to reside in neighborhoods with other Jewish residents. This has resulted in the formation of ethnic clusters in areas of second and third settlement. Outmigrants from the ghettos, largely second-generation Jews, appeared to be fleeing their ethnic heritage. But, as Oscar Handlin has pointed out, they actually were seeking a better location in which to transplant it.[45]

The form of the new, secondary "ghetto" was certainly not the same as that of its predecessor. In what has been called the "gilded ghetto,"[46] housing stock was of considerably higher quality and in better condition. There was not the customary overcrowding and poverty, and Yiddish was not as likely to be heard in the streets. But there was a feeling of ethnic belonging, fostered by the residential clustering of Jews and by the presence of ethnic institutions, like synagogues, Jewish community centers and kosher food stores, which had migrated with them. In these areas of second settlement, it was more likely than in the original ghetto that a Jewish family would have non-Jewish neighbors, although even within most of the large immigrant ghettos ethnic groups had co-existed in fairly close proximity. In the new areas, being in a Jewish neighborhood did not have to mean that everyone was Jewish, but that a sufficient number of Jewish residents (not necessarily a majority) and institutions were present to give the neighborhood a Jewish character.

In areas of third settlement, generally in the suburbs, Jewish residents were more dispersed among non-Jewish neighbors. The word "clustering" may not even seem appropriate to describe the pattern which developed after World War II. But, in the context of an entire metropolitan area, the majority of Jews preferred to live within clearly-defined suburban neighborhoods. Certain suburbs had virtually no Jewish inhabitants, perhaps because of exclusive real estate practices or because Jews preferred to live in areas where other Jews resided. Other places attracted Jewish residents and became known as "Jewish suburbs," even though Jews may have been a dispersed minority. Such areas typically contained 25 to 50 percent Jews, although some may have been as much as 80 percent Jewish at the neighborhood level.[47] Synagogues in these areas served as important foci for Jewish identity. The more mobile, automobile-oriented lifestyle of the suburbs obviated the need for proximity to Jewish neighbors and institutions, while permitting the maintenance of social networks and ethnic identity.

Post-Quota Immigration. Although the socio-geographic mobility of the American Jewish community was no longer fed by massive waves of new immigrants from Europe, sizable numbers of Jews came into the United States after 1924. The introduction of these new immigrants into the American Jewish ethnic group has been sporadic since the 1920s. In 1921, Jewish immigration peaked at 199,000 and Jews accounted for about 15 percent of the total immigration that year. After the restrictive legislation, the influx declined to 10,000 and then only 4,000 per year until the 1930s.[48] The next major Jewish immigrant wave occurred between 1937 and 1943, when almost 150,000 Jews fleeing the persecution of the Nazis entered the United States. More than 43,000 came in 1939 alone.[49] American immigration policies were not particularly responsive to the plight of European Jews during the war; many died for want of permission to enter. But, after the war, an additional 60,000 or so displaced Jews were settled in the United States. Many of the newcomers again remained in New York City, with some living in their own distinct ethnic neighborhoods, like Washington Heights in Manhattan.

A more recent wave of Jewish immigrants has come to the United States from the Soviet Union since 1971. Of the 173,000 Jews permitted to leave the Soviet Union in the 1970s, perhaps 15,000 had either directly or indirectly settled in the United States by 1977. Over 40 percent of these America-bound newcomers came to New York, but others settled in cities like Cincinnati, Detroit and Baltimore.[50] In addition, over 300,000 Jews have emigrated to the United States from Israel since its establishment in 1948.[51] In all, about 576,000 Jews arrived in the country in the 50 years after the immigration quotas were made operational, compared to almost 2.5 million in the preceding forty years.

SPATIAL PATTERNS OF LATE TWENTIETH CENTURY AMERICAN JEWS

Size and Distribution of the Jewish Population

Determining the size and distribution of America's Jewish population is not a simple task. Jews are not a racial or national-origin group and are, therefore, not enumerated in the federal census. Although a few communities have conducted formal surveys, the most common method used by Jewish communities is to count synagogue members and contributors to federated philanthropic organizations. Of course, this ignores a large body of "inactive" Jews who may comprise as much as one-half of the Jewish population. Ethnic identity thus becomes the critical issue in assessing the size of the group. If it is measured by affiliation, the available statistics are fairly accurate. If it is determined by individual self-description or some external definition, they are not. Affiliation numbers are used in this chapter because they are the best available.

American Jews in 1980 were estimated to number about 5,921,000,[52] or about 2.7 percent of the total population of the United States. Surprisingly, that percentage is one percent lower than the Jewish share of the nation's population forty years earlier. This decline has been attributed to assimilation, intermarriage, and the Jewish birth rate, which in recent years has been among the lowest of any American ethnic group.[53] The declining birth rate may be a result of increasing affluence, secularization, greater use of birth control, or other factors. In any case, it is not a positive sign for those who are concerned about the survival of the ethnic group.

Regional Distribution and Inter-regional Movement. By far the largest part of the American Jewish population lives in the northeastern region, with over half of the total residing in New York, New Jersey and Pennsylvania (Table 7.1). But, the 57.3 percent who now live in the Northeast is somewhat less than the 64 percent who lived there in 1968. This decline suggests a significant shift of the ethnic group away from this source area. A similar decline was experienced in the North Central region, which in 1930 contained 20 percent of America's Jews. While these areas were losing their Jewish population, the West and South gained Jewish population through in-migration. The South increased its Jewish population by 50 percent in ten years.

The movement from Northeast and Central U.S. to the South and West seems to parallel that of the American population as a whole. This movement is not comprised only of elderly first and second-generation Jews who are leaving the commercial/industrial centers of the urban core for the retirement communities of Florida and the Southwest, but it also includes a mobile, job-seeking, younger Jewish population which is following the migration of employment opportunities to the "Sunbelt" region. Because Jews increasingly are behaving much like the rest of American society in terms of residential mobility, it has been predicted that ". . . in an ecological sense . . . the population will become a more truly 'American population,' with all this implies in terms of assimilation and numerical visibility."[54]

TABLE 7.1. Regional Distribution of American Jews, 1980

Region	Jewish Population	Percent Distribution
Northeast	3,390,420	57.3
New England	387,235	6.5
Middle Atlantic	3,003,185	50.7
North Central	689,825	11.7
East North Central	554,490	9.4
West North Central	135,335	2.3
South	949,735	16.0
South Atlantic	811,005	13.7
East South Central	40,385	0.7
West South Central	98,345	1.7
West	890,910	15.0
Mountain	101,165	1.7
Pacific	789,745	13.3
TOTAL	5,920,890	100.0

Source: *American Jewish Yearbook*, 1981: 174.

The Urban Ethnic Group. Because Jews have been a predominantly urban ethnic group since the colonial period, it is not surprising to find that they are concentrated in metropolitan areas and especially in the urban corridor of the Northeast seaboard, often referred to as "Megalopolis." Jewish communities containing 100 or more people are widely dispersed (Figs. 7.4, 7.5, 7.6). It is clear that in spite of the strong movement to the South and West, this Northeast area continues to be the location of most Jewish communities. In other parts of the country, Jewish residents can be found in small towns, but they represent a very small percentage of the total American Jewish population. Large Jewish concentrations exist in most of the major metropolitan centers outside Megalopolis, but these communities tend to be more isolated, or "discontinuous" than the concentration in the Northeast.[55] A growing exception on a smaller scale than Megalopolis is the ribbon of Jewish communities which melt together on Florida's Atlantic coast.

In recent years, Jewish settlement patterns have become more diverse. As a result, the image of American Jews as living *only* in the Northeast has changed considerably. A study of the 1950s and 1960s showed that ". . . they were as likely to move between the equally pluralistic urban and suburban communities in the northeast as they were to emerge in the still culturally homogeneous metropolitan areas of the south and midwest."[56] The greatest increases in Jewish population in the past few decades have been in suburban areas of the Northeast, the dynamic metropolitan areas in the South and Southwest (especially in Texas and California), the Southeast in general, and the retirement areas in Florida and the Southwest.[57]

Because of the urban nature of the Jewish distribution pattern, it is more meaningful to think of the Jewish population in terms of points on the map, or "communities" rather than in terms of large areas. Maps showing area distributions, like the relative proportions of the total Jewish population residing in each state (Fig. 7.7.) are useful in a general way, but they belie the discontinuous nature of the ethnic group's distribution. Most of the interstices, the spaces between urban places, have few or no Jews living in them. Only in the Northeast and within certain metropolitan areas does some degree of continuity exist, and even this is exaggerated by the gross scale of the data units on a state or county map.

Centers of Jewish Population. By far the largest Jewish community in the United States exists, as it has always been, in New York City and its hinterland. Since data collection methods have been so unreliable, it is impossible to know exactly how many Jews live in the New York City area. A rounded figure of 2 million Jews living in New York City's five boroughs plus the suburban New York counties of Nassau, Suffolk and

TABLE 7.2. Largest Jewish Communities in the United States, 1980

Community	Jewish Population	Percent of Total United States Jewish Population
New York Metropolitan Area	2,411,300	41
in New York State	2,023,000	
in New Jersey	374,100	
in Connecticut	14,200	
Los Angeles Metropolitan Area	503,000	8
South Florida Conurbation	405,000	7
Philadelphia Area	295,000	5
Chicago Area	253,000	4
Boston Area	170,000	3
Washington, D.C. Area	160,000	3
San Francisco Bay Area	103,000	2
Baltimore	92,000	2
Cleveland	75,000	1
Detroit	75,000	1
St. Louis	60,000	1
Pittsburgh	50,000	1

Source: *American Jewish Yearbook*, 1981: 175–181.

Westchester, in 1980 is probably within appropriate limits.[58] Actually, this "community" is made up of many smaller communities in the neighborhoods, towns, and small cities of the region, but there is considerable contiguity and overlap among them. It would be improper, however, to consider the metropolitan New York Jewish population without including Jews living in adjacent northern New Jersey, southwestern Connecticut and Rockland County, New York, all of which are recognized as being within the New York conurbation. The combined statistics for all parts of this metropolitan region yield a Jewish population of over 2.4 million, making it the largest single Jewish concentration in the world. It has about 41 percent of the total American Jewish ethnic group (Table 7.2).

After New York, the next largest Jewish community is the long-established one in Los Angeles, which has more than doubled its population in thirty years. In the same range is the rapidly growing Jewish population in the contiguous communities on Florida's southeast coast, from Miami to Palm Beach. Their number in this region is now over 400,000. This figure is not very precise because in-migration to the region and the expansion of the built-up area are so dynamic, and because there are always data reporting problems when dealing with areas of high transient and seasonal population. Of the other cities shown (Table 7.2), Philadelphia, Boston, Washington and Baltimore can hardly

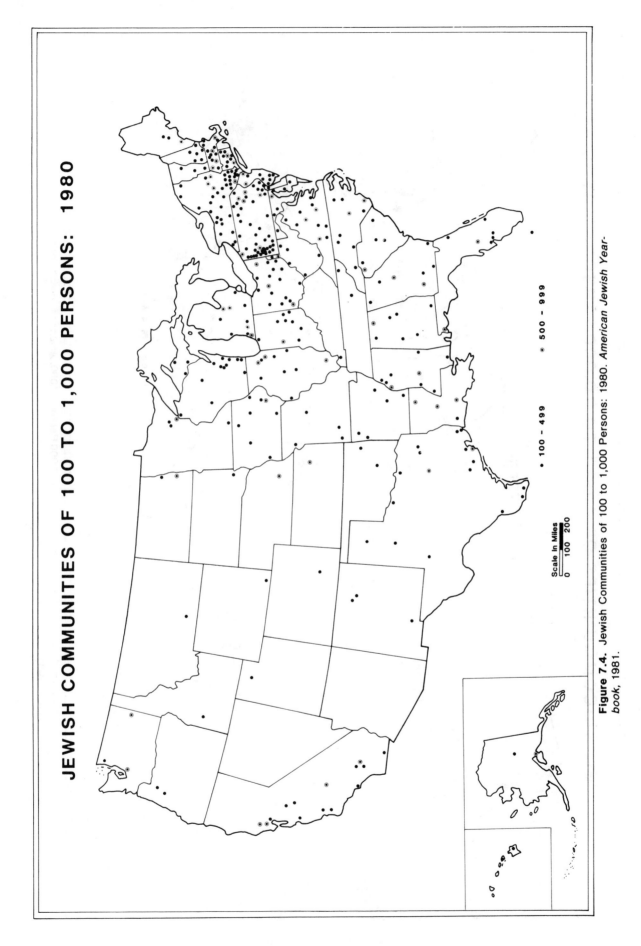

JEWISH COMMUNITIES OF 100 TO 1,000 PERSONS: 1980

⊙ 500 – 999

⊙ 100 – 499

Scale In Miles
0   100   200

Figure 7.4. Jewish Communities of 100 to 1,000 Persons: 1980. *American Jewish Year-book*, 1981.

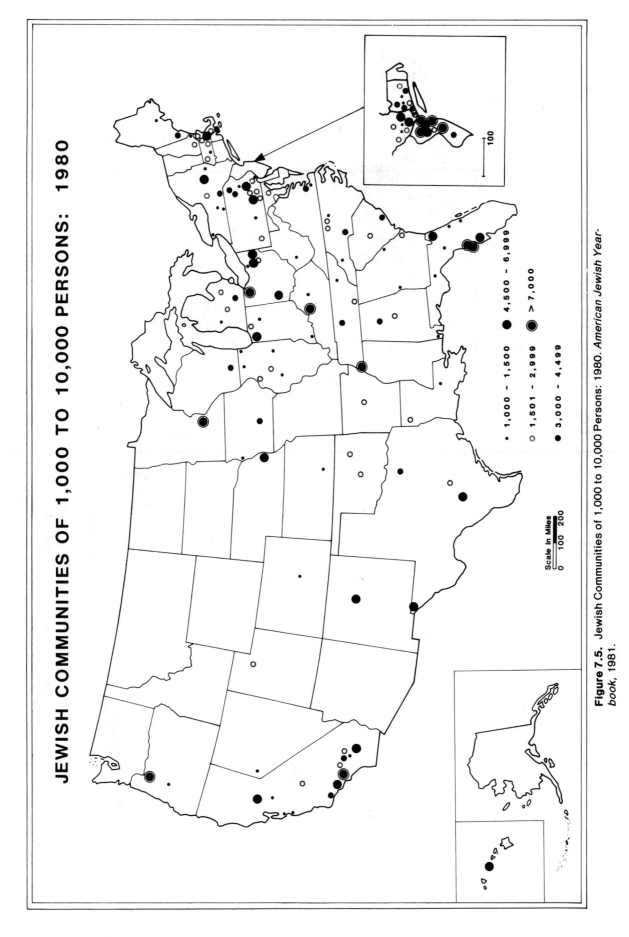

JEWISH COMMUNITIES OF 1,000 TO 10,000 PERSONS: 1980

Legend:
- 1,000 – 1,500
- 1,501 – 2,999
- 3,000 – 4,499
- 4,500 – 6,999
- > 7,000

Scale in Miles
0   100   200

Figure 7.5. Jewish Communities of 1,000 to 10,000 Persons: 1980. *American Jewish Yearbook*, 1981.

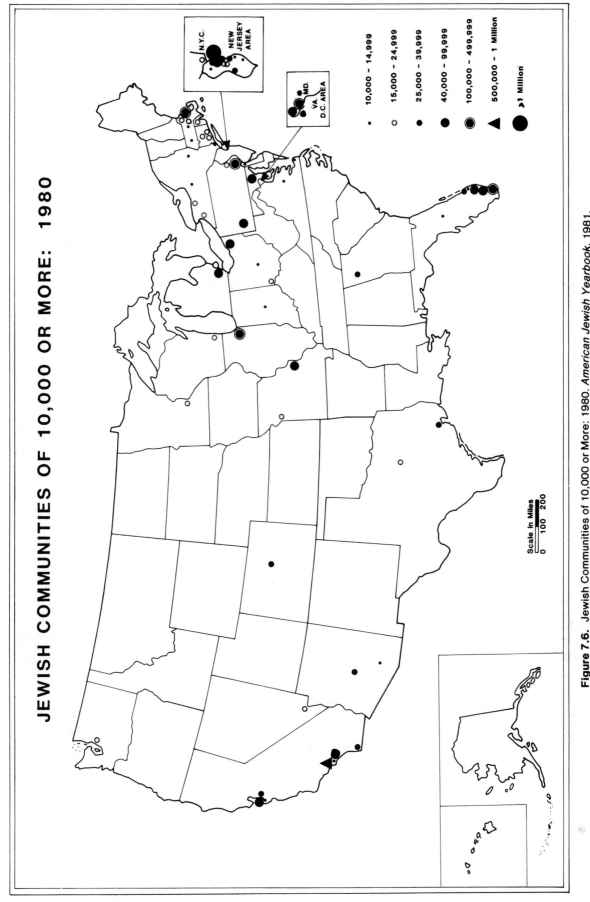

JEWISH COMMUNITIES OF 10,000 OR MORE: 1980

N.Y.C.

NEW JERSEY AREA

MD.

VA.

D.C. AREA

•	10,000 – 14,999
○	15,000 – 24,999
●	25,000 – 39,999
⬤	40,000 – 99,999
◉	100,000 – 499,999
▲	500,000 – 1 Million
⬤	>1 Million

Scale In Miles

0   100   200

Figure 7.6. Jewish Communities of 10,000 or More: 1980. *American Jewish Yearbook,* 1981.

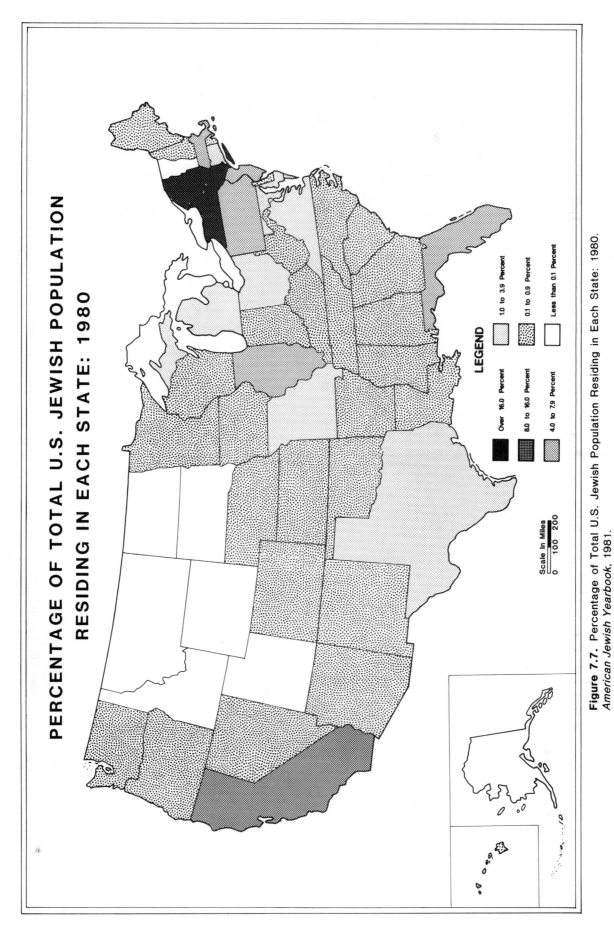

PERCENTAGE OF TOTAL U.S. JEWISH POPULATION RESIDING IN EACH STATE: 1980

LEGEND

Over 16.0 Percent

8.0 to 16.0 Percent

4.0 to 7.9 Percent

1.0 to 3.9 Percent

0.1 to 0.9 Percent

Less than 0.1 Percent

Scale In Miles
0   100   200

Figure 7.7. Percentage of Total U.S. Jewish Population Residing in Each State: 1980. *American Jewish Yearbook*, 1981.

be viewed in isolation from the megalopolitan continuity of which they, along with the Greater New York area, are part (Fig. 7.8). Other places listed are more typical of the interior American isolated concentrations, as are most of the fifteen places which have between 20,000 and 40,000 Jewish inhabitants. Roughly two-thirds of America's Jews live in five large urban communities, three of which are *not* located in the northeastern Megalopolis.

Suburbanization and Other Trends. The movement outward from the central cities of major metropolitan areas has been going on for some time, especially since World War II. But, among Jewish Americans this pattern has accelerated in recent years to a point approaching abandonment of the inner city in some cases.[59] As a result, Jews have not only been leaving the northeastern metropolitan areas, but to an even greater extent have been moving from central locations to the suburbs. In 1957, over 80 percent of the Jews in Greater New York lived within New York City. By 1980 only about 60 percent, and perhaps as little as 50 percent, remained in the city proper; the rest resided in the suburban counties. Among New York's boroughs, Brooklyn lost 41 percent and the Bronx 74 percent of their Jewish population between 1940 and 1977.[60] Similar patterns have emerged in Chicago, Detroit, Boston, and also in Minneapolis, where less than one-quarter of the Jewish community now lives within the city itself.[61]

The trends in suburbanization and migration to the Sunbelt states reflect the high rate of geographic mobility among America's Jews. The National Jewish Population Study, using 1970 data, reinforces this image of a mobile ethnic group. It found that in 1970 only two-thirds of the adult Jewish population lived in the city in which they had resided five years earlier. Twenty percent had moved within the same metropolitan area or county; another three percent had moved from another part of the same state; ten percent had moved from a different state. Among Jews in the most mobile phase of their lives, in the 25–39 age group, less than half had not moved across city lines in the previous five years. Even among those over 65, just under one-third had experienced some kind of change of residence although many of these moves were local.[62] This high and increasing degree of mobility within the ethnic group may be linked to a decline in the importance of kinship ties for many Jewish people. In terms of residential preference, economic opportunity and amenities seem to have taken priority over proximity to the extended family and even to the ethnic community. Not surprisingly, this has had a disruptive effect on the life of many local Jewish communities. They can no longer count on the long-term stability of their population and the sense of continuity which accompanied it.

Jewish Demographic Structure

The Jewish population is generally older than the American population as a whole. According to 1970–1971 figures, in the Jewish group 23 percent are under the age of 15 compared to 28 percent in the United States total population. But 25 percent of American Jews are in the 45–64 age bracket, four percent higher than in the total population. In the over-65 age group, one finds at least 12 percent of America's Jews and only 10 percent of Americans in general. A lower fertility rate and increased longevity have contributed to this situation.[63]

By now it is clear that the replacement rate for the American Jewish ethnic group is far below that of the general population. It should be noted, however, that the figures on fertility are biased in favor of the Reform and Conservative Jewish groups, as well as secular Jews. If data were available, it is probable that the Orthodox group, taken separately, would exhibit a higher fertility rate. The best information available on Jewish fertility is from the late 1960s, and it is likely that rates have remained at or even below these levels (Table 7.3).

From 1967 through 1971, the crude birth rate, the annual number of births per 1000 population was considerably lower for the Jewish population than the white population as a whole. Since the death rates for the two populations were roughly equal, the Jewish rate of natural increase (births minus deaths) was much lower than the white American rate. In fact, the Jewish population was below zero population growth, not taking into account the effects of migration. While the American population as a whole was growing slightly, the Jewish population was not growing at all through natural increase.

An even better indication of the fertility pattern of the ethnic group is the total fertility rate, which calculates the final number of children a woman can expect to have based on a persistence of the current rate of fertility in her age group. For the Jews, this rate was one child less than for women in the general white population. There is some evidence that Jewish women were waiting longer to have children, since there age-specific birth rates are similar to those of other women in their late 20s and 30s, but significantly lower in Jewish

TABLE 7.3. Population Growth Statistics, 1967–1971

Statistic	*Jewish Americans*	*All White Americans*
Crude Birth Rate	9.6	16.8
Crude Death Rate	10.0	9.5
Natural Increase	−0.4	+7.3
Total Fertility Rate	1.4	2.4

Source: S. Goldstein, *American Jewish Yearbook*, 1981: 15; and U. O. Schmelz, *American Jewish Yearbook*, 1981: 74.

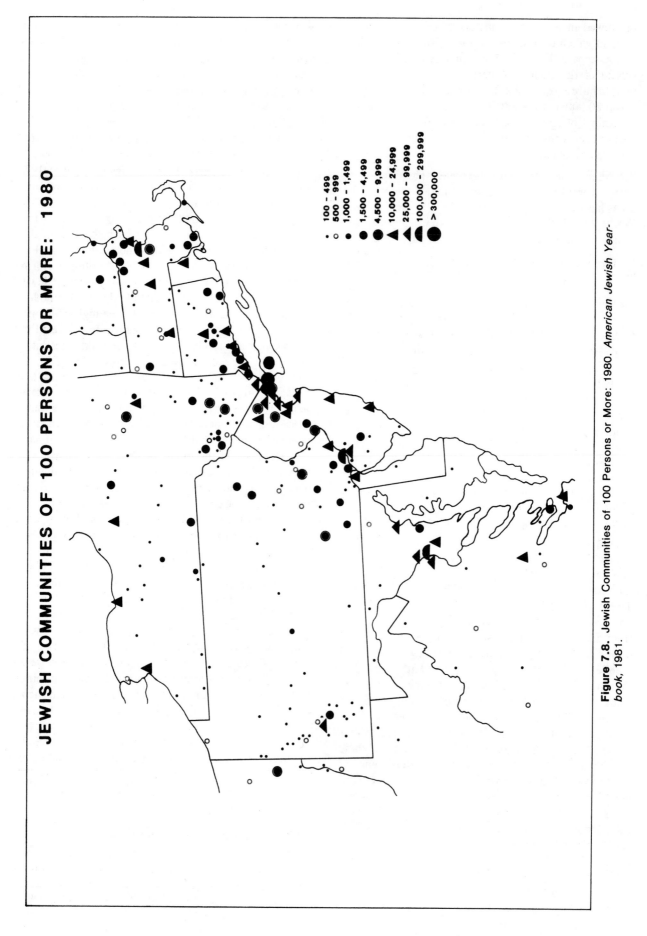

JEWISH COMMUNITIES OF 100 PERSONS OR MORE: 1980

100 – 499
500 – 999
1,000 – 1,499
1,500 – 4,499
4,500 – 9,999
10,000 – 24,999
25,000 – 99,999
100,000 – 299,999
>300,000

Figure 7.8. Jewish Communities of 100 Persons or More: 1980. *American Jewish Year-book*, 1981.

164

women under 25.[64] Finally, among Jewish women of all ages in 1973, the total average number of children ever born was 1.9, which is below the replacement rate. For Protestant women the average was 2.2, whereas for Catholic women it was 2.4.

Lower fertility is usually assumed to be related to urbanization, moderate affluence, and favorable attitudes toward family planning. While these characteristics may well apply to the highly urbanized Jewish ethnic group, other factors like minority status and traditional Jewish values may be involved as well. "Perceptions of discrimination, feelings of insecurity, and values particularly conducive to fewer children may continue to contribute to lower Jewish fertility."[65]

Education and Occupational Patterns

Jewish Americans in the twentieth century have maintained the high degree of attention to learning which has traditionally characterized Jewish culture. Levels of educational attainment are consistently higher than in the general population as a result of this emphasis. Comparisons generated by the National Jewish Population Study for 1970[66] showed that among Jews over 25 years of age only 15.6 percent had less than a high school education. About 45.5 percent of the total white population were in this category. On the other hand, 41.4 percent of the Jews had completed college, compared to only 11.3 percent of adult white Americans. Among those, 18.2 percent (26.5 percent of the males) of adult Jews had continued with graduate work, compared to 4.9 percent of the white population as a whole. The educational attainment level among Jews becomes even more striking when one considers the effects of an aging Jewish population on these figures. When only a younger age cohort, the 30–39 age group, is considered, over 70 percent of the Jewish men were college graduates and 45 percent had done some graduate work.[67]

These high levels of achievement may be attributed, in part, to the desire of first and second generation Jewish Americans to secure the futures of their children. Many of them realize the value of education for occupational mobility and economic survival, and instill that educational goal in their offspring. Since much of the push toward higher education among the Jewish population is linked to a striving for upward socioeconomic mobility, there is a strong relationship between their level of educational attainment and their occupational structure.

Jews are particularly heavily represented in the professional and technical fields, as well as in white collar managerial or administrative positions. The 1970 figures show that nearly 60 percent of adult Jews of both sexes fall into these categories, compared to less than 25 percent of the total white population. Along with clerical and sales workers, fully 88 percent of American Jewish workers are in white collar occupations. On the other hand, only 9.9 percent of the Jewish labor force have jobs in manual occupations, compared to 46.3 percent of the general white population.[68] The exception to this percentage is New York City, where as much as 27 percent of the adult Jewish males are in blue collar jobs.[69] The American Jewish tradition of mercantilism and the occupations of their parents in commercial activities have also led many Jewish students to seek business degrees and jobs in the business world. As a result, nearly one-third of the national Jewish labor force is found in the mangerial/administrative category.

The Myth of Wealth

The high levels of educational attainment and occupational status in the Jewish population suggest that Jewish Americans as a group are economically comfortable, middle and upper-middle income people. This, in fact, has been a widely held stereotype of American Jews among both non-Jews and Jews themselves. But, the statistics and stereotypes mask the existence of a substantial group of Jews living below the poverty line. One reason for the general ignorance of this phenomenon has been the traditional Jewish avoidance of public assistance. A variety of institutions have historically existed within the Jewish community to take care of Jewish poverty and illness. These institutions, however, have not been able to meet the needs of the Jewish poor in recent years, and pride often gets in the way of seeking help.[70]

Most of the known impoverished Jewish population live in two areas of high Jewish concentration: New York City and Miami Beach. A 1973 study in New York found that 15 percent of the city's Jews, or 272,000 people were at or near the poverty level. An additional 432,000 New York Jews, about one-quarter of the community, were somewhere between near-poverty and a moderate standard of living.[71] New York still has a relatively large working-class Jewish population. Of course, many of those in the poorest group are the elderly Jewish poor. They constitute about 60 percent of the poorest New York Jews. In the South Beach area of Miami Beach, 85 percent of the 40,000 poor residents, most of whom are elderly, are Jewish.[72] There is reason to believe that economic hardship, and the victimization which often accompanies it, is a fact of life for some Jews, particularly the old, in every sizable Jewish community.

SUMMARY AND PROSPECT

Jews have been a part of American society for over three hundred years. During that time, the nature of Jewish ethnicity has changed considerably, owing to the various streams of Jewish immigrants which have been infused into the ethnic group at various times, the relative pace and intensity of assimilation, the changing balance between religious adherence and secularism, and the varying degrees of spatial segregation and concentration which have marked the group's residential patterns.

Jewish ethnicity in the 1980s is a combination of religious adherence, historical-cultural attachments, and associational patterns. For some Jews, religion is at the core of their ethnicity. If they are Orthodox Jews, religion may be an integral part of their daily lives. If they are Conservative or Reform Jews, it is probably a separate and distinct aspect of their lives and the one in which they most strongly identify as Jews. For other Jewish Americans, religion itself is of little importance, but links to a Jewish heritage help them to maintain their ethnicity. For still others, the focus of ethnicity may be participation in a Jewish social network, or just living in a Jewish neighborhood in close proximity to other Jews.

Jewish immigration to the United States has occurred in waves. Generally speaking, these can be grouped into four broad periods: (1) a colonial and early nineteenth-century period dominated by a Sephardic elite, but with a sizable German-Jewish population; (2) a German-Jewish period, from the early nineteenth century until after the Civil War; (3) an Eastern European period from the 1880s to the 1920s, during which the largest contingents of new immigrants joined the ethnic group; and (4) a modern period, since the 1920s, which has been marked by an evolution of a new Jewish ethnicity, new immigration from Germany and the Soviet Union, ethnic stability, and a declining population base. These periods did not begin and end abruptly, but they do represent distinct periods in American Jewish history and the shaping of the ethnic group as it is known today.

American Jews are a decidedly urban ethnic group. While some Jewish residents can be found in very small communities just about everywhere in the United States, and some even on farms, an overwhelming proportion are located in a few large metropolitan areas, especially in the region surrounding New York City. Within these metropolitan areas, Jews at one time occupied inner-city ghettos which served an important function as buffer zones between the old world and the new. Later, they abandoned these and moved in stages outward toward peripheral suburban locations. The degree of ethnic concentration changed, but some clustering and a maintenance of social networks and institutions permitted the group to survive in its new setting. Those institutions, like the synagogue and the community center, provided foci for this continuing ethnicity.

The Jewish population in America is highly mobile and, as a result, new patterns of settlement are developing, diminishing somewhat the concentration in the Northeast. Jews are moving increasingly from the North to the Sunbelt. The Jewish population is older than the American population in general, and has one of the lowest fertility rates of any American group. American Jews are experiencing a negative rate of natural increase. This fact may have serious implications for the survival of the ethnic group.

Survival is an important issue for Jews in America. There are a number of forces working to threaten the group with eventual extinction. These are not in the form of persecution and genocide, as has been the case many times in Jewish history. While there is widespread, sometimes overt anti-Semitism in America today, rooted in ancient prejudices that are potentially damaging, it does not appear to be a major force in American society or an immediate danger. The forces which threaten Jewish survival are coming from within the group. These include: (1) a declining fertility rate and a failure to grow at a replacement rate, coupled with an aging population; (2) assimilation and resulting loss of ethnic identity; (3) secularization and a decline in the centrality of religion as an ethnic bond; and (4) intermarriage, which some see as the biggest threat of all.

Most predictions foresee a stabilization of the Jewish population at between 5.5 and 5.8 million in the near future, and then a steep decline in the size of the ethnic group. At that point, perhaps some time in the next century, the American Jewish group may be but a fraction of its current size. Among the factors which contribute to a declining population are later ages at marriage and childbearing, increasing rates of divorce and separation, an increasing level of occupational opportunity for women, and higher levels of education and secularization. While Americanization of the Jewish population will probably continue as Jews become more mobile and geographically dispersed, and interact to a greater extent with non-Jews, it has also been suggested that ". . . structural separation and the continuity of Jewish identity will persist as American Jews continue their efforts to find a meaningful balance between Judaism and Americanism."[73] Whether geographic dispersal will dilute the strength of American Jewish communities to a point below the threshold of individual community survival remains to be seen. The question of survival is not a new one for the Jewish people, but for American Jews the fulfillment of aspirations and assimilation into the American mainstream may be the ultimate threats to that survival.

NOTES

1. Will Herbert, *Protestant-Catholic-Jew* (Garden City, New York: Anchor Books, 1955): p. 182.
2. Marshall Sklare, *America's Jews* (New York: Random House, 1971): p. 27.
3. Deborah Moore, "The Emergence of Ethnicity: New York's Jews, 1920–1940" (Ph.D. Dissertation, Columbia University, 1975): p. 3.
4. Nathan Glazer, *American Judaism* (Chicago: University of Chicago Press, 1957). Chapter 6 includes a discussion of this new ethnicity.
5. Arthur Goren, "Jews," in *Harvard Encyclopedia of American Ethnic Groups,* ed. Stephen Thernstrom (Cambridge: Harvard University Press, 1980): pp. 590, 595.
6. Goren, 1980: p. 595, cites a figure of 10 percent. Liebman found that in the late 1960s there were about 205,000 Orthodox Jewish *men.* Despite the presumed higher fertility rate among the Orthodox, the average family size is probably close to that of other Jews, between 3.3 and 3.4, since they have a higher percentage of elderly as well. Calculations of the Orthodox population using these statistics yield a proportion in the range of 11 to 15 percent of American Jews. Charles Liebman, *Aspects of the Religious Behavior of American Jews* (New York: Ktav Publising House, 1974): p. 113.
7. Goren, 1980: p. 595.
8. Glazer, 1957: pp. 53–54.
9. Goren, 1980: p. 595.
10. Ibid.: p. 572.
11. Jacob Marcus, "The American Colonial Jew: A Study in Acculturation," B.G. Rudolph Lectures in Judaic Studies (Syracuse University, Syracuse, New York, 1967): p. 7.
12. Ibid.: p. 7.
13. Jacob Marcus, *Early American Jewry* (New York: Ktav Publishing House, 1975): p. 393.
14. Edwin Gaustad, *Historical Atlas of Religion in America* (New York: Harper and Row, 1967): p. 144.
15. Goren, 1980: p. 574.
16. Marcus, 1967: p. 9.
17. Selma Stern Taeubler, "The Motivation of the German Jewish Emigration to America in the Post Mendelssohnian Era," in *Essays in American Jewish History,* ed. Jacob Marcus (Cincinnati: American Jewish Archives, 1958): pp. 247–261.
18. Lee Levinger, *A History of the Jews in the United States* (Cincinnati: Union of American Hebrew Congregations, 1952): p. 177.
19. Goren, 1980: p. 571.
20. Uriah Engleman, "Jewish Statistics in the United States Census of Religious Bodies (1850–1936)," *Jewish Social Studies,* 9 (April, 1947): pp. 127–174.
21. David Ward, "Immigration, Settlement Pattern and Spatial Distribution," in *Harvard Encyclopedia of American Ethnic Groups,* ed. Stephen Thernstrom (Cambridge: Harvard University Press, 1980): pp. 496–508.
22. Jonathan Mesinger, "The Jewish Community in Syracuse, 1850–1880: The Growth and Structure of an Urban Ethnic Region" (Ph.D Dissertation, Syracuse University, 1977).
23. Leon Jick, *The Americanization of the Synagogue, 1820–1870* (Hanover: Brandeis University Press, University Presses of New England, 1976).
24. Ibid.: p. 194.
25. Goren, 1980: p. 579.
26. C. Bezalel Sherman, *The Jew Within American Society* (Detroit: Wayne State University Press, 1965): p. 61.
27. Herbert, 1955: p. 179.
28. Goren, 1980: p. 581.
29. David Ward, *Cities and Immigrants* (New York: Oxford University Press, 1971): p. 79.
30. Goren, 1980: pp. 579, 582.
31. Bernard Weinryb, "Jewish Immigration and Accommodation to American Life," in *The Jews: Social Patterns of an American Group,* ed. Marshall Sklare (Glencoe: The Free Press, 1958): p. 7.
32. Louis Wirth, *The Ghetto* (Chicago: University of Chicago Press, 1928): p. 168.
33. Sklare, 1971: p. 103.
34. Robert Park and H. A. Miller, *Old World Traits Transplanted* (Chicago: University of Chicago Society for Social Research, 1925); and T. J. Jones, *Sociology of a New York City Block* (New York: Columbia University Studies in History, Economics, and Public Law), 21, 1904.
35. Jonathan Mesinger, "Manhattan's Jewish Community: Spatial Patterns in the History of a Religion-Ethnic Group," in *Space and Religion,* eds. M. Buttner, K. Gurgel, and K. Hoheisel (Berlin: Dietrich Reimer Verlag, forthcoming 1983); Oscar Handlin, *Adventure in Freedom* (New York: McGraw Hill, 1954): p. 105.
36. Glazer, 1957: p. 81.
37. Goren, 1980: p. 581.
38. Glazer, 1957: p. 82.
39. Goren, 1980: p. 592.
40. Charles Jaret, "Residential Mobility and Local Jewish Community Organization in Chicago" (Ph.D Dissertation, University of Chicago, 1977): p. 10.
41. Sidney Goldstein and Calvin Goldscheider, *Jewish Americans, Three Generations in a Jewish Community* (Englewood Cliffs: Prentice-Hall, 1968): p. 7.
42. Judith Kramer and Seymour Leventman, *Children of the Gilded Ghetto* (New Haven: Yale University Press, 1961): p. 11.
43. Goren, 1980: p. 590.
44. Goldstein and Goldscheider, 1968: p. 9.

45. Handlin, 1954: p. 104.
46. Kramer and Leventman, 1961: pp. 11–12.
47. Glazer, 1957: p. 117; Sklare, 1971: p. 194.
48. *American Jewish Yearbook* 50 (Philadelphia: Jewish Publication Society of America, 1948–1949): p. 753.
49. Goldstein and Goldscheider, 1968: p. 37.
50. Dan Jacobs and Ellen Frankel Paul, *Studies of the Third Wave: Recent Migration of Soviet Jews to the United States* (Boulder: Westview Press, 1981): pp. 6–7.
51. Goren, 1980: p. 597.
52. *America Jewish Yearbook* (Philadelphia: Jewish Publication Society of America, 1981), 81: p. 173. This volume is the source for much of the statistical information presented in this section. Halvorsen and Newman cite a figure of 6,113,520 using other sources, but indications are that the United States Jewish population has probably never surpassed 6 million. See Peter Halvorson and William Newman, *Atlas of Religious Change in America* (Washington, D.C.: Glenmary Research Center, 1978): p. 12.
53. Sidney Goldstein, "Jews in the United States: Perspectives from Demography," in *Jewish Life in the United States: Perspectives from the Social Sciences,* ed. Joseph Gittler (New York: New York University Press, 1981): p. 40.
54. Ibid.: p. 62.
55. William Newman and Peter Halvorson, "American Jews: Patterns of Geographic Distribution and Change, 1952–1971," *Journal for the Scientific Study of Religion,* 18 (June, 1979): p. 187.
56. Ibid.: p. 192.
57. Halvorson and Newman, 1978: pp. 12, 59 (map).
58. *American Jewish Yearbook* (Philadelphia: Jewish Publication Society of America, 1981), 81: p. 179. Figures used in the remainder of this section are also from this source.
59. Jaret, 1977: p. 9.
60. Goren, 1980: p. 592.
61. Goldstein, 1981: p. 66.
62. Ibid.: pp. 69–70.
63. Ibid.: pp. 77–80.
64. Ibid.: pp. 42–45.
65. Ibid: p. 50; see also Alvin Chenkin and Maynard Miran, "Jewish Population in the United States, 1979," *American Jewish Yearbook,* 1980 (Philadelphia: Jewish Publication Society of America, 1980), 80: p. 162.
66. Fred Massarik and Alvin Chenkin, "United States National Jewish Population Study: A First Report," *American Jewish Yearbook* (Philadelphia: Jewish Publication Society of America, 1973), 74: p. 280.
67. Goldstein, 1981: p. 83.
68. Massarik and Chenkin, 1973: pp. 284–285.
69. Sklare, 1971: p. 63.
70. Naomi Levine and Martin Hochbaum, eds., *Poor Jews: An American Awakening* (New Brunswick, N.J.: Transaction Books, 1974): p. 3.
71. Levin and Hochbaum, 1974: p. 2.
72. Ibid.: p. 3.
73. Goldstein, 1981: p. 91.

8

Japanese Americans

Midori Nishi

California State University, Los Angeles

Once the largest group among Asian populations in the United States, Japanese Americans now rank third in number after the Chinese and Filipinos. With a 1980 population of 700,747 their rate of increase since 1970 has been 18.5 percent, whereas the Chinese have increased by 85.3 percent during the past decade, the Filipinos by 125.8 percent, and the Koreans by 412.8 percent.

The Japanese are highly concentrated in two states: California with 37.4 percent of the total Japanese population in the United States, and Hawaii with 34.2 percent (Fig. 8.1, Table 8.1). Seven other states have from 1.2 percent to 3.8 percent of the nation's Japanese: Washington, New York, Texas, New Jersey, Illinois, Oregon, and Colorado. Each of the remaining 41 states has less than 1 percent of the total Japanese American population.

The Japanese have experienced a dynamic settlement history with their initial concentration in the Hawaiian Islands and their pre-World War II distribution primarily in the Pacific region (Figs. 8.2 and 8.3, Table 8.1). This settlement pattern was dramatically altered with the forced evacuation of all Japanese from the designated military zone number one (largely the Pacific Coastal region) in 1942 to relocation in concentration centers and internment camps, and their subsequent dispersal and resettlement in areas outside of the Pacific military zone (Figs. 8.4 and 8.5).[1] Once the Exclusion Order was revoked in December, 1944, they rapidly returned to their familiar surroundings in the Pacific Coast region where they re-established significant settlements.[2] The nature of these settlements has notably changed in many aspects from the pre-1942 occupance.

Outside of the concentration in California and Hawaii, the remaining 28.4 percent of the Japanese in 1980 were widely dispersed throughout the United States, although Washington, New York, Illinois and Texas each had more than 10,000 Japanese. Since 1940, the sizeable gain for many states outside the three western states and Hawaii is attributable to the impact of relocation, the liberalization of immigration laws, a moderate growth rate, and an increase in the mobility of the Japanese people.

TABLE 8.1 Japanese American Population by States, 1900, 1940, 1980

	1900	1940	1980
Alabama	3	21	1,394
Arizona	281	632	4,074
Arkansas	—	3	954
California	10,151	93,717	261,817
Colorado	48	2,734	9,858
Connecticut	18	164	1,864
Delaware	1	22	426
District of Columbia	7	68	752
Florida	1	154	5,564
Georgia	1	31	3,370
Idaho	1,291	1,191	2,585
Illinois	80	462	18,550
Indiana	5	29	2,356
Iowa	7	29	1,049
Louisiana	17	46	1,482
Kansas	4	19	1,585
Kentucky	—	9	1,056
Maine	4	5	336
Maryland	9	36	4,805
Massachusetts	53	158	4,483
Michigan	9	139	5,859
Minnesota	51	51	2,790
Mississippi	—	1	687
Missouri	9	74	2,651
Montana	2,441	508	754
Nebraska	3	480	1,378
Nevada	228	470	2,308
New Hampshire	1	5	448
New Jersey	52	298	9,905
New Mexico	8	186	1,280
New York	354	2,538	24,524
North Carolina	—	21	3,186

TABLE 8.1—*cont.*

North Dakota	148	83	230
Ohio	27	163	5,479
Oklahoma	—	57	1,975
Oregon	2,501	4,071	8,429
Pennsylvania	40	224	4,669
Rhode Island	13	6	474
South Carolina	—	33	1,414
South Dakota	1	19	262
Tennessee	4	12	1,657
Texas	13	458	10,502
Utah	417	2,210	5,474
Vermont	—	3	227
Virginia	10	74	5,207
Washington	5,617	14,565	26,369
Wisconsin	5	23	2,237
West Virginia	—	3	404
Wyoming	393	643	600
Alaska			1,589
Hawaii*	61,111	157,905	239,618
Total	85,437	284,853	700,747

*Japanese American population for 1900 and 1940 was for the Territory of Hawaii. Source: Andrew W. Lind, *Hawaii's People,* 4th ed. (Honolulu: University Press of Hawaii, 1980): p. 34.
Sources: United States Bureau of Census, 1980 Census of Population, *Supplementary Reports: Race of the Population by States, 1980,* PC 80–S1–3 (Washington, D.C.: U.S. Government Printing Office, 1981); Twelfth Census, *Census of Population: 1900,* Part I (Washington, D.C.: U.S. Government Printing Office, 1901); Sixteenth Census, *Census of Population, 1940; Number of Inhabitants,* 1 (Washington, D.C.: U.S. Government Printing Office, 1942.

URBAN-RURAL DISTRIBUTION

The Japanese are highly urbanized with 89 percent classified as urban by the 1970 census compared with the United States national average of 75 percent. This distribution contrasts sharply with their mainly rural residence in earlier years.

The urbanization of the Japanese population is exemplified by their concentration in such urban areas as Los Angeles and Honolulu (Tables 8.2 and 8.3). In California, in 1970, 94 percent of the state's Japanese population lived in urban areas.

TABLE 8.3 Japanese Population in Honolulu City and Hawaii: 1896–1970

	Honolulu City	% Japanese of Total Hawaiian Population
1896	2,381	9.8
1920	24,522	22.4
1950	92,510	50.1
1960	109,066	53.5
1970*	169,025	77.8

*Represents Honolulu S.M.S.A.

Sources: Andrew W. Lind, *Hawaii's People,* 4th ed. (Honolulu: University Press of Hawaii, 1980): p. 57.

U.S. Bureau of the Census, 1970 Census of Population, *Subject Reports: Japanese, Chinese and Filipinos in the United States,* PC (2)-1G (Washington, D.C.: U.S. Government Printing Office, 1973): p. 50.

TABLE 8.2 Japanese Population in Los Angeles City and Los Angeles County: 1890–1970

	Los Angeles City	% in Conterminous* United States	Los Angeles County	% in Conterminous* United States
1890	26	1.3	36	1.7
1900	150	0.6	204	0.8
1910	4,238	5.9	8,461	11.7
1920	11,618	10.5	19,911	17.9
1930	21,081	15.1	35,390	25.5
1940	23,321	18.4	36,866	29.1
1950	25,502	18.0	36,761	25.9
1960	51,468	19.8	77,314	29.7
1970	55,485	14.4	104,078	28.1

*Excludes Hawaii and Alaska.

Sources: Compiled from reports of the U.S. Bureau of Census, Eleventh, Twelfth, Thirteenth, Fourteenth, Fifteenth, Sixteenth, Seventeenth, *1960 Census of Population, 1970 Census of Population* (Washington, D.C.: U.S. Government Printing Office).

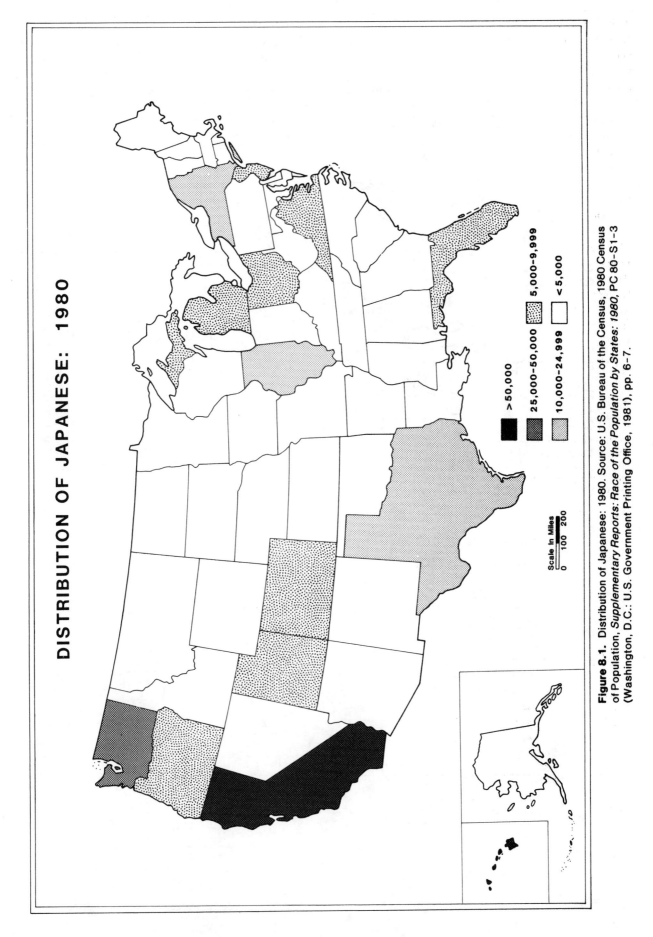

DISTRIBUTION OF JAPANESE: 1980

>50,000

25,000–50,000

10,000–24,999

5,000–9,999

<5,000

Scale In Miles
0   100   200

Figure 8.1. Distribution of Japanese: 1980. Source: U.S. Bureau of the Census, 1980 Census of Population, *Supplementary Reports: Race of the Population by States: 1980*, PC 80–S1–3 (Washington, D.C.: U.S. Government Printing Office, 1981), pp. 6–7.

DISTRIBUTION OF JAPANESE: 1900

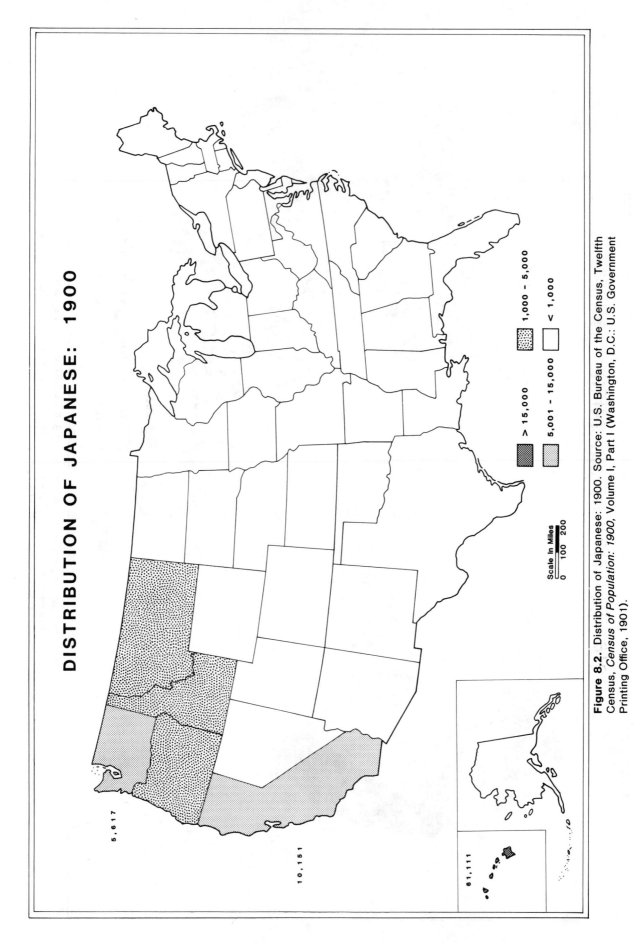

Figure 8.2. Distribution of Japanese: 1900. Source: U.S. Bureau of the Census, Twelfth Census, *Census of Population: 1900*, Volume I, Part I (Washington, D.C.: U.S. Government Printing Office, 1901).

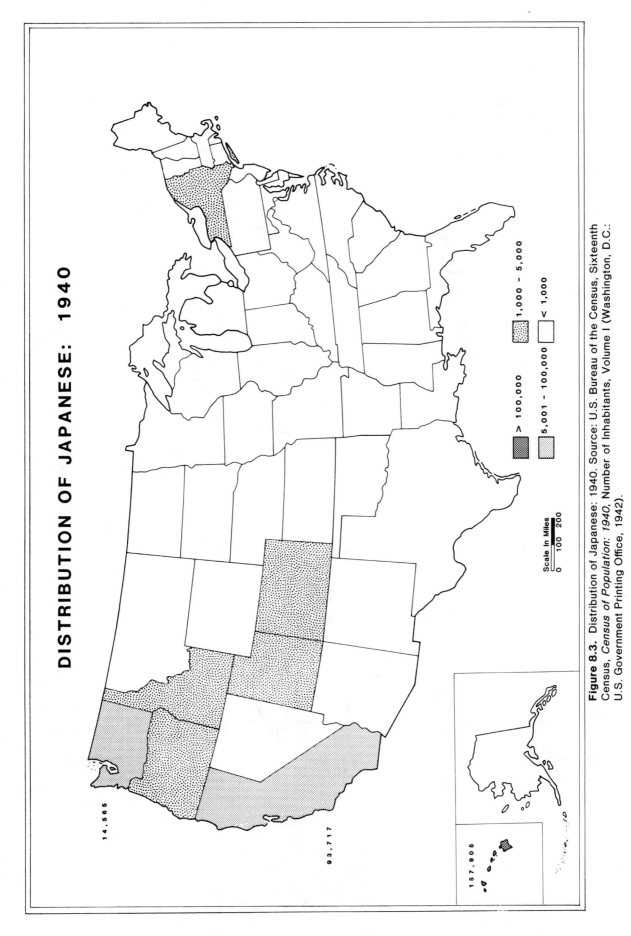

DISTRIBUTION OF JAPANESE: 1940

> 100,000

5,001 – 100,000

1,000 – 5,000

< 1,000

Scale In Miles
0   100   200

14,565

93,717

157,905

Figure 8.3. Distribution of Japanese: 1940. Source: U.S. Bureau of the Census, Sixteenth Census, *Census of Population: 1940*, Number of Inhabitants, Volume I (Washington, D.C.: U.S. Government Printing Office, 1942).

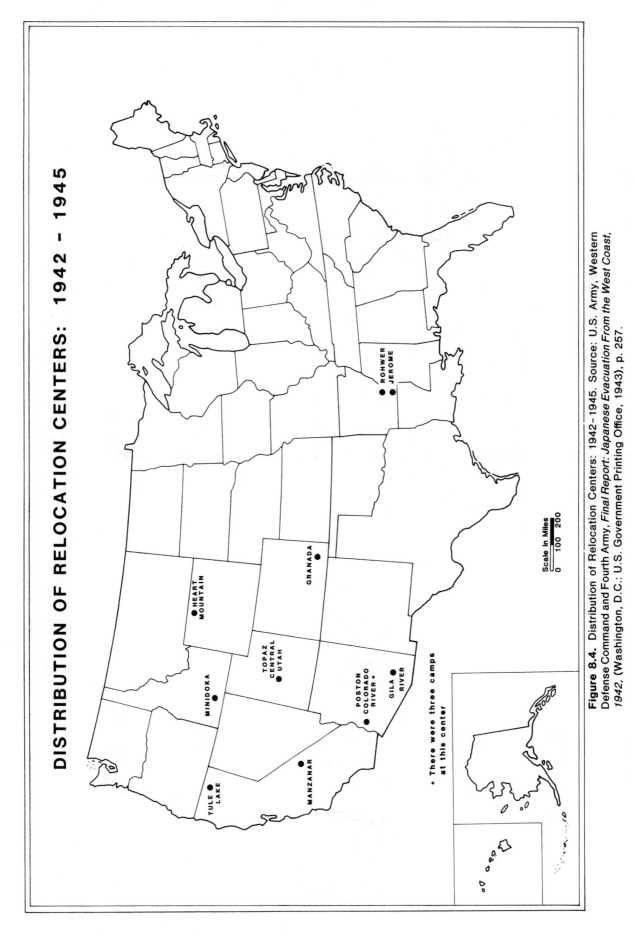

Figure 8.4. Distribution of Relocation Centers: 1942–1945. Source: U.S. Army, Western Defense Command and Fourth Army, *Final Report: Japanese Evacuation From the West Coast, 1942,* (Washington, D.C.: U.S. Government Printing Office, 1943), p. 257.

DISTRIBUTION OF RELOCATION CENTERS: 1942 – 1945

TULE LAKE

MINIDOKA

HEART MOUNTAIN

MANZANAR

TOPAZ CENTRAL UTAH

GRANADA

POSTON COLORADO RIVER *

GILA RIVER

ROHWER

JEROME

* There were three camps at this center

Scale in Miles
0 100 200

DISTRIBUTION OF INTERNMENT CAMPS: 1941 – 1946

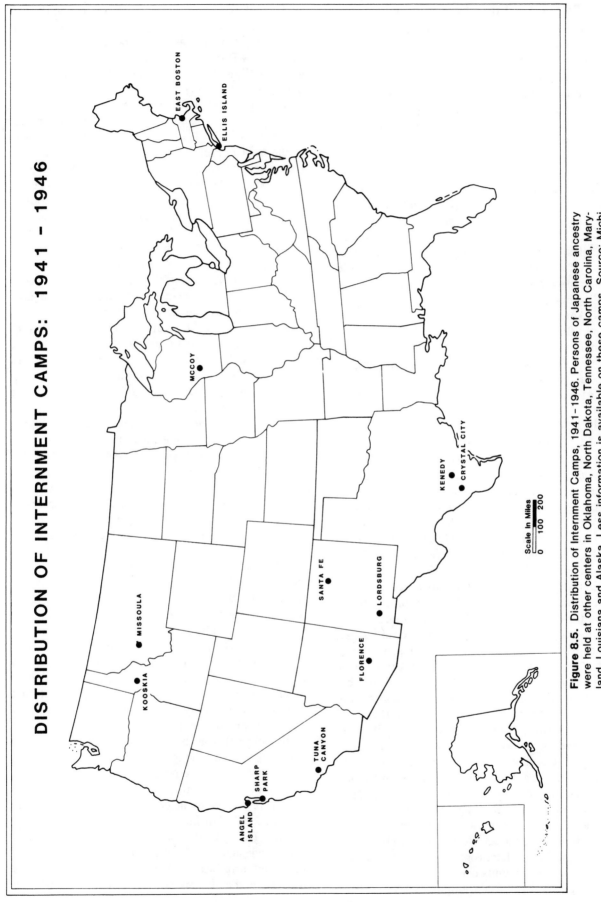

Figure 8.5. Distribution of Internment Camps, 1941–1946. Persons of Japanese ancestry were held at other centers in Oklahoma, North Dakota, Tennessee, North Carolina, Maryland, Louisiana and Alaska. Less information is available on these camps. Source: Michi Weglyn, *Years of Infamy: The Untold Story of America's Concentration Camps*, (New York: William Morrow and Company, Inc., 1976): pp. 176–177.

"Little Tokyos," or Ethno-Centered Communities

Like many minority groups, the Japanese are prone to form ethnic clusters, brought about by socio-economic forces and pressure. Historically, "Little Tokyos" or "Nihonmachi" (Japanese towns) evolved as a result of this natural affinity for one's own people. Inability to speak English brought migrants together where their native language could be spoken freely without embarrassment or conspicuousness. Such ethnic islands provided many of the needs and services which were unobtainable elsewhere.

With the emergence of a dominant American-born Japanese class, having more occupational and social mobility than the "Issei" (first generation immigrant Japanese), many of these ethnic centers have declined or lost their former identity and support base. Paradoxically the anticipated demise of "Little Tokyos" did not take place commensurate with the decline in the "Issei" generation and their replacement by progressively Americanized "Nisei," "Sansei," "Yonsei" (second, third, fourth generations). New Japanese communities have formed and some old ones have been reinforced. Their socio-cultural and economic importance has greatly increased, not only for themselves, but for the general community.

"Little Tokyo" in Downtown Los Angeles

"Little Tokyo" in the heart of downtown Los Angeles has experienced a remarkable transformation. Its inception as a Japanese community may have started in 1886–1888 when a Japanese restaurant on East First Street and a Japanese boarding house were established nearby.[3] Soon small businesses, hotels, offices, and religious and cultural institutions clustered at this location. By 1940 there were seven readily identifiable Japanese enclaves in the Los Angeles area.[4] The downtown center continued, however, to function as the leading commercial, residential, and cultural district. During the evacuation and relocation period, the district was occupied by other minorities and, in a sense, retained its ghetto-like nature. Despite Japanese reoccupance of this center in the 1950s and early 1960s, the community struggled for survival. Its future became uncertain when its deteriorating and unsafe buildings were condemned by the city. But, the determination and vitality of local community and business leaders have turned what was an ebbing tide against them into a surging wave of successful redevelopment.

A combination of local Japanese interests with their capital and an influx of big corporations from Japan who chose to invest in this blighted area have helped to promote Little Tokyo into a veritable showpiece with a bright future. Individual efforts and non-profit community organizations have contributed generously and a broadly based community participation has envolved. The Little Tokyo Redevelopment Association (L.T.R.A.), the Los Angeles City Council, and the Los Angeles Community Redevelopment Agency were all instrumental in obtaining federal funds and grants through N.D.P. (Neighborhood Development Program) and funds from H.C.D. (Housing and Community Development).

The Little Tokyo Redevelopment Project has been cited by federal officials as one of the outstanding redevelopment projects in the Nation.[5] Since 1970 some of the most impressive projects completed within the redevelopment zone of 65 gross acres or 47 net acres (eight city blocks) are the following: New Otani Hotel, Little Tokyo Towers senior citizens housing, Buddhist Temple, Christian Church, Japanese American Cultural and Community Center, a complex of shopping malls, plazas, arcades, office and bank buildings, and parking facilities. Projects planned for the 1980s include construction of residential, commercial and office buildings, a medical center, auditorium, and acquisition of land to the south and east. The new townscape's visual attractiveness capitalizes on the use of characteristic Japanese artistic and architectural features. These have been blended into basically American structural forms. Pervasive Japanese landscaping interspersed with oriental style gardens have imparted a special ambiance to this environment. Some of the complementary landscape features include Japanese style "kawara" (tile) roofs, a copy of an historic fire watch tower, "torii" style gateways, and meaningful ornamental sculptures.

Little Tokyo adjoins and shares the centrality of Los Angeles city's civic center and CBD. It also serves as a regional center for the Japanese population in southern California, although there are secondary "Little Tokyo" type communities scattered within the Los Angeles area and its suburbs[6] (Fig. 8.6). Some of the suburban "Little Tokyos" have exceeded the downtown one in the size of their Japanese population. Little Tokyo is no longer the exclusive preserve of its own ethnic group. It also serves a large non-Japanese population. Some 64 restaurants[7] are concentrated here to cater to a cosmopolitanized public taste for food and atmosphere. A diversified population is attracted by other commercial enterprises with specialty goods and services, by a variety of cultural activities, and by schools of art, dance, music, martial arts and crafts. Little Tokyo also has become a Los Angeles landmark and a tourist center (Fig. 8.7).

One highlight is the Nisei Week Festival which celebrated its 41st annual event in August, 1981. A week or two are devoted to the presentation of exhibits, tournaments, folk dancing, and various events and ceremonies. The festival culminates with a grand parade with bands and colorful floats, the naming of a Japanese American beauty queen and her attendant, and the recognition of outstanding personages. Nisei Week

176

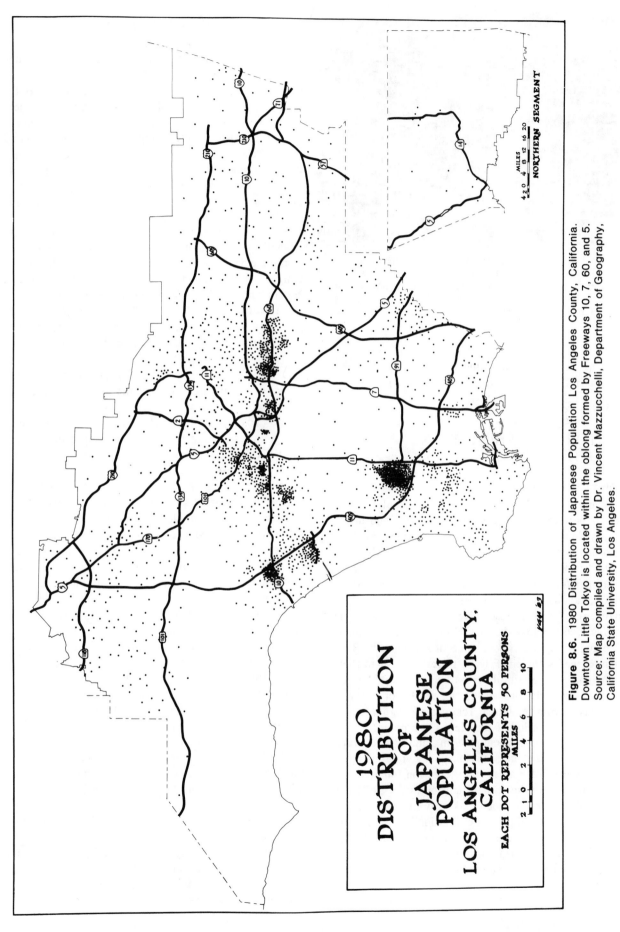

Figure 8.6. 1980 Distribution of Japanese Population Los Angeles County, California. Downtown Little Tokyo is located within the oblong formed by Freeways 10, 7, 60, and 5. Source: Map compiled and drawn by Dr. Vincent Mazzucchelli, Department of Geography, California State University, Los Angeles.

Figure 8.7. Little Tokyo in Downtown Los Angeles. Weller Court Mall, Matsuzakaya Department Store in left foreground, New Otani Hotel in left background, shops and offices to the right, Los Angeles City Hall in the background, Friendship Knot by sculptor Shinkichi Tajiri in the foreground.

Festival and a spectrum of other activites foster a strong sense of identity and cultural pride among many Japanese of different generations.

HISTORY OF MIGRATION TO THE UNITED STATES

The First Emigrants

There are a number of intriguing speculative accounts pertaining to the earliest voluntary and involuntary departures from Japan to the Americas. One recorded story was the plight of five fishermen who were cast adrift in a stormy sea and rescued by an American whaling ship captain who brought one of them, Manjiro Nakahama to Massachusetts in 1843.[8] Hikozo Hamada, also known as Joseph Heco,[9] was rescued off the shores of Japan in 1850 by a United States merchant ship and brought to sojourn in San Francisco.[10]. Both men learned sufficient English to return later to their homeland and to stimulate the beginnings of United States-Japan relationships during the historic transition period from the feudal Tokugawa Shogunate rule to the modern period of the Meiji Government.

The fall of the Shogunate in mid-19th century brought to an end the seclusion policy vigorously enforced by the Tokugawas and there soon followed the beginnings Japanese emigration overseas. In 1853 Commodore Perry's epoch making visit to Japan established official diplomatic relations between the United States and Japan. The official record of the United States Immigration Commission lists the first entry of a Japanese in 1861 (Fig. 8.8).[11]

Conditions Contributing to Japanese Migration

The Meiji Restoration in 1868 commenced a period of tremendous political, social, economic change and development within Japan. Able young Japanese students were encouraged to go to the United States to learn about western technology and American life; other young Japanese migrated in order to escape the military draft. Also, despite its rapidly growing modern industrial economy, Japan experienced severe economic problems and population pressures. Its agricultural sector suffered disproportionately, and migrants were particularly numerous from some extremely poverty stricken rural areas of southern Japan.

In 1885, for the first time, the Japanese Government officially permitted its subjects to leave the country. Complete data regarding the origins of early Japanese emigrants are unobtainable from official sources in Japan, but a study made in 1900 included source areas by prefectures from 1899 to 1903.[12] During this brief period 84,576 persons emigrated and it was estimated that 80 percent of them came to the United States. More than two-thirds of these emigrants were from rural Hiroshima, Kumamoto, Fukuoka, Yamaguchi and Nagasaki prefectures. Niigata and Wakayama prefectures were other important sources. In contrast the Kanto (Tokyo) and Kinki (Osaka) industrial districts which are at present the most densely populated and most highly industrialized areas in Japan had only a small number of emigrants (Fig. 8.9).

When news of employment in the United States reached the migrant's home community, it frequently encouraged others in the neighborhood to make the move overseas. People associated in the same home village or relatives were likely to assist each other so that the familiarity and sense of the old world village solidarity and support were transplanted to the new world settlements.

The burgeoning development of western United States starting with the discovery of gold and other abundant natural resources, the railroad construction period, the availability of enormous tracts of potential agricultural land created an insatiable demand for labor. Large American companies in order to recruit cheap labor advertised and offered inducements such as a surety, which the Japanese Government demanded under the Emigrants' Protective Law of 1896.

Passage of the Chinese Exclusion Act of 1882 curbed the large flow of Chinese emigrants and shifted the labor source to Japan. About this time the rapidly expanding sugar cane plantations in Hawaii, and fruit and vegetable farms in California, created an enormous demand for agricultural labor. Following the signing of a convention between Japan and Hawaii in 1886, thousands came as laborers for work on the plantations.

The 1907 Gentlemen's Agreement which restricted Japanese migrants as laborers caused a sharp decline

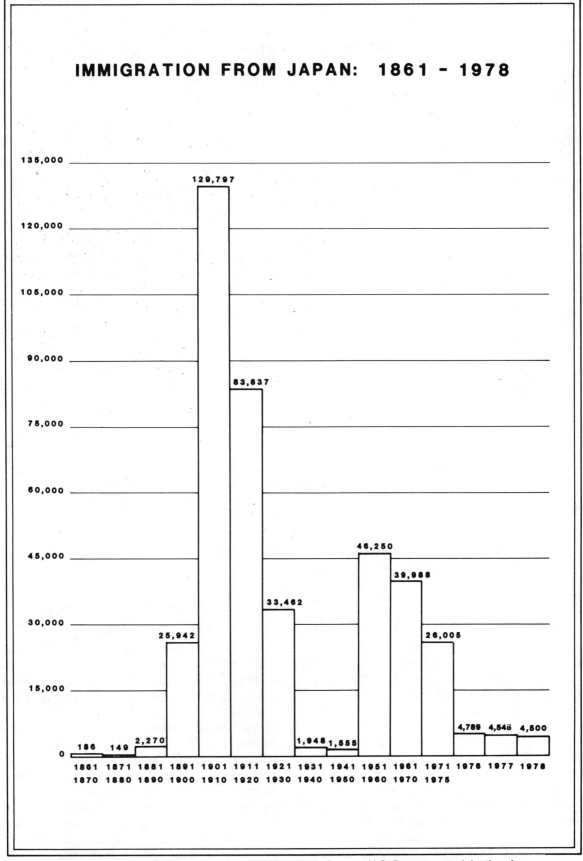

Figure 8.8. Immigration From Japan: 1861–1978. Source: U.S. Department of Justice, Immigration and Naturalization Service, *1978 Statistical Yearbook of the Immigration and Naturalization Service,* (Washington, D.C.: U.S. Government Printing Office, 1980): pp. 36–37.

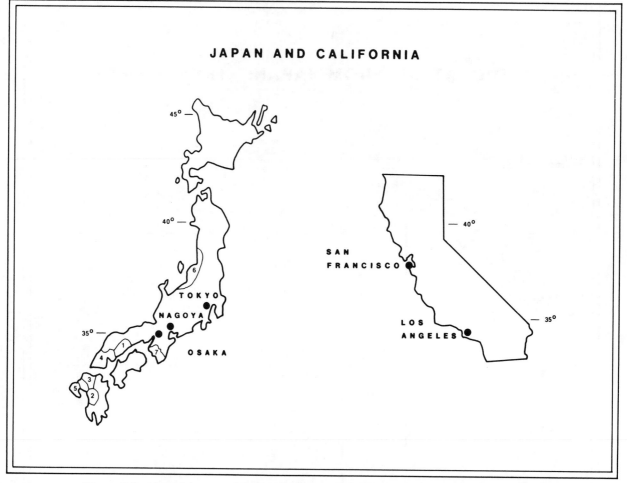

Figure 8.9. Map of Japan and California. Source Areas of Japanese Immigrants to the U.S. Between 1899 and 1903. Prefectures shown are 1. Hiroshima, 2. Kumamoto, 3. Fukuoka, 4. Yamaguchi, 5. Nagasaki, 6. Niigata, 7. Wakayama.

in migration to the United States. However, Japanese migrants already living in the United States could send for their relatives in accordance with the Agreement. There resulted an influx, largely of women, many of them designated by the term "picture bride."

The stringent Oriental Exclusion Act of 1924 with special provisions for merchants and businessmen reduced all Asian migration to a mere trickle. Because of the continuing increase in commerce and trade between Japan and the United States, Japanese merchants and businessmen have been representative migrants since then.

Not until the Walter-McCarran Act of 1952, eliminating race as a consideration, did Japanese migration make a significant upward climb. Once more in 1965, Congress passed the Immigration Act which abolished the national origins quota system. The impact of this law swelled the migration flow from many Asian countries, although the migration from Japan has been less than from other Asian countries. A booming Japanese economy, an increased standard of living, a low population growth rate, and political stability are the more apparent factors that have reduced out-migration from Japan.

SPATIAL MOVEMENT WITHIN THE UNITED STATES

By 1900 the Japanese made up nearly 40 percent of the entire Hawaii population, but in 1900, due to an outbreak of bubonic plague in Hawaii, ships loaded with Japanese immigrants were diverted from Honolulu to San Francisco. Since the major port of entry on the mainland was San Francisco, the newcomers tended to concentrate in the Bay area. Later the Japanese gradually dispersed but the majority remained in California. Next important as a part of entry was Seattle, followed by Portland. About three-fourths of the 2,000 Japanese aliens enumerated as residents of the United States in 1880 had settled near ports of entry in California and Washington.[13] Those who entered via Canada and Mexico tended to drift toward the pacific Coast states where economic opportunities were most favorable. California proved to have the strongest attraction and subsequent movements continued in that direction. Many of the earliest settlers worked as laborers on the Santa Fe or Southern Pacific railroads and became acquainted with the attractive features of southern California, including job opportunites in a new, uncrowded and steadily growing region. A sudden influx of Japanese to the Los Angeles area occurred following the disastrous San Francisco earthquake and fire. According to the 1900 census, 42 percent of the nation's alien Japanese were in California, 23 percent in Washington, 10 percent in Oregon, 21 percent in the intermontane states, and the remainder widely scattered (Fig. 8.2).

1940 Settlement Pattern

By 1940 the distribution of Japanese in the United States was regarded as essentially stabilized (Fig. 8.3). The fertile basins and valleys of the Pacific Coast states were the earliest foci of settlement, and 88.5 percent of the mainland Japanese were located in those areas. California alone accounted for 93,717 or 73.8 percent of the total Japanese population. Areas of greatest concentration were the Los Angeles Basin, followed by the Central Valley with Sacramento and Fresno as important centers, and the Bay Region with San Francisco. In Washington they settled mainly in the Puget Sound Lowland easily accessible to Seattle and Tacoma, although a large number also settled in the irrigated fruit growing valleys east of the Cascades. In Oregon, most of them lived in the Willamette Valley at no great dis-

tance from Portland. For America as a whole the so-called Japanese problem was largely a Pacific Coast phenomenon.

In the intermontane states, the Japanese were so widely dispersed that in only a few centers such as Denver and Salt Lake City was the West even conscious of them. East of the Rocky Mountains, there were a few hundred in the interior and Great Lakes cities but virtually none in the South. New York City, commonly regarded as an enormous reservoir of ethnic groups from the world at large, had less than 2,000 Japanese.

Dislocation During the War Years

During the years 1942–1946, this demographic pattern was completely disrupted. The familiar Pacific Coast agglomerations were broken up and some 120,000 persons were relocated in temporary assembly centers, ten relocation centers, and more than thirteen internment camps. The relocation centers were located mainly in the intermontane states. Unlike normal migration, this one was forced. The center locations were selected on the basis of military necessity and expediency, having little economic or geographic significance (Figs. 8.4, 8.5). The surrounding lands were generally marginal in the economic sense and devoid of any incentive for permanent settlement. Like temporary army barracks, which were their prototypes, these ugly tar-papered wooden structures were eventually abandoned (Figs. 8.10a-8.10b). Locational

Figure 8.10 A and B. Manzanar Camp. These two 1943 photographs, are a grim reminder of tarpapered barracks, watch tower, and barbed wire of Manzanar located in the Owens Valley with the east face of the Sierra Nevada Range in the background. The site is now designated a California registered historical landmark and a stone monument with a bronze plaque inscribed as the first of the 10 concentration camps stands at the former camp entrance way. Another memorial monument inscribed "Ireito" (Console the Spirit) has been erected on the cemetery grounds. Since 1969 an annual pilgrimage is conducted by Japanese Americans and special religious ceremonies are performed. Source: Photographs are by courtesy and permission of Toyo Miyatake, Inc.

changes of this proportion in an ethnic group well known for its conservative tendencies caused basic socioeconomic changes.

ECONOMIC AND OCCUPATIONAL CHANGES

Pre-1942 Rural Occupance

Farming and fishing were leading occupations during initial Japanese settlement in Hawaii and the West Coast states. Some worked on the railroads or in mining and lumber camps until they could quickly advance into more desirable employment. As common farm laborers, these hard working, enterprising people rapidly rose to farm operator or entrepreneurship status. As they acquired often poor, undeveloped land, they transformed it into productive farm land. A long and impressive list of credits go to these early Japanese farmers in their contribution to the growth in eminence of California agriculture. George Shima (Kenji Ushijima) drained swamp lands in the San Joaquin River delta and became widely known as the "Potato King."

TABLE 8.4 Employed Japanese Workers* by Occupation Group for California, Oregon, and Washington: 1940

Major Occupation Group	Number	%
Total	48,691	100.0
Professional workers	1,157	2.4
Semi-professional workers	230	0.5
Farmers and Farm managers	7,001	14.4
Proprietors, managers, and officials, except farm	5,491	11.3
Clerical, sales, and kindred workers	5,512	11.3
Craftsmen, foremen, and kindred workers	924	1.9
Operatives and kindred workers	3,517	7.2
Domestic service workers	3,541	7.3
Service workers, except domestic	3,393	7.0
Farm Laborers (wage workers) and farm formen	8,307	17.1
Farm laborers, unpaid family workers	4,832	9.9
Laborers, except farm	4,383	9.0
Occupation not reported	403	0.8

TABLE 8.5 Employed Japanese Workers* by Industry Group for California, Oregon, and Washington: 1940

Major Industry Group	Number		%	
Total	48,691		100.0	
Agriculture	22,027		45.2	
Forestry and fishing	t786		1.6	
Mining	12		0.0	
Construction	96		0.2	
Manufacturing	1,978		4.1	
Transportation	686		1.4	
Utilities and communication	20		0.0	
Trade	11,472		23.6	
Wholesale		2,190		4.5
Food stores, retail		4,972		10.2
Restaurants		2,082		4.3
Other, including filling stations		2,228		4.6
Personal services	8,336		17.1	
Domestic		4,744		9.7
Hotels and lodging places		1,335		2.7
Laundering, cleaning, and dyeing services		1,478		3.0
Misc. personal services		779		1.6
Finance, insurance, real estate	656		1.3	
Business and repair services	411		0.8	
Professional and related services	1,326		2.7	
Amusement, recreation and related services	251		0.5	
Government	126		0.3	
Non-classifiable	508		1.0	

*14 years and over, employed except on public emergency work (Tables 8.4, 8.5). Source: U.S. Army, Western Defense Command and Fourth Army, *Final Report: Japanese Evacuation From the West Coast, 1942* (Washington, D.C.: U.S. Government Printing Office, 1943): pp. 416, 407.

Kanaye Nagasawa was designated "Samurai of Fountaingrove" for his significant contribution to the state's wine industry.[14] Other important developments were made in rice growing lands and new productive varieties of rice were developed. Truck farming lands and quality truck farm products, horticulture and floriculture industries flourished. In California, in 1940, Japanese farmers held a virtual monopoly in acreage of such crops as snap beans, celery, peppers, strawberries and more than half of the acreage of artichokes, cauliflower, cucumber, tomatoes, spinach, garlic and significant production of other truck crops.[15] For the three conterminous Pacific states in 1940 the leading occupation and industry for the Japanese was farming or agriculture (Tables 8.4–8.5).

The California Alien Land Laws enacted in 1913, later amended in 1920 and 1923, deprived Japanese aliens of the right to own or lease land. As a result from 1920 to 1940, there was a marked decline in the number of Japanese in farming areas of California and decrease in acreage operated by them. This was one impetus for the movement from rural to urban settlements. As farm workers they were eager and ambitious to improve their economic, housing and living conditions and many were readily attracted to opportunities found in the cities.

Credit goes to the Japanese for their contribution to the early successful development of commercial fisheries, superior fishing techniques and equipment, canneries, and related activites along the Pacific Coast. Bainbridge Island in Puget Sound near Seattle and Terminal Island in the port of Los Angeles near San Pedro were the sites of two productive Japanese fishing communities. Because of their sensitive and strategic location near United States Navy yards, the Japanese were among the first people to suffer undue hardships and deprivation by the mercilessly swift and immediate orders for their evacuation.[16] Both were known as compact and tightly knit communities which had retained many of their old world customs. By 1931 the Japanese controlled 30 to 40 percent of the total fish catch landed at San Pedro, including 70 percent of the albacore, 75 percent of the mackerel, 35 to 40 percent of the sardines and 30 to 35 percent of the tuna.[17]

Pre-1942 Urban Occupance

The urban and rural non-farm Japanese population tended to enter into small businesses where a considerable degree of independence could be enjoyed. Their predominance in growing truck and market crops carried over into wholesale and retail marketing of these crops. In 1940 Japanese employment in wholesale and retail trades ranked second to employment in agriculture in the Pacific Coast states (Tables 8.4 and 8.5). In Los Angeles City it was estimated that approximately 75 percent of the employed Nisei in 1934 worked in some phase of produce marketing.[18] In Los Angeles County about 75 percent of all retail fruit and vegetable stands were operated by Japanese.[19] The flower business was also Japanese controlled in Los Angeles County. To a lesser extent the same chain of control from producer, wholesaler, to retailer was evident in the nursery business. With their traditional love for nature and their appreciation for beautiful gardens, the Japanese were soon engaged in contract gardening, especially in the Los Angeles area.

Some 17.1 percent of the employed Japanese workers were engaged in personal services, either as domestic day workers or resident workers. They also worked as barbers and beauticians and as employees of cleaning establishments, hotels and lodging places (Table 8.5). Outright discrimination and hostility against the Japanese by white employers both in the private and public sectors, linguistic problems, and a limited capital and economic base within the ethnic community were factors in the low employment levels in such occupations as utilities and communications, mining and construction, government services, amusement and recreation, and finance and real estate.

The timetable for the Evacuation in early 1942 allowed as little as 48 hours, a week, or a few months at the most. The swift methods employed the United States Army to transport the evacuees to Assembly and Relocation centers prevented the Japanese from adequately disposing of their properties. The economic losses in real property and personal possessions were enormous. It was an abrupt discontinuance of life styles, occupational and educational pursuits, and social contacts with the non-Japanese people. A void was created.

Present Occupational Characteristics

Striking changes in the occupational structure have taken place among the Japanese. In the professional and related services, the Japanese have made a dramatic gain from 2.7 percent employed in 1941 to 19.1 percent in 1970 (Tables 8.5, 8.6, 8.7). In 1970, approximately one-third of the Japanese males (31 percent United States born and 45 percent foreign born) were employed in the so-called upper status white-collar occupations as professionals, technical and managerial workers, a higher rate than in the total United States male (25 percent) population (c.f. United States vs. foreign born Japanese, Table 8.8, Fig. 8.11). Thirty percent of Japanese males were employed as skilled or semi-skilled blue collar workers (craftsmen, foremen and machine operators) whereas this was the largest occupational group for the total United States male (41 percent) population.

183

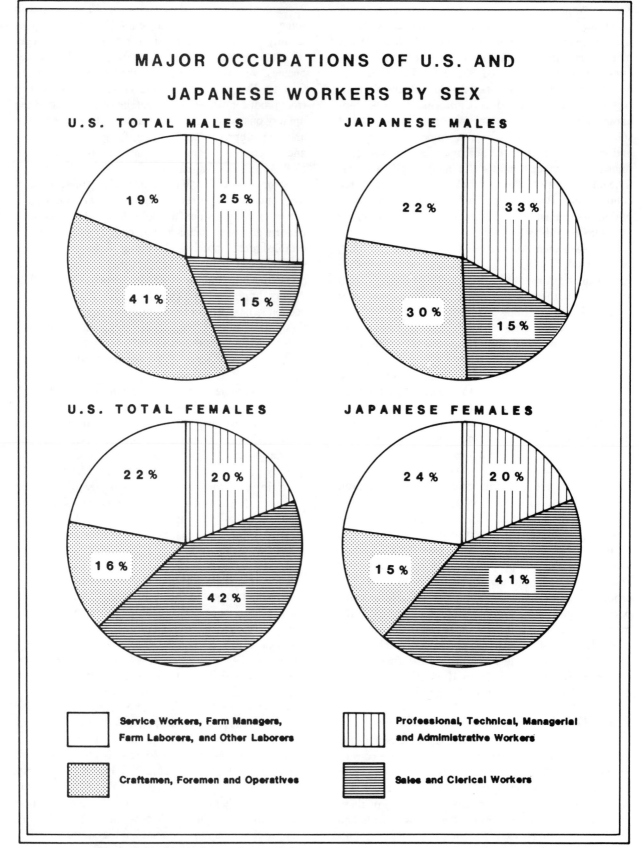

Figure 8.11. Major Occupations of U.S. and Japanese Workers by Sex. Source: U.S. Department of Health, Education and Welfare, *A Study of Selected Socio-Economic Characteristics of Ethnic Minorities Based on the 1970 Census,* Volume II: Asian Americans, Publication No. (OS) 75–121 (Washington, D.C.: D.H.E.W., July, 1974), pp. 32, 34.

TABLE 8.6 Employed Japanese Workers* by Occupation Group for the United States: 1970

Major Occupation Group		Number	%	Male	Female
	Total	263,972	100.0	147,054	116,918
Professional, technical, and kindred workers		50,083	19.0	31,530	18,544
Managers and administrators, except farm		21,738	8.2	17,263	4,475
Sales workers		16,928	6.4	8,856	8,072
Clerical and kindred workers		53,443	20.2	13,291	40,152
Craftsmen, foremen, and kindred workers		31,144	11.8	29,020	2,124
Operatives, including transport		30,860	11.7	15,131	15,729
Laborers, except farm		15,680	5.9	14,616	992
Farmers and farm managers		5,326	2.0	4,576	750
Farm laborers and foremen		4,877	1.8	3,125	1,752
Service workers, except private household		29,158	11.0	9,334	19,824
Private household workers		4,807	1.8	303	4,504

TABLE 8.7 Employed Japanese Workers* by Industry Group for the United States: 1970

Major Industry Group		Number	%
	Total	263,972	100.0
Agriculture, forestry, and fisheries		19,403	7.4
Mining		401	0.1
Construction		13,551	5.1
Manufacturing			
Durable goods		20,700	7.8
Nondurable goods		20,690	7.8
Transportation, communications, and other public utilities		14,399	5.5
Wholesale and retail trade		61,958	23.5
Finance, insurance and real estate		12,508	4.7
Business and repair services		8,779	3.3
Personal services		17,976	7.8
Entertainment and recreation services		2,327	0.1
Professional and related services		50,391	19.1
Public administration		20,889	8.0

*14 years and over (Tables 8.6, 8.7).

Source: United States Bureau of the Census, 1970 Census of Population, *Subject Reports: Japanese, Chinese, and Filipinos in the United States*, PC (2)-1G (Washington, D.C.: U.S. Government Printing Office, 1973): p. 31 (Tables 7.7, 7.8).

Regional differences are reflected in the percentage variations of Japanese employed in several occupations. In Hawaii the percentage in professional and managerial occupations is lower than the national rate whereas the percentage in skilled (craftsmen, foremen and machine operators) occupations is higher. The H. E. W. study made the observation that Asians who are in the majority in Hawaii have not faced the many and more severe discriminatory practices found elsewhere in skilled trades.[20]

In 1970, of the employed Japanese women 41 percent were either clerical or sales workers, a rate comparable to the total United States female (42 percent) working force. Another 24 percent were in service occupations, a rate again somewhat comparable to the total female (22 percent) working force. Among the foreign born Japanese women workers, there was a greater concentration in the categories of craftsmen, operatives and service workers and a smaller concentration in the professional category than for United States born Japanese. This may be related to their lack of English language skills or sufficient occupational skills.

The selectivity in recent immigration policies favoring persons with high skills and education was evident in the high proportion (53 percent) reported as professionals. Among Japanese immigrants from 1965 to 1973 clerical and sales workers comprised 17 percent and service workers another 17 percent.[21]

Underemployment was still evident in 1970 for those Japanese unable to obtain employment commensurate with their educational attainment, experience, and capabilities. The most noteworthy occupational achievements of the Japanese have been their proportionately high representation in the professions and their acceptance in positions of trust, appointments on important commissions, and in elective public offices at the local and national levels.

Japanese Americans now occupy positions which were considered almost improbable or unthinkable to aspiring, deserving and qualified persons before World War II. Judges, senators, congressmen, the governor of Hawaii, mayors, officers or officials of huge corporate businesses, military, academic and cultural institutions are among these positions. The trend toward economic diversification and social assimilation was somewhat accelerated by the demographic composition, the dislocation (evacuation) and the disruption and, to some extent, destruction of the economic and social structure built up by the Issei.

TABLE 8.8 Occupations of Japanese by Sex and Nativity: 1970

Occupations	Males % United States Born	Foreign Born	Females % United States Born	Foreign Born
Total	100	100	100	100
Professional, technical and managerial workers	31	45	21	13
Clerical and sales workers	15	13	47	19
Craftsmen and operatives	33	13	11	31
Laborers, non-farm	9	13	1	1
Service workers including domestics	4	9	18	33
Farm-related managers and workers	10	7	2	3

Source: U.S. Department of Health, Education, and Welfare. *A Study of Selected Socio-Economic Characteristics of Ethnic Minorities Based on the 1970 Census,* 2: Asian Americans, Publication No. (OS) 75–121 (Washington, D.C.: D.H.E.W., July, 1974): p. 88.

TABLE 8.9 Income Characteristics of the Japanese and U.S. Total Population: 1970

	U.S. Total	Japanese			
		U.S.	Hawaii	Calif.	Other
Income of Persons 16 Years and Over % Under $4,000					
Male	31	30	26	29	36
Female	68	58	54	58	65
% Over $10,000					
Male	25	33	33	32	31
Female	3	5	5	3	4
Income of Families					
% Under $4,000	15	10	6	9	16
% Over $10,000	47	65	71	65	54
Median Income (dollars)	9,590	12,515	13,542	12,393	11,034

Source: United States Department of Health, Education, and Welfare, *A Study of Selected Socio-Economic Characteristics of Ethnic Minorities Based on the 1970 Census,* 2: Asian Americans, Publication No. (OS) 75–121 (Washington, D.C.: D.H.E.W., July, 1974): p. 105.

A measure of the impact on the United States national as well as local economy is suggested by the number and kinds of businesses and industries held by Japanese in California, Hawaii, New York and other selected areas. A recent directory of giant companies with branches and subsidiaries in the United States indicates that 653 out of an estimated 2,000 such enterprises have their home base in Japan.[22] J.E.T.R.O. (Japanese External Trade Organization) lists in their 1981 directory 543 Japan-based firms and offices in southern California.[23] The directory lists 27 state chartered banks and agencies with their head offices in the Los Angeles downtown area. Sumitomo Bank alone lists 23 branch banks in southern California. R. C. King notes that there are more than 700 Japan-based companies employing more than 10,000 persons in California and contributing significantly to the state's economy.[24]

As yet, few Japanese Americans are known in certain fields such as the theater, film industry, sports and literary world, even though other minorities have achieved great fame and success in these areas. Proportionately there are fewer Japanese ranked at the poverty level or on welfare as compared with some other minorities or the United States' total population.

Income and Economic Well Being

The median national income for Japanese familes in 1971 was higher by almost $3,000 than for American familes in general (Table 8.9). This higher income level of Japanese familes was attributed to a higher percentage (60) of households with more than one earner, whereas for all American households the percentage was 51. The greater participation rate of Japanese women in the labor force was another factor for the higher incomes of their families. The breakdown of income data showed that almost one third (30 percent) of Japanese men, 16 years and over, earned less than $4,000 a year (almost the same as the national rate at 31 percent) while another third (33 percent) earned over $10,000 a year, higher than the national figure of 25 percent. The middle income group represented 34 percent for Japanese males whereas the national level was at 55 percent.

Among employed Japanese women, more than one-half (58 percent) were earning less than $4,000 in 1971, whereas for working women in the United States the rate was at 68 percent. On the other hand, of the Japanese working women who were earning more than $10,000, the percentage exceeded that of all American working women. Five percent of the working Japanese women earned $10,000 or more; whereas three percent of all working women in the United States earned that much.

There was a lag in income levels of Japanese males to the total United States' male population when ratios were compared of persons earning $10,000 and more to their education and occupations by age groups. However middle aged Japanese males, 45–64, ranked above all middle aged American males, 45–64 in the ratio of persons earning $10,000 and more to their education and occupations (Table 8.10). There was less than one Japanese male (0.9) earning $10,000 and more for every Japanese male with a college degree. As to the total United States male population (25–34 years old) earning $10,000 and more, there were 1.5 men for every male with a college degree. The ratio was 0.8 Japanese men for every Japanese male engaged in professional, technical, or managerial occupations; the ratio was 1.1 United States' men for every American male (Table 8.11). The data reveal less disparity between income levels, education and occupations for Japanese women when compared to women in the total population.

Historically the Japanese were under-employed in terms of their educational background, occupational skills, potential, and their economic aspirations. It was common for Nisei with American college degrees to be found in underpaid, menial, unskilled work because they were denied employment in fields for which they had been trained. Confronted with unwarranted discrimination and prejudice during much of their history in the United States, their persevering heroic uphill struggle to improve their socio-economic status deserves recognition as part of America's unique ethnic history. Apart from generalizations on the income and economic well being for this minority group over-all, further insights may be gained by a consideration of more detailed accounts of life styles for individual families at different income levels.

TABLE 8.10 Ratios of Income to Education and Occupations for the Japanese and U.S. Total Population

Ratios of Persons Earning $10,000 or More to Persons With 4 Years College or More: 1970

	Males			Females		
	25–34	35–44	45–64	25–34	35–44	45–64
U.S. Total	1.5	2.4	3.1	0.1	0.3	0.5
Japanese						
U.S.	0.9	1.8	3.4	0.1	0.4	0.8
Calif.	0.9	1.8	3.1	0.2	0.4	0.9
Hawaii*	1.6	2.7	6.0	0.1	0.6	1.1
Other	0.5	1.1	2.0	0.1	0.2	0.6

TABLE 8.11 Ratios of Persons Earning $10,000 or More to Persons in Professional, Technical and Managerial Occupations: 1970

	Males			Females		
	25–34	35–44	45–64	25–34	35–44	45–64
U.S. Total	1.1	1.5	1.6	0.2	0.3	0.4
Japanese						
U.S.	0.8	1.3	1.7	0.2	0.4	0.5
Calif.	0.8	1.3	1.8	0.3	0.5	0.6
Hawaii*	1.2	1.6	1.9	0.2	0.5	0.5
Other	0.5	1.1	1.4	0.2	0.3	0.5

*Because of cost of living differences, incomes in Hawaii are higher (Tables 8.10, 8.11).

Source: United States Department of Health, Education, and Welfare, *A Study of Selected Soci-Economic Characteristics of Ethnic Minorities Based on the 1970 Census*, 2: Asian Americans, Publication No. (OS) 75–121 (Washington, D.C.: D.H.E.W., July, 1974): p. 107

SOCIO-CULTURAL CHARACTERISTICS

Educational Attainment

As one of the better educated minorities, the Japanese heritage throughout Japan emphasized and valued education. There were those undaunted in their determination and expectation that success and acceptance would be assured by educating themselves or their children. The educational level of high school graduates and four years or more of college education for all Japanese men sixteen years and over was well above the figure for all United States' males in 1970 (Table 8.12). Although the median level of education for Japanese women was lower than for Japanese men, it was higher than the United States' total female population.

TABLE 8.12 Educational Characteristics of the Japanese and United States Total Population: 1970

	United States Total	Japanese United States	Japanese Hawaii	Japanese Calif.	Japanese Other
Schooling Completed, 16 Years of Age or Older					
Males: % 8 Years Schooling or Less	27	15	20	10	13
% High School Graduates	54	70	63	74	73
% 4 Years College or More	13	19	11	20	30
Median Schooling, Years	12.1	12.6	12.3	12.8	12.8
Females: % 8 Years Schooling or Less	25	17	24	12	14
% High School Graduates	55	67	60	74	69
% 4 Years College or More	8	11	9	11	13
Median Schooling, Years	12.1	12.4	12.3	12.6	12.4
Enrollment in School					
Total % Enrolled, 3–34 Years Old	54	59	60	61	54
% 3–4 Years Old	14	31	32	29	29
% 18–24 Years Old:					
Male	37	56	47	64	55
Female	27	48	46	53	45

Source: United States Department of Health, Education, and Welfare, *A Study of Selected Socio-Economic Characteristics of Ethnic Minorities Based on the 1970 Census,* 2: Asian Americans, Publication No. (OS) 75–121 (Washington, D.C.: D.H.E.W., July 1974): p. 70.

Most Issei who came to the United States had been exposed to the Meiji Educational System which provided for eight years of education or more (Table 8.13). First generation males, ages 21–27 years, had completed eleven years of education according to E. K. Strong's survey.[25] It is difficult to make a comparison of the United States' population with that of the Japanese emigrants on education for the early 1900s. Statistics on school attendance for ages five to twenty, and illiteracy rates for the United States population, were listed in the 1930 Census; but there were no statistics on years of schooling completed. This is corroborated by the statement made by E. K. Strong referring to the 1930 Census, "There seems to be no authoritative data as to how much education adult men have obtained."[26] E. K. Strong quotes a figure of 10.2 average school grade reached for adult men from a 1934 estimate made by Dr. David Segal of the Office of Education, United States Department of Interior.[27]

Japanese Language

Sixty-two percent of all Japanese in the United States had a mother tongue of Japanese in 1970 (Table 8.14). Remarkably high is the 28 percent of those who resided in the United States for three or more generations but maintained Japanese as their mother tongue. The Japanese language schools of the past were well attended by Nisei whose parents saw to it that they acquired both an American education followed by several hours of Japanese language instruction per school day. Their reputation for old world teaching methods and

TABLE 8.13 Median Years Schooling of the Japanese by Sex, Age, and Nativity, 25 Years Old and Over: 1970

	Total	25–44	45–64	65 and Over
Males:				
U.S. Born*	12.6	12.9	12.4	8.6
Foreign Born	12.6	16+	12.5	8.5
Females:				
U.S. Born*	12.5	12.8	12.2	7.8
Foreign Born	12.2	12.5	12.3	7.4

*Second generation only.

Source: United States Department of Health, Education, and Welfare, *A Study of Selected Socio-Economic Characteristics of Ethnic Minorities Based on the 1970 Census,* 2: Asian Americans, Publication No. (OS) 75–121 (Washington, D.C.: D.H.E.W., July 1974): p. 71.

instilling of old world values were in contradiction to the American schools, which stressed the exclusive use of English and American educational goals. Japanese language schools are still important to that segment of the population which value the second language for their children. The Japanese business executives's children, who expect to return to the highly competitive school system in Japan, may attend the Asahi schools in the United States which are designed to meet the requirements and demands of that educational system.

Japanese language courses are thriving at universities and in adult programs where there is a particular demand for them. The Modern Language Association

TABLE 8.14 Japanese Speaking Own Ethnic Language as Mother Tongue: 1970

Total	
Number Speaking Ethnic Language as Mother Tongue	366,134
% of Total Sub-Group Population	62
Native of Native Parents	
Number Speaking Ethnic Language as Mother Tongue	71,404
% of all Native of Native Parents	28
Native of Foreign or Mixed Parents	
Number Speaking Ethnic Language as Mother Tongue	181,090
% of all Native of Foreign or Mixed Parents	87
Foreign Born	
Number Speaking Ethnic Language as Mother Tongue	113,640
% of all Foreign Born	93

Source: United States Department of Health, Education, and Welfare. *A Study of Selected Socio-Economic Characteristics of Ethnic Minorities Based on the 1970 Census,* 2: Asian Americans, Publication No. (OS) 75–121 (Washington, D.C.: D.H.E.W., July, 1974): p. 64.

of America's 1980 survey listed 11,506 registrations for Japanese language courses in higher education.[28] This was a gain of 7.3 percent from 1977. In terms of percentage changes the survey showed the highest enrollment gain from 1977 to 1980 for the Arabic language at 15.9 percent; the second most high was the Chinese language at 12.9 percent; and the third was the Japanese language. There was a percentage decline in registrations for such languages as Ancient Greek, Russian and German.

Religions

The Christian church, the Buddhist temple, and the language school served as integral foci for the Japanese ethno-centered community of the past. The role of the all-Japanese Christian church or Buddhist temple continues to remain active and vital not only for religious reasons but for the social needs of the more ethnically oriented members of the community. These institutions are distinguishably bilingual in nature. Of the 41 Christian churches listed in the Southern California Japanese American Telephone Directory for 1969–1970, one-half were of the Methodist, Presbyterian, and Baptist denominations. Only one was Catholic. There were 29 Buddhist and Shinto temples listed with Hongwanji, Koyasan (Shingon), Tenrikyo, Nichiren, and Zen among the leading sects. Some examples of the Americanization process involving Buddhism are the ceremonies observing Memorial Day, the adoption of Sunday School, sutras as hymnals, the

Buddhist altar in some Japanese American homes, and the possession of many kinds of amulets for protection and good health.

Social Institutions

The Japanese are a family conscious people. Statistically, in 1970, 89 percent of young persons 18 and under were living with both parents, compared to 85 percent for the national average.[29] The integrity of the family, the priority of the family over interests of the individual, filial piety, and patriarchialism are some reminiscent Japanese values.

The Japanese ability to organize and function as a group is apparent in the network of social units and social organizations. The "kenjin-kai," an association of people from the same prefecture with concern for each others welfare, was stronger in the past, but this organization still meets, and one big event continues to be an annual picnic reunion. The Issei-founded "tan-omoshi ko," a group of closely knit members who pool some of their money to lend each other, is no longer common. The Japanese American Citizens League (J.A.C.L.), a membership largely of Nisei, has many local chapters, regional offices, and a national organization. Its concerns are with large political issues but it also sponsors local social activities, scholarships, and civic events.

There are too many of these sub-ethnic affinities to permit detailed description of their purpose and rationale. In general, these groups signify the pervasive bond of sharing a common cultural heritage and dependency on their ethnic members. Some of the clubs have their parallel or are the counterparts of American organizations such as the Optimists, sports clubs, fraternities and sororities. Some among the younger generation, presumably the most detached from old world traditions, are discovering their ancestral roots and reviving if not resurrecting "taiko" (drum) bands, family crests, and some rather exotic-special interests such as: "suiseki" (rock art), "bankei" and "sunae" (earth, sand, clay, and ground marble miniature landscape art), "rohketsu-zome" (wax-resist dye art), "kimekomi" (doll handicraft), "chigiri-e" (torn paper art), and traditional martial arts.

Age/Sex Profiles

In 1970, Japanese Americans had a smaller percentage of young people under 18 years old (29 percent) in their population compared with 34 percent for the United States as a whole. H.E.W. attributed this differential to the lower birth rate among the Sansei.[30] Another factor is a relatively high intermarriage rate particularly between Japanese women and non-Japanese men, depsite near-equal numbers of Japanese males and females in the principal age groups for marriage. The offspring resulting from these marriages may no longer be enumerated racially as Japanese by the Census Bureau. The percentage of elderly Japanese 65 years and over was 11 percent, whereas the national average was 15 percent in 1970.

Japanese females at 54 percent of the Japanese population outnumbered males at 45 percent in 1970 and the gap is widening. Sometime between 1950 and 1960 census reports, the switch from dominance of males to females took place. The higher percentage of female immigrants and the fact that women tend to out-live men have contributed to this age-sex profile (Figs. 8.12A, B, C). The larger number of Issei women clustered in the 35 to 44 age range may be attributed to the so-called war bride population. The large number of Issei women 70 to 74 years old corresponds with the peak of the picture bride migration. The impact of the 1924 Asian Exclusion Act is indicated by the diminished number of Issei in the 55 to 64 age group. The age gap betwen Issei and Nisei correlate with reduction in number of Japanese immigrants after 1924 and the baby boom of Nisei following the large Issei bride migration after the Gentlemen's Agreement Pact of 1907.

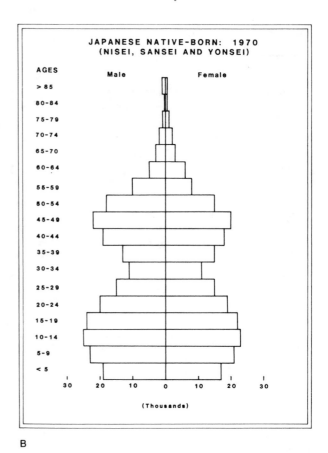

B

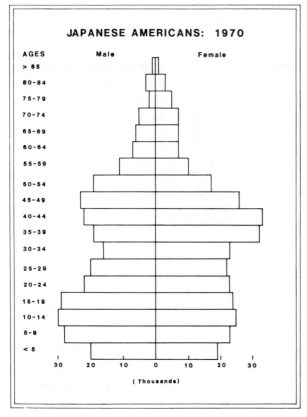

A

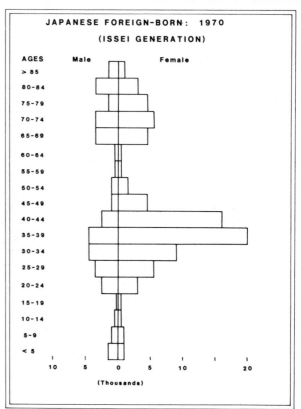

C

Figure 8.12 A, B, and C. Age/Sex Profiles of Japanese American and by Nativity. Source: U.S. Department of Health, Education and Welfare, *A Study of Selected Socio-Economic Characteristics of Ethnic Minorities Based on the 1970 Census,* Volume II: Asian Americans, Publication No. (OS) 75-121 (Washington, D.C.: D.H.E.W., July, 1974), pp. 32, 34.

CULTURAL CONTRIBUTIONS AND IMPACTS

The adoption, adaptation, and infusion of oriental art forms and architectural styles in American civilization are generally well recognized and acknowledged. Cultural borrowings were often deliberate and intentional rather than incidental or accidental by white Americans who came in contact with Japan. As early as 1799 Captain James Deveaux brought back Japanese lacquerware furnishings which were later placed in the Peabody Museum in Salem, Massachusetts.[31] Through diplomatic and trade missions, and due to many cross-cultural contacts, Americans were charmed and receptive to Japanese fine art objects. Exhibitions or expositions such as the Philadelphia Centennial in 1876, the Chicago Fair in 1893, the San Francisco Fair in 1894, and the St. Louis Fair in 1904 provided an early American exposure to Japanese art motifs, gardens, houses, shrines, pagodas, and temple architecture. In the United States, there is a wealth of the finest of Japanese cultural treasures in private collections and in libraries and museums. A vertical scroll, a folding screen, wood block prints, porcelain objects, wood and ivory carvings, bronzes, and an array of objects of art adorn the interior of many American homes and buildings.

American architecture, in particular, involves a fusion of diverse origins. For example, the California Bungalow has evolved from several sources. Such features as wide projecting roofs, verandas, woodworking and gabling have their counterparts in Japan. Also from Japan, Americans have acquired such concepts as simplicity, "shibui" or subtleness, naturalness, tranquility, and harmony, all of which are intimately associated with Japanese artistic ideals. These inspirations and overtones of Japanese design are now found throughout the United States.

In addition to its contributions to American architecture, various kinds of transplanted Japanese gardens are one of the undeniable pleasurable and meaningful contributions that Japan has made to American life and cultural landscape. Those who appreciate these gardens may have experienced the aesthetic as well as the contemplative and even spiritual value and significance that they are intended to communicate.[32] Among the most recently created of the outstanding and authentic and traditional gardens to be found in the United States are the 14 acre "Seiwa-En" (Garden of Pure, Clear Harmony and Peace) in St. Louis, Missouri, and "Sansho-En" (Garden of the Three Islands in the Chicago Horticultural Society Botanic Garden.[33] The essence of life and the environment are captured and expressed via the "bonsai" (dwarfed tree) or a tray landscape of sand, pebbles, and miniaturized objects. Symbolism is beautifully expressed in the James Irvine Garden at the Japanese

American Cultural and Community Center (J.A.C.C.) in Los Angeles (Figs. 8.13A-8.13B). Built by volunteer manpower from California Contractor's Association and the Southern California Gardeners Federation, the theme, "Seiryu-En" (Garden of the Clear Stream) represents the flow of generations of Japanese. The rushing waterfall symbolizes the hardship and struggles experienced by the Issei. The cascade of water flowing over a rocky bed then separating into two streams symbolizes the quiet and vocal Nisei and their continuing struggles. As the flow of water softens and finally rests in a pond, the symbol is of hope and tranquility for the third generation Sansei and succeeding generations.[34]

Similarly, a profoundly meaningful interpretation of Japanese Buddhism and its impression on the cultural landscape is located in Sawtelle, West Los Angeles[35] (Fig. 8.14).

Exotic Japanese foods and cooking styles have become popular and widespread in usage. Applied arts and crafts using bamboo, hand-made paper, silk, flowers, rocks and other materials have made their inroads. Authorities in literature and school children who

Figure 8.13 A and B. James Irvine Garden, Los Angeles.

191

Figure 8.14. Japanese Buddhist Temple, Los Angeles.

tural heritage. They are enthusiastically seeking their old world roots. Still there are many who no longer embrace or retain traditional traits, or do not recognize any Japanese cultural identity. There is no representative Japanese American, nor do some of the presumed stereotypes such as the "Quiet American," "Model Minority," or "Yankee Samurai" serve in that capacity. The range in degrees of assimilation and acculturation into the American mainstream runs full circle from little to fully Americanized. The cultural pluralism that enriches the lives of those who choose to fuse the best of Japanese traits into American society is a growing trend which portends a progressively complex cultural make-up in the United States.

enjoy writing "Haiku" or "Tanka" style poetry are examples of the cultural diffusion which have penetrated into a wide strata of American society. Grand "Kabuki," "Noh" (classical drama), "Gagaku" and "Bugaku" (Imperial court music and dance), "Bunraku" (puppet theater) are no longer unheard of or unkown in the United States. Such words as "shogun," "samurai," "sushi," etc. are no longer foreign terms but have crept into the American dialogue.

CULTURAL PLURALISM

There are some Japanese of the younger American born generation who have experienced a re-awakened and intensified interest in regaining their ancestral cul-

EPILOGUE

This story of the Japanese in the United States has been based on field work and on existing statistical and research data.[36] More research data may be derived by employing other methodologies such as a perceptual framework. They might add a unique perspective to this account. An intriguing viewpoint might be gained from the standpoint of Japanese American's perception of the United States or in turn white America's perception of this minority. These people are Americans. The United States is their home, destiny, and future. Because of their particular historical experience and their visibility as a minority, there is a keen sensitivity that they be regarded as Japanese Americans or Americans of Japanese ancestry. The story is still incomplete.

NOTES

1. The Pacific military zone included coastal California, Oregon, Washington, and parts of Arizona and included 89.0 percent of the Japanese population in continental United States.
2. Formal termination of Executive Order 9066 did not take place until February 19, 1976.
3. William M. Mason and John A. McKinstry, "The Japanese of Los Angeles, 1869–1920," Los Angeles County Museum of Natural History Contribution, 1 (n.p.: 1969): p. 1.
4. Downtown Little Tokyo, Boyle Heights (East Los Angeles), Westside, Olympic Boulevard area, Hollywood-Virgil districts, West Los Angeles, Harbor area.
5. Kango Kunitsugu, "Ten Years of Redevelopment: Its Progress and Expectations," Little Tokyo Redevelopment Project Newsletter (February, 1980): p. 5.
6. Gardena, West Los Angeles, Crenshaw district, Culver City area (Venice-Mar Vista), Monterey Park, Long Beach-Harbor City area, and so forth.
7. *Little Tokyo Directory* (Los Angeles: DM Little Tokyo, 1981): pp. 2–4.
8. Isamu Yonekura, "Manjiro: the Remarkable Life of a Fisherman's Son (1)," *East,* 12 (May, 1976): p. 17.
9. "Joseph Heco: The First American of Japanese Ancestry," *East,* 17 (February, 1981): p. 22.
10. Robert A. Wilson and Bill Hosokawa, *East to America: A History of Japanese in the United States* (New York: William Morrow and Company, 1980): p. 20.
11. Report of the Immigration Commission, *Immigrants in Industries,* 23 (Washington, D.C.: United States Government Printing Office, 1911): p. 5.
12. Yosaburo Yoshida, "Sources and Causes of Japanese Emigration," *Annals of the American Academy of Political and Social Science,* 34 (September, 1909): p. 159.
13. Dorothy Swaine Thomas, *The Salvage,* (Berkeley: University of California Press, 1952): pp. 8–9.
14. Terry Jones, "Samurai of the Wine Country: A Biography of Kanaye Nagasawa," *Pacific Citizen,* 81 (December 19–26, 1975): pp. A-1, C-1, 5, 8, 10–12, D-1.
15. Midori Nishi, "Changing Occupance of the Japanese in Los Angeles County, 1940–1950" (Ann Arbor, Michigan: University Microfilms, 1955): pp. 43–44.

16. Some Issei were taken into custody the very night of Pearl Harbor, December 7, 1941, and placed in internment camps without prior notice or forewarning. Some 200 families were given less than three days notice to leave the islands.

17. Kanichi Kawasaki, "The Japanese Community of San Pedro, Terminal Island, California" (unpublished Master's thesis, University of Southern California, Los Angeles, 1931): p. 31.

18. Isamu Nodera, "A Survey of the Vocational Activities of the Japanese in the City of Los Angeles" (unpublished Master's thesis, University of Southern California, Los Angeles, 1936): p. 115.

19. Estimates made by Sam Minami, Business Manager, Junior Produce Club of Los Angeles, for Tolan Committee, Hearings Before the Select Committee Investigating National Defense Migration, Part 31 (Washington, D.C.: United States Government Printing Office, 1947): p. 11724.

20. U.S. Department of Health, Education, and Welfare, *A Study of Selected Socio-Economic Characteristics of Ethnic Minorities Based on the 1970 Census,* 2: Asian Americans, Publication No. (OS) 75–121 (Washington, D.C.: D.H.E.W., 1974): p. 86.

21. *Ibid.* p. 91.

22. Estimates made by Osamu Tanaka, Los Angeles Office of Economic Salon, Ltd. and data obtained from *Economic World: Directory of Japanese Companies in the U.S.A., 1979–80* (New York: Economic Salon Ltd., n.d.).

23. Estimates made by Toshiki Saito, Public Relations Manager, Los Angeles Office of J.E.T.R.O. and data obtained from their *Directory of Japanese Firms and Offices in the Southern California Area* (March, 1981).

24. Richard C. King, "Asian Management in America," *Asian Mall,* 5, No. 11 (August, 1981): p.15.

25. Edward Kellogg Strong, *The Second-Generation Japanese Problem* (Palo Alto: Stanford University Press, 1934): pp. 185–186.

26. ———, *Vocational Interests of Men and Women* (Palo Alto: Stanford University Press, 1943): p. 709.

27. *Ibid.:* p. 710.

28. Richard I. Brod, Director, Foreign Language Programs, Modern Language Association of America, Foreign Language Registrations, Higher Education, Fall, 1980 (Preliminary Totals), Table 2 (New York: Modern Language Association of America, Fall, 1980).

29. U.S. Department of Health, Education, and Welfare, 1974. p. 44.

30. *Ibid.,* p. 31.

31. Lancaster Clay, *The Japanese Influence in America* (New York: Walton H. Rawls, 1963): p. 17.

32. Dorothy Loa McFadden, *Oriental Gardens in America: A Visitor's Guide* (Los Angeles: Douglas-West Publishers, Inc., 1976): 248 pp.

33. Designed by Dr. Koichi Kawana, lecturer in Japanese art, archichtecture and landscape design at the University of California, Los Angeles and president of Environmental Design Associates, Los Angeles.

34. Gloria Uchida, "Dedicated Volunteers Help Build J.A.C.C.C. Garden," *Little Tokyo Redevelopment Project Newsletter,* (February, 1980): pp. 7–8.

35. Donald K. Fellows, "Japanese Buddhism—Its Imprint on a California Landscape," *The California Geographer,* 13 (1972): pp. 49–58.

36. There are valuable studies done on the Japanese Americans by social scientists in their areas of expertise especially among sociologists, psychologists, anthropologists, political scientists, historians, and economists. Educators, social workers and community leaders have been contributing to the growing body of research materials and publications. Popular writers, provide objective, pro- and anti-Japanese insights on the subject. To the credit of Japanese and Asian Studies type centers and related projects, special library collections have been established and programs on Japanese studies promoted.

9

The Chinese in America

Catherine L. Brown

Clifton W. Pannell

Univ. of Georgia

INTRODUCTION

Chinese have been immigrating to the United States since the mid-1800s. Initially the migration was substantial and encouraged by economic interests in the developing West and other regions to supply labor needs. Public opinion, however, ran against Chinese immigration, and between 1882 and 1943 a series of increasingly severe immigration acts greatly reduced the legal entry of Chinese into the country. After 1943, these restrictions were eased somewhat, but it was not until 1965 that a normal national quota was granted for Chinese immigration. Consequently, and even with the increase in immigration in recent years, the Chinese have never represented more than a fraction of the total United States population.

The Chinese customarily settled in Chinatowns, especially in large cities of the West where the numbers of Chinese were substantial. These ethnic ghettos provided a measure of security, and allowed traditional customs and cultural practices to be maintained. The Chinatown ghettos also helped establish the American's view and image of the Chinese as thrifty and hardworking but also as clannish and alien, and not particularly good subjects for acculturation into the American crucible.

Over the years the Chinese have tended to leave these Chinatowns as they have achieved higher levels of education and entered professional fields or have succeeded in commercial endeavors. Even so, Chinatown is only part of the traditional picture of the Chinese in the United States. In many places where Chinese settled, Chinatowns never existed; but, social, cultural, political, and economic functions that typified Chinatown were, nevertheless, carried on. Benevolent associations, credit and commercial organizations, common surname or clan associations all have played a role in helping Chinese maintain some degree of cultural integrity and solidarity, despite the degree of clustering or dispersal of the Chinese community.

The study that follows chronicles the population growth of the Chinese in the United States, yet it emphasizes the smaller communities and groupings as the Chinese dispersed to regions other than the West. The growth and development of the Chinese community in the South is especially a subject of attention and serves to illustrate the special role of the Chinese as another minority in what was essentially a black/white bicultural society. The chapter, thus, describes and explains the evolution of the Chinese in American society outside Chinatown ghettos, a topic often neglected in studies of the growth of America's Chinese.

Maps and tabular data are used to buttress the arguments developed in the text. Newspaper accounts and census data form the bulk of the original sources consulted. A variety of secondary studies were also very useful in helping to formulate ideas advanced here.

THE ORIGINS OF PREJUDICE AND ETHNIC SOLIDARITY

Interaction of Chinese and American White

One of the hypotheses of this chapter proposes that racial prejudice, tempered by economic conditions, has greatly influenced the distribution and general characteristics of the Chinese population over time. The idea of the interplay of racial antagonism and economics, and its impact on the spatial and socioeconomic patterns of the Chinese is not unique to this study; it is a unifying theme in contemporary literature on the Chinese in America. Miller in *The Unwelcome Immigrant* established the origins of America's prejudice against the Chinese.[1] According to Miller, Americans received their first images of China through the accounts of traders, missionaries, and diplomats who had only limited access to the country and who were blinded by ethnocentric beliefs about the innate superiority of Northern European racial stock and culture. Miller argued effectively that these three groups of travellers to

China were responsible for the development of a negative Chinese stereotype predating the first large scale immigration of Chinese into the United States in the 1850s. Long before most Americans had made contact with a "genuine Chinaman" they were commonly thought to be, among other things, filthy, debased idolaters given to immoral practices so vile they could barely be discussed by decent men.

By the time the Chinese began arriving in America the image was fixed and reinforced by social Darwinism, a growing pseudo-scientific theory of the races which assumed all of the so called "colored" races to be naturally inferior to Caucasians. Miller's survey of the national press between 1850 and 1882, the year Congress passed the first Chinese exclusion bill, found that,

> The general editorial concensus . . . was that while the Chinese were not biologically suitable for the American melting pot, it would be foolish not to exploit their cheap labor before shipping them back to China.[2]

Wu noted in *Chink*, his documentary history of anti-Chinese sentiment in the United States that "racial prejudice gave way temporarily to economic necessity."[3] Kung's discussion of this echoes Wu and others; "The question of economic gain has always been a prime factor in prejudice."[4] Higham in his now classic study of nationalism and ethnic prejudice, or "nativism" as he tagged the complex of ideas represented by the two concepts, closely correlated surges of anti-ethnic movements in the U.S. with periods of economic crisis.[5] The implication of this generally accepted theory of racism and economics is that the patterns of Chinese settlement, social interaction and economic activities in the United States have been dictated by white racism, but the degree to which racist attitudes are acted upon by convention and law is determined by economic stability. In times of plenty white America is more tolerant of its minority groups than in times of economic instability when money is tight and jobs are scarce.

Another possible explanation for the manner in which the Chinese communities have evolved and sustained themselves was offered by Patterson in *Ethnic Chauvinism*.[6] According to Patterson, "ethnicity is basically a function of economic interest." He documented many Chinese settlements in South America and Asian countries to support his theory but could easily have been describing the Chinese experience in the United States. The typical Chinese immigrant is exemplified by a sojourner who is interested in the host country only for economic gain and fully intends to return home. The sojourner mentality encourages thrift and hard work, but the tendency of sojourners to form exclusive enclaves and cling to their own languages and customs provokes hostility from the host society. The self-imposed segregation of the immigrant group leads to forced segregation which further isolates them and forces them into greater internal economic cooperation.

Bonacich and Modell discussed this pattern at length in *The Economic Basis of Ethnic Solidarity*, a study of Japanese small independent businesses in the United States.[7] Bonacich and Modell concluded that hostility from the surrounding society resulted in the promotion of small independent businesses in which Japanese came to occupy a "middleman minority" position in the economic hierarchy. The middleman minority is described as an ethnic group that is an object of discrimination by the host culture but serves as a buffer group between the elites of that society and a subordinated population lower down the social scale. The buffer groups which the middleman minorities represent are usually occupied in trade and services which channel the flow of goods from producers and distributors to the laboring classes. Middlemen are considered *petit bourgeois*, not capitalists, and may come to monopolize certain areas of trade usually through concentrations of numerous small independent businesses.

The middleman concept is especially important to this study. The Chinese have traditionally exploited the middleman position wherever they have settled throughout the world. In the American South they found marginal acceptance as middlemen merchants, primarily as retail grocers in service to the black community. According to Loewen in his study of the Mississippi Delta Chinese, in the period immediately following the Civil War, white merchants who served blacks were ostracized from white society.[8] Native American blacks, on the other hand, had few acquired skills and no surviving cultural traditions or sources of capital from which to draw to provide services for themselves.[9]

The Chinese came from an area in China with a trading tradition, established their own credit associations (*hui*) which provided capital for members, and were not reluctant to serve the black population.[10] Chinese merchants found a gap in the economic system they could fill with little competition offered from either whites or blacks and without posing a threat to either group's economic position. Loewen believes that the breakdown of the Delta Chinese groups and the outmigration which was taking place by the late 1960s was the result of the breakdown of the segregated social system of the area. Like Bonacich, Modell, and Patterson, Loewen believed that ethnic solidarity was created and reinforced by economic discrimination. Once the economic function of the group was lost, it was no longer necessary or advantageous for individuals to identify with the group.

The main focus of Loewen's study was the change in status undergone by the Mississippi Delta community, as their educational attainment and economic success opened their way into white society. When the Chinese first entered the Delta, the desire of the white population to keep color lines clearly defined did not allow for the acknowledgement of a third race without a specific social classification. The following exchange between Loewen and one of his informants summed up the situation and its resolution:

"You're either a white man or a nigger, here. Now that's the whole story. When I first came to the Delta, the Chinese were classed as nigras."
"And now they are called whites?"
"That's right!"[11]

As a result of this racial definition a common pattern in the South seems to have been for Chinese to locate in black neighborhoods. This is discussed by Loewen and also noted in other studies of Chinese groups in the South. Still, the Chinese maintained social distance from the blacks and preferred to identify with the white community. The Chinese clearly had their own prejudices as well.

Interaction of Chinese and Blacks

The nature of black and Chinese relations is as important in the case of the South as the nature of Chinese and white relations, although the latter is by far the most studied. Shankman in "Black on Yellow" examined the attitudes toward the Chinese found in the national black press from 1850 to 1935 and found that in general the black press reflected white journalism in its anti-Chinese bias. Blacks accepted the negative Chinese stereotypes—opium eating, sexual perversion, heathenism—and felt threatened by them on economic grounds because they had often been thrown into competition with immigrant groups for the same types of unskilled labor. As for the South, Shankman noted, the fears of southern blacks over the possible damaging economic consequences of Chinese immigration to the region proved to be unfounded, at least for the black male. The Chinese never entered into competition with the male black wage laborer but chose instead to settle in the large cities and go into business for themselves. Chinese commercial laundries, however, probably took business from black women for whom the home laundry business was an important source of income. A hint that this may have been true of Georgia is provided by Shankman in a reference to an article in a 1892 black Savannah newspaper.[12]

SOME USEFUL SOURCES OF DATA

Miller's *Unwelcome Immigrant* and Barth's *Bitter Strength* are valuable secondary sources for the early history of Chinese immigration into the United States. Barth's study covers the period 1849 to 1870—1870 witnessing the beginning of the migration of the Chinese from the West Coast to the South and East.[13] Miller carried his study through 1882, the year the first immigration law restricting Chinese immigration was placed into effect. Both of these books contain accounts of the locational shifts of Chinese throughout the country. *The Chinese in America* by Chen is an extremely readable popular history of the Chinese from the mid-1800's to the present. Chen includes an appendix with a discussion of Chinese communities and Chinatowns by region.[14]

Sociology seems to be the only discipline to have exploited the full range of Chinese statistics collected by the United States Census since 1860. Two valuable pieces of work in this regard which have contributed to this study are Lee's *The Chinese in the United States of America*,[15] and King and Locke's "Chinese in the United States: A Century of Occupational Transition."[16] Lee's study is the first true analysis of the Chinese population in the U.S. and probably the most cited in the literature. It employs statistical data and historical information to analyze the spatial, social, and economic structure of the aggregate Chinese population and to establish a body of generalizations useful in examining individual Chinese groups.

Much of Lee's statistical analysis is limited to the 1940–1960 period. King and Locke analyzed the changes in Chinese occupational structure from 1850 to 1970. Unlike Lee who emphasizes factors internal to the Chinese community, these authors attributed changes in occupational patterns to institutionalized prejudice by law and custom. There was some attempt by King and Locke to regionalize the findings, the most significant of which being the high incidence of owner operated Chinese businesses observed in the South.

Regional Studies

Specific regional studies of the Chinese are numerous. Examples on the South include Loewen's previously mentioned study of the Mississippi Delta Chinese and an earlier article about the Mississippi group by O'Brien,[17] articles by Farrar[18] and Rhoads[19] on the Chinese in Texas; Liao's[20] thesis about the Chinese in Arkansas; articles by Ken[21] Law and Ken,[22] and Chiu[23] about the Chinese in Augusta, Georgia; Sieg's[24] account of the Chinese in Savannah, Georgia; Peabody's[25] thesis about the Chinese Labor movement in the South from 1865 to 1870; Krebs's[26] article about the Chinese issue in Alabama in 1870; Cohen's[27] article on the introduction of Chinese to Louisiana and surrounding states; and Brown's[28] analysis of the Georgia Chinese.

Newspapers

Smailes called the newspaper ". . . perhaps the most potent of all agents in the formulation and propagation of regional opinion on important issues."[29] Newspapers are probably the single most important source of primary information about the Chinese in a given place.

Contemporaneous newspaper dispatches provide information about particular events related to a region or state's Chinese and suggest newspapers played a key role in generating and reflecting public opinion about them. Tables and maps compiled from census materials provide a clear illustration of the socio-economic characteristics and distribution of the Chinese minority, but with the volume of newspaper accounts the explanation for these patterns would be lackluster and conjectural. Newspapers ranging from San Francisco's *ALTA* and the *New York Times* to the New Orleans *Times-Picayune* and *Augusta Chronicle* all proved useful in this study.

Chinatown Studies

Although many smaller Chinese communities have never established themselves in ethnic clusters, much scholarly attention has been focused on Chinatowns as concentrated ethnic communities. Some examples from geography are Murphey's[30] study of Boston's Chinatown and a special *Chinatown*[31] edition of the *China Geographer*. However, it is apparent that many of the functional organizations typically found in Chinatowns exist within a dispersed Chinese community at a smaller scale, despite the absence of a clearly definable Chinatown cluster of commercial establishments and residences.

The Chinese community may not always be spatially definable, but the institutional structure commonly found is similar to that of the bounded Chinatowns. For example, institutions such as business, social and family associations may be found organized under the auspices of a local chapter of the National Chinese Benevolent Association which is the basic political unit of a typical Chinatown. Although the Chinese communities characteristic of a region, such as the South, may differ in their economic and spatial structure from Chinese settlement patterns elsewhere in the United States, the internal social structure of the southern communities seems to vary only by degree of complexity and the number of people involved from Chinese settlement patterns elsewhere in larger cities in the United States. This finding, while it supports the hypothesis that the Chinese groups in the South differ from those Chinese groups in other regions, raises the question, "Is such a difference a matter of form, function, or some combination of the two?"

Lee developed a theory of Chinatown formation based on city size.[32] According to Lee, for a city to support a Chinatown it must have a total native population of 50,000 or more and for a Chinatown to remain viable it must have at least 260 members. Lee later modified this theory to include Chinese population within a state or service area of a Chinatown—service area being loosely defined as any distance Chinese were willing to travel to visit a given Chinatown.[33]

Lee's assumptions are based solely on comparative data for total population of those urban places with Chinatowns indexed to their total Chinese population. She attributed the lack of Chinatowns in the South to smaller city size, but other factors are clearly involved. Historic immigration patterns, nature of the economic base, the biracial culture of South, and the deliberate efforts by some Chinese communities to avoid clustering must all be considered.[34]

THE CHINESE COME TO AMERICA

The first large scale immigration of Chinese to the United States began in 1850. Most Chinese entered the country through San Francisco and remained heavily concentrated in California until the late 1860s. The majority of the early Chinese immigrants came from the southern maritime province of Guangdong. They have been variously described as "yeomen farmers," "landless laborers," "petty traders," and "hawkers" "with a tradition of hard work and thrift;" and, unlike most Chinese, with a tradition of emigration in response to domestic economic, political and/or social stress.[35] It was the custom of families who fell on hard times to send their sons abroad to find means by which to support those who remained behind. The young men who left were not considered immigrants, but sojourners, and were expected to ". . . earn money, save it, and return home as soon as possible"[36] In the mid-1800's widespread civil and economic disruption in China, coupled with the discovery of gold and stories of "work for all" in California, provided the push and pull mechanism for outmigration.[37] A flow of sojourners was generated across the Pacific which continued until 1882 when the first of a series of acts restricting Chinese immigration was passed by Congress.

Trading One Hostile Environment for Another

Prior to 1850 official and unofficial documents show fewer than 800 Chinese in the United States. Between 1850 and 1860 the number rose to 34,933 and by the 1870 census it was over 63,000 (Tables 9.1a–9.1b and Figs. 9.1–9.3). The white majority regarded this with alarm. Although the Chinese population was relatively small—less than one percent of the total population in 1870—they were a highly visible group who did not conform to the American ideal of the ideal American. Their distinctive physical characteristics, languages, and customs made them appear different in the extreme. Furthermore, the sojourners were clannish and tended to form little enclaves wherever they located, making no great attempt to acculturate because they did not expect to settle permanently. This pattern of settlement put them into direct conflict with the intense nationalism of the period which had among its

TABLE 9.1a: Chinese Population Change by Region, 1850–1980

	1850	1860	1870	1880	1890	1900	1910	1920	1930	1940	1950	1960	1970	1980
United States (Total)	758	34933	63199	105465	107475	89863	71531	61639	74954	77504	117629	237292	435062	806027
Northeast														
Total Population			137	1628	6177	14693	11688	12414	17799	19646	28931	53654	115777	217730
Absolute Change				1491	4549	8516	−3005	726	5385	1847	9285	24723	62123	101953
Percent Change				1008%	279%	138%	(29%)	6%	43%	10%	47%	85%	116%	88%
North Central														
Total Population			8	813	2351	3668	4610	6722	8078	6092	10646	18413	39343	72905
Absolute Change				805	1538	1317	942	2112	1356	−1986	4554	7767	20930	33562
Percent Change				10062%	189%	56%	26%	46%	20%	(25%)	75%	73%	114%	86%
South														
Total Population			218	922	2116	3773	3299	3900	4194	4926	10468	16839	34284	90616
Absolute Change				704	1898	1657	−474	610	294	732	5542	6371	17445	56332
Percent Change				323%	206%	78%	(13%)	18%	8%	17%	112%	61%	104%	164%
West														
Total Population	758	34933	49277	102102	96844	67729	51934	38604	44883	46840	67584	148386	245658	424776
Absolute Change			14344	52825	−5258	−29115	−15795	−13330	6279	1957	20744	80802	97272	179118
Percent Change			41%	107%	(5%)	(30%)	(23%)	(25%)	16%	4%	44%	120%	66%	73%

Source: United States Bureau of the Census, 1860–1980.

TABLE 9.1b Percent Distribution of Chinese Population by Region 1860–1980

	1850	1860	1870	1880	1890	1900	1910	1920	1930	1940	1950	1960	1970	1980
Northeast			.2	1.5	5.7	16.4	16.3	20.1	23.7	25.3	24.5	22.6	26.6	27
North Central			.01	.8	2.1	4.1	6.4	10.9	10.7	7.8	9.0	7.7	9.0	9.0
West	100	100	99	97	90.1	75.3	72.6	62.6	59.8	60.4	57	62.5	56.4	52.6
South			.3	.9	1.9	4.2	4.6	6.3	5.5	6.3	8.8	7.0	7.8	11.2

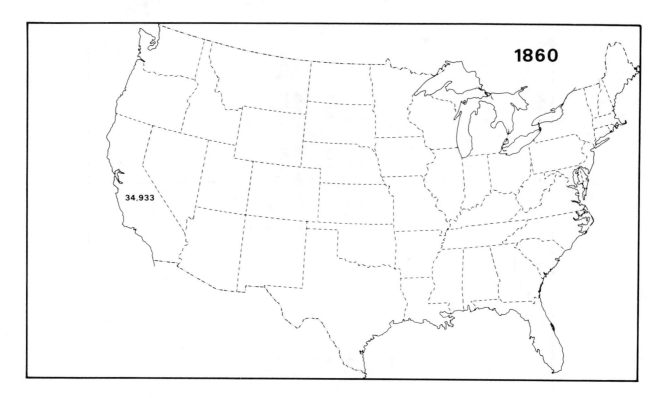

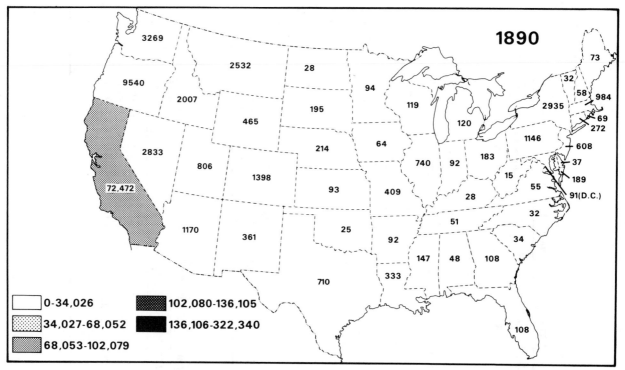

Figure 9.1. Chinese Population of the United States, 1860 and 1890. Source: U.S. Bureau of the Census, 1860; 1890.

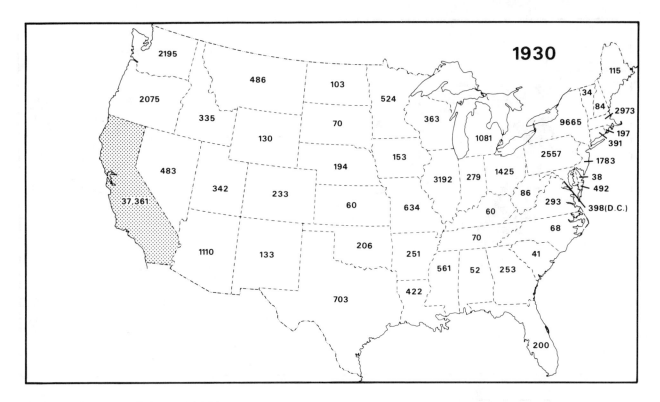

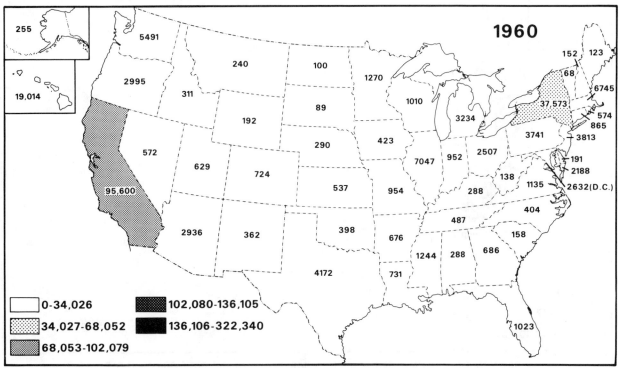

0–34,026		102,080–136,105
34,027–68,052		136,106–322,340
68,053–102,079		

Figure 9.2. Chinese Population of the United States, 1930 and 1960. Source: U.S. Bureau of the Census, 1930 and 1960.

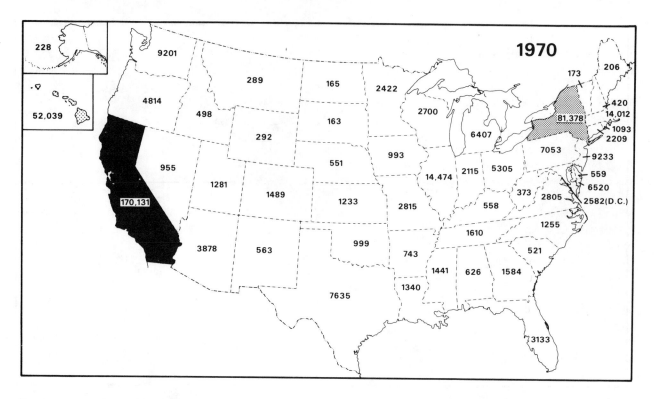

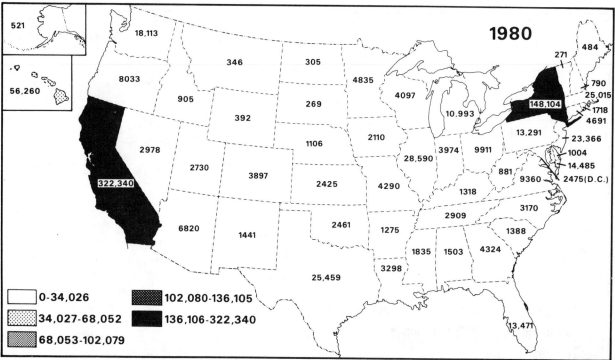

Figure 9.3. Chinese Population of the United States, 1970 and 1980. Source: U.S. Bureau of the Census, 1970 and 1980.

tenets the belief that national unity depended on a homogeneous population with common origins and traditions.[38] "The few years of Chinese occupation leave them as entirely Chinese as when they landed," complained a California correspondent for a New York newspaper, "and a century might pass before any change would be made."[39]

Nativism, ethnocentrism, and xenophobia were all variations of the nationalistic movement. The country was population hungry and needed labor, but was apprehensive about immigration. Immigrants from "superior" Northern European racial stocks had been the foundation of the American "breed" and were still welcome as a compatible and assimilable group.[40] But Chinese? For a century before the Chinese immigration began Americans had been conditioned by the accounts of travellers to China to think of the Chinese as an amorally debased, physically and mentally inferior race. This latent image surfaced quickly upon contact, its potential for discord exacerbated by the racism of the nationalistic movement. In 1852 when California's Governor denounced the Chinese as ". . . avaricious, ignorant of moral obligations, incapable of being assimilated and dangerous to the welfare of the state,"[41] he was only mildly expressing common public opinion.

The hostility toward the Chinese mounted as their numbers increased, but it was tempered by their economic utility to the region. The West had an acute labor shortage. White natives who flooded the region in search of gold created a demand for many personal services, and the capitalists who followed them needed manpower to develop their manufacturing and industrial investments. The Chinese, who were being driven from their mining claims by white prospectors, stepped in to fill the demand for labor. By 1860 there were Chinese represented in a variety of occupations. Mining companies found them to be a dependable source of inexpensive labor. There were Chinese in construction, agriculture, and manufacturing. Chinese developed California's fishing industry, performed as domestic servants, opened restaurants, boarding houses, laundries, and small stores.[42] Some were successful and returned home wealthy men. For the majority, however, life in the American West became a cycle of hard work and poverty as they eked out meager livings for themselves and their families left behind in China.[43]

As long as the Chinese were engaged in occupations which did not bring them into close competition with white labor, anti-Chinese sentiments were held in check. While the Chinese suffered acts of physical aggression during this period, much of the harassment was in the form of what might be termed "codified prejudice"—discriminatory taxes and laws which adversely affected their private lives, their business concerns, and stripped them of many constitutional rights. But, in the 1860s as mine production began to drop and the boom-town economy began to flag, the Chinese were made the scapegoats. Among the loudest of the accusers were the Irish, who, by that time, formed a sizable portion of the growing population of white organized labor. They roused public opinion by accusing the Chinese of creating the depression by working for lower wages than "decent" men could accept and sending their earnings out of the country to China.[44]

The West came to regard as sinister the frugality, industry, and strong emotional and family ties the Chinese had with their homeland. Although they were all valued traits in American culture, they were suspect in the Chinese as part of a diabolical plot to deprive white Americans of their rightful jobs and bleed the West of its wealth. In 1869 a California Senator offered this opinion:

> It is the duty of every class of men to unite to prevent the introduction of the Chinese. If they come into contact with only the common laborers to-day, tomorrow they will be in competition with the mason, the bricklayer, the carpenter and the machinist, for they are *the most frugal, industrious and ingeneous people on the face of the earth.*[45]

The Chinese also made convenient scapegoats for disease, crime, poverty, and the other social problems which plagued the rapidly expanding western cities. Support for this attack came from the social Darwinists, a group who had taken the emotionally held theory of the superiority of the white races and turned it into a popular pseudo-science. Darwin's theory of natural selection and the survival of the fittest was twisted to imply that a biological battle between the white races and the colored races would naturally lead to the elimination of the colored races within a few generations.[46] It was conceded, however, that inferior people such as the Chinese could reap havoc with the natural selection process by their sheer numbers, their penchant for vice, and their superior germs (Oriental germs were considered more potent than western germs), "sinophobes" created a grim scenario in which hoards of immoral, disease ridden Chinese interbreeding with whites led to the "mongrelization" and decline of the white race.[47]

Dispersal of the Chinese

Mayhem and murder became the order of the late 1860s and several decades thereafter as white vigilante committees were organized to rid the West of the "yellow peril." The Chinese responded to the outbreak of violence in several ways. Some returned to China; others relocated outside the United States. Another response was to withdraw from competition in the labor market. Those who stayed in the West clustered for safety in the larger cities, while the Chinese communities in smaller towns and isolated Chinese settlements disappeared.[48] The concensus among researchers is that the anonymity of the city, especially the large city, provided the Chinese an element of protection they did not have in small towns or work camps. Although the urban clusters which grew into Chinatowns lost their invisibility, Chinatown itself became a fortress against outside aggression, and it took on a political, social, and economic life of its own. Chinese who preferred to leave the West but remain in the United States began to migrate eastward. Southern migration was encouraged by a popular movement within the region to secure Chinese contract labor to supplement or replace free black labor. Just about the time the West raised the cry, "The Chinese must go!" the South issued an invitation "Let the Chinamen come."[49]

THE SOUTHERN CHINESE LABOR MOVEMENT, 1865–1870

The Southern Chinese labor movement was prompted by labor problems both real and imagined. The antebellum plantation system, the cornerstone of the South's economy, was agriculture at its worst. Its profits depended on the lavish use of a large captive work force and the destructive practice of the continual abandonment of worn out land to clear and cultivate virgin soil.[50]

With an ironic twist of fate the outcome of the Civil War bound white planters to prewar holdings and freed the slaves to mobilize and maximize their best interests. Many migrated to the less depleted "frontier" areas of Mississippi and Louisiana where productivity and wages were higher; some took up their own land; some moved to the cities giving up agricultural labor for other occupations.[51] The result was a labor shortage which affected many parts of the region, and the South launched its reconstruction effort divided over its solution. Within a few months after the close of the War the idea of replacing free blacks with "cheap" Chinese contract labor had become a popular topic of discussion.[52] One Louisiana newspaper identified the solution to the labor problem as a choice between "small farms and white labor or large farms and coolie labor . . . ," which seems to be a fair summary of at least part of the debate.[53] On the small farms and white labor side of the argument there was a group who called for a complete reorganization of the agricultural system. They urged planters to reduce the size of cultivated areas, utilize conservation methods and labor saving technology, and go out into the fields and work themselves.

This opinion was voiced by the *Norfolk Journal* in 1868 when it announced, "The planter is dead . . . we want small farmers that will till every acre of soil for themselves," and proceeded to call the Chinese ". . . tools of the demagogue's ambition," a people destined to ". . . build up the fortunes of a few" and become a

". . . thorn in the sides of the masses." The article then took a social Darwinist stance on the issue:

> We are of those who believe the noble Gothic is the one that should inhabit this continent, and the only one . . . the struggle for life that destroys the inferior classes throughout nature, will leave the Gothic race the only inhabitants of this planet. [The negro race] is wasting away, as all inferior organizations must, by law of natural selection. As the negro disappears are we to have transplanted into our midst millions and millions from that great Asiatic hive, who are to take the place of the negro as a retarder of our progress . . . the community that is cursed with Coolies will never see any peace. . . .[54]

The idea of taking the field was met with horror by the "large farms and coolie labor" group who considered field work to be the God-given responsibility of the so-called inferior races, and wished instead to recreate the Old South with a new source of servile labor. A scheme evolved whereby thousands of Chinese would be introduced into the region to compete with blacks for work. It was intended that the competition would depress wages and create a large pool of stable cheap tractable labor.

Political Issues

As might be expected, an issue with so many social and economic implications also had its political dimensions. Southerners greatly feared the potential effects of an organized black vote, and it was generally felt that blacks should be ". . . obligated to vote in the interests of their employers."[55] Chinese, on the other hand, had proven to be apolitical. It was hoped that by replacing blacks with Chinese the threat of the black vote would be reduced.[56] "The whites should make it plain to [the blacks] if they did not join in the election of Southern men of Southern feeling to public offices," stated the *Vicksburg Daily Times,* "The coolies would be brought in to drive them to the wall and make their race forever extinct throughout the land."[57]

There was also a widely circulated theory of opponents of the labor scheme that it was all some sort of northern plot devised to "punish the negro for his lack of radicalism," or reluctance to vote for northern men of northern feeling, to Southern public offices.[58] Either that or a plot by northern business interests to flood the South with cheap Chinese labor to facilitate a "return of thrift to the cotton and sugar fields" and thereby decreasing their raw material costs.[59]

The only agreement on either side of the argument was that the Chinese were an "inferior" race. The question was, did the potential economic gains of cheap Chinese labor outweigh the potential problems of introducing yet another "inferior" race into the South?

Early Experiments

As the debate raged, many private and public immigration associations were formed to promote the use of Chinese labor. One of the earliest was an Alabama agency organized in 1865 which over an unspecified period of time was responsible for contracting 500 Chinese to work in the state.[60] Some of the first Chinese who were brought into the South were from Cuba, which had been experimenting with Chinese labor since the early 1800s after the elimination of its slave labor system.[61] Records indicate that Chinese from Cuba arrived in New Orleans as early as 1866 destined for the cane fields of Louisiana but most who followed came from the western United States, or directly from China.[62]

The Memphis Proposal

In June of 1869 the Arkansas River Immigration Company was organized, and subscriptions were collected to defray the cost of importing 2,000 Chinese from Mainland China. The Governor of Arkansas was elected president of the association and issued the statement that:

> The greatest enthusiasm and unanimity prevail[ed], and that the thing [was] to be a fixed fact, if money [would] effect it. More laborers we must have . . . already the negroes are forming combinations to make their own terms with their employers next season. But these Arkansas gentlemen are determined to checkmate all such.[63]

The formation of the Arkansas River Immigration Company seems to have brought the Southern Chinese labor issue to a head. In the midst of the publicity about the activities in Arkansas a Tennessee newspaper issued an invitation to a Chinese labor convention to be held in Memphis in mid-July.[64] The meeting was well attended by representatives from all over the South. Convincing speeches by Chinese labor brokers resulted in orders being placed for thousands of Chinese contract laborers to be delivered for various states within the region.

The national press took great interest in the proceedings. "It is in this view," said the *New York Times,* "that the deliberations and measures of the Memphis Convention [will] become not only locally and commercially, but nationally important."[65] And in the weeks following the convention *The Times* prediction proved true as small town and big city newspapers across the country engaged in a spirited exchange of observations, accusations, criticism and support for the Memphis proposal. Reactions of the Eastern press were mixed although generally favorable. But, once the papers had mulled over the issue, it predicted that the Chinese would neither inundate the South nor would the small numbers likely to venture into the region decide to stay. The reason cited was the low pay scale for the South's agricultural workers which at the time was one-third to one-half the national average, and the South's outspoken desire to pay the Chinese even less.[66]

Westerners were decidedly opposed to the scheme. Although they expressed delight at the prospect of ridding themselves of their unwanted Chinese citizenry, they too had little confidence that the pittance Southern planters intended to offer as wages would ever attract the higher paid Chinese in the West. Furthermore, by this time, the Democratic and Republican parties in the West were running on anti-Chinese platforms and a fear was expressed by both parties that the Southern initiative would only trigger another wave of impoverished immigrants from China, most of whom would enter the country through Pacific ports and many of whom would end up in the West's burgeoning Chinatowns. Western Democrats were particularly irritated over southern Democrats support for Chinese labor, an interesting development in light of the fact it has been estimated that a large portion of western Democrats were transplanted southerners.[67]

The Southern Reaction

Southern response to the Memphis proposal varied; opinions ranged from vehement opposition to wholehearted approval. Rhoads in his survey of the Texas press found the state leaning toward the pro-side of the issue, but also found the Chinese maligned as ". . . miserable yellow imbecile dwarfs" as well as praised as the ". . . best, cheapest, and most reliable laborers ever known."[68] Mississippi, Louisiana, and Arkansas seem to have been the most enthusiastic of the supporters. Almost immediately after the Memphis convention, Tennessee passed a law prohibiting the entry of Chinese bondsman into the state.[69] Georgia was interested but cautioned that the economic benefits of such a scheme might not be worth the addition of another colored race to the region.[70]

Alabama soundly opposed the Chinese labor movement. Just as strongly as Arkansas' Democratic Governor had embraced the idea, Alabama's Republican Governor spoke out against it. "We do not want a superabundance of cheap labor. . . . Even in the most favorable point of view, the advantages possessed by our laboring population are limited enough."[71] He went on to express the opinion that Chinese cheap labor would be injurious to white and black workers and place the small white farmers in the same predicament they had been in during the antebellum period—unable to compete with planters who had large quantities of slave labor at their disposal. Smith also expressed the fear that the "hoards of Asia" would ". . . fill the jails with their filthy . . . disgusting vices," and, because the Chinese were known to regard themselves as sojourners, that they would save all their earnings and would ". . . not become productive members of society."[72]

Blacks were also divided over the issue. While some keenly felt the threat of losing their meager bargaining power to cheap Chinese contract labor, others were optimistic that once tested beside Chinese workers that the South would realize the blacks' true value and that the bargaining power of free black labor would be enhanced. For the most part blacks accepted the white stereotype of the Chinese as pagans given to vile excesses. Shankman noted that the primary objection blacks had toward Chinese was based on economic grounds, but they also questioned the advisability of admitting them into their Christian society.[73]

In the wake of the Memphis Convention, blacks organized their own conventions to promote their agricultural interests and discuss the threat of Chinese labor. The call to a convention held in Louisiana in November of 1869 contained this statement:

> "In view of the introduction of coolie laborers, and other dangers which threaten the colored working classes, it is hoped that colored men throughout the state will wake up and come together to protect their interests."[74]

Also contained in the statement was a plea for the Southern white power structure to offer protection for its native working class as had the North and West. In December of that year a national convention of black labor convened in Washington, D.C. and discredited the contract Chinese labor system as ". . . but a system of slavery in the new form."[75] This apparently remained a matter of concern for blacks after the Chinese labor movement lost its momentum. In 1872 the *Macon Telegraph* predicted that whichever political party positively opposed the importation of coolie labor into the South would ". . . carry the negro vote and sweep the field."[76]

The Results and Implications of the Chinese Labor Experiment

For several months following the Memphis Convention, the national press was rife with rumors of "thousands" of Chinese soon to be delivered to this Southern state or that. For example, it was reported that 30,000 Chinese laborers were ordered for use on the Georgia and South Carolina coasts; 50,000 were to be sent to Charleston; 20,000 to Tennessee; 25,000 to Mississippi; four or five "ship loads" to Key West; and 5,000 to Texas.[77] But, if any of these large groups ever materialized there are no known records which account for them. The 1870 census shows 218 Chinese in the southern region, a scant .3 percent of the nation's total Chinese population (Tables 9.1a, 9.1b and 9.2). Even smaller were the percentages of Chinese in the Northeast (.2%) and North Central (.01%). The main concentration remained in California, although there was considerable movement out of California and into other western states.

The 1870 census should be regarded with caution. Data given for occupations by state show Chinese at work in some Southern states that were reported elsewhere in the same census to have no Chinese population. On the other hand, several Southern states having a Chinese population showed no Chinese employed. Because of the obvious inconsistencies in the figures it is impossible to make any definitive statements about the distribution of Chinese among the four major categories of employment shown in Table 9.2, but the degree of concentration in services is of interest as a precursor to a trend that became more evident by the mid 1870s.

The years between the 1870 and 1880 census offer only scattered reports in newspapers, journals, and older histories available from which to gauge the success or failure of the Chinese labor movement. Somers, for example, in a post-war history of the South discussed the use of 600 Chinese on the Alabama and Chattanooga Railway and mentioned that it was a common sight in New Orleans to see Chinese strolling in small groups.[78] Crews of two or three hundred Chinese were known to be working in Texas, Mississippi, Louisiana, and Ar-

TABLE 9.2. Southern States Reporting Chinese Employed in 1870.

	Total Chinese Population	Agriculture	Personal and Professional Services	Trade and Transportation	Manufacturing and Mining
Arkansas	98		14		
Georgia	1				1
Kentucky	1		4	3	
Louisiana	71	10	27	1	10
Mississippi	16			1	
Missouri	3		1		
Tennessee	0			4	1
Texas	25	2	8	6	
Virginia	4	3			

Source: United States Bureau of the Census, 1870.

kansas, and Georgia early in the 1870s.[79] It seems likely that this would have been true for all the southern states at one time or another between 1865 and 1876—this last date admittedly being somewhat speculative. But, from these types of records it is possible to place only a limited number of Chinese at work in any one place between the 1870 and 1880 census, never hundreds of thousands as it was originally hoped by the Chinese labor proponents.

By 1880 the total number of Chinese recorded in the South was 922, an increase of only 704 from the 1870 figures (Table 9.1a). It is generally agreed that the Chinese labor movement was a failure.

Reasons for the Failure of the Chinese Labor Movement

Many reasons may be cited for the failure of the South to attract Chinese labor. Wage rates, mistreatment and misunderstanding because of the language barrier, and some shady dealings by Chinese and white contractors created problems that had not been anticipated. Planters who had been attracted to Chinese labor because, "Common gossip had it that they would work for four dollars a month, live on next to nothing, clothe themselves," and be free of the ". . . evil habit of impudence," found Chinese labor to be more expensive and demanding than the rumors allowed.[80] Actually the average pay rate expected by the Chinese was about $20 per month for Chinese from the western United States and $10–$12 per month for Chinese shipped directly from Hong Kong. Furthermore the employer was charged with the transportation costs which could range anywhere from $50 to $150 depending on the distance travelled.[81] This fee was deducted from the worker's wages but there was no 'Fugitive Free-Labor Law' to bring a contract breaker back to finish his term and the employer stood to lose a large cash investment if his workers escaped.

Those who ventured to make the investment had mixed feelings about the results, as apparently did the Chinese who contracted with them. The problem seems to have been the mistreatment of the Chinese by their employers and the cavalier attitude employers took about paying them for their work.[82] For example, the Chinese work crew for the Alabama-Chattanooga Railroad ". . . received no pay, and were fearfully abused and turned off in the swamps, where they managed to exist on roots, berries, and anything they could get. . . ."[83] One planter was said to have controlled his Chinese workers ". . . by kicking and cuffing [them] . . . at every opportunity" and ". . . by whipping their interpreter within an inch of his life."[84] The Chinese understandably took exception to this sort of treatment and either made their objections known, refused to work until the dispute was settled, or deserted as it had been feared. White employers in turn, took exception to the response of the Chinese calling them ". . . lazy . . . turbulent and unmanageable."[85] Some of the exchanges erupted into violence with the Chinese rebelling against their employers or employers using force to drive their Chinese workers away.[86] Although there were many cases reported where Chinese labor was used with success, the risk involved for both Chinese and potential employers was too great to allow the Chinese labor movement to succeed in the region. The Chinese labor issue remained open in the South until the early 1900s, but it was never again to receive the attention it had between 1865 and 1870.[87]

Chinese Settlement in the South

The Chinese were neither a boon to the South as some had hoped, nor a burden as others had predicted. Of the few who remained of the early Chinese laborers, most moved into larger cities. By the 1880s many southern cities had communities of Chinese who were engaged primarily in trade or personal services as owner operators of small groceries, laundries, and restaurants. The laundries served a white clientele, but the Chinese grocers often functioned as "middlemen" between the white community and blacks and other minority populations—Mexicans and Indians for example, in the case of Texas and Arkansas.[88]

The Chinese "middlemen" served to fill an economic gap created by the social and economic changes in the post Civil War era. The antebellum plantation economy had been relatively simple, dominated by an agricultural system which was composed of many self-sufficient plantation and farm units. The diversification of the economy after the War and the growth of urban areas created a need by blacks and whites for a variety of new services.[89] A white merchant class developed, but it had no parallel in the black community. The majority of blacks lacked the capital and skills necessary to establish their own businesses. It has also been argued that the plantation's communal social organization did not allow native blacks to develop a cultural frame of reference that included free enterprise.[90]

The Chinese, on the other hand, had capital, skills, and a cultural background which included commerce and trade.[91] Furthermore, as sojourners only temporarily in the country for economic gain, it has been postulated that they tended to be more frugal than blacks and willing to take risks.[92] In addition to the factors internal to the Chinese community which were conducive to their entry into the grocery trade, there were numerous influences from without—not the least of which was the reluctance of whites to employ Chinese in any capacity other than common labor. But ultimately it was the nature of social relations between blacks and whites in the immediate post-war period which provided Chinese with a means for economic survival in the South. Because whites considered serving blacks to be socially unacceptable and blacks were unprepared at the time to provide necessary services for themselves, there was little competition for the economic position between black consumers and white producers. The Chinese moved in to fill the gap.

Some interesting variations of this pattern include the involvement of Texas Chinese in truck gardening and the development of the dried shrimp industry by Chinese in Louisiana.[93] No doubt there are many other variations which could be cited, but the early records are poor. Given the records that do exist, however, it seems likely that these variations in early occupational representation would have accounted for only a very small percentage of the South's total Chinese population.

SETTLEMENT AND ACTIVITY PATTERN OF CHINESE

The basic pattern for Chinese settlement in the South and throughout the country where no large concentrations of Chinese were to be found was set by the late 1800s and persisted well into the 1950s. It was characterized by small urban groups engaged primarily in retail food sales (groceries and restaurants) and in the commercial laundry business. There was a Chinatown in El Paso, Texas until the 1930s, and Lee references a Chinatown in New Orleans sometime prior to 1940, although no mention of such could be found in any historical accounts of the city surveyed in the course of this research.[94]

The Chinese communities in the South, for the most part, typically were dispersed within black neighborhoods.[95] In some Southern states—Mississippi for example—this pattern was enforced by discriminatory laws.[96] In other states it was enforced by convention. In some cases, as in Georgia, there seems to have been a conscious effort by the Chinese to avoid clustering. Since many of the Chinese who came into the South had been victims of persecution in the West they preferred to keep a low profile in the community by spreading out.[97] In general, whites made the rules—written and unwritten—which determined the conditions under which Chinese were tolerated within a community, and the Chinese accommodated themselves within those limits. Every community had a slightly different way of dealing with the Chinese among them, and each Chinese group had to adjust themselves accordingly. The result, however, was the fairly uniform pattern described.

It is difficult to determine how many of the early Chinese communities faded in and out of existence in the early years. The historical documentation is poor, and even if the censuses were not questionable, small mobile groups of people can make many changes in location in the intervening years between censuses. Because the Chinese population remained almost exclusively male until the early 1900s and tended to be engaged in easy entry occupations which required a minimum of investment, they were relatively free to move at will; the successful ones perhaps returning to China and the unsuccessful moving on to find more profitable places to exploit. In the large cities, however, once a social network was established, it seems to have served to maintain community structure even though its members were in a state of flux.

The earliest communities were probably replenished by imported contract laborers who had left their plantation and construction jobs to find more lucrative employment. But as the South's demand for Chinese labor decreased, a small scale chain migration sprang up between the Southern settlements, China, and other Chinese communities in the United States.

Kinship and the Chinese Community

The extended family or clan was the basic social unit in China, kinship ties remained important to the sojourning bachelors in the United States; the pattern of migration seems to have been based largely on kinship. This is exhibited in many Chinese communities by the predominance of a few family surnames, although this is not as true of the contemporary period as it was until the 1960s.

It became the common practice for individuals when well established to send for relatives and "trans-family relations" (fictive relatives created by blood brotherhood, traditional friendships, surname similarity, geographic proximity, and marriage ties).[98] The newcomers were provided bed and board, employment, and a chance to learn a trade. The store owner was provided cheap labor and the comfort of friends and relatives. Later the original sponsor might help establish an apprentice in a store of his own. Had it not been for the persistence of the traditional Chinese family organization in the United States, the original bachelor communities might have quickly died out—but the kinship system kept them alive by the continuous addition of adult males until the early 1900s when the sex ratio began to normalize, and growth by natural increase became possible.

The occupational concentration of Chinese in particular areas has been attributed to the results of this kinship migration and apprenticeship pattern. Liao's analysis of Chinese surnames in Arkansas based on Chinese store ownership in 1949 showed that 66 percent of the stores belonged to families representing four clans. The remaining 34 percent were said to be related in some way to the predominant clans. According to Liao ". . . a Chinese who runs a store in this region without any relationships with those four clan's families could not survive for a long period."[99] Loewen in his analysis of kinship in the Mississippi Delta group also identified several dominant families although clan competition was not indicated.[100] This also proved true of Georgia, but whereas clans may be identified, there was a deliberate effort made, at least by the Savannah Chinese, to put aside clan loyalties for the advantages of internal community cooperation.[101]

Intraregional Chinese Migration

There is very little data about intraregional Chinese migration, but various studies make reference to the migration of individuals and families within the region.[102] From these references and discussions with Chinese from several southern Chinese communities the impression is gained that the social networks operating within local communities extend far beyond city and state boundaries. Communication links and intraregional population movement may provide further explanation for the early occupational concentration of Southern Chinese in food retailing. For example, Chinese from the Mississippi Delta who were almost entirely concentrated in the grocery business until the 1950s, were known to have migrated into Arkansas, Houston, Texas and Augusta, Georgia where there were high percentages of Chinese owned groceries at one time. Joe and Woo, which were common surnames in the Delta, were also found to be common in Augusta, thus adding a degree of reinforcement to the theory.

Prejudice and Hostility

So long as the Chinese remained clustered on the West Coast the stories of their persecution were reported with a modicum of sympathy by the Eastern press. But, when Chinese began appearing in Eastern cities the mood of the press changed from sympathy to antipathy. The South also viewed this voluntary eastward migration with some misgivings. Presumably contract laborers were under the control of their employers, but there could be little control over the numbers and activities of the Chinese who came to the South as free agents. Besides, after the election of 1876, the South regained its political autonomy and quickly legislated the blacks back into a state of quasi-slavery, and the Chinese were no longer perceived as economically beneficial.

Most researchers who have examined these surges of anti-Chinese sentiments agree that they were the product of racial prejudice aggravated by economic stress.[103] During times of economic crises foreigners were regarded at the national level as a threat to unity. Between individuals it was a matter of birthright and competition for scarce jobs and resources. The Chinese—the "ultimate foreigners"—bore the brunt of anti-foreign agitation.[104] A general depression between 1873 and 1877 led to the passage of America's first restrictive immigration laws in 1882, but only the Chinese were singled out as a nationality to be denied entry into the country.

There was in 1879 a brief and unsuccessful attempt by planters in Mississippi and Louisiana to revive the Chinese labor movement. The flurry of interest was stirred by a large scale outmigration of blacks to the midwest territories.[105] The action was significant enough to provoke the *New York Times* into speculating that the national movement for Chinese exclusion would make little political headway as long as the economic interest of the South could be served by Chinese immigration.[106]

National labor problems in the 1880's kept the anti-Chinese movement active even after the exclusion act was passed. The Chinese in the West were subjected to boycotts, lynchings, mass expulsions, and mass murders. Chinese businesses and residences were blown-up or burned down with little regard to the fact they might be occupied. Although the agitation was not so intense in the South and East as it was in the West, it was still manifested in some form. Take, for example, an incident in 1882 when a white woman in El Paso, Texas was presented a silver cup for attempting an armed assault on a Chinese laundryman who ventured a complaint about her refusal to pay him for his services. The event occurred in the midst of the national furor over Chinese exclusion and local commotion in El Paso over the Chinese monopoly of the laundry business. When El Paso was a male dominated frontier town, the Chinese washermen were welcome additions to the city's service sector. As more white women joined the general populace, the Chinese, who had established the commercial laundry business in the city, were accused of unfairly monopolizing an important means of their self-support. Feeling ran so high that a newspaper account of the event suggested that should other "ladies" be encouraged to shoot at Chinese there would be ". . . no more cups unless they [brought] in scalps."[107]

The Exclusion Bills

The total Chinese population of the United States increased by only several thousand between 1880 and 1890, testimony to the effectiveness of the 1882 law excluding Chinese immigration. This small gain has largely been attributed to natural increase.[108] The low birth rate indicated by this figure was the result of an abnormally high ratio of males to females, a characteristic of the Chinese population until the 1940s. The increase in the South, however, was mostly the result of internal population movements. The West lost Chinese population in 1890, both in absolute numbers and its relative share. The Northeast was the recipient for the majority of out migrants from the West, followed by the North Central and the South (Tables 9.1a and 9.1b).

For the most part the South supported the Exclusion Act. Southern protest raised after the 1882 act came primarily from those who feared the loss of the Chinese foreign cotton market should China choose to register protest against the Exclusion Act by boycotting American goods. China, however, seemed to wish to maintain its southern links and for a time New York City became a popular courting spot for Southern and Chinese economic interests—so much so that in fact *The New York Times* once observed, that "while antipathy toward blacks remained a powerful force in the south antipathy for Chinese was conspicuously absent."[109]

This relaxation of attitudes toward the Chinese lasted until 1905 when a deterioration in economic well-being generated another anti-foreign campaign.[110] This time southern support of the movement was fairly uniform.[111] The South was in agreement with the nation that the new wave of southern European immigrants in the early 1900s was not 'pure white' but tainted by Asiatic bloodstocks. A government official from North Carolina echoed a spokesman from Alabama when he called the new wave:

. . . nothing more than the degenerate progeny of the Asiatic hoards (sic) which, long centuries ago, overran the shore of the Mediterranean.[112]

The message was clear, "No foreigners need apply," especially Asians and those suspected to be of Asiatic extraction.

By the turn of the century the United States had begun to lose total Chinese population. A drop in total numbers in the West reflected the national trend, but the Northeast, North Central and South showed both absolute and relative increases due to interregional migration (Tables 9.1a–9.1b and Fig. 9.1).[113] The United States continued to show a loss in total Chinese population until 1930 (Fig. 9.2). In the South the only absolute loss occurred in 1910, but it was accompanied by a small increase in its relative share as the population continued its internal readjustments.

Changing Attitudes Toward the Chinese

Throughout the late 1910s and the 1920s the Southern press was strangely silent on the Chinese issue. Lee's survey of the national press during the 1910s and 1920s determined that by the 1920s more articles favorable to the Chinese were to be found than in earlier periods. Many of the articles related to this and other Chinese topics written during this period were published in popular periodicals.[114] It was not until the 1930s and the advent of World War II (1931–1945) that the Southerners seem to have again found the Chinese newsworthy. Initially, the hostilities roused by the War were directed toward the Japanese, but it was soon extended to include all Asians. In Georgia, in 1932, there was a brief flurry over a movement to exclude Orientals from white schools.[115] In Houston, Texas there was an effort to drive Chinese grocers out of business.[116] But by the late 1930s, the war efforts of the

Mainland Chinese had won the respect of Americans. This new image of China, coupled with the United States-Sino Alliance toward the latter part of the War, resulted in an easing of Chinese immigration restrictions in 1943 when Chinese were also granted rights to naturalization.

Rural-Urban Distribution

Table 9.3 shows the urban/rural distribution of the Chinese population from 1910 to 1970. The percent urban is high, even for the earlier periods when the general population was primarily rural. According to Lee the trend toward urbanization of the Chinese began in the 1870s. Lee provides a national estimate of 23 percent for urban Chinese in 1880 based on a sample of census data for Chinese population in cities and unincorporated places. By 1910 more than half the Chinese in the United States were urban. By region the Northeast (80%) and West (62%) had the greatest percent of urban concentration followed by the North Central (56%) and South (53%).[117]

Patterns of National Growth and Dispersal

After 1920 the total Chinese population began showing moderate increases. By 1940 the Northeast had gained 25.3 percent of the national total at the expense of the West, which had declined to a 60.4 percent share despite its large relative increases during the period (Tables 9.1a and 9.1b). Only 6.3 percent of the nation's Chinese were located in the South. Of the Southern group only 79 percent were reported having urban residences in 1940 as compared to 97 percent in the Northeast, 95 percent in the North Central, and 88 percent in the West. Data for rural farm and rural non-farm residences, however, show that majority of all Chinese in rural areas were designated as rural non-farm. The assumption is generally made that the rural non-farm population lived in small towns and had essentially urban life styles[118] (Table 9.3).

Between 1870 and 1930 Chinese occupational statistics are available only for the nation (Table 9.4), but from 1940 through 1970 data is available by regional divisions (Table 9.5). Although the categories in the earlier data sets vary somewhat from the more recent statistics and cannot be too closely compared, it is possible to characterize the 1870–1930 period and concentrated employment in services (including laundry) and trade (including proprietors and employees of retail groceries and restaurants). The significant trends in the 1870–1930 period were the rise and decline of the traditional Chinese hand laundry; the steady increase in those involved in trade; and from 1920 the trend toward representation in the professions.

1940–1970

From 1940 to 1970 (Table 9.5) the dominant trend in the changing occupational structure of the Chinese

TABLE 9.3 Percent Urban-Rural Distributions of Chinese by Region 1910–1970

	1910		1940		1970	
	urban	rural	urban	rural*	urban	rural*
Northeast	80	20	97	2	97	3
North Central	56	44	95	4	97	3
West	62	38	88	7	97	3
South	53	47	79	18	93	7

*non-farm residence

Source: United States Bureau of the Census, 1910, 1940, 1970.

TABLE 9.4 Percent Chinese Employment for the United States for Selected Major Occupational Categories 1870–1930

	1870	1900	1920	1930
Personal services	41	51	58	47
Laundry	(8)	(25)	(28)	(24)
Mining	40	3	.3	neg
Manufacturing	8	10	9	8
Agriculture	8	23	11	7
Wholesale, retail trade	2	10	16	31
Restaurant	(.4)	(.9)	(10)	(14)
Professional services	.7	.7	.9	2

Source: King and Locke, 1980.

in the United States has been the growth in professional fields. In 1940 only 3 percent of the nation's Chinese were classified in professional categories; by 1970 the figure had risen to 31 percent. Complete data are not yet available for 1980, but from a sample of state returns, it appears that the trend is continuing. By region the North Central and South have led the nation in growth in professional and technical occupations. The South increased from 2 percent to 46 percent between 1940 and 1970; the North Central from 3 percent to 51 percent; the Northeast from .4 percent to 29 percent; and the West from 3 percent to 28 percent. By absolute numbers, however, the West and Northeast surpass the South and North Central in professional employment. The percentage share for these regions is lower because the New York and San Francisco Chinatowns are principle staging areas for new immigration which dilutes the population with many unskilled workers.

The South's category of employment is distinguished from the rest of the country by its high percentage of managers and proprietors and relatively low percentage of employed in service occupations. Since 1950 the South has shown a proportion of decline in managers and proprietors to other occupations, but for the entire 1940 to 1970 period it still showed a higher proportion occupied in this category than any other region. An interesting data set available from the census,

as yet complete only for 1970, shows the percentage of self-employed Chinese in the South at 14.2 percent with 3.6 percent Chinese reported as unpaid family workers. Self-employed for the other major regional divisions were given as 8.2 percent in the Northeast, 7.8 percent in the North Central and 7.5 percent in the West; with the percentage of unpaid family workers a uniform 1.1 percent for each. Conversely the Northeast showed the highest number of wage earners at 80.6 percent followed by 75.1 percent in the West, 65.2 percent in the North Central, and 57.8 percent in the South.[119] These 1970 data support the model of the Chinese family-owned business in the South, although they give no information about specific types of self-employment. Occupational statistics for Chinese available by state for 1980 when complete will most likely show the restaurant business to be the dominant form of self-employment for southern groups.

Effects of the Relaxation of Immigration Restrictions

The 1943 revision of the Chinese Exclusion Acts gave Chinese a token annual immigration quota of 105. Further amendments to this law and other immigration laws which affected Chinese were made in the late 1940s and decade of 1950s. Finally, in 1965 an act was passed which eliminated all discriminatory legislation against Chinese immigration, and the Chinese were allowed the normal national quota of 20,000 per year.[120]

The effect of the relaxation of Chinese immigration restrictions is evident in the 1950–1980 population statistics (Tables 9.1a and 9.1b). In 1950 absolute gains for all regions were large; the South's total Chinese population increased from 10,486 in 1950 to 16,839 (Fig. 9.2) in 1960. The greatest surge of growth came, however, between 1970 and 1980 when the last discriminatory laws were repealed. In 1980 the Chinese population in the South was 90,616 placing it third behind the Northeast and West with an 11.2% of the total. The West has continued to lose relative numbers to the Northeast, and the North Central has stabilized around 9 percent (Tables 9.1a–9.1b and Figs. 9.2–9.3).

Between 1940 and 1970 the urban concentration of Chinese in the United States rose from 91 percent to

TABLE 9.5 Percent Chinese Employment by Region for Major Occupational Categories 1940–1970*

1940	United States	South	Northeast	North Central	West
Professional/Technical	3	2	.4	3	3
Managers/Proprietors	20	51	16	30	18
Sales	n/a	n/a	n/a	n/a	n/a
Clerical	11	15	5	6	16
Craftsmen	1	.4	.7	1	2
Operatives	22	12	37	26	14
Farmers/Farm Managers	1	1	.1	.2	2
Farm Labor	3	.5	.1	.06	5
Service	30	15	37	31	27
Domestic	6	2	2	2	10
Labor	2	1	.5	1	2
Others	.6	.5	.6	.2	.6

1950					
Professional/Technical	6	7	5	8	6
Managers/Proprietors	22	38	18	23	22
Sales	n/a	n/a	n/a	n/a	n/a
Clerical	11	12	5	5	16
Craftsmen	3	2	2	3	5
Operatives	16	9	25	18	12
Farmers/Farm Managers	1	2	.3	.4	2
Farm Labor	1	3	.4	.3	2
Service	32	22	41	36	28
Domestic	2	1	1	.5	3
Labor	2	4	1	3	2
Others	1	1	2	1	1

1960					
Professional/Technical	18	24	17	32	16
Managers/Proprietors	15	29	15	14	13
Sales	6	7	8	2	2
Clerical	8	6	10	3	4
Craftsmen	7	2	10	3	3
Operatives	13	6	11	11	18
Farmers/Farm Managers	.7	.6	1	.2	.1
Farm Labor	.4	.2	.6	.2	.06
Service	23	16	19	26	32
Domestic	.8	.9	.9	.4	.8
Labor	2	2	2	1	.4
Others	7	6	5	7	10

1970					
Professional/Technical	31	46	29	51	28
Managers/Proprietors	15	20	13	10	16
Sales	4	3	3	2	5
Clerical	7	5	5	3	9
Craftsmen	8	3	4	4	11
Operatives	10	6	14	5	10
Farmers/Farm Managers	.5	.5	.1	.09	.7
Farm Labor	.2	.2	.1	—	.3
Service	21	15	30	23	17
Domestic	.3	.1	.4	.2	.2
Labor	2	1	1	.9	3
Others	n/a	n/a	n/a	n/a	n/a

*Note: Columns do not total 100% due to rounding errors.
Source: United States Bureau of the Census; 1940, 1953, 1960, 1973.

97 percent. The West, Northeast, and North Central conform to the national average percentage of urban distribution with the South showing only 93 percent of its Chinese population (Table 9.3) urban. However, the majority of Chinese having rural residences were reported as rural non-farm.

Chinese communities in the South underwent many changes in the 1960s and 1970s. James Loewen observed the Mississippi groups in the processes of dispersing in the late 1960s and attributed it to the breakdown of the segregated social system. In Georgia, where discrimination against Chinese was practiced by custom but not by law, the Chinese communities appear to have begun dispersing in the late 1950s. The general trend has been for the Chinese to move out of black neighborhoods into white residential areas, and there has been an occupational shift from small business owner-operators to the white collar professions. These changes have come about as more opportunities for advancement have been opened to the Chinese and they have gained the education necessary to take advantage of them.

Change and Dispersals

In recent years with the increased immigration of Chinese to the United States two social patterns appear to have emerged. The first is composed of low income immigrants with low educational backgrounds whose knowledge of English is poor. Many of these immigrants, especially in larger cities of the Pacific coast such as San Francisco, Los Angeles and Seattle, settle in the large Chinatown communities where they are culturally protected but may often be economically exploited by their fellow countrymen. It is the continuing influx of large numbers of these poorly educated immigrants who help insure the continuation and in some cases the growth of the traditional Chinatowns.

The second pattern is composed of second, third, or fourth generation Chinese immigrants or those recent immigrants with good educational and professional qualifications. These people have either moved away from Chinatown or never lived there. Generally, they are dispersed residentially in neighborhoods appropriate to their income levels without regard to their race or ethnicity. This dual social pattern is characteristic of the large older cities with traditional Chinatowns that have persisted along with the recent dispersal. The dispersed pattern only is found in cities such as Atlanta or Houston where the bulk of the Chinese population are recently arrived, and most are well educated professionals with moderate to high incomes.

CONCLUSION

The Chinese population in the United States, although historically a small minority among the nation's ethnic immigrant groups, has received a great deal of attention. In the early period of Chinese immigration to the United States a fearful native public rallied to place obstacle upon obstacle before them to restrict their entry into the country and to make existence difficult for those who had settled. They lived within a mass of contradictions—thwarted at every turn from entering mainstream America and damned because they did not. The press kept anti-Chinese issues circulating long after immigration had all but ceased, in part, perhaps, because the titillating stories about the "evils" of Chinatown sold newspapers. It is no small irony that by the turn of the century, the Chinatowns found tourism to be an important source of income.

Over time the Chinese began to earn the grudging respect of the public. A generation of native born Chinese grew up with English as a first language and for the first time the Chinese began writing about themselves. With the barrier to communication down, America was introduced to a different view of Chinese-Americans. This fact, coupled with favorable serious academic studies of the Chinese and the effect of the Sino-American alliance of World War II, resulted in a dramatic change in popular opinion.

Today Chinese-Americans are among the most admired of United States ethnic minorities. They are as a group more educated, better employed, and enjoy higher incomes than the average citizen; and they are often lauded as a prime example of success in the "American Way." Whereas this success story is remarkable witness to the tenacity of the Chinese to overcome extreme odds, it must be remembered that the statistics are based primarily on those who were never isolated in Chinatowns or managed to escape and integrate themselves into general society. For thousands of Chinese Chinatown is still a reality. Because of the crowding, the incidence of tuberculosis, mental illness, drug abuse, and alcoholism are high; crime is increasing and juvenile street gangs are not uncommon. Chinese in these ghettos still feel the remnants of racial bias from their host cities and feel they are too often left to solve their problems alone. Despite the success of many Chinese in the United States, the reality of Chinatown for many of the first generation and recent immigrants is the American dream unfulfilled.

NOTES

1. Stuart Creighton Miller, *The Unwelcome Immigrant: The American Image of the Chinese, 1785–1882* (Berkeley: University of California Press, 1969).
2. *Ibid.*: p. 43.
3. Ching-Tau Wu, *"Chink"* (New York: World Publishing, 1972): p. 2
4. Shieu-woo Kung, *Chinese in American Life* (Seattle: University of Washington Press, 1962): p. 167.
5. John Higham, *Strangers in the Land* (New York: Atheneum, 1965).
6. Orlando Patterson, *Ethnic Chauvinism: The Reactionary Impulse* (New York: Stein and Day, 1977): p. 56.
7. Edna Bonacich and John Modell, *The Economic Basis of Ethnic Solidarity* (Berkeley: University of California Press, 1980).
8. James W. Loewen, *The Mississippi Chinese: Between Black and White* (Cambridge: Harvard University Press, 1971).
9. Thomas Sowell (ed), *Essays and Data on American Ethnic Groups* (Washington, D.C.: The Urban Institute, 1978).
10. Colin Greer, *Divided Society* (New York: Basic Books, Inc., 1974).
11. Loewen, 1971 unnumbered page.
12. Arnold Shankman, "Black on Yellow: Afro-Americans View Chinese-Americans, 1850–1935," *Phylon* 34 (March 1978): pp. 1–17.
13. Gunther Barth, *Bitter Strength: A History of the Chinese in the U.S. 1850–1870* (Cambridge: Harvard University Press, 1964).
14. Jack Chen. *The Chinese in America* (San Francisco: Harper and Row Publishers, 1980).
15. Rose Hum Lee, *The Chinese in the United States of America* (Hong Kong: Hong Kong University Press, 1960).
16. Haitung King and Frances Locke, "The Chinese in the United States: a Century of Occupational Transition," *International Migration Review,* 14 (Spring 1980): pp. 15–42.
17. Robert W. O'Brien, "Status of Chinese in the Mississippi Delta," *Social Forces,* 19 March 1941): pp. 386–401.
18. Nancy Farrar, "The Chinese in El Paso," *Southwestern Studies,* Monograph No. 23 (El Paso: Texas Western Press and Texas University Press, 1972).
19. Edward Rhoads, *The Chinese in Texas* (Austin: Texas State Historical Society, 1977).
20. P. Y. Liao, "A Case Study of a Chinese Immigrant Community" (Master's thesis, University of Chicago, 1957).
21. Sally Ken, "The Chinese Community of Augusta, Georgia, from 1873 to 1971," *Richmond County History,* 4 (1972): pp. 50–60.
22. Eileen Law and Sally Ken, "A Study of the Chinese Community," *Richmond County History* 5 (1973): pp. 23–43.
23. S. M. Chiu, "The Chinese in Augusta, Georgia," *Bulletin: Chinese Historical Society of America,* 13 (February 1978): pp. 1–5.
24. Gerald Sieg, "Georgia's Chinese Pioneers," *Atlanta Constitution,* 7 March 1965: p. 18.
25. Etta B. Peabody. "Effort of the South to Import Chinese Coolies 1865–1870" (Master's thesis, Baylor University, 1967).
26. Sylvia Krebs, "The Chinese Labor Question: A Note on the Attitudes of Two Alabama Republicans," *Alabama Historical Quarterly,* 38 (Fall 1976): pp. 214–217.
27. Lucy M. Cohen, "Entry of Chinese to the Lower South From 1865–1870: Policy Dilemmas," *Southern Studies,* 17 (Spring 1978): pp. 5–37.
28. Catherine L. Brown. "A Geographic Analysis of the Chinese in Georgia, 1865–1980" (Master's thesis, University of Georgia, 1983).
29. A. E. Smailes, "The Analysis and Delimitation of Urban Fields," *Geography,* 32 (December 1947): pp. 51–161.
30. Rhoads Murphey, "Boston's Chinatown," *Economic Geography,* 28 (1952): pp. 244–255.
31. *The China Geographer,* Special Edition on Chinatowns 4 (Spring 1976).
32. Rose Hum Lee, "The Decline of Chinatowns in the United States," *American Journal of Sociology,* 54 (March 1949): pp. 422–432.
33. Rose Hum Lee, 1960.
34. Gerald Sieg, 1965.
35. Francis L. K. Hsu, *The Challenge of the American Dream: The Chinese in the United States* (Belmont: Wadsworth Publishing Co., 1971).
36. Lee, 1960.
37. Rose Hum Lee, "Growth and Decline of Chinese Communities in the Rocky Mountains" (Ph.D. dissertation, University of Chicago, 1947).
38. Higham, 1965.
39. "The Chinese," *Alta* (San Francisco) 16 July 1869: p. 1.
40. Higham, 1965.
41. Miller, 1969.
42. Chen, 1980.
43. Lee, 1960.
44. Barth, 1964.
45. "The Chinese," *Alta* (San Francisco): p. 1.
46. "The Gothic, African, and Chinese Races," *Debow's Review* (August 1869): pp. 943–945.
47. Miller, 1969.
48. Chen, 1980.
49. Barth, 1964: p. 189.
50. James C. Banner, *A History of Georgia Agriculture: 1732–1860* (Athens, Georgia: University of Georgia Press, 1964).
51. Mildred C. Thompson, *Reconstruction in Georgia* (Columbia: Columbia University Press, 1915).
52. Vernon Lee Wharton, *The Negro in Mississippi, 1865–1890* (Chapel Hill: University of North Carolina Press, 1947).

53. Barth, 1964: p. 188.
54. "The Gothic, African, and Chinese Races,": pp. 943–945.
55. Wharton, 1947: p. 98.
56. *Savannah Morning News,* 16 July 1869: p. 2.
57. Wharton, 1947: p. 98.
58. "A Possible Phase of the Chinese Question," *Alta* (San Francisco), 18 July 1869: p. 2.
59. "Brick Pomeroy on the Chinese Question," *Alta* (San Francisco) 26 July 1869: p. 1.
60. "Coolie Labor in the South," *Alta* (San Francisco) 24 July 1869: p. 1.
61. "Coolies," *Debow's Review,* 26 (1859): p. 348; Patterson, 1977.
62. Barth, 1964; Merton E. Coulter, *The South During Reconstruction, 1865–1877* (Baton Rouge: Louisiana State University, Press, 1947).
63. "Chinamen in the South," *Alta* (San Francisco) 11 July 1867: p. 1.
64. "The Chinese," *Alta* (San Francisco)13 July 1869: p. 1.
65. "Koopmanshoop's Project," *New York Times,* 15 July 1869: p. 4.
66. *New York Times,* 12 August 1869: p. 4; Willard Range, *A Century of Georgia Agriculture* 1850–1950 (Athens: University of Georgia Press, 1954).
67. Lee, 1960.
68. Rhoads, 1977: p. 2.
69. Miller, 1979.
70. "The Chinese Labor Question," *Chronicle and Sentinel* (Augusta, Georgia) 5 August 1869: p. 2.
71. Krebs, 1976: p. 215.
72. Ibid., pp. 215–216.
73. Shankman, 1978.
74. *Chronicle and Sentinel* (Augusta, Georgia) 28 October 1869: p. 1.
75. Peabody, 1967, p. 52.
76. *Savannah Morning News,* 1 October 1872: p. 2.
77. "Chinese Laborers for the Southern States," *Chronicle and Sentinel* (Augusta, Georgia) 13 July 1869: p. 2.
78. Robert Somers, *The Southern States Since the War 1870–1970* (London: MacMillan and Co., 1871).
79. Peabody, 1967; Rhoads, 1977.
80. Wharton, 1947.
81. Barth, 1964.
82. Liao, 1957.
83. Liao, 1957: p. 19.
84. Peabody, 1967: p. 75.
85. Ibid.
86. Barth, 1964.
87. George E. Possetta, "Foreigners in Florida: A Study of Immigration Promotion 1865–1910," *Florida Historical Quarterly,* 53 (1974–1975): pp. 164–180; Peabody, 1967.
88. Loewen, 1971; Chiu, 1978; Liao, 1957; and Rhoads, 1977.
89. Thompson, 1915.
90. Sowell, 1978.
91. Greer, 1974.
92. Edna Bonacich, "A Theory of Middlemen Minorities," *American Sociological Review,* 38 (October 1973): pp. 583–594.
93. Farrar, 1972; Rhoads, 1977; and *Louisiana,* Federal Writers Project: American Guide Series, 1947.
94. Lee, 1947.
95. Loewen, 1971; Rhoads, 1977; and Brown, 1983.
96. Loewen, 1971; Ed Ritter and Helen Ritter, *Our Oriental Americans* (St. Louis: McGraw Hill Book Company, 1965).
97. Sieg, 1965.
98. Milford S. Weiss, *Valley City: A Chinese Community in America* (Cambridge: Shenkman Publishing Company, 1974): p. 36.
99. Liao, 1957: p. 23.
100. Loewen, 1971.
101. *Atlanta Constitution,* 24 July 1960: p. 10.
102. Liao, 1957; Loewen, 1976; Chiu, 1978; and Rhoads, 1977.
103. Higham, 1965.
104. Murphey, 1952: p. 249.
105. Wharton, 1947.
106. "Chinese in the South," *New York Times,* 6 May 1879: p. 4.
107. Farrar, 1972: p. 15.
108. Lee, 1960.
109. "Significant Incident," *New York Times,* 25 February 1899: p. 6.
110. Higham, 1965; and Possetta, 1974–1975.
111. Higham, 1965.
112. Lee, 1960.
113. Ibid.
114. Ibid.
115. Law and Ken, 1973.

116. Rhoads, 1977.
117. Lee, 1960.
118. Loewen, 1971; Liao, 1957; and Chiu, 1978.
119. United States Bureau of the Census, *Subject Reports, Nonwhite Population by Race, 1970* (Washington, D.C. United States Government Printing Office, 1973).
120. Betty Lee Sung, "Polarity in the Makeup of Chinese Immigrants," *Sourcebook on the New Immigration* (New Brunswick: Transaction Books, 1980).

10

The Indochinese

Alice C. Andrews
George Mason University

G. Harry Stopp, Jr.
Univ. of North Carolina at Greensboro

Since 1975, about one-half million Indochinese refugees have been resettled in the United States. Although their total number is small, and they make up only about 0.2 percent of the total 230 million Americans, their presence has been felt in all parts of the nation. Seldom has the arrival of a new ethnic group on the American scene been attended by so much publicity or by so much ambivalence on the part of the host population. As comparable recent events, there were the Hungarian influx of the late 1950s, after the failure of the abortive Hungarian revolution against communism; the Cuban flight after the Bay of Pigs; and the more recent arrival of Cuban and Haitian "boat people" on the shores of Florida. Although all these waves of immigration have had political and ethical aspects, the United States has never had to deal with a refugee movement quite like the Indochinese one. Both the Hungarians and the Cubans, for instance, fall under the general rubric of Western culture. Even the destitute Haitians, light-years away in terms of way of life, are geographically close; they come from within the Western Hemisphere. In all cases, but particularly in recent years, questions of ethics and responsibility have been aired, as well as some questions of racism and economic competition. Can the United States open its doors to an apparently never-ending stream of political and economic refugees, or are there realistic limits to the number that the country could absorb?

In the case of the Indochinese, the additional factor was the United States' involvement in the Vietnam war and the sense, not only of moral responsibility, but of guilt, engendered by the ignominious ending of that conflict. At policy-making levels, there was a feeling that the United States had to accept the refugees and make every effort to absorb them into American society. There might have been a sense of compassionate responsibility for the Hungarians and Cubans, but there was a feeling of moral obligation for the Indochinese.

ORIGINS: THE HOMELANDS

From what kind of natural environment and cultural milieu did these refugees come? This is a question of interest to cultural geographers as they begin to analyze and explain the patterns of distribution and the problems and processes of assimilation of the Indochinese into American society.

Indochina occupies the eastern part of a peninsula that separates the Indian subcontinent from China. It includes Vietnam, Laos, the Cambodia, currently called Democratic Kampuchea (Fig. 10.1). Climatically, the region is largely tropical grading to subtropical rainforest, with deciduous tropical forest in rain-shadowed parts of the interior. The influence of the monsoon is felt everywhere, and precipitation ranges from 80 inches along the coast of Vietnam to perhaps 40 inches on the plains of Kampuchea. Physiographically, the area is chiefly mountainous, but the Red River in the north and the Mekong in the central and southern parts have created large valleys and deltas of rich alluvial soil.

Much of the population lives in the valleys, the delta regions, or on the coastal plains. The major economic activity is padi rice growing. Fishing is also important, and fish and rice are the staples of diet. The major cities, such as Hanoi in the North, Hue on the central coast, and Ho Chi Minh City (formerly Saigon) in the south are also located in these densely populated areas. A different way of life prevails in the mountainous interior, where the population is less dense, more scattered, and chiefly engaged in slash-and-burn agriculture. Not only the way of life, but the ethnicity of the population differs between the two kinds of environment. In each of the three Indochinese states, the titular nationality and politically dominant majority lives in their lowland core areas, whereas various ethnic minorities, often grouped together as "hill tribes" or "montagnards," live in the outlying mountainous areas.

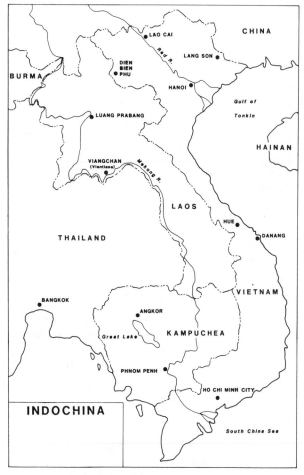

Figure 10.1. Indochina.

Laos

Laos, a landlocked mountainous state, is the smallest in population of the three. As of 1981, its population was estimated at about 3.5 million. Of these, about 48 percent are Lao and the rest are mountain tribes. About one-half are Buddhist and the rest practice animism and indigenous religions. Agricultural productivity in Laos is severely limited by the mountainous nature of the terrain and the poverty of the soil. Only about eight percent of the land is planted in rice and subsistence crops. The language of the majority is Lao, a dialect of Thai. In terms of the Laotian migration to the United States, a significant minority group is the Hmong of the central mountains.

Kampuchea

Kampuchea, formerly Cambodia, has an estimated population of about 5.6 million. No one is quite sure of the exact population today, for the Khmer (Cambodians) underwent a period of civil strife, genocide, and forced population movements in the late 1970s. The population is now less than the 6.5 million level of 1965. The massive migration out of Kampuchea during these

terrible years is the source of the Cambodian population in the United States. Kampuchea has more plains than Laos and has a short coastline. Rice is the staple crop. Khmer make up about 90 percent of the population, with 5 percent Chinese and 5 percent other minorities (the Chinese are a ubiquitous minority throughout Indochina). Religiously, the Khmer are more homogeneous than the Lao. Probably 95 percent of the population practiced Theravada Buddhism before the recent disruption of national life. At present, the country has two competing governments, both communistic.

Vietnam

Vietnam is much larger in area and many times larger in population than the two interior states. It is also the one that Americans have heard most about, and it is the source of most of our recent influx of Indochinese population. The 1981 population was about 55 million, of which 85–90 percent were Vietnamese, perhaps 3 percent Chinese, and the remainder various ethnic minorities, including Muong, Thai, Khmer, Cham, and "mountain tribesmen." In addition to being linguistically complex, it is also very diverse in its religious traditions, with elements of Buddhism, Confucianism, Taoism, animism, Islam, and Christianity.

The Red River valley in the north was the original core area of the Vietnamese state. The Viets were under Chinese rule for over a millennium. In the tenth century, after throwing off Chinese rule, they began to push southward, and by the late 1700s had occupied all present-day Vietnam. During the period 1000–1800, they were involved in many wars with the Chinese, Thai, and other neighbors. French and Portuguese missionaries began to establish outposts in the 1600s. Although they were persecuted by the Vietnamese rulers, the faith took root among the already diverse religions present. Roman Catholicism joined Confucianism which was practiced by the elite, and Buddhism which was strong in the countryside. It was the persecution of Catholic missionaries that later afforded the French a pretext for intervention in Indochina. Between 1858 and 1893, the French gradually assumed colonial control over the whole region.

Under French rule, Cambodia and Laos were essentially left to their own devices, with the French using the Vietnamese as intermediaries in ruling these remote interior regions. Vietnam was more directly under French rule and, as a result, was more influenced by it. Under French colonial rule, Confucianism, formerly the state-supported ideology, declined, while indigenous cults remained strong and French Catholicism prospered. A great variety of beliefs, however, continued to exist—particularly Buddhism. Religious syncretism was common, an example being the Cao Dai cults of South Vietnam, which were basically Buddhist with an admixture of other influences, including Christian and Chinese. Animist beliefs, traditions, and healing practices remained locally strong.

Cultural Differences

The net cultural result of French rule was a reaffirmation of national and linguistic identity and a strengthening of Buddhism in Laos and Cambodia, at least in the lowland core areas. In Vietnam the result was cultural, political, and religious fragmentation. Later on, Americans saw news coverage of Buddhist monks incinerating themselves in protest of anti-Buddhist policies of the Catholic-dominated government.

In all three countries, the basic cultural cleavage was between the majority, power-wielding people of the lowlands, who were reasonably unified linguistically if not politically, and the diverse ethnic groups who lived in the highlands. Although both groups were predominantly agricultural, the lowland peoples were padi rice farmers, whose tradition of complex social organization enabled them to maintain intricate irrigation systems. The culturally and linguistically diverse highland peoples practiced primitive swidden agriculture. The French lumped them together under the term "montagnards" and kept them separate from the lowlanders.

Later the Americans played the same role as protectors of the mountain tribes. "But where the French merely kept the highlanders sealed off from the lowlands, American Protestant missionaries brought their evangelical message to segments of the tribes."[1] The only group of the hill tribesmen who are represented in the refugee movement to the United States in really significant numbers are the Hmong of Laos. Their relationship with the Americans was the chief cause of their enforced exodus. In their case, the specific form of Christianity brought by the Americans was the Christian and Missionary Alliance denomination. It is estimated that as many as half of the Hmong refugees in the United States are Christian converts.

MIGRATION

The abrupt end of the Vietnam War in 1975 set in motion a refugee movement from Indochina that is still continuing. The first great exodus came in April and May, 1975, as American embassies in Cambodia and Vietnam closed, American forces were evacuated, and more than 150,000 fled the country by air or sea (Table 10.1). This group is often referred to as the First Wave and consisted primarily of residents of Saigon and its surroundings who had been part of the government of South Vietnam or in some way actively involved with the American presence in Vietnam. In the United States, the State Department consulted with Congress about the use of the Attorney General's parole authority for accepting evacuees from Indochina. Parole was first authorized for dependents of American citizens in Vietnam, then gradually extended to relatives, Cambodians, and "high risk" Vietnamese.

By the end of 1975, about 130,000 Indochinese, largely Vietnamese, had been resettled in the United States. Most went by way of a temporary refugee reception way-station in Guam; later similar refugee

---

TABLE 10.1 A Chronology of Early Events

1975

April 12: United States Embassy, Phnom Penh closes. Last Americans are evacuated from Vietnam in operation "Eagle Pull."

April 14: Parole is authorized for dependents of American citizens currently in Vietnam.

April 18: The President asks twelve Federal agencies "to coordinate . . . all United States Government activities concerning evacuation of United States citizens, Vietnamese citizens, and third country nationals from Vietnam and refugee and resettlement problems relating to the Vietnam conflict."

April 19: Parole is extended to include categories of relatives of American citizens or permanent resident aliens who are petition holders.

April 22: The Interagency Task Force asks civil and military authorities on Guam to prepare a safe haven estimated to be required for 90 days in order to provide care and maintenance for an estimated 50,000 refugees. The first to pass through the area arrive the following day.

April 25: The Attorney General Authorized parole for additional categories of relatives, Cambodians in third countries and up to 50,000 "high risk" Vietnamese.

April 29: The United States Embassy, Saigon, closes. Operation Frequent Wind removes last Americans and Vietnamese by helicopter from Saigon. Camp Pendleton, California opens as a refugee center prepared to care for 18,000 refugees.

May 2: Fort Chaffee, Arkansas opens as a refugee reception center prepared to care for 24,000 refugees.

May 4: Eglin Air Force Base, Florida opens as a refugee reception center prepared to accept 2,500 refugees.

May 28: A fourth stateside reception center is opened at Fort Indiantown Gap, Pennsylvania, and receives its first refugees.

July 6: Subic Bay, Philippines refugee center closes.

July 21: Principal operational responsibility for the Refugee Task Force is transferred from the Department of State to the Department of Health, Education, and Welfare.

August 1: Wake Island reception center closes.

Sept. 15: Eglin Air Force Base, Florida refugee reception center closes.

Oct. 16: The Vietnamese freighter, Vietnam Thuong Tin I, sails from Guam bound for Vietnam with 1,546 repatriates aboard.

Dec. 15: Indiantown Gap Military Reservation closes.

Dec. 20: Last 24 refugees leave Fort Chaffee resettlement center to join sponsors, and the center is closed.

---

centers were opened on Wake Island and at Subic Bay, Philippines. In the United States, refugee reception centers were opened first at Camp Pendleton, California (April 29); Fort Chaffee, Arkansas (May 2); Eglin Air Force Base, Florida (May 4), and Fort Indiantown Gap, Pennsylvania (May 29).

During 1976 and 1977, refugees continued to leave Indochina by whatever routes were open, but the numbers arriving in the United States were relatively small and manageable. Meanwhile, other countries were also accepting refugees for resettlement. Unlike the First Wave, these refugees left their homeland by whatever transportation was available. By late 1977, the plight of the "boat people," refugees who were escaping from Indochina in crowded, unseaworthy boats, was attracting world attention. In late 1977 and 1978, the Attorney General approved the entry of additional parole cases, including specified proportions of "boat cases". By this time, temporary refugee camps had been established in many "countries of first asylum."

The refugee exodus reached another peak in mid-1979, when about a half million people were in refugee camps in Thailand, Malaysia, Indonesia, and Hong Kong. Most of the outflow from Vietnam in 1978–79 was composed of ethnic Chinese, who were the subject of increased discrimination by the new Vietnamese government. Their businesses had been nationalized and they were being forced to move into New Economic Zones to develop new land. The relationship between Vietnam and the People's Republic of China deteriorated. Between 200,000 and 250,000 crossed the border from northern Vietnam into China in 1978 and were accepted for resettlement in the coastal provinces of southwest China. Thus China, like the United States, received a large number of refugees from Vietnam. Meanwhile, the exodus of ethnic Chinese from southern Vietnam was by boat, resulting in crowded conditions in the camps and in an emergency meeting of United Nations' officials.

Many Cambodians fled their country in the aftermath of the war and in the agonizing period that followed, when the victorious Khmer Rouge ordered the population out of the cities and into the countryside. In addition to the persecution of non-Communists, there was starvation and disease resulting from forced population movements and the disruption of the economy. There were also continuing troubles with neighboring Vietnam, with fighting along the border beginning in 1977. All these events contributed to a continuing outflow of Khmer from their country. In December, 1978, Vietnam invaded Democratic Kampuchea and installed a puppet regime in Phnom Penh. This triggered another exodus in 1979. These later refugees are generally referred to by the United Nations and in the refugee literature as "new Khmer".

The refugee movement from Laos, like that from Vietnam and Cambodia, began in 1975 with the collapse of the South Vietnamese government and the withdrawal of American forces from Indochina. The long-shaky monarchy in Laos was abolished and a communist Lao People's Democratic Republic was established. Many non-communist Laotians fled to Thailand. The new government launched a campaign against people who had fought against communism, chiefly the mountain tribes. Notable among these targets were the Hmong, who had fought both the Lao and Vietnamese communists and who had been closely associated with the American presence in Indochina. Many Hmong were killed. In order to avoid forcible resettlement in the lowlands, thousands of others fled across the border to Thailand, and many eventually made their way to the United States. There has been a continuing flow of refugees from Laos over the past years, due to a combination of circumstances—oppressive political control and deteriorating economy, exacerbated by such vagaries of nature as droughts and floods in 1977 and 1978.

Finally, the last major event in the refugee flow occurred when the Vietnamese government agreed to an Orderly Departure Program that began in May 1979. Under that program, over 10,000 persons left legally for resettlement abroad. These persons left on regular commercial flights or on special flights arranged by the United Nations High Commissioner for Refugees. They have emigrated chiefly to the United States and to various European countries.

Many Americans probably do not realize that the movement of Indochinese refugees into the United States is far from over, although the flow has been slowed considerably. In fiscal year 1981, 131,139 refugees from Southeast Asia were accepted into the United States (actually, more could have been accepted under the ceiling of 168,000 which had been established). The Reagan administration, after consultation with Congress, established a ceiling of 100,000 for fiscal year 1982.

By mid-1981, a large reservoir of refugees awaiting resettlement remained in the holding camps of Southeast Asia, even as more continued to come out of Indochina. Figure 10.2 shows that as of 30 June 1981, there were 169,216 Indochinese refugees in the camps, of whom 63,310 were boat people and 105,906 had escaped by land. In addition to these, there were another 24,000 in United Nations Refugee Processing Centers in Bataan, Philippines and Galang, Indonesia. Thailand, of course, is the largest recipient of refugees due to its long land border with Laos and Kampuchea; it also receives significant numbers of boat people from Vietnam.

Within Thailand, the largest number of refugees is from Laos. These are concentrated in camps along the

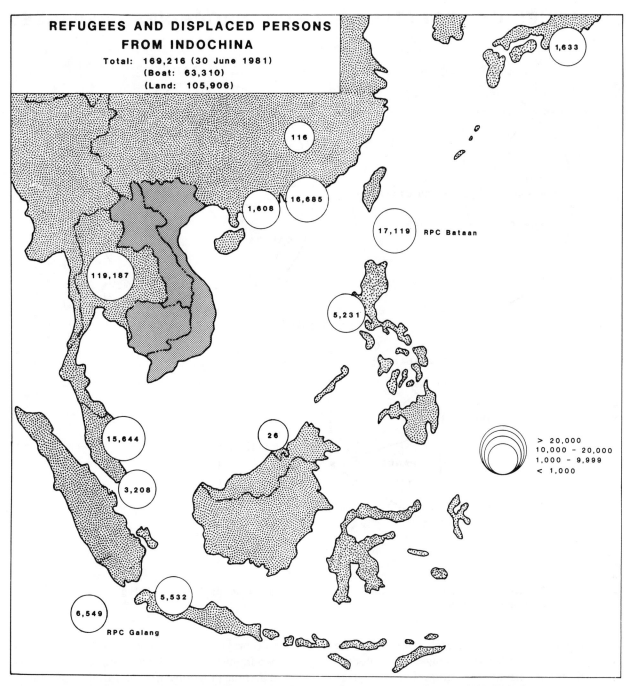

REFUGEES AND DISPLACED PERSONS FROM INDOCHINA

Total: 169,216 (30 June 1981)
(Boat: 63,310)
(Land: 105,906)

1,633

116

1,608   16,685

17,119   RPC Bataan

119,187

5,231

15,644

26

3,208

> 20,000
10,000 – 20,000
1,000 – 9,999
< 1,000

5,532

6,549

RPC Galang

Figure 10.2. Refugees and Displaced Persons From Indochina. Source: U.N. High Commission for Refugees, Geneva.

Laotian border. In mid-1981, refugees in Thailand included 100,780 Laotians, 4,080 Kampucheans, and 14,327 Vietnamese.

The refugees are moved from holding camps in the countries of first asylum to United Nations' processing centers and thence to resettlement countries. The United States has continued to take the majority of both boat cases and land cases, including a particularly large proportion of the "new" Kampuchean refugees (Fig. 10.3). Many other countries, however, are involved in the resettlement process (Table 10.2). By mid-1981

Canada had taken the second largest number, nearly 76,000. France came third with over 73,000 and Australia fourth with over 52,000. In terms of ratio of Indochinese refugees to total population, Australia has been actually the most heavily impacted country.

RESETTLEMENT POLICIES

The countries which have accepted large numbers of Indochinese, have developed resettlement policies and programs independently, and the ultimate settlement

COUNTRIES OF RESETTLEMENT FOR INDOCHINESE REFUGEES

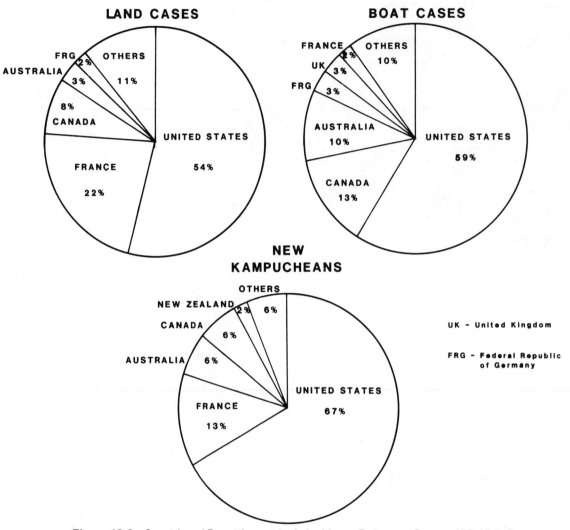

LAND CASES

FRG 2%
AUSTRALIA 3%
CANADA 8%
OTHERS 11%
FRANCE 22%
UNITED STATES 54%

BOAT CASES

FRANCE 2%
UK 3%
FRG 3%
AUSTRALIA 10%
OTHERS 10%
CANADA 13%
UNITED STATES 59%

NEW KAMPUCHEANS

OTHERS
NEW ZEALAND 2%
CANADA 6%
AUSTRALIA 6%
OTHERS 6%
FRANCE 13%
UNITED STATES 67%

UK - United Kingdom

FRG - Federal Republic of Germany

Figure 10.3. Countries of Resettlement for Indochinese Refugees. Source: U.S. High Commissioner for Refugees, Geneva.

patterns of the Indochinese in each country may be quite different. The Indochinese refugees who enter the United States are classified as refugees and are given an administrative status quite separate from that of immigrants. Canada and Australia make no legal distinction between immigrants and refugees, and make available a variety of assistance programs to all new migrants. Denmark, Holland and Sweden all make distinctions between invited and spontaneous refugees. The invited refugees are those who meet the standards of the Geneva Convention and who are invited to live in the host nation. The spontaneous refugees simply appear on the borders of the country and request admittance. The Dutch and Danes offer more programmatic support and assistance to invited refugees.

The administration of the refugee resettlement process is also housed differently from country to country.

National programs can be described as voluntary agency administered or governmental agency administered and the programs utilized are either specific to the refugees or are existing programs designed to assist all migrant or needy groups. The bulk of refugee resettlement in the United States has been carried out by a collage of voluntary agencies (VOLAGS) with financial support provided by direct grants from the Federal government (Table 10.3). This system is unique to the United States. Other countries simply assigned the refugee resettlement to existing agencies. A continuing problem in the administration of refugee programs in the United States is the fragmentation of authority at the Federal level. Authority is divided among the United States Coordinator for Refugee Affairs, the Office of Refugee Resettlement (ORR) in the Department of Health and Human Services (HHS) and the Refugee Bureau in the Department of State.

TABLE 10.2 Indochinese Refugees Cumulative Resettlement Figures Mid-1975 to Mid-1981

Resettlement Countries	Land cases	"New" Kampucheans	Boat cases
Australia	9,348	1,736	41,089
Austria	339	189	1,083
Belgium	2,381	204	1,181
Canada	23,646	1,780	50,239
China τ	2,547	—	41
Denmark	316	—	1,757
France	59,701	3,689	9,961
F.R. Germany	4,075	189	13,331
Italy	773	34	2,069
Netherlands	285	—	4,074
New Zealand	1,041	575	2,481
Norway	90	—	2,398
Sweden	—	1	2,289
Switzerland	2,515	285	4,391
U. Kingdom	758	116	14,101
U.S.A. *	147,086	18,781	226,908
Others	13,888	152	2,586
TOTAL	268,789	27,731	379,979

τ does not include some 260,000 Vietnamese who fled to China in 1978

* does not include some 130,000 Vietnamese directly resettled in the U.S.A. in 1975

Source: U.N. High Commissioner for Refugees, Geneva

The Indochinese refugee migration process presents unique challenges to host nations and this uniqueness has certainly had some effect on the policies established by host countries and therefore on the resettlement programs developed by these countries. Montero[2] points out the differences between the migration patterns of the Indochinese to the United States and those of two previous large Asian migrations, the Chinese and Japanese (Fig. 10.4). The establishment of temporary camps for refugees in Thailand and Malaysia has been especially critical in shaping the patterns of refugee resettlement in all host countries. These camps provide a host country with an opportunity to screen potential immigrants from the total refugee population and allow potential host countries to develop practical, if not necessarily more humane, entry policies and procedures. France takes this opportunity to search for refugees who speak French; they receive immigration priority. The United States takes advantage of the holding camps to delay the entry of refugees until private sponsors can be found for each refugee. For other potential host countries, the temporary camps simply localize the problem of having to deal with large masses of refugees, who might otherwise be "standing in line" on their borders awaiting entry, and provides an opportunity to control the level of immigration of Indochinese refugees.

TABLE 10.3 Indochinese Refugees Resettled in the United States and in California, by Voluntary Agency, September 1, 1980—August 31, 1981*

(ranked in descending order by percent)

VOLUNTARY AGENCY	NUMBER RESETTLED		PERCENT RESETTLED
	Total United States	California	in California
ACNS	14,314	7,050	49.3
IRC	14,735	6,517	44.2
WRRS	7,339	2,911	39.7
USCC	53,320	17,707	33.2
TF	2,585	734	28.4
AFCR	3,641	846	23.2
CWS	12,527	2,444	19.5
HIAS	3,830	637	16.6
LIRS	8,484	1,035	12.2
YMCA	2,966	218	7.3
Total	124,477	40,099	32.2

*Those classified as 'state unknown' were removed from the total resettled by each voluntary agency.

Note: IDAHO and IOWA were eliminated because none of their resettlement activities took place in California (while, on the other hand, virtually all BCRRR cases are processed through its center in California). Rav Tov and PAIRC were eliminated because neither agency resettles Indochinese refugees.

Source: calculated by the New TransCentury Foundation from a computer print-out provided by the Refugee Data Center of the American Council of Voluntary Agencies.

Source: *Kaleidoscope: The Resettlement of Refugees in the United States by the Voluntary Agencies,* by David S. North, et. al. (Washington, D.C.: New TransCentury Foundation, 1982): p. 63.

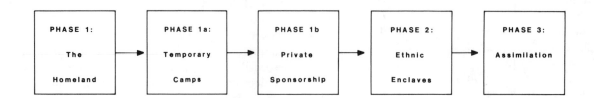

Spontaneous International Migration (S.I.M.): The Vietnamese Pattern

Earlier Immigration and Resettlement: The Chinese and Japanese Pattern

Figure 10.4. A Comparison of the Spontaneous International Migration Pattern of the Vietnamese with the Experience of Earlier Asian Immigrant Groups in the United States. Source: Darrel Montero, "The Vietnamese in America: Patterns of Socioeconomic Adaptation in *Proceedings* of the First Annual Conference on Indochinese Refugees, ed. by G. Harry Stopp, Jr. and Nguyen Manh Hung. (Fairfax, VA: C.A.R.I., George Mason University, 1979), p. 159.

REGIONAL AND LOCAL RESETTLEMENT FACTORS

The United States is a country of many regions; some culturally defined, others defined by climatic or physiographic features. Within each of these regions are sub-regions that can be significant, such as functional regions defined by urban centers and rural areas. Particular areas may be potentially productive whereas others offer little or no natural support to successful economic activity. Within even these sub-regions, certain spatial units may be identifiable as particularly positive or negative loci for Indochinese refugee resettlement. The settlement pattern of the Indochinese, whether it be a result of primary, secondary or even tertiary migration, will reflect regional and subregional influences.

The First Wave of Indochinese refugees, those who left Vietnam as the government of South Vietnam fell and the American troops withdrew, avoided the period of waiting in the temporary camps in Southeast Asia. They were transported directly to the United States and were placed in holding camps in Arkansas, California, and Pennsylvania. The First Wave refugees were primarily urban dwellers. Many were literate in more than one language, and most had worked with or for the Government of South Vietnam or the American or-

ganizations located in Vietnam.[3] First Wave refugees had two primary settlement loci, the West Coast and the Washington, D.C. region. Although the sponsor program may have prevented immediate resettlement in one of those two regions, most of the First Wave migrants chose the two locations for secondary migration. According to Dr. Nguyen Manh Hung, Director of the Indochinese Refugee Center at George Mason University and former Vice Minister of Planning for the Republic of Vietnam, these two locations possessed specific attributes that were attractive to the First Wave refugees. Washington, D.C. parallels Saigon in being a capital city, the residence of many military and governmental officials with whom the First Wave refugees had interacted in Vietnam (potential friends as well as sponsors) and a unique international community into which the Vietnamese could blend. The West Coast has a pleasant climate, an established Asian community in many cities, many large military establishments where veterans of Vietnam resided who were past acquaintances, potential sponsors and potential friends, and several large cities with international communities.

The policy of the United States government in directing resettlement of the Indochinese has not been concerned with the wishes or needs of the refugees. The conscious decision was made as the first refugees reached the United States that the new immigrants would be dispersed across the country, in contrast to the relatively uncontrolled resettlement of the Cuban refugees after the fall of the Batista government. The latter program was considered a failure because it concentrated almost all of the Cuban refugees in south Florida and radically transformed the social and economic order of that region. In the case of the Vietnamese and other Indochinese, the Federal government instructed the VOLAGS to resettle the refugees in a dispersed rather than a concentrated pattern. The availability of sponsors was the most critical determinant.

As the refugees were being resettled, research began on the regional influences on resettlement, both in preparation for resettlement and coterminous with active resettlement. In a study of regional attitudes toward the refugees, an analysis was performed to determine whether regions of the country that have a history of racial discrimination would extend those patterns to include the Indochinese. It was found that, although there might be a general dislike of the Vietnamese because of a negative emotional carryover from the Vietnam War, no specific regional discrimination against Indochinese could be detected.[4] Attitudes toward the Indochinese were particularly scrutinized among residents of the southeastern United States because of that region's history of de jure and de facto discrimination against blacks. Analysis of survey results indicated that there was very little negative feeling among Southerners for the incoming refugees and that the attitude of Southerners toward the prospect of Indochinese moving into their communities was quite similar to that of residents of other portions of the United States. This study supports the hypothesis put forth by Middleton in his model sociological study that the racist posture of many whites toward blacks in the South is specific only to blacks and does not extend into a general pattern of discrimination against any other group.[5]

Cities become the nuclei for urban regions that take on distinctive characteristics and thus become distinctive regions. Some of these characteristics may have an impact on the reactions of Indochinese refugees who resettle in cities. In a pioneering analysis of the influence of urban regionalism on the resettlement of the Indochinese in the United States, James Pisarowicz examined the interaction of region with refugees in three major American urban centers—Denver, Minneapolis and San Francisco.[6] In the study, Pisarowicz recognized five factors that could have a significant impact on the refugee resettlement pattern: 1) cultural pluralism; 2) existence of an established Asian community; 3) government programs for alien clients; 4) economic conditions within the urban region; and 5) the availability of and quality of sponsors.

For his study, Pisarowicz defined San Francisco to be culturally pluralistic, Minneapolis culturally monistic, and Denver somewhere in between. Related to this classification is the relatively large Asian community in San Francisco where over 5 percent of the population is of Asian extraction; Denver has only 0.5 percent of its population Asian; and Minneapolis only 0.2 percent. Denver and San Francisco have well developed government programs designed to handle bilingual and bi-cultural clients which have been established to work with Asians, Hispanics, and various Amerindian groups; Minneapolis has virtually no such programs. At the time of his study, Denver and Minneapolis had relatively low unemployment rates (5.5 and 5.9%), but the rate in San Francisco was quite high (9.9%).

Predictably, Pisarowicz found distinct refugee behavior patterns in the three urban regions and his results were particularly telling with regard to ethnic identity and secondary migration patterns. In a survey of Indochinese in San Francisco, the majority of refugees (93%) identified themselves as simply "Asians". A parallel survey of non-refugee San Franciscans found that all the respondents referred to the Indochinese simply as "Asians". In contrast to the reactions in San Francisco, refugees in the Denver and Minneapolis regions identified themselves as Vietnamese, Hmong or other very specific ethnic groups. Non-refugee residents of these two cities generally did not lump the refugees in with other Asians (10% in Minneapolis, 13% in Denver) but referred to them as Vietnamese (80% in Minneapolis, 68% in Denver) or simply Boat People (10% in Minneapolis). An internal settlement pattern can be implied from ethnic boundary establishment.[7] The refugees can be expected to reside in distinct Vietnamese or Hmong nodes in Denver and Minneapolis but may choose to settle in established Asian neighborhoods in San Francisco.

Goldlust and Richmond postulated that the flow of immigrants within a spatial unit will reflect not only the internal dynamics of the immigrant group but will reflect also the effect of the receiving community on the newly arrived people.[8] On a very gross level, the impact of the three cities has had differential effects on the early movement of refugees. Minneapolis at first experienced a net outflow of refugees. San Francisco became a significant magnet for refugee resettlement and very quickly experienced a net increase in refugee secondary migrants. Denver, too, lost refugees to other regions but at a much lower rate than Minneapolis. Pisarowicz found a net increase in the Hmong population in Minneapolis as a result of secondary migration. The major concentration was in the Liberty Plaza housing project, a Methodist Church residential center. This is probably a function of the tribal social organization of the Hmong, who desire to remain ethnically unique not only among other Asians but among other Indochinese.[9] The use of settlement pattern to establish and reaffirm ethnic identity is often manifested by members of peasant societies.

PATTERNS OF RESETTLEMENT

From April 1975 to January 1982, about 566,000 Indochinese were resettled in the United States. They make up a tiny minority—less than one-fourth of one percent of the total United States population. Yet, they are of geographic interest in many ways. Prior to the refugee influx, the number of Indochinese in the United States was negligible, slightly over 13,000 in January, 1975. We thus have the opportunity to observe an entirely new ethnic group as it enters the United States. The patterns of distribution are still in the formative stage and the processes of diffusion, acculturation, and assimilation are still going on.

There appear to have been four major influences on the distribution of Indochinese in the United States. They are 1) government policy, 2) the voluntary resettlement agencies (VOLAGS), 3) the location of the resettlement camps, and 4) the voluntary movements of individual refugees responding to push and pull factors in secondary migration. In addition, the tiny nucleus of Indochinese population present in 1975 cannot be ignored. Of the 13,000 Indochinese present in the United States before the refugee movement, about 18 percent lived in California and 7 percent in Texas. These two states have consistently remained first and second in number of Indochinese throughout the shifting movements of the past six years. Their Indochinese communities provided a powerful pull factor and a source of sponsors.

The government policy was one of geographic dispersal. The refugees were to be widely distributed throughout the country. This is in striking contrast to group settlement by earlier immigrants and refugees. As Linda Gordon, a demographer with the Office of Refugee Resettlement, has described it:

> "The prevailing sentiment in Congress in 1975 regarding their resettlement was that they should be dispersed widely throughout the country rather than encouraged to settle in large groups. This was to be accomplished through sponsorship of refugee families by voluntary agencies, and it was hoped that minimal Federal program assistance would be necessary. Apparently it was feared that the unpopularity of the war would carry over into an unfriendly reception for the refugees, especially if they were perceived as a drain on tax monies or if they had a perceptible impact on some local communities. The assumption of government officials and sponsoring agencies was that refugees would tend to remain in the community of first placement and sponsorship."[10]

The sponsoring agencies clearly had an important influence on the pattern of resettlement. They resettled refugees in places where they had sponsors and connections.[11] The most active agency was the United States Catholic Conference (USCC). It placed many refugees in urban areas with strong Catholic populations. For example, the heavy concentration of Vietnamese in New Orleans is largely due to the work of United Catholic Charities in that city. The Lutheran Immigration and Refugee Service (LIRS) is another active VOLAG. It placed many refugees in the northern Midwest, where the Lutheran denomination is strong. The United Hebrew Immigration and Assistance Service (HIAS) and the Tolstoy Foundation both tended to find sources of sponsors in the urban Northeast.

In addition to the nine VOLAGs who had long experience resettling immigrants, various other organizations came to participate in the Indochinese venture. The Chinese Consolidated Benevolent Association was one of these. It naturally found many sponsors in California. The Church of Jesus Christ of Latter Day Saints (Mormon) became active during the 1975 influx. By 1982, over 7000 Indochinese had been resettled in Utah, a rather high number for a state relatively small in population. Some state, county, and city agencies also became involved in providing sponsors in 1975. Their activities helped establish early resettlement nuclei that in turn attracted later migrants. The location of the resettlement camps was particularly important in the resettlement of the First Wave in 1975. Camp Pendleton, south of Los Angeles, processed more refugees than did any other single facility, and contributed to the early emergence of southern California as the most important focus of resettlement. In 1975, Pennsylvania ranked third in number of Indochinese resettled, and by 1982 it still retained fifth place. This is partially attributable to the presence of the Fort Indiantown Gap Center. The influence of the processing centers at Fort Chaffee, Arkansas, and Eglin Air Force Base, Florida, was apparent in the early distribution patterns but has diminished over time as secondary migration caused changes. The importance of the Arkansas camp is still felt however, in the large numbers of Indochinese in Texas.

The voluntary movement of individuals and groups in the current and continuing phenomenon of secondary migration will surely, in the long run, emerge as the dominant factor in the distribution of the Indochinese ethnic groups in the United States. The First Wave in 1975 had little say in regard to resettlement locations, except for a fortunate few who were either affluent enough to resettle without sponsors or were resettled directly by the American companies that had employed them in Vietnam. As soon as the refugees gained an economic foothold and began to feel more secure in America, they began to re-group, moving toward other Indochinese in the familiar clustering pattern that has characterized other immigrants. The pull toward family, friends, or simply people like themselves was very strong; the fear of isolation in non-Indochinese communities was very great. Other pull factors were economic opportunities and warmer climate.

By the beginning of 1982, the above-listed factors had been in operation for about seven years, and the resulting pattern of distribution of the Indochinese seems recognizable, if not immutable. California, the most popular original destination, has continued to attract secondary migrants and now accounts for about one-third (192,085) of all Indochinese refugees in the United States. The reasons for the concentration in California appear to be several. Before the fall of Saigon, a number of Vietnamese were flown to Travis Air Force Base in California. Later, Camp Pendleton was the first and largest of the holding centers.[12] The matter of preference is important. The Indochinese find the climate desirable and are attracted by the existing communities. It should also be noted that California was the original node of Indochinese settlement, even before the end of the war. Whatever the causes of the original clustering in California, secondary migration continues to swell the refugee population there.

Texas ranks after California in number of Indochinese, with nine percent (51,102) at the beginning of 1982. Like California, Texas had a small nucleus of Indochinese even before the great influx of 1975. It continues to attract migrants with its better job opportunities, warmer climate, and established Indochinese communities. Texas, also like California, was perceived as a very desirable location even before the refugees left Indochina. Many of these Vietnamese had been employed in their country by oil companies and other corporations with Texas ties.

In addition to California and Texas, other states with Indochinese populations of over 10,000 include: 1) the two Pacific Northwest states of Washington and Oregon; 2) Minnesota, with most of its migrants in the Twin Cities; 3) the large-population, urban-industrial states of Pennsylvania, New York, and Illinois; and 4) two southern states, Virginia and Louisiana, each with a single dominant urban nucleus of Indochinese settlement—the Northern Virginia suburbs of Washington and New Orleans, respectively.

Because of secondary migration, the present distribution pattern is more clustered than was the pattern created by the original dispersal policy in 1975. Figures 10.5 and 10.6 show the increasing concentration in California and Texas, as well as the shifting ranks of other states. Florida and Oklahoma, both owing some of their early prominence to nearness to reception centers, have been replaced by Oregon and Massachusetts in the list of the top eleven states (Table 10.4).

The distribution of each of the three Indochinese nationalities is different. "By late 1981, the composition of the Southeast Asian population in the United States was approximately 67 percent Vietnamese, 23 percent Laotian, and 10 percent Cambodian."[13] The Vietnamese pattern closely approaches the pattern already described, as the Vietnamese make up the lion's share of the total population involved. The Vietnamese were the first group to come. Their settlement pattern is perhaps more fixed by now, although secondary migration is still going on. California is by far the dominant settlement site. It has attracted about 37 percent of Vietnamese refugees arriving in the United States in 1981. The same five states received the most Vietnamese in both 1980 and 1981—California, Texas, New York, Pennsylvania and Washington.[14]

TABLE 10.4 Indochinese Refugees Top Eleven States, 12/31/75 and 12/31/81

1975 (States having more than 3,000)		%	1981 (States having more than 10,000)		%
1. California	27,199	21.0	1. California	192,085	33.9
2. Texas	9,130	7.0	2. Texas	51,102	9.0
3. Pennsylvania	7,159	5.5	3. Washington	26,272	4.6
4. Florida	5,322	4.1	4. Minnesota	23,053	4.1
5. Washington	4,182	3.2	5. Pennsylvania	21,476	3.8
6. New York	3,806	2.9	6. Illinois	21,302	3.8
7. Minnesota	3,802	2.9	7. New York	17,175	3.0
8. Virginia	3,733	2.9	8. Virginia	16,807	2.9
9. Illinois	3,696	2.9	9. Oregon	16,535	2.9
10. Oklahoma	3,689	2.8	10. Louisiana	12,769	2.3
11. Louisiana	3,602	2.8	11. Massachusetts	11,060	2.0

Source: *Report to Congress* (Washington, D.C.: Department of Health, Education, and Welfare, Task Force for Indo Chinese Refugees) March 15, 1976.
State Report on Southeast Asian Refugees, Estimated Cumulative State Totals (Washington, D.C.: Office of Refugee Resettlement, Department of Health and Human Services) December 31, 1981.

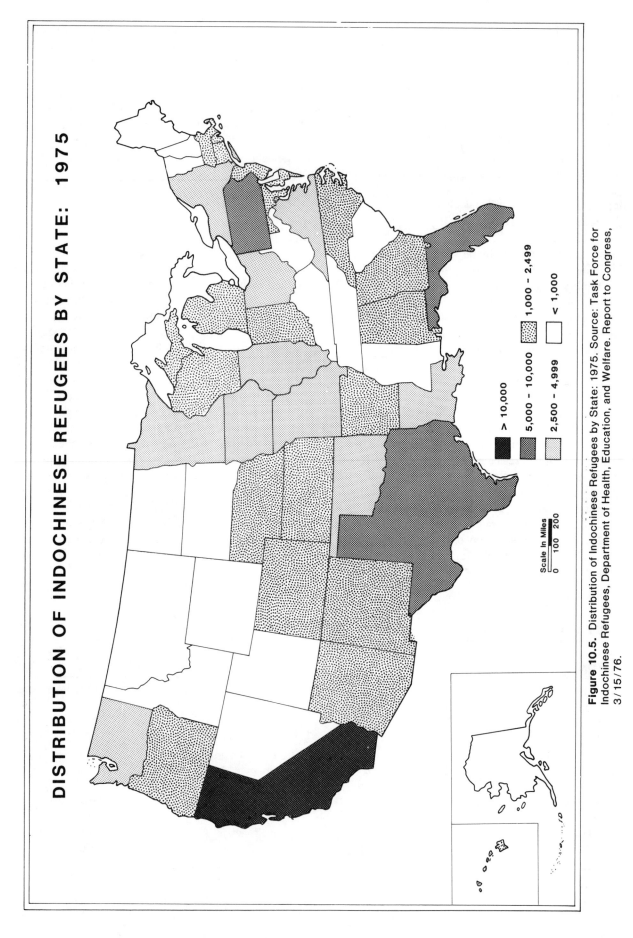

DISTRIBUTION OF INDOCHINESE REFUGEES BY STATE: 1975

> 10,000

5,000 – 10,000

2,500 – 4,999

1,000 – 2,499

< 1,000

Scale In Miles
0   100   200

Figure 10.5. Distribution of Indochinese Refugees by State: 1975. Source: Task Force for Indochinese Refugees, Department of Health, Education, and Welfare. Report to Congress, 3/15/76.

DISTRIBUTION OF INDOCHINESE REFUGEES BY STATE: 1981

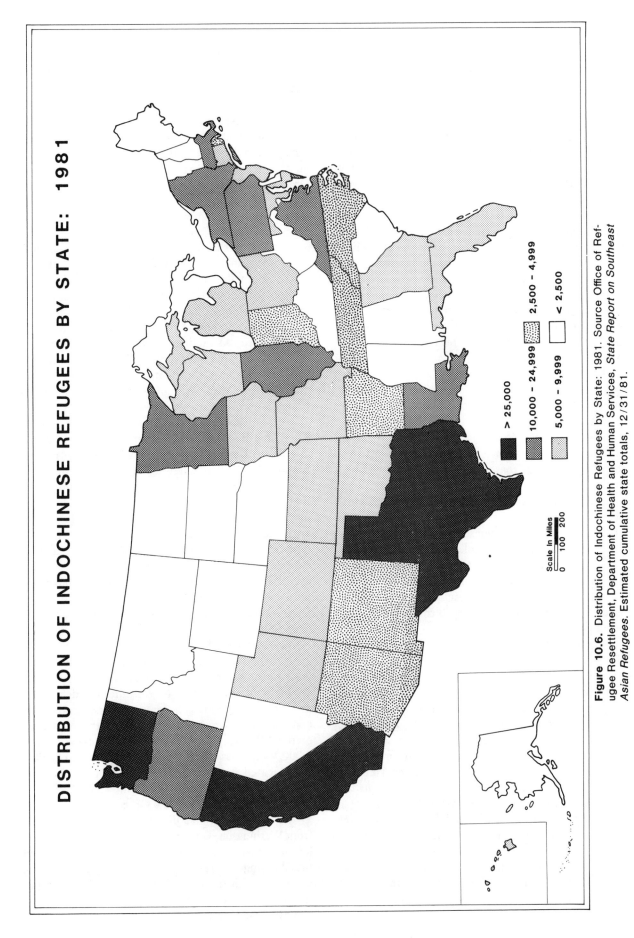

> 25,000

10,000 - 24,999

2,500 - 4,999

5,000 - 9,999

< 2,500

Scale In Miles
0   100   200

Figure 10.6. Distribution of Indochinese Refugees by State: 1981. Source Office of Refugee Resettlement, Department of Health and Human Services, *State Report on Southeast Asian Refugees.* Estimated cumulative state totals, 12/31/81.

The Cambodians, or Khmer, are fewest in number, making up only about ten percent of the total. Their resettlement pattern is quite similar to that of the Vietnamese. California and Texas rank first, and there are also concentrations in Washington, Oregon, Pennsylvania, New York, Illinois, and Virginia. The distribution pattern of the Cambodians is still in the process of formation, due to two major factors: 1) the largest number came late, in the massive outflow of "new Kampuchean" refugees in 1979 and thereafter; 2) the Khmer Guided Placement Project (also called Cambodian Cluster Resettlement project) in 1980–81. This program placed new arrivals in the following cities selected as desirable for Khmer resettlement: Atlanta, Boston, Chicago, Cincinnati, Columbus, Dallas, Houston, Jacksonville, New York City, Rochester, Phoenix, and Richmond.

The distribution pattern for refugees from Laos is somewhat different. They appear to be rather more dispersed than that of the other two groups. The largest number is again found in California, but it does not constitute such a large proportion of the total. According to figures from the Immigration and Naturalization Service for January 1980, the states that rank after California are Minnesota, Illinois, Texas, Iowa, Wisconsin, Oregon and Washington. There thus appears to be a concentration in the northern Midwest. Unfortunately, it is hard to differentiate the distribution of the Hmong from other Laotians at a national level.

At the local level of resettlement, the usual clustering pattern is clearly emerging. The Indochinese refugees are grouping themselves into ethnic neighborhoods. There are often problems of competition with the majority population or with other minority groups in regard to housing and job opportunities. Some examples of the Indochinese resettlement process in American cities illustrate the problems and the clustering process.

Detailed maps of the Indochinese population in Minneapolis-St. Paul are available[15] (Figs. 10.7, 10.8). They show that the Indochinese are rather widely distributed throughout the metropolitan area, but that there are clusters near the downtown area. Concentrations near the central business districts result from the availability of low-cost housing and from secondary migration, with the usual "pull" toward an existing community. On the other hand, the rather wide dispersal of smaller numbers of refugees throughout the Twin Cities area reflects two factors: 1) the influence of sponsors in finding housing, and 2) secondary moves of refugees who have made economic gains and can afford better housing. The Twin Cities are of particular interest because of the presence of the Hmong. St. Paul has the largest number of Hmong in the country, about 7,000. The Vietnamese tended to settle in Minneapolis,

where there are smaller numbers of Lao and Cambodians.

San Francisco's Indochinese community includes some 26,000 to 30,000 refugees; this number is projected to increase rapidly. About 2 out of 5 refugees coming in are secondary migrants. The city probably has the highest ratio of refugees to population of any city in the country. It is therefore of particular interest even though the largest concentrations in terms of total number are in southern California, with Los Angeles, Orange County, and Santa Clara County ranking ahead of San Francisco in total numbers. San Francisco's schools are heavily impacted; one out of every 15 school children is Indochinese.

The Vietnamese are the most numerous nationality, many are ethnic Chinese and speak a Chinese dialect. There are smaller numbers of Lao, Khmer, and Hmong. The residential pattern of the refugees is highly clustered in downtown San Francisco, with the majority living in Tenderloin, Chinatown, and north of the Market area. Attractions of these areas include low-cost housing, rapid turnover and high vacancy rate, and looser restrictions on the number of persons per housing unit. Clearly, the existing Asian population in San Francisco provides a powerful attraction.

New Orleans has a Vietnamese population of about 8,000, and it is continuing to grow through secondary migration. The city has what may be the largest single community of Vietnamese in the United States in an area called Versailles Gardens, an eastern subdivision that includes apartments, duplexes, and single family homes. About 3,500 Vietnamese have settled in this area, and its cultural landscape is now very Asian, with terraced vegetable gardens along the canals and Vietnamese shops and cafes on the shopping street. The overall impression is that of a Vietnamese village. The people who settled in this area were mostly poor people from villages, not the First Wave well-to-do urbanites from Saigon.

Associated Catholic Charities was the sponsoring agency and continues to be the main provider of services to the refugees in New Orleans, most of whom are Catholic. In addition to Versailles Gardens, there are three other major clusters—Algiers, Bridge City, and Harvey-Marrero. They are all on the West Bank of the Mississippi and together account for another 3,000 Vietnamese. The remaining Vietnamese, chiefly the educated and affluent, are scattered throughout the urban area. There are very few Cambodians and Lao— only a few hundred—in New Orleans.

Arlington, Virginia, directly across the Potomac from Washington, D.C., is one of the urban areas most heavily impacted by the Indochinese. As already noted, the Washington area has been a popular destination beginning with the First Wave. Within the metropolitan area Arlington has become the center of Indochinese resettlement. The migrants have resettled

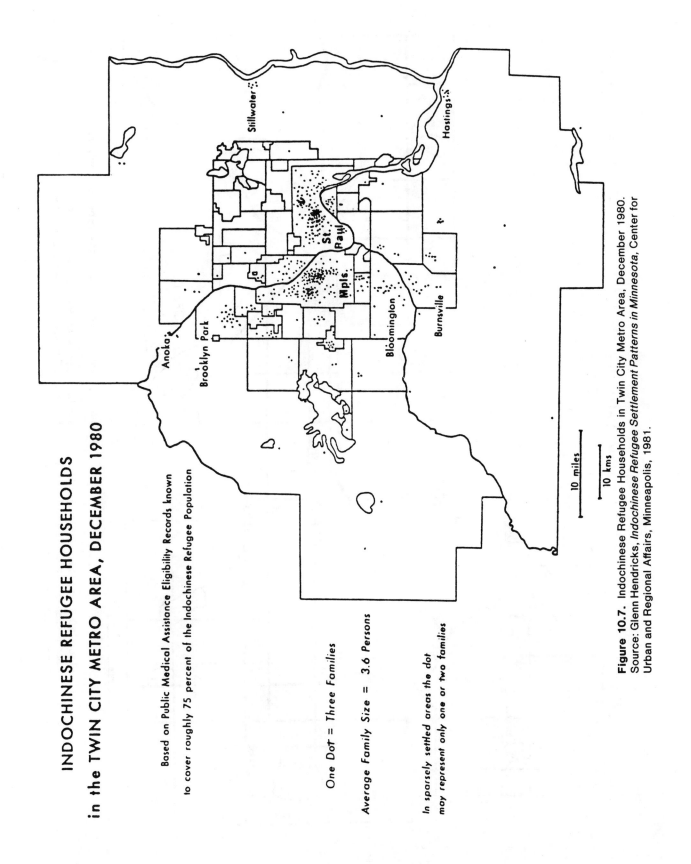

INDOCHINESE REFUGEE HOUSEHOLDS in the TWIN CITY METRO AREA, DECEMBER 1980

Based on Public Medical Assistance Eligibility Records known

to cover roughly 75 percent of the Indochinese Refugee Population

One Dot = Three Families

Average Family Size = 3.6 Persons

In sparsely settled areas the dot
may represent only one or two families

10 miles

10 kms

Stillwater

Hastings

St. Paul

Mpls.

Bloomington

Burnsville

Anoka

Brooklyn Park

Figure 10.7. Indochinese Refugee Households in Twin City Metro Area, December 1980.
Source: Glenn Hendricks, *Indochinese Refugee Settlement Patterns in Minnesota*, Center for
Urban and Regional Affairs, Minneapolis, 1981.

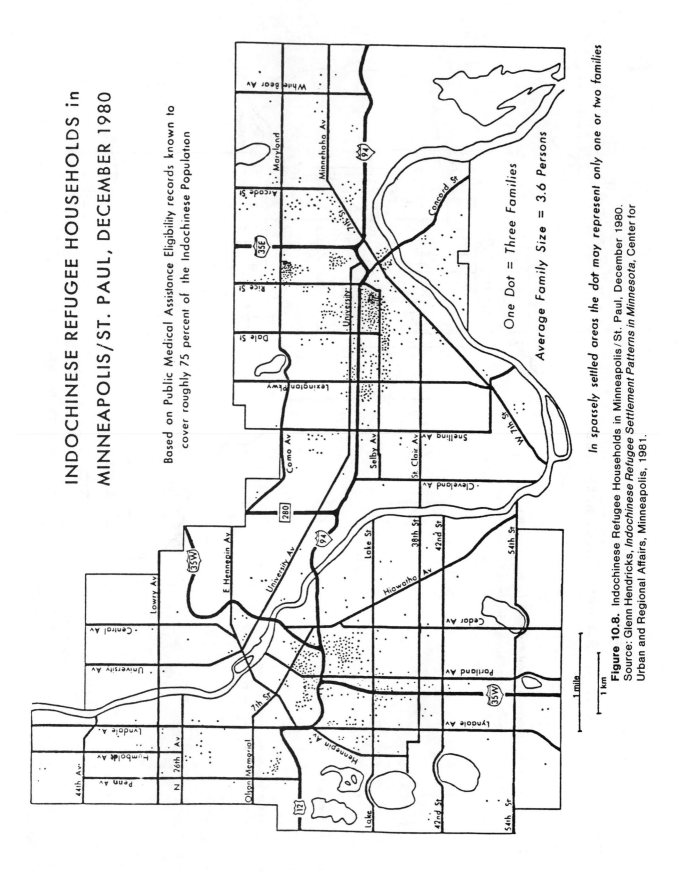

Figure 10.8. Indochinese Refugee Households in Minneapolis/St. Paul, December 1980. Source: Glenn Hendricks, *Indochinese Refugee Settlement Patterns in Minnesota*, Center for Urban and Regional Affairs, Minneapolis, 1981.

primarily in older, low-rise apartment complexes which have relatively low rental rates and are accessible to good public transportation. Most are located in South Arlington, in the Glencarlyn, Wakefield, and Claremont areas. Some are located, however, in North Arlington in the Westover, Buckingham, Clarendon, and Rosslyn areas. They tend to be clustered ethnically; the Vietnamese generally are not co-located with the Lao and Cambodians. The secondary migrants are generally reunited with friends and relatives in the refugee clusters. The apartments are frequently overcrowded, as extended families move in together and pool their resources to pay the rent. This arrangement may be considered by the residents as temporary, but "temporary" may mean a year or more. The impact on the county is particularly evident in the school population. The 1:14 ratio of Indochinese school children to total school enrollment is the highest in the country.

Small businesses operated by the Indochinese are scattered among shopping centers throughout Arlington. One center, the Clarendon commercial area—has so many shops operated by Indochinese that it is sometimes referred to as "Little Saigon" and "Arlington's Mekong Delta." The businesses tend to reflect the owners' ethnic heritage and have distinctive store fronts and merchandise.

MUTUAL ASSISTANCE ASSOCIATIONS

As the Indochinese settled into United States communities, they began to seek information about their new homeland that would help them adjust to the social, cultural and economic patterns of the United States. Quite often the information they sought was also a call for assistance. They needed to know how to obtain housing, where to obtain employment, where English language training was available, and where other Indochinese were located. Some of this information was provided by the sponsor and, where religious or civic organizations coordinated efforts to provide sponsors for refugees, there were institutionalized assistance and information centers established that could answer most of the questions offered by the refugees and could, in many cases, provide the needed service on the spot. These organizations were in touch with local public assistance and information programs, and often served as the representatives of local educational or social service agencies to the refugee community.[16]

For many of the refugees the need for information and service was closely related to a need to re-establish ethnic identity and to establish new social networks within their own ethnic community as these communities were formed and grew with resettlement.[17] The manifestation of this need became the Indochinese

Mutual Assistance Associations (IMAA), consisting of corporate organizations within local communities. Local names of organizations reveal something of the purpose and nature of the organizations and include: Vietnamese Founder Kings Commemoration Committee, Cambodian Religio-Cultural Association, the Hmong Family Association, Lao Friendship Association, and Vietnamese American Friendship Association. The IMAAs generally have a community-wide interest in providing information and assistance to the refugees but they can be treated as five different types of associations: religious, political, self-help, professional (lawyer, doctor, merchant), and student.[18] Some of the IMAAs are linked by a national organization. This is particularly true and well developed among the professional and religious groups, but most are the result of local initiative and need and remain quite independent of any but local control.

The IMAAs that have developed strong national organizations have certain goals in mind requiring national coordination of efforts. The various groups of lawyers are trying to obtain American Bar Association recognition of Indochinese credentials and are seeking Federal support of retraining programs for Indochinese lawyers. The dental organizations have already obtained a limited acceptance of their Indochinese credentials, and medical doctors with European credentials (and many Vietnamese have these) can be accepted into the practice of medicine in the United States. Many of the local organizations do not aspire to any national goals and serve only their local community.

Two types of service are offered by all IMAAs—access to language training programs (both English, primarily for adults, and the native language, primarily for children), and information in the refugee's native language in the form of a newsletter. Vinh reports over 400 IMAAs in the United States and just over 100 newsletters, all in the native language of the local community.[19] The newsletters vary in format. Some are simply mimeographed on 8 1/2 × 22 paper, some are typeset and printed as small newspapers. These newsletters are the chief source of news about other refugee communities in the United States and in other countries and they feature stories about current events in Indochina. They also serve to re-enforce ethnic awareness among the refugee communities by featuring articles about traditional holidays, religious ceremonies and celebrations.

The IMAAs are the primary mechanism for maintaining ethnic credibility and awareness in the refugee communities, and have certainly become important segments of the refugee communities in the United States. If the results of a survey of Vietnamese refugees in Tulsa, Oklahoma can be considered indicative, the Indochinese refugees in the United States depend extensively on members of their own community for assistance in all matters as they adjust to the new life in their new home. When such assistance is sought, it is quite often located through the cooperation and guidance of a local IMAA. Many of the more affluent acculturated Vietnamese are active in various Asian-Pacific Heritage Associations.

SECONDARY MIGRATION

The Indochinese refugees in the United States are, by definition, not willing emigrants from their homeland nor are they particularly well informed or properly prepared immigrants in this country. For the vast majority of refugees, international travel of any kind is not only a new experience but it is an activity about which many have never thought of or imagined. Certainly many of the First Wave of refugees had experienced international travel and, even if they had not experienced the variety of lifestyles necessitated by such travel, they had read or heard about foreign cultures. This group was able to move from resident to emigrant to immigrant relatively painlessly. Subsequent waves of refugees from Indochina which were comprised mainly of members of the middle and lower economic strata of Vietnam, Cambodia and Laos; were not able to do so. This was particularly true for the Hmong and other groups of isolated tribespeople for whom much of their own country was quite foreign.

The first refugees left Vietnam with at least a general destination in mind. Most of the First Wave were residents of Saigon and, for them, the only logical place in which to relocate was another capital city. The Primate City concept is particularly well developed in Third World countries and the residents of Saigon expected that only capital cities could provide them with the cultural accouterments, economic opportunities, and lifestyle to which they had become quite accustomed. Washington, D.C. thus became a primary resettlement focus for the First Wave of Indochinese refugees in the United States and the suburbs of Washington quickly established large refugee communities within months of the Fall of Saigon in 1975.

The sponsor program developed by the State Department played a large role in the original resettlement pattern of Indochinese refugees in the United States. It was a particular factor in limiting the initial choices of the refugees. There were, at the Fall of Saigon, two significant foci of potential refugee sponsors in the United States. Many military and diplomatic personnel lived in the Washington, D.C. area. These people served as sponsors for their counterparts who sought asylum in the United States with the First Wave.

Secondary migration and subsequent secondary resettlement have been significant activities among the Indochinese refugees in the United States. Secondary migration among the Indochinese refugees has developed at least some preliminary patterns that can be recognized. Some of the migration and resettlement patterns are very general and apply to all Indochinese refugees, but some are nationality or ethnic group specific. Whatever the impetus, secondary migration has been an important factor in developing the current pattern of residence characteristic of the Indochinese refugees.

A survey of Vietnamese refugees residing in the Washington, D.C. metropolitan area indicated a series of factors that determine the locational choices of these refugees. In that survey, carried out among a population of predominately First Wave refugees, approximately 40 percent of the Vietnamese wanted to move from the Washington region and gave as their reasons for wanting to leave: (1) warmer weather (64%), (2) better job opportunities (29%), and (3) extended family ties (7%). The potential migrants had specific destinations in mind as they pondered moving. These included:[20] California (29%), Texas (29%), any warmer climate (29%), and Louisiana (13%).

Gordon recognized similar patterns of secondary migration in her national study and indicated California, Texas, Louisiana, Oregon, and Colorado as target states. States with sizeable refugee populations that registered refugee declines included Florida, New York, Oklahoma, Ohio, Maryland, Missouri and Indiana. These states had refugee population losses of 13 to 31 percent from January 1976 to January 1979.[21]

These figures indicate a general tendency to move from northern states to states with milder climates and, at least in the case of the Vietnamese in Washington, D.C., "any warmer climate" is indeed a potential target of secondary migration. Gordon's study introduces an anomaly to this general pattern with Florida, a Sun Belt state, losing refugees and Colorado, with a much colder climate, gaining refugees during her study period. The reasons for these discrepancies can be discovered if the Indochinese as separate national and ethnic entities are examined.

The Vietnamese represent the largest subset of the Indochinese refugees and should be examined as two further subsets; (1) The First Wave refugees tended to be educated, skilled and urban-oriented, (2) The subsequent Vietnamese tended to be rural, poorly educated, and at best, semi-skilled. The Washington, D.C. region received many of the First Wave immigrants and, as a result, the study in 1979 reflected the attitudes of that group more accurately than it did for any other segment of the refuge population. In that study, 72 percent of the respondents were white collar workers or students in Vietnam. Among that group, specific secondary migration goals were overwhelmingly urban Sun Belt centers such as Houston (28%), Dallas (23%), and Los Angeles (26%). An unpublished survey conducted among the Vietnamese in and around Lancaster, Pennsylvania, indicated a preference for coastal Louisiana (19%), coastal or rural Texas (24%), and the Pacific coast and farming regions (26%).

In general, the Cambodians have tended to follow the secondary migration patterns of the uneducated, semiskilled Vietnamese. Those who settled originally in the South or Southwest have tended to stay, and those who did not intend to migrate toward those regions. The Laotians, however, indicate a quite different pattern of secondary migration, indicative of a separate set of settlement forces. While California is a primary resettlement node for the Laotians, other primary loci included Colorado, Minnesota, Illinois, Oregon and Pennsylvania. The tendency to move to ethnic clusters is apparently very important among the Laotians and may be a result of their relatively small numbers, even among the Indochinese refugee population. Certainly for the distinct ethnic groups such as the Hmong, the primary resettlement factor is the nearness of other Hmong. A bimodal settlement pattern including southern California and Colorado has resulted.

HEALTH CONSIDERATIONS

The arrival of large numbers of refugees from Southeast Asia in the United States has presented a number of health-related problems. The group includes people of all ages (Fig. 10.9). Basically there are two subjects of concern, both of considerable interest to medical geographers. One is the incidence of disease among the refugees and the potential for the diffusion of new and dangerous diseases into the United States. The other is the problem of health care delivery for the

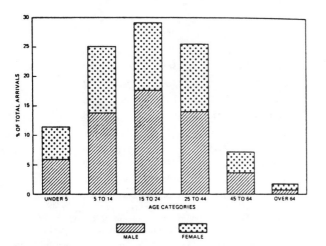

REFUGEES — Indochinese refugee arrivals in the United States, 1980

Figure 10.9. Refugees-Indochinese refugee arrivals in the United States, 1980. Source: Centers for Disease Control, *Morbidity and Mortality Weekly Report*, Vol. 29, No. 54 (September, 1981), Annual Summary 1980, p. 116.

newcomers and the difficulties that are posed by cultural differences in approaches to health and disease.

Refugees go through a medical screening process in the camps in Southeast Asia and a more thorough one when they arrive in the United States. Data gathered by the Center for Disease Control show that gastrointestinal disorders and intestinal parasites are very common. Hookworm is the most common intestinal parasite, but there are many others. Although many of these parasitic infections are new to American doctors, they do not pose a public health hazard inasmuch as adequate sewage disposal interrupts transmission.

Another common problem is conjunctivitis. In the summer of 1980, acute hemorrhagis conjunctivitis (AHC) was observed in a significant proportion of Southeast Asian refugees entering California. AHC is a rather severe form of this common eye disease; it was first identified in Western Africa in 1969 and there have been large epidemics in a number of Asian countries since then. Because AHC, transmitted by a virus, is extremely contagious, there was concern lest it be introduced into the United States. Epidemics usually occur, however, in densely crowded humid areas with poor hygenic conditions, such as the holding camps in Southeast Asia. The CDCs adjudged the possibility of secondary spread in the United States to be negligible. Screening procedures in the camps in Thailand and Singapore were intensified, and the number of cases imported into the United States was minimized.

Two diseases that aroused particular concern were malaria and tuberculosis. The United States has been malaria-free since the 1940s, but each year some imported cases occur, brought back from Africa or Asia by travelers. The number of such cases has risen dramatically since 1975, with most of the increases accounted for by the Indochinese refugees. The concern has been to detect and treat such cases rapidly, lest the disease spread. Fortunately, chloroquine and primaquine have been effective in controlling the disease. Recently, medical authorities have diagnosed a number of cases of congenital malaria in babies born to refugees, so surveillance for malaria continues in second-generation Indochinese.

Tuberculosis has proven to be the greatest health threat posed by the refugees, and this situation has received a great deal of alarmist attention in the press. The influx of immigrants from Asia and Latin America has caused a reversal in the long-standing trend of steady decline in tuberculosis rates.

The Centers for Disease Control have carefully monitored the incidence of TB among the refugees and reported that 3,895 Indochinese refugees were treated for tuberculosis in 1979 and 1980. Of these, over 85 percent had entered the United States in 1979 and 1980. The incidence rate at the time of entry was 1,138 cases per 100,000 refugees (Table 10.5). The incidence

TABLE 10.5 Estimated prevalence of tuberculosis at the time of entry and annual incidence after entry among Indochinese refugees, United States, 1979–1980

Age Group (years)	Prevalence of Tuberculosis at Entry*	Incidence of Tuberculosis after Arrival†	Incidence of Tuberculosis in the United States, Excluding Refugee Cases, 1980
0–4	197.0	438.5	4.9
5–14	173.1	301.1	1.4
15–24	736.5	293.1	4.5
25–44	1,840.1	488.3	10.3
45–64	4,059.3	768.6	18.4
65+	6,833.5	1,584.9	30.2
All ages	1,137.8	407.4	11.3

*Cases per 100,000.
†Cases per 100,000 per year.
Source: *Morbidity and Mortality Weekly Report* 30, No. 48 (Washington, D.C.: Centers for Disease Control, Department of Health and Human Services), December 11, 1981: p. 603.

among the refugees was about 100 times higher than among the rest of the United States population of all ages (Fig. 10.10). The influence of TB case rates among Indochinese on overall rates in the United States is shown in Table 10.6.

Indochinese refugees accounted for about 7 per cent of the tuberculosis cases added to the case registers in the two-year period 1979–1980, but there was considerable geographic variation. In St. Paul, for example, refugees accounted for 60 percent of new tuberculosis cases and in Minneapolis for 38 percent. In five California urban areas (Orange County, Long Beach, San Francisco, Sacramento, and San Diego) Indochinese accounted for 30 to 50 percent of the new cases. Other heavily impacted cities were Wichita, Seattle, and Denver.

The Indochinese, who make up only a tiny fraction of the U.S. population, are screened for tuberculosis both in the Asian camps and after arrival. Because they are quickly treated and monitored, they pose a minimal health hazard, much less than the more numerous illegal immigrants from Latin America.

A dramatic health problem unique to the Indochinese was reported during 1981. During that year 38 cases of sudden unexpected death during sleep occurred among refugees, all but one among men. Thirty-three of the victims were from Laos, of whom 25 were Hmong, four were Vietnamese, and one was Kampuchean. These events pose a medical puzzle that will take some time to solve.

Health care delivery for the new immigrants has been a major concern of resettlement agencies. After the initial screening for dangerous disease and the routine immunization of children, what then? Many of the immigrants qualify for Medicaid, at least for a time. Others find the high cost of American health care a serious problem. The arrival of a baby in an American

TABLE 10.6 The 10 states and 10 major urban areas in which refugees accounted for the largest percentage of tuberculosis cases, United States, 1979–1980

Area	Refugees with Tuberculosis	Estimated Percentage of Cases Added To Registers
States		
1. Utah	53	36
2. Minnesota	149	34
3. Washington	289	33
4. Colorado	112	32
5. Kansas	20	27
6. Oregan	103	23
7. Nevada	25	22
8. California	1,348	17
9. Idaho	9	15
10. Iowa	23	14
Metropolitan Areas		
1. St. Paul, MN	68	60
2. Wichita, KS	41	55
3. Orange County, CA	368	50
4. Long Beach, CA	60	42
5. Seattle, WA	106	38
6. Minneapolis, MN	37	38
7. San Francisco, CA	283	33
8. Sacramento, CA	82	30
9. Denver, CO	49	30
10. San Diego, CA	133	30

Source: *Morbidity and Mortality Weekly Report* 30, No. 48 (Washington, D.C.: Centers for Disease Control, Department of Health and Human Services), December 11, 1981: p. 604.

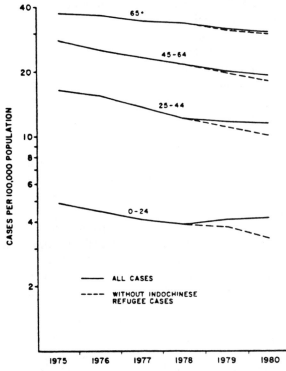

Tuberculosis case rates, by age group, United States, 1975-1980

Figure 10.10. Tuberculosis Case Rates by Age Group, United States, 1975–1980. Source: Centers for Disease Control, *Morbidity and Mortality Weekly Report*, Vol. 30, No. 48, (December 11, 1981), p. 605.

hospital can pose a serious financial problem for most refugees.

Even when free or inexpensive health care is available, refugees are often slow in seeking medical advice. A Denver study showed that four-fifths of the refugees surveyed wait at least five days after the onset of illness to seek professional care and nearly three-fourths fail to follow up after they have consulted a doctor. Differing cultural norms play a major role in these problems of health care delivery. Among the Hmong, for instance, the sense of time as a continuum, rather than something neatly divided into hours, is a serious problem in keeping medical appointments and taking medication at proper intervals.

Indochinese often have different concepts as to the origins of disease. They may relate illness to the Oriental idea of "balance," symbolized by the Yin-Yang duality. If a person is sick, something is out of balance and must be set right. Some customs have caused serious misconceptions on the part of their new American neighbors. Coin-rubbing is a traditional Vietnamese practice for respiratory ailments. Sometimes the chest of a child is rubbed so vigorously with a coin that bruises appear, thereby leading to misinterpretation of the practice as child abuse.

PROBLEMS IN ACCULTURATION

What have been the greatest problems in acculturation for the Indochinese? Ask this of almost any of the welfare workers, ESL (English as a Second Language) teachers, refugee coordinators, or others who have been involved in refugee resettlement and you get the same answer: jobs, housing, and education (especially language). This seems to be a very American set of priorities, especially in the recessionary atmosphere of the early 1980s. They are not always in the same order. Some refugee workers will add others: health, especially mental health; lack of acceptance by, and occasionally conflict with, their new American neighbors; and breakdown of family ties in the new environment. This last usually occurs when children, particularly teenagers, acquire new American value systems as rapidly as they acquire the English language, jeans as a standard uniform, and a taste for hamburgers and coke.

One problem, very geographic and related to all these others, is transportation. Public transportation is a must for the new arrivals until they can save enough money to buy a car, which is one of the prominent dreams or goals. Hence low-cost apartments on public transport lines acquire added importance.

Jobs are not only important but are controversial. The refugee resettlement agencies have stressed the urgency for immediate employment. Many refugees, finding that it was possible to live on welfare while learning English and going to school, have put education first and jobs second. This brings them into confrontations with the VOLAGS, the state and local agencies, and the sponsors. During the early period, when the federal government allowed up to 36 months on public assistance, some Indochinese refugees were finding it possible to get a community college education, and even to make substantial progress towards a bachelor's degree, before their eligibility for benefits expired. This changed in 1982 when the maximum period for benefits was cut to 18 months.

As to the kinds of jobs filled by Indochinese refugees, they have settled into slightly different economic niches in different regions and cities. In general, most of them have gone into service occupations, serving as everything from waitresses and dishwashers to dry cleaners and hairdressers. Many start out at the bottom rung on minimum wages and work their way up, becoming proprietors and entrepreneurs of restaurants, beauty salons, dry cleaning establishments, and all kinds of stores.

In the very early days, after 1975, there were bizarre occupational adjustments as generals or cabinet ministers became doormen or waiters and doctors worked as orderlies. These situations have been changed over time. Mutual assistance organizations and VOLAGS have helped professionals retrain, so that many professionals such as doctors, dentists, and professors have re-entered their professions. It has been more difficult for lawyers, trained in a totally different legal system.

SUMMARY

The arrival of the Indochinese refugees in the United States has added an almost entirely new element to the American ethnic mix within a very short time span. By far the largest number of new immigrants are Vietnamese. It is important to note, however, that we are dealing with not just one, but several ethnic groups who have been lumped together under the term Indochinese.

The nature of the movement of these people has often been very dramatic, symbolized by the helicopter flights from the roof of the United States Embassy during the final hours before the fall of Saigon and, later on, the hazardous voyages of the boat people. The movement, on the whole has been highly unselective, as most forced migrations are. The mix has varied during different time frames; but, the Indochinese minority, as it now exists, includes people of all ages, social strata, educational levels, and occupations.

In many ways the emerging patterns of Indochinese resettlement in the United States are illustrative of classic migration theory. The initial force was a systematic policy of dispersed settlement, implemented by the government agencies at all levels and by the VOLAGS. Unlike earlier immigrant groups, who settled in or near points of entry or in enclaves of ethnic similarity, the Indochinese were originally dispersed all over the United States. An opposing force, resulting in secondary migration, has been the desire of the refugees to rejoin family and friends, find a supportive ethnic community with a network of MAA's, and maximize the benefits offered by the various government entities.

The major barrier to rapid assimilation has been language. Once that difficulty is overcome, acculturation proceeds very rapidly, particularly among the young. The problems are, however, many: jobs, housing, language skills, transportation, finances, formal education, lack of proper working skills, health, and last but not least, cultural deprivation and loneliness. The Indochinese, nevertheless, have adapted very rapidly in comparison to other groups in the past. In particular, higher education is being used to a remarkable degree to accelerate assimilation.

The processes of resettlement are far from complete. The geographic pattern is not yet distinct, and push-and-pull factors are still very much in operation. The strength of secondary migration forces suggest, however, that the initial pattern of wide dispersal is giving way to the more usual pattern of clustering.

NOTES

1. John K. Whitmore, "Cultural and Religious Patterns," *An Introduction to Indochinese History, Culture, Language, and Life,* ed. John K. Whitmore (Ann Arbor, Michigan: Center for South and Southeast Asian Studies, University of Michigan, 1979): p. 26.
2. Darrel Montero, "The Vietnamese Refugees in America: Patterns of Socioeconomic Adaptation," *Proceedings* of the First Annual Conference on Indochinese Refugees, eds. G. Harry Stopp, Jr., Nguyen Manh Hung (Fairfax, Virginia: Citizens Applied Research Institute, George Mason University, 1979): p. 119.
3. Han T. Doan, "Vietnamericans and Their Acculturation Process," (Paper presented at the 72nd Annual Convention of the American Sociological Association, Chicago, Illinois, 1981): p. 4.
4. Barbara S. Cotter and Patrick R. Cotter, "American Attitudes Toward Indo-Chinese Refugees: The Influence of Region", *Proceedings* of the First Annual Conference on Indochinese Refugees, eds. G. Harry Stopp, Jr., Nguyen Manh Hung (Fairfax, Virginia: Citizens Applied Research Institute, 1979): p. 16.
5. R. Middleton, "Regional Differences in Prejudice," *American Sociological Review,* 41 (October, 1976): pp. 94–117.
6. James A. Pisarowicz, "Indochinese Refugee Experiences in Three American Cities," *Proceedings* of the First Annual Conference on Indochinese Refugees, eds. G. Harry Stopp, Jr., Nguyen Manh Hung (Fairfax, Virginia: Citizens Applied Research Institute, 1979): pp. 167–180.
7. G. Harry Stopp, Jr., "Cultural Brokers and Social Change in An American Peasant Community," *Peasant Studies,* 5 (July 1976): pp. 18–22.
8. J. Goldlust and A. H. Richmond, "A Multivariate Model of Immigrant Adaptation," *International Migration Review,* 8 (Fall, 1974): pp. 193–225.
9. George M. Scott, Jr., "The Hmong Refugees of San Diego: Initial Strategies of Adjustment," *Proceedings* of the First Annual Conference on Indochinese Refugees, eds. G. Harry Stopp, Jr., Nguyen Manh Hung (Fairfax, Virginia: Citizens Applied Research Institute, 1979): pp. 78–85.
10. Linda Gordon, "Settlement Patterns of Indochinese Refugees in the United States," *INS Reporter,* 28 (Spring, 1980): pp. 6–10.
11. Gail Paradise Kelly, *From Vietnam to America* (Boulder, Colorado: Westview Press, 1977): p. 155.
12. *Ibid.:* p. 153.
13. Linda Gordon, "Southeast Asian Refugees in the United States: Dispersal and Concentration," (Paper presented to the annual meeting of the Southwest Social Sciences Association, San Antonio, Texas, March 17–20, 1982): p. 7.
14. *Ibid.*
15. Glenn Hendricks, *Indochinese Refugee Settlement Patterns in Minnesota* (Minneapolis, Minnesota: Center for Urban and Regional Affairs, 1981).
16. S. Jenkins and B. Morrison, "Ethnicity and Service Delivery," *Proceedings* of the 1977 Conference of the American Orthopsychiatric Association (New York: American Orthopsychiatric Association, 1977): p. 215.
17. K. A. Skinner and Glenn L. Hendricks, "The Shaping of Ethnic Identity Among Indochinese Refugees," *The Journal of Ethnic Studies,* 7 (Fall, 1979): pp. 19–26.
18. Ha Ton Vinh, "The Plight of Indochinese Mutual Assistance Associations in the United States," (Paper presented at the Workshop on Refugee Problems sponsored by the Kennedy Foundation, Washington, D.C., January 14, 1982): p. 6.
19. Nguyen Manh Hung, "Vietnamese in America," (Paper given to the Annual Meeting of the Virginia Political Science Association, Norfolk, Virginia, May, 1980).
20. Alice C. Andrews and G. Harry Stopp, Jr., "The Indochinese Diaspora: Some Preliminary Geographic Observations," *Proceedings* of the First Annual Conference on Indochinese Refugees, eds. G. Harry Stopp, Jr., Nguyen Manh Hung (Fairfax, Virginia: Citizens Applied Research Institute, 1979): pp. 181–196.
21. Linda Gordon, 1980, p. 7.

11

Rural Ethnic Islands

Allen G. Noble
University of Akron

A majority of the immigrants to the United States came in search of economic opportunity. For most, this meant the possibility of acquiring land and hence many came to unoccupied, or sparsely settled areas. Others went to urban centers. The various Homestead Laws of the middle 19th century attracted the immigrants toward the heretofore unsettled lands (except for Native Americans), where they might secure ownership simply by occupying and improving the land. Immigration agents for railroads, and even states, facilitated the movement.

The immigrants moved thousands of miles into new territory. It was only natural that they sought the security, protection and support of their own cultural group. For example the Germans, one of the large foreign national groups to migrate to the United States, sought out existing German settlements. A checkerboard pattern of settlement emerged in which various ethnic groups clustered together, each maintaining its own identity.

Through continued settlement and use of the land specific groups became identified with certain regions in the United States. Today, many of these cultural areas can still be identified by the character of the landscape. These rural ethnic settlements are generally distinguished as being *ethnic provinces* or *ethnic islands/folk islands* depending on their size in terms of population and area. Ethnic provinces are used to refer to larger areas that frequently contain several thousands or millions of persons. Such identifiable provinces in the United States include blacks in the South, Hispanics in the Southwest, and Native Americans in Oklahoma and the Southwest. In contrast, ethnic islands are smaller in area and population, but are more numerous and include a wider array of ethnic groups. The American Midwest is a good example of where numerous ethnic islands appear on the landscape.

Since most of the major groups comprising ethnic provinces are discussed elsewhere in this text, this chapter will devote discussion primarily to rural ethnic islands. Emphasis will be placed on how the various

groups modified the American landscape particularly with regard to the structures (i.e. houses, barns) they erected. Specific groups to be included are the Germans, Belgians, Swedes, Cajuns, Finns, Norwegians, Amish and Mormons.

CHARACTERISTICS OF ETHNIC ISLANDS ON THE CULTURAL LANDSCAPE

One of the distinguishing characteristics of many European ethnic islands in the United States is the sense of community. It has been so strong within many ethnic groups that the internal divisions which characterized the group in its European setting were established in the New World, even in the face of unfriendly reception from surrounding groups belonging to other nationalities. Peter Munch has shown for Norwegian settlements in Vernon County, Wisconsin, that old country ties remained among the strongest influences affecting later settlements.[1] In Vernon County, although Norwegians are the dominant settlers, at least three sub-strata can be identified. On Coon Prairie in the northern part of the county, most of the Norwegians came from around Gudbrandsdal and Lake Mjösa in eastern Norway, whereas settlers in the southern part of the county originated in west Norway (Fig. 11.1). Intermediate between these settlements are Norwegians with ties to the southwest coast of Norway. The persistence of the separate identities of the first two groups is all the more interesting because both came in 1850 to Vernon County from a single earlier settlement in Dane County, Wisconsin.[2] Norwegians from the Flekkefjord area did not commence settling Vernon County until about 1880 and hence were forced to those lands located between the two earlier Norwegian settlements.

In the 19th century and earlier, ethnic communities usually were easy to identify and some were quite well-known, but in the 20th century forces of change have been at work. Some communities have dwindled; others

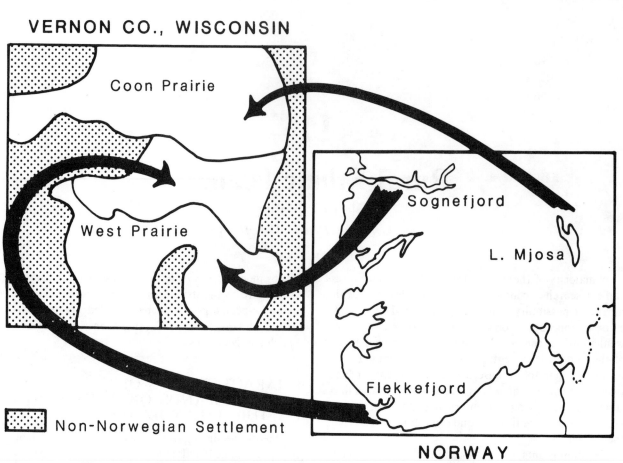

VERNON CO., WISCONSIN

Coon Prairie

West Prairie

Sognefjord

L. Mjosa

Flekkefjord

NORWAY

Non-Norwegian Settlement

Figure 11.1. Selective migration of Norwegians to Vernon County, Wisconsin (after Munch).

have expanded. Some groups found themselves in the path of suburban expansion and their members sold off the land and turned to urban occupations. The cohesiveness of the ethnic group weakened and its identity has, in some cases been lost. Furthermore strenuous attempts have been made to assimilate the children. Often the immigrant parents enthusiastically supported the process, so their children might gain the full benefits from complete participation in the affairs of the new country. The rate of assimilation varied with a number of factors including the difficulties of language, the physical accessibility of the group, the strength of opposing institutions (such as the presence of ethnic clergymen) and, above all, the size of the ethnic community.

In many places the ethnic identity of the settlers persisted, even though modified by time. Not everywhere, but in many places, a series of rural ethnic islands can be identified where the original cohesiveness of the group has not been lost. The mosaic of immigrant settlement never has been studied in its entirety, but for restricted regions, a few attempts have been made to identify ethnic territories. The literature on the geographical extent of ethnic settlement has been reviewed by Raitz.[3]

The most comprehensive investigation of ethnic territories was made for the state of Wisconsin by George W. Hill using data from 1905.[4] Hill's map, executed at the level of the individual township, attempted to identify every ethnic settlement in the state in a system encomposing twenty-three nationality groups and a "mixed" category when no single nationality reached 80 percent of the total. The pattern revealed by Hill's map is literally one of a checkerboard of ethnic settlements.

The geographer is interested in many aspects of these ethnic islands: the process by which the immigrants chose the place of settlement; the types of areas they sought and those they attempted to avoid; the techniques and systems of cultivation they brought, and how these were modified in the new environments; the different perceptions of the environment held by immigrants of other ethnic communities, and above all; the alterations each immigrant group made on the appearance of the countryside by the structures it erected.

Building Structures of Rural Ethnic Islands

If in sufficient numbers, all ethnic groups stamp their imprint on the land, especially if they are the initial settlers. Because each group followed the guidelines of its traditions, the structures erected, in large part, were quite similar to one another, and yet quite distinct from the structures of other ethnic groups.

Figure 11.2. A German Bank barn, Summit County, Ohio (Photo by A. G. Noble, 1976).

One conspicuous rural building, the German Bank barn, familiar to many Americans because of its widespread distribution as well as its distinctive appearance illustrates this principle. Although there are important variations in the basic structure,[5] all German Bank barns are at least two stories high and have a distinctive overhanging second story forebay (Fig. 11.2). Barns of this type are found in great numbers in southeastern Pennsylvania, where German settlement in cohesive groups was first introduced into North America (Fig. 11.3). Elsewhere, the presence of surviving German Bank barns indicates either the pathways of German movement from the southeastern Pennsylvania hearth or the location of later German settlements without a direct connection to the earlier hearth (Fig. 11.3). No other nationality built this type of barn, so that today it always functions as an indicator of German occupation and original settlement,[6] and the major routes of movement out of the southeastern Pennsylvania can be clearly traced by its presence (Fig. 11.3). In parts of the Shenandoah Valley over one-half of all barns are of this type. Another route of migration leads directly west, tying the German settlements of Pennsylvania to those of the Midwest. Independent concentrations show up in Wisconsin and southern Ontario.

The German Bank barn is only one structure which provides a clue to ethnic settlement. Many other nationalities erected distinctive barn types. Dutch, English and French barns are well-known. Houses, too, have distinct ethnic connections, although because houses change appearance more frequently than barns, house types are more difficult to identify.

The cultural landscapes characterizing some ethnic islands have not been examined at all by scholars despite their distinctive character. Such is the case with the Belgian settlements in Door County, Wisconsin (Fig. 11.4).

French-speaking Walloon settlers began to occupy the heavily forested, but fertile soils, of the gentle dip slope of the Niagara cuesta in the southern Door peninsula between 1853 and 1857.[7] The dense forest cover, combined with scattered swamps, effectively isolated the Belgian settlement from its neighbors. Although two or three attempts have been made to document the history of this settlement, only one serious effort has been made to examine the distinctive structures which still characterize the area.

In 1979 geographers Charles F. Calkins and William G. Laatsch looked at the outdoor oven.[8] Fifteen surviving ovens were documented in their study. Most

Figure 11.3. German Bank Barns. Percent of German Bank Barns to all barns, 1975.

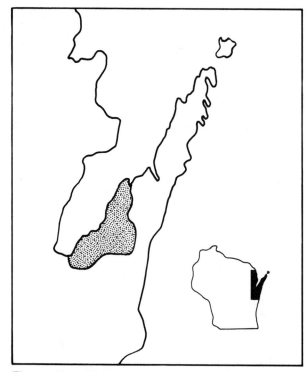

Figure 11.4. Distribution of Belgian settlement area in Door County, Wisconsin.

Figure 11.5. Belgian house, summer kitchen and outdoor oven extension, Door County, Wisconsin (Photo by A. G. Noble, 1980).

were extensions of the summer kitchen, a feature of most Door County Belgian farmsteads. Both the oven and the summer kitchen were normally constructed of blocks of local Niagara limestone. The domed oven was sometimes covered by a wooden roof structure (Fig. 11.5). The baking chamber of the oven was formed of bricks and resembled those of other French-speaking groups.[9] Careful attention was given to the size of the

244

Figure 11.6. Typical Belgian brick house, Door County, Wisconsin. (Photo by A. G. Noble, 1980).

The privy also illustrates the architectural distinctiveness of ethnic settlements. In most rural communities the privy is situated at some convenient distance to the rear of the house, but usually away from other buildings. On the Belgian farmsteads the privy usually occupies the ell formed by the bakeoven and the rear gable wall of the summer kitchen (Fig. 11.8). Here it takes maximum advantage of the heat radiated by the oven, as well as the shelter afforded from winter winds. A further advantage may be that for most of the way only a single pathway need be shoveled after a snowstorm, thus reducing effort. Both the privy and the summer kitchen-bakeoven face in opposite directions, so that despite proximity, functions are kept quite separate.

Another small outbuilding apparently unique to the Belgian community, is the diminutive chapel on each farmstead (Fig. 11.9). Just large enough for two or three persons to worship, the chapel reflects the strong

Figure 11.7. Belgian log barn, Door County, Wisconsin.

baking chamber, since it governed the effectiveness of the facility. Hence, great uniformity in structural form and size is found in these ovens.[10]

A similar kind of tradition-enforced uniformity also pervades the other Belgian structures, although perhaps with not quite so much exactness. The house dimensions and form vary, but all have the unmistakeable stamp of Belgians construction (Fig. 11.6). The underlying structure may be of log or timber frame, set on a limestone foundation, but the facing is of brick from local clays. The exterior frequently is ornamented with mortar decorations (large gable-placed stars are popular), stone quoins, window hoods and frames, and even cobblestone panels (Fig. 11.6). The barns, in contrast, are constructed of hewn logs with half notching (Fig. 11.7). Clay chinking keeps out the frigid winds which blow off Green Bay in the winter season. The form of the barns, an elongated rectangle with off-set, double wagon doors and a series of smaller man-size doors, is close to that of the Quebec Long Barn of the St. Lawrence Valley.[11] Further study will be necessary to provide the points of differentiation of the barns of these two Gallic areas and peoples.

Figure 11.8. On this Door County Belgian farmstead, the privy is snugly fitted into the ell between the outdoor oven and the rear gable wall of the summer kitchen. Note the limestone construction of the latter. (Photo by A. G. Noble, 1980).

Figure 11.9. Typical Door County Belgian farm chapel (Photo by A. G. Noble, 1980).

Roman Catholic heritage of these people. The chapels, which may be frame or stone, measure about 6' long by 4' wide and are universally covered by a gable roof of shingles or metal. The single door is in the gable and the diminutive altar and figure of the Virgin rests against the opposite gable wall.

The combination of distinctively decorated brick house, elongated log barn, limestone summer kitchen with bakeoven extension, unusual privy location and the tiny chapel unmistakeably mark the Belgian homestead. Unfortunately, no one has yet seen fit to examine the buildings of this ethnic group in detail. Nor have the methods of construction, attitudes towards the structures, or approaches to building been analyzed. Consequently, some intriguing questions remain to be answered. Why did the Belgians seek out an environment so unlike that of their native country? What adjustments were necessary for them to accommodate themselves to the new, harsher surroundings? What was the process by which the settlers took up building with hewn logs, which had not previously been a part of their tradition in Belgium? Obviously the Belgian community in Wisconsin is a potentially rewarding subject for future study.

SELECTED ETHNIC ISLANDS

Cajuns in Southern Louisiana

In southern Louisiana, a distinctive group occupies a rather large area (Fig. 11.10). Although this group might be considered an ethnic province, it will be discussed in this chapter since the Cajuns are not included elsewhere in this text. The Cajuns first entered Louisiana in 1754 in flight from Acadia (the term *Cajun* is corruption of the word *Acadien*), where they were expelled by the British at the beginning of the French and Indian War.[12] Many of the early Acadians settled around St. Jacques de Cabanocey (now St. James Parish), located to the west of the city of New Orleans. Through time, the Cajuns diffused throughout the lower Louisiana bayou landscape.

The southern Louisiana bayou environment is, of course, quite different from that of the Door County cuesta. Consequently, certain design features are altered in the two locations. Conserving heat, as demonstrated in the Wisconsin Belgian privy location, is not an important consideration, but providing ventilation and protection from dampness and insects is of paramount concern. Hence, houses are raised up on short pillars or piers of cypress wood. This raises the sills of the house from contact with the damp ground, provides a barrier to termites and other pests, and permits circulation of air beneath the floor of the house.

The standard folk house of this area bears the name of Creole house despite the fact that most of its builders have been Cajuns.[13] Creole is the term applied to the

French culture which evolved in Louisiana from the initial settlers who came directly from France or from the St. Lawrence Valley, Florida or the French Caribbean colonies, especially Santo Domingo. Generally speaking, Creole architecture is associated with established plantation areas, whereas the structures of the Cajuns are those of small scale farmers. In reality, Creole and Cajun building forms are similar enough that a broader term, such as "French buildings" could be applied to both. Rather than using the name of Creole house, it would be more appropriate to call the basic or standard house of French Louisiana by the name of Grenier House (Fig. 11.11) and thus avoid the confusion between Cajun and Creole. While forms are similar, construction methods are better differentiated, perhaps because of the difference in affluence of the two groups. Cajuns, who lived on the river levees but close to the bayou swamps, used a mixture of Spanish

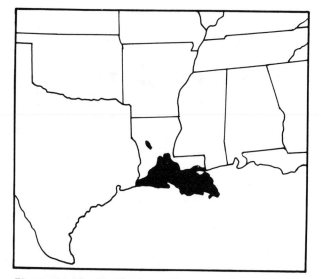

Figure 11.10. Distribution of French settlement area in Louisiana.

Figure 11.11. The Grenier House.

246

moss, mud, and sometimes, calcined seashells called *bousillage* which was used as in-filling between hewn, vertical timbers. As economic levels increased, early Cajuns turned to the abundant resources of bayous for cypress wood to use as cladding. They found the cypress to be durable, resistant to insects, slow to rot, easy to saw and work with simple hand tools, straight-grained and thus easy to split, unlikely to warp even when used "green," and difficult to burn.[14] A paragon of woods!

Creole builders, while they occasionally employed *bousillage* in the early period, were much more likely to use bricks as wall nogging.[15] Furthermore, their houses might be raised on brick foundations or brick piers, and often in the more elaborate examples, had full lower stories of brick. Many of the later, and most of the larger, Creole houses had prominent hipped roofs, whereas the Cajun houses employed primarily the gable roof. Both appear to stem from a single New World French building tradition, although the details of that development are not yet clearly defined.

The Grenier house is the standard French house of rural Louisiana. Its most distinctive feature and the one from which it derives its name, is the attic which projects forward over the open, front *galerie* or verandah. Among other early ethnic groups, the front porch is usually clearly an afterthought, tacked on to the main structure and having a separate roof. The *grenier,* however, is clearly a part of the original design of the French house, as is the *galerie.* Together they provide a profile which distinctively marks the Grenier house.

William Knipmeyer has demonstrated by examining typical floor plans that an evolutionary sequence exists among Grenier houses from single room houses with an outside stairway on the galerie to houses of eight to ten rooms with rear stairway.[16] William Ruston has suggested that the former are typical of Cajun buildings, whereas the latter are of Creole origin.[17]

Not quite as common as Grenier houses, but nevertheless still important in rural French Louisiana are Shotgun and Double Shotgun houses. The Shotgun house (Fig. 11.12) is as distinctive as the Grenier house but in a much different way. It consists of a single file of rooms which permits maximum cross ventilation of the house, a desirable feature during the long hot and humid summers of the region. Folk traditions insist that the house derives its name from the fact that the doors of each room are in line, and hence a shotgun fired through the front door would pass through the house and out the back door, despite the fact that many Shotgun houses do not possess in-line doors. Folk myths die hard!

Double Shotgun houses have been given the name of Bungalows, which is unfortunate since it causes confusion with other, rather similar appearing houses found in other parts of the country, but from much different origins. In French Louisiana the "bungalow" is a one-story structure derived by placing two single Shotgun houses together to achieve a larger building suitable for larger families. That this is its origin is clear from the fact that some Double Shotgun houses have no interior doorway connecting the two halves of the house, an inconvenience remedied in most later buildings of the type.

The combination of Grenier, Shotgun and Double Shotgun houses differentiates the French agricultural settlements of Louisiana. These house types could never be confused with those of the Wisconsin Belgian farmers. Not only are the houses in Louisiana quite different, so are the barns and out-buildings, as well as the arrangement of the structures. Barns are small, gable-entry buildings, consisting of a central space with one or two flanking areas. On occasion a rear shed will also be found. The most distinctive feature of the Cajun barn is the recessed entryway (Fig. 11.13). Out-buildings include corn cribs, chicken houses, chicken roosts, and now-and-then, an outdoor bake oven.

Figure 11.12. A Shotgun House, near Donaldsonville, Louisiana, 1978. This particular house is somewhat wider than normally found. (Photo by A. G. Noble).

Figure 11.13. A Cajun Barn.

The farm properties are rectangular, with the house close to the road and the barn and out-buildings behind. Because of the narrow aspect of the farm property, the buildings are not placed to form a barnyard as is frequently the case with the Wisconsin Belgian farmsteads.

Both the Wisconsin Belgian and the Louisiana French settlements show adjustments of building design to local environmental conditions which are quite different from one another.

Finns in the Upper Midwest

Of the two groups, Finns and Norwegians, the buildings of the former are the better known. Finns entered the United States in numbers only toward the end of the 19th century and at the beginning of the 20th. Finnish immigration peaked in the 1920s when nearly 17,000 emigrated, but their total number of immigrants is considerably smaller when compared to those of Norway. Migration was highly localized. One-half of all migrating Finns came from the province of Vaasa, particularly from South Ostrobothnia and most ended up in the vicinity of Lake Superior (Fig. 11.14).[18] Because they came so late, the Finns found only the poorest land unoccupied. Nevertheless, such land closely resembled what they had left behind, and there was much more of it available and at very low cost. The principal difficulty standing in the way of effective settlement was clearing the land of its natural forest cover. Use of pine logs as building material helped in the process of land clearing.

Building with squared, hewn logs is one of eight distinctive features which, according to Mather and Kaups, make up the Finnish cultural landscape of the Lake Superior basin.[19] Other investigators have identified other characteristics. For example, Alanen and Tishler note that the typical farmstead consists of a cluster of buildings placed in a rough courtyard arrangement.[20] In the earliest of these, all the structures are of log, but in later farmsteads houses are built of dimension lumber, but the barns and outbuildings continue to be built of log.

Great variety is found in house design, but a three-rooms-in-line plan (Fig. 11.15) is one of the most common,[21] owing its origins to ancient Baltic center hearth houses. Finnish settlers often built these houses one or two units at a time, so that sometimes the entire house never was completed. A two room log house was about as common as the three, even in Finland.[22]

Certain other characteristics identify the Finnish house. Logs are hewn in a quite distinctive fashion, square on both inside and out with the top remaining convex and the bottom hewn concave so that a tight fit of wall logs is achieved. The fit is so close that little or no chinking is required between the logs, a desirable feature in the biting cold winters of both Finland and the northern Midwest. In those instances when chinking was required, a layer of moss or a strip of cloth was often used. Also helping to produce firmly built walls is the use of corner notching techniques such as the double notch and the full dove-tail, both of which permit tight fits.

Two quite distinctive structures mark the typical Finnish farmstead. One is the *sauna* and the other is the *riihi* or grain drying barn. The presence of numerous barns and outbuildings, also characterize the Finnish farmstead.[23] Some barns house livestock; others house hay; still others, the riihi, have the very specialized function of grain drying and threshing. These barns were never widely built in America because the climate of the northern Midwest was drier than that of Finland and hence the need for a closed drying facility was eliminated, or at least greatly reduced.[24] The most unusual feature of the riihi was a large, chimneyless stove

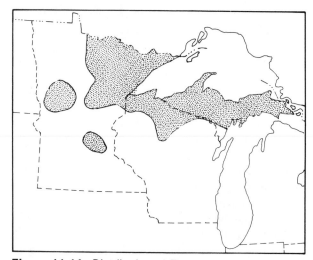

Figure 11.14. Distribution of Finnish settlement area in the Great Lakes region.

Figure 11.15. A Finnish three room house. The ladders on the roof and the small enclosed entryway are typically Finnish. Old World Wisconsin outdoor Ethnic Museum, (Photo courtesy of Marty Perkins).

248

of brick and stone, in which wood was burned to dry out the grain. The combination of wood burning amidst great quantities of easily combustible grain and straw meant that riihi fires were always a danger. To reduce the risk, the riihi was kept outside the farmstead, away from other buildings.[25]

The sauna, the other distinctive building of a Finnish farmstead, was also a potential fire hazard and consequently it, too, was built somewhat apart. The log sauna initially was a single room, windowless structure containing a set of stepped benches and a stove of unmortared field stone. Smoke from the stove, which had no chimney, was allowed to escape through small wall vents or roof flues.[26] The fire was burned primarily to heat igneous and metamorphic rocks piled on the top of the stove. The heated rocks then provided the energy to keep the sauna interior hot for extended periods. Water was ladled onto the rocks to reduce the temperature if it became too hot and at the same time to increase the sensation of heating.

The original, one-room sauna was replaced at an early date on many farms by a larger, two-room structure in which the new room functioned as a dressing area. These structures typically measured 8–10 feet wide by 15–18 feet long (Fig. 11.16), and added both a chimney for ventilation and small windows for interior light. The entrance door remained on the gable, but now led into the dressing room rather than into the stove room.

The sauna building received the same meticulous crafting as the Finnish log house. The logs were carefully hewn so as to fit together with virtually no chinking. Double notching or full dovetail notching was employed to ensure the sound, tight structure required to conserve the heat of the sauna. Pine logs were preferred for the sauna because they were little affected by the great temperature changes associated with the sauna.[27] Most important was that the timber be left untreated, neither painted nor even oiled, so that the maximum moisture could be absorbed by the wood.

The Norwegians

Early Norwegian migration to the United States began in 1825 when approximately 50 Norwegians emigrated. The Norwegian immigration started rather slowly but gathered momentum in the 1860s and continued through the 1920s with the peak immigration periods occurring in the 1880s and 1900s when slightly less than 400,000 came to America during these two decades. From 1825 to the present, a total of more than 850,000 Norwegians have migrated to the United States.

After initially forming a colony called the "Kendall Settlement" in Orleans County, New York, Norwegians began moving westward after 1834. The Fox River region, near Ottawa in La Salle County, Illinois formed the early nucleus of this Norwegian migration. Through time, Norwegians established other settlements in Wisconsin, Minnesota, Iowa, and elsewhere in the Midwest and West.

Norwegians are much more widely scattered than the Finns (Fig. 11.17). They came in greater numbers and at an earlier period of time, so that their farmsteads occupied better land, often initially in prairie openings in the forest. Later on, towards the West, all of the land on which they settled was treeless prairie. Thus, they were spared part of the rigorous ordeal of clearing land. They built with logs, nevertheless, because their folk traditions encouraged it and timber was plentiful and cheap. Surprisingly, little has been written about Norwegian vernacular architecture and, perhaps because of the widely disbursed nature of their ethnic islands, little attempt has been made to consciously

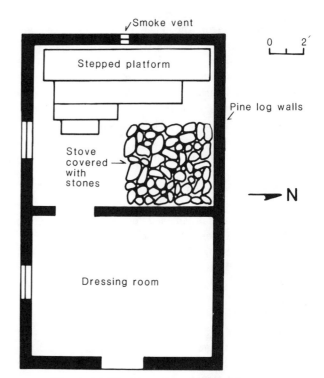

Figure 11.16. Floor plan of a Finnish sauna.

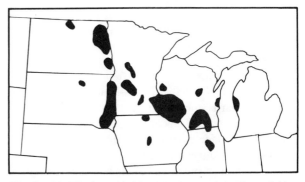

Figure 11.17. Areas of greatest concentration of Norwegians in the northern Midwest.

preserve their folk architecture. One of the difficulties in locating examples of early Norwegian structures, is that Norwegians frequently settled on easily accessible land of high quality, so that in time they prospered and rebuilt with more modern, less traditional buildings. Alternatively, they sold their land to non-Norwegians if prices were right.

The Norwegians used many of the same log techniques as the Finns. They hewed log walls on both inside and out and they hewed each log to be convex on top and concave on the bottom. They further chamfered the top and bottom edges of each log so as to make chinking easier and for appearance sake.

Although definitive evidence is not yet available, it appears that the American Norwegian houses were quite different from the American Finnish. Some one-story, three-room houses of the Baltic type may have been built. More common, however, was a dwelling which can be called a Norwegian Gallery house. Its name is derived from the long narrow, second story gallery or *sval,* which runs along one side of the house (Fig. 11.18). The *sval* is reached by a direct flight of stairs at one end. In many instances the space beneath the *sval* has been boarded in to create a narrow room on the first floor to complement the two original rooms which are of unequal size. The first floor rooms are replicated by two unequal-sized rooms on the second. Sometimes the roof of the house is assymmetrical in order to incorporate the *sval.*[28]

One of the very few detailed descriptions of a Norwegian Gallery house in the American Midwest can be found in the works of Richard Perrin.[29] His description of the John Bergen house confirms that these structures are derivations of those found in Norway,[30] as well as in Sweden.[31] Preserved in the Old World Wisconsin Outdoor Ethnic Museum is another Norwegian Gallery dwelling (Fig. 11.19), known as the Andrew Kvaale house. The plan of this house is not exactly that of a Scandinavian gallery house, but it is close.[32] The *sval* is incomplete; no outside stairway is present, and the lower level of the *sval* is partially closed in. But, other features of the structure are faithful to its predecessors: logs are right fitting, with little or no chinking, hewn in the Scandinavian fashion, and locked at the corners with full dovetail notching. A few other Norwegian Gallery houses have been described, mostly in Wisconsin, due to the efforts of the Old World Wisconsin staff.[33]

So little research has been attempted on American Norwegian buildings that virtually nothing can be said about the barns and outbuildings of the typical Norwegian farmstead. They are, of course, constructed of logs held in place by saddle notching or half dovetail notching. In contrast, houses employ double notching or full dovetail,[34] much like Finnish houses. One of the more unusual outbuildings on the Norwegian farm is

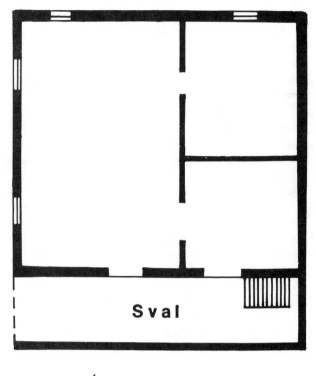
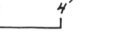

Figure 11.18. Floor plan of a Norwegian Gallery house.

Figure 11.19. A modified Norwegian Gallery house. The Sval is to the right. Old World Wisconsin Outdoor Ethnic Museum, 1979 (Photo by A. G. Noble).

the *stabbur* or granary. As with many of the structures of the Finns and Norwegians, most existing stabburs have been covered over with siding, or otherwise modified. For this reason many undoubtedly go undetected. The modifications to the Norwegian stabbur at Old World Wisconsin have been better documented than for most such structures (Fig. 11.20).

The rural architecture of the Norwegians in America has not been studied adequately. Not only do the basic

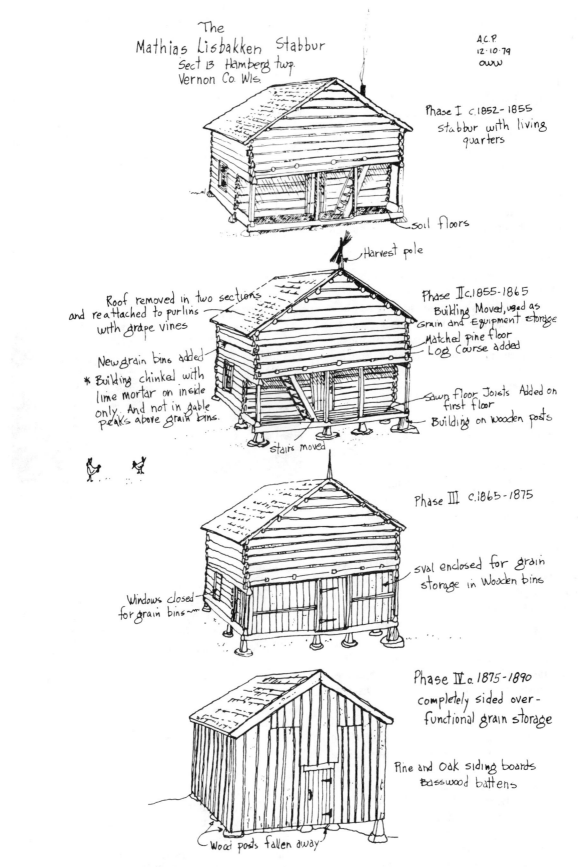

The
Mathias Lisbakken Stabbur
Sect 13 Hamberg twp.
Vernon Co. Wis.

A.C.P.
12·10·79
aww

Phase I c.1852-1855
Stabbur with living
quarters

soil floors

Harvest pole

Roof removed in two sections
and reattached to purlins
with grape vines

New grain bins added
* Building chinked with
lime mortar on inside
only. And not in gable
peaks above grain bins.

stairs moved

Phase II c.1855-1865
Building Moved, used as
Grain and Equipment storage
Matched pine floor
Log Course added

Sawn floor Joists Added on
first floor
Building on wooden posts

Phase III c.1865-1875

sval enclosed for grain
storage in Wooden bins

Windows closed
for grain bins

Phase IV c.1875-1890
completely sided over-
functional grain storage

Pine and Oak siding boards
Basswood battens

Wood posts fallen away

Figure 11.20. Stages in the Modification of the Lisbakken Stabbur. (Source: Alan C. Pope, 1980: 3; Used by permission).

251

types remain to be located and identified, but the place which these structures occupied in the life of the settlers needs to be documented as well.

The Amish

Amish immigration to America occurred in two peak periods, during 1727 to 1770 and from 1815 to 1860.[35] Because of persecution in Europe, the Amish were reluctant to keep formal records of their members; therefore, official documentation of the arrival date of the first Amish to America remains unknown. However, some may have arrived as early as 1710. Evidence exists, however, to indicate that in 1727 a ship landed in Philadelphia which contained several Amish names on its passenger list.[36] In 1737 another ship landed which is often referred to as the "first Amish ship" since the numerous families aboard can definitely be established as being Amish.[37] The early journeys to America were difficult and many Amish were reluctant to leave their native Switzerland. These early Amish established settlements in Berks, Chester, and Lancaster counties in southeastern Pennsylvania. It is estimated that during the eighteenth century only about 500 Amish emigrated to America.[38]

During the nineteenth century, the second wave of Amish immigration occurred, many were from Alsace, Lorraine, Bavaria, and Waldeck and they contributed to the establishment of other communities in America such as those in Ohio (Holmes, Stark, Wayne, and Fulton counties); Indiana (Adams, Allen, Daviess, Elkhart, and LaGrange counties); Illinois (Woodford and Tazewell counties): Iowa (Henry and Washington counties): New York (Lewis County): Maryland (Somerset County); and in Waterloo and Perth counties in Ontario, Canada.[39] Near the end of the nineteenth century, "the 1890 U.S. *Census of Religious Bodies* reported twenty-two Old Order Amish congregations with 2,038 baptized adult members in nine states."[40] Total population in 1890 was estimated to be 3,700. By 1920 the Amish had 83 districts and an estimated population of 14,000; by 1950 the districts had grown to 197 and a population of 33,000, and as of 1979, there were a total of 526 districts and 85,783 persons.[41] Districts vary in size, but most are small. Some of the largest districts average about 35 households. Of the 85,783 Amish persons, approximately 80 percent are located in Ohio (29,137), Pennsylvania (22,570), and Indiana (16,628).[42]

The Amish who are scattered in a series of ethnic islands from Pennsylvania to beyond the Mississippi River (Fig. 11.21), cling to tradition tenaciously. One consequence is that they continue to need large, two-story barns to house their draft animals as well as other livestock. Barns on all farms are more susceptible to fire than houses and on Amish farms the risk is even greater, since they oppose the use of lightning rods on

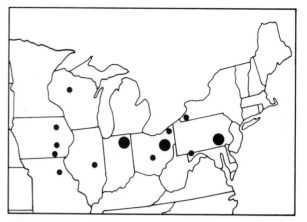

Figure 11.21. Distribution of Amish settlements in northeastern United States.

Figure 11.22. Straw stack beside a typical Sweitzer barn. Holmes County, Ohio, 1981 (Photo by A. G. Noble).

religious grounds as an interference with God's will.[43] Consequently, barns are replaced much more frequently than houses. Thus, even in the newly settled areas of the Midwest where Amish families have taken over non-Amish properties, the Sweitzer barn gradually establishes the Amish cultural landscape.

The Amish construct Sweitzer barns (Fig. 11.22) of the type built in southern Germany or Switzerland, the area of the group's origin. Newly designed barn types, such as Pole barns, Wisconsin dairy barns, or Round Roof barns, are noticeably lacking in Amish areas. Furthermore, traditional practices such as stacking straw from threshed grain outside in the barnyard (Fig. 11.22) or shocking of corn in the fall are maintained. Certain smaller structures found in Amish areas also help to contribute to the sense of a traditional landscape. Thus, one finds windmills (Fig. 11.23), because the Amish do not believe in using electrical power; privies, because water normally cannot be made available within the house; board fences, often white-washed;[44] a multiple bird house perched high on a pole; and gardens, in front of or close beside the farmhouse rather than behind it.[45] Other typical features closely related to the kitchen garden are the larger "patch" for potatoes and other vegetables consumed in large quantities in the house, and the fruit orchard.[46]

The most typical house associated with the Amish is the Four-Over-Four (Fig. 11.24), a type common in southeastern Pennsylvania.[47] Elsewhere, this house type is less often encountered for three reasons. First, the Amish often purchased farmsteads of earlier non-Amish settlers and occupied the existing houses thereon. Second, the Amish normally have large families and additions are often made to the original houses. With enlargement, the houses are modified so that their original type is sometimes difficult to identify from the outside. Apparently only one floor plan of an Amish house has ever been published.[48] It suggests a structure which has grown by accretion rather than by careful adherence to a preconceived plan traditionally acceptable to the ethnic group.

Finally, on many Amish farmsteads two houses are found (Fig. 11.25). These may be entirely separate structures, the obviously newer one being the smaller of the two. Sometimes the two houses are connected by a closed passageway. The rationale for two houses on the farmstead lies in the practice among the Amish of retiring from farming at a relatively early age and turning the active direction of the farm over to the youngest son. Upon retirement, the parents move to a newly built house on the family homestead. Sometimes instead of building a separate, or nearly separate house, the existing dwelling is simply enlarged to include a private set of rooms for the older generation. When a separate dwelling is built, it is referred to as the "grandfather or gross-dawdy" house. Such an arrangement is a strong confirmation of the traditional outlook of Amish society.

The Mormons

Besides the Amish, another group also oriented to religion but in a quite different fashion, are the Mormons. Beginning just before the middle of the 19th century, Mormon settlers occupied a series of desert oases in the intermontane West. Gradually settlement was spread by extending irrigation works until the areas coalesced to form a large Mormon cultural region. Donald Meinig has delimited the Mormon culture region in terms of core, domain, and sphere (Figure 11.26).[49] The Wasatch Oasis, which extends approximately 65 miles in a north-south direction forms the core of the Mormon region. The central cities of the core are Salt Lake City and Ogden. Surrounding the core is the domain where Mormon culture values are dominant, but Gentile intrusion has occurred, thereby lessening the Mormon homogeneity of the area. In the sphere, Mormon culture is present, but it is less intense and Mormons reside as minorities or nucleated enclaves within the region.

Figure 11.23. Amish farmstead in Holmes County, Ohio, 1978. Note the windmill, the board fence and the buggy, all typical of Amish landscapes (Photo by A. G. Noble).

Figure 11.24. An Amish farmstead, Holmes County, Ohio 1978. Typical elements include the Sweitzer barn, a Four-Over-Four house, the grandfather house, and board fences (Photo by A. G. Noble).

Figure 11.25. The grandfather is to the left, separate but connected to the older, main house by a common porch. Holmes County, Ohio, 1978 (Photo by A. G. Noble).

The Mormons tended to settle in small farm villages rather than on isolated, individual farmsteads.[50] Three reasons probably explain this variance from the usual American practice. First, was the apprehension of Indian attack which made group settlement sensible. Second, was the need to organize farmers to construct, maintain and protect, at the lowest cost possible, the irrigation facilities upon which settlement depended. Finally, the clustering of settlers was encouraged by church leaders in order to maintain the religious discipline and spirit of the Mormons. Thus, the cultural landscape of the Mormons is that of small villages rather than individual farmsteads. Richard Francaviglia has identified ten significant factors which delimit the Mormon village,[51] although other writers suggest a shorter list.[52]

Among the most important and distinctive features are the uniformly very wide streets running at right angles to each other and set in accord with cardinal compass points. They divide each village into spacious, square blocks.[53] Allowing for local idiosyncracies, the villages have a uniform plan related to that of "the city of Zion" decreed by Mormon church leaders. As Lowry Nelson notes, the Mormon village was in part, "motivated by a sense of urgent need to prepare a dwelling place for the Saviour at His Second Coming."[54] The large blocks permitted, not only the Mormon house to be located in the village, but the farmstead as well.

The houses of the Mormons are invariably small, partly a reflection of the relatively recent settlement of the area, partly because of the modest living standards afforded by the desert oases, and partly due to the frugality and communal quality of Mormon life. That lifestyle requires a large portion of income to be donated to the church and its social welfare work. One survey of a Mormon village in 1923 showed the mean number of rooms per house to be 4.5 and the median only 3 rooms.[55]

Considerable variety in house types exists, but the most often encountered earlier structure is a two-room, one story, gable-roofed house with gable chimneys, and often a rear extension[56] (Fig. 11.27). Secondary features include, very little roof overhang, a general absence of decorations, and sometimes double front doors. A very high percentage of these houses are composed of adobe brick,[57] a logical material in the dry, unforested lands of the intermontane West. The use of adobe continued in Utah until the construction of rail lines in 1875 making coal deposits easily available as a fuel for making kiln fired bricks.[58]

Another group of houses are characterized by central hallways. Of these, some belong to the I house type, others are Four-Over-Four houses.[59] Regardless of type, the houses invariably are done in Greek Revival architectural style. A very high percentage of all Mormon houses constructed between 1860 and 1890 adhered to this style. Earlier this style was the dominant one in

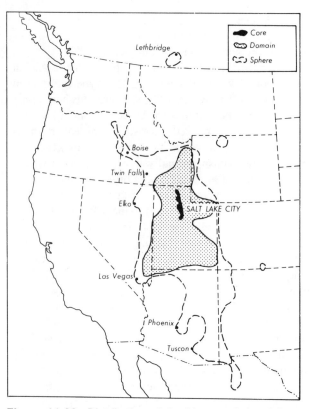

Figure 11.26. Distribution of the Mormon Cultural Area (after Meinig).

Figure 11.27. A Mormon house built of adobe brick.

midwestern and eastern United States when the Mormons left those areas. Thus the Mormons brought the idea of the Greek Revival house to Mormonland "and their self-imposed isolation kept other styles out until late in the 1800s."[60]

During this period, adobe was superceded by brick as the major building material. Since population was rapidly expanding at this time, predominance of brick structures has come to be recognized as one of the characteristics of the Mormon settlement area.[61]

Figure 11.28. Transverse barn typical of Mormonland.

Very much in contrast to the neat and simple adobe and brick buildings are the rest of the structures, including plank-sided barns (Fig. 11.28), open hay sheds, hay derricks (Fig. 11.29) and rough "Mormon fences" of irregular vertical boards nailed to horizontal rails (Fig. 11.29). All of these features are unpainted and often quite ramshackled, giving a strong, yet erroneous impression of a relict landscape.

Generations of western travellers have remarked on the distinctiveness of the Mormon landscape, a quality probably due to its desert oasis location. Even the trees, Lombardy poplars, are a product of the Mormon occupance.[62] The cultural landscapes of other ethnic groups are not quite so easily perceived by casual observers. Nonetheless they do exist and are important in local areas. Since the settlements of the various ethnic groups are scattered, they form a distinctive checkerboard of ethnic islands strewn across America.

Figure 11.29. The hay derrick is one of the most distinctive features of the Mormon landscape, Strawberry Valley, 1974 (Photo by A. G. Noble).

NOTES

1. Peter A. Munch, "Segregation and Assimilation of Norwegian Settlements in Wisconsin," *Norwegian-American Studies and Records,* 18 (1954): pp. 102–140.
2. *Ibid.:* p. 112.
3. Karl B. Raitz, "Ethnic Maps of North America," *Geographical Review,* 68 (July, 1978): pp. 335–350.
4. George W. Hill, "The People of Wisconsin According to Ethnic Stocks, 1940," *Wisconsin's Changing Population* (Madison: Bulletin of the University of Wisconsin No. 2642), 1942.
5. Charles H. Dornbusch and John K. Heyl, *Pennsylvania German Barns* (Allentown: Pennsylvania Folklore Society, Monograph No. 21), 1956.
6. Allen G. Noble and Gayle A. Seymour, "Distribution of Barns in Northeastern North America," *Geographical Review,* 72 (April, 1982): 155–170.
7. Hjalmar R. Holand, *Wisconsin's Belgian Community* (Sturgeon Bay, Wisconsin: Door County Historical Society), 1933.
8. Charles F. Calkins and William G. Laatsch, "The Belgian Outdoor Ovens of Northeastern Wisconsin," *Pioneer America Society Transactions,* 2 (1979): p. 1–12.
9. Fred B. Kniffen, "The Outdoor Oven in Louisiana," *Louisiana History,* 1 (1960): 20–35; Michel Lessard and Huguette Marquis, *Encyclopedie de la Maison Quebecoise* (Montreal: Les Editions de l'Homme, 1972): pp. 620–625.
10. Calkins and Laatsch, 1979: p. 4.
11. Eric Arthur and Dudley Whitney, *The Barn: A Vanishing Landmark in North America* (New York: New York Graphic Society, 1972): pp. 114–141.
12. William F. Rushton, *The Cajuns: From Acadia to Louisiana* (New York: Farrar Straus Giroux, 1979): pp. 67–68.
13. William B. Knipmeyer, *Settlement Succession in Eastern French Louisiana* (Ann Arbor: University Microfilms International, 1956): p. 88.
14. Rushton, 1979: p. 174.
15. Knipmeyer, 1956: p. 99.
16. *Ibid.:* p. 120–123.
17. Rushton, 1979: p. 183–184.
18. Cotton Mather and Matti Kaups, "The Finnish Sauna: A Cultural Index to Settlement," *Annals of the Association of American Geographers,* 53 (December, 1963): p. 498–499.
19. *Ibid.:* pp. 500–501.
20. Arnold R. Alanen and William H. Tishler, "Finnish Farmstead Organization in Old and New World Settings," *Journal of Cultural Geography,* 1 (Fall/Winter, 1980): pp. 66–81.
21. Richard W. E. Perrin, "Log Houses in Wisconsin," *Antiques,* 89 (June, 1966):p. 869.
22. Nils E. Wickberg, *Finnish Architecture* (Helsinki: Otava Publishing Company, 1959): p. 16.
23. Eugene Van Cleef, "The Finn in America," *Geographical Review,* 6 (September, 1918): p. 192.
24. Matti Kaups, "A Finnish Riihi in Minnesota," *Journal of the Minnesota Academy of Science,* 38 (Spring and Summer, 1973): p. 66.
25. *Ibid.:* p. 69.
26. Matti Kaups, "A Finnish Savusauna in Minnesota," *Minnesota History,* 45 (Spring, 1976): p. 15.
27. *Ibid.:* p. 12.
28. Perrin, 1966: p. 870.
29. Richard W. E. Perrin, "John Bergen's Log House," *Wisconsin Magazine of History,* 44 (Autumn, 1960): pp. 12–14.
30. John Lloyd, "The Norwegian Loftehus," in *Shelter and Society* ed. Paul Oliver (New York: Frederick A. Praeger, 1969).
31. Thomas Paulsson, *Scandinavian Architecture* (Newton, Mass.: Charles T. Branford, 1959).
32. Alan C. Pape, "Kvaale House: Architectural Analysis Report" (Unpublished internal report), Eagle Wisconsin: Old World Wisconsin Outdoor Ethnic Museum, n.d.).
33. Alan C. Pape, "Lisbakken Stabbur: Architectural Analysis Report: (Unpublished internal report), Eagle, Wisconsin: Old World Wisconsin Outdoor Ethnic Museum, 1980): p. 3.
34. Lawrence R. Brandt and Ned E. Braatz, "Log Buildings in Portage County, Wisconsin: Some Cultural Implications," *Pioneer America,* 4 (January, 1972): p. 37.
35. John A. Hostetler, *Amish Society* (3rd ed. Baltimore: John Hopkins University Press, 1980): p. 50.
36. *Ibid.:* p. 56.
37. *Ibid.*
38. Ibid.: p. 65.
39. *Ibid.*
40. *Ibid.:* p. 98.
41. *Ibid.:* p. 99.
42. *Ibid.:* p. 100.
43. Maurice A. Mook and John A. Hostetler, "The Amish and Their Land," *Landscape,* 6 (Spring, 1957): p. 25.
44. *Ibid.*
45. *Ibid.* p. 24.
46. John A. Hostetler, *Amish Society* (2nd ed. Baltimore: Johns Hopkins University Press, 1968): p. 98.
47. Richard Pillsbury, "Patterns in the Folk and Vernacular House Forms of the Pennsylvania Culture Region," *Pioneer America,* 9 (July, 1977): pp. 12–31.
48. Hostetler, 1968: p. 178.
49. Donald W. Meinig, "The Mormon Culture Region: Strategies and Patterns in the Geography of the American West, 1847–1964," *Annals of the Association of American Geographers,* 55 (June, 1965): pp. 191–220.

50. Richard V. Francaviglia, *The Mormon Landscape* (New York: AMS Press, Inc., 1978).
51. ———, "The Mormon Landscape: Definition of an Image in the American West," *Proceedings of the Association of American Geographers,* 2 (1970): p. 59–61.
52. Richard H. Jackson, "The Use of Adobe in the Mormon Culture Region," *Journal of Cultural Geography,* 1 (Fall/Winter, 1980): p. 82.
53. Lowry Nelson, *The Mormon Village* (Salt Lake City: University of Utah Press, 1952): p. 25.
54. *Ibid.*: p. 28.
55. *Ibid.*: p. 99.
56. Joseph E. Spencer, "House Types of Southern Utah," *Geographical Review,* 25 (July, 1945): p. 448.
57. Richard H. Jackson, "Religion and Landscape in the Mormon Cultural Region," in *Dimensions of Human Geography: Essays on Some Familiar and Neglected Themes,* ed. Karl W. Butzer (Research Paper #186, Chicago: University of Chicago, Department of Geography, 1978): pp. 113–114.
58. Jackson, 1980: p. 85.
59. Richard V. Francaviglia, "Mormon Central-Hall Houses in the American West," *Annals of the Association of American Geographers,* 61 (March, 1971): p. 65.
60. Jackson, 1978: p. 114.
61. Francaviglia, 1970: p. 59.
62. Austin E. Fife, "Folklore of Material Culture on the Rocky Mountain Frontier," *Arizona Quarterly,* 13 (Summer, 1957): p. 107.

12

Urban Ethnic Islands

Donald J. Zeigler
Old Dominion University

Stanley D. Brunn
University of Kentucky

American cities have long been destinations for immigrants from all parrts of the world. Many early Europeans settled in urban places, and they continue to be the foci for recent ethnic groups arriving from Latin America and Asia. As a result, urban areas in the United States are characterized by a rich diversity of ethnic nationalities, and the mix of ethnic groups has played and continues to play an important role in American history.

Each large American city contains varying proportions of two or more ethnic nationalities. The total number of cities with Italian, German, Irish, English, Scottish and Polish ethnic populations is larger than those with French, Dutch, Portuguese, Japanese, and Chinese origins. All, however, contribute to the rich diversity of urban America. Mapping the spatial patterns of ethnic groups reveals that some nationalities are spread through urban areas; others exist in two or three concentrations; still others live in small islands. Over the years, the process of acculturation and assimilation has changed the size and shapes of these ethnic cores, archipelagos, and islands.

This chapter will examine the historical ethnic settlement processes in the U.S., urban settlement concentrations, and the ethnic mixes in selected cities. Following this look at the ethnic geography of urban America three salient features of ethnic America (the foreign language press, foreign language broadcasting and ethnic festivals) are investigated. These characteristics are associated primarily with urban settlements where most of the first, second, and third generations live.

THE THREE WAVES OF IMMIGRATION

The spatial patterning of ethnic minorities in the United States and their cultural attributes is closely related to the history of American immigration. This history can be divided into three major immigrant waves which rolled across the American landscape displacing the native American population in many places and forging a new American identity. The first wave of immigrants was composed of peoples from western and northern Europe, most importantly from the British Isles and Germany. This period of immigrant history began with the founding of Jamestown in 1619 and extended until about 1870. The real surge of immigrants to a youthful American nation, however, did not begin until the 1840s when more than one-and-one-half million people arrived in the United States. With this swelling tide, mass immigration began. Western and northern European nationalities continued to migrate to the United States throughout the nineteenth and twentieth centuries, but beginning in 1870 eastern and southern Europeans began accounting for a larger share of new arrivals. These new nationalities constituted the second wave of immigrants which by the 1890s accounted for over 50 percent of the new arrivals. The second wave immigration ended in 1921 when Congress enacted the first quota system to regulate the overall number of immigrants the nation would accept and the proportions which could originate from any particular country. The quota system, the Great Depression, and World War II put a damper on immigration until the start of the third wave of immigrants during the 1960s when the national quota system was replaced with a system more favorable to Latin American immigrants. For the first time in the 1960s, immigrants from Latin America outnumbered immigrants from Europe. The third wave, therefore, has seen a surge of legal and illegal arrivals mostly from Latin America on a permanent and temporary basis. Mexico, Cuba, Puerto Rico and more recently Central American countries have been the origins of most of these Latin American immigrants.

259

These three waves overlap and were compounded by immigrant streams from Asia during the second and third periods. Initially, Asian immigrants came from China and Japan. More recently they have come from India, Pakistan, South Korea, Taiwan, the Phillipines, Vietnam, Iran and some Arab-speaking Middle Eastern countries. During the 1970s, 1.4 million Asians immigrated to the United States as compared with 1.8 million Latin Americans and .7 million Europeans. The historical era initiated by each wave has been characterized according to the origin of the group of immigrants which rode the crest of the wave into American society, and each wave of immigrants has contrasted, sometimes sharply, with its predecessor wave in language, religion, customs, and economic background, as well as other important aspects of culture. The history of each wave helps to explain the changing geographic patterns of American ethnic groups and the present status of ethnic America.

IDENTIFYING ETHNIC GROUPS

The decennial censuses of population make it possible to determine the country of birth of first generation immigrants, known as "foreign born" population, and the country of the parents' birth for second generation immigrants, known as the "native population of foreign or mixed parentage." Despite some difficulties arising from the directive to use national boundaries existing at the time of the census, the fact that foreign nativity data have been collected in so many censuses reflects the importance of ethnicity in American culture. The melting pot hypothesis has been almost institutionalized by the census which, in essence, has equated the ethnic population of the United States with first- and second-generation immigrants only. Third, fourth, and further generations, as far as the census has been concerned, have not been differentiated from the mainstream of society.

With the 1980 Census, ethnicity data were collected by asking a different set of questions. Such a change in the questions signals a change in American culture and its view of ethnicity. It is no longer possible to define a foreign stock population as it was defined by the Census Bureau in the past. First generation immigrants will still be identifiable through a question on nativity. Replacing the question which made it possible to identify the native population of foreign or mixed parentage is a question asking "What is your ancestry?"

The 1980 Census also uses a more refined racial classification and singles out populations of Hispanic origin for detailed statistical data. What does this change in the questions indicate about American culture? First, it suggests that second-generation immigrants, that is, descendants of original immigrant groups, should not be categorized as foreign stock but

as native stock, suggesting, perhaps, the task of assimilation is easier today than it has been in the past. Second, it illustrates the importance of the third wave immigrants, that is, immigrants from Latin America and Asia and their descendants. Just as previous Census questionnaires were designed to maximize information about European immigrant groups, the 1980 questionnaire was designed to maximize information about Latino immigrant groups. Third, it sets the stage for equating ethnicity with race or ancestry rather than nativity. Both of these concepts span generations, rather than being restricted to only two—the original immigrants and their descendants. Do these new definitions, particularly with reference to ancestry, indicate that Americans are so comfortable with their stock pot character that citizens are no longer reluctant about expressing their ancestry on a national questionnaire? Is this question, in fact, a response of American society to what some believe is an ethnic renaissance in the United States?

Overall, the questions asked betray American heritage as a nation of immigrants and are concerned with minority populations. Only six questions, other than the person's name, were asked of every American in the 1980 Census of Population: Two of the six questions solicited information about minority ethnic status. One concerned race, the other Hispanic origin. In addition, several questions included on the long form, which was mailed to every sixth household, solicited information about the place of birth, citizenship status, language, and ancestry. As these data are analyzed it will become possible to gain a clearer picture of the ethnic complexion of an immigrant nation in which, as Sowell notes, there are no real minorities because there is no majority.[1] The American population is a composite of ethnic strains defined on the basis of nationality, race, and religion. No single group has even constituted a majority of the population. In response to the question about ancestry in 1980, over 130 different backgrounds were identified, but none constituted more than a quarter of the population. English ancestry was identified by 49,598,000 people and German ancestry by 49,224,000, followed by Irish, Afro-American, and French.

The percentage of the population that was identified as first generation immigrants, that is, the foreign born population, increased from 4.7 percent in 1970 to 6.2 percent in 1980 (Table 12.1). The national averages, however, mask much regional variation, particularly the contrast between the Sunbelt states and the Northeastern quadrant of the country. In 1970, only New York, the traditional gateway to America, had more than 10 percent of its population foreign born. By 1980, five states had exceeded 10 percent, and New York's first place ranking had been usurped by California with a population that was almost 15 percent foreign born (Figure 12.1). All Sunbelt states experienced relative

Table 12.1 Selected Ethnic Characteristics of U.S. Population

Source: Selected Statistics from the U.S. Bureau of Census, 1980 Census Report "Provisional Estimates of Social, Economic, and Housing Characteristics, PHC80–S1–1; and *1970 Census of Population, Characteristics of the Population,* 1973.

State	1980 Pop. (in 000s)	1980 % Foreign Born	1970 % Foreign Born	1980 % Non-English Speakers
Ala.	3,890	1.0	.5	1.9
Alaska	400	3.9	2.5	12.0
Ariz.	2,718	6.0	4.3	19.7
Ark.	2,286	0.9	.4	1.8
Calif.	23,669	14.8	8.8	22.5
Colo.	2,889	3.8	2.7	10.7
Conn.	3,108	8.5	8.6	14.2
Del.	595	3.4	2.8	5.7
Fla.	9,740	10.9	8.0	13.1
Ga.	5,464	1.7	.7	2.6
Hawaii	965	14.0	9.8	25.6
Ida.	944	2.3	1.8	5.3
Ill.	11,418	7.3	5.7	11.8
Ind.	5,490	1.9	1.6	4.8
Ia.	2,913	1.7	1.4	3.1
Kans.	2,363	2.0	1.2	4.8
Ky.	3,661	0.9	.5	1.8
La.	4,204	2.1	1.1	9.8
Maine	1,125	3.8	4.3	11.4
Md.	4,216	4.6	3.2	6.2
Mass.	5,737	8.4	8.7	13.0
Mich.	9,258	4.4	4.8	6.7
Minn.	4,077	2.7	2.6	5.5
Miss.	2,521	0.9	.4	2.0
Mo.	4,917	1.8	1.4	3.1
Mont.	787	2.3	2.8	5.5
Neb.	1,570	1.9	1.9	4.9
Nev.	799	6.7	3.7	9.4
N.H.	921	4.2	5.0	10.3
N.J.	7,364	10.3	8.9	15.7
N.M.	1,300	4.2	2.2	38.2
N.Y.	17,557	13.4	11.6	19.3
N.C.	5,874	1.5	.5	2.6
N.D.	653	2.3	2.9	11.6
Ohio	10,797	2.7	3.0	5.1
Okla.	3,025	1.8	.8	3.7
Ore.	2,633	4.2	3.1	5.6
Pa.	11,867	3.6	3.8	6.9
R.I.	947	8.8	7.9	16.5
S.C.	3,119	1.4	.5	2.5
S.D.	690	1.4	1.6	7.0
Tenn.	4,591	1.0	.5	1.8
Tex.	14,228	6.0	2.8	22.2
Utah	1,461	3.5	2.8	7.5
Vt.	511	4.2	4.2	6.8
Va.	5,346	3.2	1.5	4.4
Wash.	4,130	5.8	4.5	6.6
W.Va.	1,950	1.1	1.0	2.3
Wisc.	4,705	2.7	3.0	5.6
Wyo.	471	1.9	2.0	6.1
United States	226,505	6.2	4.7	10.9

in the foreign born population, and states with major ports of entry or adjacent to source regions of immigrants experienced the sharpest growth rates. California saw its percentage of first generation immigrants increase from 8.8 percent to 14.8 percent, Hawaii from 9.8 percent to 14.0 percent, Texas from 2.8 percent to 6.0 percent, and Florida from 8.0 percent to 10.9 percent. Three Northeastern states with traditionally large ethnic populations also experienced relative increases: New York, New Jersey, and Rhode Island. Most other states of the Northeast saw a relative decline in first generation immigrants as did many states of the interior such as Wisconsin, North and South Dakota, Montana, and Wyoming. What will be interesting to watch is the migration history of first generation immigrants which initially settled in the Frostbelt to see whether they are attracted to the growth centers of the Sunbelt as many native born Americans have been.

CULTURAL MOSAIC OR MELTING POT?

A classic debate in ethnic geography is whether the United States population can best be described as an ethnic mosaic or an ethnic melting pot. The mosaic analogy suggests that immigrant groups, particularly after the start of mass immigration in the 1840s, have had difficulty in becoming part of the mainstream of American culture. According to this school of thought ethnicity in the United States surfaces as relatively easily identifiable rural and urban ethnic islands of unmeltable Americans. The melting pot analogy, on the other hand, suggests that American culture is quick to assimilate newcomers so that in a few generations ethnic Americans are indistinguishable from the population as a whole. According to this school of thought, ethnicity is quickly snuffed out by the business of daily American life. Only selected cultural traits are salvaged from the flotsam of old world tradition to become a part of popular American culture. The melting pot idea has been around since the founding of the Republic. The clergyman, Jedidiah Morse, who defined geography for generations of American school children in the decades after 1789 postulated an idea that is still being tested by the contemporary generation of social scientists. He noted in his *The American Geography:* "The time . . . is anticipated when the language, manners, customs, political and religious sentiments of the mixed mass of the people who inhabit the United States, shall have become so assimilated, as that all nominal distinctions shall be lost in the general and honourable name of Americans."

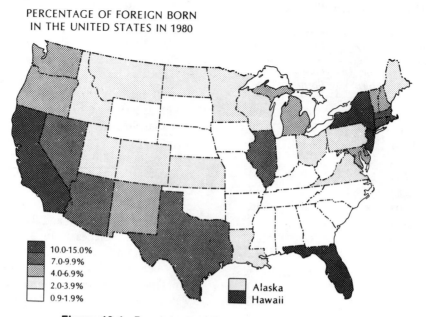

PERCENTAGE OF FOREIGN BORN
IN THE UNITED STATES IN 1980

10.0-15.0%
7.0-9.9%
4.0-6.9%
2.0-3.9%
0.9-1.9%

Alaska
Hawaii

Figure 12.1. Percentage of Foreign Born in the United States in 1980.

What is known today is that the melting pot analogy may pertain to some ethnic groups but not to others. The United States remains, for instance, much more of a mosaic of racial types than a melting pot. Ethnicity defined by racial divides has prevented the black population of the United States from melting into the mainstream of American culture. Religion, until recently, has also proven an impediment to assimilation. The Catholic population of the United States, whether from Ireland, southern or eastern Europe, and the Orthodox population have long been discriminated against because of divergent religious beliefs. Some American ethnic groups, in other words, have been more meltable than others. Some have even suggested that rather than a melting pot, American society should be seen as a "stock pot" since neither melting pot nor cultural mosaic seems to accurately describe the nature of ethnic America.

If inter-ethnic marriages are the litmus test of the melting pot hypothesis, then ancestry data should provide a first approximation of the extent to which various ethnic groups have melted into the mainstream of American culture. Table 12.2 lists the nationalities which were designated in 1979 as ancestry groups by at least 650,000 Americans. In all, over 179 million Americans reported at least one foreign nationality when asked "What is your ancestry?" Of those 179 million, 46 percent reported a combination of nationalities. These groups have been arranged in order of descending percentage of mixed ancestry. Almost 89 percent of those listing Scottish as their ancestry listed another nationality as well. So mixed have they become that to speak of Scottish Americans as a single group camouflages the variegated background of most

Americans of Scottish descent. Among blacks, at the other extreme, only 7 percent acknowledged being of mixed parentage. Those groups which are more than one-third of mixed ancestry are all, with the exception of the American Indian, from western and northern Europe. These nationalities represent the first wave of immigrants from Europe. Ancestry groups which are between one-third and two-thirds of mixed ancestry are all from eastern and southern Europe. They represent the second wave of immigration. Given these two categories one might conclude that the only correlate of mixed heritage in the United States is the number of generations which have elapsed since the initial immigration. Immigrant groups which arrived first, save Afro-Americans, are "melting pot" Americans whereas immigrants who arrived later are headed toward "melting pot" status.

Among some groups less than one-third of their members report mixed ancestry. Of those in Table 12.2, the only two which can claim recency of immigration as an explanation for their "purity" are the Spanish, almost all of whom are from Latin America, and the Filipinos. The other groups in this category strongly contradict the melting pot hypothesis. Blacks arrived in the American colonies as early as any European group, yet only a fraction report mixed heritage. Similarly, the Chinese and Japanese who immigrated to the United States by the tens of thousands during the first two decades of the twentieth century have not experienced the same degree of success at melting into the dominant society. The stratification evidenced in Table 12.2 may be understood on the basis of two factors: (1) immigration history, with the earliest arrivals

262

TABLE 12.2 Ethnic Groups* in the United States Reporting Multiple Ancestry 1979

Ancestry Group	Percent Reporting Multiple Ancestry
More than two-thirds of the following groups reported mixed ancestry.	
Scottish	88.6
Dutch	83.2
Welsh	82.3
American Indian	79.3
Irish	77.7
French and French Canadian	76.0
Swedish	75.1
Swiss	74.6
Danish	73.8
English	71.3
Norwegian	70.1
German	66.8
Between one-third and two-thirds of the following groups reported mixed ancestry.	
Hungarian	66.5
Austrian	64.0
Lithuanian	61.9
Polish	58.5
Slavic	58.4
Russian	56.8
Czechoslovakian	53.2
Italian	48.0
Portuguese	47.9
Greek	42.7
Less than one-third of the following groups reported mixed ancestry.	
Filipino	31.3
Chinese	23.4
Japanese	22.3
Spanish	21.9
Afro-American	7.0

*Ancestry Claimed by more than 650,000 Americans.

Source: U.S. Bureau of the Census, *Current Population Reports,* 1982.

TABLE 12.3 Median Age of Selected Ancestry Groups in the United States (in years)

	Single Ancestry	Multiple Ancestry
English	40.4	27.1
Scottish	43.5	32.2
Irish	39.0	25.7
French	36.2	24.5
Dutch	39.3	27.5
German	37.1	23.0
Italian	42.3	17.7
Polish	46.0	20.3
American Indian	29.2	23.4

Source: U.S. Bureau of the Census, *Current Population Reports,* 1982

the melting process has begun much more recently for them.

Some contrasts also exist in the concentration of European ancestry groups in metropolitan areas (Table 12.4). Among single ancestry groups, the Spanish, Italians, and Poles are the most metropolitan; the English and French are the least. Italians and Poles are the most metropolitan among those with mixed ancestry whereas those with mixed American Indian and mixed Dutch heritage are the least metropolitan. Significant differences appear in the groups that are in SMSAs exceeding one million and those with less than one million. The Poles, Italians, and Spanish are the most numerous and the American Indians, Dutch, French, and Scots the least. The single and multiple ancestry Poles, Italians, and Spanish are also the most numerous in central cities. These areas contain the smallest percentage of French, English, Scots, Germans, and American Indians.

On a national scale, the first wave of immigrants are less concentrated in metropolitan areas than the second wave of immigrants. In terms of specific ethnic groups, the Poles and Italians whether they be single or multiple ancestry, are more concentrated in large and small metropolitan areas than those with English, French, German, Irish, and Scottish ancestries. The second wave of immigrants are also more likely to be concentrated in the central cities than immigrant groups with ancestries in northern and western Europe. The single ancestry Spanish populations are concentrated in central cities of large or small metropolitan areas. Table 12.4 reveals the sorting out that has occurred and continues to occur in metropolitan America. Central cities and fringe areas are occupied by varying mixtures of first, second, and third wave immigrant groups. A cross-section of the ethnic populations in any metropolitan area at any time reveals varying residential patterns. Populations that may have existed in the central city in one decade may now have been replaced by a new wave of immigrants in another.

having more opportunities for intermarriage and (2) race, with black and oriental groups exhibiting the least inter-ethnic marriage.

The contrast between first and second wave immigration is also evident in Table 12.3. This table contrasts the median age of individuals claiming single ancestry with those claiming multiple ancestry. Whether the ancestry group is very young, as the American Indians, or relatively old, as the Scottish, the median age of the single ancestry group ranges between 7 and 26 years older than the multiple ancestry group. Second wave immigrants, represented by the Italians and Poles, exhibited the youngest population among the multiple ancestry groups. The data indicate

TABLE 12.4 Geographic Distribution of Ancestry Groups (by Percent)

Single Ancestry Groups	Metropolitan	SMSAs of One Million	In Central Cities of SMSAs of 1 Mill.+	Outside Central Cities of SMSAs of 1 Mill.+	In SMSAs of Under One Million	Nonmetropolitan
English	57.2	27.1	7.8	19.2	30.1	42.8
French	58.4	24.7	7.4	17.4	33.7	41.6
German	61.3	32.2	8.7	23.5	29.1	38.7
Irish	62.6	36.1	12.4	23.7	26.5	37.4
Italian	86.3	58.2	20.4	37.8	28.1	13.7
Polish	83.2	59.9	23.6	36.3	23.3	16.8
Scottish	62.9	30.4	10.3	20.1	32.5	37.0
Spanish	84.4	54.6	30.9	23.7	29.8	15.6
Other	76.4	48.3	27.5	20.8	28.1	23.6

Multiple Ancestry Groups	Metropolitan	SMSAs of One Million	In Central Cities of SMSAs of 1 Mill.+	Outside Central Cities of SMSAs of 1 Mill.+	In SMSAs of Under One Million	Nonmetropolitan
American Indian & Other	56.1	24.8	7.7	17.7	31.2	43.9
Dutch & Other	57.7	24.3	5.0	19.2	33.4	42.3
English & Other	66.6	34.1	7.8	26.3	32.5	33.4
French & Other	66.8	32.3	8.7	23.6	34.5	33.2
German & Other	67.1	37.0	8.7	28.2	30.1	32.9
Jewish & Other	65.6	33.9	8.1	25.8	31.7	34.4
Italian & Other	80.9	50.4	11.6	38.8	30.5	19.1
Polish & Other	80.7	52.2	15.5	36.8	28.5	19.3
Scottish & Other	65.4	32.1	7.1	25.0	33.3	34.6

Source: U.S. Bureau of the Census, *Current Population Reports*, 1982

URBAN SETTLEMENT PATTERNS

The 1970 Census of Population contains data that provides insights into urban settlement features of first- and second-generation ethnic groups. An examination of their continent of origins reveals some underlying similarities as well as some contrasts (Table 12.5). The foreign stock population is a decidedly urban population. First and second generation immigrants are far more likely to reside in urban settings, in urbanized areas, and in central cities than the population as a whole. The passage of generations, however, seems to break the grip of central cities on immigrants. Second generation immigrants (native of foreign or mixed parentage) are not so concentrated in urban settings as are first generation immigrants (foreign born). More than 9 out of 10 of the foreign born reside in urban settings as compared with slightly more than 7 out of 10 of the total population.

About one-half of the total foreign born population resides in central cities of SMSAs. This compares with 31 percent of the total population and 37 percent of the native population of foreign or mixed percentage

(second generation). The second generation more closely approximates the total population than the foreign born population in terms of the percentage that resides in the central city.

European, Asian, and Latin American first generation immigrants exhibit very little variation in their preference for urban settings. More than 9 out of 10 first generation immigrants from all three continents live in urbanized areas or other urban places. Only in terms of the percent residing in central cities of SMSAs do first generation European ethnic groups differ markedly from Asian and Latin American ethnic groups. Only 48 percent of first generation European immigrants reside in central cities, whereas 58 and 59 percent of Asian and Latin American groups, respectively, reside in central cities.

European, Asian, and Latin American second-generation immigrants parallel the first generation immigrants in their urban settlement patterns, but the second generation in all cases tends to be less concentrated in urbanized areas and central cities than the first generation. Again, second generation Europeans are less

TABLE 12.5 Comparative Urban Settlement Patterns of First and Second Generation Ethnic Groups in the United States: 1970

	Percent Urban	Percent in Urbanized Areas	Percent in Central Cities
Total Population	73	58	31
Native of Native Parentage	71	55	30
Native of Foreign or Mixed Parentage	84	74	37
Foreign Born	91	83	50
First Generation Immigrants:			
European Nationalities	90	83	48
Asian Nationalities	93	84	58
Latin American Nationalities	94	87	59
Canadians	85	73	33
Second Generation Immigrants:			
European Nationalities	84	74	36
Asian Nationalities	90	78	46
Latin American Nationalities	88	75	49
Canadians	79	64	28
First Generation European Immigrants:			
Greece	97	90	62
Italy	95	88	52
Ireland	94	90	62
U.S.S.R.	94	89	61
Poland	94	89	60
Lithuania	93	87	56
Yugoslavia	91	86	53
Hungary	91	86	50
France	89	80	45
United Kingdom	88	78	35
Czechoslovakia	86	79	43
Germany	86	76	40
Sweden	82	70	39
Netherlands	81	70	30
Switzerland	81	70	33
Denmark	80	67	33
Norway	79	66	39
First Generation Asian and Latin American Immigrants:			
Cuba	99	97	58
China	97	91	72
Japan	89	78	50
Mexico	88	74	51

Source: U.S. Bureau of the Census, *1970 Census of Population,* 1973, Table 97.

markedly concentrated in central cities than are Asians and Latin Americans.

Movement toward national averages for the total population seems to be taking place at the same rate for ethnic groups from all continents. Only Asian second generation immigrants seem to be slightly less likely to break the bonds of urban living, with high percentages still residing in urban settings in general and urbanized areas in particular even among second generation immigrants.

Eastern and southern European first generation immigrants (foreign born) are more concentrated in urban settings than are western and northern European ethnic groups. Only the Irish and the Czechoslovakians seem to be exceptions to this rule. Foreign born Irish remain concentrated in urban settings in similar percentages to Greeks, Italians, and Poles, whereas foreign born Czechoslavakians tend to be less concentrated in urban settings when compared with other first wave and second wave immigrants. Norwegians and Danes are the least urbanized of any European ethnic group. Overall, all foreign born European immigrant groups are far more urban than the population as a whole.

TABLE 12.6 Estimated Numbers of Persons with Non-English Backgrounds in the United States by Language and Age Groups, Spring 1976 (numbers in 1,000's)

	Total	5 & Under	6–18	19+
Total	27,985	2,224	3,032	20,730
Selected European Languages	22,475	1,766	4,263	16,446
French	1,932	83	303	1,546
German	2,735	70	286	2,378
Greek	542	41	88	412
Italian	2,931	99	296	2,336
Polish	1,498	24	87	1,387
Portuguese	489	29	77	383
Russian	228	x	17	209
Scandinavian Lang.	661	x	29	624
Spanish	10,609	1,384	3,022	6,203
Yiddish	852	26	58	768
Selected Asian Languages	1,842	220	301	1,321
Chinese	537	57	81	399
Filipino Lang.	522	69	103	351
Japanese	439	30	40	370
Korean	194	15	31	128
Vietnamese	150	30	46	74
Arabic	190	26	22	143
Navajo	159	22	54	83
Other Languages	3,319	191	391	2,738

x Less than estimated 15,000 persons

NOTE: Detail may not add to total shown due to rounding

SOURCE: *Survey of Income and Education,* conducted by the U.S. Bureau of the Census, Spring 1976. U.S. HEW/Education Division, National Center for Education Statistics, Bulletin 78 B-5, July 26, 1978, Table 1a.

The first generation immigrants from China and Cuba are among the most urbanized ethnic groups. The Cubans, a very recent group, have high percentages in both central cities and the urban fringe. Of the ethnic groups listed in Table 12.5, the Chinese have the highest percentages residing in central cities. Detailed 1980 Census data, when released, will reveal whether new immigrant groups from Central America and Southeast Asia are also highly concentrated in urban areas, especially in central cities.

THE ETHNIC PRESS

Immigrant groups often differ from other Americans in a multitude of cultural traits, especially in terms of their language. In 1976, there were an estimated 28 million persons in the United States with non-English backgrounds (about 13 percent of the total population) (Table 12.6). Nearly 11 million of these people speak Spanish, which alone accounts for almost half of the European languages spoken in the United States.

The aging of the three immigrant waves is evident in the number of children with non-English backgrounds in each language group. Whereas only 13 percent of the German speaking population is 18 and under, this age group accounts for 51 percent of the Vietnamese population, 42 percent of the Spanish population, and 33 percent of the Fillipino/Tagalog population. The age structure of these ethnic groups help to explain the trends in ethnic printing and broadcasting.

Ethnic islands are very often linguistic islands, and the language of immigrant groups manifests itself in both the spoken and written world.[2] In fact, the appearance of an ethnic press, typically a foreign language press, is one of the universal concomitants of immigration to the United States, a country where freedom of the the press is almost sacrosanct. Robert Park[3] found in 1922, for instance, that in New York City even the smallest of the immigrant groups had established a periodical of some kind. Roucek,[4] in surveying the status of the press in the 1940s found that newspapers in the United States were being printd in 39 different tongues. Even though the nature of the publications has changed since then, a tabulation of the entries appearing in the 1982 editions of *Ayer Directory of Publications, Editor and Publisher International Yearbook,* and *The Media Encyclopedia* showed that newspapers were published in 39 ethnic languages in the United States. Examples of these newspapers range from widely circulated Spanish language dailies such as Miami's *Diario Los Americas* to bi-monthly publications such as Chicago's *Samostigna Ukraina.* Examples of America's foreign language newspapers are presented in Table 12.7.

Focusing on ethnicity rather than language, Wynar in 1972[5] identified 43 ethnic groups which supported their own periodicals. Of these only 45 percent were in the native language whereas almost one-third were published totally in English. Wynar was able to list 903 ethnic publications (Figure 12.2). The Jewish press can be seen to account for about one-fifth of the total, but these Jewish periodicals appear in a number of different languages, most notably Yiddish, Hebrew, and English. Ukrainian and German publications rank in second and third place. In terms of circulation, however, the largest ethnic presses are Spanish and Jewish.

Indicative of the contemporary economic climate and technological milieu under which the Spanish language press is evolving, it is characterized by fewer publications with larger circulations. Older ethnic groups on the other hand are characterized by a greater number of publications each of which has a declining number of subscribers as the traditional European ethnic groups abandon the periodicals which their parents and grandparents so actively supported. While the

TABLE 12.7 Selected Ethnic Newspapers in the United States

ETHNIC GROUP	NEWSPAPER	PLACE OF PUBLICATION	CIRCULATION
Arabic	The News Circle	Glendale, CA	5,000
	American-Arab Message	Highland Park, MI	3,000
	New Al-Hoda	New York, NY	9,500
Armenian	Hoosharar	New York, NY	8,000
Bulgarian	Makedonska Tribuna	Indianapolis, IN	2,300
Chinese	Chinese Times	San Francisco, CA	11,000
	The China Post	New York, NY	20,000
Croatian	Nasa Nada	Chicago, IL	6,200
Czech	Czechoslovak Daily Herald	Berwyn, IL	8,700
	Hospodar	West, TX	6,500
Danish	Den Danske Pioneer	Chicago, IL	3,600
Estonian	Vaba Eesti Sona	New York, NY	4,000
Finnish	Raivaaja	Fitchburg, MA	2,100
French	Journal Francais d'Amerique	San Francisco, CA	15,000
	France-Amerique	New York, NY	20,000
German	California Staats-Zeitung	Los Angeles, CA	16,500
	Der Deutsch-Amerikaner	Mt. Prospect, IL	10,000
	Milwaukee Deutsche Zeitung	Milwaukee, WI	169,000
Greek	The Hellenic Chronicle	Boston, MA	38,000
Hebrew	Hadoar Hebrew Weekly	New York, NY	4,500
Hungarian	Californiai Magyarsag	Los Angeles, CA	7,500
	Amerikai-Kanadai Magyar Elet	Chicago, IL	15,600
Iranian	The Iran Times	Washington, DC	50,000
Italian	Il Progresso Italo-Americano	New York, NY	75,000
	The Echo	Providence, RI	25,000
	Italian Tribune	Newark, NJ	25,000
Japanese	Rafu Shimpo	Los Angeles, CA	21,000
	Kashu Mainichi	Los Angeles, CA	7,000
	Itokubei Mainichi	San Francisco, CA	8,500
	North American Post	Seattle, WA	2,000
Korean	New Korea	Los Angeles, CA	3,000
Latvian	Latvian News Laiks	Brooklyn, NY	12,000
Lithuanian	Lithuanian Daily News Naujienos	Chicago, IL	26,400
	Dirva	Cleveland, OH	4,000
	Garsas	Wilkes-Barre, PA	5,000
Norwegian	Nordish Tidende	Brooklyn, NY	10,000
Polish	Dziennik Zwiazkowy	Chicago, IL	25,000
	Am-Pol Eagle	Buffalo, NY	26,000
	Straz	Scranton, PA	10,000
Portuguese	Voz de Portugal	Hayward, CA	5,500
	Luso-Americano	Newark, NJ	12,000
Roumanian	Solia	Detroit, MI	2,150
Russian	Russian Daily Life	San Francisco, CA	3,000
	Russky Golos	New York, NY	3,000
Serbian	American Srbobran	Pittsburgh, PA	10,000
Slovak	Jednota	Middletown, PA	3,700
Slovene	Prosveta	Hinsdale, IL	25,000

Sources: *Ayer Directory of Publications*, 1982. *The Media Encyclopedia*, 1982. *Editor and Publisher International Yearbook*, 1982.

TABLE 12.7—*cont.*

Spanish	La Opinion	Los Angeles, CA	43,000
	La Voz Hispana De Colorado	Denver, CO	10,000
	Diario Las Americas	Miami, FL	62,000
	El Continental	El Paso, TX	18,000
	The Laredo Times	Laredo, TX	19,500
Swedish	Norden	Brooklyn, NY	1,400
Turkish	Hurriyet	New York, NY	5,800
Ukrainian	Svoboda	Jersey City, NJ	17,000
	Samostigna Ukraina	Chicago, IL	1,000
Yiddish	Jewish Forward	New York, NY	35,000
	Der Yid	Brooklyn, NY	18,000

ETHNIC GROUPS WITH 25 OR MORE PUBLICATIONS 1972

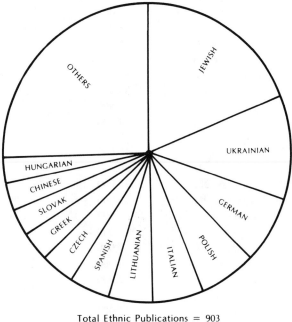

Total Ethnic Publications = 903
Source: Wynar, 1972.

Figure 12.2. Ethnic Groups with 25 or More Publications 1972.

Jews, Ukrainians, Spanish, and other ethnic groups shown on the graph can all boast several dozen publications, some minorities support only one or two. Minorities with one publication and a circulation of less than 1000 include Cossacks, Luxembourgers, and the Welsh.

What are the functions of the foreign language press which account for its virtual ubiquity among first-generation immigrant groups and its persistance in a country which is reluctant "to view language and ethnicity as consonant with modern social development."[6] In general, it serves to both insulate and assimilate successive waves of immigrants into American culture.

First, it provides a medium of communication for groups whose native language is not English and whose origins are not in the United States. Even as English is mastered among first- and second-generation immigrants, the language of comfort and security is often the native tongue. Second, it serves to publish news of the home country which would otherwise be unavailable. The Italian press, for instance, gives priority to news from Italy rather than the non-Italian world.[7] Third, it aids the process of assimilation by offering information and advice on lifestyles in a new country. Silverman, for instance, has called the Yiddish press one of the two "most powerful Americanizing (agencies) operative on the Jewish scene."[8] The other is the public school. Fourth, it provides a vehicle for promoting social cohesion, ethnic activities, and mutual support networks.

The spatial and temporal dimensions of foreign language publishing in the United States are closely associated with immigrant history and the settlement geographies of ethnic Americans. The 1982 *Media Encyclopedia* lists, by place of publication, 33 languages in which newspapers are published. Those states, which served as gateways for immigrants from Europe, from Latin America, and from Asia, have also become the locus of the majority of foreign language presses. The ethnic press in New York publishes in 20 foreign languages, in California 12, and in Illinois 10. These three states, and particularly the New York, Chicago, and Los Angeles metropolitan areas, are clearly the capitals of the foreign language publishing industry in the United States. The American South, the Great Plains, the Northern Rockies, and the Great Basin region, on the other hand, are areas which support almost no foreign language newspapers.

Five foreign languages in the United States are spoken by more than 800,000 persons five years of age and older: Spanish, Italian, German, French, and Polish.[9] These languages represent the Romance, Germanic, and Slavic language groups. By place of pub-

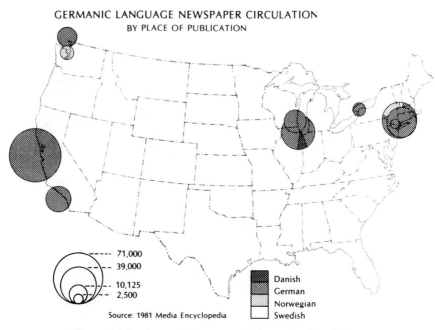

GERMANIC LANGUAGE NEWSPAPER CIRCULATION
BY PLACE OF PUBLICATION

Figure 12.3. Germanic Language Newspaper Circulation.

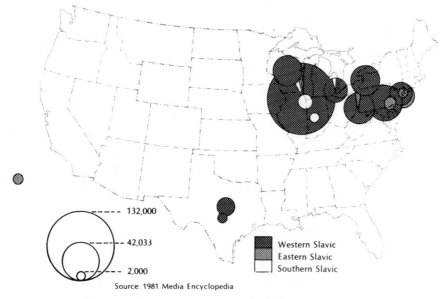

Figure 12.4. Slavic Language Newspaper Circulation.

lication, the newspapers listed in *The Media Encyclopedia* are mapped out in Figures 12.3, 12.4, 12.5 according to available circulation statistics. The languages which dominate these maps are the languages which are the most frequently spoken in the United States.

The Germanic language press is dominated by the German language itself; it is today restricted to a handful of major metropolises (Figure 12.3). It was a German newspaper, however, that initiated foreign language publishing in the United States. The short-lived *Philadelphia Zeitung* was published by Benjamin Franklin in 1732.[10] Its successor, begun in 1739, attained a circulation of 4000 and served to unite an archipelago of German ethnic islands in New York, Pennsylvania, Virginia, the Carolinas, and Georgia.[11]

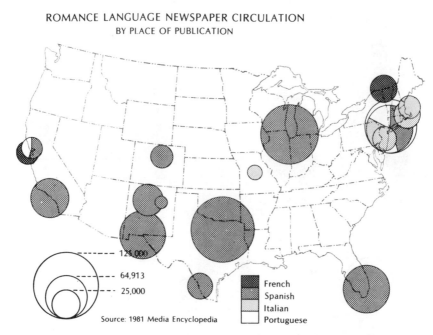

Figure 12.5. Romance Language Newspaper Circulation.

The first German language daily in the United States appeared in 1834[12] and the number of German publications peaked in 1893 at close to 800 when they accounted for over two-thirds of all foreign-language publications in this country.[13] As German-Americans and their Scandinavian counterparts have been successfully integrated into American culture, their patronage of foreign language newspapers has diminished.

The Norwegian press is even smaller than the German press and is restricted to two centers, Seattle and New York, quite distant from the original province of Norwegian settlement in the west north central states. From 1847 when the first Norwegian daily was founded in Norway, Wisconsin, through the 1870s, Illinois, Wisconsin, and Minnesota spawned a thriving Norwegian press catering to first- and second-generation immigrants. Today the locational pattern reflects two or more recent chapters in Norwegian immigrant history. In the 1880s, the focus of immigration switched to the Pacific Northwest where both land and opportunities were abundant, and to New York City and other Northeastern ports where Norwegian seamen jumped ships by the thousands. The immigrant communities in Seattle and New York are not as many generations removed from the original immigrants and are now the only major Norwegian language publishing centers.

Slavic language publications appear to have a larger circulation than Germanic language publications (Figure 12.4). The Slavic nationalities constituted the second wave of immigration to the United States. Not only did they arrive later than many western and southern European groups, but their full assimilation was hampered by their different cultural, linguistic, and

religious traditions. These eastern European nationalities did not start arriving in large numbers until the 1870s and 1880s when the growth centers of the United States were the heavy industrial cities of the northeastern quadrant of the century. Conspicuous is the concentration of Slavic publications in that northeastern section, a distributional pattern that mirrors Slavic settlement patterns. In 1970, 80 percent of the first- and second-generation Slavic population lived in the Northeast and North Central census regions. Equally conspicuous on the map is the predominance of the Western Slavic languages, primarily Polish but also including some Czech and Slovak publications. Polish immigration dramatically increased after 1870 and during the succeeding decade Polish language newspapers appeared to serve ethnic communities in Buffalo, Detroit, Toledo, Philadelphia, Pittsburgh, and several smaller cities.[14] By 1888, the first successful Polish language daily had been founded in Milwaukee. The only significant area of Slavic language-publishing outside the Northeast is the Austin and Waco area of Texas where several Czech language newspapers serve the Czech-American population of the Texas prairies.

Romance language publications are dominated by Spanish (Figure 12.5). The recency of this immigrant wave and the settlement patterns of Hispanic immigrants are reflected in the size and distribution of the proportional circles appearing on the map. Over one-fifth of the population of New Mexico, California, and Texas are non-English speakers, a fact which helps to explain the growth of the Spanish language press in these states. In addition to the Hispanic borderland, two northern metropolises, Chicago and New York, are major foci of Hispanic settlement and Spanish language publishing.

The *Miami Herald* has included a Spanish language section since 1976 and one of the major Spanish language dailies in the United States was founded in Miami in 1954. New York, Los Angeles, El Paso, and Laredo also have Spanish language dailies.

Like the Spanish press, the Italian and Portuguese presses mirror the settlement patterns of immigrants. Italian newspapers are especially important in the Northeast whereas Portuguese newspapers are to be found in New York, San Francisco, and the San Joaquin Valley area of California. The absence of a Portuguese press in New England reflects the inadequacy of data sources. Massachusetts, Connecticut, and Rhode Island are major centers of Portuguese settlement and the number of Portuguese and Azorean immigrants to this area actually increased during the 1970s.

Except for the Spanish, the number of Romance, Germanic, and Slavic language publications is declining. As circulation drops off, publication frequency is typically reduced and the publication is ultimately terminated. In 1983, for instance, *The Jewish Daily Forward,* published in New York City, became a weekly rather than a daily publication. The *Forward* was the last of the nation's Yiddish dailies. The trend in foreign language dailies portends a dismal future for many foreign language presses. According to the *Ayer Directory of Publications,* their number declined from 71 in 1963 to only 28 in 1982. In two decades it has been more than halved. Daily newspaper circulation has historically been confined to urban centers where there is a high density of ethnic Americans. As the density of ethnic Americans thins out, daily newspapers become less practical, and as the number of first- and second-generation immigrants diminishes, as it has for European nationalities, the use of the mother tongue in ethnic publications becomes less readable.

The future of the foreign language press may not be so bleak as these trends indicate. A recent survey of 13 ethnic groups in Cleveland found that more than half of them read more than one ethnic newspaper, and 30 percent read at least one ethnic magazine.[15] So long as there are immigrants to the United States there will be foreign-language presses.

Presses serving European immigrants of the first and second waves have also declined, but presses serving Latin American and Asian immigrants have grown. Just as the *Philadelphia Zeitung* provided a medium for the dissemination of news and information to the German ethnic islands of Pennsylvania and surrounding states, the news-oriented Spanish language press may soon serve the entire Hispanic community in the United States. In 1981 the Gannett newspapers acquired *El Diario-La Prensa,* New York's Spanish daily.

It foresees a nationwide information network serving Hispanic communities around the country using satellites to transmit full pages of news to any member newspaper of the network.[16] Already the Chinese language *World Journal* is transmitted from San Francisco to New York via satellite and Hong Kong's *Sing Tao* is transmitted across the Pacific to the United States and Canada. By taking advantage of modern technology, the emerging ethnic presses may more efficiently serve the needs of a far-flung archipelago of ethnic islands.

The future of the established foreign-language presses may be as bright as the future of the emerging foreign language presses if they can make the transition to *ethnic* presses serving the needs of third-, fourth-, and fifth-generation immigrants who neither know the mother tongue nor care about events in the "old country," but who do take pride in their ethnic heritage. In 1979, 58 million Americans identified their ancestry as German, 44 million as Irish, 14 million as Scottish and French, and 10 million as Italian, to name only a few.[17] By tapping only a fraction of these enormous markets, the foreign language press may be able to take advantage of the trend to "narrow-casting" and make the transition to an ethnic press. As the editor of the *Irish American* has stated: "Our readers are losing touch with Ireland as a country and are becoming more atuned to their Irish identity. There are fewer people who have ever been to Ireland, an even fewer who have come from there. I think the press has to adapt itself to this new audience—an audience of third and fourth generation Americans."[18] This transition may mean publishing an increasingly larger proportion of the news and features in English. Many smaller presses have already made the transition to English as witnessed by the *Voice of the Basques* published in Boise, Idaho, the *Cape Verdean* published in Lynn, Massachusetts, *Luxembourg News of America* published in Mount Prospect, Illinois, and *Malta News* published in Windsor, Ontario. The largest Spanish language daily in the United States is debating whether to become a bi-lingual newspaper since 57 percent of the nation's Hispanic population speaks both Spanish and English.[19] Many newspapers have already succumbed to pressures for more English-language coverage. The *Jewish Forward,* for instance, includes an English language section which runs to about one-third of the newspaper. Nevertheless, a recent survey of 13 ethnic groups in Cleveland found that more than half read more than one ethnic newspaper and 30 percent read at least one ethnic magazine.[20]

Continuing immigration to the United States, advances in communications technology, the undiminished diversity of foreign languages in which newspapers are published, and the so-called ethnic revival in the United States may contribute to the sustenance of a press serving the needs of American ethnics. It may be totally foreign-language press, in some instances, serving the needs of recent immigrants, or it may be an English-language press which sustains the comradery of ethnicity long after the native language has disappeared. Whatever the future of the foreign-language press, it has been an important part of American culture although a neglected theme in American cultural geography.

ETHNIC BROADCASTING

Radio broadcasting targeted at ethnic minorities is another activity that distinguishes American ethnic islands from the mainstream of English-speaking culture. Since listening to radio does not require the ability to read, its appeal is even broader than the foreign language press. Unlike the autonomous press, however, most foreign language radio programs are broadcast over stations whose clientele is primarily English-speaking. For the most part, they are limited to only a few hours per week. Ethnic broadcasting serves to create a point of contact with other members of an American ethnic community and to preserve ties with the country of origin. Warshauer[21] notes its function as a source of entertainment for linguistic minorities who are geographically isolated from their homeland and culturally isolated from the dominant society. Musical programming has dominated ethnic radio just as it has English language radio.

In 1941, twenty years after the birth of radio broadcasting, Roucek[22] reported that 205 radio stations in the United States were broadcasting in 26 foreign languages. At that time he predicted the eventual disappearance of foreign language broadcasting in the United States. Twenty years later, in 1960, 1340 stations were broadcasting in 39 foreign languages according to data compiled by the Language Resource Project,[23] which also found that the number of stations airing at least a few hours of foreign language programs had increased at a rate commensurate with radio programming in general. In 1976, radio stations nationwide were broadcasting to at least 40 different ethnic groups.[24] Grame,[25] in his field of investigation, found radio broadcasts in 56 languages. In New York alone, he found 36 ethnic groups with programs of their own, and in San Francisco he found 18. During the past four decades, the diversity of foreign language broadcasting does not seem to have diminished. What has diminished has been the number of hours of many foreign language broadcasts. There remain only 8½ hours of Chinese, 2¼ hours of Norwegian, 2 hours of Dutch, 1½ hours of Lithuanian, 1½ hours of Armenian, 1¼ hours of Swiss, and ½ hour of Romanian radio programs per week in the United States. While the number of hours of radio broadcasting for some European languages is declining, programs in new languages are appearing. In some American cities there are now programs in Hindu, Punjabi, Haitian, Pakistani (Urdu), Filipino, and Tagalog. Some of the ethnic groups with comparatively limited broadcast time are listed in Table 12.8.

The major foreign language broadcasts have fared much better. In 1960, five languages accounted for 88 percent of the total number of broadcast hours per week: Spanish, Italian, Polish, German, and French (Table 12.9). These five tongues along with English are the nation's most common household languages. In 1981, they continued to dominate foreign language broadcasting and all but one of the five had actually increased in broadcast time over the preceding score of

SPANISH LANGUAGE RADIO BROADCASTING 1982

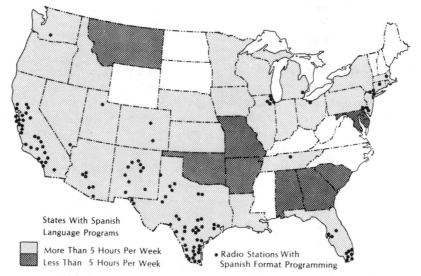

States With Spanish Language Programs

More Than 5 Hours Per Week
Less Than 5 Hours Per Week

• Radio Stations With Spanish Format Programming

Figure 12.6. Spanish Language Radio Broadcasting, 1982. Source: *Broadcasting Cable Yearbook*, 1982.

TABLE 12.8 Selected Ethnic Radio Programming (in Hours)

Basque		*Haitian*	
Elko, NV	1–½	Bronx, NY	1
Buffalo, WY	1	New York, NY	1
Boise, ID	1	*Hindi*	
Chinese		New York, NY	2
San Francisco, CA	7–½	*Norwegian*	
New York, NY	1	Decorah, IA	1
Czech.		Northfield, MN	¾
Foley, AL	½	Williston, ND	½
Cedar Rapids, IA	4	*Pakistani*	
New York, NY	2	Fort Collins, CO	1
Bellaire, OH	2	Cleveland, OH	1
Cleveland, OH	½	Bellingham, WA	1
Dallas, TX	½	*Romanian*	
Gonzales, TX	17	Detroit, MI	½
Hillsboro, TX	2	*Russian*	
LaGrange, TX	8	Nome, AS	5
Rosenberg-Richmond, TX	8	Chicago, IL	¾
Temple, TX	1	*Swedish*	
Filipino/Tagalog		Rockford, IL	1
Delano, CA	12–½	Northfield, MN	¾
Santa Rosa, CA	1	Colquet, MN	½
Hilo, HI	18–½	Holdrege, NB	½
Honolulu, HI	33	Jamestown, NY	2
Kahului, HI	11–½	*Ukrainian*	
Kealakekua, HI	1	Jenkintown, PA	2–½
Lihue, HI	10	Zaraphath, NJ	1–½
Wailuku, HI	18	Chicago, IL	1
Finnish		New York, NY	1
Clouquet, MN	1	Utica, NY	1
Lake Worth, FL	½	Struthers, OH	1
Ironwood, MI	1	Takoma Park, MD	½
Ishpeining, MI	1	Trenton, NJ	½
		Auburn, NY	½
		Montrose, PA	½

Source: Wasserman, Morgan, 1976.

years. In 1981, 143 radio stations in the United States were listed by the *Broadcasting-Cable Yearbook* as Spanish-format stations airing at least 20 hours per week of Spanish-language programs.[26] In addition, there were about 2000 hours per week of Spanish programming on English language stations throughout the country. Figure 12.6 depicts the widespread influences of Spanish language radio broadcasting. All but eleven states have at least some Spanish language programming even if it is only a few hours per week. The concentration of the Spanish speaking population is accentuated by the galaxy of radio stations with Spanish format programming which corresponds with the so-called Hispanic borderland. The first and second generation Spanish-speaking populations from Cuba, Mexico, Puerto Rico, and more recently South America

TABLE 12.9 Foreign Language Radio Programming in the United States (Hours per Week)

	1960[1]	*1981*
Spanish	3,802.50	12,000.00[2]
Italian	608.95	329.10[3]
German	215.75	288.00[3]
French	225.50	316.20[3]
Polish	509.00	537.90[3]

[1]M. E. Warshauer, "Foreign Language Broadcasting," 1966.
[2]T. C. Grame, *Ethnic Broadcasting in the United States,* 1980 (estimate for 1977).
[3]B. J. Fike, (ed.), *The Media Encyclopedia,* 1981.

(in southern Florida) and Central America (in southern California) have increased in Miami, San Antonio, Phoenix, and Los Angeles. Accompanying the rapid Hispanic growth of these and smaller cities has been an increase in the number of stations and number of hours of Spanish format programming.

Like Spanish, the number of hours of German, French, and Polish broadcasting also has increased since 1960. By 1981, German language broadcasts had increased by 33 percent to 288 hours per week. French broadcasts by 40 percent to 316 hours per week; and Polish broadcasts by 6 percent to 538 hours per week. Italian language broadcasts, on the other hand, had declined by 46 percent. By comparison, Spanish remains the giant of the industry and exhibits the most widespread geographic distribution, although at the regional scale, other languages may take on considerable importance. Two languages whose patterns of radio broadcasting are highly concentrated are French and Portuguese. Both languages evidenced healthy rates of growth in broadcast time during the 1960s and 1970s.

In 1970, the foreign stock population of French numbered 343,000 (excluding French Canadians) and of Portuguese 318,000. If it is possible to explain the geographic distribution of foreign language programming by reference to the foreign stock population, then these states should also be the locus of the majority of French and Portuguese broadcasting. In fact, the pattern of Portuguese broadcasting is as concentrated as the settlement pattern (Figure 12.7). Eighty-seven percent of first- and second-generation Portuguese immigrants were concentrated in the five states of Massachusetts (108,919), California (98,275), Rhode Island (35,730), New Jersey (17,335), and Connecticut (15,218). In 1981, these five accounted for virtually all radio broadcast time, about 135 hours per week, an increase of about one-fifth since 1960. In New England, Portuguese programming has been reinvigorated by a resurgence of immigration from Portugal and the Azores during the 1970s. In the San Francisco-San Joaquin Valley area of California, the Portuguese early established themselves in the dairy industry. Today, this area of California and several satellites to the north and south serve as one of the two major markets for Portuguese broadcasting.

The pattern of French broadcasting in Figure 12.7 casts some doubt on the hypothesized correlation between the most recent immigrants and foreign language radio. First- and second-generation French immigrants numbered only 25,000 more than Portuguese immigrants in 1970, but French settlement patterns were more dispersed. The five leading states were California (63,449), New York (56,861), New Jersey (22,152), Illinois (19,266), and Pennsylvania (18,484), all of which are highly urbanized. Together they accounted for only 53 percent of the French foreign stock. Likewise, the pattern of French radio broadcasting is more dispersed. None of the top five states in French stock population account for any more than a token number of hours. In fact, only three of the five states have any French programming at all. The leading states in broadcast hours, as depicted in Figure 12.7, are Louisiana, Georgia, Kansas, and Maine. The presence of French programming in Maine and the rest of New

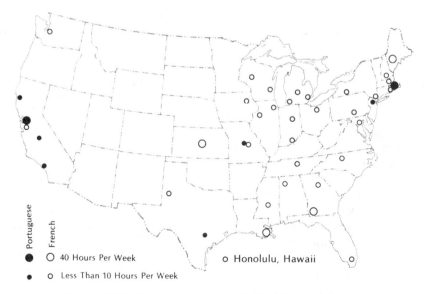

FOREIGN LANGUAGE RADIO BROADCASTING:
FRENCH AND PORTUGUESE 1981

Portuguese French

● ○ 40 Hours Per Week

• ○ Less Than 10 Hours Per Week

○ Honolulu, Hawaii

Figure 12.7. Foreign Language Radio Broadcasting: French and Portuguese, 1981. Source: *Broadcasting Cable Yearbook*, 1981.

England is easily explained by the French Canadian immigrants who are difficult to identify in the Census reports since they are included among Canadian immigrants as a whole. In 1970, more than 600,000 first- and second-generation Canadians resided in Massachusetts and Maine; the majority undoubtedly originated from Quebec. Unexplained by the recent immigration of French-speaking people, however, is the largest center of French language broadcasting, Louisiana. Here the rural isolation of the French ethnic island has preserved the cultural and linguistic heritage longer than in the urban areas where more recent immigrants have settled. Urban French ethnic islands have lost their linguistic identity more rapidly than rural French ethnic islands. The French Cajuns have been sequestered in Louisiana since the 1750s and today support a significant radio industry. Still, one might expect the French Canadian arrivals in the industrial cities of southern New England to command, given their numbers, more than the few hours of broadcast time that characterize Massachusetts, Rhode Island, and Connecticut.

The contrast between the Cajuns of Louisiana and the French Canadians of New England illustrates the importance of urban influences in evaluating the melting pot hypothesis. The rural Cajuns are many generations removed from their original immigrant groups, yet they maintain a cultural and linguistic identity that makes foreign language broadcasting a successful enterprise. The urban French Canadians of New England, on the other hand, began arriving in the industrial cities of Massachusetts and Rhode Island only in the late 1800s, yet they have not been nearly so successful as the Cajuns in maintaining the French language, a fact reflected in the underrepresentation of New England in French language broadcasting.

One trend which augurs well for the future of ethnic broadcasting, whether or not it be in a foreign tongue, is the appearance of "narrow-casting," programming aimed at particular audiences. Satellite transmission and extensive land lines make it possible to reach a nationwide audience of ethnic islands, unifying the various overlapping archipelagoes of immigrant groups whose second, third, and further generations have dispersed across the American landscape. In 1981, according to the *Broadcasting-Cable Yearbook,* the Spanish International Network and three regional networks provided information for Spanish language stations in the United States. In addition, eleven stations in New England were linked by the French Program Group of New England. The networking of information, whether by radio or television, should encourage ethnic renaissance, accentuate group identity, and a feeling of group consciousness among scattered ethnic islands. According to Grame,[27] ethnic broadcasting has "passed through the eye of the storm" into an era when demands for uniformity are giving way to demands for "multiformity."

ETHNIC FESTIVALS AND ETHNIC ORGANIZATIONS

Festivals of all sorts are a large and growing business in the United States today. Many of these festivals are devoted to ethnic themes and are designed to glorify ethnic cultures, to buttress group identity, and to educate outsiders about the contributions of various nationalities. While most ethnic groups have traditionally participated in church and family festivities as a matter of course, public ethnic festivals seem to be dependent on the willingness of an ethnic group to expose itself to outsiders, and on the willingness of outsiders to partake of ethnic culinary, artistic, and musical delights. In general, there must be a mutual respect between the ethnic group and society-at-large before public festivities can become successful community-wide events. This respect can often take many years to develop which may explain why, unlike the cultural traits of ethnic groups previously discussed, ethnic festivals have not often been staged by recent immigrants. Unfortunately, by the time this mutual respect has been developed, the group may have become so acculturated that there is little interest in showy festivities to impress the public. For many, ethnic festivals serve as much to revive ethnic customs as to maintain them. They become transient islands of ethnicity that glorify the ethnic past.

Is it possible to explain the locations of ethnic festivals by reference to the settlement patterns of immigrant groups and their descendants? Only in part. Most immigrants of Slavic nationalities who have settled in the United States exhibit a decidedly urban-oriented settlement pattern. The industrial cities of the northeastern United States, in particular, have become the locus of sizeable urban ethnic islands. In these urban settings, however, it is a rarity to find a public ethnic festival. Rather, the Slavic festivities are usually sheltered within religious institutions and are seldom aimed at the larger society. The Slavic groups who established themselves on the frontier during the late 1800s, however, have maintained their identity without the acculturating forces inherent in an urban area. Most Slavic festivals today are found in the plains states from North Dakota to Texas as depicted in Figure 12.8. Even though these states account for the fewest Czechs and Poles, they have been able to glorify their ethnicity in these rural areas more than have their counterparts in the cities.

Festivals and fairs in honor of the Scots' heritage are held in 25 large cities and small towns throughout the country.[28] San Diego, Atlanta, St. Paul, Syracuse, and Juneau hold them as do the small towns of Minden,

Figure 12.8. Slavic Festivals in the United States. Source: Wasserman, Morgan, 1976.

NE; Mt. Pleasant, S.C.; Coeur d'Alene, ID; Highland, MI; and Dunedin, FL.

Scandinavian festivals are held in areas of heaviest initial settlement, a pattern strikingly different from festivals staged by the Slavics and Scots. Small towns and large cities in Minnesota, Wisconsin, Michigan, and the Dakotas are the sites for most of these. Minneapolis and St. Paul, major centers for second and third generation Scandinavians, hold Swedish, Norwegian and Danish festivals annually.

In contrast to the large number of festivals held to unite the above named groups and the Greeks (14 festivals), Dutch (13), and Irish (9), there are fewer festivals to link smaller ethnic groups in order to pay tribute to their accomplishments and culture. Syrian-Lebanese festivals are held only in Toledo, OH and Providence, RI; Basque festivals in Elko, NV and Sun Valley, ID; Portuguese in Fall River, MA; and Hungarian in Los Angeles. Belgian-Americans celebrate a festival in St. Paul and Cornish Americans in Central City, CO. Many of these smaller ethnic groups do, however, piggy back on pan-ethnic festivals such as Milwaukee's Holiday Folk Fair which provides a focal point for large numbers of Germans and Poles as well as small numbers of Dutch Indonesians.

An intriguing question that arises in mapping the sites of ethnic festivals and fairs is why so many appear in rural areas. Have rural ethnic islands been able to retain and maintain their homogeneity and sense of ethnicity longer than urban islands? Or are rural farming communities with their seasonal slow-downs in activity more suited to festivals than urban communities which run on the same schedule year around? Perhaps, the resurgence of ethnic identification and

pride will give rise to festivals in those metropolitan areas which have been homes to the majority of Slavic and Scandinavian nationalities. Recent immigrant groups such as the Cubans, Korean, Vietnamese, and Filipinos are mainly in large cities where some ethnic diversity already exists; many of these same cities have a history of supporting nationalistic groups.

The transience of the ethnic festival contrasts sharply with the permanence of ethnic organizations in the United States. Wynar[29] lists 73 ethnic groups in the United States which maintain their own organizations, both religious and secular. Some have large memberships, such as the Ukrainian National Association with 89,000 members and the Dutch Immigrant Society with 10,000. Even the Manx-Americans may belong to seven different organizations devoted to the preservation of Manx ethnic identity! New immigrant groups also organize, witness the growth of the Muslim Student Association on college and university campuses since the mid-1970s. The Pakistani Students Association of America, and the Organization of Arab Students in the United States and Canada are other examples of student organizations set up along national lines.

Wynar sees ethnic organizations as fulfilling needs of the ethnic group that are not met by established social institutions. They may serve cultural, political, social, fraternal, special interest, welfare, educational, or scholarly functions within the ethnic system. Wynar maintains that the greater the "cultural disparity" between the immigrant group and society-at-large, the greater the number of ethnic organizations. He asserts that "the survival of ethnic communities and an ethnic 'life' is largely a result of the continued existence of ethnic organizations and their various activities that insure the continuation of the ethnic society."[30]

The distribution of these ethnic organizations often reflects the distribution of the groups themselves. Seldom are organization locations a perfect mirror of areas of concentration, however. The maps in Figure 12.9 compare the patterns of the Irish, Norwegian, Finnish, and Greek American organizations. New York City appears on all maps and assumes the importance of a capital city for Irish and Greek Americans. Similary, the District of Columbia has become a major locus of ethnic organizations. Despite the fact that Washington, D.C. has been neither a traditional port of entry nor a major industrial center, it has attracted ethnic organizations because of its role as the major political control point in the United States just as New York has been the major economic control point. Outside of the Northeast, cities that appear on these four maps are located primarily in the Midwest. Detroit, Chicago, and Minneapolis-St. Paul appear as major ethnic control points in the American ethnic system. Greek-American organizations seem to be most concentrated, Finnish-American organizations seem to be most dispersed. Los Angeles and San Francisco, while not major loci for European ethnic organizations, are important control points for immigrant groups from Central America, Southeast Asia, and the Pacific Islands. Los Angeles and Long Beach have ethnic islands of Guamanians, Tongans, and Samoans, and serve as sites for the organizations that serve these ethnic islands. These headquarters of ethnic American society provide a focus for ethnic identity at the local, state, and national levels. They serve to give cohesion to increasingly far-flung groups and they give many ethnic Americans a visibility that they might not otherwise enjoy.

ETHNIC MIXES IN SELECTED CITIES

Research on ethnic minorities by geographers and other social scientists has revealed a high degree of persistence in the regional patterning of most ethnic groups.[31] Most of this research, however, has focused on only the largest ethnic groups such as the Irish, Germans, Italians, and Polish. It has also tended to center on a few major cities, especially the large cities of the industrial Northeast and Middle West. As a result a plethora of case studies exists on urban ethnic processes in New York, Philadelphia, Boston, Cleveland, Pittsburgh, and Chicago. In 1970, 22 out of 243 Standard Metropolitan Statistical Areas (SMSAs) contained more than half of the foreign stock population even though they had only about 30 percent of the total population[32]. Fourteen of these metropolitan areas were in the northeastern quadrant of the country and all but three of the remainder were in California. These met-

ropolitan areas include the largest urban settlement nodes in the United States.

Because of size and regional biases, the largest cities and northeastern cities are often used to develop models of ethnic neighborhood development and mobility. Much less is known about the ethnic geographies of most Sunbelt cities and about small and medium-sized metropolitan areas elsewhere in the United States. The latter part of this chapter will focus, therefore, on the ethnic mixes in eight cities ranging from 119,000 to 786,000 population in 1980, including representative cities from all regions of the United States: Erie, Pennsylvania; Providence, Rhode Island; Norfolk, Virginia; Birmingham, Alabama; Omaha, Nebraska; Portland, Oregon; Milwaukee, Wisconsin; and San Antonio, Texas.

Residential segregation has long been used as an indicator of the amount of assimilation that has taken place among ethnic groups over a period of time. Stanley Lieberson's early work on the assimilation of ten ethnic groups in ten Northeastern and Middle Western cities in 1930 is a case in point. He used the spatial distribution of ethnic groups, citizenship, year of arrival, intermarriage, and ability to speak English. He concluded that "the differential residential segregation of American cities is an important factor in the assimilation of ethnic groups. Segregation is not only a significant dimension of assimilation but, further, the magnitude of a group's segregation appears to influence other aspects of the group's assimilation."[33] In the same study Lieberson assessed the impact of residential segregation on the occupational composition of eight European groups in 1950. His conclusion supported Hawley's notion that residential disperson was a prerequisite for assimilation.[34] Segregation and differences were accentuated in these early works with attempts to show how social and spatial assimilation could explain what was happening to the patterns of ethnic groups. Alternative models or conceptual designs based on contrasting rates and patterns of individual groups and their settlement histories were given less importance in explaining segregation and persistence.

The ethnic mosaic of the eight cities listed above can be explored in two ways. One is to examine the single and multiple ancestry of residents. The second is to investigate which groups reside in relative spatial isolation from other ethnic groups and which share residential spaces with other ethnic groups. Both investigations will shed light on the ethnic patterns of minor ethnic groups in medium and small sized metropolitan areas in the United States.

In regards to ancestry mixes, the patterns are not too dissimilar from those associated with the cultural regions in which the cities are located. Smaller percentages of residents with a single ancestry are associated either with long histories of European ethnic

NORWEGIAN-AMERICAN ORGANIZATIONS

GREEK-AMERICAN ORGANIZATIONS

IRISH-AMERICAN ORGANIZATIONS

FINNISH-AMERICAN ORGANIZATIONS

Number of Ethnic Organizations:

○ 1
○ 2
○ 3-5
● 6-10
● 11-15
◉ 16-20

Source: Wynar, 1975.

Figure 12.9. Number of Ethnic Organizations.

TABLE 12.10 Single and Multiple Ancestry of Persons in Selected Cities: 1980

	Pop. (000's)	Single Ancestry	Eng.	Germ.	Irish	Ital.	Polish	Nor.	Swed.	Span.	French	Port.	Russ.
						Percent Single Ancestry							
Erie, PA	119	52.0	4.1	11.0	3.7	7.0	10.3		.9	1.1			
Providence, RI	157	65.8	4.6	1.3	22.0	19.5	1.6			5.8	3.1	5.1	1.4
Norfolk, VA	267	56.4	11.4	3.8	3.1	1.1	.7			2.3	.8		
Birmingham, AL	284	68.0	12.3	1.8	3.2	.1				.7			
Omaha, NE	314	48.0	4.5	11.0	5.0	2.0	2.5		1.5	2.3			
Portland, OR	365	45.0	8.7	8.5	3.8	1.4		1.6	1.4	2.1			
Milwaukee, WI	636	61.3	2.0	17.0	1.9	1.5	8.4	.7		4.1			
San Antonio, TX	786	71.4	5.0	5.0	2.0		.8			53.7			

	Multiple Ancestry	English & Other	German & Other	Irish & Other	Italian & Other	French & Other	Polish & Other
			Percent Multiple Ancestry				
Erie, PA	40.5	9.7	23.8	18.1	5.8	3.0	7.8
Providence, RI	23.9	7.9	3.4	10.6	6.3	6.0	1.9
Norfolk, VA	40.0	9.5	9.3	10.9	1.5	3.2	1.0
Birmingham, AL	12.1	5.2	3.4	7.5			
Omaha, NE	43.7	12.6	23.4	19.8		4.8	3.2
Portland, OR	41.0	17.1	17.6	15.3	1.7	5.8	1.2
Milwaukee, WI	29.7	5.3	19.7	8.2	1.8	4.3	7.4
San Antonio, TX	19.4	7.1	2.7	8.1	8.4	2.7	

Source: *1980 U.S. Census of Population and Housing, Census Tracts, Selected Cities,* Tables 7 and 9.

in-migration or those that never had a large ethnic population from Europe or Latin America. Cities where the percentages of single ancestry are very high, have large numbers of blacks (Milwaukee and Birmingham) or inhabitants of Spanish origin (San Antonio). Those with a German single ancestry are industrial centers in the Northeast and Middle West (Milwaukee, Omaha, and Erie). Italians are an important part of the single ancestry population especially in Providence; Irish are also an important segment of this city's ethnic composition. Polish ancestry residents are noteable in the populations of Erie and Milwaukee. In San Antonio, over one-half of the residents are of a single ancestry Spanish background. What becomes apparent in the populations of the single ancestry groups is that in most cities listed in Table 12.10, there are very few residents who have such a background. Probably the few who have a Norwegian, Swedish, Portuguese, or French single ancestry are older and have lived in the same city for several decades.

What the assimilation and mixture of ethnic groups in a city over time leads to are residents who have a multiple ancestry. The number of intermarriages can be expected to vary among ethnic groups. In terms of the eight cities in Table 12.10, the percentage having a multiple ancestry ranges from only 12 percent for Birmingham to 44 percent for Omaha. Birmingham, as an industrial inland city, has a very small ethnic population: there are, outside of those with an English heritage, few residents of single or multiple ancestry. San Antonio, like Birmingham, has a small percentage of the population with a multiple ancestry, in large part because of its very large population with origins in Mexico and other Central American and West Indian nations. Those with French, German, Irish, and Italian multiple ancestries are few. Erie, Norfolk, Omaha, and Portland have 40 percent or more of their population with a multiple ancestry. The mixes of English, German, Irish, Italians, and Polish vary. Milwaukee and Providence also have small but sizable numbers in five different ethnic ancestries.

It becomes further apparent in examining the percentages in Table 12.10 that multiple ancestries of those with Irish and German backgrounds are more numerous than those with Italian, French, or Polish backgrounds. The smaller percentages in most cases also reflect the smaller numbers of these three ethnic groups in the eight cities. What does not appear in the above tables are ethnic groups with relatively small numbers in these cities. Birmingham has 2695 Italians; 1391 French, 1407 Scots, 336 Swedes, 335 Polish, and 240 Greeks of a single ancestry, together these account for only about 2 percent of the city's population. San Antonio, a city dominated by residents of Spanish origin, has 4800 Italians and 4200 French of single ancestry.

279

Erie, a very ethnically diverse city has 975 Swedes, 708 Russians, 686 Hungarians, 568 French, 315 Greeks, 298 Scots, 279 Ukranians, 191 Dutch, and 140 Portuguese of single ancestry. Milwaukee has 4716 Norwegians, 3500 French, 2398 Swedes, 2289 Russians, 2200 Hungarians, 1800 Greeks, 1500 Dutch, 950 Scots, 780 Ukranians, and 147 Portuguese of single ancestry in 1980. San Antonio, a city dominated by residents of Spanish origin, has 4000 Italians, 1900 Scots, 1200 English, 1100 Russians, 847 Norwegians, 535 Hungarians, 477 Greeks, 190 Portuguese, and 172 Ukranians.

URBAN ETHNIC GEOMETRIES

The distribution of ethnic groups within a city or metropolitan region may exhibit any number of geometrical forms. Small concentrations or pockets around ethnic churches, schools, clubs, businesses, or organizations may be conceptualized as ethnic "islands." A series of these large and small islands throughout a metropolitan area may be thought of as an "archipelago," with the main islands most often located in the central city and out islands farther away, possibly even in the suburbs. Ethnic groups that grow and remain concentrated over time may occupy so large an area as to be considered a "continent." Linear growth along major thoroughfares radiating out from islands and continents may form "peninsulas" of urban ethnicity.

Agocs has proposed a typology of ethnic communities based on their distinctive geometrical patterns within a metropolitan area. Ethnic communities within the central city may be ghettos, immigrant reception centers, urban villages, or more dispersed and integrated residential communities, which she describes as "small islands of ethnic concentration remaining in neighborhoods that had passed to other groups."[35] Immigrant reception centers are described as closely-knit, self-contained neighborhoods inhabited primarily by first generation immigrants, whereas urban villages are described as neighborhoods inhabited primarily by second generation immigrants and their children. Ethnic communities in the suburban zone, according to Agocs, may be transplanted communities, new suburban settlements, or more dispersed ethnic communities which are interactional than territorial.

Definitions of ethnic geometries within the city are most easily derived from studies of individual ethnic groups. To what extent, however, do these ethnic geometries overlap? When ethnic Americans sort themselves out in residential space do they choose to associate with fellow ethnics, other ethnics, or non-ethnics? According to Izaki,[36] few studies have been carried out on the "spatial correspondence of the residential patterns among different groups" probably as a result of limited data and the complexity of a task involving so many

variables. The geographical study by Jones on Australian cities is an exception.[37] For examining ethnic patterns within American cities, census tracts provide a useful, albeit less than ideal, geographic base. Unfortunately, data for only the major racial categories (whites, blacks, Asian and Pacific Islanders, and so forth) and the Hispanic population are available at the block level, making it difficult to discern small concentrations of ethnic Americans and the intratract overlap among different ethnic groups. Within any one tract there may be one or two dominant groups in combination with any number of minor groups. Detailed large scale mapping is needed to discern the interdigitation of ethnic groups within a city and whether groups reside side by side, overlap in their cores or on their peripheries, or are completely isolated from other Americans, whether ethnic or not.

Some insight into the ethnic mixtures of tracts in selected cities can be obtained by examining Table 12.11. What is depicted are examples of the dominance of ethnic groups in seven cities. Four contrasting patterns are evident: single dominant groups in the city's tracts, and two, three, and four dominant groups. Shared tract residences are revealed in those with more than one dominant ethnic group.

The ethnic profile of a city can be discerned by examining the column mixes in Table 12.11 (two or three dominant groups), or by studying the columns themselves. Some cities clearly have single dominant groups in many of their tracts, e.g., the Italians and Poles in Erie, the Poles and Germans in Milwaukee, and the Spanish-origin population in San Antonio. While several cities have one or two dominant groups, there are others with a rich European heritage. Erie has one dominant group, the Germans, and the mixture of Germans, Italians, Irish, and English in other tracts. Similar mixtures exist among the Germans, English, Irish and Scandinavian populations in Portland, Oregon. Examples exist where two, three, and four of these groups reside side by side.

Another way of examining the mixes in cities is by the ethnic groups most likely to live within the same tracts. There are a number of cities where the English and Irish, and the English, Irish, and Germans live in the same tracts. Omaha, Portland, and Norfolk are examples. Germans, Poles, and Italians live in similar tracts in Erie, Omaha, and Milwaukee. The advantage of the ethnic "map" on Table 12.11 is that it reveals the varying degree of mixes that can and do occur within cities. A more detailed examination of a dozen different ethnic groups would demonstrate the presence of varying degrees of residential separateness and integration in insular, peninsular, and archipelagic forms.

Our findings support Izaki's finding that there is diversity in the mixes of ethnic groups at the district and census tract level. He found in San Francisco that

TABLE 12.11 Examples of Dominant Ethnic Groups in Same Census Tracts for Selected Cities

	Erie	Providence	Norfolk	Omaha	Portland	Milwaukee	San Antonio
Single Dominant							
English			X				
Germans	X					X	
Italians		X					
Poles		X					
Portuguese							
Spanish							X
Two Dominant							
English & Germans	X			X	X		X
Germans & Irish				X			
Germans & Italians	X						
Poles & Germans	X			X		X	X
Poles & Italians	X						
Three Dominant							
Germans, English & Irish			X	X	X	X	X
Germans, English & Italians		X					
Germans, Italians & Poles	X						
Four Dominant							
German, English, Polish, Irish							X
German, English, Italian, Irish	X				X		
German, Norwegian, Irish, English					X		
German, Swedish, Irish, English					X		
Irish, Italian, German, Poles				X		X	
Irish, Italian, French, German		X				X	
Irish, Italian, Portuguese, German		X					

Source: Derived from *1980 U.S. Census of Population and Housing, Census Tracts, Selected Cities,* Tables 7 and 8.

"Whites, Japanese, and Chinese form one strongly related group whereas another group consists of Latinos, Filipinos, and American Indians. All seven groups associated with at least one other group."[38] He also discovered that "most districts in San Francisco are comprised of two or three ethnic groups which dominate particular discrete census tracts within a district. Consequently, the degree of correspondence among these groups has been reduced. For this reason, the analysis by census tract is probably more accurately and more closely expresses a realistic appraisal."[39]

CONCLUSIONS

With only a few notable exceptions, ethnic minorities in the United States have chosen to reside in the cities which have served as ports of entry or centers of economic opportunity. Within these cities groups have formed conspicuous urban ethnic islands that have developed their own cultural institutions, and that support networks to nurture their sense of separateness from the dominant society. The foreign language press has become a universal concomitant of ethnic settlement in the United States dating back to 1732. With the advent of commercial radio in the 1920s, foreign language broadcasting aimed at ethnic audiences experienced an age of growth that for many languages, particularly those most frequently spoken at home, has continued until the present day. Nevertheless, there has been a decline in cohesiveness among many first and second wave ethnic groups, now many generations removed from the mother country and the mother tongue. The result has been a diminution of support for many foreign language newspapers and radio programs. As third wave immigrants provide the support for new foreign language publications and broadcasts, older ethnic groups must decide whether their insular identity has been so totally submerged in the mainstream of the dominant society that the need for avenues of ethnic communication is gone. In popular American culture, the search for individual identity has seen a proliferation of special interest groups, advocacy organizations, and other communities that operate independently of a territorial base. Just because islands of ethnicity disintegrate as territorial entities does not mean that the sense of community must also dissolve.

In fact, given the ease of transportation and communication in today's world, even mobile, melting-pot Americans can maintain contact with spiritual cousins of the same ethnic background. This may mean a transition from foreign-language communication to English, but the ethnic press and ethnic radio, supported by regional and national networks, can survive. In essence, nationwide archipelagoes of ethnic Americans can take advantage of the trend toward narrow-casting, remain in touch with those of similar interests, and use their ethnic heritage as one of the factors that makes them unique in our pluralistic society.

European-, Latin American-, and Asian-Americans continue to be a vital part of American culture and a conspicuous part of the American landscape. When the third wave of immigration will crest or what group will constitute the fourth wave are open questions, but the future of the United States is as likely to be colored by generations of new immigrants as has its past. What needs to be further investigated is if third wave immigrants from Latin America and Asia will conform to the same models as their European counterparts. Another chapter in the ethnic geography of the United States that begs to be written is a treatment of the wave of students that has turned almost all college and university campuses in the United States into mosaics of global cultures. Many of these students remain in the United States to make their own contributions to ethnic America. Those that return home are replaced by new arrivals, guaranteeing at least semi-permanent ethnic islands on most campuses. The 1980 Census has made available a multitude of statistical data on race, Hispanic origin, nativity and ancestry which promises a decade of fruitful ethnic research. Other data from ethnic organizations and field surveys are needed to provide an understanding of America as a cultural mosaic, as a melting pot, or as a stock pot of ethnic groups.

The evolution of urban ethnic islands is one of many spatial processes that bears watching to see how new immigrants and their descendants sort themselves out between central cities and suburbs, and to see whether different forces shape the geometries of ethnic islands in Subelt cities versus Frostbelt cities. It may be that residential contrasts will not be as sharp as demonstrated by previous ethnic groups in Northeastern and Middle Western cities.[40,41,42,43] Contrasts among regions and among ethnic groups may be so strong as to defy a universal model of ethnic assimilation. Agocs makes a case for pluralistic theories of ethnic evolution when she states:

> "There may be little point in hypothesizing uniform patterns of ethnic group development and persistence, or of assimilation.[44,45] It is more likely that each ethnic community differs from every other in mode and rate of development, under the influences of many different variables, not all which are part of the experience of other groups. Not of the least important of these influences upon ethnic settlement patterns, for example, is historical accident; the timing and circumstances of immigration of groups into a particular city, and the locations of their original settlement areas. The pluralistic theoretical perspective that is developing in ethnic and minority studies may sensitize researchers to what is unique in the experience of each ethnic group, as the search for general patterns continues."[46]

Pluralistic theories seem entirely consonant with our pluralistic society and spatial pluralistic theories seem entirely consonant with the renaissance of regionalism in America. The ethnic future will evolve from the conflict between forces encouraging cultural standardization and forces maintaining cultural distinction. At the individual level the ethnic future will be shaped by our personal decisions to cast off the cultural baggage of our immigrant forebears, to maintain the practices and values of our ethnic heritage, or to resurrect an ethnic identity that individuals may never have known, even as children.

NOTES

1. Thomas Sowell, *Ethnic America: A History* (New York, Basic Books, 1981).
2. Donald J. Zeigler, "Printing in Tongues: The Foreign Language Press in the United States" (Paper presented at the annual meeting of the Association of American Geographers, Denver, Colorado, April 26, 1983).
3. Robert E. Park, *The Immigrant Press and Its Control* (New York: Harper and Row, 1922).
4. Francis J. Brown and Joseph Roucek (eds), *One America* (New York: Prentice Hall, 1945).
5. Labomyr R. Wynar, *Encyclopedia Directory of Ethnic Organizations in the United States* (Littleton, Colorado: Libraries Unlimited, 1975).
6. Joshua A. Fishman, *Language Loyalty in the United States* (The Hague: Mouton, 1966).
7. Charles Jaret, "The Greek, Italian and Jewish American Ethnic Press," *Journal of Ethnic Studies,* 7 (1979): pp. 47–70.
8. David W. Silverman, "The Jewish Press: A Quadrilingual Phemononon," in M. E. Marty et al. (eds), *The Religious Press in America* (New York: Holt, Rhinehart, and Winston, 1963): pp. 123–172.
9. U.S. Bureau of the Census, "Ancestry and Language in the United States: November, 1979," *Current Population Reports,* Series P-23, 116 (Washington, D.C.: U.S. Government Printing Office, 1982).
10. Carl Wittke, *The German Language Press in America* (New York: Haskell House, 1973).
11. Park, 1922: p. 254.
12. Ibid.: p. 252.
13. Wittke, 1973: p. 282.

14. Jan Kowalik, *The Polish Press in America* (San Francisco: R & E Research Associates, 1978): p. 4.
15. Leo W. Jeffres and K. Kyoon Hur, "The Forgotten Media Consumer—The American Ethnic," *Journalism Quarterly,* 57 (1980): pp. 10–17.
16. Andrew Radolf, "Gannet Acquires El Diario-La Prensa," *Editor and Publisher,* September 5, 1981: pp. 10 and 29.
17. U.S. Bureau of the Census, 1982.
18. Nina Kessler, "Ethnic Newspapers Speak to Interests of Their Readers," *Advertising Age,* September 22, 1980.
19. Radolf, September 5, 1981.
20. Jeffres and Hur, 1980.
21. Mary Ellen Warshauer, "Foreign Language Broadcasting," in J. A. Fishman (ed), *Language Loyalty in the United States* (The Hague: Mouton, 1966): pp. 75–91.
22. Joseph Roucek, "Foreign Language Broadcasts," in F. J. Brown and J. Roucek (eds), *One America* (New York: Prentice Hall, 1945): pp. 384–391.
23. Warshauer, 1966.
24. Paul Wasserman and Jean Morgan (eds), *Ethnic Information Sources in the United States* (Detroit: Gale Research, 1976).
25. Theodore C. Grame, *Ethnic Broadcasting in the United States* (Washington, D.C.: Libarary of Congress, 1980): pp. 73, 109–130.
26. *Broadcasting/Cable Yearbook* (Washington D.C.: Broadcasting Publications, 1981 and 1982).
27. Grame, 1980.
28. Wasserman and Morgan (eds), 1976.
29. Wynar, 1975.
30. Ibid.: p. xviii.
31. David Ward, "Immigration: Settlement Patterns and Spatial Distribution," in S. Thernstrom (ed), *Harvard Encyclopedia of American Ethnic Groups* (Cambridge, Mass.: Harvard University Press, 1980): pp. 496–508.
32. Ronald J. McAlister and Joel Smith, "The Distribution of the Foreign Stock Population in Selected Metropolitan Areas: 1970," *Sociology and Social Research,* 62 (1978): pp. 213–214.
33. Stanley Lieberson, "The Impact of Residential Segregation on Ethnic Assimilation," Social Forces, 40 (1961): p. 57.
34. Amos H. Hawley, "Dispersion versus Segregation: Apropos of a Solution of Race Problems," *Papers, Michigan Academy of Science, Arts, and Letters,* 30 (1944): p. 674.
35. Carol Agocs, "Ethnic Settlement in a Metropolitan Area: A Typology of Communities," *Ethnicity,* 8 (1981): p. 137.
36. Yoshiharu Izaki, "The Residential Correspondence Between Japanese and Other Ethnic Groups in San Francisco," *Geographical Review of Japan,* 54 (1981): p. 115.
37. L. F. Jones, "Ethnic Concentration and Assimilation: An Austrialian Case Study," *Social Forces,* 45 (1967): pp. 412–423.
38. Izaki, 1981: p. 122.
39. Ibid.: p. 123.
40. Stanley Lieberson, "Suburbs and Ethnic Residential Patterns," *Journal of Sociology,* 67 (1962): pp. 673–681.
41. N. Kantowitz, *Ethnic and Racial Segregation in the New York Metropolis* (New York: Praeger, 1973).
42. Avery M. Guest and J. Weed, "Ethnic Residential Segregation: Patterns of Change," *American Journal of Sociology,* 81 (1976): pp. 1088–1111.
43. Avery M. Guest, "The Suburbanization of Ethnic Groups," *Sociology and Social Research,* 64 (1980): pp. 497–513.
44. A. M. Greeley, *Ethnicity in the United States: A Preliminary Reconnaissance* (New York: Wiley, 1974).
45. W. M. Newman, *American Pluralism: A Study of Minority Groups and Social Theory* (New York: Harper and Row, 1973).
46. Agocs, 1981, p. 146.

SELECTED BIBLIOGRAPHY

Ayer Directory of Publications (Bala Cynwyd, Pennsylvania: IMS Press, 1982).

Broadcasting/Cable Yearbook (Washington, D.C.: Broadcasting Publications, 1981 and 1982).

Darroch, A. G. and W. G. Marston, "The Social Class Basis of Ethnic Segregation: The Canadian Case," *American Journal of Sociology,* 77 (November, 1971): pp. 491–510.

Editor and Publisher International Yearbook (New York: Editor and Publisher, 1982).

Fike, Beverly J. (ed), *The Media Encyclopedia: The Working Press of the Nation,* 1, *Newspaper Directory* (Chicago: National Research Bureau, 1981 and 1982).

Kiang, Y. C., "The Distribution of Ethnic Groups in Chicago," *American Journal of Sociology,* 74 (1968); pp. 292–295.

Lieberson, Stanley, *Ethnic Patterns in American Cities* (Glencoe: The Free Press, 1963).

Miller, Wayne Charles, *A Handbook of American Minorities* (New York: New York's University Press, 1976). Olson, James Stuart, *The Ethnic Dimension in American History* (New York: St. Martin's Press, 1976).

Sugg, John F., "Diario: Paper With New Clout," *Advertising Age,* February 15, 1982: pp. 26–28.

Thernstrom, Stephen, *Harvard Encyclopedia of American Ethnic Groups* (Cambridge, Mass.: Harvard University Press, 1980).

U.S. Bureau of the Census, *1970 Census of Population,* 1, *Characteristics of the Population* (Washington, D.C.: Government Printing Office, 1973).

———, *1980 Census of Population, Supplementary Report: Provisional Estimate of Social, Economic, and Housing Characteristics,* PHC80–S1–1 (Washington, D.C.: Government Printing Office, 1982).

———, *1980 Census of Population* (Washington, D.C.: Government Printing Office, 1983).

———, *Census of Population and Housing, Census Tracts.* Birmingham, AL, PHC-2–93.

———, *1980 Census of Population and Housing, Census Tracts: Erie, PA,* PHC-2–148, 1983.

———, *1980 Census of Population and Housing, Census Tracts: Milwaukee, WI,* PHC-2–243, 1983.

———, *1980 Census of Population and Housing, Census Tracts: Norfolk-Virginia Beach-Portsmouth, VA,* PHC-2–265, 1983.

———, *1980 Census of Population and Housing, Omaha, NE-IA,* PHC-2–272, 1983.

———, *1980 Census of Population and Housing, Census Tracts: Portland, OR-WA,* PHC-2–290, 1983.

———, *1980 Census of Population and Housing, Census Tracts: Providence-Warwick-Pawtucket, RI-MA,* PHC-2–293, 1983.

———, *1980 Census of Population and Housing, Census Tracts: San Antonio, TX,* PHC-2–319, 1983.

U.S. Department of Health, Education, and Welfare, Education Division, National Center for Education Statistics, *Bulletin* 78 B-5, July 26, 1978.

Ward, David, *Cities and Immigrants* (New York: Oxford, 1971).

Webber, M., "Order in Diversity: Community Without Propinquity," *Cities and Space: The Future Uses of Urban Land,* edited by L. Wingo (Baltimore: Johns Hopkins Press, 1963): pp. 23–54.